D1804979

C++ for Lazy Programmers

Quick, Easy, and Fun C++ for Beginners

Will Briggs

Apress®

C++ for Lazy Programmers: Quick, Easy, and Fun C++ for Beginners

Will Briggs
Lynchburg, VA, USA

ISBN-13 (pbk): 978-1-4842-5186-7 ISBN-13 (electronic): 978-1-4842-5187-4
https://doi.org/10.1007/978-1-4842-5187-4

Managing Director, Apress Media LLC: Welmoed Spahr
Acquisitions Editor: Steve Anglin
Development Editor: Matthew Moodie
Coordinating Editor: Mark Powers

Cover designed by eStudioCalamar

Cover image by Raw Pixel (www.rawpixel.com)

Distributed to the book trade worldwide by Springer Science+Business Media New York, 233 Spring Street, 6th Floor, New York, NY 10013. Phone 1-800-SPRINGER, fax (201) 348-4505, e-mail orders-ny@springer-sbm.com, or visit www.springeronline.com. Apress Media, LLC is a California LLC and the sole member (owner) is Springer Science + Business Media Finance Inc (SSBM Finance Inc). SSBM Finance Inc is a **Delaware** corporation.

For information on translations, please e-mail editorial@apress.com; for reprint, paperback, or audio rights, please email bookpermissions@springernature.com.

Apress titles may be purchased in bulk for academic, corporate, or promotional use. eBook versions and licenses are also available for most titles. For more information, reference our Print and eBook Bulk Sales web page at http://www.apress.com/bulk-sales.

Any source code or other supplementary material referenced by the author in this book is available to readers on GitHub via the book's product page, located at www.apress.com/9781484251867. For more detailed information, please visit http://www.apress.com/source-code.

Printed on acid-free paper

To my favorite C++ programmer and the love of my life;

To the little one who first inspired her to study at home so she wouldn't go mommy-crazy;

And to the boy who's already programming.

Table of Contents

About the Author

Will Briggs, PhD, is a professor of computer science at the University of Lynchburg in Virginia. He has over 20 years of experience teaching C++, 12 of them using earlier drafts of this textbook, and more than that teaching other languages including C, LISP, Pascal, PHP, PROLOG, and Python. His primary focus is teaching of late while also doing research in artificial intelligence.

About the Technical Reviewer

Michael Thomas has worked in software development for over 20 years as an individual contributor, team lead, program manager, and vice president of engineering. He has over 10 years of experience working with mobile devices. His current focus is in the medical sector using mobile devices to accelerate information transfer between patients and health-care providers.

Acknowledgments

Special thanks to

- Dr. Kim McCabe, for advice on publishing
- Dr. Zakaria Kurdi, for advice on publishing
- Apress
- Microsoft
- The makers of GIMP (the GNU Image Manipulation Program)
- Pixabay.com and contributors, especially David Mark/12019 (Chapter 2, beach), Free-Photos (Chapter 2, pug), Andi Caswell/andicaz (Chapter 6, scones), joakant (Chapter 11, tropical fish), Gerhard Janson/Janson_G (Ch12, ufo), 13smok (Chapter 12, alien sign), Prawny (Chapter 12, splat), Elliekha (Chapter 12, haunted house), pencil parker (Chapter 12, candy), and Robert Davis/rescueram3 (Chapter 12, pumpkin photos)
- Wikimedia Commons
- OpenClipArt.org and contributors, especially Firkin (Chapter 2, flamingo)
- Flickr, especially Speedy McZoom (Chapter 12, jack-o-lantern art)
- FreeSounds.org and contributors, especially Razor5 (Chapter 2, techno music), robbo799 (Chapter 2, church bells), alqutis (Chapter 12, hovercar), Berviceps (Chapter 12, splat), mistersherlock (Chapter 12, Hallowe'en graveyard), matypresidente (Chapter 12, water drop), Osiruswaltz (Chapter 12, bump), mrose6 (Chapter 12, echoed scream), and robcro6010 (Chapter 12, circus theme)

- Chad Savage of Sinister Fonts for Werewolf Moon (Chapter 12)
- Lazy Foo' Productions
- StackOverflow.com
- Einar Egilsson of cardgames.io for images of card games, Nicu Buculei (`http://nicubunu.ro/cards`) for card images, and "Nanami Kamimura" for Montana image

Introduction

Surely there's no shortage of C++ intro texts. Why write yet another?

I'm glad you asked.

Ever since moving from Pascal to C++ (back when dinosaurs roamed the Earth), I've been underwhelmed by available resources. I wanted something quirky and fun to read, with sufficient coverage and fun examples, like the old *Oh! Pascal!* text by Cooper and Clancy.

It's about time we had this again. Even a perfectly accurate text with broad coverage gives you nothing if you fall asleep when you read it. Well, nothing but a sore neck.

But the other reason, of course, is to promote laziness.

We all want our projects to be done more quickly, with less wailing and gnashing of teeth. Sometimes, it's said, you have to put your nose to the grindstone. Maybe, but I like my nose too well for that. I'd rather do things the easy way.

But the easy way isn't procrastinating and dragging my feet: it's to find something I love doing and do it so well that it feels relatively effortless. It's producing something robust enough that when it does break down, it tells me exactly what the problem is, so I don't have to spend a week pleading with it to explain itself. It's writing code that I can use again and again, adapting it to a new use in hours instead of days.

You'll benefit from this book if you're a beginning programmer or one who hasn't yet learned C++ or its descendants like Java or C#; if you already know a C++-like language, you can go a little faster.

Here's what you can expect:

- A pleasant reading experience.
- Adequate coverage.
- Games, that is, use of the SDL graphics library, which makes it easy to get graphics programs working quickly and easily. It isn't fair that Python and Visual Basic should get all the eye candy.[1] The SDL

[1]"Eye candy": things that look good on the screen. See *The New Hacker's Dictionary*, available at time of writing at `www.catb.org/jargon/`.

library is used through Chapter 12. After that we'll use more standard (but less visually interesting) I/O, so we can also get practice with the more common console programs.

- ...and an easy introduction to SDL's graphical magic, using the SSDL library (see below).
- Sufficient examples, and they won't all be about actuarial tables or how to organize an address book. (See "pleasant reading experience" earlier.)
- Antibugging sections throughout the text to point out common or difficult-to-trace errors - and how to prevent them.
- Compatibility with g++ and Microsoft Visual Studio.
- Compliance with C++17, the latest standard, and the nice goodies it provides.
- For g++ programmers, instructions on using g++, the ddd/gdb debugger system, and Makefiles; for Visual Studio, use of the debugger and project files.
- An appreciation of laziness.
- A cool title. Maybe I could have tried to write a "For Dummies" book, but after seeing *Bioinformatics for Dummies* I'm not sure I have what it takes.

Why SDL?

It's surely more enjoyable to make programs with graphics and WIMP[2]-style interaction than to merely type things in and print them out. There's a variety of graphical libraries out there. SDL, or Simple DirectMedia Layer, is popular, relatively easy to learn, portable between platforms, and fast enough for real-world work, as evidenced by its use in actual released games (Figure 1).

[2]WIMP: window, mouse, icon, pointer. What we're all used to.

Figure 1. *A game of Freeciv, which uses the SDL library.*

Why SSDL?

...but although SDL is *relatively* simple, it's not simple enough to start with on day 1 of programming with C++. SSDL (*Simple* SDL) saves you from needing to know things we don't get to until Chapter 14[3] before doing basic things like displaying images (Chapter 2) or even printing a greeting (Chapter 1). It also hides the initialization and cleanup code that's pretty much the same every time you write a program, and makes error handling less cumbersome.

You may want to keep using SSDL as is after you're done with this book, but if you decide to go on with SDL, you'll find you know a lot of it already, with almost nothing to unlearn: most SSDL function names are names from SDL with another "S" stuck on the front. We'll go into greater depth on moving forward with SDL in Chapter 29.

[3]Pointers.

Software You Will Need

Your compiler, plus various free SDL libraries (SDL2, SDL2_Image, SDL2_TTF, and SDL2_Mixer), my free SSDL library, and (for Chapter 2, and whenever you need it) a deluxe graphics editing package. I use GIMP, which is free, and at time of writing is available from `www.gimp.org`.

SSDL is available at `www.apress.com/9781484251867`, as is my sample code.

In Unix, you may choose to install the GNU Free Fonts library, or msttcorefonts, Microsoft Core Fonts for the Web. Look for `ttf-mscore-fonts` and `fonts-freefont-ttf` (Debian and Ubuntu systems) and `gnu-free-fonts-common` and `msttcore-fonts-<something or other>` (Red Hat and Fedora), remembering that systems differ, standards change, and Unix is hard. But if you're using Unix, you knew that. I use Microsoft Core Fonts for the Web in the example programs.

Programming with sound may not be practical over remote connections, because of the difficulty of streaming sound. If using Unix emulation, you might check the emulator's sound capabilities – say, by playing a video.

If this is for a course…

C++ for Lazy Programmers covers through pointers, operator overloading, virtual functions, templates, exceptions, STL – everything you might reasonably expect in two semesters of C++.

The SSDL library does take a small amount of time, but the focus is firmly on writing good C++ programs, with SSDL there just to make the programs more enjoyable. How many labs or projects do you have in which it's hard to stop working because it's so much fun? It may not happen with *all* these problems, but I do see it happen.

SDL also gives a gentle introduction to event-driven programming.

In the first 12 chapters, there is emphasis on algorithm development and programming style, including early introduction of constants.

After Chapter 12, the examples are in standard I/O, though SDL is still an option for a few exercises and is used in Chapter 21 and (briefly) Chapter 26.

A normal two-semester sequence should cover approximately

- Semester 1: The first 12 chapters, using SDL; Chapter 13, introducing standard I/O. With some exceptions (& parameters, stream I/O), this looks a lot like C, and includes variables, expressions, functions, control structures, arrays, and stream I/O.
- Semester 2: Chapters 14–22, using standard I/O, covering pointers, character arrays, classes, operator overloading, templates, exceptions, virtual functions, multiple inheritance (briefly), and a taste of the Standard Template Library using vectors and linked lists.

Subsequent chapters cover material that wouldn't easily fit in two semesters, including more of the Standard Template Library, history of C++, C programming, and a few more esoteric topics.

Online Help

Here are some sites to go to for more information, with URLs correct at time of writing.

SDL: `www.libsdl.org`; click "Wiki." You'll find a reference for SDL functions.

SDL's helper libraries `SDL_Image`, `SDL_Mixer`, and `SDL_TTF`: `www.libsdl.org/projects/SDL_image/`, `www.libsdl.org/projects/SDL_mixer/`, and `www.libsdl.org/projects/SDL_ttf/`. In each case, click Documentation. You'll find references for their functions. If the web sites have changed, doing a web search for the name of the library (`SDL_image`, for example) should get you there.

Legal Stuff

Visual Basic, Visual Studio, Windows, Windows Vista, Excel, and Microsoft are trademarks of the Microsoft Corporation. All other trademarks referenced herein are property of their respective owners.

This book and its author are neither affiliated with nor authorized, sponsored, or approved by Microsoft Corporation.

Screenshots of Microsoft products are used with permission from Microsoft.

CHAPTER 1

Getting Started

Most programs in the first half of this book use the SDL and SSDL libraries,[1] on the theory that watching colorful shapes move across the screen and shoot each other is more interesting than printing text. Don't worry; when you're done, you'll be able to write programs both with and without this library – and if I have anything to say about it, you'll have had fun doing it. Let's see how it goes.

A simple program

It's wise to start small. Fewer things can go wrong.

So we'll start small here with a simple program that writes "Hello, world!" on the screen. We'll take it line by line to see what's in it. (In the next section, we'll compile and run it.)

Example 1-1. "Hello, world!" is a classic program to start off a new language with. (I think it's a law somewhere.)

```
//Hello, world! program, for _C++ for Lazy Programmers_
//  Your name goes here
//  Then the date[2]
```

[1]SDL provides graphics, sound, and friendly interaction including mouse input. SSDL, standing for *Simple* SDL, is a "wrapper" library that wraps SDL's functions in easier-to-use versions. Both libraries are described in more detail in the Introduction. Don't worry; I don't read introductions either.

[2]From here on, I'll be putting the title of the text, rather than name and date, because that's more useful for textbook examples. Ordinarily name of programmer and date are better for keeping track of what was done and who to track down if it doesn't work.

W. Briggs, *C++ for Lazy Programmers*, https://doi.org/10.1007/978-1-4842-5187-4_1

```
//It prints "Hello, world!" on the screen.
//    Quite an accomplishment, huh?

#include "SSDL.h"


int main (int argc, char** argv)
{
      sout << "Hello, world!  (Press any key to quit.)\n";

      SSDL_WaitKey ();       //Wait for user to hit any key


      return 0;
}
```

The first set of lines are comments. **Comments** look like this – `//Something on a line after two slashes` – and are there just for you or for someone who later tries to understand your program. It's best to be kind to yourself and your maintainers – help them easily know what the program's doing, without having to search and figure it out.

Next we have an `include` file. Some language features are built into the C++ compiler itself, like the comment markers `//` and `#include`. Other things are in libraries; they'll only be loaded if needed. In this case, we need to know how to print things on the screen using the SSDL library, so we load the include file `SSDL.h`.

Next we have the main program. `main ()` is special: it's what that tells the compiler, "This is what we're doing in the program; start here." The `int` at the start and the weird sequence `int argc, char** argv` we'll get in Chapter 26 under "Command-line arguments." Same for the `return 0;` at the end. For now, we always put these things in. If not, the C++ gods will punish us with incomprehensible error messages.

In this case, `main ()` only does two things.

First, it prints `"Hello, world"` using the `sout` object, pronounced "S-out."

Second, it calls `SSDL_WaitKey ()`, which waits for you to hit a key before ending the program. Otherwise the program closes before you have a chance to see its message.

We return `0` because `main ()` has to return something, largely for historical reasons. In practice we almost never care what `main` returns.

The curly braces `{}` tell `main ()` where to start taking action and where to end: whatever you want the computer to do when it runs the program goes between the curly braces.

The compiler is very picky about what you type. Leave off a `;` and the program won't compile. Change capitalization on something and C++ won't recognize it.

If you're curious what this program would have looked like without SSDL, see Chapter 29. It's not for the fainthearted beginner, but later it should make perfect sense.

Extra "Hello, world!" is often the first program a beginner writes in a new language. Although it was originally a simple example in C – the language C++ is descended from; more on that in Chapter 25 – the practice of writing this as the first program has spread. Here's "Hello, world!" in BASIC:

```
10 PRINT "Hello, world!"
```

Not bad, huh?

This is what it looks like in APL. APL (A Programming Language) has been described as a "write-only" language because it's said you can't read the programs you wrote yourself. APL requires symbols such as □, ∇, and ρ.

```
□←'Hello, world!'
```

Although those look easier than C++'s version, C++'s is neither the longest nor the toughest. I'll spare you the long ones to save trees (an example for the language Redcode took 158 lines, which may be why you've never heard of Redcode), but here's one of the tough ones, from a purposefully difficult language sometimes called BF.

```
++++++++++++++++[>++++>++++++>+++++++>+++>++<<<<-]>
++++++++.>+++++.+++++++..+++.>>----.>.<<+++++++.<.>
-----.<---.--------.>>>+.
```

More "Hello, world!" examples, at time of writing, can be found at `http://helloworldcollection.de/`.

Spacing

One thing the compiler *doesn't* care about is spacing. As long as you don't put a space inside a word, you can put it wherever you like. You can break lines or not as you choose; it won't care, as long as you don't break a `//comment` or a `"quotation"`.

Example 1-2. A blatant instance of evil and rude[3] in programming

```
//Hello, world! program, for _C++ for Lazy Programmers_
//It prints "Hello, world!" on the screen.
//Quite an accomplishment, huh?
//           -- from _C++ for Lazy Programmers_

             #include "SSDL.h"

                 int main (int argc, char** argv) {
     sout <<
"Hello, world!  (Press any key to quit.)\n";

                 SSDL_WaitKey ();     //Wait for user to hit any key

return 0;
     }
```

The compiler won't care about spacing – but the poor soul that has to understand your 500-page program will! Example 1-2's spacing would be a cruel thing to do to the people who later maintain your code.

Readability is a Good Thing.[4] The programmer struggling to figure what you meant may very well be you a few days after writing it. Most of the expense in software development is programmer time; you won't want to waste yours trying to decipher your own code. *Make it clear.*

[3]"Evil and rude" is a technical term meaning, essentially, "maliciously awful." See *The New Hacker's Dictionary*, currently online at `www.catb.org/jargon`, for other terms in programmers' slang.

[4]Good Thing: hacker slang for something that's completely wonderful and everybody knows it (or should).

Tip Make your code clear *as you write it*, not later. Readable code helps with development, not just future maintenance.

To help with clarity, I have things in Example 1-1, like initial comments, `#include`, and `main ()`, separated by **`blank lines`**. It's sort of like writing paragraphs in an English paper: each section is its own "paragraph." Blank lines increase readability.

I also break lines in sensible places and indent in a way that makes the program easy to read. The default **`indentation`** is the left margin. But if something is contained in something else – as the `sout` statement is contained in the main program – it gets indented one tab, or a few spaces.

This is like outline format for a paper, or like the layout of a table of contents (Figure 1-1). What's contained in something else is indented slightly. What's in Example 1-2 breaks the rule because `#include "SSDL.h"` isn't part of the comment above it, so it shouldn't be indented relative to it. `int main (int argc, char** argv)` isn't part of `#include "SSDL.h"`, so it shouldn't be indented either.

```
int main (int argc,
          char** argv)
{
        sout << "Hello, world!\n";

        SSDL_WaitKey ();

        return 0;
}
```

```
My wonderful paper

        Part One

        Part Two
                Reasons Part One is wrong
                    a.  Why those reasons fail
                    b.  Reassurance it's right
                Reasons Part Two is way better

        Conclusion
```

Figure 1-1. *Like an English paper outline, a C++ program is indented, with subparts indented relative to what they're parts of*

By contrast, the `sout` statement in Example 1-1 *is* contained in `main`, so it gets indented a little.

You'll have plenty of examples of clear indenting as you read on.

Golden Rule of Spacing

When something is part of what comes previously,

    it should be indented (like this).

When it's independent, it maintains the same indentation level.

Creating an SSDL project

...in Visual Studio

The easiest way to start is to

1. Make a copy of a working project folder. The source code has one named `basicSSDLProject`. It knows where to find SDL and SSDL in the source code, so keep your copy in the same location.
2. Rename it appropriately (`hello`, perhaps?).
3. Open its solution (`.sln`) file.[5]

If you want to make it from scratch, see instructions in source code.

Extra The first time you start up Visual Studio, it may ask you what default environment you'll want. Your answer is C++.

It may now take significant time setting up your profile. Don't worry; it's a one-time thing: you won't have to wait for it again.

If you make a mistake, you can fix it once you're in: select Tools ➤ Import and Export Settings ➤ Reset all settings.

[5]If you get a dialog box asking if you want to "Retarget Projects," just accept the defaults and press OK. This happens if your machine and my machine have slightly different versions of a Windows library.

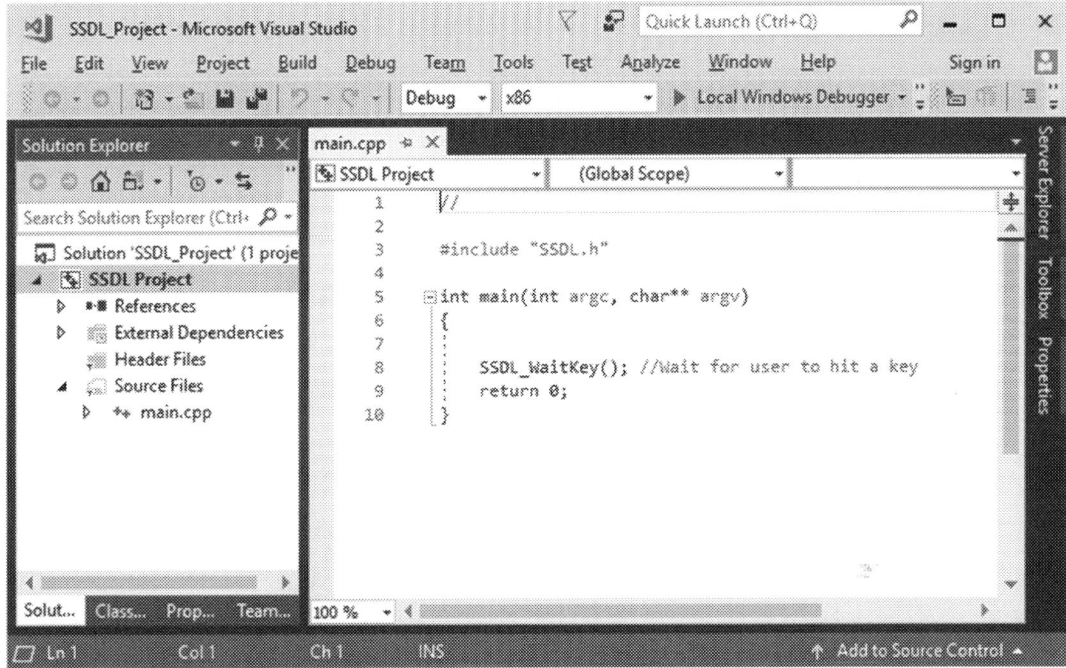

Figure 1-2. *An SSDL project. Click the triangle arrows next to SSDL Project on the right and then Source Files and then double-click main.cpp to see the main program's (incomplete) contents*

Compiling your program

Your program doesn't do anything yet, so you'll want to give it some content. For now, you might type in the Hello, world! program from Example 1-1.

Maybe you'll make some typos.

If so, the editor may warn you by putting a squiggly red line under what it objects to. Wave your mouse pointer over the offending portion and it'll give a hint as to what went wrong (though that hint may not always be clear).

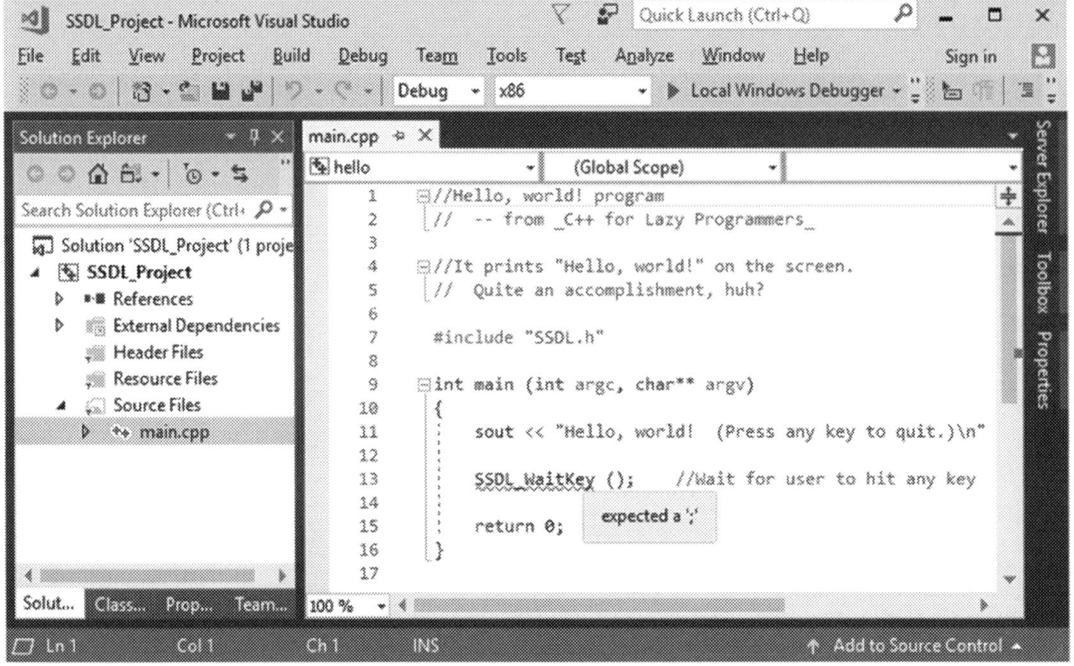

Figure 1-3. *Visual Studio highlights – and correctly identifies – an error*

Helpful as this is, though, you can't be certain the editor is correct. You won't know for sure if there are errors till you try to compile and run.

To compile your program, go to Build ➤ Build Solution. To run it, go to Debug ➤ Start without debugging.

Alternately, click the green arrow or triangle near the top of the window (see Figure 1-2 or Figure 1-3 again).

If your program doesn't compile, it will give you a list of errors. Sometimes it's clear what the messages mean, sometimes not. Here's a typical set, using "..." to make them briefer. In this case, I forgot a ; and misspelled SSDL_WaitKey:

```
c:\...\main.cpp(13): error C2146: syntax error: missing ';' before
identifier 'SDL_WaitKey'
c:\...\main.cpp(13): error C3861: 'SDL_WaitKey': identifier not found
```

As time goes by, you'll understand more of what obscure error messages mean. For now, compare the program you typed to Example 1-1, and repair any differences, until you get this successful result. (The program actually prints white on black, unlike what's shown in Figure 1-4 and some subsequent examples. Books, big black squares of ink, not a good mix.)

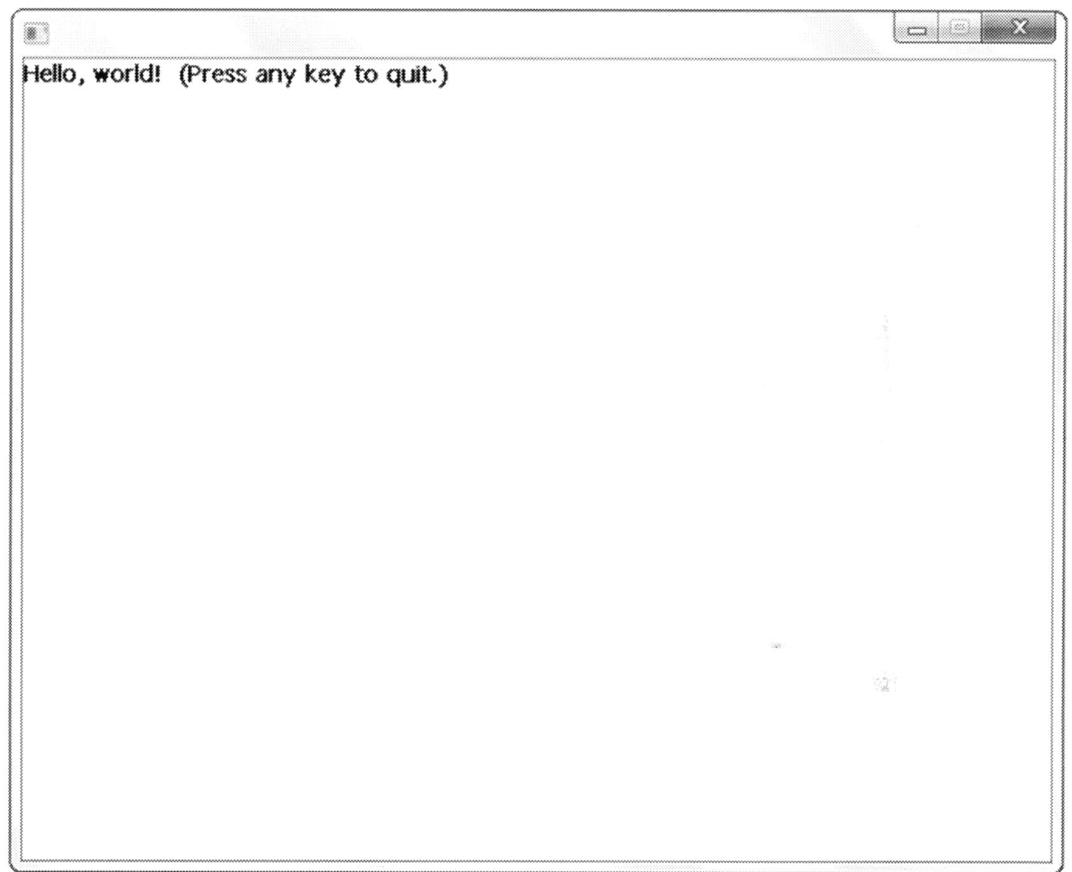

Figure 1-4. *Hello, world! running*

When it runs, hit any key to end it. (We often use the Escape key, since SSDL's set up to recognize Escape as a signal to quit, but any key will do for `SSDL_WaitKey`.)

Extra In Visual Studio, if you try to run an uncompiled program, you may see this dialog box:

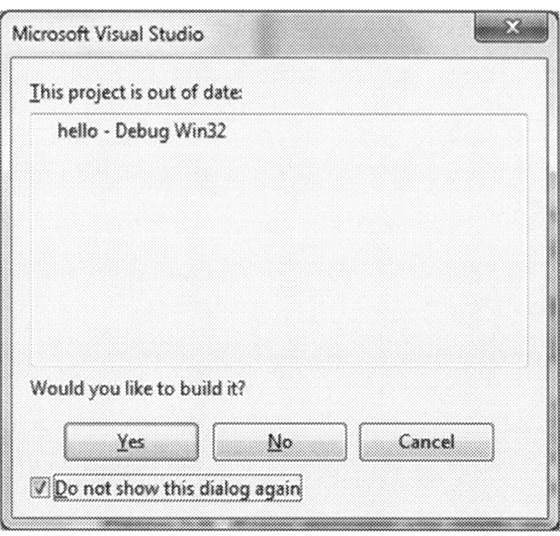

If so, click "Do not show this dialog again" as shown, and click "Yes." This means that it will always try to recompile before running if needed.

If there are errors, you'll likely see this box:

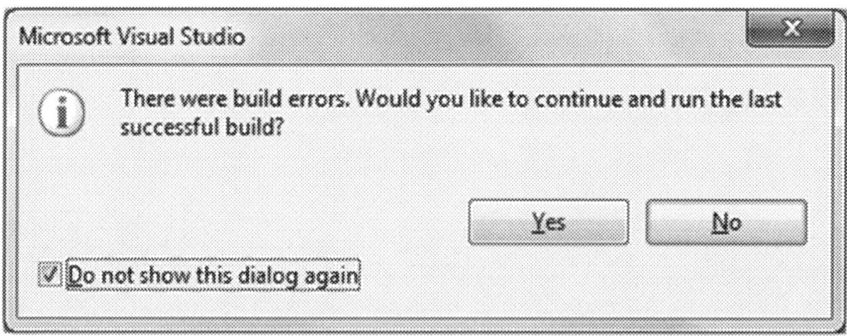

Click "Do not show this dialog again," and say no. (Otherwise when you make changes, it will go back to previous versions to find one that works, rather than your latest copy. Confusing!)

If you do want to see the dialog boxes again – say, if you hit "Yes" when you meant "No" – you can fix it through the menus: Tools ➤ Options ➤ Projects and Solutions ➤ Build and Run, and reset the "On Run…" blanks to what you want.

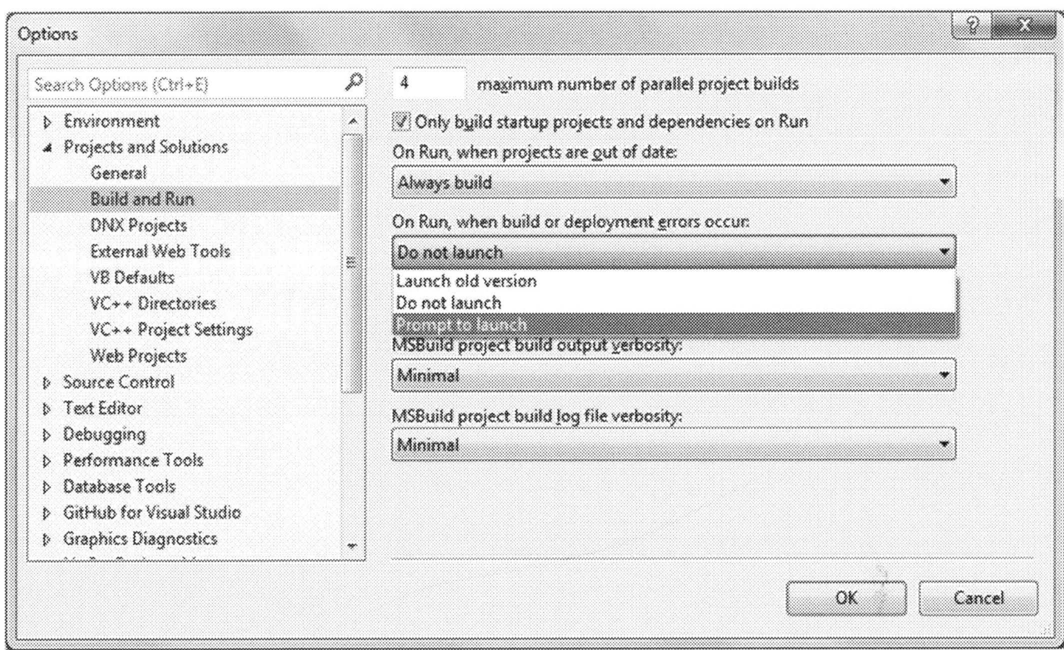

The files you created

Look through your folder now. (Access it through Windows Explorer or by opening its folder in Windows, whichever you like.) You should see something like Figure 1-5. (The layout may be different.)

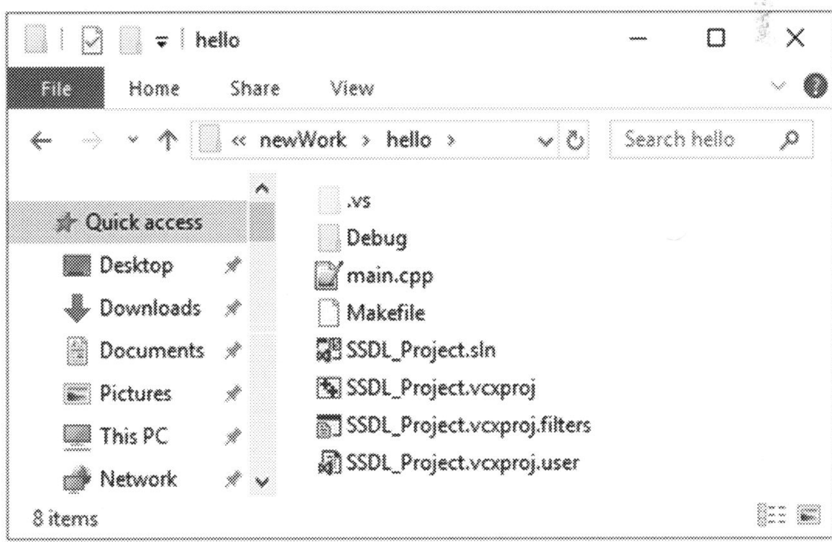

Figure 1-5. *Files in your project folder*

Extra If the files you see are named SSDL_Project rather than SSDL_Project-dot-something, I ***VERY STRONGLY RECOMMEND*** that you change this so you can see the "file extensions" after the dot. It's not essential, but it's often helpful to see what kind of file you're working with!

To do that, in the View tab of a folder, select Options ➤ Change folder and search options (Windows 8 or earlier: Organize Menu ➤ Folder and Search Options).

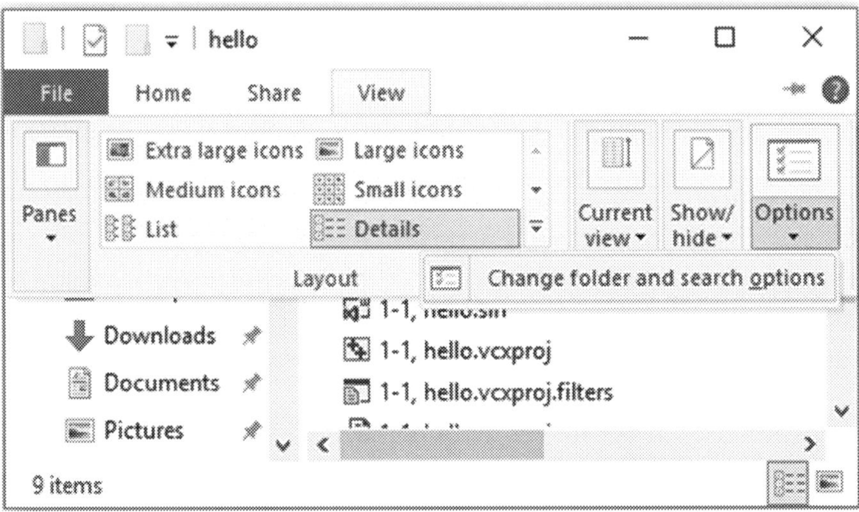

You should get a box that says Folder Options.

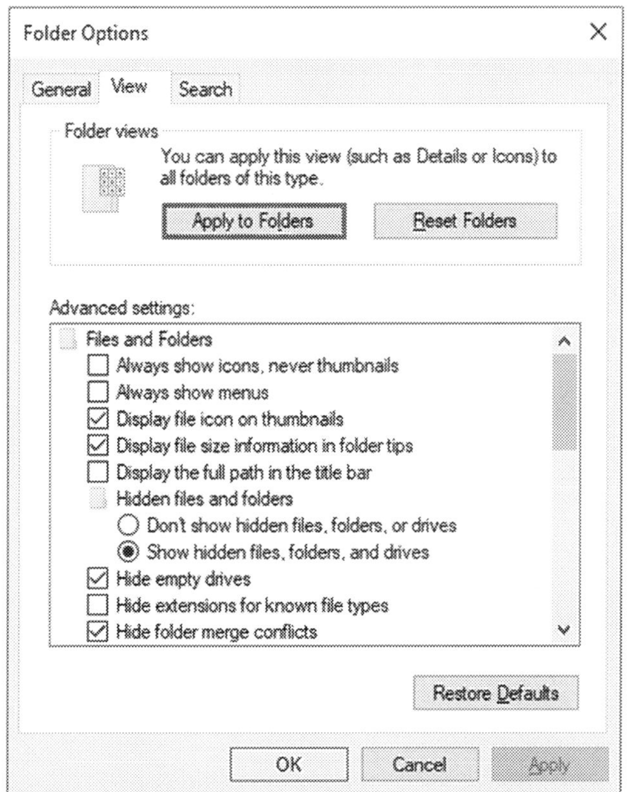

Select the View tab of the Folder Options box. Once there, uncheck Hide extensions for known file types; and select Show hidden files, folders, or drives. (The latter enables you to erase some things later that are bulky, don't need to be stored, and are not otherwise visible.)

Important files in your folder include

- `hello.sln`, the "solution" file: The main file that knows where the other files are.
- `hello.vcxproj`, the "project" file: It knows that the program is stored in `main.cpp` and a few other things. You can't compile without it.

- `main.cpp`, your program.
- The Debug (or, sometimes, `x64`) folder, which contains your executable.

Tip You can erase the Debug, .vs, and x64 folders, and .sdf or .ncb files if any. Visual Studio will re-create them as needed. This is important if space is crucial, for example, if you plan to send the folder by email.

If you can't see the `.vs` folder, then Show hidden files, etc., as shown in the preceding image.

Reopening your project

If your computer is set up properly, you can double-click `hello.sln` to start Visual Studio and reopen what you were working on. (Double-clicking on other things might not open all the files you need.) You can also open the compiler and drag `hello.sln` into the main window, ignoring the text that's already there. Or you can go through the menus: File ➤ Open ➤ Project/Solution.

Tip Reopen the `.sln` file, not the `.vcxproj` or `.cpp` files.

Antibugging

In the "Antibugging" sections, we'll consider things that can go wrong and how to repair or prevent them.

Here are some of the common or difficult problems you'll find using Microsoft Visual Studio (or other compilers, for that matter):

- **Visual Studio asks you to log in with a Microsoft account and you're in a rush.** Notice the line "Not now, maybe later."
- **It can't open an include file or a `.lib` file.** In the error messages, it may say something like

  ```
  fatal error C1083: Cannot open include file: 'SSDL.h': No such
  file or directory
  ```

  or

  ```
  1>LINK : fatal error LNK1104: cannot open file 'sdl2_ttf.lib'
  ```

  The most likely explanation at this point is that your project folder isn't in the right place in the source code repository. Make sure it's in the same place as the `basicSSDLProject` folder. If you know what you're doing and chose a different setup, be sure the Additional Include Directories and Additional Library Directories contain valid paths to SDL's and SSDL's include and library folders.
- **It's happy to accept your edits, but doesn't offer you an option to compile; or if it does, the edits don't seem to have any effect.** The problem is likely that you didn't open the `.sln` file, but instead

opened `main.cpp` (or some other file). Visual Studio needs its `.sln` file. Close the file you're working on (saving it someplace so you can use those edits!) and reopen by double-clicking the `.sln` file.

- **You type something in that it should recognize, but the editor doesn't color it the way you'd expect, or puts a squiggly red line under it.** Usually it will recognize `return` and `void`, and color them to show it knows they're keywords. You may have a typo. Or the editor may be confused. Recompile to be sure.
- **It says the `.exe` file cannot be opened for writing.** You're probably still running the program; it can't overwrite the program because it's in use. Kill the program and try again.
- **It gives some other error message and won't finish building.** Often, trying again is enough to make it work.
- **It's taking forever to finish running the program.** You can be patient or kill it through Windows Task Manager. If it keeps happening, it's a good bet there's a problem with your program. (Or is it waiting for you to give it a response?)
- **You read a complaint about Windows SDK:**

  ```
  C:\...\Microsoft.Cpp.WindowsSDK.targets(46,5): error
  MSB8036: The Windows SDK version <some number or other>
  was not found. <More details.>
  ```

  or else it just fails before attempting to compile.

  Solution: right-click the project (not the solution or `main.cpp`), select Retarget Projects, and agree to what it says.

Extra Zip Files

You may want to email someone your project; or you may want to store it compactly.

The usual way is to right-click the folder and select Add to Zip (or Add to `<folder name>.zip`); or right-click the folder, select Send to... ➤ Compressed Folder. Then you can attach it to an email, if that's your plan.

However you do it, be sure you first erase (if they exist) `Debug`, `.vs`, any `.ncb` or `.sdf` files, to save space. Especially `Debug`: if you don't, some mail programs won't send the attachment.

...with g++

g++[6] has much to recommend it: free, open source, and when someone says "*Real* programmers use Unix," you don't have to duck your head. But it doesn't have its own environment or editor. On Unix, you might use **vi/vim** (I'm not that "real," but maybe you are), **emacs**,[7] or some other editor. If you're doing this through a windowing environment, you'll likely find getting started relatively painless. If not, you can find instructions online. Good luck!

Tip Unix and Windows disagree on how to end a line. If you move a file designed on one system to the other and read it, you may see everything apparently jammed on one line, or sporting a `^M` at the end of each line.

If it's a Windows file displayed in Unix, you can just ignore the funny symbols. If it's a Unix file and you're in Windows, try Notepad++ or Microsoft's WordPad. For a program to convert to your preferred format, see "Cool command-line tricks" below.

I'll leave the details of the editor and how to get around the operating system to other sources[8] and go straight to compiling. The easiest way is to make a copy of the `basicSSDLProject` folder found in the book's source code repository to use as your new project (try `cp -R`) and follow the instructions in `README.txt`.

---

[6]If g++ isn't installed or isn't working, see Appendix A: Setting up SDL and SSDL - problems.

[7]For a quick start with emacs, you might try A Guided Tour of Emacs currently at `www.gnu.org/software/emacs/tour/`. For an even quicker start, go to "Basic editing commands" and skip over the first table.

[8]I recommend UNIX Tutorial for Beginners currently at `www.ee.surrey.ac.uk/Teaching/Unix/`. Up through Tutorial 4 should be fine for now. Or search for your own.

The files you created

In your new folder, type `ls` or `dir` at the prompt. You'll see some files, possibly `a.out`

```
main.cpp main.cpp~ main.o #and a bunch of other stuff
```

`a.out` is the executable program. `main.cpp` is the code you wrote to make it. `main.cpp~` is a backup file your editor may make of your `.cpp` file. `main.o` is an "object" file g++ may build on the way to creating your program. If you see it – you may not – it's perfectly safe to delete it: `rm main.o`

To delete all the things listed here that you don't need, type `make clean`.

Cool command-line tricks

- **Repeating a command.** Often at the command prompt, you can hit up arrow to repeat the last command, or several times to repeat an earlier command. If that doesn't work, ! followed by the first few letters of the command may repeat the last instance of it.
- **Converting code from the Windows world into Unix and back.** If you care to, you can find an online converter, or (if it's installed) use this command:

  ```
  dos2unix < windowsfile.txt > unixfile
  ```

  To go the other way, use `unix2dos`.

Extra `tar` Files

Want to stuff that directory into a single file for mailing or storage? After erasing any bulky files you don't want (`make clean`), go up a directory (`cd ..`) and `tar` it:

```
tar -czvf project1.tar.gz project1 #for a directory named
project1
```

You should now have a file `project1.tar.gz`, suitable for sending as an attachment by your favorite mailer.

To unstuff it, put it wherever you want to put it (ensuring there isn't already a `project1` directory there, to prevent overwrite) and say

```
tar -xzvf project1.tar.gz
```

Unix installations vary; you may have to change the command slightly – but that works as is on many machines.

Antibugging

- **You run the program, and it never stops.** It might be waiting for some input (like hitting a key to continue), or it might have gone into la-la land forever. You can kill it with Ctrl-C (hold Ctrl down and hit C).
- **It stops with the message** `Segmentation fault: core dumped`. This means, more or less, "Something bad happened." For now, just remove the core file (`rm core`) and look in the program for the problem.

How not to be miserable

These are problems you may encounter no matter what compiler you're using:

- **You get about a zillion errors.** This doesn't mean you did a zillion things wrong. Sometimes one error confuses the compiler so much it thinks everything that came later is wrong. For this reason, it's wise to **fix the first error first**. It may eliminate a hundred subsequent error messages.
- **The line the error's on looks fine.** Maybe the problem is on the previous line. The compiler couldn't tell what was wrong until the next line, so it reported the error later than you'd have expected. This often happens with missing **;**'s.
- **You get warnings, but the program's still ready to run. Should you?** There are errors, and there are warnings. The compiler can still generate the program if it only gave warning, but an error prevents compilation. You can ignore warnings, but they're often good hints as to something that really does need fixing.

- **Every program you write! it seems, starts out full of errors. You wonder if you're stupid.** If so, well, so are the rest of us. I might be able to get a Hello, world! program working the first time. Anything longer, forget it.

And here's the big one:

- **You made a mistake and the program, which had been doing mostly OK, now won't work at all.** Whenever you make a significant change (significant meaning "enough you're scared you might not be able to undo it")...
    - Windows: Go to the folder that has your project in it (`.sln` file, `.vcxproj`, .cpp, all of it); copy it; paste it (skipping any file it won't let you copy – it'll be something you don't care about anyway), thus creating a backup.
    - Unix: Copy your `.cpp` file by saying something like `cp main.cpp main.cpp.copy1`. You could also copy the entire directory with `cp -R`.

  A trail of backup copies is absolutely essential for big projects. I urge you to go ahead and get into practice now. If not...you've worked 6 months on your project. You did something that made it crash, or refuse to compile, or give the wrong output; worse yet, you did it yesterday and you've done several updates since. Wouldn't it be nice to go back to yesterday's code and get the almost working version, rather than recreating 6 months of work? Backup copies are what every programmer, lazy or not, needs.

Golden Rule of Not Pulling Your Hair Out

Make backup copies as you edit your program. *Lots* of them.

EXERCISES

1. Using your compiler, type in the Hello, world! program, and get it working.
2. Write another program to print the lyrics of a song on the screen.
3. Take the Hello, world! program and deliberately introduce errors: take out semicolons or curly braces; break a quote in the middle; try several different things. What kind of error messages do you get? Some will likely make sense (as in, "`missing ';' before '}'`"); others may not. The number of errors really doesn't tell you how many mistakes there are.
4. Clean up your folder (i.e., remove those extra, bulky files) and compress it.

Shapes and the functions that draw them

Let's have a look again at that blank window you created the first time you ran an SSDL program.

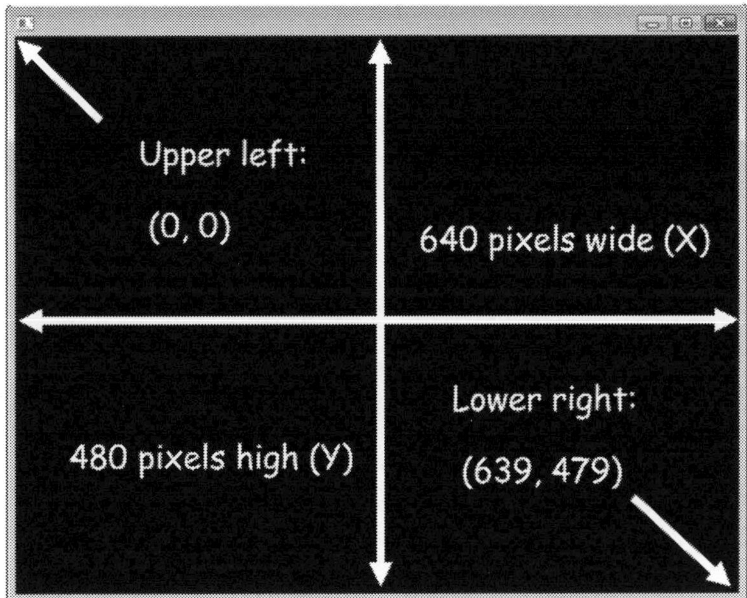

Figure 1-6. *Dimensions of the basic SSDL window*

Locations of shapes we put into this window are in (X, Y) coordinates (see Figure 1-6). The upper left corner is (0, 0); the lower right is (639, 479) – so the Y coordinates go *down* the page, not up. There are 640 locations going across (0 through 639 inclusive) and 480 going down. Each (X, Y) location is called a "pixel" (picture element).

This section shows some things you can do.

Example 1-3. Program to draw a dot at the center of the screen

```
// Draw a dot at the center of the screen
//              -- from _C++ for Lazy Programmers_

#include "SSDL.h"

int main (int argc, char** argv)
{
        //draws a dot at the center position (320, 240)
        SSDL_RenderDrawPoint (320, 240);

        SSDL_WaitKey ();

        return 0;
}
```

Example 1-3 draws a dot at location (320, 240). (It won't be as big as in Figure 1-7, but I wanted it to show up, so I enhanced it.)

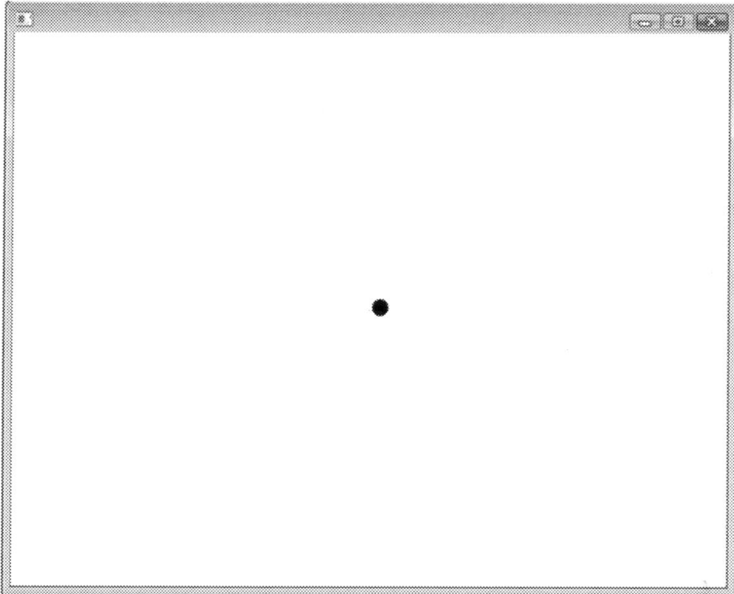

Figure 1-7. *Drawing a dot at the center of the screen*

Functions for other basic shapes are listed in Table 1-1. `int` means integer, that is, whole number. The function descriptions of form `void <function-name> (<bunch of stuff>);` are called "prototypes": precise descriptions of how to call the function – its name and what kind of values it expects between the `()`s.

Table 1-1. *Common SSDL drawing functions*

`void SSDL_RenderDrawPoint (int x, int y);`	draws a dot at (x, y)
`void SSDL_RenderDrawLine (int x1, int y1, int x2, int y2);`	draws a line from (x1, y1) to (x2, y2)
`void SSDL_RenderDrawCircle (int x, int y, int radius) ;`	draws a circle with this radius, centered at (x, y)
`void SSDL_RenderFillCircle (int x, int y, int radius) ;`	draws a filled circle with this radius, centered at (x, y)
`void SSDL_RenderDrawRect (int x1, int y1, int w, int h);`	draws a box with (x1, y1) as its top left corner and with width w and height h
`void SSDL_RenderFillRect (int x1, int y1, int w, int h);`	draws a filled box with (x1, y1) as its top left corner, with width w and height h

The notation is worth paying attention to. `SSDL_RenderDrawPoint` takes two integers for its two arguments x and y. `SSDL_RenderDrawLine` takes four: x1, y1, x2, y2, and so on.

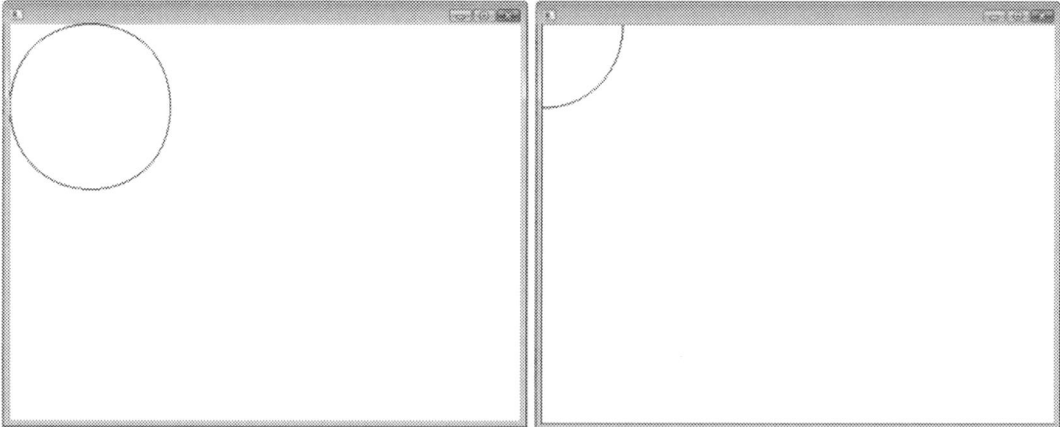

Figure 1-8. *On the left, a program with `SSDL_RenderDrawCircle (100, 100, 100);` on the right, a program with `SSDL_RenderDrawCircle (0, 0, 100);`. The one on the right illustrates "clipping": SDL simply not showing things that are outside the viewing area*

This line of code, for example, makes a circle near the top left (see Figure 1-8, left image): `SSDL_RenderDrawCircle (100, 100, 100);`

And this one gives you one *centered* on the top left (Figure 1-8, right), so you can only see a quarter of it: `SSDL_RenderDrawCircle (0, 0, 100);`. Not showing what would be outside the viewing area is called "clipping."

To make an interesting design, you'll need to plan ahead. We'll have a section on planning ahead more generally soon, but for now, you might make a storyboard, like movie producers or comic makers, for whatever design you want to make.

You may want graph paper as in Figure 1-9. (See also the source code.)

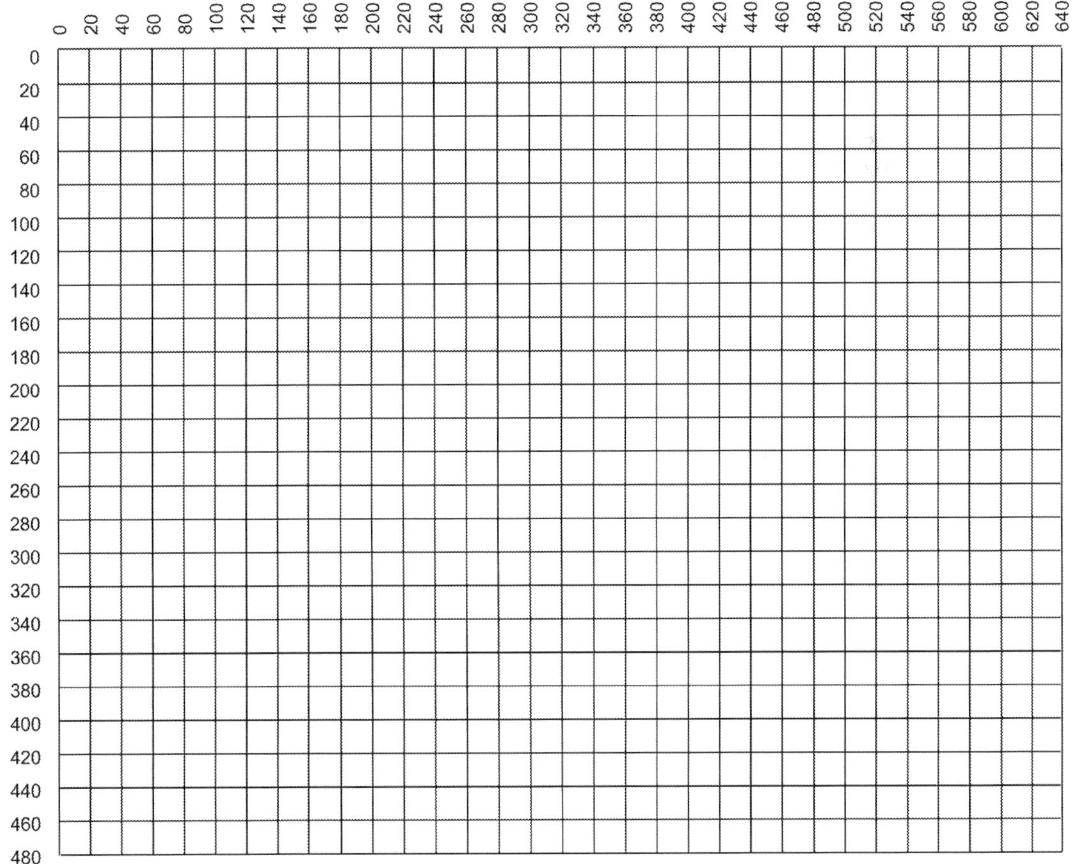

***Figure 1-9.** A graph of the viewing area for designing what you want to display*

I decided to make a bug face: big eyes, big head, antennas. So I drew what I wanted (Figure 1-10).

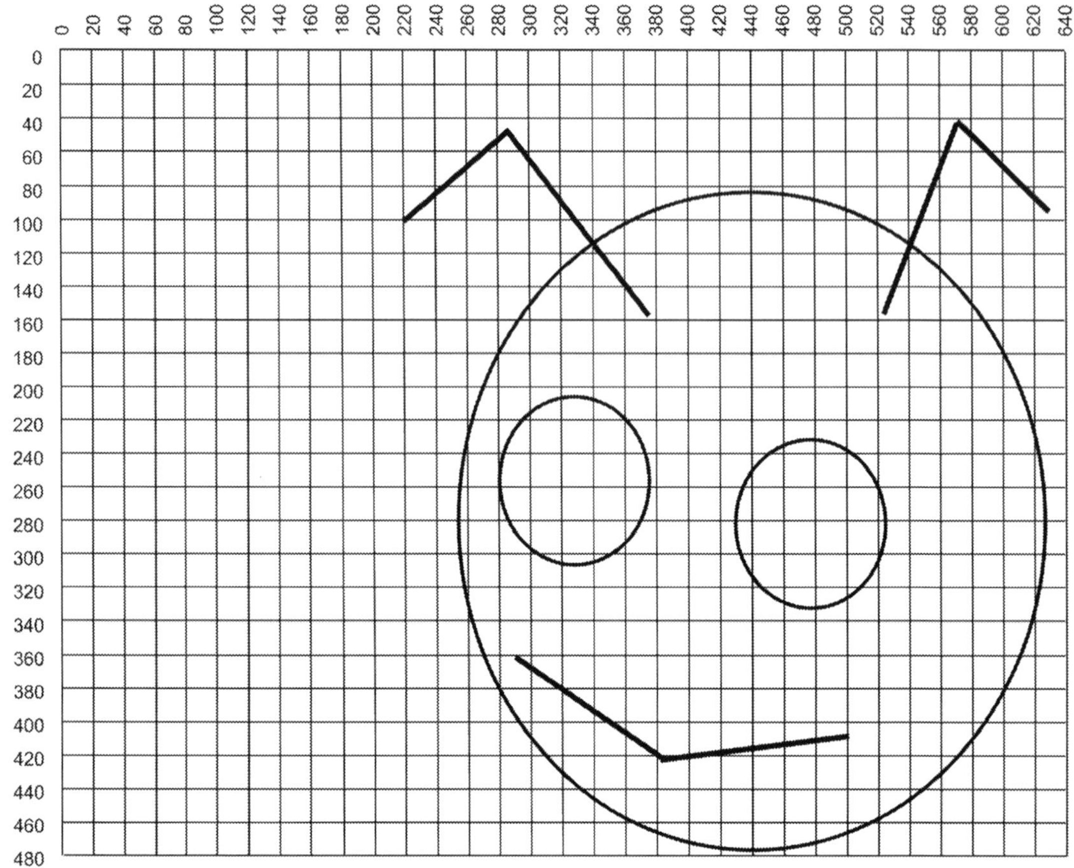

Figure 1-10. *Drawing for the bug head program*

I can now eyeball the locations. The center of the left eye is around (320, 250), and its radius is roughly 45; the big circle's center is around (430, 250), and its radius is about 150; and so on.

My program is in Example 1-4. I made several mistakes initially as I wrote it – confusing diameter with radius; reading the graph lines wrong. You will too. If you don't, well, that's true resume fodder.

Example 1-4. A bug's head

```
//Bug's head example
//      -- from _C++ for Lazy Programmers_

//Program to draw a cartoonish bug's head on the screen
```

```
#include "SSDL.h"

int main (int argc, char** argv)
{
      SSDL_RenderDrawCircle (430, 250, 200);  //draw the bug's head

      SSDL_RenderDrawCircle (320, 250,  45);  //the left eye
      SSDL_RenderDrawCircle (470, 270,  45);  //the right eye

      SSDL_RenderDrawLine (360, 140, 280, 40);//left antenna
      SSDL_RenderDrawLine (280,  40, 210, 90);

      SSDL_RenderDrawLine (520, 140, 560, 40);//right antenna
      SSDL_RenderDrawLine (560,  40, 620, 80);

      SSDL_RenderDrawLine (290, 350, 372, 410);//the smile
      SSDL_RenderDrawLine (372, 410, 490, 400);

      SSDL_WaitKey ();                        //Wait for user to hit a key

      return 0;
}
```

The resulting output is shown here.

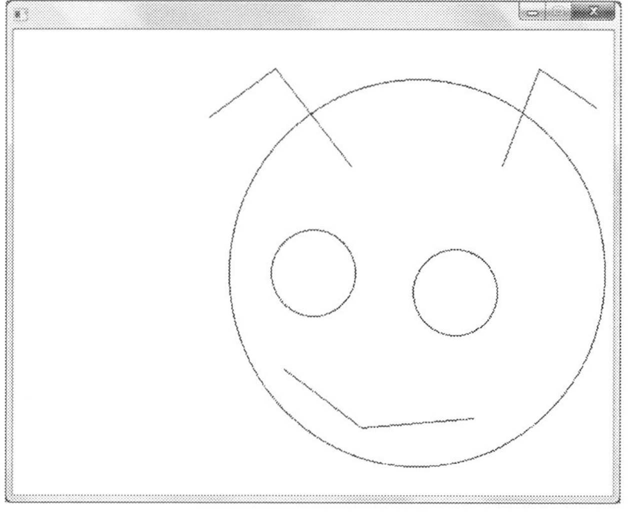

Notice how I rigorously documented in comments the purpose of everything I'm doing. Suppose I hadn't put those comments in:

```
//Program to draw a cartoonish bug's
//  head on the screen
//  -- from _C++ for Lazy Programmers_

#include "SSDL.h"

int main (int argc, char** argv)
{
      SSDL_RenderDrawCircle (430, 250, 200);
      SSDL_RenderDrawCircle (320, 250,  45);
      SSDL_RenderDrawCircle (470, 270,  45);
      SSDL_RenderDrawLine (360, 140, 280, 40);
      SSDL_RenderDrawLine (280,  40, 210, 90);
      SSDL_RenderDrawLine (520, 140, 560, 40);
      SSDL_RenderDrawLine (560,  40, 620, 80);
      SSDL_RenderDrawLine (290, 350, 372, 410);
      SSDL_RenderDrawLine (372, 410, 490, 400);

      SSDL_WaitKey ();

      return 0;
}
```

What a nightmare! You come back in a few months to reuse or upgrade this program, see the code, and think, what the heck was I doing? Which line does what?

Then you try to run it, and...your system administrator has upgraded compilers or libraries, and the program no longer works. (It's a well-known fact that software rots; at least, *something* makes your programs stop working over time.) You have a nonworking program, and it will take detective work to identify what the parts are.

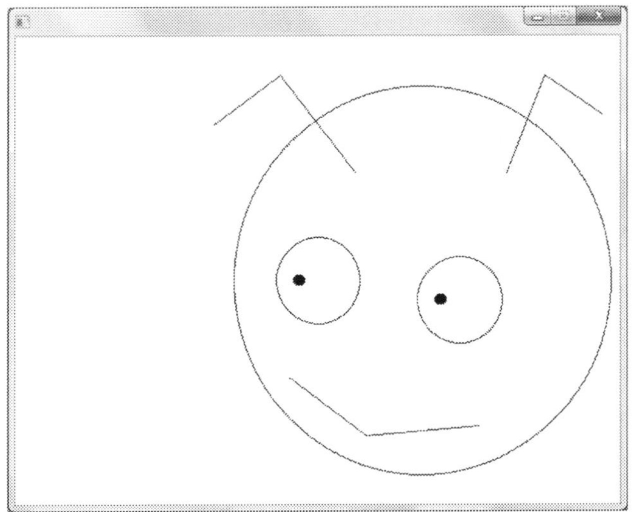

Better to comment, so you can understand, maintain, and update your program as needed. In Example 1-5 I decide to add pupils to the eyes. It's easy to figure where they go, given the commenting.

Example 1-5. A bug's head, with pupils in the eyes

```
//Bug's head example
//      -- from _C++ for Lazy Programmers_

//Program to draw a cartoonish bug's head on the screen
//Uncomment the "pupil" lines to see the pupils too

#include "SSDL.h"

int main (int argc, char** argv)
{
      SSDL_RenderDrawCircle (430, 250, 200);      //draw the bug's head

      SSDL_RenderDrawCircle (320, 250,  45);      //the left eye
      SSDL_RenderFillCircle (300, 250,   5);      // ... and its pupil
      SSDL_RenderDrawCircle (470, 270,  45);      //the right eye
      SSDL_RenderFillCircle (450, 270,   5);      // ... and its pupil
      ...
}
```

Antibugging

- **You call an SSDL function, but it has no effect.** At this point the most likely guess is that it's drawing things outside the viewing area, so you can't see them. The best way to determine what's wrong is to examine the arguments you gave and be sure they're reasonable.
- **(For Visual Studio) You can't remember exactly how to call a function, and you don't want to look it up.** That's no bug, but it is a reality, and it shows admirable laziness, so let's roll with it. You can sometimes get a hint as you type

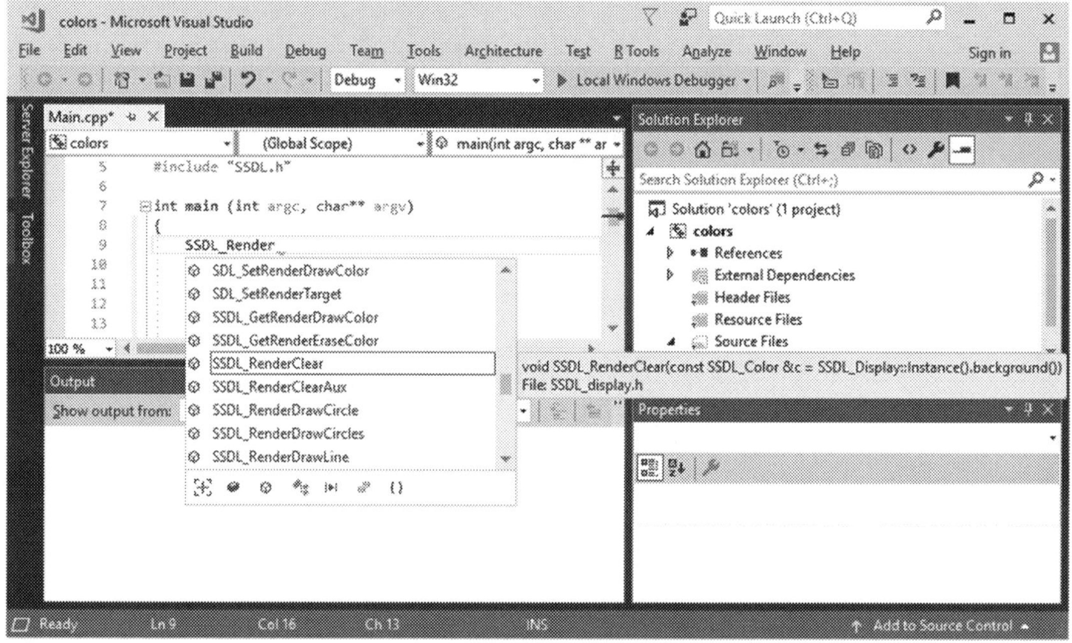

or, when you open the parentheses, it may give you a description of the function or what it expects

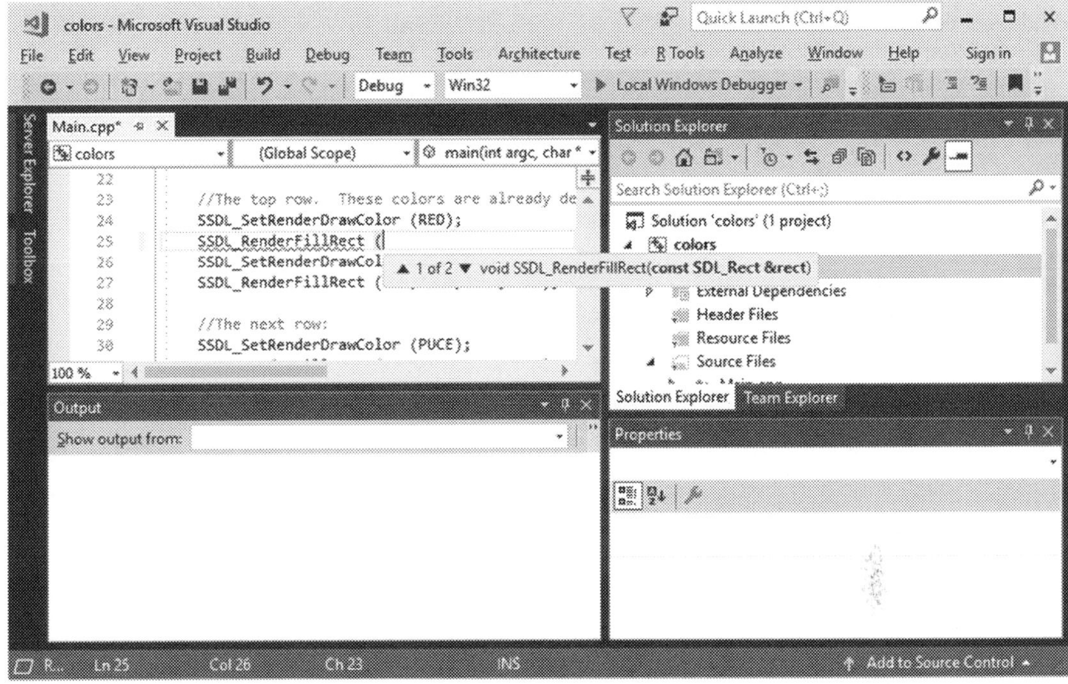

...and sometimes it won't show up. Or it puts the red squiggly lines on things that are perfectly OK. You can try retyping the line or compiling the code – one of those will usually do it.

EXERCISES

1. Design something of your own, and write a program to show it on the screen.
2. Draw a cube as seen not quite straight on, like the one shown here.

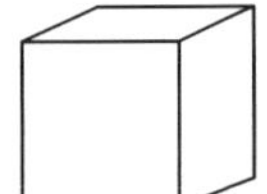

`const`s and colors

Naturally we'll want to color our shapes too.

Colors on computers come in three parts: red, green, and blue. In our library they range from 0 (lowest) to 255 (highest). So black is 0, 0, 0; white is 255, 255, 255; red is 255, 0, 0 (red at max, the others at zero). Other combinations make other colors. You can use a web site like www.colorpicker.com to find the red, green, blue components of a color you want.

You can use a few colors built into SSDL (BLACK, WHITE, RED, GREEN, or BLUE) or create your own color thus:

```
const SSDL_Color MAHOGANY = SSDL_CreateColor  (192,  64,   0);
```

Here, SSDL_Color MAHOGANY says we're creating a color and naming it MAHOGANY. SSDL_CreateColor (192, 64, 0) gives it the numbers we want.

Colors don't change, so we'll use C++'s const keyword to emphasize this and prevent them from changing by mistake. Constants are written in ALL CAPS to make it obvious to the reader of the program that they don't change. (You get used to it, and it's unmistakable.)

To use the color in the next thing drawn or printed, do this:

```
SSDL_SetRenderDrawColor (RED);    //Draw things in RED, from now
                                  // till the next call to this function
```

To clear the screen, either do this:

```
SSDL_RenderClear (BLACK);         //erase the screen and make it BLACK
```

or this:

```
SSDL_SetRenderEraseColor (DARK_GREY);
SSDL_RenderClear ();
```

Example 1-6 uses built-in and new colors to draw boxes on the screen.

Example 1-6. Use of colors to paint some rectangles

```
//Displays boxes of colors
//    -- from _C++ for Lazy Programmers_

#include "SSDL.h"

int main (int argc, char** argv)
{
```

```
    SSDL_SetWindowTitle ("Four squares in different colors");

    //We'll use 3 built-in colors, and 3 new ones
    const SSDL_Color PUCE       = SSDL_CreateColor (127,  90,  88);
    const SSDL_Color MAHOGANY   = SSDL_CreateColor (192,  64,   0);
    const SSDL_Color DARK_GREY  = SSDL_CreateColor (100, 100, 100);

    //Make a dark grey background
    SSDL_SetRenderEraseColor (DARK_GREY);
    SSDL_RenderClear ();

    //We'll have two boxes across, and two down

    //The top row. These colors are already defined in SSDL.h.
    SSDL_SetRenderDrawColor   (RED);
    SSDL_RenderFillRect       (   0,    0, 100, 100);
    SSDL_SetRenderDrawColor   (GREEN);
    SSDL_RenderFillRect       (100,   0, 100, 100);

    //The next row, using new colors
    SSDL_SetRenderDrawColor    (PUCE);
    SSDL_RenderFillRect        (    0, 100, 100, 100);
    SSDL_SetRenderDrawColor    (MAHOGANY);
    SSDL_RenderFillRect        (100, 100, 100, 100);

    //Program's end.
    //Have to set the color back to white here,
    //  or we'll get mahogany text!
    SSDL_SetRenderDrawColor (WHITE);
    sout << "Hit any key to end.\n";

    SSDL_WaitKey();

    return 0;
}
```

And here are functions relevant to colors and clearing the screen. Some of these prototypes don't precisely match the descriptions in the appendices: the descriptions are simplified, but close enough.

`SSDL_Color SSDL_CreateColor (int r, int g, int b);`[9]	create and return a color. Max values for (r)ed, (g)reen, and (b)lue are 255
`void SSDL_SetRenderDrawColor (SSDL_Color c);`[10]	set subsequent drawing, including text, to use color c
`void SSDL_SetRenderEraseColor (SSDL_Color c);`	set erasing (including clearing of the screen) to use color c
`SSDL_Color SSDL_GetRenderDrawColor ();`	return current drawing color. For example: `const SSDL_Color FOREGROUND = SSDL_GetRenderDrawColor();`
`SSDL_Color SSDL_GetRenderEraseColor ();`	return current erasing color
`void SSDL_RenderClear ();`	clear the screen to current erasing color
`void SSDL_RenderClear (SSDL_Color c);`	clear screen to color c

Some functions (the ones returning `void`) don't calculate a value for you; they just do something (like drawing a shape, clearing the screen, or setting a color). Others, like `SSDL_CreateColor ()`, have the job of calculating an answer. This one finds a color, so its "return type" is not `void`, but `SSDL_Color`.

We will cover functions and return types further in Chapter 7.

[9]You can also give an optional fourth argument, "alpha," that can make the color transparent:

```
SSDL_Color SSDL_CreateColor (int r, int g, int b, int alpha);
```

Alpha ranges from 0 (completely transparent) to 255 (completely opaque). For example,

```
const SSDL_Color GHOSTLY_GREY =SSDL_CreateColor (100, 100, 100, 128);
```

gives us a color that is about halfway transparent.

We won't use this, since we rarely want transparent geometric shapes, and the PNG format we'll use for images allows transparency without any special handling. But it's there if you want to experiment.

[10]Some of these functions have their descriptions simplified to be understandable based on what we've covered so far. The correct versions are in Appendix H – but simplified is fine for now.

EXERCISES

1. Add color to a program you wrote to draw figures on the screen or to another program from this book.
2. Make a scene for your favorite holiday: an orange scary face for Halloween, a green Christmas tree, or get wild with Holi, the Festival of Colors.
3. Make the screen flash a variety of colors by alternating calls to `SSDL_RenderClear` with calls to `SSDL_WaitKey`.
4. Write the names of several colors, each written in that color ("RED" written in red, etc.).

Text

`sout`, escape sequences, and fonts

You can print multiple things with the SSDL library's `sout` – not just text but also numbers.

```
sout << "The number pi is " << 3.14159 << ".\n";
sout << "...and the number e is "
     << 2.71828
     << ".\n";
```

How you space the lines in your program doesn't change what's printed; the line ends when you reach the `\n` character, the "end of line" character. The only reason for spacing the lines of code one way rather than another is for clarity's sake. (The preceding version looks fine to me.)

But the spacing inside the quotes *does* matter. Note the space I put after the word "is": if you don't put it, your first line of output will look like this:

```
The number pi is3.14159.
```

There are other **escape sequences**, a.k.a. "escape codes": special characters that start with \:

- `\t`, the tab character, which takes you to the next tab stop. The tab stops are arranged at 0, 8 spaces, 16 spaces, and so on. (Since most of our fonts are variable-width, we can't expect 8 I's or 8 M's to be the same width as 8 spaces; it will be approximate.)
- `\"`, the " character. If we just put " in your text, like so– `"Quoth the raven, "Nevermore""` – C++ would be confused by the extra "'s. So we write it like this instead:

  `"Quoth the raven, \"Nevermore.\""`
- `\\`, the \ character. (Because a single \ character has C++ trying to figure out what escape sequence you're starting.)

For all available escape sequences, see Appendix E.

You may also decide where on the screen you want the text to appear. Here's how to **set the cursor** at X position 100, Y position 50:

```
SSDL_SetCursor (100, 50);
```

And you can change the **font and font size**. Font files must be in TTF (TrueType Font) format; C++ expects them to be in the same folder as your project.

```
const SSDL_Font FONT = SSDL_OpenFont ("myFont.ttf", 18);  //my font; 18 point
SSDL_SetFont (FONT);
```

If you want to use a font that comes with the system, one in the standard fonts folder, you can use this call instead:

```
const SSDL_Font FONT =   SSDL_OpenSystemFont ("verdana.ttf", 18);
                                                        //Verdana font; 18 point
SSDL_SetFont (FONT);
```

You can see available fonts from Microsoft Windows/Microsoft Core Fonts for the Web by looking in Microsoft Word or (at time of writing) at `https://en.wikipedia.org/wiki/Core_fonts_for_the_Web`. The filenames aren't always obvious, for example, what shows up as "Bookman Old Style" in Microsoft Word is actually four files: `bookos.ttf`, `bookosb.ttf`, `bookosbi.ttf`, and `bookosi.ttf` – corresponding to normal, bold, bold italic, and italic.

In Unix, you can likely get a list of installed fonts with this command: fc-list. They'll probably be in /usr/share/fonts or a subfolder thereof.

The SDL2_ttf library is happy to make a font you give it italic, bold, whatever, but it can't compete with human artists. Where possible, use the enhanced version that comes in the font, as with Timer_New_Roman_Bold.ttf or timesbd.ttf for Times New Roman Bold.[11]

Example 1-7 illustrates use of these features.

Example 1-7. Using escape sequences, cursor, and fonts to print a poem

```
//Prints an excerpt from Sir Walter Scott's _The Lady of the Lake_
//      -- from _C++ for Lazy Programmers_

#include "SSDL.h"

int main (int argc, char** argv)
{
    //Window setup
    SSDL_SetWindowTitle ("Hit any key to end");
                                      //Always tell user what's expected...

    //We'll be using the classic Times New Roman font...
    //  so load it, and tell SSDL to use it
    const SSDL_Font FONT = SSDL_OpenSystemFont ("times", 18);
    SSDL_SetFont (FONT);

    SSDL_SetCursor (0, 50);                   //Skip down the page 50
                                              //pixels to start


    //And now, the poem (or part of it)
    sout << "from The Lady of the Lake\n";
```

[11]If you can't, there's a function TTF_SetFontStyle, which can generate the new style (though it may look a little ragged), and which is called thus:

```
TTF_SetFontStyle (myFont, TTF_STYLE_BOLD); //bold
```

or

```
TTF_SetFontStyle (myFont, TTF_STYLE_BOLD | TTF_STYLE_ITALIC); //bold italic
```

The available styles are TTF_STYLE_BOLD, TTF_STYLE_ITALIC, TTF_STYLE_UNDERLINE, TTF_STYLE_STRIKETHROUGH, and the default, TTF_STYLE_NORMAL.

```
    sout << "\tby Sir Walter Scott\n\n";
                                //Here, tab over for author's name, then
                                // double space at the end of the line

    sout << "\"Tis merry, 'tis merry, in Fairy-land,\n";
    sout << "\tWhen fairy birds are singing,\n";
    sout << "When the court cloth ride by their monarch's side,\n";
    sout << "\tWith bit and bridle ringing...\"\n";

    //End when user hits a key
    SSDL_WaitKey ();

    return 0;
}
```

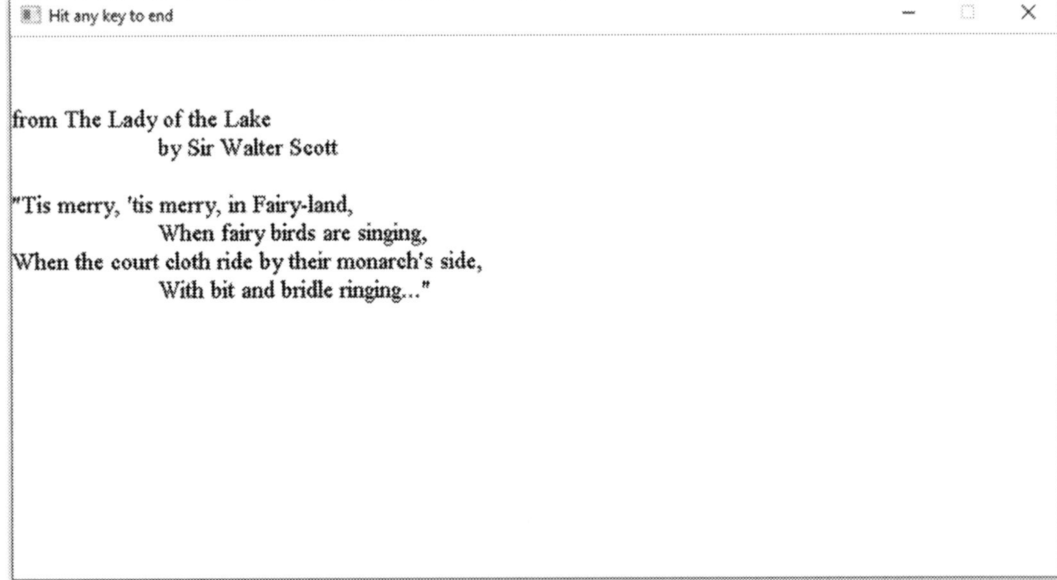

`void SSDL_SetCursor (int x, int y);`	position the cursor at x, y for the next use of `sout` or `ssin`
`SSDL_Font SSDL_OpenFont (const char* filename, int point);`	creates a font from filename for a TrueType font, and point
`SSDL_Font SSDL_OpenSystemFont (const char* filename, int point);`	same, but loads from the system fonts folder
`void SSDL_SetFont (const SSDL_Font& f);`	use `f` as the font for text

SSDL_RenderText, SSDL_RenderTextCentered

We can combine the setting of the cursor and font and the printing into one statement (and center text as well) with the following two function calls. This is convenient when the goal is not just to dump a bunch of text but to precisely determine its appearance and location. If you don't specify the font, it will use whatever font you were already using.

```
const SSDL_Font fontForYear = SSDL_OpenSystemFont ("verdana.ttf", 14);
SSDL_RenderText ("When did King Sejong publish the Korean alphabet?", 0, 0);
                                          //didn't specify font; use old one here

SSDL_RenderText (1446, 500, 0, fontForYear); //...use new font here
                                          //Year was 1446. Print at
                                          location 500, 0.
```

If you say `SSDL_RenderTextCentered`, the location you give will be the center of the text, not its left side.

`void SSDL_RenderText (T thing, int x, int y, SSDL_Font font = currentFont);`	print `thing` (which may be any printable type) at position x, y, using font if specified, otherwise using current font
`void SSDL_RenderTextCentered (T thing, int x, int y, SSDL_Font font = currentFont);`	print `thing`, as above, centered on x, y

The end-of-line character will take you to the next line if it's in the text you're printing – still centered if it's SSDL_RenderTextCentered; still indented to the position you specified if not – but the tab character is not supported.

Example 1-8 shows these features in use (see the lines in bold).

Example 1-8. An adaptation of Example 1-6 to include labels

```
//Displays boxes of colors, labeled
//      -- from _C++ for Lazy Programmers_

#include "SSDL.h"

int main (int argc, char** argv)
{
      SSDL_SetWindowTitle ("Two colored squares, with labels");

      //We'll use 3 built-in colors, and 3 new ones, counting
      const SSDL_Color PUCE      = SSDL_CreateColor(127,  90,  88);
      const SSDL_Color MAHOGANY  = SSDL_CreateColor(192,  64,   0);
      const SSDL_Color DARK_GREY = SSDL_CreateColor(100, 100, 100);

      //Make a dark grey background -- another way to do it
      SSDL_RenderClear (DARK_GREY);

      //We'll have two boxes across
      //First box:
      SSDL_SetRenderDrawColor     (RED);
      SSDL_RenderFillRect        (  0,   0, 100, 100);
      SSDL_SetRenderDrawColor (WHITE);
      SSDL_RenderTextCentered ("RED", 50, 50);       //dead center of
                                                     //  red square

      //Second box:
      SSDL_SetRenderDrawColor (GREEN);
      SSDL_RenderFillRect (100,   0, 100, 100);
      SSDL_SetRenderDrawColor (WHITE);
      SSDL_RenderTextCentered ("GREEN", 150, 50); //dead center of
                                                  //  green square
```

```
    //Report number of colors, thus demonstrating non-centered text
    SSDL_RenderText              ("Number of colors:  ", 0, 100);
    SSDL_RenderText              (2, 150, 100);    //We showed 2 colors,
                                                  //  so we print "2"

    //Note sout still has its cursor up at the top:
    //  SSDL_RenderText* doesn't use or alter the cursor
    //Therefore "Hit any key to end" still shows at top of screen
    sout << "Hit any key to end.\n";

    SSDL_WaitKey();

    return 0;
}
```

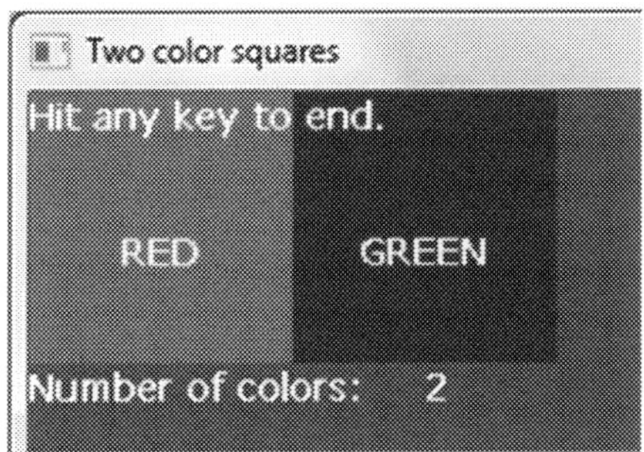

The image here shows the output. Two things to note:

- sout doesn't notice where things were printed with SSDL_RenderText and SSDL_RenderTextCentered; they do not affect the cursor. So sout still starts at the top of the page.
- SSDL_RenderTextCentered only centers things left to right; it doesn't pay attention to y values. To make the labels truly centered in the box, we'd have to calculate the Y position or just guess. The default font is 14 point; half of 14 is 7, so we could subtract that from the true center of the box in the Y direction, 50, and pass 50-7 for the y argument into SSDL_RenderTextCentered. If we care.

EXERCISES

1. Put some appropriate text into the program you wrote in the previous section (or one of the earlier examples). For example, you could give the bug's head something to say.
2. Print a long poem or text, page by page, using `SSDL_WaitKey`. Use an appropriate font and size.
3. Make up some statistics – isn't that how it's usually done? – and use the `\t` character to line up a table, like so,

```
Character              Coolness
=========        ===============
Greta Garbo                 83%
Humphrey Bogart             87%
Marilyn Monroe              98%
me, if I were               99%
     in the movies
```

4. Draw a stop sign: an octagon with STOP written in the middle.
5. Draw a yield sign: an inverted triangle with YIELD in the middle.

CHAPTER 2

Images and Sound

Enough of these line drawings: let's have something pretty.

Images and changing window characteristics

Let's start by displaying an image, using the code in Example 2-1.

Example 2-1. Displaying an image

```
//Program to show an image on the screen
//            -- from _C++ for Lazy Programmers_

//Simple version

#include "SSDL.h"

int main (int argc, char **argv)
{
      //Show image
      const SSDL_Image BEACH = SSDL_LoadImage ("beach.jpg");
      SSDL_RenderImage(BEACH, 0, 0);

      SSDL_WaitKey();

      return 0;
}
```

This program loads an image called beach.jpg and shows it at location 0, 0 on the screen.

That's it.

W. Briggs, *C++ for Lazy Programmers*, https://doi.org/10.1007/978-1-4842-5187-4_2

C++ will look for the picture in the same folder as `a.out` (g++) or as the `.vcxproj` file (Visual Studio). If we have more than one image, the folder may get messy. Let's put those images in a subfolder named `media` and load an image thus:

```
const SSDL_Image BEACH = SSDL_LoadImage ("media/beach.jpg");
```

...where `media/` means "inside the folder named media."[1]

You can at present load an image in GIF ("jiff"), JPG ("J-peg"), BMP ("bitmap"), or PNG ("ping") formats or in LBM, PCX, PNM, SVG, TGA ("targa"), TIFF, WEBP, XCF, XPM, or XV formats.

If you have another format, try loading it in GIMP or some other graphics editor and saving/exporting as JPG or PNG. I recommend PNG because it supports transparency.

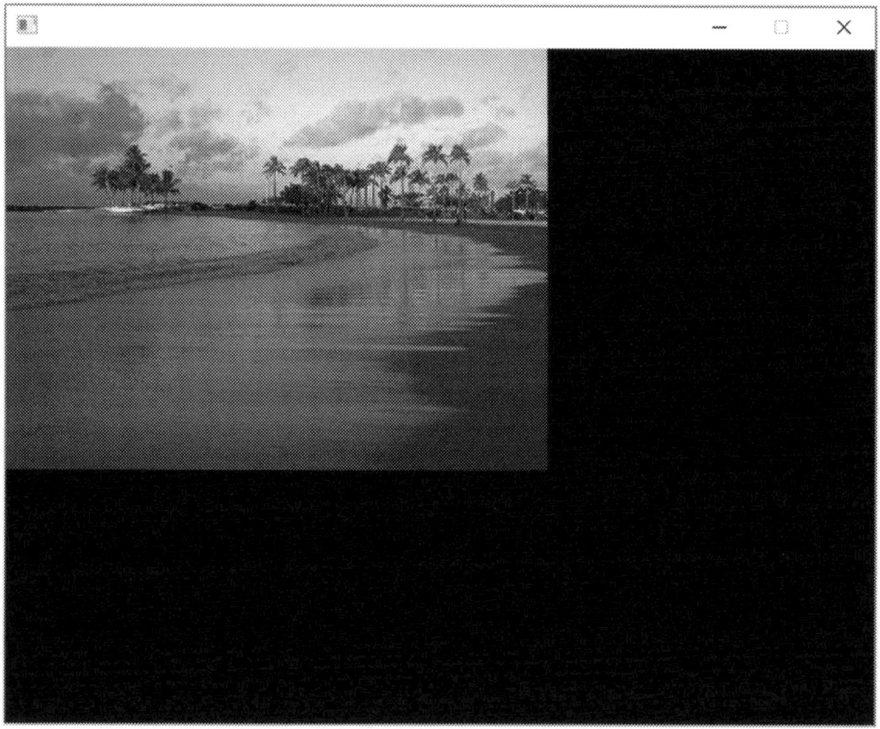

Figure 2-1. *Displaying an image*

[1]Yes, experienced Windows users, that's really a / not a \. This will work in Windows and Unix, and portability between operating systems is a Good Thing. (You can also use the escape sequence \\. But / is nicer.)

You may be wondering as you see the result in Figure 2-1: can we scale the image? Yes: `SSDL_RenderImage(BEACH, 0, 0, 640, 480);` would make it a 640x480 image. But stretching it might make the image fuzzy, so let's resize the window to fit the image instead.

First, we'll find out how big it is. If you load it in GIMP, the top bar will tell you:

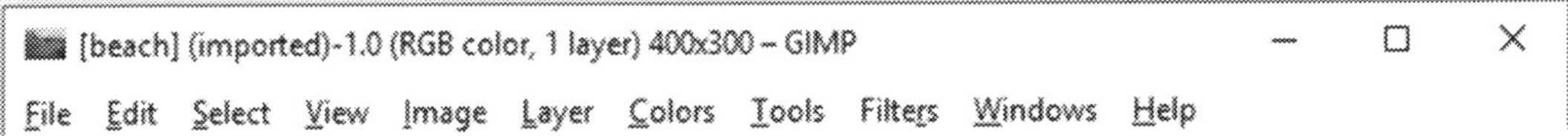

Unix users can say `exiv2 beach.jpg`. If `exiv2` isn't installed, talk nice to your system administrator.

Windows users can right-click the file in its folder and select Properties and then the Details tab. You'll see the Width and Height listed as shown in Figure 2-2.

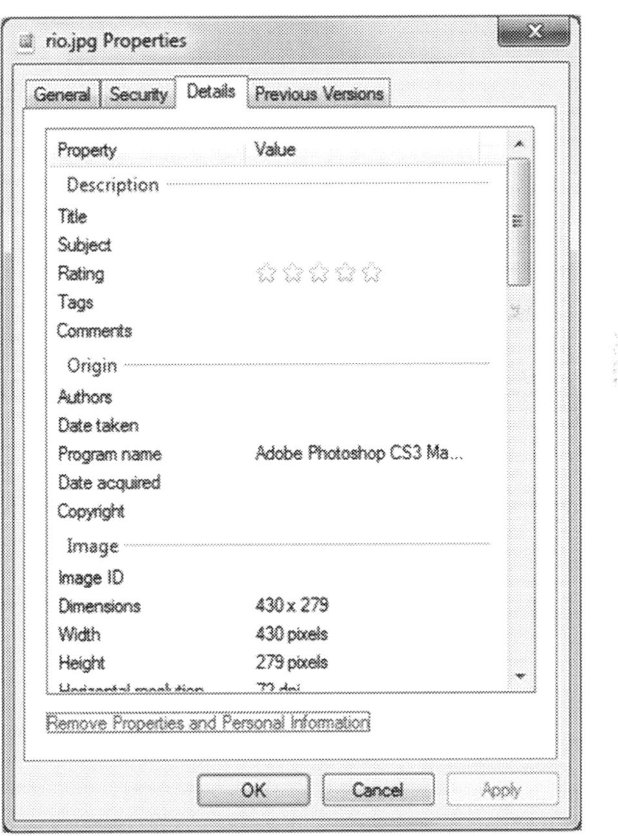

***Figure 2-2.** Properties for an image in Microsoft Windows*

However we get the info, we'll tell the program to make the window this same size, giving it parameters of width and height in that order:

```
SSDL_SetWindowSize (400, 300);
           //make a 400x300 window
```

Since we're trying to make things cooler, let's also add a label to the window itself:

```
SSDL_SetWindowTitle ("My trip to the beach ");
```

This puts `My trip to the beach` on the top bar of the display window. The code is in Example 2-2; the result is in Figure 2-3.

Example 2-2. Displaying an image, resized and titled

```
//Program to show an image on the screen
//            -- from _C++ for Lazy Programmers_

#include "SSDL.h"

int main(int argc, char **argv)
{
      //Set window parameters
      SSDL_SetWindowSize  (400, 300); //make a 400x300 window
      SSDL_SetWindowTitle ("My trip to the beach");

      //Show image
      const SSDL_Image BEACH = SSDL_LoadImage("media/beach.jpg");
      SSDL_RenderImage(BEACH, 0, 0);

      SSDL_WaitKey();

      return 0;
}
```

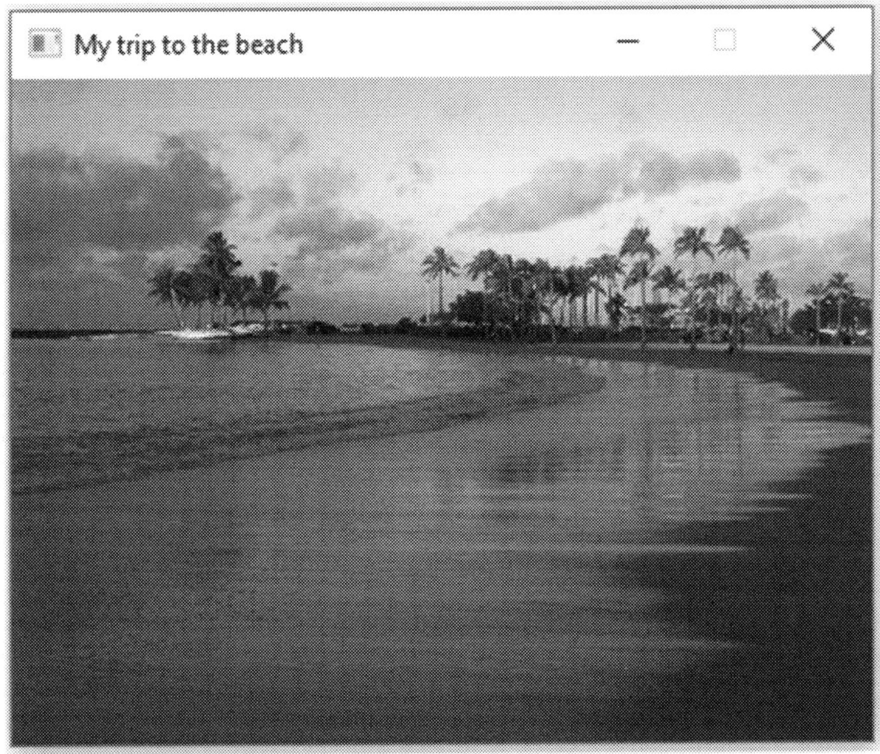

Figure 2-3. *A titled window resized to show an image with no extra space*

In Table 2-1 are prototypes for our new functions related to images and window properties.

Table 2-1. Some SSDL image and window functions

`SSDL_Image SSDL_LoadImage (char* filename);`	load the image named `filename`, and provide an `SSDL_image`
`void SSDL_RenderImage (SSDL_image img, int x, int y);`	show the image `img` at position `x, y`, using `img`'s width and height
`void SSDL_RenderImage (SSDL_image img, int x, int y, int width, int height);`	show the image `img` at position `x, y`, specifying width and height
`void SSDL_SetWindowSize (int width, int height);`	resize the window
`void SSDL_SetWindowTitle (char* title);`	give the window a `title`
`int SSDL_GetWindowHeight ();`	return window height
`int SSDL_GetWindowWidth ();`	return window width

The last two functions return integers, just as `SSDL_CreateColor` returns an `SSDL_Color`, so we can use them wherever it makes sense to put an integer. Adding this line to our program

```
//Make a label in the middle, centered
SSDL_RenderTextCentered  ("BALI? BORA BORA? BEAUTIFUL, WHEREVER!",
                    SSDL_GetWindowWidth()  / 2,
                    SSDL_GetWindowHeight() / 2);
```

gives us the result in Figure 2-4.

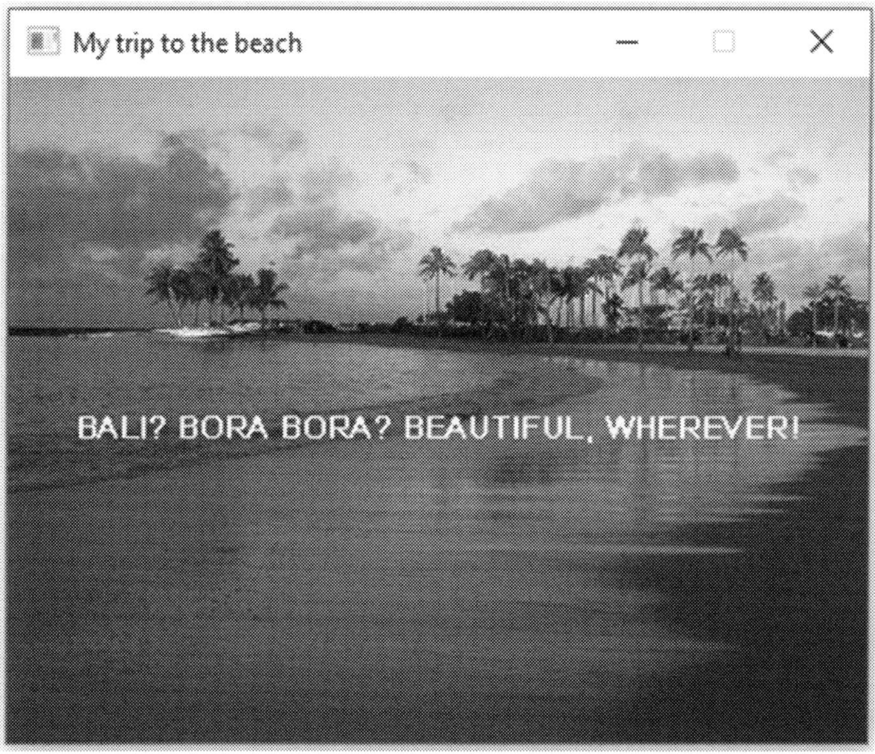

Figure 2-4. *Centered text using `SSDL_GetWindowWidth`, `SSDL_GetWindowHeight`*

Antibugging

The usual problem in this chapter, whether it's a crash or something not being visible, is

- An image didn't load, or
- A font didn't load

Here are possible culprits:

- **Folder location.** Files should be in the same folder as your `a.out` or `.vcxproj` file or in a subfolder as specified, like `media/`.
- **Spelling errors.** If you're like me, you *will* get names misspelled. When debugging the preceding program I misspelled `beach.jpg` as `myImage.jpg`. Go figure.
- **(Microsoft Windows) You can't tell what kind of file it is.** You can't see the file extension, so you can't tell if it's .jpg, .png, or something very different that SDL can't use (see Figure 2-5).

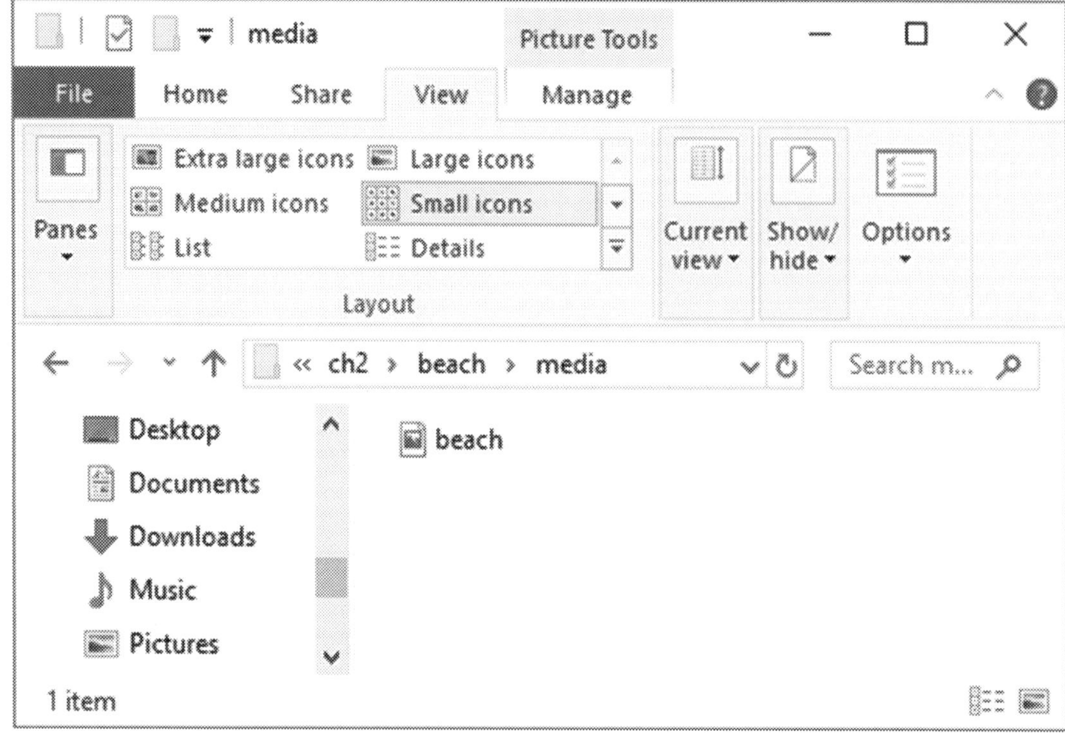

Figure 2-5. *An unidentified file type in Microsoft Windows*

Solution: un-hide extensions for known file types (see Chapter 1, "The files you created").

- **The file is corrupted or has features your image loader can't handle.** One trick is to load up the file in a graphics editor. If it loads, save it in a different format or with different export options, and try the new file.
- **It's loading, but is being pasted off screen.** Try putting it at position 0, 0 and see if it becomes visible.
- **It's none of those things. What can you do?**

If a new feature (say, images) is giving trouble, I can make, or copy from source code, a program that only does that one feature and make sure it works.

When it does, I add something else that makes it more like the final version I want. Once that works, I add another change, and another, each time making a backup of the last working program, so that if I mess up the new version I can go back to what I just had.[2]

For me, this trail of backups is essential to getting new features working.

Multiple images together

Pasting multiple images is easy with the SDL library – you just put them on the screen in order from back to front, and you're there. And if they're partly transparent, all the better.

You can find images with transparency like the one in Figure 2-6 by doing an Internet image search, requiring the file type to be PNG. Paste it after the BEACH background, and it should show up, with the background showing through the transparent parts. The result is in Figure 2-7.

```
//Load images
const SSDL_Image BEACH     = SSDL_LoadImage("media/beach.jpg");
const SSDL_Image FLAMINGO  = SSDL_LoadImage("media/flamingo.png");

//Paste in the background image, and the flamingo
SSDL_RenderImage(BEACH,      0,   0);
SSDL_RenderImage(FLAMINGO,   0, 175);
```

Figure 2-6. *A PNG with transparency*

[2]Remember the **Golden Rule of Not Pulling Your Hair Out** from Chapter 1: keep lots of backup copies as you make changes.

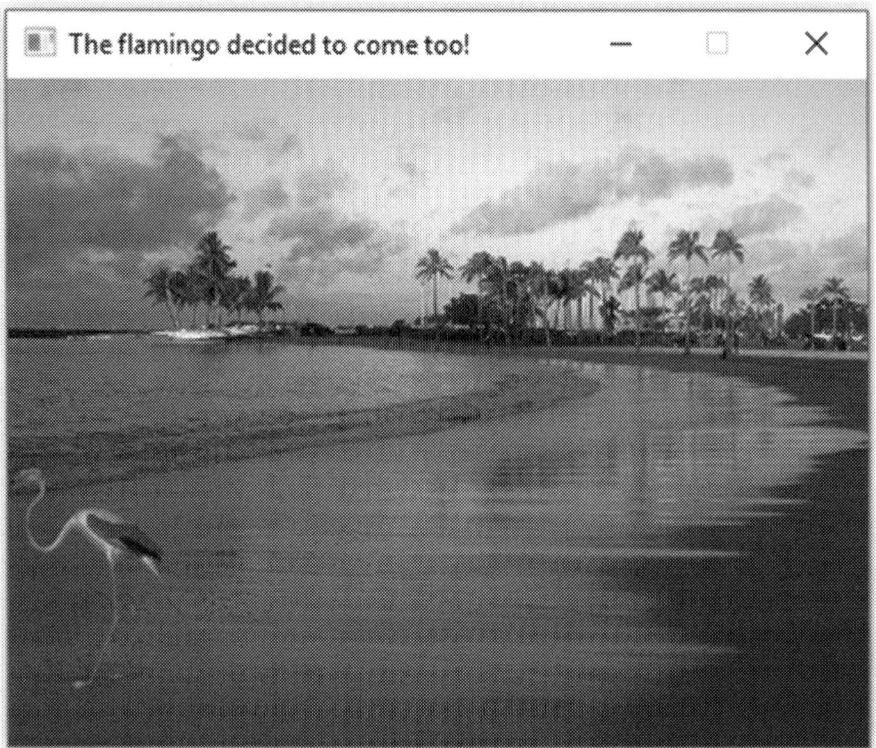

Figure 2-7. *A partly transparent image pasted onto a background*

Adding transparency with GIMP

My flamingo image came with no background. You may have your heart set on something in a photo, like the adorable puppy in Figure 2-8 – but you just want the puppy, not the background. Here's the easiest way I know to make the background transparent and keep the pup.

Figure 2-8. *A JPG image*

Be warned: unless you're a true artiste, the resulting image may look ragged around the edges.

Load your image in a deluxe graphics editor. I use GIMP in my examples, but if you prefer another program, go for it.

Next, tell GIMP you want to allow transparency. Under the Layer menu, select Transparency ➤ Add Alpha Channel. What's an alpha channel? Alpha is how transparent a pixel is. Adding the channel means transparency is possible. Figure 2-9 shows how this might look.

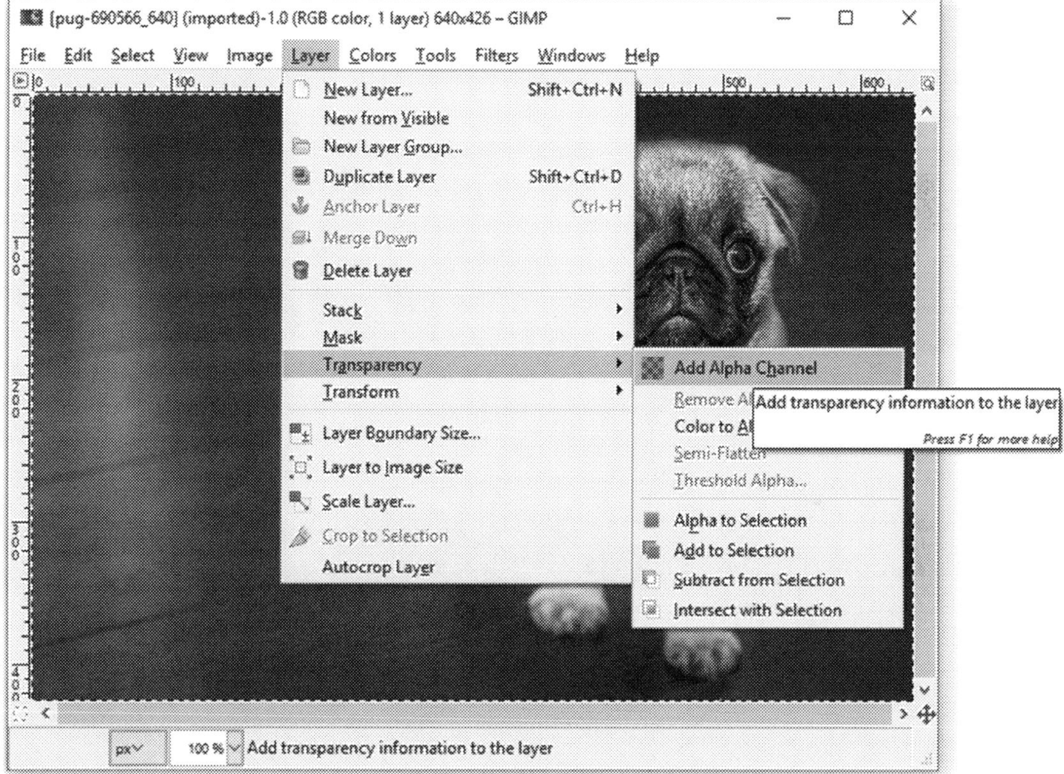

***Figure 2-9.** Adding transparency in GIMP*

Now we'll remove the background, leaving a transparent area instead. You'll need what GIMP calls the "Fuzzy Select Tool" (see Figure 2-10), which selects an area of similar color (in this case, the colors in the floor). The tool looks like a fairy godmother's wand. Don't ask me how I know that.

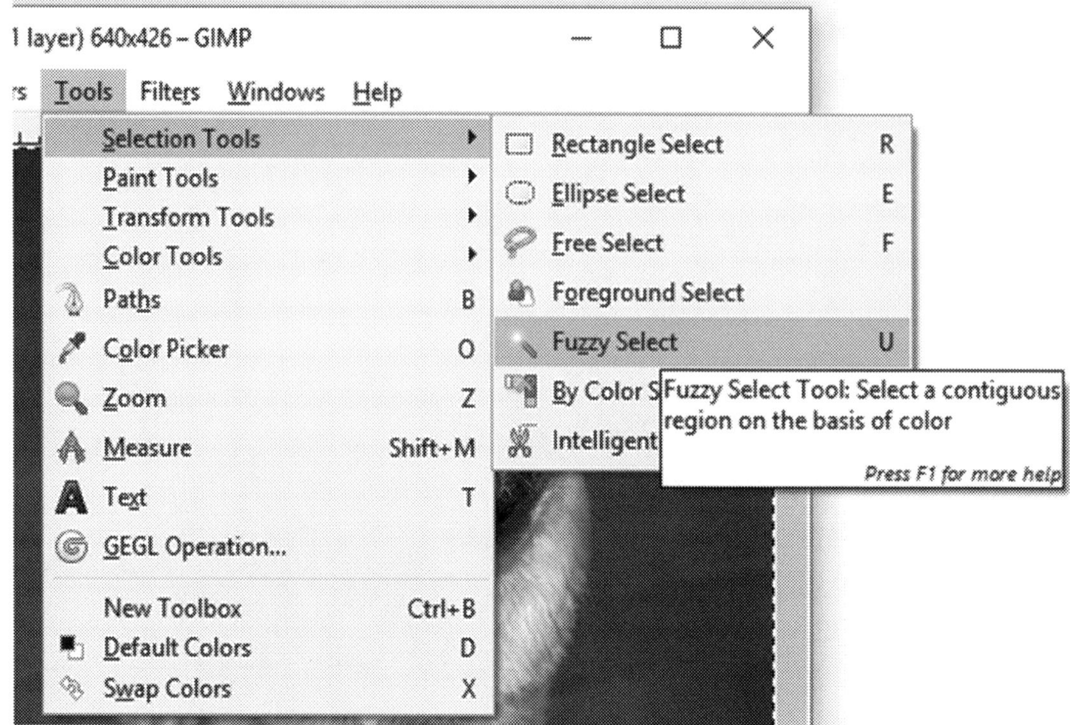

Figure 2-10. *The Fuzzy Select Tool*

Click the wand on parts of the background, and hit delete. In GIMP, you should see a checkerboard pattern, which means you're seeing *through* the image to whatever's behind. You can also clean up with Rectangle Select, other Selects, or the Eraser, and, if you like, Crop to Selection, Scale Image, whatever. Figure 2-11 shows how it might look.

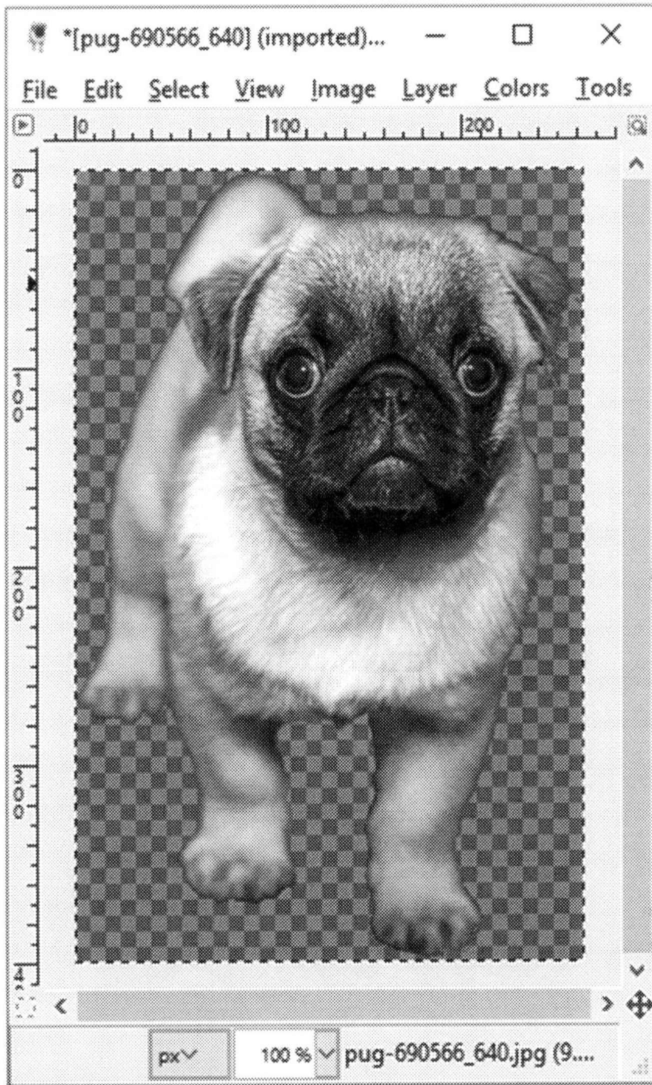

Figure 2-11. *An image with transparent background. I also cropped it*

When you're done admiring your handiwork, save – no, *export*[3] – into PNG format (which, unlike JPG, supports transparency), and use the result in your program, as I do in Example 2-3.

[3]Graphics editors don't let you *save* in useful formats; saving is for their own format. You have to *export* instead.

Example 2-3. Multiple images, with transparency. Output is in Figure 2-12

```
//Program that pastes two images onto a background
//            -- from _C++ for Lazy Programmers_

#include "SSDL.h"

int main (int argc, char **argv)
{
      //Set window parameters
      SSDL_SetWindowSize(400, 300);     //make a 400x300 window
      SSDL_SetWindowTitle("Pup dog and flamingo at the beach");

      //Load images
      const SSDL_Image BEACH   =SSDL_LoadImage("media/beach.jpg");
      const SSDL_Image FLAMINGO=SSDL_LoadImage("media/flamingo.png");
      const SSDL_Image PUPPY   =SSDL_LoadImage("media/pupdog.png");

      //Paste in the background image, and the flamingo
      SSDL_RenderImage(BEACH,      0,   0);
      SSDL_RenderImage(FLAMINGO,   0, 175);
                               //I'll increase flamingo's size
                               // from 81x100
                               // to 81x120 -- make it taller
                               // and move it a little (175->155)
                               // just for grins
      SSDL_RenderImage(PUPPY, 320, 225, 50, 75);
                               //puppy goes on bottom right
                               //She's bigger than I want, so I
                               // make her 50x75. It's better to
                               // resize when making the image, but
                               // this works too

      SSDL_WaitKey ();

      return 0;
}
```

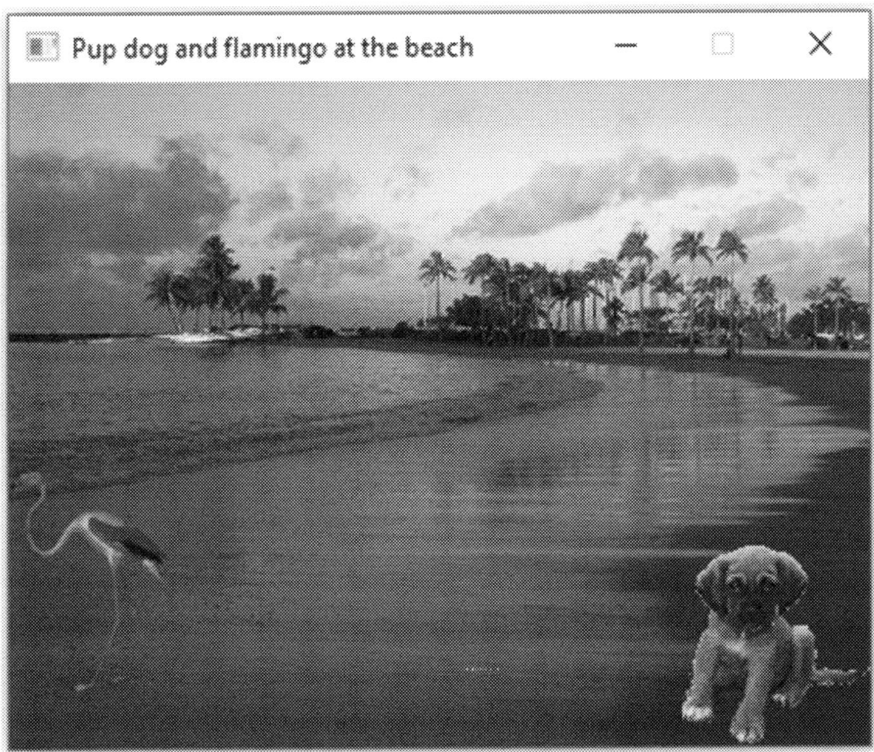

Figure 2-12. *Two transparent images pasted onto a background*

EXERCISES

1. Make a slide show of all the fabulous locations visited by pup dog and flamingo (or by your own dog or your yard gnome). If you want to have the slides progress automatically, as opposed to waiting for the user to hit a key, you can use `SSDL_Delay`. When the program hits an `SSDL_Delay`, it stops for the given amount of time before continuing:

```
SSDL_Delay (3000); //waits 3000 milliseconds, or 3 seconds
```

Sound

Sound is also easy in SSDL. I know what you're thinking: "I'll be the judge of that." But you'll agree, unless your sound decides not to load and the program crashes.

There are two kinds of sounds: those that play continuously in the background and annoy the user to death, called "music," and those that occur with particular events such as collisions, called "sounds." Bottom line: background sound is music; sound effects are sounds.

We can only have one music running at a time, but multiple sounds are fine. The main things you can do with either type are load it, play it, pause or resume it, and halt it. The format we'll usually be using is WAV, but music can also be in MP3. (If you have a sound file in another format and SSDL can't handle it, look for an online converter.)

The most common functions are here; a more complete listing is in Appendix H. When you see a parameter with a default value given, like `repeats` in `SSDL_PlaySound (SSDL_Sound s, int repeats=0)`, this means that if you leave out that argument, it uses the default:

```
SSDL_PlaySound (mySound, 2);      //repeat sound twice after you play it
SSDL_PlaySound (mySound);         //repeat sound 0 times after playing it --
                                  // that's the default
```

`SSDL_Music SSDL_LoadMUS (char* filename) ;`	load music from `filename`
`void SSDL_PlayMusic (SSDL_Music m, int numTimesToPlay=-1);`	play music for specified number of times; -1 means repeat forever
`void SSDL_PauseMusic () ;`	pause music
`void SSDL_ResumeMusic() ;`	unpause music
`int SSDL_VolumeMusic (int volume=-1);`	set the volume, which should be 0 to `MIX_MAX_VOLUME` (which is 128), and return the new volume. If volume is -1, it only returns the volume
`void SSDL_HaltMusic () ;`	halt music
`SSDL_Sound SSDL_LoadWAV (char* file);`	load sound from file. Despite the name, it can be in WAV format or other supported formats. See online documentation on SDL2_mixer for details
`void SSDL_PlaySound (SSDL_Sound sound, int repeats=0);`	play this sound, plus specified number of repeats. If repeat is -1, it repeats forever

(continued)

void SSDL_PauseSound (SSDL_Sound snd) ;	pause sound
void SSDL_ResumeSound (SSDL_Sound snd);	unpause sound
int SSDL_VolumeSound (SSDL_Sound snd, int volume=MIX_MAX_VOLUME);	set volume of sound, from 0 to MIX_MAX_VOLUME, which is 128; return the volume. If volume argument is -1, it only returns the volume
void SSDL_HaltSound (SSDL_Sound snd);	halt sound

You can often find sounds online: do a web search for "free WAV" or some such. Copy what you need into your media folder.

Example 2-4 shows a simple program that plays music and hits a gong when you hit a key.

Example 2-4. A simple music and sound program

```
//Program to play sounds
//            -- from _C++ for Lazy Programmers_

#include "SSDL.h"

int main(int argc, char** argv)
{
      //Initial window setup
      SSDL_SetWindowTitle("Simple sound example");

      //Load our media
      SSDL_Music music=SSDL_LoadMUS("Media/457729__razor5__boss-battle-2-0.wav");
      SSDL_Sound bell = SSDL_LoadWAV("Media/321530__robbo799__church-bell.wav");

      //Start the music
      SSDL_VolumeMusic(int(MIX_MAX_VOLUME*0.50));
                               //play music at 50% volume,
                               //  because...that was LOUD.
```

```
    SSDL_PlayMusic      (music, SSDL_FOREVER);
                                  //...looping continuously
                                  //SSDL_FOREVER means -1

    sout << "Hit a key to hear the bell.\n";
    SSDL_WaitKey();
    SSDL_PlaySound(bell);

    sout << "Hit another key to end.\n";
    SSDL_WaitKey();

    return 0;
}
```

Antibugging

Almost anything that goes wrong with a sound will make the program crash. Prime suspects are having the filename wrong, or in the wrong folder, and using a nonsupported file type.

EXERCISES

1. Make your own music video; complete with lyrics, images, and sound; and play it. You'll need to time the delay between slides; see Exercise 1 in the previous section.
2. Playf a song, adding a gong or some other annoying sound to every (say) fourth beat.

CHAPTER 3

Numbers

Numbers are what makes the computer's world go 'round, so let's examine ways to get the computer to handle those numbers for us.

Variables

Variables might seem like the letters we use in algebra – y=mx+b, that sort of thing – but in C++, they're just places to store numbers (among other things). Example 3-1 shows what it looks like when we create variables.

Example 3-1. Variable declarations for my *American Idol* obsession

```
int main (int argc, char** argv)
{
    int    seasonsOfAmericanIdol              = 17;
                            //after a while you lose track
    float  hoursIveWatchedAmericanIdol        = 424.5F;
                            //missed half an episode, dang it
    double howMuchIShdCareAboutAmericanIdol   = 1.0E-21;
                            //1x10 to the -21 power
    double howMuchIDoCareAboutAmericanIdol    = 0.000000000000001;[1]
                            //So why'd I watch it if I don't care?
    ...
}
```

This gives us an integer variable; a float variable, which can take decimal places; and two double variables, which can take twice as many decimal places. (How many depends on the machine you're on.)

[1]I'm lining up the ='s, you'll notice. Neatness makes for easier reading.

W. Briggs, *C++ for Lazy Programmers*, https://doi.org/10.1007/978-1-4842-5187-4_3

The trailing F on 324.5F means that it's a float, not a double, value. (If you don't specify, it's a double.) If you get these confused, you may get a warning from the compiler. To prevent that warning, I use double generally and forget the F.

1.0E-21 is how C++ writes $1.0x10^{21}$.

You can think of the main function as containing locations with these names, each of which can store a value of the appropriate type (see Figure 3-1).

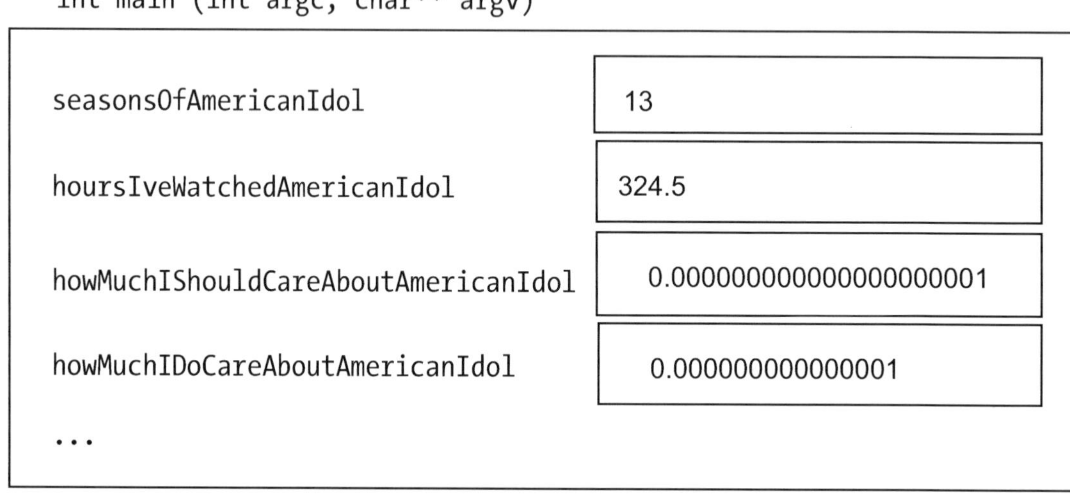

Figure 3-1. *Variables storing values in* `main`

We gave these variables values as soon as we made them, on the same line. We didn't have to, but it's good practice. It's disappointing when you find that the number of dollars in your bank account is -68 million or so, because you didn't tell the computer what value to initialize it with, and it just happened to start with a very inappropriate number in that space.

Golden Rule of Variables

Initialize them.

It's also good to make descriptive names like those in Figure 3-1. It's frustrating to search through code trying to find out what "z" or "x" means. But you know exactly what seasonsOfAmericanIdol means.

Variable names start with letters (possibly preceded with _'s), but after that they can have numerals in them. Capitalization matters: `temp` and `Temp` are different variables.

Extra Variable and constant names *should* be descriptive and *shouldn't* be the same as any of the built-in keywords in C++ (`const`, `int`, `enum`, etc.).

By convention, C++ constants are written in ALL CAPS to SCREAM at the programmer that this is a CONSTANT, not a variable, value. To separate words jammed together, use _: `MAX_LENGTH`, for example.

How do you think it got its name?

Conventions for variable names are flexible. I tend to use "camel case" variables: when you jam words together to make a variable, capitalize all but the first: `firstEntry`, `minXValue`. I reserve initial capitals for created types like `SSDL_Image`. Initial _'s are for the compiler's own identifiers. There are other conventions; whatever convention you use, it's best to be clear as possible.

Constants

We've already made constants with SSDL types:

```
const SSDL_Color MAHOGANY   = SSDL_CreateColor     (192,  64,   0);
const SSDL_Font  FONT       = SSDL_OpenSystemFont ("times", 18);
```

As you might expect, you can also do this with built-in types:

```
const double PI = 3.14159265359;
```

It's a good idea for anything that must not change. (PI does come to mind.)

There's also an easy-on-the-fingers option for integer types:

```
//Location and dimensions for a box we might draw
enum {BOX_LEFT=100, BOX_TOP=50, BOX_WIDTH=200, BOX_HEIGHT=100};
```

This gives us four constant values and is easier than writing

```
const int BOX_LEFT  =100;
const int BOX_TOP   = 50;
const int BOX_WIDTH =200;
const int BOX_HEIGHT=100;
```

For more uses of enum, see Chapter 10.[2]

Tip enums are a quick, easy way to declare constant values (as long as they're whole numbers).

When to use constants, not literal values

When should you use a constant symbol like BOX_LEFT, and when should you use a literal value, like 100? The answer is almost always: use the constant rather than the bare literal value. There are two reasons.

One is clarity, as shown previously. You're going back through your program, and you see (let's say) a reference to 7. Seven what? Days in the week? The number of deadly sins? The age you were when you wrote your very first program? You'll have to do detective work to figure it out, especially if there's more than one 7 in your program. Detective work is not for the lazy. Better to document it with a clear name.

The other reason is that you may find that the number you were using was wrong. For example, there are by convention seven deadly sins, but using bare numeric literals like 7 is a pretty deadly sin in programmer terms. So maybe that enum {NUMBER_OF_DEADLY_SINS = 7}; needs to be updated to 8. If you used this enum, you've got one line to change. If you put 7 all through your program, you'll have to go through figuring which 7's to change and which ones to leave alone. Too much work.

[2]There are maybe too many ways to declare constant values in C++: const, enum, constexpr, inline constexpr, static const...but we'll get to that later.

The bottom line is clarity. We won't go back to the bug-face program in Chapter 1 and replace the numbers with `consts`, because it would make the program *harder* to follow: each value is unique, and naming it doesn't make it clearer. (We have comments to show what it means anyway.) But the bug-face program is the exception. Generally, values should be named.

Golden Rule of Constants

Any time it's not blindingly obvious what a numeric literal value is for, define it as a constant symbol, in ALL CAPS, and use that name whenever you refer to it.

Math operators

Whether you're using the `float` and `double` types or the `int` type, these are the arithmetic operators you can do in C++ (Table 3-1).

Table 3-1. *The arithmetic operators*

Operator	Meaning
+	addition
-	subtraction, negation
*	multiplication
/	division
%	modulus

They're used as you might expect: `2.6+0.4` or `alpha/beta` or `-2*(5+3)`.

Integer division

Back before you learned fractions, when you only used whole numbers, the result was always a whole number: 5 divided by 2 was 2, with a remainder of 1. It's the same for C++'s integer division: `5/2` gives you not `2.5` (that's a floating-point value), but another integer, 2.

This can be confusing. `1/2` sure looks like it should be `0.5`, but since `1` and `2` are integers, `1/2` has to be an integer too: `0`.

In keeping with the way we divide integers, C++ also provides %, the modulus operator, which means "divide and take the remainder." `5%2` gives us `1`, the remainder after dividing 5 by 2. % only works with `int`s. We'll see more of % in Chapter 8, in the section on random numbers.

Assignment (=) operators

We've been using = already:

```
const SSDL_Color MAHOGANY    = SSDL_CreateColor  (192,  64,   0);
int     seasonsOfAmericanIdol = 13;
```

Constants can't be changed past that first line or they wouldn't be constant, but variables can vary whenever you like:

```
x = 5; y = 10;
x = 10;              //I changed my mind: put a 10 in X, replacing the 5

seasonsOfAmericanIdol = seasonsOfAmericanIdol + 1; //Another year! Yay!
```

The latter means take whatever number is in that `seasonsOfAmericanIdol` memory location; add 1 to it; put the resulting value back into that same place.

It can also be written this way:

```
seasonsOfAmericanIdol += 1;
```

They mean the same thing: add 1 to `seasonsOfAmericanIdol`.[3]

It works for other arithmetic operators: `-=`, `*=`, `/=`, and `%=` are all defined the same way.

[3] If you want to add 1, rather than some other number, there's a special "increment" operator just for that:

```
++seasonsOfAmericanIdol;
```

We'll see that again in Chapter 5, along with "decrement" (`--`).

A diving board example

Now let's put this into practice with a program that uses math for sport (Example 3-2). Someone's going off the diving board. We'll make second-by-second images of the character as it plunges toward the water.

Example 3-2. A program to show a diver's path, using enums and math operators

```
//Program to draw the path of a diver
//            -- from _C++ for Lazy Programmers_

#include "SSDL.h"

int main(int argc, char** argv)
{
      SSDL_SetWindowTitle("Sploosh!  Hit a key to end");

      //Stuff about the board
      enum {BOARD_WIDTH = 60, BOARD_THICKNESS = 8, BOARD_INIT_Y =20};
      SSDL_RenderDrawRect(0, BOARD_INIT_Y,
            BOARD_WIDTH, BOARD_THICKNESS);

      //...the water
      enum { SKY_HEIGHT = 440 };
      SSDL_SetRenderDrawColor(BLUE);
      SSDL_RenderFillRect(0, SKY_HEIGHT,
            SSDL_GetWindowWidth(),
            SSDL_GetWindowHeight() - SKY_HEIGHT);
                                          //height is
                                          //  window height - sky height

      //...the diver
      enum {WIDTH = 10, HEIGHT = 10};//Dimensions of the "diver"
      enum {DISTANCE_TO_TRAVEL = 20};//How far to go right each time
      enum {FACTOR_TO_INCREASE =  2};//Increase Y this much each time

      enum { INIT_X = 50, INIT_Y = 10 };
      int x = INIT_X;                  //Move diver to end of board
      int y = INIT_Y;                  //and just on top of it
```

```
    const SSDL_Color DIVER_COLOR = SSDL_CreateColor(200, 150, 90);
    SSDL_SetRenderDrawColor(DIVER_COLOR);

    //Now draw several images, going down as if falling, and right
    //Remember x+=DISTANCE_TO_TRAVEL means x=x+DISTANCE_TO_TRAVEL
    //      ...and so on

    SSDL_RenderFillRect(x, y, WIDTH, HEIGHT);
    x += DISTANCE_TO_TRAVEL;  //go right the same amount each time,
    y *= FACTOR_TO_INCREASE;  // down by an ever-increasing amount

                              //Same thing repeated several times
    SSDL_RenderFillRect(x, y, WIDTH, HEIGHT);
    x += DISTANCE_TO_TRAVEL; y *= FACTOR_TO_INCREASE;

    SSDL_RenderFillRect(x, y, WIDTH, HEIGHT);
    x += DISTANCE_TO_TRAVEL; y *= FACTOR_TO_INCREASE;

    SSDL_RenderFillRect(x, y, WIDTH, HEIGHT);
    x += DISTANCE_TO_TRAVEL; y *= FACTOR_TO_INCREASE;

    SSDL_RenderFillRect(x, y, WIDTH, HEIGHT);
    x += DISTANCE_TO_TRAVEL; y *= FACTOR_TO_INCREASE;

    SSDL_RenderFillRect(x, y, WIDTH, HEIGHT);
    x += DISTANCE_TO_TRAVEL; y *= FACTOR_TO_INCREASE;

    //end program
    SSDL_WaitKey();
    return 0;
}
```

Things to notice:

- I initialize all variables, as always.
- No bare numeric literals in any calculation or variable initialization: it's CONSTANTS all the way.
- I'm repeating the same pair of lines six times – seriously? Is that lazy? We'll have a better way in Chapter 5.

Figure 3-2 is the result.

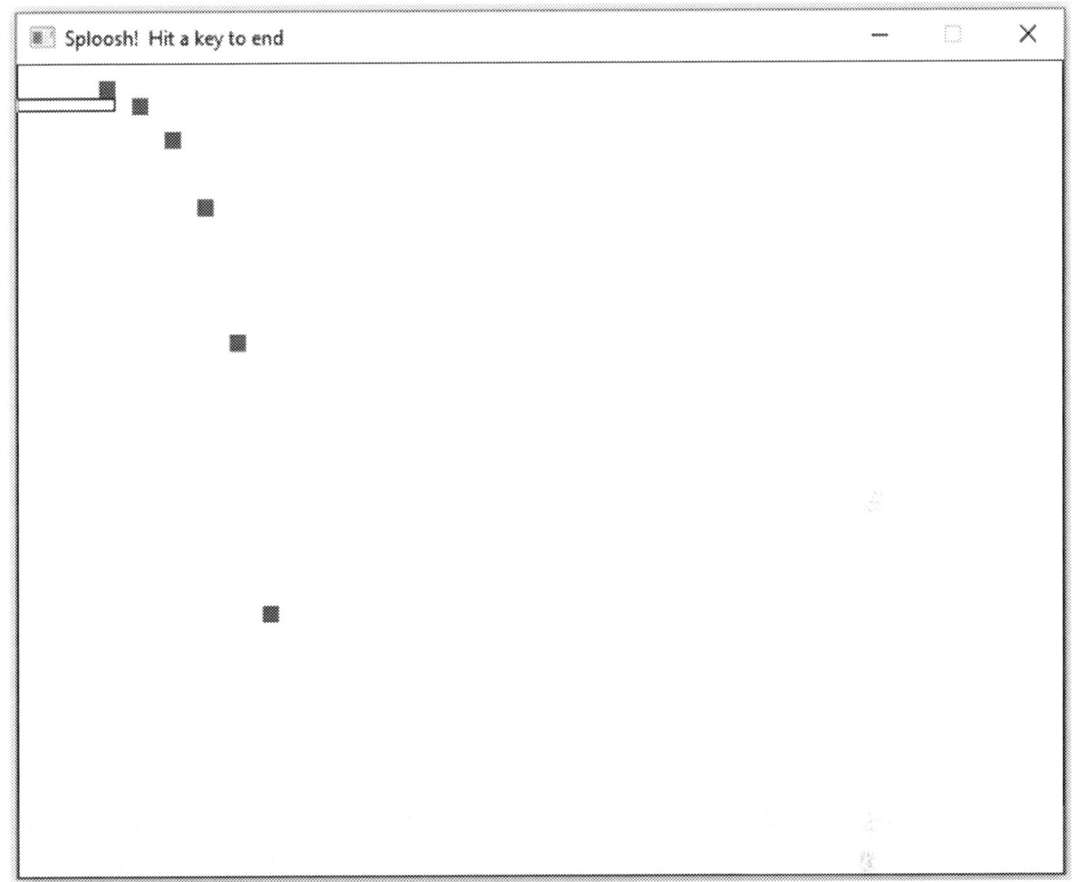

Figure 3-2. *A program that shows the path of a diver into the water*

That worked, and in some small sense evokes the terror I feel when I go off the high dive.

The no-worries list for math operators

Let me now give a sort of "no worries" list: things C++ will handle naturally enough you won't need to memorize anything for them.

- **Precedence.** Consider a math expression, `2*5+3`. In C++, as in algebra class, we'd do the multiplying before the adding: this means `(2*5)+3` = `13`, not `2*(5+3)` = `16`. Similarly, in `8/2-1`, we divide before subtracting. In general, do it the way that makes sense to you, and it'll be right. If not, use parenthesis to force it to go your way: `8/(2-1)`.
- **Associativity.** In `27/3/3`, which division comes first? Is it done like `27/(3/3)` or `(27/3)/3`? Arithmetic operations are performed left to right. Assignment is done right to left: `x=5+2` requires you to evaluate the `5+2` before doing anything to the `x`.

Precise details of precedence and associativity are in Appendix B.

- **Coercion.** If you want to cram a variable of one type into another, C++ will do it:

```
double Nothing = 0;     //Nothing becomes 0.0, not 0
int  Something = 2.7;    //ints can't have decimal places, so
                         // C++ throws away the .7;
                         // Something becomes 2. No rounding, alas
```

  Also, if you mix integers and floating-point numbers in a calculation, your result will be the version with the most information, that is, floating point. `10/2.0`, for example, gives you `5.0`.

EXERCISES

1. Accumulate this sum for as far as you're willing to take it: 1/2 + 1/4 + 1/8 + 1/16 +..., using +=. Do you think if you did it forever you would reach a particular number? Or would it just keep getting bigger? The ancient philosopher Zeno of Elea would have an opinion on that (`https://en.wikipedia.org/wiki/Zeno%27s_paradoxes`, at time of writing). But he'd be wrong.

"You can't get there from here." —Zeno. Sort of.

2. Make a program to have a box move across the screen in 0.1-second jumps – like the diver moves, but showing each successive position 0.1 seconds later (use `SSDL_Delay`), clearing the screen at every jump, so it looks like it's really moving. Or make the delay shorter for a better illusion of motion.

Built-in functions and casting

Now I want to make a geometric figure – a 5-pointed star – but unlike in Chapter 1, I don't want to draw it on graph paper; I want the computer to figure it out for me.

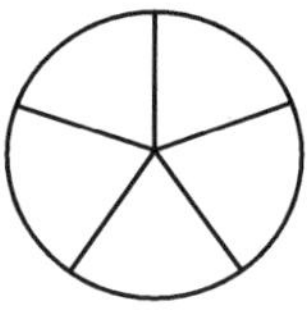

If I think of it as inscribed in a circle...I probably know the center, so what I need calculated is the points at the edges. Each point is 1/5 of the way further around the circle than the previous, so if a circle is 360 degrees, the angle between them is 360/5 degrees. If you use radians rather than degrees – like C++ – that's $2\pi/5$ or $\frac{2}{5}\pi$ radians between the points.

SDL uses x, y coordinates, so we'll need a way to get that from the angle. We can do that using the picture in Figure 3-3. Since sine of the angle θ is the y distance divided by radius (if math isn't your thing, trust me), the y distance = RADIUS * sin (θ). Similarly the x distance is RADIUS * cos (θ).

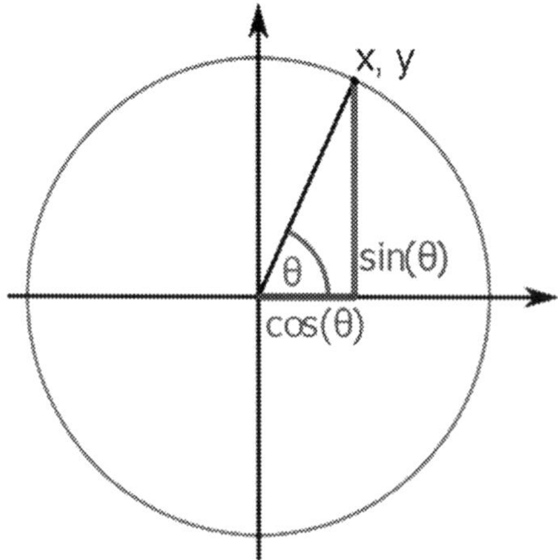

Figure 3-3. *Sine and cosine as related to x and y*

The `sin` and `cos` functions, like most C++ math functions, have their prototypes in an include file called `cmath`,[4] added to our program thus:

```
#include <cmath>
#include "SSDL.h"
```

System include files (those that come with the compiler) have `<>`'s not `""`'s and come *before* library include files.

This program is meant to draw a line from center to edge, turn 1/5 of the way around the circle and do it again, and keep going for a total of five lines.

Example 3-3. A star using `sin` and `cos` functions

```
//Program to make a 5-point star in center of screen
//              -- from _C++ for Lazy Programmers_

#include <cmath>
#include "SSDL.h"
```

[4]Include files inherited from C++'s ancestor C, under current conventions, start with a "c": `cmath` and `cstdlib`, for example.

```
int main(int argc, char** argv)
{
      const double PI = 3.14159;

      //Starting out with some generally useful numbers...

                        //Can't initialize enums with functions or
                        // calculations -- so must use const here
      const int CENTER_X=SSDL_GetWindowWidth() /2; //center of screen
      const int CENTER_Y=SSDL_GetWindowHeight()/2;
      enum { RADIUS = 200 };
      enum { NUMBER_OF_POINTS = 5 };

      //angle information...
      double angle = 0;          //angle starts at 0
      const double ANGLE_INCREMENT = (2 / NUMBER_OF_POINTS) * PI;
                              //increases by whole circle/5 each time

      //...now we make the successive lines
      int x, y;                  //endpt of line (other endpt is center)

      x = CENTER_X + int(RADIUS * cos(angle));          //calc endpoint
      y = CENTER_Y + int(RADIUS * sin(angle));
      SSDL_RenderDrawLine(CENTER_X, CENTER_Y, x, y);    //draw line
      angle += ANGLE_INCREMENT;                         //go on to next

      x = CENTER_X + int(RADIUS * cos(angle));          //calc endpoint
      y = CENTER_Y + int(RADIUS * sin(angle));
      SSDL_RenderDrawLine(CENTER_X, CENTER_Y, x, y);    //draw line
      angle += ANGLE_INCREMENT;                         //go on to next

      x = CENTER_X + int(RADIUS * cos(angle));          //calc endpoint
      y = CENTER_Y + int(RADIUS * sin(angle));
      SSDL_RenderDrawLine(CENTER_X, CENTER_Y, x, y);    //draw line
      angle += ANGLE_INCREMENT;                         //go on to next

      x = CENTER_X + int(RADIUS * cos(angle));          //calc endpoint
      y = CENTER_Y + int(RADIUS * sin(angle));
      SSDL_RenderDrawLine(CENTER_X, CENTER_Y, x, y);    //draw line
      angle += ANGLE_INCREMENT;                         //go on to next
```

```
        x = CENTER_X + int(RADIUS * cos(angle));              //calc endpoint
        y = CENTER_Y + int(RADIUS * sin(angle));
        SSDL_RenderDrawLine(CENTER_X, CENTER_Y, x, y);        //draw line
        angle += ANGLE_INCREMENT;                              //go on to next

        //end program
        SSDL_WaitKey();
        return 0;
}
```

Figure 3-4 shows the result. What is going on here?

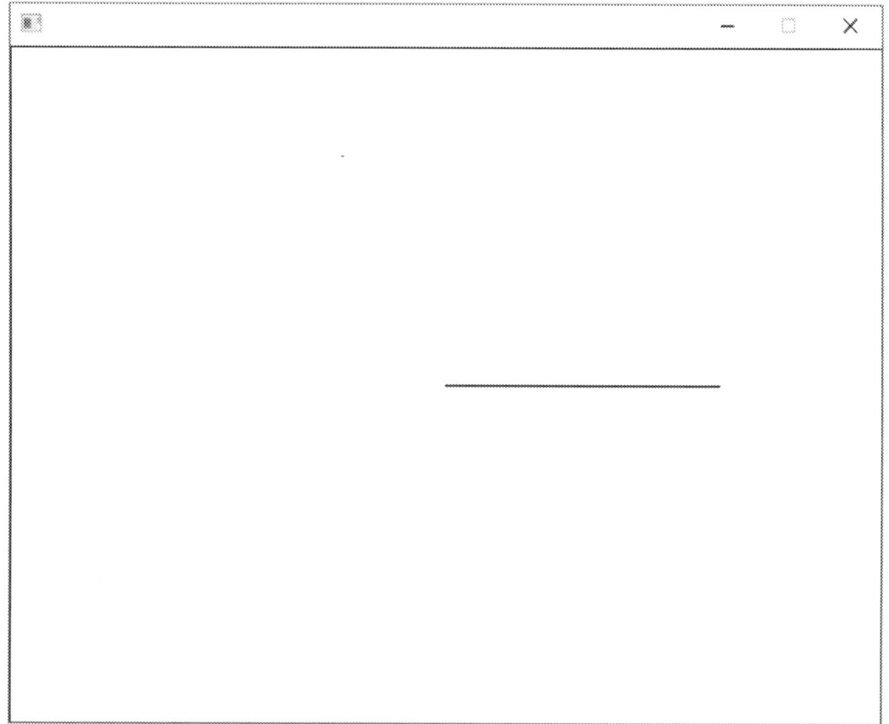

Figure 3-4. *A 5-pointed star – at least, it was supposed to be*

This will be a breeze to debug once we've covered the debugger in Chapter 9, but for now, we'll just have to channel Sherlock Holmes. That line never changes, which means `angle` never changes, which must mean `ANGLE_INCREMENT` is 0. Why would it be 0?

Because operators deal with the types we give them, look at that calculation: (2/NUMBER_OF_POINTS)*PI. The first thing to do is divide 2 by NUMBER_OF_POINTS, or 5. Since both are integers, we do integer division: 5 goes into 2 zero times (with a remainder of 2, for what it's worth), so 2/5 gives us zero. Zero times PI is zero. So ANGLE_INCREMENT is zero.

We needed floating-point division.

One way is to force 2 and 5 to be float or double. You can do this by saying

```
double (whatEverYouWantToBeDouble)
```

This is called **casting**.

This won't work

```
double (2/NUMBER_OF_POINTS)
```

because that divides 2 by 5, gets 0, and converts the 0 to 0.0. It's still doing integer division.

Any of the following will work. As long as one of the arguments is double or float, you'll get a result with decimal places.

```
double (2)/NUMBER_OF_POINTS
2/double (NUMBER_OF_POINTS)
2.0 / NUMBER_OF_POINTS
```

So changing the beginning of main to what you see in Example 3-4 repairs the problem.

Example 3-4. A new beginning to main to make Example 3-3 work

```
int main(int argc, char** argv)
{
    ...

    //angle information...
    double angle = 0;              //angle starts at 0
    const double ANGLE_INCREMENT=(2/double(NUMBER_OF_POINTS))*PI;
                                   //increases by whole circle/5 each time
    ...
```

Figure 3-5 shows the result.

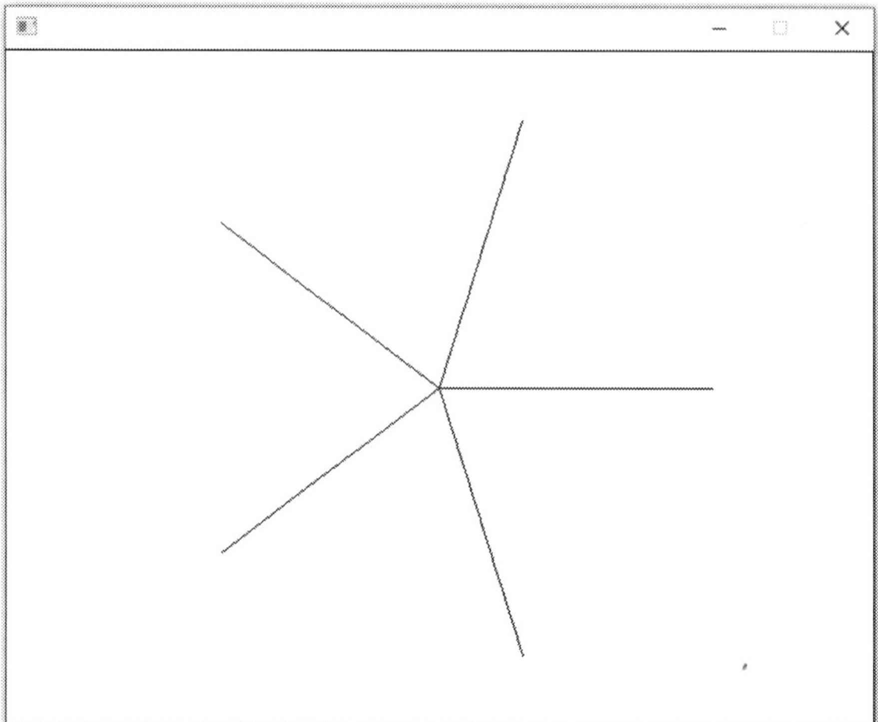

Figure 3-5. *A 5-pointed star*

It's not vertical, it seems. Exercise 1 is about turning it straight.

Other commonly useful mathematical functions include `asin` and `acos` (reverse sine and cosine), `pow` (raising a number to a power), `abs` (absolute value), and `sqrt` (square root). See Appendix F for more.

Antibugging

- **You call a value-returning function, but it has no effect.** Here's an example with a function we saw earlier:

  ```
  SSDL_GetScreenWidth();
  SSDL_RenderTextCentered (320, 240, "Blastoff!");
  ```

Sure, you called SSDL_GetWindowWidth()...but you never did anything with the result! C++ is happy to let you waste time by calling functions and not using what they give you. (It's sort of a "let the programmer shoot self in the foot, and laugh" language.) If you want to use the value, refer to it wherever you wanted that value

```
SSDL_RenderTextCentered(SSDL_GetScreenWidth ()/2,
                        SSDL_GetScreenHeight()/2,
                        "Blastoff!");
```

or put it in a variable or constant for later use

```
const int SCREEN_WIDTH  = SSDL_GetScreenWidth ();
const int SCREEN_HEIGHT = SSDL_GetScreenHeight();
SSDL_RenderTextCentered (SCREEN_WIDTH/2, SCREEN_HEIGHT/2,
                         "Blastoff!");
```

- **You divided two integers to get a floating-point number between zero and one, but you got zero.** See Example 3-3 in this section. One of those operands of the / symbol should be cast to float or double.
- **You get a warning about conversion between types.** You can ignore it, but to make it go away, cast the offending item to what you wanted. Then the compiler will know it was intentional.

EXERCISES

1. Adjust the star in Example 3-4 so that the star's top point is straight up.
2. Here's how to get system time in seconds:

```
#include <ctime>
...
int timeInSeconds = int⁵ (time (nullptr));
```

[5]We cast to int to avoid that conversion warning mentioned in the preceding "Antibugging." The time function returns a time_t (whatever that is); we'll force it to be an int.

Use % and / operators to find the current time in hours, minutes, and seconds. The hours may be off due to what time zone you're in; you can adjust appropriately.

3. (Harder) Make a clock face: a circle with numbers 1–12 in appropriate places.
4. ...and, having done 2 and 3, make a clock face that shows the current time.

CHAPTER 4

Mouse, and if

In this chapter we'll get mouse input, and the art of making decisions, computer style.

Mouse functions

Example 4-1 shows a program to detect where you clicked the mouse and report the result. Amazing, huh? Thus, we introduce three mouse functions: SSDL_GetMouseX, SSDL_GetMouseY, and SSDL_WaitMouse.

Example 4-1. A program to capture and show a mouse click. Excitement!

```
//Program to get a mouse click, and report its location
//            -- from _C++ for Lazy Programmers_

#include "SSDL.h"

int main(int argc, char** argv)
{
    sout << "Click the mouse and we'll see where you clicked.\n";

    //Get the mouse click
    SSDL_WaitMouse();                    //wait for click...
    int xLocation = SSDL_GetMouseX(),
        yLocation = SSDL_GetMouseY();    //and get its X, Y location

    //Print the mouse click
    sout << "The X position of your click was " << xLocation << "\n";
    sout << "The Y position of your click was " << yLocation << "\n";

    //End the program
    sout << "\n\nHit a key to end the program.\n";
```


W. Briggs, *C++ for Lazy Programmers*, https://doi.org/10.1007/978-1-4842-5187-4_4

```
    SSDL_WaitKey();

    return 0;
}
```

At this point

```
int xLocation = SSDL_GetMouseX(),
    yLocation = SSDL_GetMouseY();    //and get its X, Y location
```

your program allocates space to store two integers, xLocation and yLocation, and puts a value in each.

And at this point the program prints them (Figure 4-1).

```
//Print the mouse click
sout << "The X position of your click was " << xLocation << "\n";
sout << "The Y position of your click was " << yLocation << "\n";
```

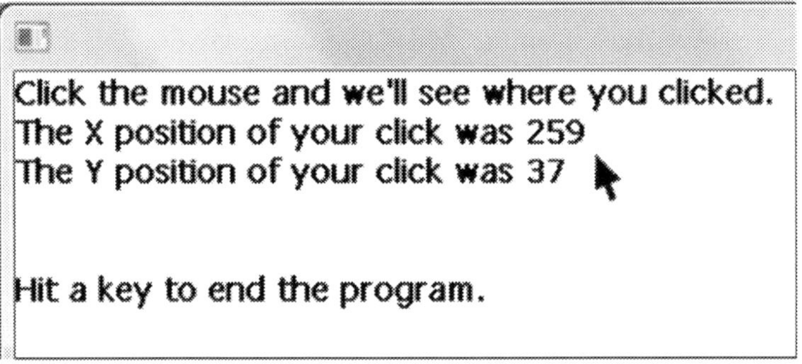

Figure 4-1. *Reporting a mouse click*

In Table 4-1 are the prototypes for the new mouse functions.

Table 4-1. *Basic mouse functions in SSDL*

`int SSDL_GetMouseX ();`	returns the X position of the mouse pointer
`int SSDL_GetMouseY ();`	returns the Y position of the mouse pointer
`void SSDL_WaitMouse ();`	waits for any mouse button to be clicked

Extra Where should you declare variables?

Putting them here

```
int main (int argc, char** argv)
{
    int xLocation;                          // X and Y location
    int yLocation;                          // of mouse
    sout << "Click the mouse and we'll see where you clicked.\n";
    //Get the mouse click
    SSDL_WaitMouse ();                     //wait for it...
    xLocation = SSDL_GetMouseX ();        // and get its X and Y
    yLocation = SSDL_GetMouseY ();        // location
    ...
```

instead of here

```
int main (int argc, char** argv)
{
     sout << "Click the mouse and we'll see where you clicked.\n";
     //Get the mouse click
     SSDL_WaitMouse ();                          //wait for it...
     int xLocation = SSDL_GetMouseX ();          // and get its X and Y
     int yLocation = SSDL_GetMouseY ();          // location
     ...
```

is an old-fashioned way of doing things, from when C++ was still just plain C. Some prefer it, because the variables are always easy to find: they're at the top! I don't, because

- I start looking for them where they're set or used, not at the top.
- I prefer to initialize them to useful values when possible (and in this case, that couldn't happen until after the `SSDL_WaitMouse` call).
- As this example shows, it leads to a need for more commenting.

The old way's not wrong, but "declare as late as possible" seems lazier.

Antibugging

- **The numbers reported for the mouse click don't have anything to do with where you actually clicked.** And your code looks like this:

```
int  xLocation = SSDL_GetMouseX (),
     yLocation = SSDL_GetMouseY ();  //Get the X, Y location
SSDL_WaitMouse ();                   //wait for click...
```

Thing is, SSDL_GetMouseX/SSDL_GetMouseY don't get a mouse *click* location; they just get a location. So here's what happens:

```
1. Program gets the mouse X, Y location
2. You move the mouse where you want it while the program waits
3. You click
```

So it gets the location *before* you move the mouse where it should go. No wonder it's wrong! Rearrange it thus:

```
1. You move the mouse where you want it while the program waits
2. You click
3. Program gets the mouse X, Y location
```

That looks like this in code:

```
SSDL_WaitMouse ();                  //wait for click...
int  xLocation = SSDL_GetMouseX (),
     yLocation = SSDL_GetMouseY (); //Get the X, Y location
```

EXERCISES

1. Write a program that lets you click twice to draw a line between your two mouse clicks.
2. Write a program that lets you click once to set the center of a circle, then again for a point on the edge of that circle; then it draws the circle.

if

So, how can I determine if the mouse is in a particular area of the screen?

```
enum {HALF_SCREEN_WIDTH = 320};

if (xLocation < HALF_SCREEN_WIDTH)
      sout << It's on the left side of the screen.\n";
else
      sout << "It's on the right side of the screen.\n";
```

If `xLocation` is less than `HALF_SCREEN_WIDTH`, the program will tell us it's on the left, else on the right.

The `else` part is optional. You can have the program report if `xLocation` is on the left, and say nothing if it's on the right:

```
if (xLocation < HALF_SCREEN_WIDTH)
      sout << "It's on the left side of the screen.\n";
```

Note The general form of the `if` statement is

`if` (<condition>) <action 1> [`else` <action 2>]

where things in *<pointy brackets>* are blanks you'd fill in with something else, and anything in *[square brackets]* can be omitted. This is called "Backus-Naur form," and it's the conventional way to describe programming language structures.

The `if` statement does exactly what it looks like: if *condition* is true, it does *action 1*, else it does *action 2*.

Naturally the `if` statement's condition must be something that can be true or false. It's often one of the true or false expressions in Table 4-2.

Table 4-2. *Using comparison operators in C++*

Condition	Meaning
X<Y	X is less than Y
X<=Y	X is less than or equal to Y
X>Y	X is greater than Y
X>=Y	X is greater than or equal to Y
X==Y	X is equal to Y. (X=Y, using a single =, means "store the value of Y in X.")
X!=Y	X is not equal to Y

You can also have the `if` part or the `else` part contain multiple actions:

```
if (xLocation < HALF_SCREEN_WIDTH)
{
       int howFarLeft = HALF_SCREEN_WIDTH - xLocation;
       sout << "It's this far left of the middle of the screen: "
            << howFarLeft << "\n.";
}
else
{
       int howFarRight = xLocation - HALF_SCREEN_WIDTH;
       sout << "It's this far right of the middle of the screen: "
            << howFarRight << "\n.";
}
```

The curly braces ({}) cause the compiler to bundle the actions within together and consider them one thing (the `if` action or the `else` action). If you declare a variable inside the {}'s – why not? – the variable only has definition within those {}'s; outside them, if you refer to it, the compiler will tell you it's never heard of it: "`howFarLeft` not declared in this scope," or some such.

Note the indenting. Things contained in the `if`, whether in {}'s or not, are part of the `if` statement and are therefore indented relative to it – just as what's contained in `main`'s {}'s is indented relative to it. Not doing this drives other programmers crazy:

```
if (xLocation < HALF_SCREEN_WIDTH)
{
int howFarLeft = HALF_SCREEN_WIDTH - xLocation;
sout << "It's this far left of the middle of the screen:";
sout << howFarLeft << ".\n";
}
```

Fortunately, your programmer-friendly editor will indent code for you: hit Enter at the end of a line, and it'll take you where the next line should start. Unless (say) you forgot a semicolon and it got confused.

Extra There are different styles of layout for `if`. Here's a good way to string together `if` statements to handle exclusive options:

```
if      (x < 0)          sign = -1; //it's positive
else if (x > 0)          sign = +1; //it's negative
else                     sign = 0;  //it's 0
```

Here's a common variation for `if` statements using { }'s:

```
if (xLocation < HALF_SCREEN_WIDTH) {
                   //"Egyptian" brackets, so called
                   // because they look like where
                   // the Egyptian's hands are in
                   // Figure 4-2

                   // I'd guess the Bangles' song
                   // "Walk Like an Egyptian" gave
                   // us this bit of silliness,
                   // but who knows
   int howFarLeft = HALF_SCREEN_WIDTH - xLocation;
   sout << "It's this far left of the middle of the screen: ";
   sout << howFarLeft << ".\n";
}
```

The writer saved a line by putting the first { on the line with the condition. But it's harder to scan the left margin now and ensure that all the { }'s are matched. I won't say it's wrong, but I think you'll make fewer errors if you put each { and } on a line by itself.

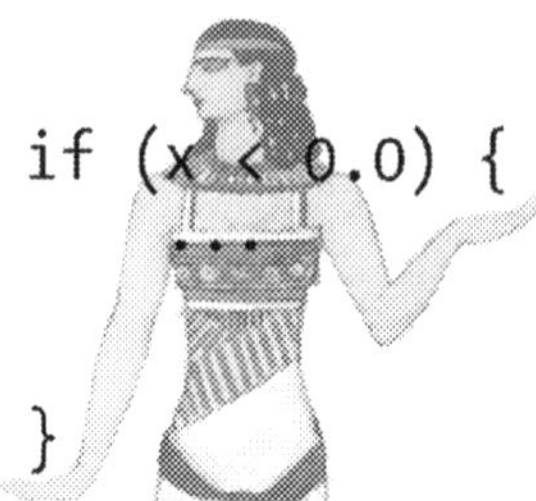

Figure 4-2. *Where "Egyptian brackets" got the name*

Coercion and `if` conditions (`int`'s dirty little secret)

You probably won't mean to use something other than a true or false condition inside the ()'s of an `if` statement...but what if you did?

```
int x;
...
if (x) ...;
```

As it happens, C++ considers 0 to mean false and all other integers to mean true. So if `x` is 0, the `if` statement fails; otherwise, it executes.

If you meant to do that and it's clear, OK. But sometimes it sneaks up on us, as we see in the following "Antibugging" section.

Combining conditions with &&, | |, and !

There's something else we can do with conditions: combine them. Consider these expressions:

- `X>0 && X<10`. The "&&" is read as "and." This means `X` is more than `0` *and* less than `10`.
- `X<=0 || X>=10`. The "||" is read as "or." This means `X` is either `0` or less, or it's `10` or more.

- `! (X<0)`. The "`!`" is read as "not." This means it isn't true that `X` is less than `0`. (You need the `()`'s. If you type `! X < 0`, C++'s precedence rules make it interpret this as `(! X) < 0`. Go figure.)

The odd look of these operators (why "`&&`" rather than "`&`" or "and"?) is a historical artifact. You get used to it.[1]

So, to adapt the earlier example, here's a way of seeing if the mouse click stored in `xLocation` and `yLocation` is in the upper left of the screen:

```
if (xLocation < HALF_SCREEN_WIDTH && yLocation < HALF_SCREEN_HEIGHT)
    sout << "That's in the upper left quadrant.";
```

Antibugging

- **The condition always fails or always succeeds, though you're sure it shouldn't.** Like this:

  ```
  //Cinderella must leave the dance at midnight.
                                          //Does she have time?
  int minutesLeftTillMidnight = 32400; //3 p.m. --
                                          //plenty of time!

  if (minutesLeftTillMidnight = 0)      //Warn her if time's up
        sout << "It's midnight! Cinderella, get home now!\n";

                                         //Print time left
  sout << "You have " << minutesLeftTillMidnight
       << " minutes left.\n";
  ```

  This reports she has 0 minutes left – which is wrong! – and if she did, shouldn't it have warned her to go home?

  The problem is the condition. `minutesLeftTillMidnight = 0`, as we know, means store 0 in `minutesLeftTillMidnight`. So we alter the variable when we shouldn't.

[1] We also have single & and single | as operators (see Chapter 26) – but that's another matter.

But we're not done yet! Now the `if` statement must decide whether the condition is true. No problem: `0` is false, and we just got a zero value between the parentheses, so the `if` doesn't fire and Cinderella, despite losing all her time, doesn't get her warning.

We meant `minutesLeftTillMidnight == 0`. This is the **double-equals error**. It has its own name because everybody does it.

Solution: try not to, and don't hit yourself when you do. The compiler may warn you. It's a Good Thing to notice compiler warnings.

- **It does the action in the `if`, even if the condition is false.** The problem may be that you put a `;` after the condition.

  ```
  if (2+2==5);
     sout << "Orwell was right: the Party even controls math!\n";
  ```

  `;` signals that the statement you're working on is over. C++ interprets the preceding code as: if `2+2==5`, do nothing (since nothing is what comes next, before the `;`). After that, print that Orwell was right.

  Solution: remove the first `;`.

- **It does the later actions in the `if`, even if the condition is false.**

  ```
  if (2+2==5)
     sout << "Orwell was right: the Party even controls math!\n";
     sout << "2+2==5 if I say it does!\n";
  ```

  This code will print

  ```
  2+2==5 if I say it does!
  ```

Since there are no {}'s, C++ doesn't bundle those two `sout` statements together as the things to do if the condition succeeds; it interprets the statement as: if the condition succeeds, print that Orwell was right. Then, whatever happens, print `2+2==5`. Solution:

```
if (2+2==5)
{
   sout << "Orwell was right: the Party even controls math!\n";
   sout << "2+2==5 if I say it does!\n";
}
```

The last two problems were exacerbated by *correct* indenting, which made it look like everything was OK. The editor can help prevent that:

Tip When using a programmer-friendly editor, if you find yourself correcting the editor's indenting, it may have found a punctuation error. You can trace the weird indenting back to the problem.

- **You can't figure which `if` an `else` goes with.**

```
if (TodayIsSaturday)
      if (IAmAtWork)
            sout << "I need a life.\n";
      else
            sout << "Life is good.\n";
```

What do we do if today isn't Saturday? Print "Life is good."? Which `if` does the `else` go with? Indenting doesn't matter to the compiler. The compiler needs a clear rule, and here it is: *the* `else` *always goes with the most recent* `if`. In this case, "Life is good." is printed if `TodayIsSaturday` is `true` but `IAmAtWork` is false. If today isn't Saturday, the code prints nothing.

This ambiguity is called the **`dangling else problem`**, and most languages solve it just as C++ does here.

- **It's still giving incorrect results, and it looks like this:**

  ```
  if (x > y && z)      //If x is bigger than both y and z...
  ```

  That reasoning works in human language, but C++ needs what's on each side of the && to be a true or false condition you want evaluated. The statement will compile, but C++ will understand it to mean "if x > y is true, and z is also true, that is, if z is nonzero," which is not what I meant.

  This fixes my problem:

  ```
  if (x > y && x > z) //If x is bigger than y AND
                      //x is bigger than z
  ```

EXERCISES

1. Write code to report whether the square root of some X is greater than 1.
2. Given two integers, report what order they're in (correct order, reverse order, or equal).
3. Given a numeric score for a grade, 0–100, print whether it's an A, B, C, D, or F.
4. Write an `if` statement that will print whether a mouse click is in the upper left quarter of the screen, the upper right, the lower left, or the lower right.
5. Write code that will print "Out of range!" if X is less than 0 or greater than 8 – and will force it to be in range (by changing X to 0 if it's too small and to 8 if it's too big).

Boolean values and variables

If we can use true or false values in our `if` statements, can we also store them for later reuse? Sure. Here's one:

```
bool isRaining = true;  //bool means "It's got to be true or false;
                        //nothing else allowed"
```

and here is how you might use it:

```
if (isRaining) sout << "I need an umbrella.\n";
```

Tip I usually start bool variable names with is, so it's obvious the value should be true or false.

The possible values for a Boolean variable are – wait for it – true and false.

You can also calculate these values in expressions, as you can with int or double or float variables:

```
bool isTooHotForGolf = (temperature > 85);
```

but if you prefer to use an if, that also works:

```
bool isTooHotForGolf;
if (temperature > 85) isTooHotForGolf = true; else isTooHotForGolf = false;
```

Why would you want Booleans? For convenience and clarity. Suppose you want to find out if it's a good day for golf, but you're really finicky. You can say

```
if (windSpeed < 10 &&
    (cloudCover > 50 && (temperature > 75 && temperature < 85) ||
    (cloudCover < 50 && (temperature > 60 && temperature < 75)))
                  //Aaaigh!  What does this mean?
```

or you can initialize some bool variables and say

```
if (isCalm && ((isCloudy && isWarm) || (isSunny && isCool)))
                  //Cloudy & warm or sunny & cool -- as long as it's calm
```

I think I've proved my point.

Extra George Boole (1815–1864) is the founder of modern symbolic logic, that is, using symbols as variables that can be true or false.

Prior to Boole, there certainly was an understanding of logic, but people were unsure that you could express logical expressions without reference to the meaning and not run the risk of error. (Many might have a hard time trusting that, say, "p and q implies p," but wouldn't have any problem with "If it's raining and cold, it's raining.") Even Boole was cautious: in the introduction to his book *The Mathematical Analysis of Logic*, he anticipated arguments that what he was doing was a really bad idea, but suggested it might not be totally useless. He was right: it was a resounding success, and the computer in front of you as you program is evidence of it.

EXERCISES

1. Wait for a mouse click, and set a Boolean variable to true if the X is greater than the Y. Report whether it was by printing a message on the screen.
2. Get two mouse clicks, and set Boolean variables for whether the second is to the right of the first and whether it's below the first. Then report the second's relation to the first as north, northeast, east, southeast, or whatever's correct.

A hidden object game

Somewhere in a field of rocks is a fossilized ammonite (Figure 4-3). We'll make a game to train budding paleontologists: click on the screen, and if you get the fossil, you win.

Figure 4-3. *An image to search. The fossil's in there somewhere...*

What we need is a sort of imaginary "bounding" box around it: if I click in the box, I win; elsewhere, I lose. It's too hard to guess the coordinates of the box. Maybe I can draw a box on the image, (Example 4-2) and if it looks wrong, adjust. My wrong guess is in Figure 4-4.

Example 4-2. Drawing a box on the screen to find the bounding box we want for part of the image

```
//Program to draw a box around a fossil, to find its coordinates
//            -- from _C++ for Lazy Programmers_

#include "SSDL.h"

int main (int argc, char** argv)
{
  //Resize window to fit the background image.
  SSDL_SetWindowSize (500, 375);              //image is 500x375
  SSDL_SetWindowTitle("A box to enclose the fossil -- hit a key to end");
```

```
  //Load up the world to find fossil in
  const SSDL_Image BACKGROUND = SSDL_LoadImage("media/ammonitePuzzle.jpg");
  SSDL_RenderImage (BACKGROUND, 0, 0);

  //Draw a box where we think he is. Is it right?
  SSDL_SetRenderDrawColor (WHITE);          //a *white* box, for visibility
  //arguments below mean: left x, top y, width, height
  SSDL_RenderDrawRect (375, 175, 80, 50);   //my guess

  //End program
  SSDL_WaitKey ();

  return 0;
}
```

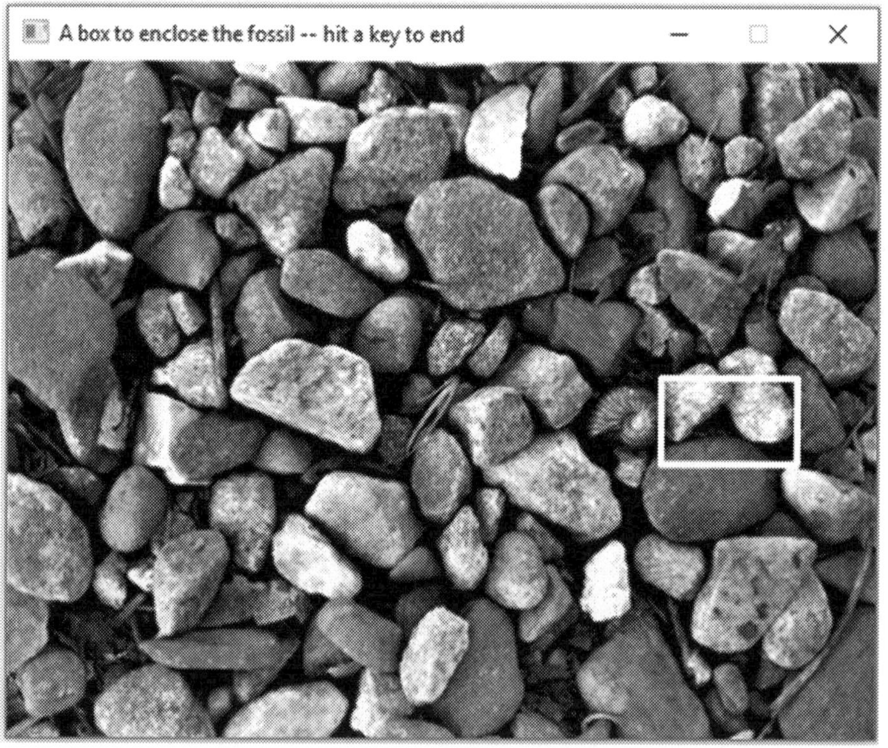

***Figure 4-4.** Looks like the bounding box for the ammonite needs some changes. (I adjusted the lines' thickness to make it easier to see)*

After some playing around I get a new bounding box, the one that results in Figure 4-5:

```
SSDL_RenderDrawRect (335, 180, 45, 35); //corrected numbers
```

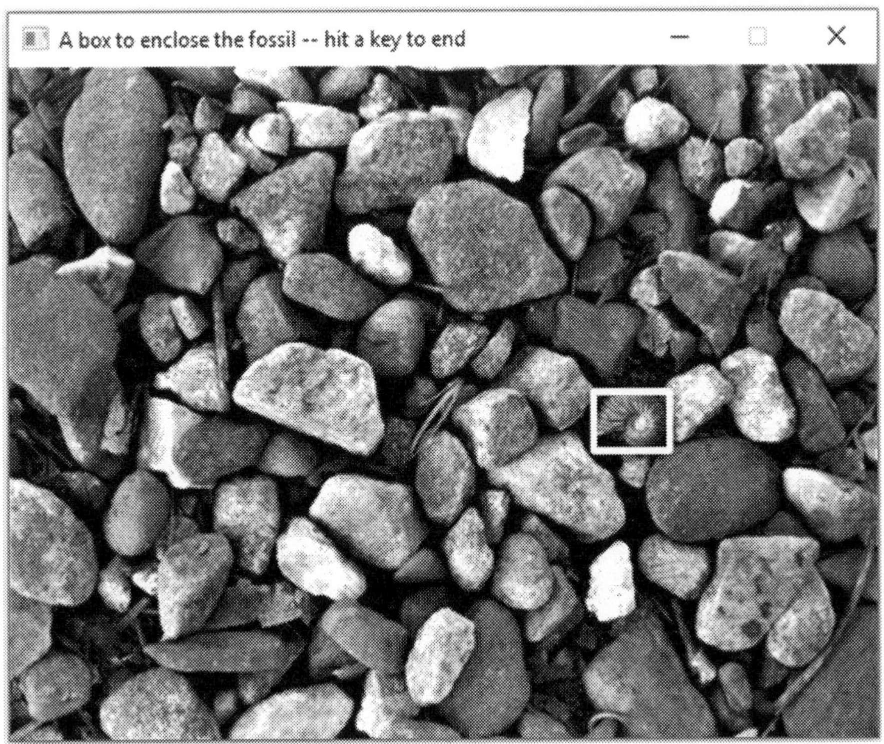

Figure 4-5. *The bounding box is correct*

So now we'll have a program (Example 4-3) that detects whether a mouse click is inside that box. It uses a couple of Boolean variables; and it flashes the bounding box in red and white if you lose.

Example 4-3. My fossil hunt game: trying to find an object with a mouse. Figure 4-6 shows possible output

```
//Program to find a fossil in a field of stones
//            -- from _C++ for Lazy Programmers_

#include "SSDL.h"

int main (int argc, char** argv)
{
    //Set up window
```

```
enum {PICTURE_WIDTH=500, PICTURE_HEIGHT=375}; //size of the picture
enum {WINDOW_WIDTH =500, WINDOW_HEIGHT =430}; //size of program window
                                              //(has extra room
                                              //  for messages)
SSDL_SetWindowTitle ("My fossil hunt: a hidden-object game");
SSDL_SetWindowSize (WINDOW_WIDTH, WINDOW_HEIGHT);

//Load up the world to find the fossil in
const SSDL_Image BACKGROUND=SSDL_LoadImage("media/ammonitePuzzle.jpg");
SSDL_RenderImage (BACKGROUND, 0, 0);

//Print instructions to the user.
SSDL_SetCursor (0, PICTURE_HEIGHT);
sout << "Where's the ammonite?  Click it to win.\n";

//Get that mouse click.
SSDL_WaitMouse ();

//Redraw what's on screen
SSDL_RenderClear ();
SSDL_RenderImage (BACKGROUND, 0, 0);

//See where we clicked, and report if the fossil was found
//I got these numbers by running the searchBox program
enum {BOX_LEFT = 335, BOX_TOP = 180, BOX_WIDTH=45, BOX_HEIGHT=35 };

int x= SSDL_GetMouseX(), y = SSDL_GetMouseY();

//Is X between left side of box and right? Is Y also within bounds?
bool isXInRange = (BOX_LEFT < x && x < BOX_LEFT+BOX_WIDTH );
bool isYInRange = (BOX_TOP  < y && y < BOX_TOP +BOX_HEIGHT);

if (isXInRange && isYInRange)
   sout << "You found the ammonite! Here's your Ph.D.\n";
else
{
   sout << "You lose.\n";
```

```
        //Now we'll flash where the fossil was
        SSDL_RenderImage (BACKGROUND, 0, 0);[2]
        SSDL_SetRenderDrawColor (RED);
        SSDL_RenderDrawRect (BOX_LEFT, BOX_TOP, BOX_WIDTH, BOX_HEIGHT);
        SSDL_Delay (250); //250 msec, or 1/4 sec

        SSDL_RenderImage (BACKGROUND, 0, 0);
        SSDL_SetRenderDrawColor (WHITE);
        SSDL_RenderDrawRect (BOX_LEFT, BOX_TOP, BOX_WIDTH, BOX_HEIGHT);
        SSDL_Delay (250); //250 msec, or 1/4 sec

        SSDL_RenderImage (BACKGROUND, 0, 0);
        SSDL_SetRenderDrawColor (RED);
        SSDL_RenderDrawRect (BOX_LEFT, BOX_TOP, BOX_WIDTH, BOX_HEIGHT);
        SSDL_Delay (250); //250 msec, or 1/4 sec

        SSDL_RenderImage (BACKGROUND, 0, 0);
        SSDL_SetRenderDrawColor (WHITE);
        SSDL_RenderDrawRect (BOX_LEFT, BOX_TOP, BOX_WIDTH, BOX_HEIGHT);
        SSDL_Delay (250); //250 msec, or 1/4 sec
    }

    //End program
    sout << "Hit a key to end.";

    SSDL_WaitKey ();

    return 0;
}
```

[2]Do I really have to post the background each time? Any time SSDL updates the screen – by a call to `SSDL_Delay`, `SSDL_WaitKey`, `SSDL_WaitMouse`, or otherwise – it may then lose what it updated so it won't show up on the next update. Or it may not. I'm reposting the background to be sure.

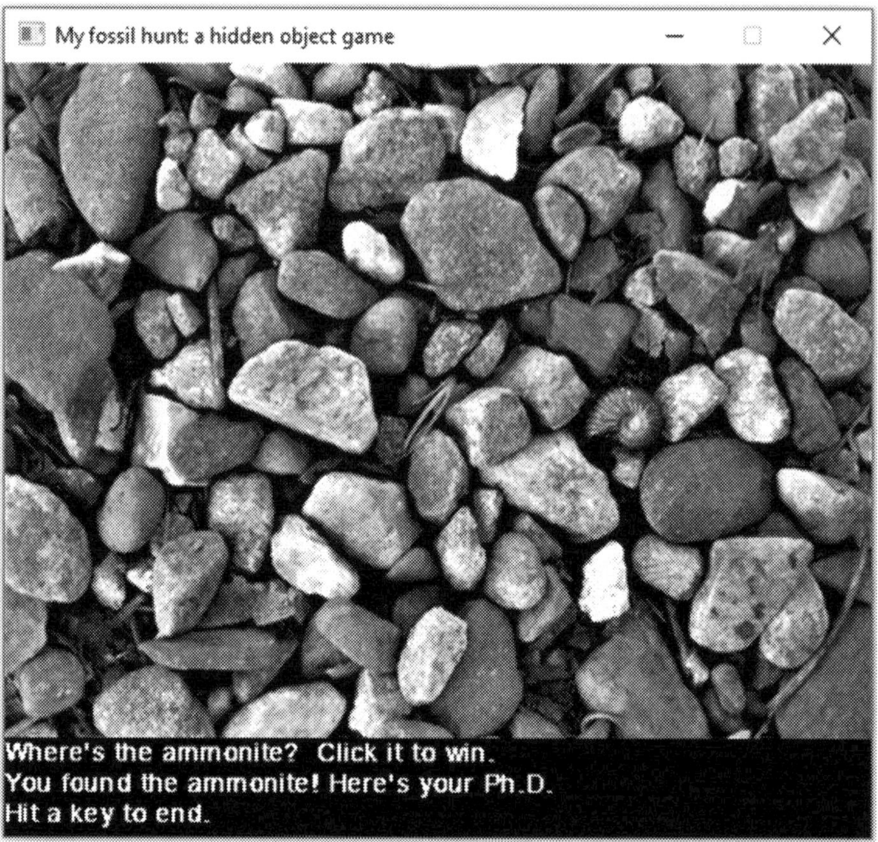

Figure 4-6. *The completed fossil hunt game*

EXERCISES

1. Write a program that displays a box, waits for a mouse click, and tells you whether you clicked within the box.

   To make it more fun, put up a roughly square image of something interesting. I like Spam. Special thanks to the creative people who made "Find the Spam" (`www.smalltime.com/findthespam/`) for this surreal game.

2. Make a hidden object game: the user must click on the objects you provide (have two or more) in order to win. You can require the user to do it in order. A click on something that *isn't* one of the objects, or the correct object in order, ends the game in a loss.

   You may consider each object to be a square area on the screen.

3. Write a program that draws a bubble wherever you clicked. Always the same size bubble…but it won't let you put one *partly* on the screen. If you click too close to an edge, it moves the bubble away from the edge enough that it does not cross the edge. You might also add a sound effect when you create a bubble.

CHAPTER 5

Loops, Input, and `char`

In this chapter we'll look at repeated actions, input, and things to do with the character type.

Keyboard input

Consider this code:

```
int ageInYears;
sout << "How old are you? "; ssin >> ageInYears;
```

This prints the query about age, then waits for keyboard input. If the user enters a number, that number is stored in `ageInYears`. (Anything else is likely to give `ageInYears` a 0 value.) `ssin`[1] waits for you to hit Enter before it processes input, so backspacing is allowed.

`ssin` uses the same font and cursor as `sout`; they are both part of SSDL.

You may note how the << arrows go: with `sout`, they go from the value to the output; with `ssin`, they go from the input to the variable.

This is as good a time as any to introduce a new basic type: `char`, or character. Examples of chars include 'A' and 'a' (which are distinct), '?', '1', ' ' (the space character), and '\n'. Here is some code that uses a `char` variable:

```
char answer;
sout << "Are you sure (Y/N)? "; ssin >> answer;
if (answer == 'y')
    sout << "Are you *really* sure?\n";
```

[1] I could have called it `sin` and waited for the puns to start, but `sin` already means something in C++: the sine function. "S-in" might be a good way to pronounce it.

W. Briggs, *C++ for Lazy Programmers*, https://doi.org/10.1007/978-1-4842-5187-4_5

You can also chain things you're reading in with >>:

```
ssin >> firstThingReadIn
     >> secondThingReadIn;
```

Whether reading chars or numbers of whatever, ssin skips whitespace (spaces, tabs, and returns); so you can type what you want with spaces between, and it can handle it.

Example 5-1 shows a sample program that finds ways to insult you no matter what your response. Figure 5-1 shows a sample session.

```
Let's see if you can handle the truth.
How old are you? 20
The truth is you are OLD.
Hit any key to end.
```

Figure 5-1. *Insulting the world, one person at a time*

Example 5-1. A program using ssin

```
//Program to insult the user based on input
//              -- from _C++ for Lazy Programmers_

#include "SSDL.h"

int main (int argc, char** argv)
{
    int ageInYears = 0;

    sout << "Let's see if you can handle the truth.\n";
    sout << "How old are you? "; ssin >> ageInYears;

    bool isOlder = (ageInYears >= 20);
    //Seriously? Well, 20 *is* old if you're a computer program

    if (isOlder) sout << "The truth is you are OLD.\n";
    else         sout << "You're not old enough. Sorry, kid.\n";

    sout << "Hit any key to end.\n";
```

```
    SSDL_WaitKey ();

    return 0;
}
```

Antibugging

- **You get a string of error messages like this**[2]:

```
main.cpp: In function 'int main(int, char**)':
main.cpp:11:39: error: no match for 'operator<<' (operand
types are 'std::istream' {aka 'std::basic_istream<char>'}
and 'int')
     sout << "How old are you? "; ssin << ageInYears;
                                  ~~~~~^~~~~~~~~~~~~
main.cpp:11:39: note: candidate: 'operator<<(int, int)'
<built-in>
main.cpp:11:39: note:   no known conversion for argument
1 from 'std::istream' {aka 'std::basic_istream<char>'} to
'int'
In file included from /usr/include/c++/8/string:52,
                  from /usr/include/c++/8/bits/locale_
                  classes.h:40,
                  from /usr/include/c++/8/bits/ios_
                  base.h:41,
                  from /usr/include/c++/8/ios:42,
                  from /usr/include/c++/8/istream:38,
                  from /usr/include/c++/8/sstream:38,
                  from ../../external/SSDL/include/SSDL_
                  display.h:26,
                  from ../../external/SSDL/include/
                  SSDL.h:27,
                  from main.cpp:4:
```

[2]This is from the g++ compiler. Visual Studio gave me three lines and clearly identified << as the problem. Nice!

```
/usr/include/c++/8/bits/basic_string.h:6323:5: note:
candidate: 'template<class _CharT, class _Traits,
class _Alloc> std::basic_ostream<_CharT, _Traits>&
std::operator<<(std::basic_ostream<_CharT, _Traits>&, const
std::__cxx11::basic_string<_CharT, _Traits, _Alloc>&)'
     operator<<(basic_ostream<_CharT, _Traits>& __os,
     ^~~~~~~~
```

and then literally pages more. Good luck decoding that.

It all came from one error: the >>'s went the wrong way on an `ssin` statement. It should have been `ssin << ageInYears`. Compilers sometimes get confused.

You may get another flood of errors if you try to `ssin >> "\n"`, or something else that isn't a variable.

EXERCISES

1. Write a program for converting degrees Fahrenheit to degrees Centigrade, using the formula C = (F-32)*(5/9). Make it interactive, that is, ask the user for the temperature to convert.
2. Write a program that identifies what generation you're in (`Gen Z`, `millennial`, etc.), based on the age or year of birth the user inputs. You get to pick the ranges.
3. The Body Mass Index (BMI) tells you if you're heavy, thin, or in the middle. (It's imprecise, but if nothing else, maybe I could convince my grandmother I won't starve if I don't take seconds.)

   Officially, these are the ranges:

underweight	less than 18.5
normal weight	18.5–25
overweight	25–30
obese	30+

So: write a program to calculate the user's BMI. The formula is

$$BMI = weight\ in\ kg / (height\ in\ meters)^2$$

If you're in a country that uses English units, you'll also need this information: 1 kg = 2.2 pounds; 1 meter = 39.37 inches.

4. Have the user enter two single-digit numbers and return their sum. But here's the twist: the numbers entered are in base 16. In base 16, we use 'A' to represent 10, 'B' for 11, 'C' for 12, and so on to 'F' for 15. You can give the result in base 10.

5. Write a program that asks the user for two times (such as 1:06 or 12:19) and prints the difference neatly (11:03, for example, or 0:40, but not 13:0 or -12:70).

6. Instead of asking the user for the two times, in the previous example, *measure* the two times that the user hits the return key, getting the current system time like so:

   ```
   long long int myTime = time (nullptr);
   ```

   This gives you time in seconds since midnight, January 1, 1970 (on systems I know). You'll need to `#include <ctime>`.

while and do-while

The program can do something *if* a condition is true…or it can do something *while* a condition is true.

Here's a loop to determine how many times you can divide a number by 10 before you get 1. (This will be the same as the number of digits in the number if you print it.)

```
int digits = 0;
while (number > 1)    //while we haven't reached 1
{
    number /= 10;     //divide it by 10
    digits += 1;      //that's one more digit!
}
```

In Backus-Naur form (BNF), the `while` statement is

`while` (<condition>) <action>

As long as the condition is true, the while loop will execute the action. When it stops being true, the loop ends, and the program moves on to whatever comes after.

There's a variation on `while`, exactly the same except that it checks the condition *after* doing the action: `do-while`. Its BNF form is

do <action> `while` (<condition>)

and an example is

```
do
{
      sout << "Ready to rumble (Y/N)? "; ssin >> answer;
}
while (answer != 'n' && answer != 'y');
      // while answer isn't yes or no, ask again and again

if (answer == 'y')
      ...//rumble!
```

That wouldn't work as a `while` statement

```
while (answer != 'n') ...
```

because you don't know what `answer` is until you've asked at least once.

The bottom line is that `do-while` does the action at least once (before testing the condition), whereas `while` *might* quit before taking any action at all. We usually use `while`, but sometimes `do-while` is the very thing we need. Thus, we have the Golden Rule of Loops.

Golden Rule of Loops (Version 1)

If you want the loop to execute at least once, use `do-while`.

If it makes any sense for it to execute zero times, use `while`.

Loops with SSDL

There's something I didn't tell you about SSDL. It doesn't update the screen every time you draw or print. To save update time, it puts this off till it has a reason to wait on the user: an `ssin` statement, or an `SSDL_WaitKey` or `SSDL_WaitMouse`. The following loop, which is intended to show you `"Move mouse to right half of screen to end."` until you move the mouse to the right, will never update the screen:

```
while (SSDL_GetMouseX() < WHERE_IT_IS)
{
    SSDL_RenderClear ();
    SSDL_SetCursor (0, 0);
    sout << "Move mouse to right half of screen to end.";
}
```

SSDL also doesn't check for things that make it quit the program - hitting Escape or clicking the X to kill the window - until it's waiting on you. So the preceding code won't let you quit the program either.

The fix is the same for both problems: call the function `SSDL_IsQuitMessage`. It updates the screen, checks for input messages (mouse clicks, keystrokes), and returns whether there's been a command to quit.

```
while (! SSDL_IsQuitMessage () && SSDL_GetMouseX() < WHERE_IT_IS)
{
    SSDL_RenderClear ();
    SSDL_SetCursor (0, 0);
    sout << "Move mouse to right half of screen to end.";
}
```

Here's the ready-to-rumble do-while loop from earlier, adapted to allow the user to quit easily:

```
do
{
     sout << "Ready to rumble (Y/N)? "; ssin >> answer;
}
while (!SSDL_IsQuitMessage () && answer != 'n' && answer != 'y');
```

Extra We could ask the user to type 1 for yes and 2 for no if we wanted to expose ourselves as user-hostile throwbacks to the 1970s and never get hired again. (What does 2 have to do with "no"?) It's much easier on the user to remember that *"n"* means no.

If there are more options to choose than yes and no – say, your program manipulates files, Opening, Saving, and Renaming – it's still **user-friendly** to give options with letters (O, S, and R) rather than numbers.

How to make your programs easy to interact with is the subject of one sub-field of computer science: human-computer interaction.

break and continue

break means leave the loop immediately. Here's a version of the preceding while loop, now using break. You decide which way's clearer.

```
while (SSDL_GetMouseX() < WHERE_IT_IS)
{
    if (! isQuitMessage ()) break;
    SSDL_RenderClear ();
    SSDL_SetCursor (0, 0);
    sout << "Move mouse to right half of screen to end.";
}
```

continue means skip the rest of this iteration of the loop and go back to the top. I rarely use it.

Some programming-style mavens are horrified by break and continue. They think you should be able to look at the loop's continuation condition and see immediately under what circumstance the loop can end – essentially, that these keywords reduce clarity. I think they're right that clarity is crucial, but I'm not sure break is the problem. Certainly if your loop was 50 lines long, it would be tedious to examine it for breaks. But I think the solution is not to have loops 50 lines long. Simple is good.

Antibugging

- **The program won't end, and you can't even kill the program.** You're probably stuck in a loop, but what do you do to restart? If Ctrl-C doesn't work, try these:
    - Visual Studio: Debug ➤ Stop Debugging, or hit the reddish square for stop near the top of the window.
    - MinGW: Kill it with Task Manager.
    - Unix: If you don't even have a command prompt, hit Ctrl-Z in the command window to get it.

      There are two commands that can help us. `ps` lists active processes:

      ```
      PID TTY          TIME CMD
      14972 pts/0    00:00:00 bash
      15046 pts/0    00:00:00 bash
      15047 pts/0    00:00:01 a.out
      15054 pts/0    00:00:00 ps
      ```

      `kill -9 <process-id>` means something like "I tried, but I can't find a nice way to end this process, so just kill it."

      `a.out` is what we're trying to kill, but if we ran it with a script like `runx`, we'll want that gone too. It's probably the most recent shell command, some command with "sh" in its name. (Get the wrong one and you may kill your terminal. Oops.) This command will kill it and its dependent process `a.out`.

      ```
      kill -9 15046
      ```

- **The loop repeats forever, and you can't quit.** The problem is it isn't checking for quit messages. Make your loop condition look like this:

```
while (! SSDL_IsQuitMessage () &&
                ...whatever else you want to check...  )
```

or, if it's a do-while,

```
do
{
        ...
}
while (! isQuitMessage () && ...);
```

The loop repeats forever until you hit quit; or it does something forever that you wanted done a few times.

Consider under what condition you will break the loop. It must be that it's never met:

```
int rectanglesDrawn = 0;
while (!SSDL_IsQuitMessage () &&
                rectanglesDrawn < MAX_RECTANGLES)
{
        SSDL_RenderDrawRect (...);
}
```

The loop never incremented `rectanglesDrawn`...so no matter how many you draw, the loop doesn't end. This line should do it:

```
        ...
        rectanglesDrawn += 1;
}
```

- **The loop repeats forever, or won't repeat when it should.** It's easy to get confused when the loop has a combination of conditions:

```
do
{
        if (isQuitMessage ()) break;

        sout << "Answer Y or N: "; ssin >> answer;
}
while (answer != 'n' || answer != 'y');
```

This may look right, but it actually says: keep looping while the answer is not yes *or* not no. Well it's always either not yes *or* not no! Suppose it's yes: then "not no" is true, so it keeps going. Suppose it's no: then "not yes" is true, so it keeps going. So it loops forever.

The solution is to keep going while it's not yes, *and* it's also not no – while it's a nonsensical answer like `'7'` or `'X'`.

```
do
{
      if (isQuitMessage ()) break;

      sout << "Answer Y or N: "; ssin >> answer;
}
while (answer != 'n' && answer != 'y');
```

EXERCISES

1. Make your own music player: put buttons marked "Music on" and "Music off" near the bottom of the screen, and turn sound on or off appropriately when the user clicks on the boxes.

2. Write a program that draws a bubble wherever you click. The bubble's size should depend on how long since the last mouse click. Use the Internet to read up on the function `SDL_GetTicks()`.

3. Update Exercise 1 from the end of the previous chapter – the hidden object game – so the user can click on the hidden objects in any order.

4. (Harder; requires geometry) Consider the perimeter of a triangle which is centered on a point and whose endpoints are "R" away from that center.

   Now consider if it were a square, or a pentagon, or something with N sides (Figure 5-2). What will the perimeter look like when N is large?

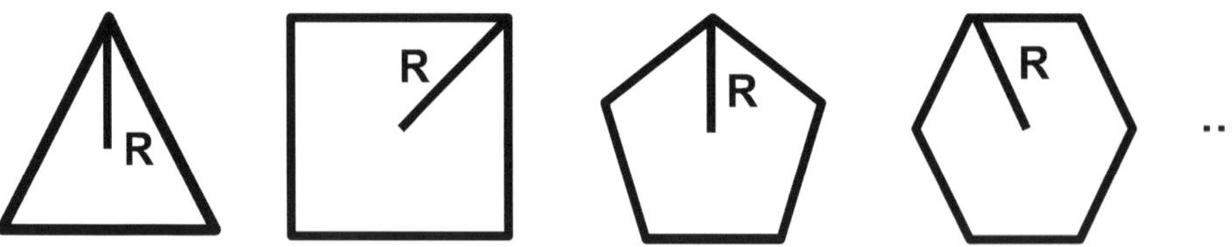

Figure 5-2. *Polygons for Exercise 4*

Write a program that finds, given some R, the perimeter of a regular N-sided polygon, where N is large. Divide that perimeter by 2R. How much does it look like the value you know for π?

for loops

A for loop is a loop that counts through a range. Here's a simple one:

```
for (int count=0; count < 10; count += 1)
    sout << '';          //print these numbers, separated by spaces
```

and here's its output:

```
0 1 2 3 4 5 6 7 8 9
```

In Backus-Naur form, a for loop is

for (<initialization>; <continuing-condition>; <increment>)

<action>

Let's look at that piece by piece.

The **initialization** section – `int count=0` – is done before the loop starts. As you can see, you can declare variables in it. The variables are only visible inside the loop.[3]

As long as the **continuing condition** is true, the loop continues.

At the end of each time through the loop, each "iteration," C++ does the **increment** part. This could be anything, but it usually increments an index variable (i.e., the variable we're using to count with).

[3]Some compilers aren't up to speed on this, and let the variables stay defined after the loop. Solution: declare the variable before the loop. Better yet, upgrade your compiler.

The order that the computer does the sections is

1. do <initialization section>
2. is <continuing-condition> true? If not, leave the loop
3. do <action>
4. do <increment-section>
5. go back to step 2

Increment operators

We often find we need to add 1 to a variable (or subtract 1). C++ provides operators for this. Here are two examples:

```
++y; //adds 1 to y. This is called "increment."
--x; //subtracts 1 from x. This is called "decrement."
```

Most computers have a built-in instruction to add 1 and another to subtract 1 – so we're telling the compiler to use them. It's efficient.

We often do this in for loops, like so:

```
for (int count=0; count < 10; ++count)
    sout << count << ' ';
```

We can also use decrement operators:

```
for (int count=10; count > 0; --count) //A countdown, 10 to 1...
    sout << count << ' ';
sout << "Liftoff!\n";
```

You can increment by other amounts, though it's unusual:

```
for (int count=2; count <= 8; count += 2) //2 4 6 8...
    sout << count << ' ';
sout << "Who do we appreciate?\n";
```

There's another type of increment, called "post-increment," and a corresponding post-decrement. It looks like this: `count++`, not `++count`. You won't notice the difference unless you put the expression on the right side of an = or as an argument to a function.

Pre-increment: Y = ++X means X = X+1; Y = X. That is, add 1 to X, then use the value of X (copy it to Y).

Post-increment: Y = X++ means Y = X; X = X+1. That is, use the value of X (copy it to Y), *then* add 1 to X.

An example: averaging numbers

Suppose you want to average a list of ten numbers, taken from the user. I know: how exciting. But we can't play games *all* the time; people will start thinking programming is too much fun and pay us less. Here's my plan:

```
tell the user what we're doing

total = 0              //so far, nothing in the total...

for ten times
      get a number from the user
      add that to the total

average = total/10.0  //floating-point division, for a floating-point answer
                      //better not use int division -- remember what happened
                      //  in Example 3-3 (drawing a star), when our division
                      //  answers kept showing up as zeroes...
print average
```

Example 5-2 puts it into code.

Example 5-2. A program to average numbers, using a for loop

```
//Program to average numbers
//            -- from _C++ for Lazy Programmers_

#include "SSDL.h"

int main (int argc, char** argv)
{
    enum {MAX_NUMBERS = 10};
```

```
    sout << "Enter " << MAX_NUMBERS
         << " numbers to get an average.\n";

    double total = 0.0;

    //Get the numbers
    for (int i = 0; i < MAX_NUMBERS; ++i)
    {
        double number;

        sout << "Enter the next number:  ";
        ssin >> number;

        total += number;
    }

    //Print the average
    double average = total / MAX_NUMBERS;
    sout << "The average is " << average << ".\n";

    sout << "Hit any key to end.\n";
    SSDL_WaitKey ();

    return 0;
}
```

The keywords break and continue work in for loops just as they do in while and do-while loops:

```
int howMany = 0; //how many numbers did we add to total?

for (int i = 0; i < MAX_NUMBERS; ++i)
{
      int number;
      sout << "Enter a number: "; ssin >> number;

      if (number == NUMBER_THAT_SHOULD_BE_SKIPPED)
            continue;      //go back to start of loop

      if (number == NUMBER_THAT_MEANS_WE_SHOULD_END)
            break;          //leave loop NOW
```

```
        total += number;
        ++howMany;
}
```

...and are as frowned on by purists, on the grounds of clarity.

So we now have three kinds of loops. You know how to decide between while and do-while – the Golden Rule of Loops, earlier in this chapter. What about for loops?

By convention and by reason, we use for loops when we're counting through a range – when we know what we're counting from and to. Thus, we have the final Golden Rule of Loops.

Golden Rule of Loops (Final Version)

If you know in advance how many times you'll do it, use `for`. Otherwise:

If you want the loop to execute at least once, use `do-while`.

If it makes any sense for it to execute zero times, use `while`.

Antibugging

- **Later actions are done once, not many times**. A common problem. Example:

  ```
  //Code to print several powers of 2
  int product = 1;
  sout << "Here are several successive powers of 2: ";
  for (int i = 0; i <10; ++i)
        sout << product << '';
        product *= 2;
  ```

  I forgot the {}'s. I assumed the code would do this:

  ```
  for i goes from 0 through 9
        print product
        multiply product by 2
  ```

but it actually does this:

```
for i goes from 0 through 9
      print product
multiply product by 2
```

Solution: let your editor indent for you as you go, thus catching the error.

- ***No* action gets repeated.**

```
for (int i = 0; i < N; ++i);      //This loop prints
                                    only one *
      sout << '*';
```

There's an extra ; at the end of the first line.

- **Your loop goes one step too far.**

```
for (int i = 0; i <=4; ++i) ...
```

The last time through, ++i makes i equal 4. But if you wanted four entries, you just got 5: 0, 1, 2, 3, 4. Solution: use < for the condition. To be sure you have the right range, do a walkthrough. Or always use the form

```
for (int i = 0; i < howManyTimes; ++i) ...
```

Tip For loops almost always start at 0 and use <, not <=, for the continuation condition: `i < howManyTimes`, not `i <= howManyTimes`.

EXERCISES

1. Adapt Example 3-3/Example 3-4 (drawing a star) so that it asks the user for the radius, center, and number of points – and uses a loop rather than repeating code to draw the lines.
2. Write a program which asks the user for an integer and a power to raise it to, and prints the result.

3. Write a program like the average program in Example 5-2, but let it provide not average, but maximum.
4. Print the first 20 square integers: 1, 4, 9, 16, and so on.
5. Draw a graph of some function (sine is a good one). Add X and Y axes and appropriate labels.
6. Write a program to ask the user for N times (times as in 2:30), summing to get total hours and minutes.
7. Write a program which has the user guess a number (that number can be a constant in the program) and keeps taking guesses until the user runs out of turns – you decide how many – or gets it right. Then it reports success or failure. You'll need a Boolean variable `isSuccess`.

chars and cctype

Example 5-3 compares two input characters.

Example 5-3. A program to compare characters

```
//Program to tell if two letters are in alphabetical order
//            -- from _C++ for Lazy Programmers_

#include "SSDL.h"

int main(int argc, char** argv)
{
    char char1, char2;

    sout << "Give me a letter: "; ssin >> char1;
    sout << "Give me another: ";  ssin >> char2;

    if (char1 < char2)
        sout << "You gave me two characters in order.\n";
    else if (char1 > char2)
        sout << "They are in reverse order.\n";
```

```
    else
        sout << "They are identical.\n";

    SSDL_WaitKey();

    return 0;
}
```

It mostly works. It's a little strange that 'a' comes after 'Z.' But that's how the computer thinks of it: lowercase letters, a–z, come after the uppercase range. The precise ordering of the characters was decided in 1967 and is maintained by the American National Standards Institute (ANSI). A complete listing of this American Standard Code for Information Interchange (ASCII) codes is in Appendix C.

I'd rather my comparison ignore capitalization. Here's one way: convert it to uppercase.

```
char myChar           = 'b';
char upperCaseVersion = myChar - 'a' + 'A';
```

It looks weird, but...to get the lowercase version of `'b'`, we do this: subtract `'a'` first. This gives us a difference of `1`, of course. We then add this `1` to `'A'`, which gives us `'B'`. This will work for any lowercase letter.

What if we aren't sure it's lowercase? We can use an `if` statement to be sure.

```
if (myChar >= 'a' && myChar <= 'z') //it's lower case -- fix it
    upperCaseVersion = myChar - 'a' + 'A';
else                                //it's not -- leave it alone
    upperCaseVersion = myChar;
```

This is so useful we'll want to do it again and again. Fortunately, the makers of C and C++ agree. They've given us a suite of functions for handling capitalization and a few other qualities of characters; these are found in the include file `cctype`. Table 5-1 shows a few; for more such functions, see Appendix F.

Table 5-1. Some useful functions regarding capitalization

`int islower (int ch);`	return whether `ch` is lowercase. (Non-letter characters are not lowercase)
`int isupper (int ch);`	return whether `ch` is uppercase. (Non-letter characters are not uppercase)
`int tolower (int ch);`	return the lowercase version of `ch`. If `ch` is not a letter, it returns `ch`
`int toupper (int ch);`	return the uppercase version of `ch`. If `ch` is not a letter, it returns `ch`

These functions existed in the C, the language C++ grew out of. This explains something that looks odd: we're dealing with characters, but the type is not `char` but `int`! Well, characters are integers, in a way, so this is tolerable, if not absolutely clear.

The other odd thing about these functions is similar: `islower` and `isupper` return `int`. Shouldn't they return `true` or `false`? Yes, but since C++ interprets `0` as `false` and other integers all as `true`, `int` will serve, as in this code snippet:

```
if (isupper (myChar))
    sout << "You have an upper-case letter.\n";
```

Example 5-4 uses `toupper` to compare characters without regard to case.

Example 5-4. Example 5-3, using true alphabetical order rather than simple ASCII order

```
//Program to tell if two letters are in alphabetical order,
// regardless of upper or lower case
//              -- from _C++ for Lazy Programmers_

#include <cctype>
#include "SSDL.h"

int main(int argc, char** argv)
{
      char char1, char2;

      sout << "Give me a letter: "; ssin >> char1;
      sout << "Give me another: ";  ssin >> char2;
```

```
    if      (toupper(char1) < toupper(char2))
            sout << "You gave me two characters in order.\n";
    else if (toupper(char1) > toupper(char2))
            sout << "They are in reverse order.\n";
    else
            sout << "They are identical.\n";

    SSDL_WaitKey();

    return 0;
}
```

Here's a piece of code that doesn't quite work:

```
sout  << "The upper-case version of '" << char1
      << "' is ' << toupper (char1) << ".'\n";
```

If we run this, the output will be something like

```
The upper-case version of 'a' is '65.'
```

The problem is that `toupper` returns not `char` but `int` – so `sout` prints that `int`. Here's the fix: casting.

```
sout  << "The upper-case version of '" << char1
      << "' is '" << char (toupper (char1)) << ".'\n";
```

Extra So far we've seen these types:

`int double float bool char`

Some can have modifiers. For example, a `long double` has more decimal places than a regular `double`; how many is compiler-dependent. `int` can be preceded by the keywords `signed`, `unsigned`, `short`, `long`, or `long long` (I guess the word "humongous" was taken), as in `unsigned long int`. As you can imagine, `short` and `long` refer to how big the number can be. `int` may be omitted: `unsigned short x;` or `long y`. If not specified, an `int` is `signed`.

Suffixes on the literal values – as in "5.0F" or "42U" – are there to tell the compiler "this is a `(f)loat`, not a `double`"; "this is `(u)nsigned`"; and so on. Suffixes can be lowercase.

If a `char` is not specified as `signed` or `unsigned`, it is up to the compiler to decide which it is. It shouldn't matter. `chars` are always the same size, allowing for $2^8 =$ 256 possibilities, which is more than enough for the conventional character set.

`wchar_t` ("wide character") is a larger character type, used when 256 characters aren't enough, that is, for international characters.

If you want to know just how big an `int`, `long int`, and so on can be, you can find out using `#include <climits>`, which defines constants for maximum and minimum values for the various types. You can get the size of one of these in bytes with `sizeof`: `sizeof (int)` or `sizeof (myInt)`, where `myInt` is an `int`.

If you store values that are too big, they'll wrap around: instead of a too large positive number, you'll get a negative number. This is almost never a problem. If it is, use a `long int` or a `long long int`.

For a complete list of basic types, see Appendix D.

EXERCISES

1. Write a program to help you determine whether the creature you just saw was a fairy, a troll, a dwarf, and elf, or some other magical creature, assuming you carried your laptop into the Enchanted Forest. You pick the distinguishing features of each type of creature. A session might start something like this:

```
Welcome to the Enchanted Forest.
This creature you have seen:
Does it have wings (Y/N)? Y
...
```

   The user should be able to type either 'y' or 'Y' and either 'n' or 'N' to answer. (If the user types something that doesn't make sense, you can assume that means "no.")

switch

Consider this `if` statement, which prints whether a letter is as vowel, semivowel, or consonant.

```
//Print classification of letters as vowel, semivowel, consonant
if      (toupper (letter) == 'A') sout << "vowel";
else if (toupper (letter) == 'E') sout << "vowel";
else if (toupper (letter) == 'I') sout << "vowel";
else if (toupper (letter) == 'O') sout << "vowel";
else if (toupper (letter) == 'U') sout << "vowel";
else if (toupper (letter) == 'Y') sout << "semivowel";
else if (toupper (letter) == 'W') sout << "semivowel";
else                              sout << "consonant";
```

It will work, but there's a shorter way.

In BNF, a **switch** statement is

switch (<expression>)

{

*case <value>: <action>**

...

[default: <action>]*

}

The * means "as many copies as you want, maybe zero."

What this does: the expression in the parentheses is evaluated. (It has to be something you can count by – integers or characters. No floats, no doubles.) If it matches a particular value, the computer goes to that *case <value>* and executes whatever actions come after that. If you specify a default action, that's what happens if the expression doesn't match anything.

So here's that same piece of code, using a `switch` statement:

```
//Print classification of letters as vowel, semivowel, consonant
switch (toupper (letter))
{
```

```
    case 'A':
    case 'E':
    case 'I':
    case 'O':
    case 'U':   sout << "vowel";
                break;
    case 'Y':
    case 'W':   sout << "semivowel";
                break;
    default:    sout << "consonant";
}
```

If `letter` matches 'A' (for example), it does whatever actions it finds after case 'A'. In this example, the next action it finds is `sout << "vowel";`. It keeps going till it finds `break`, which, just as before, means "leave this structure" – so at that point it leaves the `switch` statement. (Nobody will gripe at you for using `break` in this way; `switch` needs it.)

I usually include a `default` in a `switch` statement to handle unexpected values that might arise from errors.

Antibugging

- `switch` **does what you wanted to do for that value...then it does the options that follow as well.** This is the most common error with `switch`: forgetting the `break`. Solution: go back and put `break`s between the different options you wanted (in the preceding code, vowel, semivowel, and consonant).
- **The compiler complains something about case labels and variables.** This code has that problem:

  ```
  switch (myChar)
  {
  case 'P':
        int turns = MAXTURNS;
        playGame (turns);
        break;
  ...
  }
  ```

It doesn't like initializing a variable as part of a `switch`. No problem: we'll just put {}'s around the area that needs the variable:

```
switch (myChar)
{
case 'P':
      {
            int turns = MAXTURNS;
            playGame (turns);
            break;
      }
...
}
```

EXERCISES

1. Write and test a function that, given a number, prints the associated ordinal: that is, for 1, print 1st, for 2, print 2nd, for 3, print 3rd, and for everything else, print the number plus "th."
2. Menus are a time-honored (old-fashioned) way of getting user input. Make a menu offering to draw for the user a circle, or a line, or maybe some other shape, then draw the selected shape.

CHAPTER 6

Algorithms and the Development Process

Let's step back from the details of C++ and think about something in the big picture: specifically, the need for thinking about the big picture. In the rest of life, doesn't planning help? You wouldn't build a house or cook a meal without a plan. (Heating soup in the microwave doesn't count.)

In programming, the plan is called an *algorithm*: a sequence of steps, to be executed in order, that leads to a goal.

Adventures in robotic cooking

Imagine if we can get our computer to make biscuits: the fluffy kind – like scones, but not sweet (Figure 6-1). A computer can follow instructions, but they must be clear.

Figure 6-1. *(Left) Biscuits improperly made are often of use to the construction industry. At least you'll think so once you try to eat them. (Right) What I'm hoping to make instead*

W. Briggs, *C++ for Lazy Programmers*, https://doi.org/10.1007/978-1-4842-5187-4_6

I get out a bowl, and...what goes in biscuits, anyway? You got me. Flour should help. Don't they put eggs in biscuits? and milk? Tell the robot to dump some flour in a bowl, put in a couple of eggs and a glug of milk, mix it up hard as it can, roll them, and put them in the oven.

They'll come out hard as bricks, of course. Our robo-chef put eggs in – my grandmother would laugh at that – and mixed them way too much. I should have made a solid plan first.

Tip Write the algorithm before the program, even for simple tasks.

Exactly what should I have told it to do? Here's one way:

```
1 cup/250 mL all-purpose flour
1/2 tsp/3 mL salt
1/8 cup/30 mL cold shortening
1/3 cup/80 mL milk
```

```
Heat oven to 450° F/ 230° C
Mix dry ingredients
Mix in shortening just till it's distributed
Mix in milk
Form into balls
Bake in the oven
```

Oven heated? Check. The robot can mix the dry ingredients. Let it take a cup of flour, and mix in the salt and baking soda. The cup will overflow as the robot mixes them. Why didn't it put the flour into a bowl? I didn't tell it to.

Next, it will mix in the shortening, then the milk. Of course, we'll get a wet mess. Then it will form the mess into balls – how many? I didn't say. Is two OK? Then it puts the seeping mess in the oven, at which point it falls through the rack onto the bottom...I didn't tell it to use a tray either. And I never told it to take the biscuits out! Got a fire extinguisher handy?

The steps weren't specific enough. For example, I told it to mix, but didn't tell it that one of the steps in that is to put things into a bowl. We need more detail. **Stepwise refinement** is how to solve that problem: write down what needs doing, then break that step into sub-steps, then break *those* into sub-steps, until the steps are simple enough a computer can handle them.

Tip Refine your algorithm till it's obvious how each line converts to C++.

Let's try again:

```
1 cup/250 mL all-purpose flour
1/2 tsp/3 mL salt
1/8 cup/30 mL cold shortening
1/3 cup/80 mL milk

Heat oven to 450° F/ 230° C
Mix dry ingredients:
      Put dry ingredients into a large bowl
      Mix them
Mix in shortening just till it's distributed
      Cut shortening into small bits (half-centimeter sized)
      Put shortening into the large bowl
      Mix just till it's distributed
Mix in milk
      Put milk into the large bowl
      Mix till it's distributed
Form into balls
      Get a cookie sheet
      While there is dough left
       Put flour on your hands so the dough won't stick
         Take out dough the size of a baby's fist
         Put it on the cookie sheet, not touching any others
Bake in the oven
      Put the cookie sheet in the oven
      Wait till the biscuits are golden brown on top
      Take the cookie sheet and biscuits out
```

Good. Now we're done. It's a tediously detailed algorithm, but if we're going to get a computer to understand, we have to break it down till it's obvious – to a computer! – what the steps mean.

Is it time-consuming to write all that detail? Not as time-consuming as puzzling out this type of detail while writing code, getting it wrong, debugging, and starting again and again. Experts agree: time spent planning ahead *reduces* programming time spent overall. For that reason, lazy programmers use this rule:

Golden Rule of Algorithms

Always write them.

Extra Lady Ada Lovelace (1815–1852) and Charles Babbage (1791–1871) – see Figure 6-2) – are credited with being the world's first computer scientists. Too bad computers hadn't been invented yet.

Figure 6-2. *Charles Babbage; Lady Ada Lovelace*

Babbage certainly tried. He got the British government to fund his Difference Engine, which was meant to be a mechanical calculator, and then his Analytical Engine, designed as a mechanical computer. (In those days, government funding of research was nearly unheard of. Maybe that's why it was called "the Age of Invention.") Machine parts weren't of sufficient refinement at the time, and the project failed.

Lovelace, daughter of the poet Lord Byron, took an interest in Babbage's machine and understood the nature of the programs it ran or, rather, would have run if it had existed. "The Analytical Engine has no pretensions to originate anything," she said. "It can do whatever we know how to order it to perform." This is sometimes used as an objection to the concept of artificial intelligence.

Writing a program, from start to finish

Let's apply this planning ahead thing to a real, if small, programming task.

Here are the steps we might go through to create the program:

- Identify requirements.
- Write the algorithm.
- ...and do a walkthrough; if there are errors, go back to a previous step.
- Convert the algorithm to valid C++ code.
- Compile it.
- Test it; if there are errors, go back to a previous step.

Requirements: What do we want to do?

I want to make a series of concentric circles, such that each circle is half the area of the one outside it, as in Figure 6-3. We'll keep going till they start to blur (maybe when the radius is around 1 pixel).

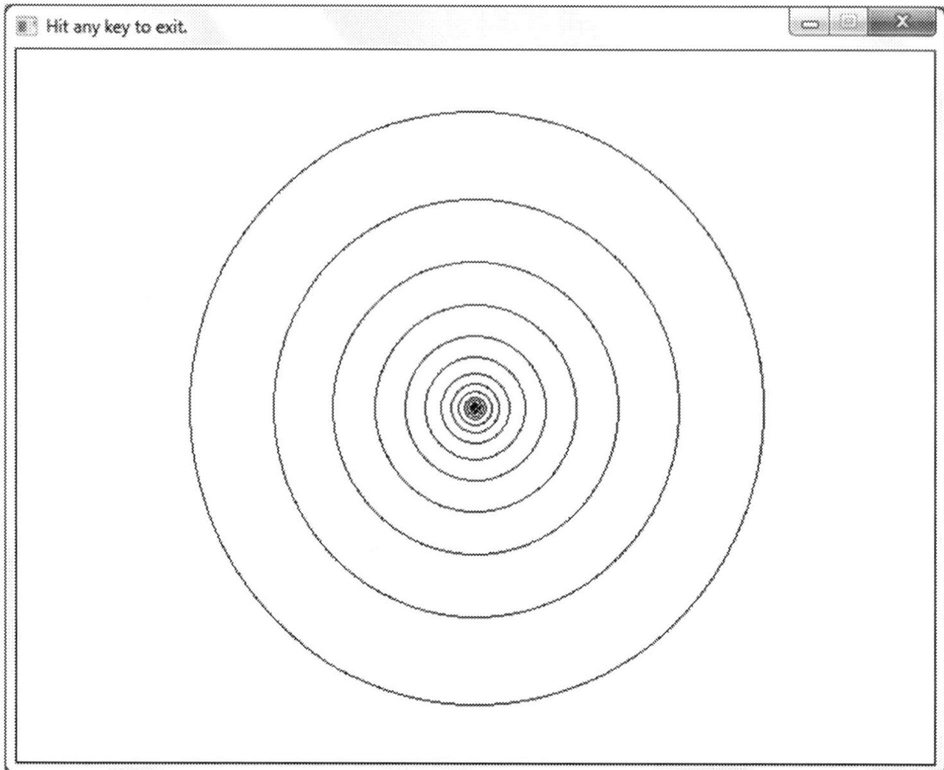

Figure 6-3. *A program that makes concentric circles, each half the area of the next bigger one*

Ready to start coding? Not yet. First we'll make a plan, as discussed in the previous section.

Algorithm: How do we do it?

So what should happen at runtime?

```
draw the first circle
draw the second
keep going until the circle's too small to see -- radius 1, I'd suppose
```

(Too obvious? I find that programming goes much more easily when I state the obvious, write it down, and try to refine it.)

Tip State the obvious, especially when just starting.

Not specific enough yet. We don't know how to draw the circles because we don't know the radii.

We can pick the outermost circle's radius arbitrarily; I'll say it's 200.

The second...I want the area to be half that of the first. Remember the formula for the area of a circle: π radius^2. To get a halved area, we'll need next circle's area = first circle's area / 2. This works out to be that the next radius is the first radius / $\sqrt{2}$.

Here's the amended algorithm.

```
draw the first circle, with radius 200...
```

No – I didn't say where! Try again:

```
draw the first circle at center of screen, with radius 200
draw the second circle at center of screen, with radius 200/√2
draw the third circle at center of screen, with radius 200 / √2 /√2...
```

Too complicated.

We *could* use variables. We'll start the value for radius at 200 and change it every time:

```
start radius at 200
draw a circle at center of screen, with this radius
divide radius by √2 to get a circle with half the area as before
keep going until the circle's too small to see -- radius 1, I'd suppose
```

That "keep going" sounds like we need a loop. We don't know how many times we'll do it, but it's least once, so by the Golden Rule of Loops, it's a do-while.

```
start radius at 200
do
      draw a circle at center of screen, with this radius
      divide radius by √2
while radius > 1  (quit when circle's too small to see)
```

This is specific enough. Do you need to go to this trouble every time you write a program? Pretty much. As time goes by and your skills improve, you can specify less detail. But I still write out the steps for anything I'm not certain of.

Walkthrough: Will it do it?

Will it work? Another thing I do is trace through the code, seeing what it does, and confirm that it does what I want.

First, radius is set to 200. The area is $\pi\ 200^2$. We draw a circle with that radius.

Next, radius is set to what it was divided by $\sqrt{2}$. The area is $\pi\ (200/\sqrt{2})^2 = \pi\ 200^2/2$, which is half the first area; that's what I wanted. We draw the new circle.

Next, radius is set to what it became divided by $\sqrt{2}$. The area is $\pi\ (200/\sqrt{2}/\sqrt{2})^2 = \pi\ 200^2/4$, which is 1/4 the first area. Good. We draw the new circle.

Seems OK.

As programs get more complex, it'll be even more useful to do walkthroughs to verify the algorithms. Why spend time getting a program to compile, if we aren't even sure it does what we want? I'm too lazy for that.

Coding: putting it all into C++ (plus: commenting the lazy way)

To create the program I start the usual way: I tell the reader exactly what I'm doing at the top of the file. Then I put the algorithm right into `main`, as comments.

```
//Program to draw 5 concentric circles
// Each circle is twice the area of the one inside it
//              -- from _C++ for Lazy Programmers_

#include "SSDL.h"

int main (int argc, char** argv)
{
      //start radius at 200
      //do
      //            draw a circle at center of screen, with this radius
      //            divide radius by sqrt (2)
      //while radius > 1 (quit when circle's too small to see)
}
```

The cops didn't arrest me for putting the algorithm right there into the editor, so I guess I'll keep going.

Tip Include the algorithm in the program, after //'s, and you've already written most of your comments.

The editor can help turn text into comments quickly. (This is also useful for making troublesome bits of code stop generating errors: put 'em in comments till you're ready to deal with them.)

In emacs, highlight the region, then select C++ ➤ Comment out region to comment it; hit tab to indent. If you're in a nongraphical version of emacs, highlight the region by hitting Ctrl-space at one end of the region, then move the cursor to the other end. Ctrl-c Ctrl-c will comment it, and tab will indent.

(Note that final cool emacs tip too: highlight a region and hit tab, and emacs indents the region all at once.)

In Visual Studio, clicking the Comment out button will turn the highlighted code into comments. (It looks like parallel horizontal lines and is highlighted at the top right of Figure 6-4.)

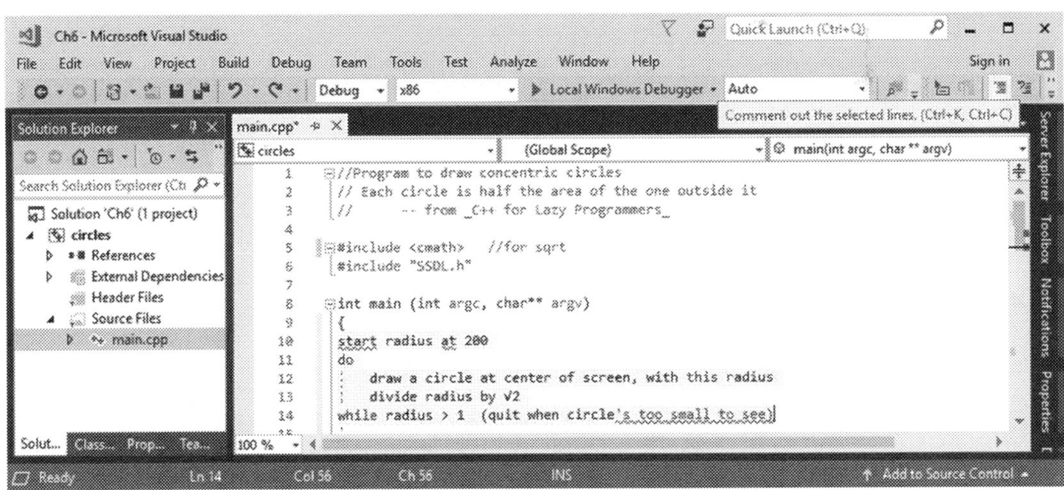

***Figure 6-4.** The Visual Studio window, with the Comment out button highlighted (top right)*

Figure 6-5 shows the commenting.

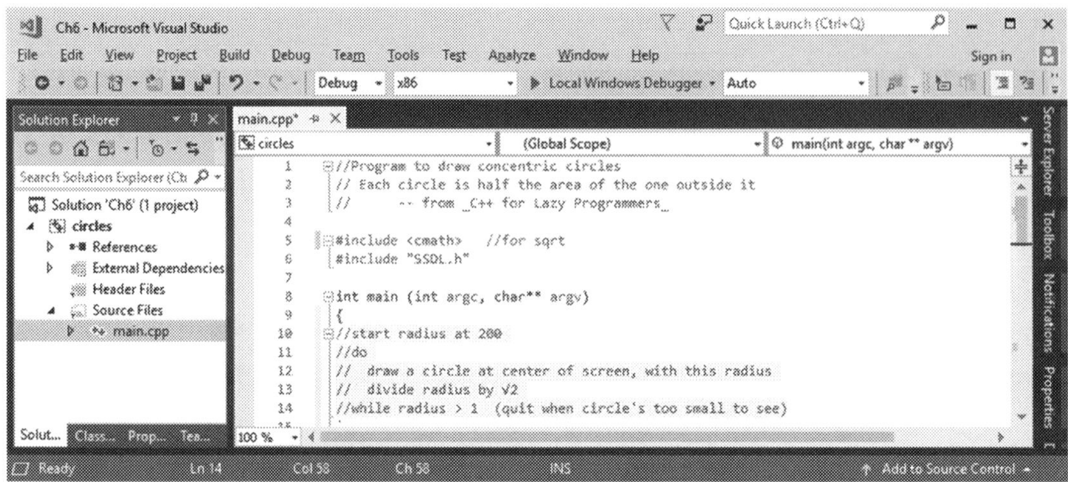

Figure 6-5. *The code, commented out*

Now you can hit tab to indent the region.

Sometimes, if an editor does the commenting for you, it will use a style of commenting we haven't covered yet: bracketing the comments in /* and */. That works too.

May as well code the easy parts first: the declaration of radius and the loop.

```
int main (int argc, char** argv)
{
    double radius = 200.0;       // start radius at 200

    do
    {
        //draw a circle at center of screen, with this radius
        //divide radius by √2
    }
    while (radius > 1.0);        //quit when circle's too small to see

    return 0;
}
```

Now put the middle steps in code, keeping the algorithm as comments:

```
int main (int argc, char** argv)
{
    double radius = 200.0;      // start radius at 200
    do
    {
        //draw a circle at center of screen, with this radius
        SSDL_RenderDrawCircle (CENTER_X/2, CENTER_Y/2, int (radius));

        radius /= sqrt (2);       //divide radius by √2
    }
    while (radius > 1);           //quit when circle's too small to see

    return 0;
}
```

Looks like we need the center point:

```
int main (int argc, char** argv)
{
    const int CENTER_X = SSDL_GetWindowWidth();
    const int CENTER_Y = SSDL_GetWindowHeight();

    double radius = 200.0;      // start radius at 200
    do
    {
        //draw a circle at center of screen, with this radius
        SSDL_RenderDrawCircle (CENTER_X/2, CENTER_Y/2, int (radius));

        radius /= sqrt (2);       //divide radius by √2
    }
    while (radius > 1);           //quit when circle's too small to see

    return 0;
}
```

Put some friendliness at the program's start, and our usual wrap-up, and we have our program complete and already commented (Example 6-1).

Example 6-1. A program to draw concentric circles, each half the area of the one outside it

```
//Program to draw concentric circles
// Each circle is half the area of the one outside it
//            -- from _C++ for Lazy Programmers_

#include <cmath>   //for sqrt
#include "SSDL.h"

int main (int argc, char** argv)
{
    SSDL_SetWindowTitle ("Hit any key to exit.");

    const int CENTER_X = SSDL_GetWindowWidth();
    const int CENTER_Y = SSDL_GetWindowHeight();

    double radius = 200.0;      // start radius at 200
    do
    {
        //draw a circle at center of screen, with this radius
        SSDL_RenderDrawCircle (CENTER_X/2, CENTER_Y/2, int (radius));

        radius /= sqrt (2);      //divide radius by √2
    }
    while (radius > 1);          //quit when circle's too small to see

    SSDL_WaitKey();

    return 0;
}
```

Note how the program is broken by blank lines into the major steps from the algorithm. This isn't a requirement, but it's not a bad idea.

EXERCISES

1. Write an algorithm to find the average of three numbers.
2. Write the corresponding program for Exercise 1.
3. Write an algorithm, then a program, to draw a *filled* circle, by drawing many circles with radii ranging from 0 to some radius R. It doesn't have to look completely filled.
4. Write the algorithm for a program to draw the Australian flag, the New Zealand flag, the Ethiopian flag, a Scandinavian flag, or some other flag using shapes you can draw with SSDL. Concentrate on what makes a coherent subtask, or a repeated subtask.

CHAPTER 7

Functions

In this chapter, we get the number one way to not get lost in pages of code till your eyes go blurry: functions.

Functions that return values

Consider how things are done in a candy factory. It has machines to make things we want. Each machine has things it needs piped in, and the thing it produces piped out. Want a candy bar? Activate the machine, give it its inputs, and it'll provide the result (see Figure 7-1).

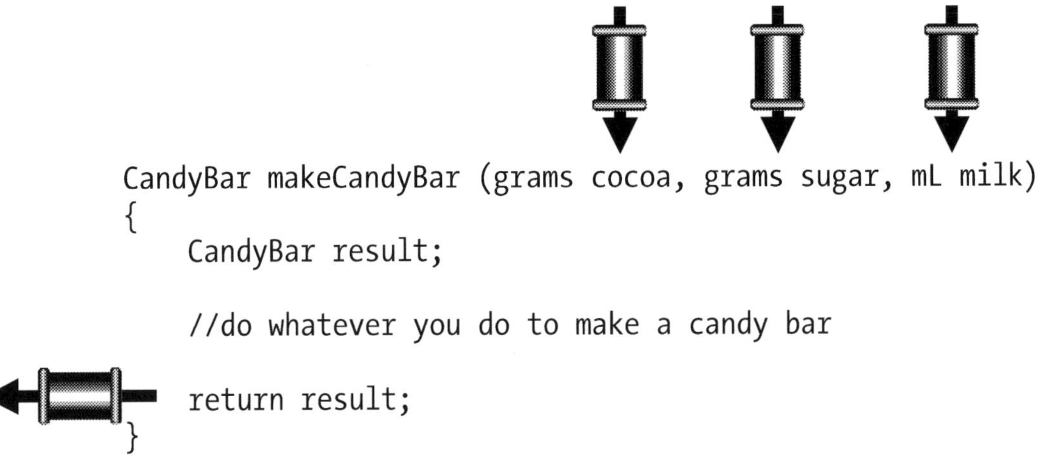

Figure 7-1. *Structure of a "makeCandyBar" machine*

We have "machines" too (called "functions"): `SSDL_CreateColor`; `SSDL_WaitKey`; `sin` and `cos`. `SSDL_CreateColor`, for example (Figure 7-2), takes in three `int`s and returns an `SSDL_Color`.

W. Briggs, *C++ for Lazy Programmers*, https://doi.org/10.1007/978-1-4842-5187-4_7

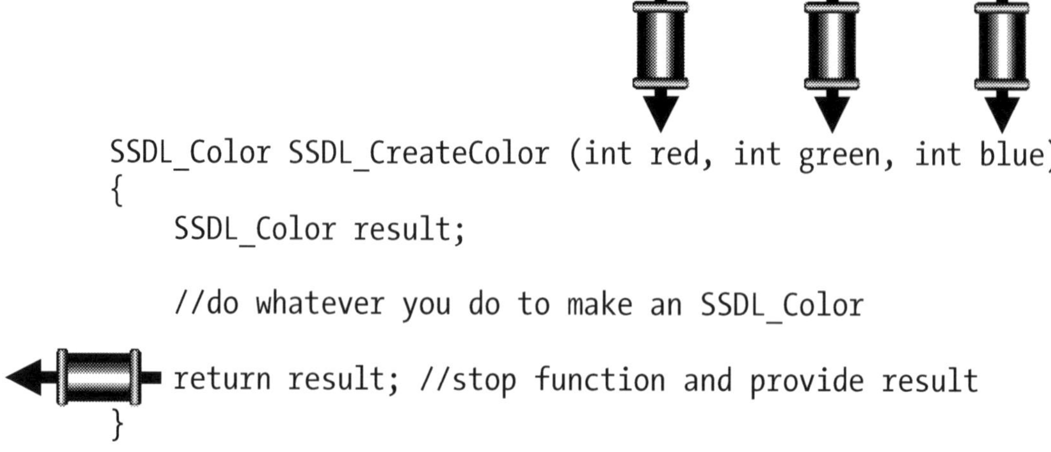

Figure 7-2. *Structure of the SSDL_CreateColor function*

BNF for a function is

<return type> <name> (<parameters, separated by commas>) //"header"
{
*<thing to do -- variable declaration, action, whatever>**
}

where a *<parameter>* is a *<type>* plus a *<name>*: `int red`, for example.

The top line is the **function header**; the rest is the **function body**. We often copy the top line and put a `;` at the end, for a precise description of how we interact with the function (its inputs and its outputs):

```
SSDL_Color SSDL_CreateColor (int red, int green, int blue);
```

This is a **prototype**, and was seen in previous chapters where library functions were described. It's useful not just for programmers learning but for the compiler (read on).

Now to make our own function. Here's the prototype (top line) for something to average 3 `int`s. (In this parameter list, I omit the names of the parameters; you can do that in the prototype as long as it's doesn't hurt clarity.) The body is in Figure 7-3.

```
int average (int, int, int);      //function prototype
```

```
int average (int a, int b, int c)//function header
{                                 //start function body
    int result;

    result = (a+b+c)/3;

    return result; //stop function and provide result
}                                 //end function body
```

Figure 7-3. *The* `int average (int, int, int)` *function*

We made the function, so let's use it. To use it means store its value in a variable, print it, send it to another function (see the upcoming example)...do *something* with the result; else there was no point in calling it.

```
int myAverage = average (1, 2, 12); //A "function call"
```

OK, that works. Instead of `int` literals, we could give it variables:

```
int i = 1, j = 2, k = 12;
int myAverage = average (i, j, k);
```

...or constants, or expressions – anything with appropriate values:

```
int otherAverage = average (DAYS_PER_WEEK, 14/2, sqrt(144));
```

What we can't do is declare the variable between the parentheses like so:

```
int i = 1, j = 2, k = 12;
int myAverage = average (int a, int b, int c); //NO -- won't compile!
```

C++ reads something of form *<function name> (<parameter list, separated by commas>);* and thinks: I know what that is – it's a prototype! It may then get confused (like here) as to why you're setting an `int` equal to a function prototype. It may just say, OK, I see the prototype, and go on. But one thing's for sure: it *won't* call the function.

Tip When calling a function, keep type information out of the ()'s. Type information is for prototypes.

Extra Some purists prefer only one return statement per function – not

```
if (condition)
    return this;
else
    return that;
```

but

```
if (condition)
    result = this;
else
    result = that;

return result;
```

This relates to easily tracing through the function and verifying correctness. As we go through examples in the coming chapters, you can see what you think.

Here's a function to make a grayscale equivalent of a given color, described as red, green, and blue components. It'll do this by averaging the red, green, and blue and applying the average to each component to create and return an `SSDL_Color`. First, the prototype

```
SSDL_Color greyscale (int r, int g, int b);
        //Gets a greyscale color for a given r, g, b
```

and now the function body

```
SSDL_Color greyscale (int r, int g, int b)
       //Gets a greyscale color for a given r, g, b
{
       int rgbAverage = average (r, g, b);
```

```
    SSDL_Color result
        = SSDL_CreateColor (rgbAverage, rgbAverage, rgbAverage);

    return result;
}
```

I used the function average from earlier. *This is a Good Thing.* Code reuse is how avoid doing the same work again and again, making fresh mistakes each time.

Golden Rule of Code Reuse

If you already wrote code to do something, don't write it again. Put it in a function and call that function.

Example 7-1 shows a program that makes use of what we've done (output is in Figure 7-4). Note that the structure of the program got a little more complicated. Before it was

```
//initial comments
#include "SSDL.h"
constants if any
main
```

but now it's

```
//initial comments
#include "SSDL.h"
constants if any
function prototypes[1]
main
function bodies
```

The compiler reads the prototypes before it gets to any code that might have a function call and thus can ensure that the calls are correct (spelled right, right parameters, right use of return value).

[1]We could put function *bodies* up here too...but people like main as the first function so it's easy to see quickly what the program is mainly about.

Example 7-1. A program to make and use grayscale colors

```
//Program to change some colors to greyscale
//              -- from _C++ for Lazy Programmers

#include "SSDL.h"

//Prototypes go here

int average(int, int, int);
//Averages 3 ints
SSDL_Color greyscale(int r, int g, int b);
//Gets a greyscale color for a given r, g, b

int main (int argc, char** argv)
{
    sout    << "Some colors you know turned to black-and-white. "
            << "Hit any key to end.\n";

                //By now the compiler knows that greyscale
                // takes 3 ints and returns an SSDL_Color, but doesn't
                //know how to do the greyscale...

    SSDL_SetRenderDrawColor (greyscale (255, 255, 255));
    sout << "WHITE\n";
    SSDL_SetRenderDrawColor (greyscale (255,   0,   0));
    sout << "RED\n";
    SSDL_SetRenderDrawColor (greyscale (  0, 255,   0));
    sout << "GREEN\n";
    SSDL_SetRenderDrawColor (greyscale (  0,   0, 255));
    sout << "BLUE\n";
    SSDL_SetRenderDrawColor (greyscale (181, 125,  41));
    sout << "MARIGOLD\n";
    SSDL_SetRenderDrawColor (greyscale ( 50, 205,  50));
    sout << "LIME GREEN\n";

    SSDL_WaitKey ();

    return 0;
}
```

```
//Function bodies come after main, by convention

int average(int a, int b, int c)
//Averages 3 ints
{
    return (a + b + c) / 3;
}

SSDL_Color greyscale(int r, int g, int b)
//Gets a greyscale color for a given r, g, b
{
    int rgbAverage = average(r, g, b);

    SSDL_Color result
        = SSDL_CreateColor(rgbAverage, rgbAverage, rgbAverage);

    return result;
}

                    //...and now the compiler has all the information
                    // it needs about greyscale (and anything else)
```

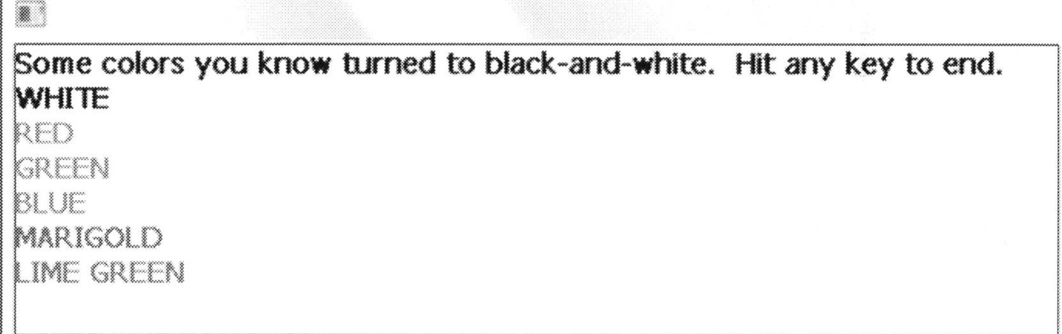

Figure 7-4. *Several bright colors, converted to monochrome by* `SSDL_Color greyscale (int r, int g, int b);`

EXERCISES

1. Write and test a function to get the screen's aspect ratio, that is, width divided by height.

2. Write an algorithm for, then write and test, the distance formula, $\sqrt{(x2-x1)^2+(y2-y1)^2}$

Functions that return nothing

Some functions don't return a value but do something else – draw a picture, or print text, perhaps.

Consider a function to draw not a rectangle or circle, like we already have, but a cross. With no points for originality, we'll name it `drawCross`.

What inputs will it need, so it can get started? It'll need to know *where* to draw the cross, so that's an x and a y. It'll also need to know size, the distance from center to ends. This will work for the prototype:

```
void drawCross (int x, int y, int distanceToEnds);
```

The return type is `void`, meaning "I don't return anything." The meanings of the parameter names are blindingly obvious, which is a Good Thing.

Example 7-2 shows a sample program to use the `drawCross` function. Output is in Figure 7-5.

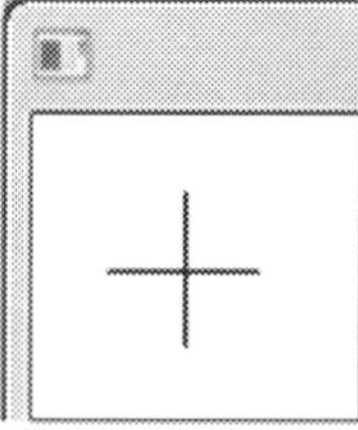

Figure 7-5. *Output from Example 7-2*

Example 7-2. A program that uses a function to draw a cross. The order of arguments sent in determines the order received: `crossX` is sent to `x`, `crossY` to `Y`, and `size` to `distToEnds`

```
//Program to draw a cross on the screen
//            -- from _C++ for Lazy Programmers_

#include "SSDL.h"

void drawCross  (int x, int y, int distToEnds);

int main(int argc, char** argv)
{
    int crossX = 40, crossY = 25, size = 20;

    drawCross (crossX, crossY, size); //draw a cross

    SSDL_WaitKey();

    return 0;
}

void drawCross (int x, int y, int distToEnds)
//draw a cross centered at x, y, with a distance to ends as given
{
   SSDL_RenderDrawLine (x-distToEnds, y, x+distToEnds, y);//draw horizontal
   SSDL_RenderDrawLine (x, y-distToEnds, x, y+distToEnds);//draw vertical
}
```

When using functions, I find it helpful to draw diagrams of what functions are active and what parameters and variables they have.

First, C++ creates an instance of the main function (Figure 7-6).

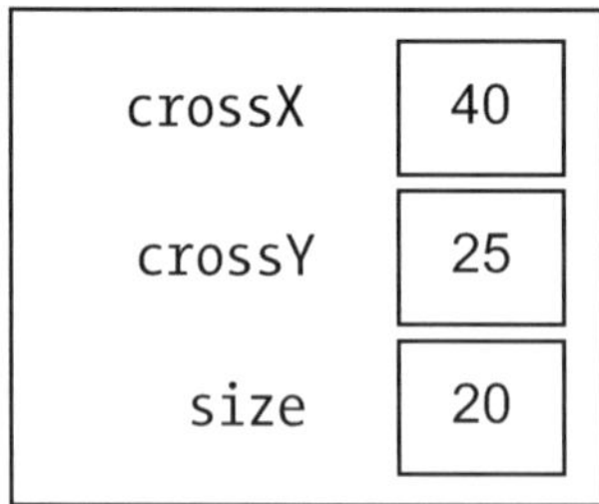

Figure 7-6. *main, in Example 7-2*

When main gets to this line

```
drawCross (crossX, crossY, size);
```

C++ creates a copy of drawCross, with its parameters (and any other variables it has), and copies the values in (Figure 7-7). This is why it doesn't matter whether main's arguments passed in and drawCross's parameters have the same names. Each function uses its own set of names.

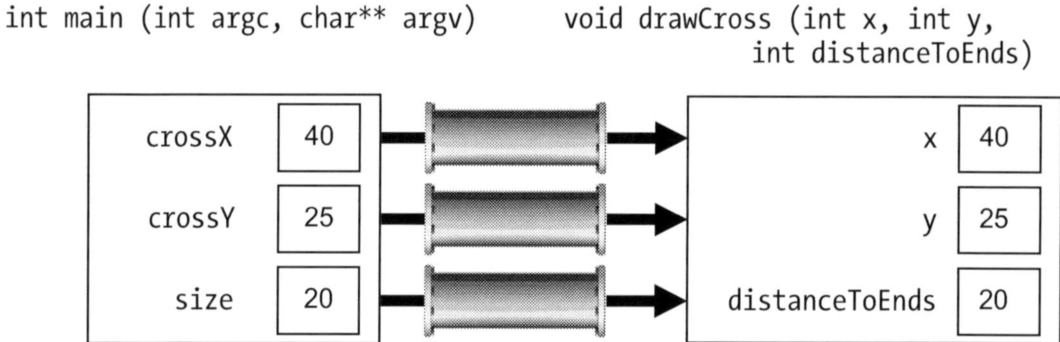

Figure 7-7. *main, calling drawCross and copying in values*

When our call to drawCross is finished, it's erased and we're back in main (Figure 7-8).

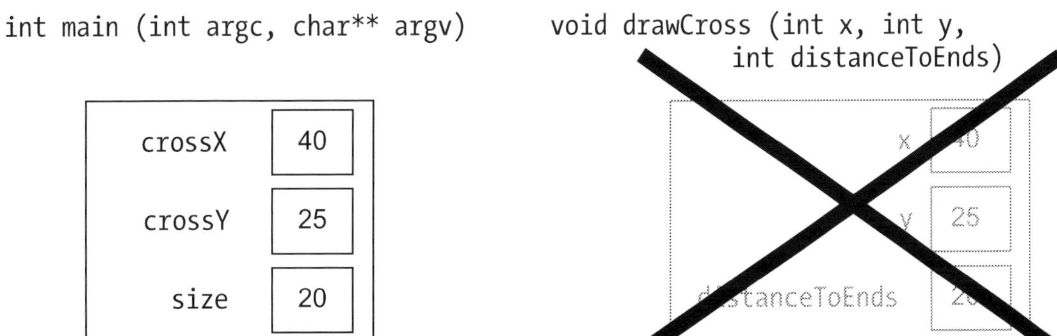

***Figure 7-8.** Leaving `drawCross` and returning to `main`*

We can reuse `drawCross` as often as we like, just as we can `SSDL_RenderDrawPoint`, `SSDL_RenderDrawCircle`, and so on.

Example 7-3. Calling function `drawCross` multiple times. Output is in Figure 7-9.

```
int main(int argc, char** argv)
{
    drawCross( 40, 40, 20); //draw three crosses
    drawCross( 80, 30, 15);
    drawCross(110, 50, 40);

    SSDL_WaitKey();

    return 0;
}
```

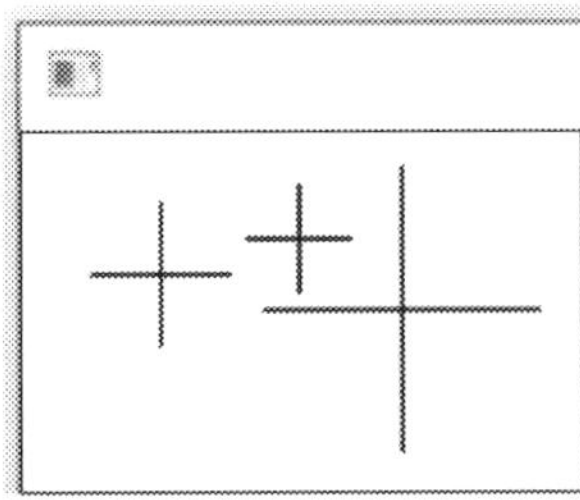

***Figure 7-9.** Output from Example 7-3*

Global variables

Some find this workaround: instead of passing in parameters, they'll make their variables *global* (meaning "not inside anybody's {}'s), rather than *local* (inside main's {}'s, or drawCross's, or someone's).

```
//Program to draw a cross on the screen
//            -- from _C++ for Lazy Programmers_

#include "SSDL.h"

//GLOBAL VARIABLES: THE EIGHTH DEADLY SIN
int       x = 40, y = 40;
int       distanceToEnds = 20;

//Prototypes
void drawCross  ();

int main (int argc, char** argv)
{
    //draw three crosses
    drawCross();
    x =  80; y = 30; distanceToEnds = 15; drawCross();
    x = 110; y = 50; distanceToEnds = 40; drawCross();

    SSDL_WaitKey();

    return 0;
}

void drawCross ()
//draw a cross centered at x, y, with distance to ends, all global
{
    SSDL_RenderDrawLine (x-distanceToEnds, y, x+distanceToEnds, y);
    SSDL_RenderDrawLine (x, y-distanceToEnds, x, y+distanceToEnds);
}
```

Easy, huh?

Not really. There are three drawbacks.

1. **It's hard to read and write.** `drawCross` will draw a cross, but where? You have to look inside the body to find out: it draws it at (x, y). What are `x` and `y`? Look at the top; they're (40, 40). Then look back in `main` to see how they've changed. And hope there's not some other function that *also* uses `x` and `y` for something else and changed their values. To be certain, you'll have to look through *all* the code. Try that with a 500-page program. Aaaigh!

2. **It's the devil to debug.** Looking all over the program to find what screwed up a variable is hard work. We try to break programs into relatively independent parts (functions), with parameter lists to specify clearly how those parts interact. This reduces the scope of where to look for an error. It also helps with group projects: different programmers can work on different functions, with minimal interference with each other's work. This is called **`modularity`**.

3. **Programmers who have to maintain your code will hate you.** Not as if you snubbed them, but as if you egged their cars and insulted their mothers. They don't want to inherit the debugging disaster.

4. For some offenses, I hear, **Santa won't bring you any presents.** For worse ones, he actually *takes* your presents. This is one of the latter kind.

Golden Rule of Global Variables

Just say no.

Antibugging

- **It's not calling the function.** You may have put type information in, so the compiler thinks it's a prototype. Take the type info out.
- **You call a value-returning function, but it has no effect.** See Chapter 3, "Built-in functions," Antibugging section - same problem, same solution.

- **You get an error, something like "no local function definitions allowed."** If something's missing a closing }, the compiler may think you're still in one function when you start another. Be sure the {}'s are balanced. A good reason to avoid Egyptian brackets (see Chapter 4).

  To prevent this, when starting a function body, put both {}'s in place at the same time. If you do, the function will probably compile, even if it doesn't do anything yet. Such an empty function is called a "stub." It's common to have them in unfinished programs.

- **It skips the latter part of the function**, as here:

```
int value (char letter) //score letters in a word game.
                        //Q, K are best
{
   return 1;            //default score is 1

   if (toupper (letter) == 'Q' || toupper (letter) == 'K')
       return 5;
}
```

  This always returns 1. The reason is that first `return` didn't just establish a return value, but also stopped the function: it won't go on to run the `if`.

  Solution: recognize `return` as the last thing a function does.

- **No matter what parameters you give, the function always does the same thing.** Be sure they aren't being reset inside the function (see the next section, "How to write a function in four easy steps").

- **You repeat a function by having it call itself.** That's not an error, but it's not the best practice. Suppose you want to play a game multiple times:

```
void playGame ()
{
      ...
      //now let's play again:
      playGame ();
}
```

Thinking from the perspective of the diagrams in the previous section...when you call a function, C++ creates a copy, which it keeps until the function is done. What happens when you're on your umpteenth game here? You get umpteen copies of the function (see Figure 7-10), and each one requires memory. If "umpteen" becomes *very* large, it'll crash the program.

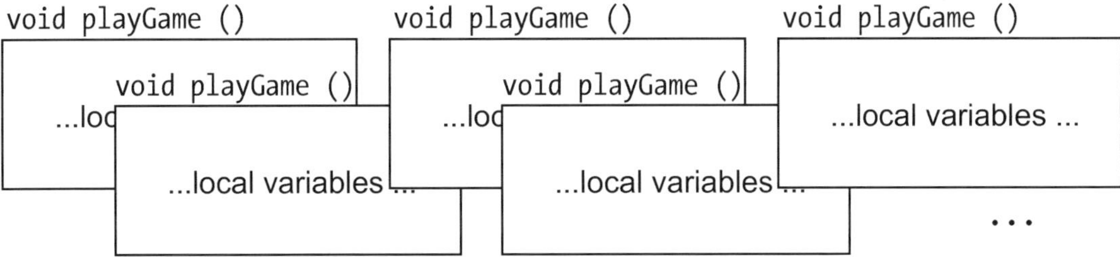

Figure 7-10. *Multiple "recursive" (self-calling) copies of a function*

Better solution: use a loop.

EXERCISES

1. Write an algorithm for, then write and test, a function to draw a triangle at some location specified by parameters.
2. Write an algorithm for, then write, a program to display the flag of Greece. You'll at least want these two functions: `drawCanton` (the upper left) and `drawStripes`.
3. Write an algorithm for a function to draw the Australian flag (as in the last exercise in Chapter 6). Then, using functions appropriately, write that program. You'll want a function `drawStar` to draw any of the stars you see on the flag, which means it should be able to handle either 5- or 7-pointed stars. You won't fill in the stars, but just do a rough outline (see Figure 7-11), unless you can think of a trick.

   Wikipedia is a good source for flag specifications.

Figure 7-11. *The Australian flag, simplified for Exercise 3*

How to write a function in four easy steps (and call it in one)

I recommend using these steps for *every function you write* till you're certain you have functions nailed:

1. Put this after `main`, using your own function name and comment.

```
<return type> greaterNumber ()//Returns the greater of two numbers
{
    <return type> result;

    return result;
}
```

2. What kind of value does it return? Whatever it is, use that for the return type.

```
double greaterNumber ()       //Returns the greater of two numbers
{
    double result;

    return result;
}
```

If the function doesn't return anything, skip all the `return` stuff and make its type `void`:

```
void drawCross ()
{
}
```

3. What information will the function need to get started?

   Say you're the `greaterNumber` function and I'm `main`. I say to you: give me the greater number! You say, I can't - I need more information! Well, what information do you need?

   You need the numbers. They go in the ()'s. You need to specify their types (`int`, `double`, `char`, etc.).

```
double greaterNumber (double num1, double num2)
                                        //Returns greater of 2 numbers
{
    double result;

    return result;
}
```

4. How does the function do its work?

   a. Put the algorithm inside the function as comments. Skipping this step is a bad idea unless you really know what you're doing.

```
double greaterNumber (double number1, double number2)
                              //Returns the greater of two numbers
{
    double result;

    //let result be the bigger of number1, number2

    return result;
}
```

b. Write valid C++ to do the task.

```
double greaterNumber (double number1, double number2)
                             //Returns the greater of two numbers
{
    double result;

    //let result be the bigger of number1, number2
    if (number1 > number2)
        result = number1;
    else
        result = number2;

    return result;
}
```

5. How do I use the function?

a. Copy the top line, put it above `main`, and end with a semicolon (see below).

b. Call the function, and (if it isn't `void`) store the result or use it.

```
double greaterNumber (double number1, double number2);
                             //Returns the greater of two numbers

int main (int argc, char** argv)
{
    ...
    bigNum = greaterNumber (20, 30);
```

Let me now give some notes on what can go wrong.

In Step 3, where do the values for the parameters come from? They're provided by `main` when we call the function, as in Examples 7-1, 7-2, and 7-3. Since they're sent in from `main`, we would *not* do this:

```
double greaterNumber (double number1, double number2)
                             //Returns the greater of two numbers
{
    double result;
```

```
    sout << "Enter two numbers: ";
    ssin >> number1;  //WRONG. It erases the numbers main gave us!
    ssin >> number2;

    ...

    return result;
}
```

or this:

```
double greaterNumber (double number1, double number2)
                        //Returns the greater of two numbers
{
    double result;

    number1 = 12;       //WRONG. It erases the numbers main gave us!
    number2 = 25;

    ...

    return result;
}
```

Another thing we won't need: printing. We almost never have a function to print something (unless it's named "print"). We return the value and let `main` decide what to do with it. (Think if, in the program for drawing a star in Example 3-3, `sin` and `cos` printed "The result of this function is..." every time you called them, covering up your star with text.)

```
double greaterNumber (double number1, double number2)
                        //Returns the greater of two numbers
{
    double result;

    ...

    sout << "The bigger number is " << result;
                      //WRONG. We're supposed to *return*, not *print*

    return result;
}
```

EXERCISES

1. Write an algorithm for, then write and test, the pow function. (`pow (a, b)` returns a^b.) To make it easier, assume only integer values for the exponent: you can calculate `pow (3, 2)`, but not `pow (3, 2.1)`.
2. Write an algorithm for, then write and test, a function that, given a positive integer, returns the sum of all numbers up to that integer. For example, given a 5, it should return 1+2+3+4+5 = 15.
3. Write an algorithm for, then write and test, a function `log` which, given a positive integer number and an integer base, returns $\log_{base}$ (number). $\log_{base}$ (number) is defined as how many times you can divide number by base before getting to 1. For example, 8/2 gives 4, and 4/2 gives 2, and 2/2 gives 1; that's 3 divisions; so $\log_2 8$ is 3. We won't worry about fractional parts: $\log_2 15$ is also 3, because (using integer division) 15/2 is 7, 7/2 is 3, and 3/2 is 1.

Why have functions, anyway?

Till now we've started with the function and then made use of it. Let's look now at writing a larger program and deducing what functions we need – the more usual approach.

Consider how we might write a program to show a comic, frame by frame. To make the drawing easy, we'll use stick figures that talk but don't move. We'll have four frames, showing one at a time.

We start our algorithm:

```
write the dialog for the left character
draw the line from the left character's head to the dialog
draw the left character's head
draw the left character's body
draw the left character's left arm
draw the left character's right arm
draw the left character's left leg
draw the left character's right leg
write the dialog for the right character
write the line from the right character's head to the dialog
...
```

Argh! That's a lot of writing. This isn't C++ *for Programmers Who Want Carpal Tunnel Syndrome*! And when we start coding, we'll find that extra typing is the least of our worries. Twice as much code means five times as many opportunities for error. (This may not be mathematically sound, but based on experience, it's conservative.)

As covered in the previous chapter, you write your algorithm, do a walkthrough, write the program, and run it. Then you find an error – say, the dialog's in the wrong place – and fix it. In *one* of the frames. The other frames, you forget to fix. More errors.

Better to follow the Golden Rule of Code Reuse from earlier: put that dialog-drawing code in a function and call as needed.

We'll therefore bundle the algorithm (and, later, the code) into functions to enable code reuse.[2] Here's what `main` might look like:

```
main program:
      give the window a title
      draw frame 1; wait for user to hit a key
      draw frame 2; wait for user to hit a key
      draw frame 3; wait for user to hit a key
      draw frame 4; wait for user to hit a key
```

Did I cheat? I didn't actually say how to *do* anything. Well, that's not quite true: I said how to do *everything*! Just not in detail. That's no sin as long as I give that detail in another function – perhaps one named `draw frame`:

```
draw frame:
      clear the screen
      draw left character and its dialog
      draw right character and its dialog
```

Again, I put off most of the work! (What do you expect, from a lazy programmer?) But it's fine: `draw frame` is a coherent task. As long as `draw character` and `draw dialog` work, we'll be OK.

[2]Taking a chunk of information and labeling it for reuse is *abstraction*: an essential way of keeping yourself sane in large programming projects.

```
draw character:
      draw head as a circle
      draw body, a line
      draw arms, two lines
      draw legs, two lines
draw dialog
      draw line
      draw the text
```

The process we went through – starting with the main program, writing its subtasks, then writing subtasks of subtasks, and so on, until we get down to specifics we know how to write in C++ (drawing lines, circles, and text) – is called *top-down design,* and it's how we write programs. (Purists who want to point out other software engineering techniques here are right, but you gotta start somewhere.)

We still need detail, but I'll leave that for now, because I want to talk about how we decide what pieces of code should be made into functions.

For one thing, I should make code into a function if the code is **repeatable**. `draw character` is likely to be repeated. Making it into a function means it *can* be repeated (as we see in the `main program`).

The preceding examples (`draw character`, etc.) are also **coherent** tasks – like functions we've already seen, such as `sqrt`, `sin`, `SSDL_RenderText`, and so on. Why not a function `SSDL_RenderPrintSin,` to "find the sine of an angle and print it on the screen"? It takes longer to describe, and that's a tipoff it'll be less generally useful. (How often do *you* want to print sines?) Better to break it into functions each of which does *one* thing.

Another criterion is that a function should be **short enough to understand**. If it's too big to see on the screen, it's too big to follow what it's doing as you write and debug it. Once it's more than a screenful, break it into subtasks.

Golden Rule of Functions Make code into a function if it is repeatable, forms a coherent task, or is part of another function that's getting to be more than a screenful long.

Extra Psychologists have[3] measured the mind's ability to be aware of multiple things at once and determined that one can think of approximately seven items at a time. For example, read these digits, then look away from the page and see if you can repeat them.

5 7 16 19 28 29 32

Now try doing it with this sequence of numbers. Having a little trouble?

5 7 16 19 28 29 32 3 8 12 26 32 14 19 7 50 2 19 18 33 25 11 36 41 1

The point is that you can't keep arbitrarily long sets of data in your mind at one time. A version of the main program spanning hundreds of pages – or even one – is too long to understand.

We have the algorithm. Since it has functions, let's decide on each new function's parameters with the help of the third question from "How to write a function": what does each function need to get started? `draw Frame` draws a frame; it'll need the dialog. There are two parts to that: the left character's dialog and the right character's. Since the stick figures don't move, that should be all.

```
main:
      give the window a title
      draw frame 1 (left char's dialog, right char's dialog);
      wait for user to hit a key
      draw frame 2 (left char's dialog, right char's dialog);
      wait for user to hit a key
```

[3]George A. Miller. "The Magical Number Seven, Plus or Minus Two." *The Psychological Review*, 1956, vol. 63, pp. 81-97. The application of this to things that aren't sequences of digits - like I'm doing right now - has been condemned as urban legend material, on the grounds that the precise number of items one can keep in mind varies by type of cognitive task (`www.knosof.co.uk/cbook/misart.pdf`, at time of writing). True enough - but even if it does vary, there is a limit.

```
        draw frame 3 (left char's dialog, right char's dialog);
        wait for user to hit a key
        draw frame 4 (left char's dialog, right char's dialog);
        wait for user to hit a key
```

`draw dialog` requires the dialog (duh), so we'll pass that in. It'll also need to know where to put it (left character's area, or the right's).

`draw character` is always the same except for position, so that's all it needs.

Here, therefore, is the final algorithm. There's a lot of code reuse; good. The graph paper representation I used to help me draw is in Figure 7-12.

```
draw frame (left char's dialog, right char's dialog):
        draw character (left x, left y);
        draw dialog    (left x, left y, left char's dialog)
        draw character (right x, right y);
        draw dialog    (right x, right y, right char's dialog)

draw character (x, y)
        draw head as a circle
        draw body, a line
        draw arms, two lines
        draw legs, two lines

draw dialog (x, y, dialog)
        draw line
        draw the text
```

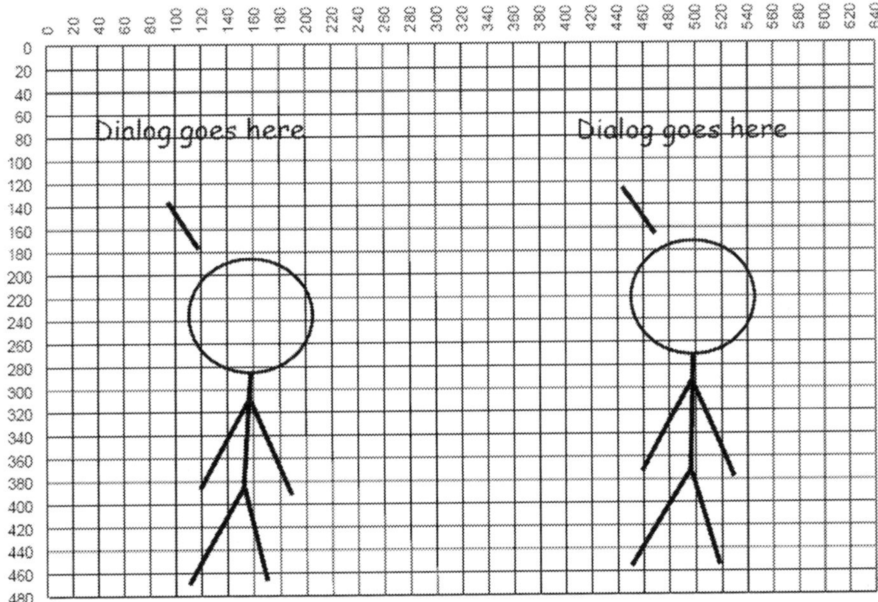

Figure 7-12. *Graph paper to plot out a cartoon frame*

The program is in Example 7-4. It turned out that `wait for user to hit a key` was more than a bare call to `SSDL_WaitKey()`: for user-friendliness I wanted a prompt, and I wanted it nicely placed. The task is repeated and tedious to write, so following the Golden Rule of Code Reuse, it gets its own function. Output is in Figure 7-13.

Example 7-4. A program to do a 4-panel cartoon

```
//Program to display a 4-panel comic strip with stick figures.
//            -- from _C++ for Lazy Programmers_

#include "SSDL.h"

//function prototypes
void drawFrame    (const char* leftDialog, const char* rightDialog);⁴
void drawCharacter(int x, int y);
void drawDialog   (int x, int y, const char* dialog);
void hitEnterToContinue (); //wait for user to hit Enter
```

[4]We've seen parameters of type `const char*` in SSDL function prototypes related to text (e.g., `void SSDL_SetWindowTitle (const char* text)`). We'll get to the true meaning of `const char*` in Chapter 14. For now, just think of it as meaning "text."

```
int main (int argc, char** argv)
{
    //Set up:  window title and font
    SSDL_SetWindowTitle ("My own 4-panel comic");
    const SSDL_Font COMIC_FONT = SSDL_OpenSystemFont("comic.ttf",18);
    SSDL_SetFont (COMIC_FONT);

    //Now the four frames
    drawFrame  ("Somebody said something really nasty\nto me "
                "on Internet.\nSo I put him in his place.",5
                "Maybe it's not a him.\nMaybe it's a her.  "
                "You never know.");
    hitEnterToContinue();

    drawFrame  ("OK, her.  Whatever.  She kept saying\nall this "
                "stuff about how superior\nshe was.  I found "
                "a spelling error and\ntold her she can't even "
                "spell so she\nshould just shut up.",
                "If it's a her.  It *might* be a him.\nThe point "
                "is we just don't know.");
    hitEnterToContinue();

    drawFrame  ("The *point* is, he went on a rant about\nhow you "
                "can spell things like \"b4\"\nand so on in l33t, "
                "and I told him l33t\nis for lusers -- with a u, "
                "you know.\nThen he told me I misspelled \"loser.\"",
                "If it's a him.  It could be both.\nSometimes "
                "married people\nshare accounts.");
    hitEnterToContinue();

    drawFrame  ("You're making me crazy!",
                "Can I have the URL for that forum?\nI'm not "
```

[5]It's called "string literal concatenation": if you jam "quoted" "things" together with only whitespace between, C++ will interpret them as one "quoted thing". This helps us break lines neatly wherever we like. Nice!

This has no effect on how lines break when *printed*; for that, we use \n.

```
                "done yet.");
    hitEnterToContinue ();

    return 0;
}

void drawFrame (const char* leftDialog, const char* rightDialog)
//draw a cartoon's frame, given dialog for each of two characters
{
    const int LEFT_X  =   0, LEFT_Y  = 20;
    const int RIGHT_X = 320, RIGHT_Y = 40;
    //right character is drawn a little lower
    //it doesn't look so much like a mirror image

    SSDL_RenderClear ();      //clear background to black
    drawCharacter    (LEFT_X,  LEFT_Y);
    drawDialog       (LEFT_X,  LEFT_Y,  leftDialog);
    drawCharacter    (RIGHT_X, RIGHT_Y);
    drawDialog       (RIGHT_X, RIGHT_Y, rightDialog);
}

void drawCharacter (int x, int y)
//draw a stick-figure character, with its dialog at the top.
// The upper-left corner of it all is x, y.
{
    enum {HEAD_RADIUS = 45};

    SSDL_RenderDrawCircle (x+140, y+195, HEAD_RADIUS);  //draw head

    SSDL_RenderDrawLine   (x+142, y+240, x+140, y+340); //draw body,
                                                         //slightly angled

    SSDL_RenderDrawLine   (x+142, y+260, x+115, y+340); //draw arms
    SSDL_RenderDrawLine   (x+142, y+260, x+165, y+342);

    SSDL_RenderDrawLine   (x+140, y+340, x+100, y+420); //draw legs
    SSDL_RenderDrawLine   (x+140, y+340, x+157, y+420);
}
```

```
void drawDialog (int x, int y, const char* dialog)
//Draw the dialog for a character, with a line connecting
// it to the character.  x, y is the upper-left corner of
// the whole set (dialog plus character)
{
    //line linking character to dialog
    SSDL_RenderDrawLine (x+90, y+100, x+112, y+130);
    //dialog itself
    SSDL_RenderText (dialog, x+20, y);
}

void hitEnterToContinue()
{
      //How far up to put the "Hit a key" message
      const int BOTTOM_LINE_HEIGHT = 25;

      //More succinct than "Hit any key to continue but not
      // Escape because that ends the program"
      SSDL_RenderTextCentered("Hit Enter to continue",
            SSDL_GetWindowWidth() / 2,
            SSDL_GetWindowHeight() - BOTTOM_LINE_HEIGHT);

      SSDL_WaitKey();
}
```

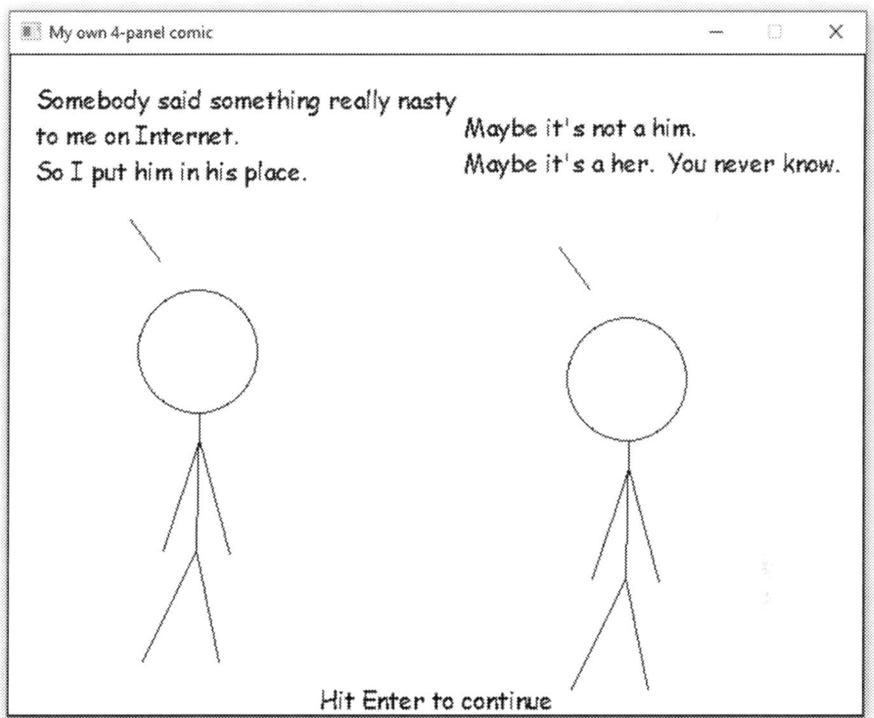

Figure 7-13. *Frame 1 of the 4-panel cartoon program. The other frames are similar except way funnier*

EXERCISES

1. Write your own multi-panel cartoon: first the algorithm (you'll need it fer sure!), then the functions.

2. On the Japanese holiday of Tanabata, people celebrate by writing wishes on vertical strips of paper (*tanzaku*) and tying them to bamboo. Write a program to make several *tanzaku* on the screen, writing text vertically as in Figure 7-14.

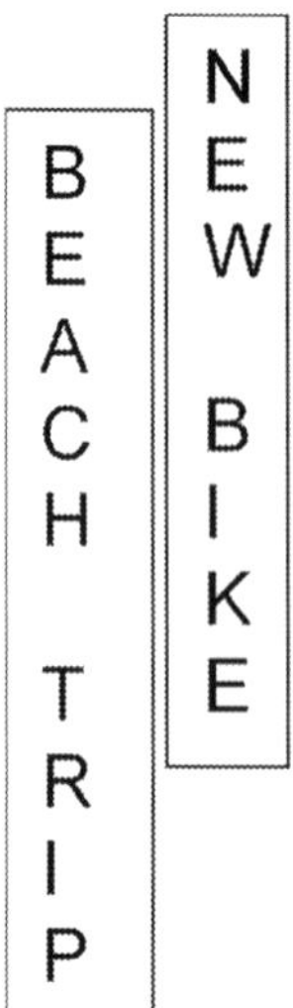

Figure 7-14. *Tanzaku for Exercise 2*

CHAPTER 8

Functions (Continued)

More things about functions: random number functions, Boolean functions, parameters that change, and the scope (visibility) of variables.

Random numbers

> *Anyone who considers arithmetical methods of producing random numbers is, of course, in a state of sin.*
>
> —John von Neumann, inventor of FORTRAN (Goldstine, 1972)

Random numbers aren't just useful for games. They're useful for simulations – predicting the average behavior of some system – and for scientific computing. You can tell people that why you're studying them. It isn't for games. Honest.

But computers are orderly machines. They can't really make random numbers, as von Neumann knew. I suppose you could drop one and see how it lands, but then how will you play solitaire on it?

Making a random number generator

So what we'll do is make a sequence of numbers that *look* random to a human observer – but they'll actually be perfectly predictable, if you know how the computer is doing it.

In Example 8-1, the `%` operator, called "modulus," means "divide and take the remainder." So `36%10`, for example, gives us 6, because if you divide 36 by 10, the remainder is 6.

Remember from Chapter 3 that `A += B` means `A = A+B`; `*=` and `%=` are defined similarly.

W. Briggs, *C++ for Lazy Programmers*, https://doi.org/10.1007/978-1-4842-5187-4_8

Example 8-1. A random number generator

```
int rand () //Return a pseudo-random integer
{
	static unsigned int seed = 76;
	static const unsigned int INCREMENT  = 51138;
	static const unsigned int MULTIPLIER= 21503;
	static const unsigned int MODULUS    = 32767;

	seed += INCREMENT;
	seed *= MULTIPLIER;
	seed %= MODULUS;

	return seed;
}
```

The `static` keyword here means that these variables will be created once, the first time the function is called, and will remain there as long as the program is running. Ordinarily variables local to a function are re-created each time the function is called. But we want `seed` remembered time to time, so we can get a different answer for each call, based on what happened previously. We'll also make the `consts` `static`, so they won't have to be reinitialized each time we call the function.

Suppose seed starts at, oh, 76. Add that `INCREMENT`; multiply it by `MULTIPLIER`; then divide by `MODULUS` and take the remainder. What's the new value? You can't do that in your head?

Neither can anyone else. If you call this again and again, you'll get a sequence of large numbers that you can't predict without doing the math. It looks random; it isn't: 21306 20152 10309 31100...

Usually we don't want such big numbers though. No problem: we can easily get them down to a manageable range. Here are some examples:

```
int numberLessThanTen = rand()% 10;
```

This gives us a number in the range 0 through 9 – since the maximum remainder after you divide by 10 is 9.

```
int oneThroughTen = rand()%10 + 1;
```

Now we have 1 through 10: 7 3 10 1 6...

That's how it's done.

There's one other thing we need. Do we always want to start with the same number, 76? If we do, we'll get an apparently random sequence of numbers...but it will always be the *same* sequence! If we're making a card game, say, those cards we pick will always be in the same order.

You may have seen a game that *asks* for a seed. If one of the options is "Select game" and you can give it a number, what you're doing is initializing the seed for the random number generator. Example 8-2 amends the code to support this.

Example 8-2. A complete random number generator

```
unsigned long int seed;           //Current random number seed

void srand (unsigned int what)  //Start the random number generator
{
    seed = what;
}

int rand ()                     //Return a pseudo-random integer
{
    static const unsigned int INCREMENT = 51138;
    static const unsigned int MULTIPLIER= 21503;
    static const unsigned int MODULUS   = 32767;

    seed += INCREMENT;
    seed *= MULTIPLIER;
    seed %= MODULUS;

    return seed;
}
```

You call `srand` (s for "seed"? for "start"? Either works for me) to start your sequence. Subsequent calls to `rand` get the next number in the sequence, and the next, and so on.

Now, this has a serious drawback: the variable `seed` is declared outside any function. That means any function in the entire program can mess it up. We avoid using global variables whenever we can – but in this unusual case, there's no other good way to do it: `srand` and `rand` both need access.

I'm on the naughty list now for sure. Sorry, Santa.

Using the built-in random number generator

Good news: other programmers besides you have wanted to use pseudo-random numbers! So the functions shown in Example 8-2 come with your compiler. Here's how to use them:

```
#include <cstdlib>  //for srand, rand

int main (int argc, char** argv)
{
      srand (someNumber); //start random number generator
      ...
```

cstdlib stands for "C standard library." cstdlib gives us rand, srand, and other functions.

Of course, I'm not too happy with that someNumber thing. Where does it come from? We can always make the user select the game by typing in a seed. It'll work, but it's more work on the user.

Better: get the number from the computer. But how can we be sure it gives us a different one each time?

Consult the clock.

Every time you restart the program, it's a different time. If we can give srand a number based on the time, we'll get a different sequence each time.

Here's how.

```
#include<cstdlib>    //for srand, rand
#include<ctime>      //for time

int main (int argc, char** argv)
{
      srand ((unsigned int) time (nullptr));
      ...
```

ctime contains a function time that returns the number of seconds since midnight January 1, 1970, Greenwich Mean Time. We don't care about the starting point, but we do care that the answer will be different each second – so we'll get different games.

It returns the time as a time_t, which is some kind of int. srand wants unsigned int; we convert it so the compiler won't give us a warning.

Don't worry what nullptr means; we'll get to that later.

Golden Rule of srand

Call it *once*, thus: `srand (time (nullptr));`

If you call it multiple times, you'll reset the "random" number sequence multiple times -- and the first several "random" numbers you get (until the second changes) will be identical. Call it once; that's all you need.

Now, as an example, let's try a program that rolls a couple of dice, as in a craps game, and tells how you did. On the first try, if you get 2, 3, or 12, you lose. 7 or 11 wins. Any other number is your "point" for more betting.

Algorithm:

```
main:
      start things up with srand
      roll 2 dice
      print what you rolled
      print what happens to your bet
      wait for user to hit a key
```

How do we roll a die? A reasonable question.

```
roll die:
      pick a random number 1 to 6.
```

How do I do that? As earlier: divide by the range and take the remainder, then add 1.

```
roll die:
      return rand () % 6 + 1
```

The program is in Example 8-3; output is in Figure 8-1.

Example 8-3. A program to do a craps roll, illustrating srand and rand

```
//One step in a game of craps
//          -- from _C++ for Lazy Programmers_

#include <ctime>            //for time function
#include <cstdlib>          //for srand, rand
#include "SSDL.h"
```

```
enum { SIDES_PER_DIE = 6 };

int rollDie ();          //roll a 6-sided die

int main (int argc, char** argv)
{
    srand ((unsigned int) (time (nullptr)));
                              //This starts the random # generator
                              //It gets called once per program

    SSDL_SetWindowTitle ("Craps roll");

    sout << "Ready to roll?  Hit a key to continue.\n";
    SSDL_WaitKey ();

    int roll1 = rollDie (), roll2 = rollDie ();
    sout << "You rolled a " << roll1 << " and a " << roll2;

    switch (roll1 + roll2)
    {
    case  2:
    case  3:
    case 12: sout << " -- craps.  You lose the pass line bet.\n";
        break;
    case  7:
    case 11: sout << " -- natural.  You win the pass line bet.\n";
        break;
    default: sout <<", so " << roll1 + roll2 << " is your point.\n";
    }

    sout << "Hit a key to end.\n";
    SSDL_WaitKey();

    return 0;
}

int rollDie () { return rand() % SIDES_PER_DIE + 1; }
```

```
Craps roll
Ready to roll? Hit a key to continue.
You rolled a 5 and a 2 -- natural. You win the pass line bet.
Hit a key to end.
```

Figure 8-1. *Output of the craps program, Example 8-3*

Antibugging

When you're debugging a program, **you may want to get the same sequence of pseudo-random numbers every time**: if something goes wrong, you want it to go wrong the same way each time so you can fix it. If so, replace `srand (time (nullptr))` with `srand (someInteger)` until it's debugged.

Now, something that can go wrong:

- **You get the same random number over and over.** Here's a common cause early on: you keep calling `srand (time (nullptr))`. Or maybe you didn't call it at all. The fix: call `srand` *once*, at the start of the program.

EXERCISES

1. On paper, write what you think a sequence of 20 coin flips might be. Then write a program that flips coins and tells the user what the results are. Output might look like this:

   ```
   How many coins do you want to flip? 20

   Here are the results: HTTHTHHHTTHHTTTTTHHT

   That's 9 heads and 11 tails.
   ```

   Did the sequence look the way you expected?

2. How many times do you need to roll a 6-sided die before you roll a 6? Write an algorithm for, then write and test, a program to roll until it does, and report the number of times it needed.

   Now do it a thousand times, and report the average.

3. Play against the computer, or against another player, with a dreidel, until someone is out of gelt. You can find the rules on Wikipedia or elsewhere.

4. Welcome to *The Price Is Right*, and come on down! Our task this time is to find the correct answer to the classic "Monty Hall" problem.

You have a choice between doors 1, 2, or 3. Behind one is a Porsche and clear title to a South Pacific island; behind the other two are week-old pizza, a goat, and box mac and cheese. Hard as it is to pass up mac and cheese, you have your heart set on the Porsche and the island.

You pick a door. The host then opens one of the other doors, one with no prize behind it. (If you picked wrong, he opens the only other door without a prize. If you picked right, he selects a prize-less door at random.) He offers you the chance to switch.

Should you?

Write a program that will simulate the entire process, and do it a large number of times. (What's a reasonable large number? You decide.) Be sure to do each part, all the way down to identifying the door the player switches to and comparing that to the door with the prize behind it. (Simplifying the problem may be valid, but simplifications can trip you up. Also, it's interesting to find a way to identify the door switched to.)

What percentage of the time do you win if you switch? If it's 50% or close, it must not matter.

So, did it matter?

Extra The Monty Hall problem is a classic probability problem popularized at one point by Marilyn vos Savant, the high-IQ author of the "Ask Marilyn" column in *Parade* Magazine. She gave the correct answer…then wrote more columns as people kept writing in. A grade-school class tried running the scenario several times (without a computer, presumably) to find the answer. Several mathematics professors, giving their names and affiliations, wrote to ask her to recant, with such comments as "You blew it!" and "You are the goat!" How embarrassing – for them.

Boolean functions

We've had functions to return true or false values before: `isupper`, for example, in Chapter 5. Here's how I'd write it (Example 8-4).

Example 8-4. My own `isupper`, a Boolean function

```
bool isupper (char ch) //returns whether ch is an upper-case letter
{
    bool result;

    if (ch >= 'A' && ch <= 'Z')
        result = true;
    else
        result = false;

    return result;
}
```

So if `ch` is in the uppercase range, it returns `true`, otherwise `false`. On the other hand, in Example 8-5's version… if `ch` is in uppercase range, it returns `true`, otherwise `false`. They do exactly the same thing.

Example 8-5. My own `isupper`, a cooler version (I think)

```
bool isupper (char ch) //returns whether ch is an upper-case letter
{
    return ch >= 'A' && ch <= 'Z';
}
```

Which do you prefer? I like the short one. Pick the one you find clearest. Different strokes for different folks.

EXERCISES

1. Write a function `inRange` which, given a number and a lower and upper bound, tells if the number is between the bounds. As is usually the case, it won't print anything, but will return its answer. `main` can do the printing.
2. Write an algorithm, then code, for a function which puts boxes on the screen for "YES" and "NO" and another that waits for a mouse click and returns true if the YES box was clicked, false if NO was clicked, and continues to wait if the click is outside both boxes. Then make a program that demonstrates these functions' use.
3. Using the previous exercise, design and write a program to determine whether the creature you just saw was a fairy, troll, dwarf, elf, or some other magical creature, as in Exercise 1 in the "`chars` and `cctype`" section of Chapter 5. You pick the distinguishing features of each type of creature.

& parameters

What if you want your function to provide more than one value? To alter a variable you have? You can only return one thing from a function.[1]

In the analogy of the candy-making machine, you can only spit out one product. That being the case, we need a different kind of machine: one that takes in a confection and changes it (bakes it, frosts it, whatever).

The function I want is one that can swap values: `swap (x, y)` should make `x` be what `y` was, and `y` be what `x` was. Here's my first attempt:

```
void swap (int arg1, int arg2)
{
    arg1 = arg2; arg2 = arg1;
}
```

[1]Until Chapter 20.

Trace this through. Here are the states of these variables as we go through this process. Assume the values are initially 5 and 10 (Figure 8-2).

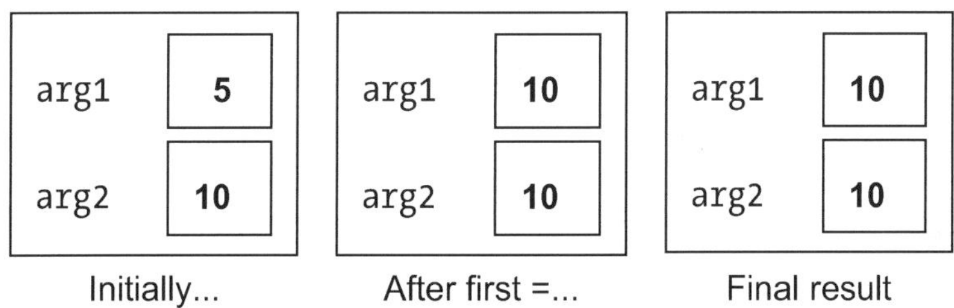

***Figure 8-2.** What happens with `swap`: first attempt*

A variable is like a box that contains a value, but only one. If you wanted to swap what was in your hands, how would you do it? You'd find a place to put one of the objects – a temporary holding area. If the computer's going to swap, it'll need a third place too: a temporary variable. This should work (see Figure 8-3.)

```
void swap (int arg1, int arg2)
{
    int temp = arg1; arg1 = arg2; arg2 = temp;
}
```

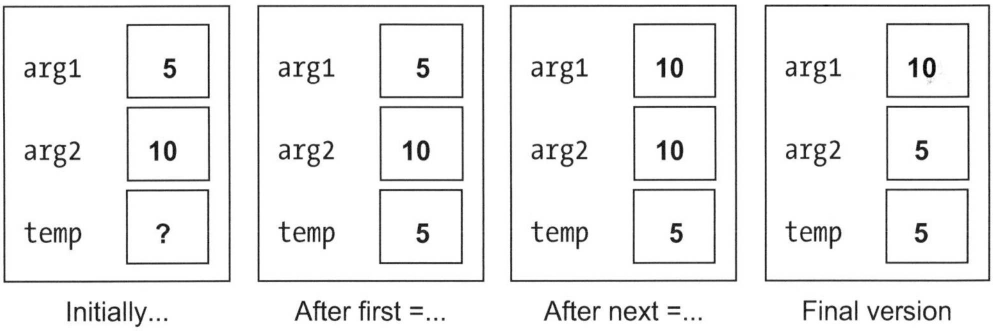

***Figure 8-3.** `swap`: second attempt*

Now let's see what happens when we call it.

```
int main (int argc, char** argv)
{
    int x=5, y=10;

    swap (x, y);

    ...
}
```

We begin with main (Figure 8-4).

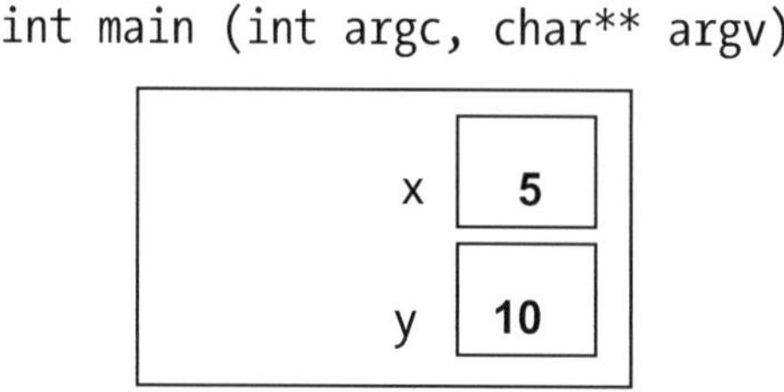

Figure 8-4. *main before calling swap*

Then we call swap. The compiler creates an instance of the swap function – the variables it contains, and anything else it needs to know, copying arguments from main into the parameters (Figure 8-5).

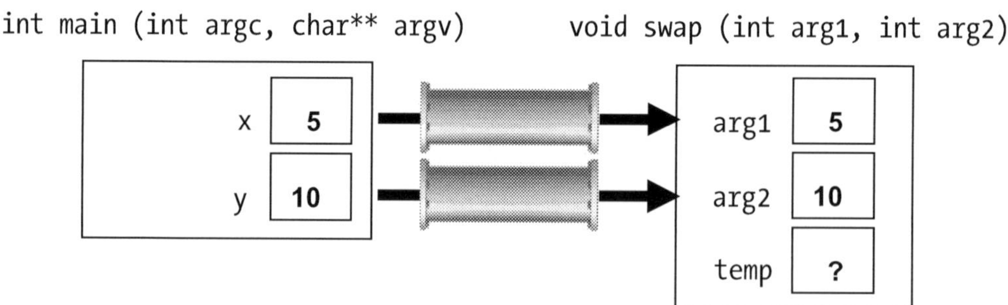

Figure 8-5. *swap begins*

We go through the same process as before, successfully swapping arg1 and arg2 (Figure 8-6).

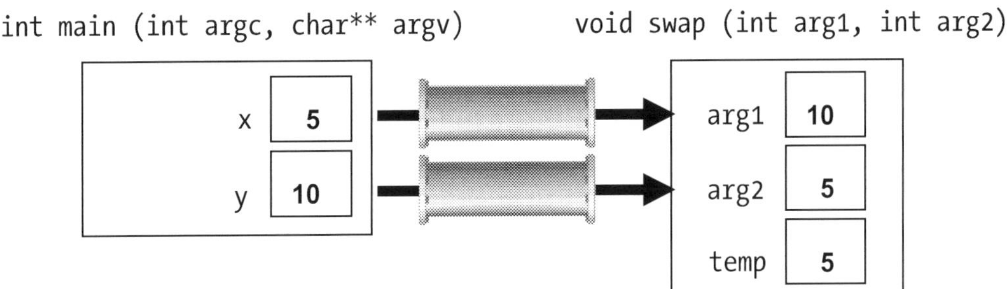

Figure 8-6. *swap completes*

Now we're done with swap, so it can go away (Figure 8-7).

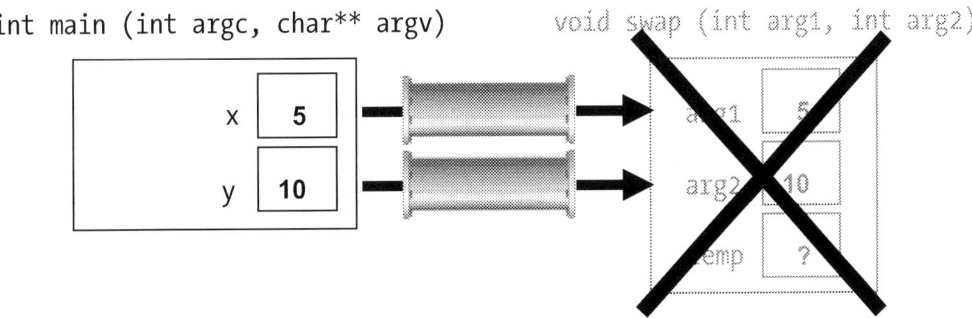

Figure 8-7. *swap goes away*

I suppose that was fun and all, but...weren't we supposed to be changing x and y in main?

Instead, we altered swap's local variables arg1 and arg2. When swap went away, so did they.

The solution is to put & after the type in the parameter. This makes arg1 and arg2 not copies of what's passed in, but temporary aliases: arg1 *is* x, as long as we're in the call to swap. A for ampersand, A for alias.

```
void swap (int& arg1, int& arg2)
{
    int temp = arg1; arg1 = arg2; arg2 = temp;
}
```

Calling the function (Figure 8-8)...

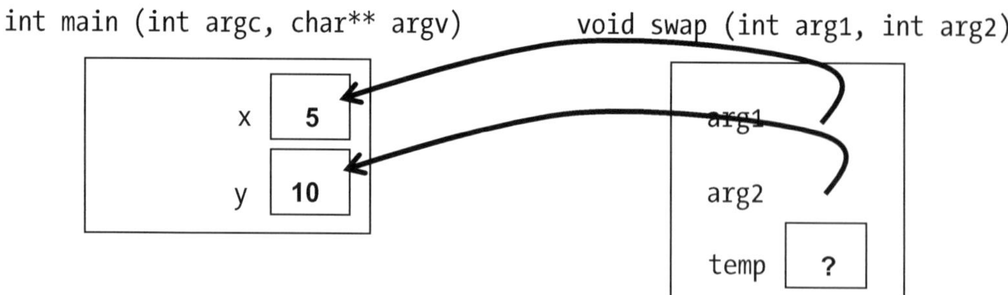

Figure 8-8. *Calling* swap*, with & parameters*

Since arg1 *is* x and arg2 *is* y, what we do to arg1 and arg2, we really do to x and y. So x and y really get changed (Figure 8-9).

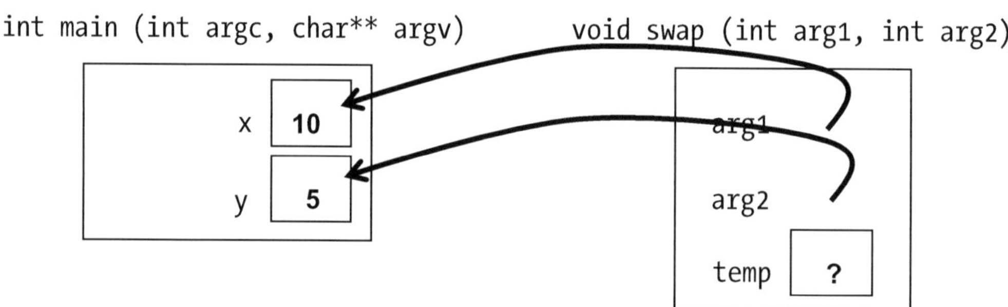

Figure 8-9. swap *actually swaps now!*

The function is finished and goes away (Figure 8-10), with x and y swapped.

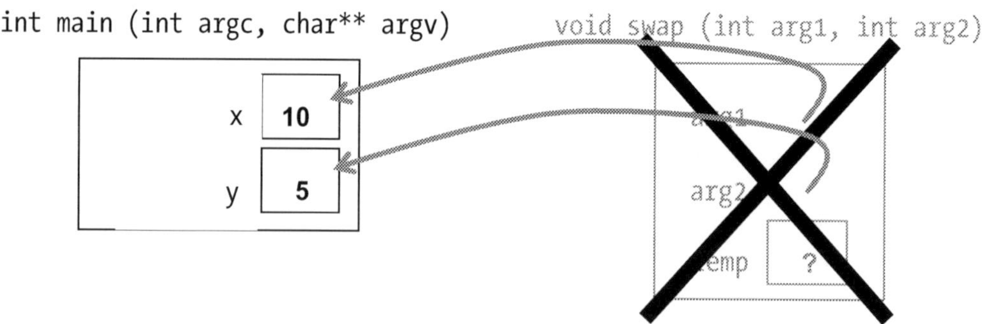

Figure 8-10. swap *complete (and correct)*

So when should you get a value from a function with &, and when do you use a `return` statement? For now, if you have exactly one value to return, use `return`. If you have multiple values, you need a parameter list with &'s.

Golden Rule of Function Parameters and `return` (Version 1)

If the function provides no information to the calling function, its return type is `void`.

If it provides one piece of information, its return type is the type of that piece.

If it provides multiple pieces, its return type is `void`, and those pieces are provided through the parameter list using &.

Antibugging

- **The function seems to change its parameters; but when you leave the function, they're unchanged.** This came from forgetting the &. A common, and maddening, mistake.

EXERCISES

1. Write the algorithm for, and write, a function to generate a random location on the screen and provide it to the function that calls it. Then use it to fill the window with stars (dots) at random locations. Run it a few times to make sure you don't always get the same pattern.
2. Write a function to make a color darker. Here's how: cut the red, the green, and the blue each in half. This means you'll have to do it to the red, green, and blue `int` values, not to the `SSDL_Color` provided by `SSDL_CreateColor`. Then use this function to make a sequence of dots of progressively darker value. Ask the user the initial values.

3. Write a function to solve the quadratic formula. The solutions are $\left(b+\sqrt{b^2-4ac}\right)/2a$ and $\left(-b+\sqrt{b^2-4ac}\right)/2a$ (the – sign before the b is the difference). This amounts to either 2 solutions, or 1 solution (if both solutions are the same), or 0 solutions (if the thing we take the square root of, $b^2 - 4ac$, is negative). So provide the main program with the solutions *and* a parameter saying how many solutions there are. (If there are 0, the contents of the solutions won't matter.)

Identifier scope

The **scope** of an identifier (i.e., a variable name, a function name, or some other defined name) is the area in which it has meaning.

Consider the `swap` example. In the diagrams, we saw `x` and `y` as inside `main` (since they were); we saw `arg1`, `arg2`, and `temp` as inside `swap` (since they were). Variables inside functions can't be seen - or interfered with - by other functions. That means outside code *can't* mess them up. That's modularity: keeping separate things separate, mostly for security.

To look further at scope, consider Example 8-6.

Example 8-6. A program to draw some angles

```
//Program which takes you through successive angles
//          in 30-degree increments
//          -- from _C++ for Lazy Programmers_

#include <cmath> //for sin, cos
#include "SSDL.h"

enum { LINE_LENGTH = 200};
enum { CENTER_X = 320, CENTER_Y = 240 };

const float PI = 3.14159F;
```

```
double degrees2Radians (double angle); //conversion
void   drawAngle       (double angle); //draw 2 lines,
                                       //given angle between

int main (int argc, char** argv)
{
    SSDL_SetWindowTitle ("See some angles.  "
                         "Hit a key to go between frames.");

    double currentAngle = 0.0;

    while (! SSDL_IsQuitMessage () && currentAngle < 360.0)
    {
        static const double ANGLE_INCREMENT = 30.0;2

        SSDL_RenderClear();         //clear screen

        SSDL_SetCursor (0, 0);      //draw angle
        sout << "Angle:  " << currentAngle << "\n";
        drawAngle (currentAngle);

        SSDL_WaitKey ();            //wait for user

        currentAngle += ANGLE_INCREMENT;
                                    //go on to next angle
    }

    return 0;
}

//converts degrees to radians -- since 180 degrees = PI radians
double degrees2Radians (double angle) {      return angle * PI / 180; }

void drawAngle (double angle)
{
    //length of base of a right triangle is hypotenuse * cos(angle)
    //length of vertical is hypotenuse * sin (angle)
```

[2]If I'm going to put this const inside the loop, which I do for clarity, I can make it static so that, like the consts in Example 8-1, it stays till the program ends. More efficient than recreating and reinitializing in each iteration of the loop.

```
    //sin and cos expect radians, so we must convert
    int base     = int (LINE_LENGTH*cos(degrees2Radians (angle)));
    int vertical = int (LINE_LENGTH*sin(degrees2Radians (angle)));

    //draw horizontal line...
    SSDL_RenderDrawLine (CENTER_X, CENTER_Y,
                         CENTER_X+LINE_LENGTH, CENTER_Y);

    //then we'll add the base to the center X, to get the ending X
    //and  we'll add the vertical to center Y, to get the ending Y

    //draw line elevated by given angle
    SSDL_RenderDrawLine (CENTER_X, CENTER_Y,
                         CENTER_X+base, CENTER_Y-vertical);
    //Why -vertical, not +vertical?  Because positive y is down
}
```

As Figure 8-11 illustrates, definitions can go into the pairs of curly braces, but they can't come out. (Sort of like a duck blind: if you're in the blind, you can see things outside, but they can't see you.) Everybody can see LINE_LENGTH, CENTER_X, CENTER_Y, and PI, since they're outside everything, and definitions can always go in; so drawAngle can use CENTER_X and so on, and degrees2Radians can use PI. Nobody can see base and vertical except their owner drawAngle, because they can't leave the {}'s in which they're declared. Similarly, nobody can see currentAngle except main, and ANGLE_INCREMENT can only be seen inside the while's {}'s.

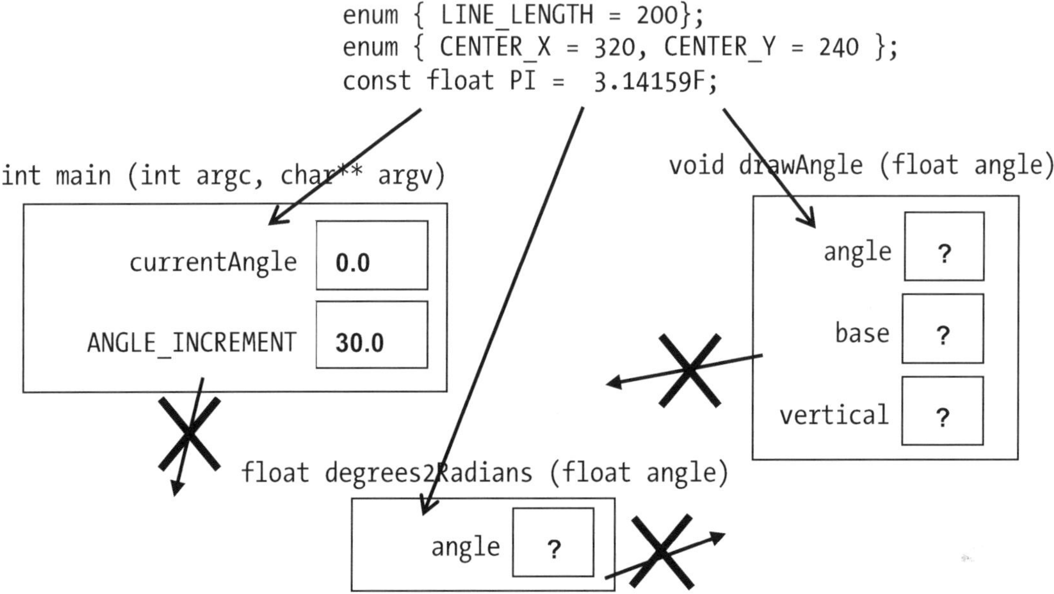

Figure 8-11. *Identifier scope. Definitions outside {}'s can be seen inside them; definitions inside can't be seen outside. Attempts to reference them get something like "identifier not found" or "not declared"*

So how do functions share information? Through parameter lists and `return` statements.

Golden Rule of Identifier Scope

Identifiers can't be seen outside of the {}'s where they were declared.

A final note on algorithms

Through our exercises, we've continued to write algorithms for whatever we do, as suggested in Chapter 6. I won't keep putting the reminder in, but I'll make a blanket statement now: it's best to get into the habit. It feels lazy to skip the step, but it's more work overall, so the lazy thing is: solve the problem of how to do it in the algorithm-writing step. Then coding it can be relatively easy.

CHAPTER 9

Using the Debugger

The debugger lets you step through the program, line by line or function by function, seeing the values of variables so you can tell what goes wrong. Good idea, right?

I think so.

A flawed program

To cover useful debugger commands, let's use the debugger to repair the flawed program in Example 9-1. It's intended to draw a US flag: a sort of a groovy, hand-made looking version with hollow stars as in the picture. (To do a better job, we'd use an image from a file – but for now I want to use, and debug, a star-writing function.) The design is illustrated in Figure 9-1.

Example 9-1. A buggy program to draw the US flag. Output is in Figure 9-2

```
//Program to draw Old Glory on the screen
//      -- from _C++ for Lazy Programmers_

#include <cmath> //for sin, cos
#include "SSDL.h"

const double PI = 3.14159;

//Dimensions1
const int HOIST                   = 400; //My pick for flag width
                                         //Called "A" in Figure 9-1
const int FLY                     = int (HOIST * 1.9);    //B
const int UNION_HOIST             = int (HOIST * 0.5385); //C
```

[1]Dimensions courtesy of the US government, from 4 USC § 1, available at uscode.house.gov.

W. Briggs, *C++ for Lazy Programmers*, https://doi.org/10.1007/978-1-4842-5187-4_9

```
const int UNION_FLY                = int (HOIST * 0.76);    //D

const int UNION_VERTICAL_MARGIN    = int (HOIST * 0.054);  //E and F
const int UNION_HORIZONTAL_MARGIN  = int (HOIST * 0.063);  //G and H

const int STAR_DIAMETER            = int (HOIST * 0.0616); //K

const int STRIPE_WIDTH             = HOIST/13;             //L
```

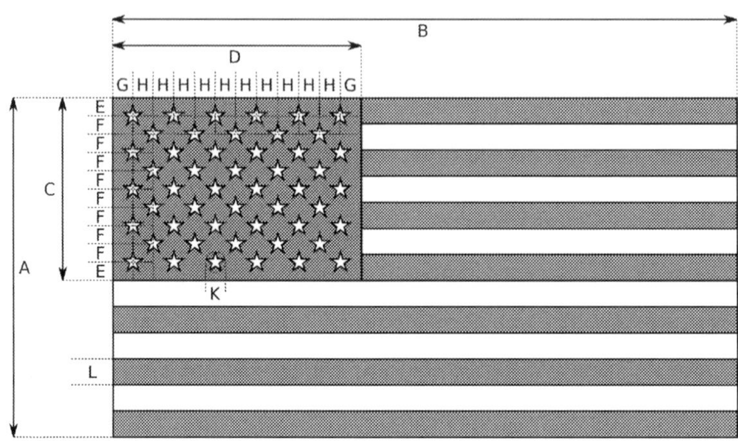

***Figure 9-1.** Designing the US flag*

```
//Colors²
const SSDL_Color RED_FOR_US_FLAG   = SSDL_CreateColor (179, 25, 66);
const SSDL_Color BLUE_FOR_US_FLAG  = SSDL_CreateColor ( 10, 49, 97);

void drawStripes    ();             //the white and red stripes
void drawUnion      ();             //the blue square
void drawStar       (int x, int y); //draw a star centered at x, y

//draw a row of howMany stars, starting with the x, y position,
// using UNION_HORIZONTAL_MARGIN to go to the right as you draw
void drawRowOfStars (int howMany, int x, int y);
```

[2]Colors from the US State Department: eca.state.gov/files/bureau/state_department_u.s._flag_style_guide.pdf.

```
int main (int argc, char** argv)
{
    SSDL_SetWindowTitle ("Old Glory");
    SSDL_SetWindowSize  (FLY, HOIST);

    drawStripes ();
    drawUnion   (); //draw the union (blue square)

    SSDL_WaitKey();

    return 0;
}

void drawStripes ()
{
    SSDL_SetRenderDrawColor (RED_FOR_US_FLAG);
    SSDL_RenderFillRect (0, 0, FLY, HOIST); //first, a big red square

    //Starting with stripe 1, draw every other stripe WHITE
    SSDL_SetRenderDrawColor (WHITE);
    for (int stripe = 1; stripe < 13; stripe += 2)
        SSDL_RenderFillRect (0, stripe*STRIPE_WIDTH,
                             FLY, STRIPE_WIDTH);
}

//draw a row of howMany stars, starting with the x, y position,
// using UNION_HORIZONTAL_MARGIN to go to the right as you draw
void drawRowOfStars (int howMany, int x, int y)
{
    for (int i = 0; i < howMany; ++i)
    {
        drawStar (x, y); x += 2*UNION_HORIZONTAL_MARGIN;
    }
}

void drawUnion ()
{
    SSDL_SetRenderDrawColor (BLUE_FOR_US_FLAG);
    SSDL_RenderFillRect (0, 0, UNION_FLY, UNION_HOIST);
```

```
    //draw the blue box

    SSDL_SetRenderDrawColor (WHITE);
    int y = 1;  //What's the y position of the current row of stars?
    for (int i = 0; i < 4; ++i) //Need 4 pairs of 6- and 7-star rows
    {
        drawRowOfStars (6, UNION_HORIZONTAL_MARGIN, y*UNION_VERTICAL_MARGIN);
        ++y;

        //The 2nd row is staggered right slightly
        drawRowOfStars (5,
                2*UNION_HORIZONTAL_MARGIN,
                y*UNION_VERTICAL_MARGIN);
        ++y;
    }
    //...and one final 6-star row
    drawRowOfStars (6, UNION_HORIZONTAL_MARGIN,
                       y*UNION_VERTICAL_MARGIN);
}

void drawStar (int centerX, int centerY)
{
    const int RADIUS = STAR_DIAMETER/2;
    enum { POINTS_ON_STAR = 5 };

    int x1, y1, x2, y2;
    double angle = PI/2;     //90 degrees: straight up vertically
                             //90 degrees is PI/2 radians

    x1 = int (RADIUS * cos (angle));  //Find x, y point at this angle
    y1 = int (RADIUS * sin (angle));  // relative to center

    for (int i = 0; i < POINTS_ON_STAR; ++i)
    {
        angle += (2 * PI / 360) / POINTS_ON_STAR;
                                          //go to next point on star
```

```
        x2 = int (RADIUS * cos (angle));//Calculate its x,y point
        y2 = int (RADIUS * sin (angle));// relative to center

        SSDL_RenderDrawLine (centerX+x1, centerY+y1,
                             centerX+x2, centerY+y2);

        x1 = x2;                        //Remember the new point
        y1 = y2;                        //  for the next line
    }
}
```

***Figure 9-2.** A buggy US flag*

That could have gone better. The stars are almost invisible dots. Even the stripes are off: note how the blue union square doesn't line up with that middle red stripe; and the bottom red stripe is too big.

What debugger will you use? If you're using Microsoft Visual Studio, it's built in. For Unix I recommend `ddd`, a friendly, graphical interface to the `gdb` debugger. MinGW does not support `ddd` at this point, so I recommend `gdb` itself: text-based but standard and readily available.

As you go through upcoming sections…it's easiest to remember things if you do them yourself, so I strongly recommend you load this program from the book's sample code and follow along, doing the same things as in the book.

Breakpoints and watched variables

Let's start by examining dimensions to see why the stripes don't line up. What dimensions? `STRIPE_WIDTH` seems relevant! So does `UNION_HOIST`, which is the height of the blue square, and `HOIST`, the height of the whole thing.

Being globally defined, they're set by the time the program starts. We can stop on the first line and inspect them.

Visual Studio

Be sure you compiled in Debug mode, not Release mode. You should see Debug, not Release, in the line of symbols and drop-down boxes under the menu bar (see Figure 9-3). If not, you'll know when the debugger commands don't work.

Click the off-white bar left of `main`; a sort of red stop sign appears, as in Figure 9-3. (OK, it's a red dot. But "stop sign" is easier to remember.)

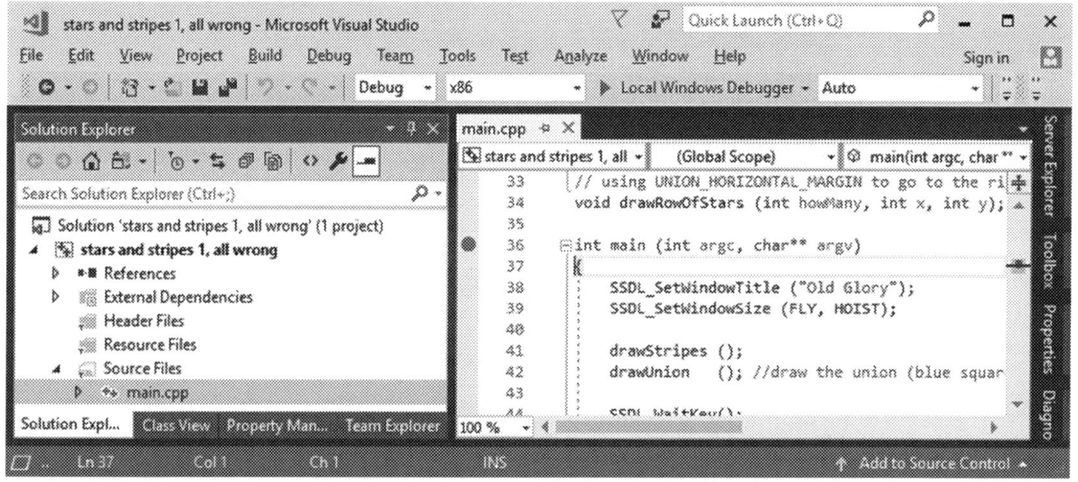

Figure 9-3. *Setting a breakpoint in Microsoft Visual Studio*

Start the program.

Visual Studio didn't like where my breakpoint was, so it moved it down a line. No problem. The yellow arrow means "This line is next." It's about to start `main`. So it's already done the initial constant declarations. Let's see what it made.

On the lower left corner of the Visual Studio Window, you probably see something like in Figure 9-4: a window with tabs for Autos, Locals, and so on. (If you don't, try Window ➤ Reset Window Layout on the menu bar.)

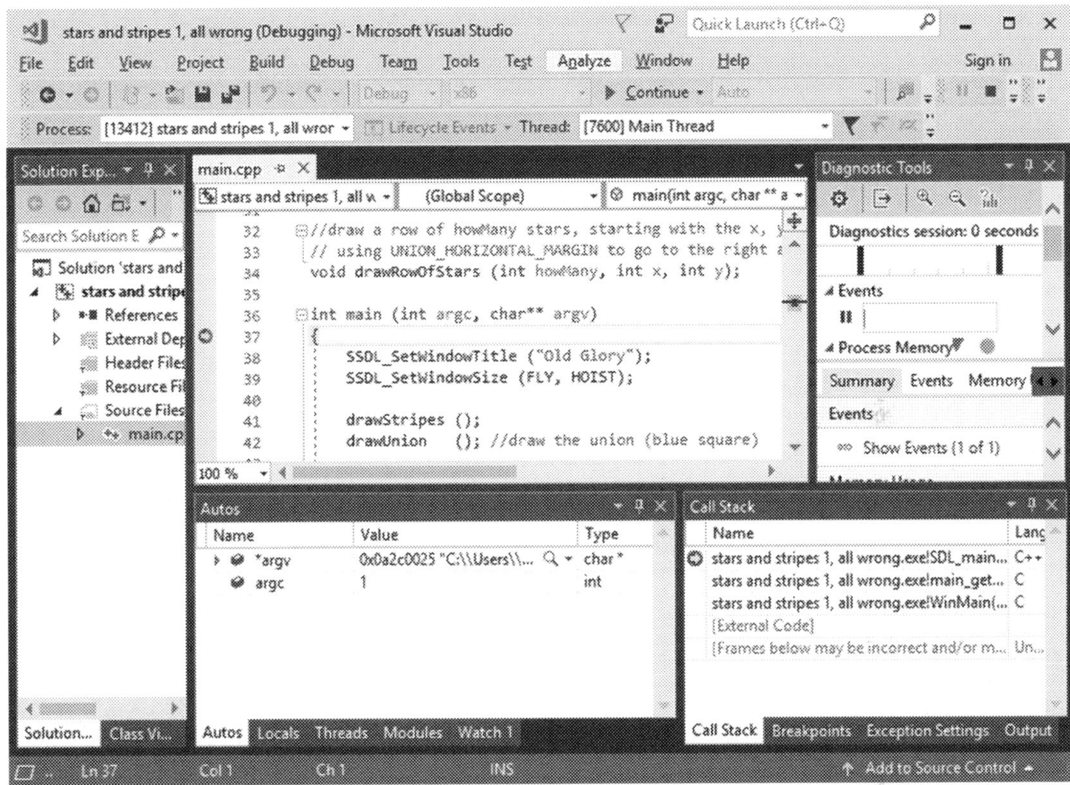

***Figure 9-4.** Starting a debugger session in Microsoft Visual Studio*

Autos are things Visual Studio thinks you might want to see. It's wrong this time: I'm not worried about `argv` and `argc`.

Locals are local variables; we don't have any.

Watch 1 is a place where we can watch the values of variables. Click that tab. You can now click under "Name" and give the name of something you want to see. Try `STRIPE_WIDTH`, then `UNION_HOIST` and `HOIST`.

These are the numbers we need (trust me). Click on the breakpoint to delete it and proceed to the section "Fixing the stripes."

ddd

To debug the program `a.out`, with ddd in Unix, go to its folder and type `./dddx`. If there is no `dddx`, copy it from the `basicSSDLProject` folder you've been using.

Highlight `main`. (If you don't see any code, check the "Antibugging" section.) On the top row of controls, find the stop sign icon labeled "Break"; click that. A stop sign appears on the line, meaning, the program will stop here when it runs. You should see something like Figure 9-5.

In the bottom window with the `(gdb)` prompt, the command `break main` should appear. ddd is a training wheels interface, always telling you what gdb command you just chose. This way you learn gdb as you go.

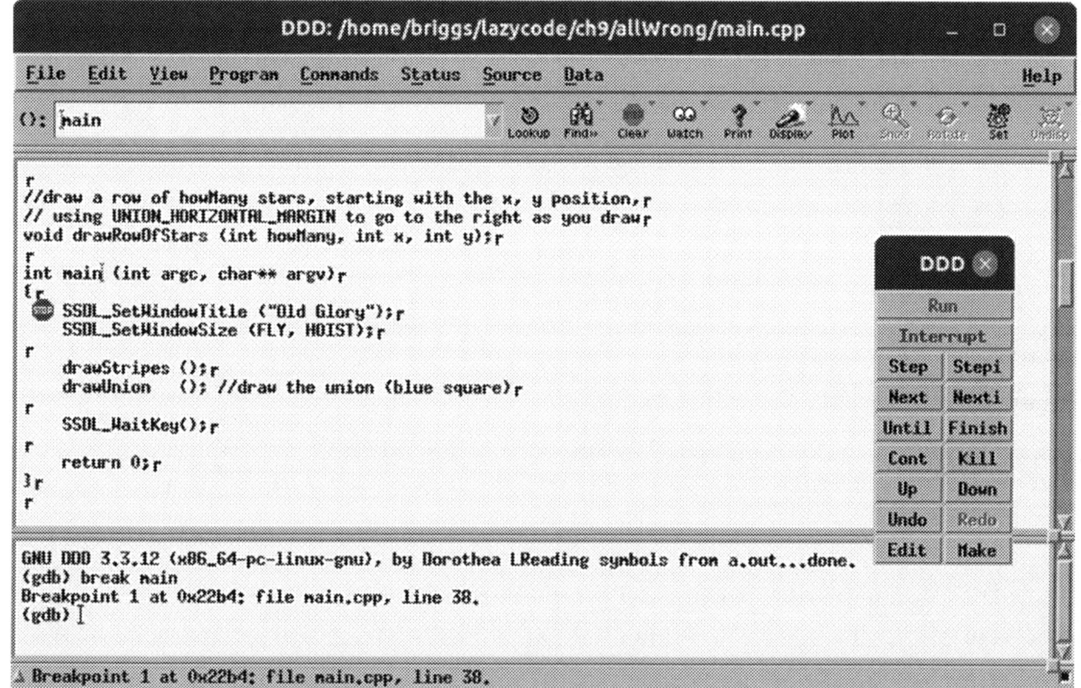

Figure 9-5. *The ddd interface to the gdb debugger*

To run, click Run on the menu on the right, or type `run` at the `(gdb)` prompt. `print STRIPE_WIDTH` and so on at the prompt to get the values of `STRIPE_WIDTH`, `HOIST`, and `UNION_HOIST`.

Clicking on the breakpoint may delete it. If not, `delete <breakpoint number>`. See the gdb window for the breakpoint number. To quit, type `quit`.

gdb

Go to the program's folder and type ./gdbx (Unix) or bash gdbw (MinGW). If there is no such file, copy it in from the basicSSDLProject folder you've been using.

To make the program stop on that first line, I type break main (Unix) or break SDL_main (MinGW). When I run the program, it'll break there and I can examine the values.

To start the program, type run. To see the values, type print: print STRIPE_WIDTH; print HOIST; print UNION_HOIST.

To end gdb, type quit.

Fixing the stripes

Now we have the numbers; let's make some sense of them.

A stripe should be 1/13 of the FLY. 400/13, by my calculator, is 30.76 something; STRIPE_WIDTH, being an int, is only 30. So that's right. There should be 7 stripes covered by that UNION_HOIST: the stripes cover 7*30 = 210 pixels, but the UNION_HOIST is HOIST*7/13 = 215.

The problem is that we're doing integer division and losing decimal places.

I'll make the fix of making the FLY not 400, but something divisible by 13. STRIPE_WIDTH was 30 here; 13*30 = 390. Let's see what amending this will do. Change the initialization of HOIST:

```
const int HOIST                        = 390;  //My pick for flag width
```

and run again. The stripe problem is fixed!

Going into functions

The star problem requires further digging. So restore your breakpoint at main and start the debugger again.

Visual Studio

Looking at the Debug menu: you can Step Over (execute) a line (selecting Step Over, or hitting F10; Function-F10 on some keyboards). As you do, the yellow arrow goes down a line, executing the line as it goes.

When you're down to `drawUnion`, you want to Step *Into* (F11/Function F-11) that function.

Using F10 and F11, go into `drawRowOfStars`, then `drawStar`, until you get to the for loop, as in Figure 9-6. The Call Stack, lower right, shows what function you're in (its top line) and how you got there (lines beneath).

If you don't see the Locals window, click the Locals tab.

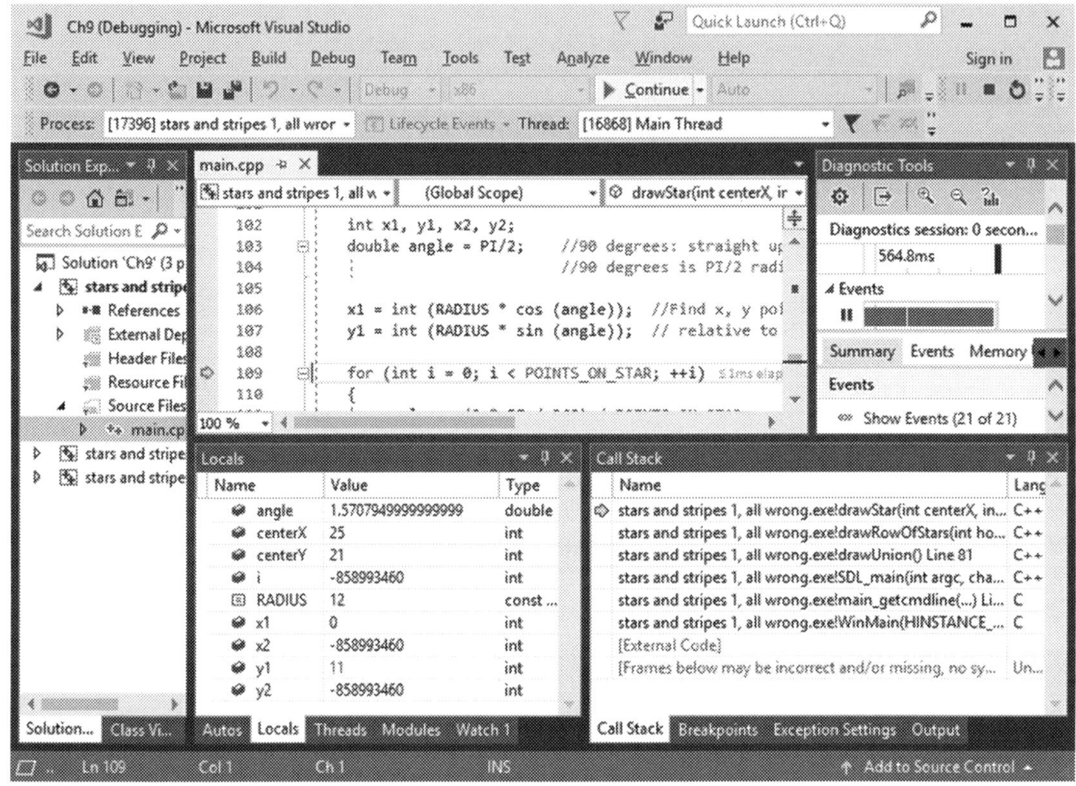

Figure 9-6. *The Locals window in Microsoft Visual Studio*

Nothing looks obviously wrong. Let's go on to `SSDL_RenderDrawLine`. Wasn't angle supposed to change more than that? In the Watch 1 window, type or paste `(2 * PI/360)/POINTS_ON_STAR`: the debugger will calculate it for you.

ddd

In the "DDD" menu on the right, Next takes you to the next line, and Step steps into a function. The arrow on the left shows what line you're about to execute. Use Next to go to `drawUnion`. When there, Step into that function.

Using Next and Step, go into `drawRowOfStars`, then `drawStar`, until you get to the for loop.

At this point it makes sense to find out what the variables are. Under the Data menu, select Display Local Variables. You may need to make the Data area visible: View ➤ View Data Window. Figure 9-7 shows the result.

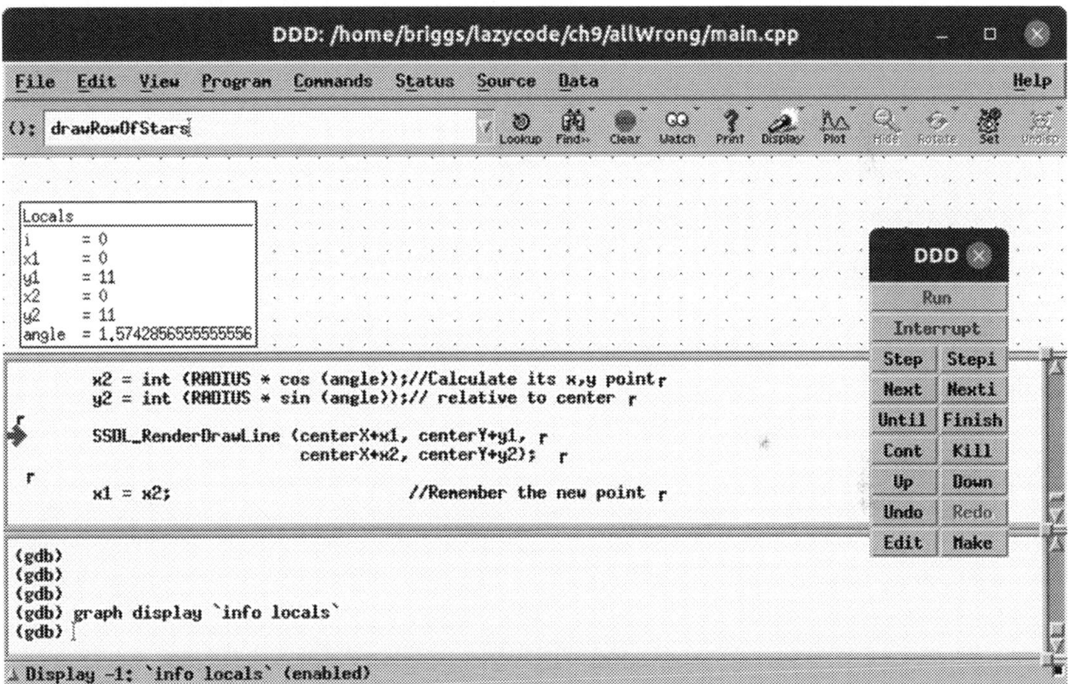

***Figure 9-7.** Displaying local variables in ddd*

Nothing looks obviously wrong. Let's go on to `SSDL_RenderDrawLine`. Wasn't `angle` supposed to change more than that? `print (2 * PI/360)/POINTS_ON_STAR` at the gdb prompt and see what you get.

gdb

To go further in the program, you can type next (or n) to go to the next line, and step (or s) to step into a function. (Enter repeats the last command.) As you progress, it will print the current line so you know where you are. Use these commands to go into drawUnion, then through drawStar, until you get to the for loop.

You may want to put a breakpoint in case you need to come back to this line. break will put one on the current line. break drawStar will break at the start of the function. Just for grins, try that now, and type run. Then continue, or cont, or c, to get back to the breakpoint.

delete <number of breakpoint> deletes the breakpoint; delete deletes them all.

To print local variables, enter info locals.

Nothing looks obviously wrong. Let's go on to SSDL_RenderDrawLine. Wasn't angle supposed to change more than that? print (2 * PI/360)/POINTS_ON_STAR and see what you get.

Fixing the stars

(2 * PI/360)/POINTS_ON_STAR was supposed to take us to the next point on the star. Isn't a fifth of a circle bigger than 0.00349? It should be a circle divided by 5. That's 360°/5, or, in radians, 2π/5, but that's not what the formula says. Looks like I mangled degrees together with radians. There's our problem, so here's our fix.

```
angle += (2 * PI)/POINTS_ON_STAR;       //go to next point on star
```

When we recompile and run, we get a flag with the stars drawn as pentagons. At least they have five sides!

The program tells the computer to go five steps around the circle, each time drawing a line covering 1/5 of that distance. Isn't that what a pentagon, not a star, does?

To draw a star, don't go 1/5 of the way around the circle. Go 2/5 of the way. Let's try that:

```
angle += 2*(2 * PI)/POINTS_ON_STAR; //go to next point on star,
                                    //   2/5 way around circle
```

Now the stars are there, but upside down. I think of 90 degrees as straight up, but with SDL we have increasing Y going *down* the screen. Is that the problem? I'll try starting at -90 degrees and see what happens.

```
float angle = -PI/2;            //-90 degrees -- straight up vertically
```

The result is in Figure 9-8. Much better.

Figure 9-8. *The flag with actual stars*

Wrap-up

For a summary of common debugger commands, see Appendix G.

Antibugging

- **(ddd/gdb) There's no file.** Maybe you forgot to `make` it! Or you made it for Unix but are debugging it with MinGW, or the reverse.
- **It just sits there, giving no prompt.** It may be waiting for input. Click on the program's window and give it what it needs.
- **You're looking at some file you didn't write.** It's the compiler's code, or a library's.

  Visual Studio: Step out (Shift-F11) of the function(s) you're in to get back to your own code. Or set a breakpoint in your code and Continue (F5).

  `ddd/gdb`: `up` will take you up to the calling function; do this enough and you'll see what part of your code you were in. Then set a breakpoint where you like and `continue`.

Extra The GNU ("guh-NOO") Free Software Foundation (`www.gnu.org`) was formed in 1984 to provide free software for the Unix operating system. It's since expanded its mission, and people may use GNU Public License as a licensing agreement when they want to freely share their work.

This is how we get not only ddd and gdb but also g++, GIMP, and other cool stuff.

GNU often applies funny names to things, and GNU itself is no exception. GNU is an acronym: it stands for "GNU's Not Unix."

Bottom-up testing

We looked at top-down design in Chapter 7: start with `main`, then write the functions it calls, then the functions *they* call, until done.

Bottom-up testing is a natural corollary. It's sometimes too hard to test the whole program at once. Suppose you're doing economic forecasting with a program of many functions: correlations, compound interest, predicted GDP, and a lot of hand-waving (Figure 9-9).

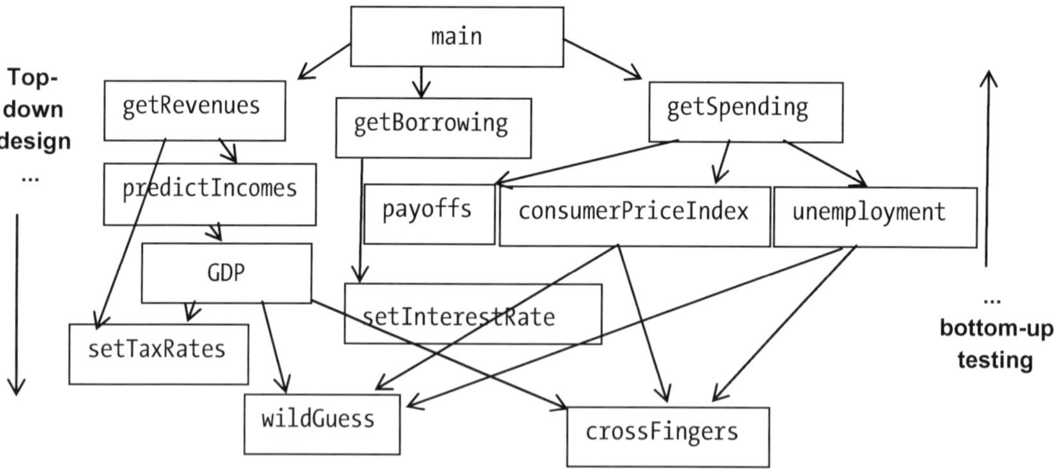

Figure 9-9. *A complicated mess to debug.* `main` *calls three functions,* `getRevenues`*,* `getBorrowing`*, and* `getSpending`*, and they call lots of others*

You run the program, and it tells you

```
The nation will be bankrupt in -2 years.
```

That can't be right. But which function has a problem? `main`? `consumerPriceIndex`? `wildGuess`? You can't get that information from a bare "-2"!

You need to know that you can trust every function. So you take the ones at the bottom (`wildGuess` and `crossFingers`), the ones that don't call the others but are called, and test them until you're confident.

Then you test the ones that call them.

And the ones that call them...all the way up to `main`.

More on antibugging

Here are more hints on getting working programs:

- **Make plenty of backups.** If it's a large or difficult project, a trail of them, so you can backtrack if something screws up.
- **Keep functions modular (no global variables).**
- **Display the information you need.** In the preceding example, the answer "-2" for the years until an event was clearly wrong, but otherwise wasn't informative.
- The biggest problem in testing often is you just don't know what values are in your variables. Here are two common fixes:
    - **Use the debugger.**
    - **Use lots of print statements.** If a variable has a value, then just while debugging, print it. Clearly labeled: not

      ```
      sout << growthRate;
                     //so 0.9 gets printed. What does it mean?
      ```

      but

      ```
      sout << "growthRate is " << growthRate << ".\n";
      ```

That's longer, but it's better than struggling to remember what the numbers you see, mean. Working blindly to fix an error you can't identify is too much work. Better to *see* the problem so you can fix it.

- **Don't let it get your gumption.** In *Zen and the Art of Motorcycle Maintenance,* author Robert Persig warns of things that suck out your "gumption," your ability to solve or even focus on problems with your bike. Or your English essay. Or whatever.

  In programming, too, you can lose gumption. You just found a bug you thought you'd resolved, and the program's useless till you fix it, so now you're too frustrated to do anything but mope. I've been there, recently.

  I once spent two working days tracking down what turned out to be misplaced parentheses. That's *it*? Tiny parentheses? They *are* tiny, but they were a big problem, because I couldn't go on till they were fixed.

  I just said "Whew!" and went on to the next issue.

  If you can suspend self-evaluation when there's an error and get back to the problem, you're on your way.

- **If you make stupid errors...**See "gumption". Stupid errors are the *best* kind, because they're easy to fix. The hard ones are the subtle ones. Everyone makes stupid errors.

- **If you're just no good at this...**Everyone feels that way in the beginning. I did. You wouldn't expect to be fluent in a new language after a few weeks of study, and C++ is way cooler than any mere spoken language.

- **Do it quick.** If you want to do something right, you probably have to do it wrong first. So go ahead and do it wrong. It's quicker to fix a broken program than stare at a screen till enlightenment strikes.

EXERCISES

No exercises yet – just be sure and use your debugger of choice in subsequent chapters!

CHAPTER 10

Arrays and enum

In this chapter, sequences (arrays) of values, enumeration types, weather data, and board games are discussed.

Arrays

"If you don't like the weather in these parts," the old-timer said with a twinkle in his eye, "wait a few minutes."

Let's find out if he's right: we'll take 10 temperatures at 1-minute intervals and see the variation. I'll start like this:

```
double temp1; sout << "Enter a temperature: "; sin >> temp1;
double temp2; sout << "Enter a temperature: "; sin >> temp2;
double temp3; sout << "Enter a temperature: "; sin >> temp3;
```

That's getting old fast. Maybe there's a better way to store 10 numbers. Here it is:

```
enum {MAX_NUMBERS = 10};

double temperatures[MAX_NUMBERS]; //an array of 10 doubles
```

The BNF syntax for an array is *<base type> <name of array>* `[`*<array size>*`];` where *<base type>* is what you want an array of and *<array size>* is how many you want. Array size should be `const int` or `enum`.

Now we have an array of `temperatures`, starting with the 0th and ending with the 9th. If we started with 1, we'd go through 10...but C++ starts counting at 0.

To use one of the array's elements, just say which

```
temperatures[3] = 33.6;
sout << temperatures[3];
```


W. Briggs, *C++ for Lazy Programmers*, https://doi.org/10.1007/978-1-4842-5187-4_10

Since temperatures is an array of double, you can use temperatures[3] anywhere you can use a double – since that's exactly what it is.

Note that here the number in the [ ]'s is not the array size – that's in the declaration only! – but which element you want. This "index" should be some countable type like int or enum. We commonly use variables of type int:

```
//Get the numbers
for (int i = 0; i < MAX_NUMBERS; ++i)
{
      sout << "Enter a temperature: ");
      ssin >> temperatures[i];
}
```

For loops are a natural way to process arrays because they can easily go through each element. This loop starts at 0 and keeps going as long as i is less than 10 (MAX_NUMBERS), so we'll be seeing temperatures[0], temperatures[1], and so on up through temperatures[9] – all 10.

This isn't how we're used to counting, but you get used to it: an array of N elements starts with the 0th and ends with the $N\text{-}1^{th}$. Maybe you'll soon be starting your to-do lists with 0.

Example 10-1 is a complete program for reading in and spitting back out temperatures.

Example 10-1. Reading/writing a list of numbers using an array

```
//Program to read in and print back out numbers
//              -- from _C++ for Lazy Programmers_

#include "SSDL.h"

int main (int argc, char** argv)
{
    enum {MAX_NUMBERS = 10};

    sout << "Enter " << MAX_NUMBERS
         << " temperatures to make your report.\n\n";

    double temperatures [MAX_NUMBERS];
```

```
    //Get the numbers
    for (int i = 0; i < MAX_NUMBERS; ++i)
    {
        sout << "Enter the next temperature: ";
        ssin >> temperatures[i];
    }

    //Print the numbers
    sout << "You entered ";
    for (int i = 0; i < MAX_NUMBERS; ++i)
        sout << temperatures[i] << ' ';

    sout << "\nHit any key to end.\n";

    SSDL_WaitKey ();

    return 0;
}
```

We usually initialize our variables. Here's how to do that with an array:

```
//where MAX_NUMS = 4...
double Numbers[MAX_NUMS] = {0.1, 2.2, 0.5, 0.75};[1]
                                          //uses an "initializer list"
```

Unfortunately, the bracketed list only works at initialization time: we can't later set `Numbers` to a bracketed set of values. We'll have to do it one element at a time, possibly using a for loop.

I needn't put `MAX_NUMS` in the `[]`'s because C++ can count the initialization list and figure out the size:

```
double temperatures[] = {32.6, 32.6, 32.7, 32.7, 32.7,
                         32.7, 32.7, 32.7, 32.7, 32.7};
    //I think the old guy was messing with us
```

[1]Omit the = if you like: `double Numbers[] {0.1, 2.2, 0.5, 0.75};`.

If you give too few values, it fills in the rest with 0's[2]:

```
double temperatures[MAX_NUMS] = {};//If it's really 0's,
                                   // I hope we're using Fahrenheit
```

Arrays' dirty little secret: using memory addresses

Arrays aren't stored in memory the same way other variables are.

An array variable is actually an address: the address of a chunk of memory that contains the elements. When you declare an array, this makes the computer do these things: allocate the array variable (left in Figure 10-1); allocate a chunk of memory to store the elements (right in Figure 10-1); and put the address of the 0th element, that is, the start of that chunk, in your new array variable.[3]

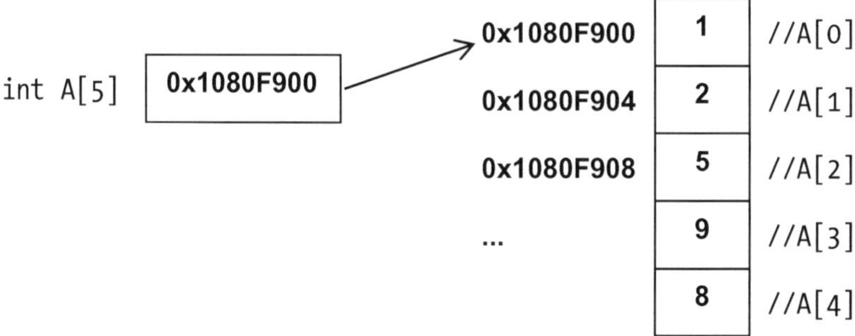

Figure 10-1. *How arrays are stored in memory*

This scheme is why C++ starts with array index 0. To calculate the address of the `i`th element, it adds `i*sizeof(int)`, that is, `i` times the size of a `int`, whatever that is, to the location of the address. If you started at 1, it would have to add `(i-1)*sizeof(int)`. C++, and even moreso its ancestor C, prefers to do things as efficiently as possible even if it sacrifices a little clarity in the process.

So, in Figure 10-1, where is the array size stored? How can I check if I need it later?

[2]"Zero initialization." If the members of your array are of a type that has 0 (or 0.0!), they'll be set to that.

[3]In this illustration, I write the addresses in "hexadecimal," that is, base 16, which is conventional. The reason it goes up by 4 each row is that I'm assuming `int` takes up 4 memory locations, that is, 4 "bytes." None of this matters here, but I don't want the C++ gods to laugh at my diagram.

I can't. C++ uses array size when it allocates the memory, but after that, if you want that number – say, to be sure you're not going too far in the array – you have to keep track of it yourself. If you declare an array of five elements and try to access the 5th element (which, since C++ uses 0-based counting, doesn't exist), *it lets you*. This means you are reading a chunk of memory that's being used for something else.

It's even worse if you write to that chunk of memory, as in `A[5] = 0`. If you do, you may overwrite data that makes up some other variable.

Antibugging

- **Your loop goes one element too far in the array.** I'd bet the less than operator is to blame. Change

  ```
  for (int i = 0; i <= N; ++i)
  ```

  to

  ```
  for (int i = 0; i < N; ++i)
  ```

- **A variable's value changes, but you didn't tell it to.** You may have used an index too big for an array and thereby overwritten a *different* variable.

- **Your program crashes (stops running).** In Unix, you get `Segmentation fault: core dumped`. In other venues, you may get a window that says "<your program> has stopped working," or (in Visual Studio) "Exception thrown."

  A likely cause at this point is...using an index too big for the array.

EXERCISES

In the following, be sure to use the debugger if something goes wrong:

1. Write a program that gets from the user all seven daily high temperatures and daily lows for the week and tells the user which day had the lowest low and the highest high.
2. Make the same program, but don't ask the user: initialize the array using {}'s.

3. Given an array of chars (use {}'s to initialize), report if the characters are in alphabetical order.
4. Read in a list of integers, and print them out in reverse.

Arrays as function parameters

When we want to pass a variable to a function, we essentially lift the declaration (without the semicolon) and use that to define the parameter: that is, we'd declare x with `int x;`, so if we want to send x into function f, we write `void f(int x);`.

We do the same with arrays.

```
void f (int myArray[ARRAY_SIZE]);
```

Example 10-2 shows a function to find the smallest temperature in our array.

Example 10-2. `lowestTemp`, taking an array and returning its smallest element

```
double lowestTemp(double temperatures[MAX_NUMBERS])
//returns lowest entry in temperatures
{
    double result = temperatures[0];

    for (int i = 0; i < MAX_NUMBERS; ++i)
        if (temperatures[i] < result)
            result = temperatures[i];

    return result;
}
```

It's called thus:

```
sout << "The lowest temp was " << lowestTemp (temperatures);
```

It isn't possible, based on what we know so far, to make a function return an array. For now we'll just pass them in as parameters.

Array parameters that change, or don't

I don't have to use the & with an array, even if I want to change the array's contents. Here's why.

Remember that an array variable isn't really all the different elements; it's the address of the 0th. If you don't use &, you can't alter it – and that's no problem: we don't want to alter the *address*, we only want to alter the *contents* – and they weren't the thing passed in! Alter them to your heart's content – your alterations will be there when the function returns.

You might say, "Doesn't that violate security? What if the called function alters them, and they shouldn't have been altered?" Good point. Here's the fix:

```
double lowestTemp (const double temperatures[ARRAY_SIZE])
//returns lowest entry in temperatures
{
        ...
```

Declaring the parameter as `const` ensures that `lowestTemp` can't change it. A good habit to get into.

Array parameters and reusability

Another important implication of how arrays are stored is that since C++ doesn't care how big your array is, when you pass it to a function, it totally ignores the size given between the `[]`'s. Put it in or leave it out; C++ doesn't care. *This means the same function can be used for any array of the same base type, regardless of size.*

Here's a version of `lowestTemp` that doesn't restrict you to a particular size.

```
double lowestTemp (const double temperatures[], int arraySize)
//returns lowest entry in temperatures
{
      bool result = temperatures[0];

      for (int i = 0; i < arraySize; ++i)
          ...
}
```

Now let's be even more flexible. As Chapter 7 suggests, it's good to make your functions general, versatile, and thus reusable. There's no reason the function we just called `lowestTemp` would work only with temperatures. Think of it more generally, and you can use it again in another program. Code reuse, yay.

Example 10-3. `minimum`, a function that can be used for any `double` array, any size

```
double minimum(const double elements[], int arraySize)
//returns lowest entry in elements
{
    double result = elements[0];

    for (int i = 0; i < arraySize; ++i)
        if (elements[i] < result)
            result = elements[i];

    return result;
}
```

Antibugging

- **The compiler complains about "invalid conversion from int to int*" or "int to int[]" on a function call.** It's saying it expected an array but got a single value. But didn't we give it an array? In this example

  ```
  minimum (temperatures[NUMTEMPS], NUMTEMPS);
  ```

  ...I didn't. I gave it the `NUMTEMPS`th temperature, whatever that is.

  This problem is a confusion over two uses of [ ]'s: when declaring, what goes between the [ ]'s is array size. At all other times, it's which element we want to access.

  Since the array's name is `temperatures`, not `temperatures[NUMTEMPS]`, I'll pass that in: `minimum (temperatures, NUMTEMPS);`.

Golden Rule of []

What goes between the [ ]'s in an array reference is which element you want. (Except at the time of declaration. Then it's the array size.)

EXERCISES

In these exercises, remember to use your favorite debugger if something goes wrong:

1. Write a `maximum` function to correspond to `minimum` in Example 10-3, and use these to find the range in a given array of temperatures – thus answering the question the chapter started with, of how quickly the weather is changing. If the range is more than half a degree, print "You're right; the weather really does change quickly here!"
2. For a month of temperatures, report the highest high, the lowest low, and the day with the biggest gap between.
3. Write a program that will graph the high and low temperatures for a given month (you'll want to initialize the array using {}'s; it'll be too much work to type them each time), displaying X and Y axes for day and temperature and putting dots to mark the data points. You'll definitely want to write the algorithm first for this one.

Enumeration types

In preparation for using playing cards, or colored pieces in a board game, or months of the year...let's look over `enum` again. There are two things about them we haven't made use of yet:

1. They can create new types.
2. The symbols you put between the { }'s are ordered by default.

In BNF, an `enum` declaration is `enum` *[<typename>]* `{`*<list of values>*`};`. It's just that till now we've always omitted the typename.

If you don't specify, the values start at 0 and increase by 1 each time: for example,

```
enum Suit {CLUBS, DIAMONDS, HEARTS, SPADES}; //Playing card suit
```

is equivalent to

```
const int CLUBS    = 0;
const int DIAMONDS = 1;
const int HEARTS   = 2;
const int SPADES   = 3;
```

but is way easier to write, and also creates a new type `Suit` so you can declare variables of that type:

```
Suit firstCardSuit = HEARTS, secondCardSuit = SPADES;
```

What *is* `firstCardSuit`, really? It's really a `Suit`! But, yes, it is very much like an `int`. Why not just make it an `int`? Clarity: when you declare an `int`, it's not clear if you really meant it as a suit for cards. If you declare it as a `Suit`, it's obvious.

With the naming convention used in this book, new types we create are capitalized (like `Suit`, but unlike `int`: types built into the standard are lowercase).

We can also declare

```
enum Rank {ACE=1, JACK=11, QUEEN, KING}; //Playing card rank
```

We didn't specify a value for `QUEEN`, so it keeps counting from `JACK`: `QUEEN` is 12, `KING` is 13.

`enum` values are meant more as labels than numbers, so though you can assign to `enum` variables (=) and compare them (==, <, <=, etc.), you can't easily do math with them: you can't use ++, --, +=, -=, *=, /=, or %=. You can't print them with `sout` or read them with `ssin`. You can't assign `int`s into them (`myRank = 8` won't compile). So what good are they?

Sometimes you don't need to do those things.

If you must do math, there's a workaround. Need to give `myRank` a value of 8? Use casting:

```
myRank = Rank (8);
```

Need to go on to the next? Casting again:

```
myRank = Rank (myRank+1);
```

What if you want to print it? There's no way the compiler would know *how* we want a Suit printed, so we'll tell it (Example 10-4).

Example 10-4. A function for printing playing card suit

```
void print(Suit suit) //prints a Suit
{
	switch (suit)
	{
	case CLUBS   : sout << 'C';      break;
	case DIAMONDS: sout << 'D';      break;
	case HEARTS  : sout << 'H';      break;
	case SPADES  : sout << 'S';      break;
	default      : sout << '?';      break;
	}
}
```

I find not having to declare long lists of consts such a plus I have no reservations about using enums. Though I do wish you could use ++ with them.

enum class

There's a more modern way (C++11 and later) to do enum. Say enum class Suit instead of enum Suit, and for security's sake, the compiler won't let you refer to the values without Suit:: preceding; or go from Suit to int without casting. So

```
for (int s = CLUBS; s <= SPADES; ++s) //for all possible cards, do...
    for (int r = ACE; r <= KING; ++r) ...
```

must be written as

```
for (int s = int (Suit::HEARTS); s <= int (Suit::SPADES); ++s)
    for (int r = int (Rank::ACE); r <= int (Rank::KING); ++r)...
```

This is way more typing, but prevents accidental, weird uses of the values (int daysLeftTillVacation=QUEEN – huh?) and name conflicts (say, if you had two enum types, each having a member named RED). You decide if it's worth it.

Antibugging

C++ doesn't care one whit if your variable of some `enum` type goes beyond the values you listed:

```
r = Rank (-5000);
```

The solution is to, well, not do that.

EXERCISES

1. Declare an enumeration type for chess pieces: king, queen, bishop, knight, rook, and pawn.
2. Declare an enumeration type for the planets in the Solar System. Earth is the third planet, so adjust your numbering so that `EARTH` is 3, and all other planets are also correctly numbered.
3. Write a function `printRank` which, given a `Rank`, prints it appropriately – as `A, 2, 3, 4, 5, 6, 7 8, 9, 10, J, Q, or K`. This and the next exercise will be useful in Chapter 19's card game examples.
4. Write a function `readRank` which returns the `Rank` it reads in using the same format as in Exercise 3. Yes, it's an issue that some input is numbers and some is letters – so what type variable will you need to handle both?
5. Write a function to play music of these styles: SPOOKY, CARNIVAL, and ALIEN (or whatever styles you like). Pass in an `enum` parameter to tell it which style.

   Write another that picks which style to use, based on what box the user clicks.

   ...and another which draws boxes for the user to click.

   Put 'em together to make a music player.

Multidimensional arrays

Not all arrays are simple lists. You can have an array in two or more dimensions.

Here's an array for a Tic-Tac-Toe (noughts and crosses) board: a 3x3 grid. Each square can contain an X, an O, or nothing.

```
enum {MAX_CLMS = 3, MAX_ROWS = 3};
enum class Square { EMPTY, X, O };
Square board[MAX_ROWS][MAX_CLMS];
```

To set the square in row 1, column 2, to X, we say

```
board[1][2] = Square::X;
```

and to check the `row`th, `clm`th square, we say something like

```
if (board[row][clm] == Square::X) ...
```

Figure 10-2 shows how C++ arranges the array in memory. First, we have the 0th row, with all its columns, from 0 to the last column; then the 1st row; then the 2nd.

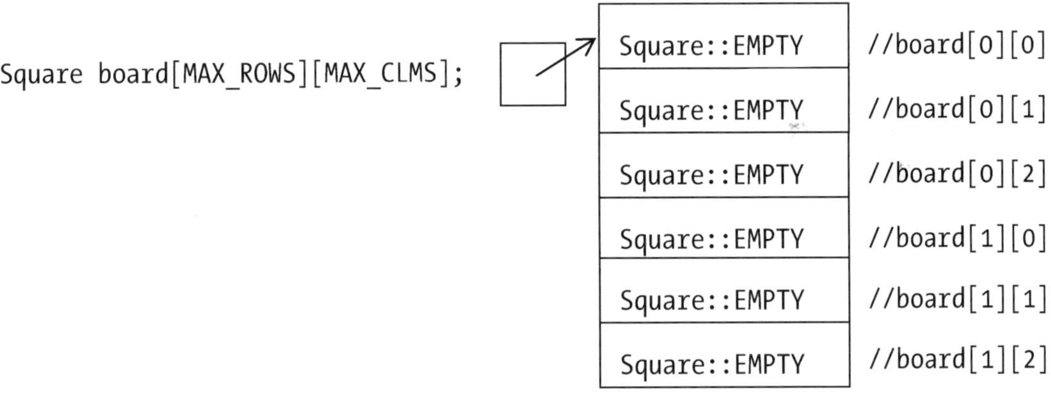

Figure 10-2. *How 2D arrays are arranged in memory. (I omit the actual addresses this time to emphasize that we don't have to know them.)*

Each row has `MAX_CLMS` squares, so to get to `board[1][2]`, C++ calculates that it's 1∗`MAX_CLMS`+2 = 5 squares down. Counting 5 down from the initial element in Figure 10-2 takes us to `board[1][2]`, which is what we wanted.

Displaying the board

What are the two basic steps of drawing a board?

```
draw the board itself (the grid)
draw the X's and O's on the board
```

Drawing the grid is just making some lines, and is simple enough I won't spend time on it here. We can break down drawing the X's and O's piecemeal as we're used to doing.

```
for every row
      draw the row
```

How do we draw the row? Let's refine that.

```
for every row
      for every clm
            draw the square
```

And how do draw the squares? Last refinement:

```
for every row
      for every clm
            if board[row][clm] contains X draw an X
            else if it has an O draw an O
```

Example 10-5 is the resulting program. Output is in Figure 10-3.

Example 10-5. Initializing and displaying a Tic-Tac-Toe (noughts and crosses) board

```
//Program to do a few things with a Tic-Tac-Toe board
//              -- from _C++ for Lazy Programmers_

#include "SSDL.h"

//Dimensions of board and text notes
enum { MAX_ROWS     =   3, MAX_CLMS     =   3 };
enum { ROW_WIDTH    = 100, CLM_WIDTH    = 100 };
enum { BOARD_HEIGHT = 300, BOARD_WIDTH = 300 };
                  //enough room for 3x3 grid, given these widths
enum { TEXT_LINE_HEIGHT = 20 };
```

```
//A Square is a place in the TicTacToe board
//No enum class: I got tired of typing "Square::"
enum Square { EMPTY, X, O };

//Displaying the board
void display(const Square board[MAX_ROWS][MAX_CLMS]);

int main(int argc, char** argv)
{
    //Shrink the display to fit our board
    // allowing room for 2 lines of text at the bottom;
    // set title
    SSDL_SetWindowSize     (BOARD_WIDTH,
                            BOARD_HEIGHT + TEXT_LINE_HEIGHT * 2);
    SSDL_SetWindowTitle("Hit any key to end.");

    //Colors
    SSDL_RenderClear       (SSDL_CreateColor(30, 30, 30)); //charcoal
    SSDL_SetRenderDrawColor(SSDL_CreateColor(245, 245, 220)); //beige

    //The board, initialized to give X 3 in a row
      Square board[MAX_ROWS][MAX_CLMS] =
        { {EMPTY, EMPTY,     X},
          {EMPTY,     X, EMPTY},
          {    X,     O,     O} };

    display (board);            //display it

    //Be sure the user knows what he's seeing is the right result
    SSDL_RenderText("You should see 3 X's diagonally, ",
                    0, MAX_ROWS * ROW_WIDTH);
    SSDL_RenderText("and two O's in the bottom row.",
                    0, MAX_ROWS * ROW_WIDTH + TEXT_LINE_HEIGHT);

    SSDL_WaitKey();

    return 0;
}
```

```
void display(const Square board[MAX_ROWS][MAX_CLMS])
{
    //Make 'em static: loaded once, and local to the only function
    // that needs 'em. What's not to like?
    static const SSDL_Image X_IMAGE = SSDL_LoadImage("media/X.png");
    static const SSDL_Image O_IMAGE = SSDL_LoadImage("media/O.png");

    //draw the X's and O's
    for (int row = 0; row < MAX_ROWS; ++row)
        for (int clm = 0; clm < MAX_CLMS; ++clm)
            switch (board[row][clm])
            {
            case Square::X: SSDL_RenderImage(X_IMAGE, clm*CLM_WIDTH,
            row*ROW_WIDTH);
                break;
            case Square::O: SSDL_RenderImage(O_IMAGE,clm*CLM_WIDTH,
            row*ROW_WIDTH);
            }

    //draw the lines for the board:  first vertical, then horizontal
    //doing this last stops X and O bitmaps from covering the lines
    enum { LINE_THICKNESS = 5 };

    SSDL_RenderFillRect(CLM_WIDTH     - LINE_THICKNESS / 2, 0,
                        LINE_THICKNESS, BOARD_HEIGHT);
    SSDL_RenderFillRect(CLM_WIDTH * 2 - LINE_THICKNESS / 2, 0,
                        LINE_THICKNESS, BOARD_HEIGHT);
    SSDL_RenderFillRect(0, ROW_WIDTH  - LINE_THICKNESS / 2,
                        BOARD_WIDTH, LINE_THICKNESS);
    SSDL_RenderFillRect(0, ROW_WIDTH*2- LINE_THICKNESS / 2,
                        BOARD_WIDTH, LINE_THICKNESS);
}
```

To write the parameter list for `display`, we copy the definition of `ticTacToeBoard` between the `()`'s.

But unlike with 1D arrays, you can't leave out the numbers between the `[]`'s willy-nilly. As we saw in Figure 10-2, `MAX_CLMS` is used by C++ to determine memory locations of the elements. You could leave out the *first* dimension, but that doesn't make it clearer, so I don't.

Figure 10-3. *A Tic-Tac-Toe board*

Note Example 10-5 doesn't just show the appropriate output; it prints what the output should be. Is this overkill?

I don't think so. It's a lot easier to see what the outcome should be on the screen than to search the code for it. In Chapter 18 we'll see even lazier ways of testing.

Arrays of more than two dimensions

In the previous example, our array was 2D. Can we have 3D arrays? 4D? You can have as many dimensions as you're likely to want.

To initialize a 3D array with an initializer list, use another set of nested {}'s.

But the only uses I've found for 3D arrays are the 1971 text-based "Star Trek" game (going between "quadrants" fighting Klingon ships) and 3D Tic-Tac-Toe. I've never found a use for 4D arrays. If you find one, don't tell me. There are things I don't want to know.

Antibugging

- **Things in your 2D array are going into the wrong places.** That could result from using `row` when you mean `clm` or `clm` when you mean `row`.

  The best prevention is to be consistent in what you call rows and columns: don't use `row`, `clm` sometimes, `x`, `y` sometimes, and `i`, `j` sometimes. Always use `row`, `clm`. You can also use `row1`, `clm1`, or `rowStart`, `clmStart`, but always something with `row` or `clm` in the name.

EXERCISES

In these and subsequent exercises, remember to use the debugger if something goes wrong:

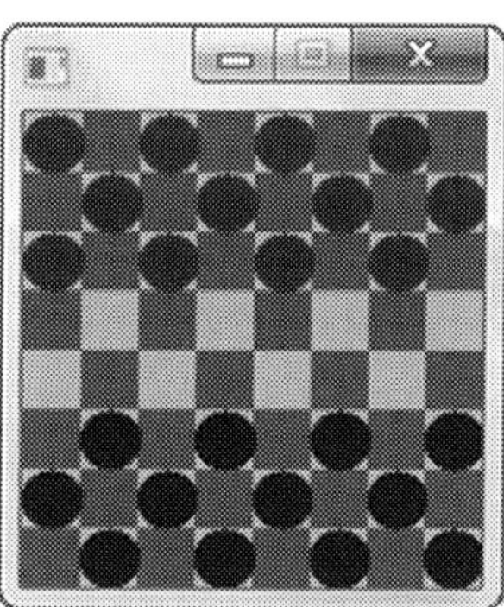

1. Make a checkerboard: eight rows, eight columns, alternating light and dark squares.
2. Put the pieces on the checkerboard for the initial game configuration: alternating squares, as shown.
3. For the checkerboard, make a function which counts the checkers of a given color and returns the count.

4. . . .and now a function which determines which side has more pieces. If neither has more, it can return `EMPTY`.

5. Write a function which takes a checkerboard, the location of a piece, and a direction `LEFT` or `RIGHT` (use `enum`), and returns whether that piece can move in that direction. A piece can move one square diagonally forward to an empty square or two squares diagonally forward, jumping an opponent's piece, to an empty square.

6. (Harder) In the game Memory, you have (say) eight pairs of cards, each pair showing an identical image. They're dealt face down in a 4x4 grid; the player picks two and turns them face up, and if they're identical, those two cards are taken away. You win by finding all matching pairs in relatively few turns.

   Make a program to play the game. (Definitely write the algorithm first.) Let the user click a pair of cards; show the cards by replacing the "card back" image with the "card front" images; wait for the user to see the card fronts (use `SSDL_Delay`); and then, if there's a match, replace the images with nothing and increment the player's score; else replace them again with the "card back" image. Play different sounds depending on whether there was a match. Repeat till all cards are matched or the player has exceeded some maximum number of turns.

   You will need code for recognizing mouse clicks in a box area.

7. (Harder) Write a complete Tic-Tac-Toe game. For the computer moves, you could just pick a random location for the next move. Or you could go for something tougher, and make the computer figure out what a good move would be.

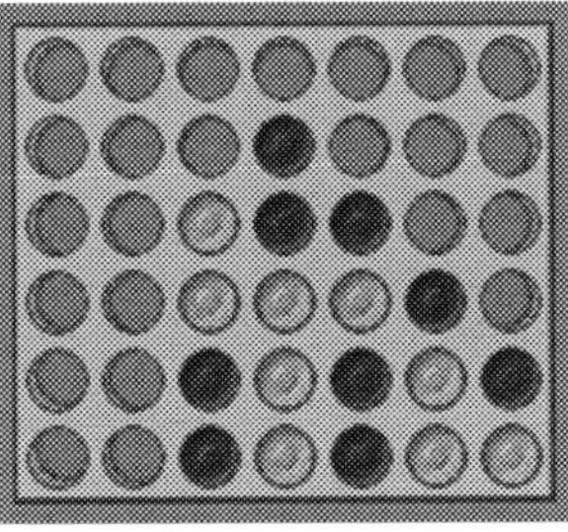

8. (Hard) Play Connect Four. In this game, you have an initially empty grid, and players alternate putting tokens into the top row. A token automatically falls far as it can: it can't go past the bottom row and can't go into a square that's occupied. The winner is the one who gets four in a row in any direction.

CHAPTER 11

Animation with structs and Sprites

Time to make some movies. We'll need a few more features.

structs

A **struct** is a way of bundling information.

```
struct <name>
{
      <variable declaration>*
};
```

For example, here's a type we've needed for a while: a geometric point. It has two parts, x and y.

```
struct Point2D
{
      int x_, y_;
};
```

(The trailing _'s are a convention meaning "member of something else." We'll see why that's worth bothering with in Chapter 16.)

This version's even better: we'll build default values right into the `struct`. 0 is a good default.

```
struct Point2D
{
      int x_=0, y_=0;
};
```


W. Briggs, *C++ for Lazy Programmers*, https://doi.org/10.1007/978-1-4842-5187-4_11

Now we can declare points using our new type:

```
Point2D myCircleLoc; //location for a circle that moves. Its x_
                     // and y_ members are both 0 since we made
                     // that their default
```

You can initialize a struct the same way you would an array: with an initializer list.

```
Point2D myCircleLoc = {0, 5}; //start at position x_=0,y_=5.
                              //omit the = if you want
Point2D otherLoc    = {3};    //overriding x_ to be 3; y_ becomes 0
```

To get at the parts of a Point2D, use ". ":

```
myCircleLoc.x_ += AMOUNT_TO_MOVE_X;
myCircleLoc.y_ += AMOUNT_TO_MOVE_Y;
SSDL_RenderDrawCircle (myCircleLocation.x_, myCircleLocation.y_,
                       RADIUS);
```

That should do it.

Why have structs?

- **Clarity**. It's easier to think of a point as, well, a point than as an X and a Y.
- **Shorter parameter lists**. Your function to detect whether a mouse click is within a box need no longer have 6 parameters, as in

  ```
  bool containsClick (int x, int y,
                      int xLeft, int xRight,
                      int yTop,  int yBottom);
  ```

  but 3, as in

  ```
  bool containsClick (Point2D p,
                      Point2D upperLeft, Point2D lowerRight);
  ```

- **Arrays of structs**. Suppose you want multiple objects in your universe (seems likely!). Each has an X, Y location. How can you make an array of these? Bundle X and Y into a Point2D, and have an array of that:

```
Point2D myObjects[MAX_OBJECTS];
```

To initialize them, you can use the {} initializer lists:

```
Point2D myObjects[MAX_OBJECTS] = {};
                        //go with defaults: every point is {0, 0}
```

or

```
Point2D myObjects[MAX_OBJECTS] = {{1, 5}, {2, 3}}
                        //each point specified
```

Example 11-1 uses this new type. Output is in Figure 11-1.

Example 11-1. Staircase program, illustrating `struct Point2D`

```
/Program to draw a staircase
//              -- from _C++ for Lazy Programmers_

#include "SSDL.h"

struct Point2D  //A struct to hold a 2-D point
{
    int x_, y_;
};

int main (int argc, char** argv)
{
    //Setup
    enum {WINDOW_WIDTH=400, WINDOW_HEIGHT=200};
    SSDL_SetWindowSize  (WINDOW_WIDTH, WINDOW_HEIGHT);
    SSDL_SetWindowTitle ("Stairway example:  Hit a key to end");

    enum {MAX_POINTS        = 25};
    enum {STAIR_STEP_LENGTH = 15};

    Point2D myPoints [MAX_POINTS];

    int x = 0;                          //Start at lower left corner
    int y = WINDOW_HEIGHT-1;            // of screen
    for (int i = 0; i < MAX_POINTS; ++i) //Fill an array with points
    {
```

```
        myPoints[i].x_ = x;
        myPoints[i].y_ = y;

        //On iteration 0, go up (change Y)
        //On iteration 1, go right
        // then up, then right, then up...

        if (i%2 == 0)                   //If i is even...
            y -= STAIR_STEP_LENGTH;
        else
            x += STAIR_STEP_LENGTH;
    }

    for (int i = 0; i < MAX_POINTS-1; ++i) //Display the staircase
        //The last iteration draws a line from point
        // i to point i+1... which is why we stop a
        // little short.  We don't want to refer to
        // the (nonexistent) point # MAX_POINTS.
        SSDL_RenderDrawLine (   myPoints[i  ].x_, myPoints[i  ].y_,
                                myPoints[i+1].x_, myPoints[i+1].y_);

    SSDL_WaitKey();

    return 0;
}
```

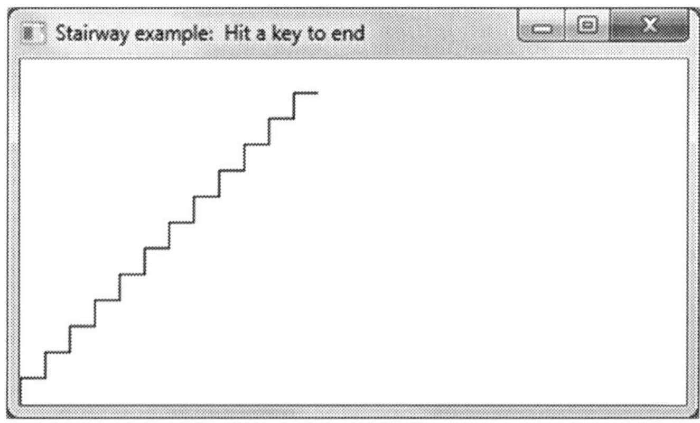

Figure 11-1. *Staircase program*

Cool struct tricks

The initializer list is more versatile with `struct`s than with arrays.

```
myPoint = {5,5};        //can use the {} initializer with =,
                        // any time, unlike with arrays

doSomethingWithPoint ({10,10}); //or pass it in as a parameter

struct Box
{
    Point2D upperLeft_, Point2D lowerRight_;
};

bool containsClick (Point2D where, Box boundingBox);

...
containsClick(mousePoint, {{5,5},{10,10}});
                 //Box expected as 2nd argument? Here's one!
                 //A Box is 2 Point2D's, so this works.
```

EXERCISES

1. Write and test the `containsClick` function given previously (the one taking a `Point2D` and a `Box`).

2. Make an array of `Point2D`'s, and set the value of each with this function:

```
Point2D pickRandomPoint (int range)
{
   Point2D where;

   where.x_ =
     rand()%range + rand()%range + rand()%range;
   where.y_ =
     rand()%range + rand()%range + rand()%range;

   return where;
}
```

   Graph them, and notice: are they evenly distributed? This shows something about what happens when you sum random numbers.

Making a movie with `struct` and `while`

Think how movies are made. You see one still frame after another, but they come so quickly they look like one continuous, moving image.

We'll do the same thing. A real movie has a specific speed – frames per second – so the rate of movement is always the same. We'll tell C++ to keep a constant frame rate too.

Here's a rough version:

```
SSDL_SetFramesPerSecond (70); //Can change this,
                              //  or leave at the default of 60

while (SSDL_IsNextFrame ())
{
      SSDL_DefaultEventHandler ();

      SSDL_RenderClear ();       //first, erase previous frame

      //display things (draw shapes and images, print text, etc.)

      //update variables if needed

      //get input, if relevant...
}
```

`SSDL_IsNextFrame` waits for enough time to pass to get to the next frame in our movie. It also refreshes the screen. It will do 60 frames per second unless we change that with `SSDL_SetFramesPerSecond`. If the user tried to quit by killing the window or hitting Escape, `SSDL_IsNextFrame` returns `false` and the loop ends.

But something's going to have to check for those quit messages. Before, we used `SSDL_WaitKey`, `SSDL_WaitMouse`, and `SSDL_Delay`, each of which checked for certain events: keystrokes or mouse clicks for the first two and quit messages in all cases. Since we aren't using them now, something else must check for quit messages.

That something is `SSDL_DefaultEventHandler`. Here it is:

```
void SSDL_DefaultEventHandler ()
{
    SDL_Event event;

    while (SSDL_PollEvent (event))
        switch (event.type)
```

```
        {
        case SDL_QUIT:    //clicked the X on the window? Let's quit
            SSDL_DeclareQuit(); break;
        case SDL_KEYDOWN: //User hit Escape? Let's quit
            if (SSDL_IsKeyPressed (SDLK_ESCAPE)) SSDL_DeclareQuit();
        }
}
```

An SDL_Event is a struct that stores information on any kind of event SDL recognizes. SSDL_PollEvent gets the next available event, if any, failing if there is none; but if one is found, it stores the information in event, and the switch statement decides how to process it.

Let's use it in a program (Example 11-2) to make a ball move back and forth across the screen – whoo-hoo! Output is in Figure 11-2.

Example 11-2. A ball moving back and forth across the screen

```
//Program to make a circle move back and forth across the screen
//              -- for _C++ for Lazy Programmers_

#include "SSDL.h"

enum {RADIUS = 20};      //Ball radius & speed
enum {SPEED  =  5};      // ...move 5 pixels for every frame

enum class Direction { LEFT=-1, RIGHT=1 };
//Why -1 for left?  Because left means going in the minus direction.
//See where we update ball.x_ in the main loop for how this can work

struct Point2D
{
    int x_=0, y_=0;
};

struct Ball                 //A ball is an X, Y location,
{                           //and a direction, left or right
    Point2D   location_;
    Direction direction_;
};
```

```
int main (int argc, char** argv)
{
    SSDL_SetWindowTitle ("Back-and-forth ball example.  "
                         "Hit Esc to exit.");

    //initialize ball position; size; rate and direction of movement
    Ball ball;
    ball.location_.x_  = SSDL_GetWindowWidth ()/2;
    ball.location_.y_  = SSDL_GetWindowHeight()/2;
    ball.direction_    = Direction::RIGHT;

    enum { FRAMES_PER_SECOND = 70 };
    SSDL_SetFramesPerSecond(FRAMES_PER_SECOND);

    while (SSDL_IsNextFrame ())
    {
        SSDL_DefaultEventHandler ();

        //*** DISPLAY THINGS ***
        SSDL_RenderClear ();    //first, erase previous frame

        //then draw the ball
        SSDL_RenderDrawCircle (ball.location_.x_, ball.location_.y_,
                               RADIUS);

        //update variables
        //update ball's x position based on speed
        // and current direction
        ball.location_.x_ += int(ball.direction_)*SPEED;

        //if ball moves off screen, reverse its direction
        if      (ball.location_.x_ >= SSDL_GetWindowWidth())
            ball.direction_ = Direction::LEFT;
        else if (ball.location_.x_ <                      0)
            ball.direction_ = Direction::RIGHT;
    }

    return 0;
}
```

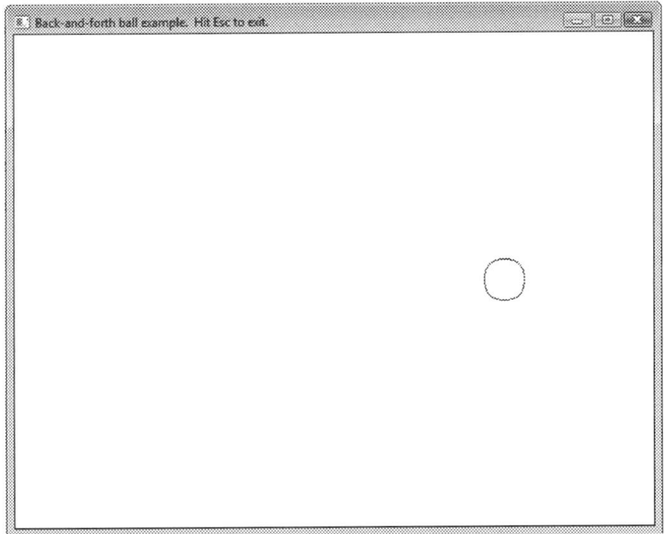

Figure 11-2. *A ball moving back and forth across the screen*

What if we want more than one object moving? We can have an array of `Balls` and use for loops to initialize them, display them, and so on.

`main`'s getting a little long, so in keeping with the "no more than one screenful of code per function" principle I'll put several tasks in their own functions. Example 11-3's output is in Figure 11-3.

Example 11-3. An example with multiple moving balls

```
//Program to make circles move back and forth across the screen
//              -- for _C++ for Lazy Programmers_

#include "SSDL.h"

enum {RADIUS = 20};      //Ball radius & speed
enum {SPEED  =  5};      // ...move 5 pixels for every frame

enum class Direction { LEFT=-1, RIGHT=1 };
//Why -1 for left?  Because left means going in the minus direction.
//See where we update ball.x_ in the main loop for how this can work

struct Point2D
{
    int x_=0, y_=0;
};
```

```
struct Ball              //A ball is an X, Y location,
{                        //and a direction, left or right
    Point2D   location_;
    Direction direction_;
};

//Ball functions
void initializeBalls (      Ball balls[], int howMany);
void drawBalls       (const Ball balls[], int howMany);
void moveBalls       (      Ball balls[], int howMany);
void bounceBalls     (      Ball balls[], int howMany);

int main (int argc, char** argv)
{
    SSDL_SetWindowTitle ("Back-and-forth balls example.  "
                         "Hit Esc to exit.");

    //initialize balls' position, size,
    //  and rate and direction of movement
    enum {MAX_BALLS = 3};
    Ball balls [MAX_BALLS];
    initializeBalls (balls, MAX_BALLS);

    enum {FRAMES_PER_SECOND = 70};
    SSDL_SetFramesPerSecond(FRAMES_PER_SECOND);

    while (SSDL_IsNextFrame ())
    {
        SSDL_DefaultEventHandler ();

        //*** DISPLAY THINGS ***
        SSDL_RenderClear ();    //first, erase previous frame
        drawBalls (balls, MAX_BALLS);

        //*** UPDATE  THINGS ***
        moveBalls (balls, MAX_BALLS);
        bounceBalls(balls, MAX_BALLS); //if ball moves offscreen,
                                       // reverse its direction
    }
```

```
    return 0;
}

//Ball functions

void initializeBalls (Ball balls[], int howMany)
{
    for (int i = 0; i < howMany; ++i)
    {
        balls[i].location_.x_ = i * SSDL_GetWindowWidth ()/3;
        balls[i].location_.y_ = i * SSDL_GetWindowHeight()/3
                                  + SSDL_GetWindowHeight()/6;
        balls[i].direction_   = Direction::RIGHT;
    }
}

void drawBalls  (const Ball balls[], int howMany)
{
    for (int i = 0; i < howMany; ++i)
        SSDL_RenderDrawCircle (balls[i].location_.x_,
                               balls[i].location_.y_, RADIUS);
}

void moveBalls  (Ball balls[], int howMany)
//update balls' x position based on speed
// and current direction
{
    for (int i = 0; i < howMany; ++i)
        balls[i].location_.x_ += int (balls[i].direction_)*SPEED;
}

void bounceBalls(Ball balls[], int howMany)
{
    //if any ball moves off screen, reverse its direction
    for (int i = 0; i < howMany; ++i)
        if      (balls[i].location_.x_ >= SSDL_GetWindowWidth())
            balls[i].direction_ = Direction::LEFT;
```

```
        else if (balls[i].location_.x_ <  0)
            balls[i].direction_ = Direction::RIGHT;
}
```

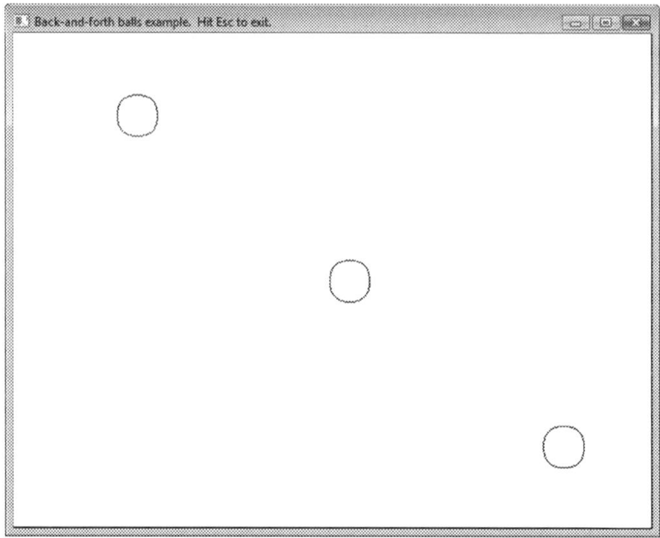

Figure 11-3. An example with multiple moving balls

EXERCISES

1. Make the balls capable of moving in other directions. A ball is no longer just an X, Y location and a direction; it's an X, Y location and an X, Y velocity. Each time you go through the main loop, you'll update the location based on the velocity:

   ```
   for (int i = 0; i < MAX_BALLS; ++i)
   {
      balls[i].location_.x_ +=
                     balls[i].velocity_.x_;
      balls[i].location_.y_ +=
                     balls[i].velocity_.y_;
   }
   ```

   The velocity's X component is always reversed when it hits a left or right wall – same for the velocity's Y if it hits the floor or ceiling. It's OK to use `Point2D` for `velocity_`, or you can create a new `struct` for it.

   Add sound effects whenever a ball hits a wall.

2. Now let's add gravity. Velocity doesn't just change each time you hit a wall; it changes in each iteration of the loop, like so:

   ```
   for (int i = 0; i < MAX_BALLS; ++i)
       balls[i].velocity_.y_-= GRAVITY;
                   //adjust velocity for gravity
   ```

   Now the balls should move more realistically.

3. Now add friction. Whenever a ball hits a wall, its velocity is not exactly reversed; instead, it's reversed, but it's a little smaller than it was. This will make the balls slower after each collision.

Sprites

Enough circles – let's move images.

We already have images, but they just sit there. Sprites are mobile images: they can move, rotate, flip, and other things. Here are the basics.

You create a sprite much as you do an image:

```
SSDL_Sprite mySprite = SSDL_LoadImage ("filename.png");
```

You can now set its location with `SSDL_SetSpriteLocation` and its size with `SSDL_SetSpriteSize`.

Here I use sprites to put a fish in the middle of the screen – maybe I'm going to make a video aquarium – and print some information about it using other sprite functions. The sprite-related code is highlighted. Output is in Figure 11-4.

Example 11-4. Program to draw a fish, using a sprite

```
//Program to place a fish sprite on the screen
//              -- from _C++ for Lazy Programmers_

#include "SSDL.h"

int main (int argc, char** argv)
{
    //Set up window characteristics
    enum { WINDOW_WIDTH = 600, WINDOW_HEIGHT = 300 };
```

```
SSDL_SetWindowSize(WINDOW_WIDTH, WINDOW_HEIGHT);
SSDL_SetWindowTitle ("Sprite example 1.  Hit Esc to exit.");

//initialize colors
const SSDL_Color AQUAMARINE(100, 255, 150); //the water

//initialize the sprite's image and location
SSDL_Sprite fishSprite = SSDL_LoadImage("media/zitronen.png");
SSDL_SetSpriteLocation (fishSprite, WINDOW_WIDTH/2, WINDOW_HEIGHT/2);

//*** Main loop ***
while (SSDL_IsNextFrame ())
{
    //Look for quit messages
    SSDL_DefaultEventHandler ();

    //Clear the screen for a new frame in our "movie"
    SSDL_RenderClear (AQUAMARINE);

    //Draw crosshairs in the center
    SSDL_SetRenderDrawColor (BLACK);
    SSDL_RenderDrawLine (0,               WINDOW_HEIGHT/2,
                         WINDOW_WIDTH,    WINDOW_HEIGHT/2);
    SSDL_RenderDrawLine (WINDOW_WIDTH/2, 0,
                         WINDOW_WIDTH/2, WINDOW_HEIGHT);
    //and print the statistics on the fish
    SSDL_SetCursor (0, 0);  //reset cursor each time or
    // the messages will run off the screen!
    sout << "Sprite info\n";
    sout << "X:\t"
         << SSDL_GetSpriteX      (fishSprite) << '\n';
    sout << "Y:\t"
         << SSDL_GetSpriteY      (fishSprite) << '\n';
    sout << "Width:\t"
         << SSDL_GetSpriteWidth  (fishSprite) << '\n';
    sout << "Height:\t"
         << SSDL_GetSpriteHeight(fishSprite) << '\n'\b;
```

```
        //Show that fish
        SSDL_RenderSprite (fishSprite);
    }

    return 0;
}
```

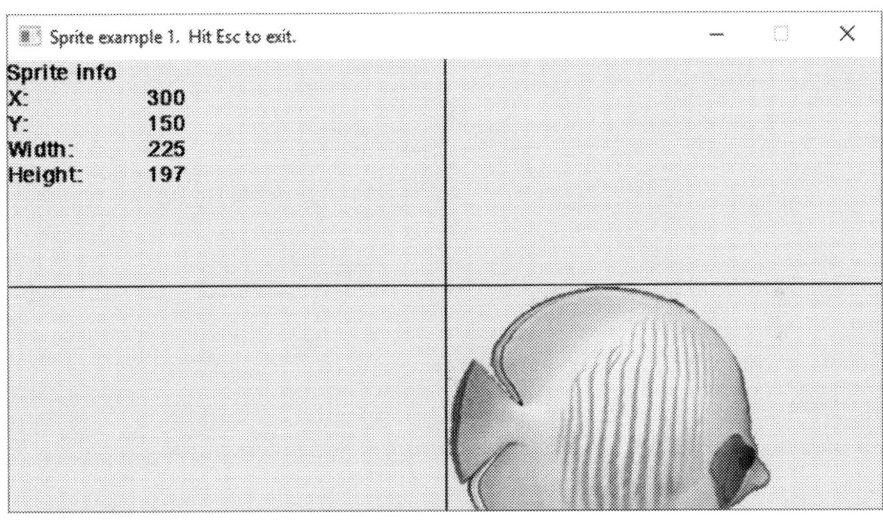

Figure 11-4. *A sprite and some of its current specs*

The fish is too big for the screen. According to the program, its width is 225 and its height is 197. We can use SSDL_SetSpriteSize to resize,[1] giving us a result like Figure 11-5:

```
enum {FISH_WIDTH = 170, FISH_HEIGHT = 150};
SSDL_SetSpriteSize     (fishSprite, FISH_WIDTH, FISH_HEIGHT);
```

[1]It's more efficient to set this in your graphics editor, but I want to show how to resize in SSDL if need be.

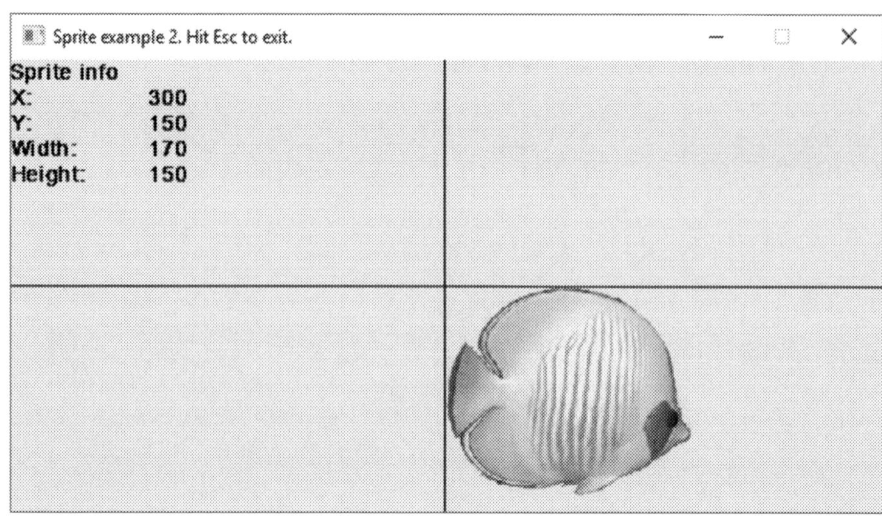

Figure 11-5. *A sprite, resized*

Now I want it centered. The x, y location I gave it *is* in the center...but that's the upper left corner of the image.

Here is the call to offset the sprite so it's centered on the point we gave as its location.

```
SSDL_SetSpriteOffset (FISH_SPRITE, FISH_WIDTH/2, FISH_HEIGHT/2);
```

If it still looks off-center, I can play with the numbers to get a different offset.

I won't repeat the entire program, but Example 11-5 shows the lines that changed to resize and center the sprite. The result is in Figure 11-6.

Example 11-5. Code to resize and center a sprite

```
int main (int argc, char** argv)
{
    ...

    //Init size and offset. Image is offset so fish looks centered.
    enum {FISH_WIDTH = 170, FISH_HEIGHT = 150};
    SSDL_SetSpriteSize     (fishSprite, FISH_WIDTH, FISH_HEIGHT);
```

```
    //This offset looks right on the screen, so I'll use it:
    SSDL_SetSpriteOffset   (fishSprite,
                            FISH_WIDTH/2, int(FISH_HEIGHT*0.45));
    ...

    return 0;
}
```

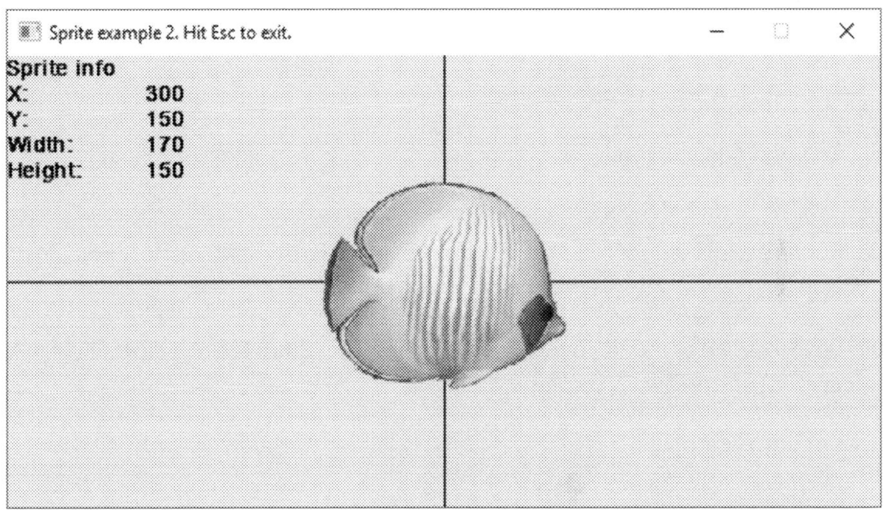

Figure 11-6. *A sprite, resized and centered*

You can do other things with sprites: rotate, flip horizontally or vertically, or use only part of your original image. (Table 11-1 has more.) You can also do anything to them you can do with an image – for example, `SSDL_RenderImage (mySprite)`. This will ignore the sprite's other characteristics (position, size, etc.) and only use the image aspects.

And now that you have this, you can (almost) make your own arcade games.

Table 11-1. *Common sprite commands. For a complete list, see Appendix H*

`SSDL_Sprite mySprite = SSDL_LoadImage ("image.png");`	this is how to create one
`void SSDL_SetSpriteLocation (SSDL_Sprite& s, int x, int y);`	set sprite's location on screen
`void SSDL_SetSpriteSize (SSDL_Sprite& s, int w, int h);`	...and its size
`void SSDL_SetSpriteOffset (SSDL_Sprite& s, int x, int y);`	...its offset
`void SSDL_SetSpriteRotation (SSDL_Sprite& s, double angle);`	...its angle of rotation
`void SSDL_RenderSprite (SSDL_Sprite s);`	draw sprite at its current location
`int SSDL_GetSpriteX (SSDL_Sprite s);`	return sprite's x position on screen
`int SSDL_GetSpriteY (SSDL_Sprite s);`	...and its y

Antibugging

- **The sprite doesn't show up.** Here are likely reasons:
  - The image didn't load: you're looking in the wrong folder, made a typo in the file name, or are using a bad or incompatible image.
  - It showed up, but it's off screen. What numbers do you get from `SSDL_GetSpriteX` and `SSDL_GetSpriteY`? Be sure they're in range.

EXERCISES

1. Make a video aquarium: a background, and fish that move back and forth (facing whatever direction they go, so you'll need `SSDL_SpriteFlipHorizontal`).
2. Do Exercise 2 or 3 from the previous section (bouncing balls), but instead of drawing circles, use an image of a basketball. Let the basketballs spin as they go.

CHAPTER 12

Making an Arcade Game: Input, Collisions, and Putting It All Together

In this chapter we'll make our own 2D arcade games, putting together what we've got so far for a time-wasting experience to make others goof off so we can shine. Or something like that. The new things we need are better mouse and keyboard interaction, and collisions of objects.

Determining input states

Mouse

We already can wait on a mouse click and get its coordinates...but arcade games wait for no man.

Suppose we want our weapon to fire continuously if a mouse button is down. We need a way to detect that the button is depressed, without stopping to wait. This'll do it:

`int SSDL_GetMouseClick ();`	return 0 if no button is depressed; SDL_BUTTON_LMASK (left button depressed), SDL_BUTTON_MMASK (middle), or SDL_BUTTON_RMASK (right)

W. Briggs, *C++ for Lazy Programmers*, https://doi.org/10.1007/978-1-4842-5187-4_12

As in

```
if (SSDL_GetMouseClick () != 0)//mouse was clicked
{
      x = SSDL_GetMouseX(); y = SSDL_GetMouseY();
      //do whatever you wanted to do if mouse was clicked
}
```

Before getting to an example, let's see how to check the state of the keyboard.

Keyboard

`ssin` waits for you to hit Enter. That won't work for arcade games: we want to know whether a key is pressed as soon as it's hit. The function `SSDL_IsKeyPressed` tells if a given key is down – any key, including the ones not associated with letters, like Shift and Control.

`bool SSDL_IsKeyPressed (SDL_Keycode key);`	Returns whether key is currently pressed

Though many key values this function accepts match what you'd expect ('0' for the 0 key, 'a' for the A key – but not 'A' for the A key), it's not always obvious, so it's best to go with their official names. At time of writing a complete list is at wiki.libsdl.org/SDL_Keycode; a few are listed in Table 12-1. Example 12-1 shows how you might use them.

Table 12-1. *Selected key codes for SDL*

SDLK_1	SDLK_F1	SDLK_ESCAPE	SDLK_LEFT	SDLK_LSHIFT
SDLK_2	SDLK_F2	SDLK_BACKSPACE	SDLK_RIGHT	SDLK_RSHIFT
...	...	SDLK_RETURN	SDLK_UP	SDLK_LCTRL
SDLK_a		SDLK_SPACE	SDLK_DOWN	SDLK_RCTRL
SDLK_b				
...				

Example 12-1. A program to detect control keys, shift, caps lock, space bar, and F1

```
//Program to identify some keys, and mouse buttons, being pressed
//      -- from _C++ for Lazy Programmers_

#include "SSDL.h"

int main (int argc, char** argv)
{
    while (SSDL_IsNextFrame ())
    {
        SSDL_DefaultEventHandler ();

        //Display
        SSDL_RenderClear ();    //Clear the screen
        SSDL_SetCursor (0, 0);  //And start printing at the top

        sout << "What key are you pressing? ";
        sout << "Control, Shift, Caps lock, space, F1? \nIt's ";

        if (SSDL_IsKeyPressed (SDLK_LCTRL))    sout << "Left ctrl ";
        if (SSDL_IsKeyPressed (SDLK_RCTRL))    sout << "Right ctrl ";
        if (SSDL_IsKeyPressed (SDLK_LSHIFT))   sout << "Left shift ";
        if (SSDL_IsKeyPressed (SDLK_RSHIFT))   sout << "Right shift ";
        if (SSDL_IsKeyPressed (SDLK_CAPSLOCK))sout << "Caps lock ";
        if (SSDL_IsKeyPressed (SDLK_SPACE))    sout << "Space bar ";
        if (SSDL_IsKeyPressed (SDLK_F1))       sout << "F1 ";
        sout << "\n";

        if (SSDL_GetMouseClick () == SDL_BUTTON_LMASK)
            sout << "Left mouse button down\n";
        if (SSDL_GetMouseClick () == SDL_BUTTON_RMASK)
            sout << "Right mouse button down\n";
    }

    return 0;
}
```

Antibugging

- **You're hitting a function key, but nothing happens.** On some keyboards you have to hold down the Fn key as well.
- **You're hitting multiple keys at once but only some show up;** or **you're hitting a key and it won't register mouse buttons.** Keyboard "ghosting" is losing keypresses because the keyboard can only handle so many at once. It may also lose mouse clicks. At time of writing, if you care, you can test your keyboard and mouse at `https://keyboardtester.co/`.

  You're probably safe using Control, Shift, and Alt with other keys - that's expected.

Events

Sometimes we don't care if a mouse button is up or down at the moment, but just that it has been clicked. Maybe you get one shot from your BFG per mouse click. Or maybe you're using the mouse to click a control or turn sound on or off, as in the program shown by Figure 12-1:

```
while (SSDL_IsNextFrame ())
{
    myEventHandler ();                              //handle events

    if (SSDL_GetMouseClick ()) toggleSound (); //not gonna work

    ...
}
```

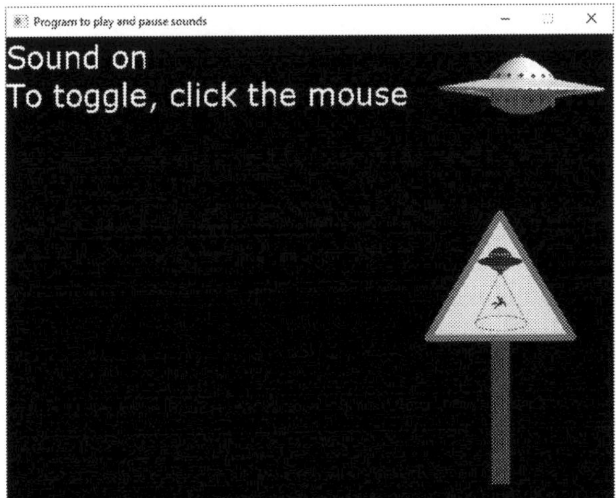

Figure 12-1. *A program that uses mouse clicks to toggle sound*

Thing is, computers are fast. Suppose your mouse click takes a tenth of a second. At 60 frames per second, sound will turn on and off *six times* before you release the button, and it's only good luck if it ends up the way you wanted.

What we need is an **event**: a message that comes from the operating system telling the program, something happened you may care about. In this case, a mouse click.

We already handle quit events and keystroke events in SSDL_DefaultEventHandler:

```
void myEventHandler ()
{
    SDL_Event event;

    while (SSDL_PollEvent (event))
        switch (event.type)
        {
        case SDL_QUIT:    SSDL_DeclareQuit();
            break;
        case SDL_KEYDOWN: if (SSDL_IsKeyPressed (SDLK_ESCAPE))
                              SSDL_DeclareQuit();
            break;
        }
}
```

You can find out about the various supported events on the SDL Wiki site, but at this point we only want SDL_MOUSEBUTTONDOWN. With it we can make our own event handler and use it to determine if the music should be toggled (Example 12-2).

Example 12-2. Making your own event handler

```
void myEventHandler (bool& mouseClicked)
{
    SDL_Event event;
    mouseClicked = false;   //We'll soon know if mouse was clicked

    while (SSDL_PollEvent (event))
        switch (event.type)
        {
        case SDL_QUIT:              SSDL_DeclareQuit();
            break;
        case SDL_KEYDOWN:           if (SSDL_IsKeyPressed (SDLK_ESCAPE))
                                        SSDL_DeclareQuit();

            break;
        case SDL_MOUSEBUTTONDOWN: mouseClicked = true; //It was!
            break;
        }
}

//and the following in main:

    while (SSDL_IsNextFrame ())
    {
        bool mouseWasClicked;
        myEventHandler (mouseWasClicked);

        if (mouseWasClicked) toggleSound ();

        ....
```

This way of thinking – event-driven – is at the core of programming such important operating systems as Windows, iOS, and Android.

Cooldowns and lifetimes

Suppose we want an effect to linger a moment after something happens. Maybe there's a visual effect that should be there for a second (its "lifetime") after a mouse click creates it; then it vanishes. Or maybe the BFG has to wait a while before you can fire again, however madly you click - a "cooldown" period.

We'll have an integer `framesLeftTillItsOver` which, when the mouse is clicked, gets set to the number of frames you want to delay.

This sort of reasoning won't do:

```
while SSDL_IsNextFrame ()
    handle events

    SSDL_RenderClear ()
    draw things
    if framesLeftTillItsOver == 0 && mouseWasClicked
        draw the visual effect
```

When you draw the effect, `SSDL_RenderClear` erases it on the very next iteration!

We must distinguish *changing the state* of the visual effect (from on to off) from *drawing* it; they're separate actions. This will work:

```
while SSDL_IsNextFrame ()
    handle events

    SSDL_RenderClear ()
    draw things including, if it's on, the visual effect
      (consider it to be on if framesLeftTillItsOver > 0)

    if effect is on (that is, framesLeftTillItsOver > 0)
        -- framesLeftTillItsOver; //1 frame closer to disappearance
    else if mouseWasClicked
        framesLeftTillItsOver = HOWEVER MANY FRAMES WE WANT IT TO LAST
```

Tip As a good rule of thumb, inside that main animation loop have three separate sections: handling events, drawing things, and updating variables. The order doesn't matter, as they'll all get done eventually; what does matter is that you don't do drawing in the update section or check events in the draw section and so on.

In Example 12-3, when you click the mouse, the program puts a splatter image wherever you click. One second later it drops the image and lets you click again.

Example 12-3. Using a visual effect with specified duration: splatter on the screen

```
//Program that makes a splat wherever you click
//      -- from _C++ for Lazy Programmers_

#include "SSDL.h"

void myEventHandler (bool& mouseClicked);

int main (int argc, char** argv)
{
    SSDL_SetWindowTitle ("Click the mouse to see and hear a splat; "
                         "hit Esc to end.");

    const SSDL_Sound SPLAT_SOUND =
        SSDL_LoadWAV ("media/445117__breviceps__cartoon-splat.wav");

    //Set up sprite with image and a size, and offset its reference
    // point so it'll be centered on our mouse clicks
    SSDL_Sprite splatSprite = SSDL_LoadImage("media/splat.png");

    enum { SPLAT_WIDTH=50, SPLAT_HEIGHT=50 };
    SSDL_SetSpriteSize  (splatSprite, SPLAT_WIDTH,   SPLAT_HEIGHT);
    SSDL_SetSpriteOffset(splatSprite, SPLAT_WIDTH/2, SPLAT_HEIGHT/2);

    while (SSDL_IsNextFrame ())
    {
        static int framesLeftTillSplatDisappears = 0;
        enum { SPLAT_LIFETIME = 60 };        //It lasts one second

        //Handle events
        bool isMouseClick;
        myEventHandler (isMouseClick);

         //Display things
        SSDL_RenderClear();
```

```
        if (framesLeftTillSplatDisappears > 0)
            SSDL_RenderSprite(splatSprite);

        //Update things: process clicks and framesLeft
        if (framesLeftTillSplatDisappears > 0) //if splat is active
            --framesLeftTillSplatDisappears;   // keep counting down

        else if (isMouseClick)      //if not, and we have a click...
        {
                                    //Reset that waiting time
            framesLeftTillSplatDisappears = SPLAT_LIFETIME;

                                    //Play splat sound
            SSDL_PlaySound (SPLAT_SOUND);

            SSDL_SetSpriteLocation  //move splat sprite to
                (splatSprite,       // location of mouse click
                 SSDL_GetMouseX(), SSDL_GetMouseY());
        }
    }

    return 0;
}

void myEventHandler (bool& mouseClicked)
{
      //exactly the same as in Example 12-2
}
```

EXERCISES

1. Adapt the program in Example 12-3 to allow multiple splatters to exist at once: you can fire every second, but each splatter lasts 5 seconds.

2. A *particle fountain* is a set of particles continually generated, going in various directions. This is how flames can be generated in computer games, and rainstorms. You can also make a bubble fountain or a sparkler.

Let each particle start at the same location; draw the particle with `SSDL_RenderDrawPoint`; give it an initial random velocity; and if you want it to look more flame-like, use gravity, but in reverse: flame particles tend to fly upward rather than downward over time. Finally, when a particle has existed for some number of frames, reset it to its starting point and let it go again.

Collisions

There's one more thing we need before making our own games: collisions.

Collisions are easy with SSDL sprites.

`int SSDL_SpriteHasIntersection (const SSDL_Sprite& a, const SSDL_Sprite& b);`	return whether sprites a and b overlap

As in

```
if (SSDL_SpriteHasIntersection (robotSprite, playerSprite)
    playerDead = true;
```

Collisions *are* easy with sprites, but not always accurate. Since your sprite probably has a big chunk of itself transparent, you may find that SDL thinks two sprites are colliding even if the visible parts aren't touching. No reasonable person would consider the candy and the Hallowe'en basket in Figure 12-2 (a) to be in collision – but SSDL would.

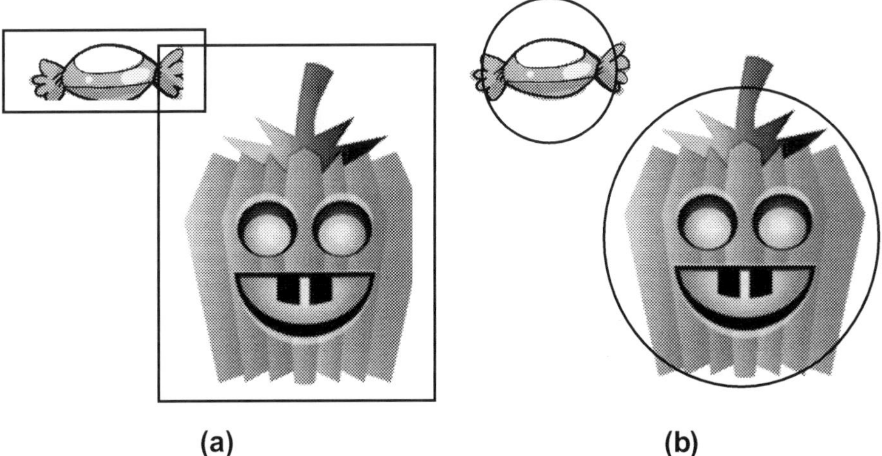

Figure 12-2. *Collisions between sprites, as evaluated by `SSDL_SpriteHasIntersection` (a) and by the circle-based method of Example 12-4 (b)*

There's a cheap, easy fix in Example 12-4. We find the distance between two points (which will probably be the centers of the sprites) and consider a collision to have happened if that distance is less than the sum of the radii `aSize` and `bSize` we give to our objects – that is, if bounding circles intersect.

Use whichever method fits your sprites best.

Example 12-4. A simple collision function, based on circles

```
bool inCollision (Point2D A, Point2D B, int aSize, int bSize)
{
      float aToBDistance = distance (A.x_, A.y_, B.x_, B.y_);
      return (aToBDistance < aSize + bSize);
}
```

The big game

The rest of this chapter is about creating the arcade games: first mine, then yours.

I have in Examples 12-5 through 12-9 a game for catching Hallowe'en candy in the basket. If you catch enough, you win; miss too many and you die. It has sounds, a background, silly graphics, keyboard interaction (uses arrow keys), and to show use of the mouse, I allow the user to toggle a heads-up display showing stats on misses and catches.

To illustrate specifying the lifetime of an effect, a floating "Yum!" message appears for a moment when you catch candy. Output is in Figure 12-3.

Example 12-5. Falling candy program, part 1 of 5

```
//Program to catch falling Hallowe'en candy
//      -- from _C++ for Lazy Programmers_

#include <cmath> //for sqrt
#include "SSDL.h"

//dimensions of screen and screen locations
enum {SCREEN_WIDTH=675, SCREEN_HEIGHT=522}; //dimensions of bkgd

enum {CANDY_START_HEIGHT = 15};  //where candy falls from

enum {MARGIN             = 25};  //As close to the left/right edges
                                 // of the screen as moving objects
                                 // are allowed to get

enum {BOTTOM_LINE        = 480}; //Where last line of text is printed
                                 //on instruction & splash screens

//dimensions of important objects
enum { CANDY_WIDTH  = 60, CANDY_HEIGHT  = 20 };
enum { BASKET_WIDTH = 70, BASKET_HEIGHT = 90 };

//how many candies you can catch or miss before winning/losing
enum {MAX_CAUGHT         = 10,  MAX_MISSED= 10};
                                 //If you change this, change
                                 // printInstructions too
                                 // because it specifies this

//fonts for splash screens and catch/miss statistics
enum {SMALL_FONT_SIZE  = 12,
      MEDIUM_FONT_SIZE = 24,
      LARGE_FONT_SIZE  = 36};

const SSDL_Font SMALL_FONT
    = SSDL_OpenFont ("media/Sinister-Fonts_Werewolf-Moon/Werewolf Moon.ttf",
                     SMALL_FONT_SIZE);
```

```
const SSDL_Font MEDIUM_FONT
    = SSDL_OpenFont ("media/Sinister-Fonts_Werewolf-Moon/Werewolf Moon.ttf",
                MEDIUM_FONT_SIZE);
const SSDL_Font LARGE_FONT
    = SSDL_OpenFont ("media/Sinister-Fonts_Werewolf-Moon/Werewolf Moon.ttf",
                LARGE_FONT_SIZE);

//how far our victory/defeat messages are from left side of screen
enum { FINAL_SCREEN_MESSAGE_OFFSET_X = 40 };

//background
const SSDL_Image BKGD_IMAGE
    = SSDL_LoadImage("media/haunted-house.jpg");

//sounds and music
const SSDL_Music BKGD_MUSIC
    = SSDL_LoadMUS("media/159509__mistersherlock__halloween-graveyd-short.mp3");
const SSDL_Sound THUNK_SOUND
    = SSDL_LoadWAV("media/457741__osiruswaltz__wall-bump-1.wav");
const SSDL_Sound DROP_SOUND
    = SSDL_LoadWAV("media/388284__matypresidente__water-drop-short.wav");

//structs
struct Point2D { int x_=0, y_=0; };

using Vector2D = Point2D;[1]

struct Object
{
    Point2D     loc_;
    int         rotation_     = 0;
```

[1]using newTypeName = existingType; makes newTypeName an alias for the existingType. Use it for clarity as needed.

The old style of this, which you may see sometimes, is typedef existingType newTypeName;.

```
    Vector2D    velocity_;
    int         rotationSpeed_ = 0;

    SSDL_Sprite sprite_;
};

//major functions called by the main program
bool playGame            ();

//startup/ending screens to communicate with user
void printInstructions   ();
void displayVictoryScreen();
void displayDefeatScreen ();

int main (int argc, char** argv)
{
    //set up window and font
    SSDL_SetWindowTitle ("Catch the falling candy");
    SSDL_SetWindowSize  (SCREEN_WIDTH, SCREEN_HEIGHT);

    //prepare music
    SSDL_VolumeMusic (int (MIX_MAX_VOLUME * 0.1));
    SSDL_PlayMusic   (BKGD_MUSIC);

    //initial splash screen
    printInstructions ();

    //The game itself
    bool isVictory = playGame ();

    //final screen:  victory or defeat
    SSDL_RenderClear (BLACK);
    SSDL_HaltMusic   ();

    if (isVictory) displayVictoryScreen ();
    else           displayDefeatScreen  ();

    SSDL_RenderTextCentered("Click mouse to end",
                            SCREEN_WIDTH/2, BOTTOM_LINE, SMALL_FONT);
```

```
    SSDL_WaitMouse();               //because if we wait for a key, we're likely
                                    // to have left or right arrow depressed
                                    // when we reach this line... and we never
                                    // get to read the final message

    return 0;
}

//// Startup/ending screens to communicate with user ////

void printInstructions ()
{
    enum { LINE_HEIGHT = 40 };
    SSDL_SetRenderDrawColor (WHITE);
    SSDL_RenderTextCentered ("Catch 10 treats in ",
              SCREEN_WIDTH/2,             0, MEDIUM_FONT);
    SSDL_RenderTextCentered("your basket to win",
              SCREEN_WIDTH/2, LINE_HEIGHT   , MEDIUM_FONT);
    SSDL_RenderTextCentered ("Miss 10 treats and",
              SCREEN_WIDTH/2, LINE_HEIGHT*3 , MEDIUM_FONT);
    SSDL_RenderTextCentered("the next treat is YOU",
              SCREEN_WIDTH/2, LINE_HEIGHT*4 , MEDIUM_FONT);

    SSDL_RenderTextCentered ("Use arrow keys to move",
              SCREEN_WIDTH/2, LINE_HEIGHT*6 , MEDIUM_FONT);
    SSDL_RenderTextCentered("left and right",
              SCREEN_WIDTH/2, LINE_HEIGHT*7 , MEDIUM_FONT);

    SSDL_RenderTextCentered ("Click mouse to",
              SCREEN_WIDTH/2, LINE_HEIGHT*9 , MEDIUM_FONT);
    SSDL_RenderTextCentered("toggle stats display",
              SCREEN_WIDTH/2, LINE_HEIGHT*10, MEDIUM_FONT);

    SSDL_RenderTextCentered ("Hit any key to continue",
              SCREEN_WIDTH/2, BOTTOM_LINE,    SMALL_FONT);

    SSDL_WaitKey      ();
}
```

```
void displayVictoryScreen ()
{
    //sound and picture
    static const SSDL_Sound VICTORY_SOUND
        = SSDL_LoadWAV("media/342153__robcro6010__circus-theme-short.wav");
    SSDL_PlaySound(VICTORY_SOUND);
    static const SSDL_Image GOOD_PUMPKIN
        = SSDL_LoadImage("media/goodPumpkin.png");
    SSDL_RenderImage(GOOD_PUMPKIN, SCREEN_WIDTH / 4, 0);

    //victory message
    SSDL_SetRenderDrawColor(WHITE);
    SSDL_RenderText ("Hooah!"  ,
                     FINAL_SCREEN_MESSAGE_OFFSET_X, SCREEN_HEIGHT/4,
                     LARGE_FONT);
    enum { LINE_DISTANCE_Y = 96 }; //an arbitrarily chosen number...
    SSDL_RenderText ("You won!",
                     FINAL_SCREEN_MESSAGE_OFFSET_X,
                     SCREEN_HEIGHT/4+LINE_DISTANCE_Y,
                     LARGE_FONT);
}

void displayDefeatScreen ()
{
    //sound and picture
    static const SSDL_Sound DEFEAT_SOUND
        = SSDL_LoadWAV("media/326813__mrose6__echoed-screams-short.wav");
    SSDL_PlaySound(DEFEAT_SOUND);
    static const SSDL_Image SAD_PUMPKIN
        = SSDL_LoadImage("media/sadPumpkin.png");
    SSDL_RenderImage(SAD_PUMPKIN, SCREEN_WIDTH / 4, 0);

    //defeat message
    SSDL_SetRenderDrawColor (WHITE);
    SSDL_RenderText ("Oh, no!", FINAL_SCREEN_MESSAGE_OFFSET_X,
                     SCREEN_HEIGHT/4, LARGE_FONT);
}
```

So far we have the general outline of the program. I put a lot of information into the `Object` struct: position, velocity, sprite information, and rotation. Some isn't always needed - only candy rotates, for example - but having only one type of `Object` keeps things simpler.

Example 12-6. Falling candy program, part 2 of 5

```
///////////////////// Initializing /////////////////////////

void resetCandyPosition(Object& candy);

void initializeObjects (Object& basket, Object& candy, Object& yumMessage)
{
    //load those images
    SSDL_SetSpriteImage(candy.sprite_,
                        SSDL_LoadImage("media/candy.png"));
    SSDL_SetSpriteImage(basket.sprite_,
                        SSDL_LoadImage("media/jack-o-lantern.png"));
    SSDL_SetSpriteImage(yumMessage.sprite_,
                        SSDL_LoadImage("media/yum.png"));

    //two images are the wrong size; we resize them.
    SSDL_SetSpriteSize (candy.sprite_,   CANDY_WIDTH,  CANDY_HEIGHT);
    SSDL_SetSpriteSize (basket.sprite_, BASKET_WIDTH, BASKET_HEIGHT);

    //move 'em so they're centered on the coords we set for them
    SSDL_SetSpriteOffset(candy.sprite_,
                         CANDY_WIDTH/2,  CANDY_HEIGHT/2);
    SSDL_SetSpriteOffset(basket.sprite_,
                         BASKET_WIDTH/2, BASKET_HEIGHT/2);

    //put the objects in their starting positions
    basket.loc_.x_ = SCREEN_WIDTH / 2;
    basket.loc_.y_ = SCREEN_HEIGHT - BASKET_HEIGHT/2;
    SSDL_SetSpriteLocation(basket.sprite_,
                           basket.loc_.x_, basket.loc_.y_);
    resetCandyPosition(candy);
    //We don't care about yumMessage position till we make one
```

```
    //And set velocities
    //basket's can't be specified till we check inputs
    enum { CANDY_SPEED = 11 };           //11 pixels per frame, straight down
    candy.velocity_.y_ = CANDY_SPEED;    //11 per frame straight down
                                         //Increase speeds for faster game
    yumMessage.velocity_ = { 1, -1 };    //Up and to the right

    //And rotational speeds
    candy.rotationSpeed_ = 1;            //Candy spins slightly
}

/////////////////////////// Drawing /////////////////////////////

//Display all 3 objects (2 if yumMessage is currently not visible)
void renderObjects (Object basket, Object candy, Object yumMessage,
                    bool showYumMessage)
{
    SSDL_RenderSprite (basket.sprite_);
    SSDL_RenderSprite ( candy.sprite_);
    if (showYumMessage) SSDL_RenderSprite (yumMessage.sprite_);
}

void renderStats(int Caught, int Missed)
{
    //Stats boxes, for reporting how many candies caught and missed
    SSDL_SetRenderDrawColor(BLACK);
    enum { BOX_WIDTH = 90, BOX_HEIGHT = 25 };
    SSDL_RenderFillRect(0, 0,                           //Left box
        BOX_WIDTH, BOX_HEIGHT);
    SSDL_RenderFillRect(SCREEN_WIDTH - BOX_WIDTH, 0, //Right box
        SCREEN_WIDTH - 1, BOX_HEIGHT);

    //Statistics themselves
    SSDL_SetRenderDrawColor(WHITE);
    SSDL_SetFont(SMALL_FONT);

    SSDL_SetCursor(0, 0);                               //Left box
    sout << "Caught: " << Caught;
```

```
    SSDL_SetCursor(SCREEN_WIDTH - BOX_WIDTH, 0);      //Right box
    sout << "Missed: " << Missed;
}
```

resetCandyPosition starts the candy at the top of the screen, with a random X location. It's called in initializeObjects and again in handleCatchingCandy and handleMissingCandy.

renderStats prints how many pieces you've caught or missed, on two black boxes used to make those stats easier to read.

Example 12-7. Falling candy program, part 3 of 5

```
//////////////// Moving objects in the world ///////////////////

void resetCandyPosition (Object& candy)  //When it's time to drop
                                         // another candy...
{
    //Put it at a random X location
    candy.loc_.x_ = MARGIN + rand() % (SCREEN_WIDTH - MARGIN);
    candy.loc_.y_ = CANDY_START_HEIGHT;    //at the top of the screen

    SSDL_SetSpriteLocation(candy.sprite_, candy.loc_.x_, candy.loc_.y_);
}

void moveObject(Object& object)
{
    object.loc_.x_ += object.velocity_.x_; //Every frame, move object
    object.loc_.y_ += object.velocity_.y_; //  as specified
    SSDL_SetSpriteLocation(object.sprite_, object.loc_.x_, object.loc_.y_);

                                           //...and spin as specified
    object.rotation_ += object.rotationSpeed_;
    object.rotation_ %= 360;               //angle shouldn't go over 360
    SSDL_SetSpriteRotation(object.sprite_, object.rotation_);
}
```

```
void moveBasket(Object& basket, int basketSpeed)
{
    //Let user move basket with left and right arrows
    if (SSDL_IsKeyPressed (SDLK_LEFT )) basket.loc_.x_ -= basketSpeed;
    if (SSDL_IsKeyPressed (SDLK_RIGHT)) basket.loc_.x_ += basketSpeed;

    //..but don't let the user touch the sides of the screen
    if (basket.loc_.x_ < MARGIN)
        basket.loc_.x_ = MARGIN;
    if (basket.loc_.x_ > SCREEN_WIDTH - MARGIN)
        basket.loc_.x_ = SCREEN_WIDTH - MARGIN;

    //Tell the sprite about our changes on X
    SSDL_SetSpriteLocation(basket.sprite_,
                           basket.loc_.x_, basket.loc_.y_);
}
```

moveObject is called on both the candy and the Yum! message, as they both move on their own. The player controls the basket, so that needs its own moveBasket function. moveBasket checks the state of the left and right arrows with SSDL_IsKeyPressed and moves the basket accordingly, ensuring with MARGIN that it doesn't go off screen.

Example 12-8. Falling candy program, part 4 of 5

```
////////What happens when a candy is caught or missed ////////

//Some math functions we need a lot...
int sqr(int num) { return num * num; }

double distance(Point2D a, Point2D b)
{
    return sqrt(sqr(b.x_ - a.x_) + sqr(b.y_ - a.y_));
}

//Circular collision detection, better for round-ish objects
bool inCollision(Point2D a, Point2D b, int aSize, int bSize)
{
    return (distance(a, b) < aSize/2 + bSize/2);
}
```

```
//Detect and handle collisions between basket and candy,
// and update numberCaught
bool handleCatchingCandy (Object basket, Object& candy, Object& yumMessage,
                          int& numberCaught)
{
    if (inCollision (basket.loc_, candy.loc_, CANDY_WIDTH, BASKET_WIDTH))
    {
        SSDL_PlaySound (THUNK_SOUND);

        ++numberCaught;

        resetCandyPosition (candy);

        yumMessage.loc_.x_    = basket.loc_.x_;
        yumMessage.loc_.y_    = basket.loc_.y_;

        return true;
    }
    else return false;
}

//Detect and handle when candy goes off bottom of screen,
// and update numberMissed
void handleMissingCandy (Object& candy, int& numberMissed)
{
                                   //you missed it: it went off screen
    if (candy.loc_.y_ >= SCREEN_HEIGHT)
    {
        SSDL_PlaySound (DROP_SOUND);

        ++numberMissed;


        resetCandyPosition (candy);
    }
}
```

If the basket and candy collide, handleCatchingCandy resets the candy to the top of the screen; positions the Yum! message wherever the basket is; and returns true so main will know to start the countdown framesLeftTillYumDisappears, keeping the Yum! visible for a second.

If the candy falls to the bottom of the screen – if it's missed – handleMissingCandy resets the candy to top of the screen. Either way, the statistics are appropriately updated.

Example 12-9. Falling candy program, part 5 of 5

```
///////////////////// Events /////////////////////

void myEventHandler(bool& mouseClicked)
{
    SSDL_Event event;

    while (SSDL_PollEvent(event))
        switch (event.type)
        {
        case SDL_QUIT:             SSDL_DeclareQuit(); break;
        case SDL_KEYDOWN:          if (SSDL_IsKeyPressed(SDLK_ESCAPE))
                                       SSDL_DeclareQuit();
                                   break;
        case SDL_MOUSEBUTTONDOWN: mouseClicked = true;
        }
}

///// ** The game itself ** ////

bool playGame ()
{
    bool isVictory          = false;      //Did we win?  Not yet
    bool isDefeat           = false;      //Did we lose? Not yet
    bool letsDisplayStats   = true;       //Do we show stats on screen?
                                          //  Yes, for now

    int numberCaught = 0,                 //So far no candies
        numberMissed = 0;                 //  caught or missed
```

```
 //Initialize sprites
Object basket, candy, yumMessage;
initializeObjects (basket, candy, yumMessage);

//Main game loop
while (SSDL_IsNextFrame () && ! isVictory && ! isDefeat)
{
    enum {FRAMES_FOR_YUM_MESSAGE = 60};
    static int framesLeftTillYumDisappears = 0;

    //Handle input events
    bool mouseClick = false; myEventHandler (mouseClick);
    if (mouseClick) letsDisplayStats = !letsDisplayStats;

    //Display the scene
    SSDL_RenderImage(BKGD_IMAGE, 0, 0);
    renderObjects (basket, candy, yumMessage,
                   framesLeftTillYumDisappears>0);
    if (letsDisplayStats) renderStats (numberCaught, numberMissed);

    //Updates:

    //Move objects in the scene
    enum { BASKET_SPEED = 7 };     //7 pixels per frame, left or right
    moveBasket(basket, BASKET_SPEED);
    moveObject(candy); moveObject(yumMessage);

                                            //Did you catch a candy?
    if (handleCatchingCandy(basket, candy, yumMessage, numberCaught))
        framesLeftTillYumDisappears = FRAMES_FOR_YUM_MESSAGE;

    if (numberCaught >= MAX_CAUGHT)
        isVictory = true;
    else                                    //...or did it go off screen?
    {
        handleMissingCandy (candy, numberMissed);
        if (numberMissed >= MAX_MISSED)
            isDefeat = true; //You just lost!
    }
```

```
        //Update yum message
        if (framesLeftTillYumDisappears > 0)  //if yumMessage is active
            --framesLeftTillYumDisappears;    //  keep counting down
    }

    return isVictory;
}
```

The main loop stops when we get victory or defeat. It's divided into the events section, the display section, and the update-things section. In the events section, this statement

```
if (mouseClick) letsDisplayStats = ! letsDisplayStats;
```

toggles whether the stats are displayed on the screen, if you get a mouse click.

Handling the Yum! message is distributed appropriately: it's displayed just like the other objects, but its lifetime is continually counted down in the Updates section.

***Figure 12-3.** The Hallowe'en candy game in action*

Antibugging

- **You've got a feature that's supposed to display for a while but never shows up.** Something like the splat from earlier in this chapter. Maybe your code looks like this:

```
while (SSDL_IsNextFrame ())
{
    ...
    if (mouseClick)
    {
        framesLeftTillSplatDisappears = SPLAT_LIFETIME;
        while (framesLeftTillSplatDisappears > 0)
        {
            //display the splat
            --framesLeftTillSplatDisappears;
        }
    }
    ...
}
```

  It displayed, all right - again and again, till `framesLeftTillSplatDisappears` was 0 - all in 1/60 of a second! It displayed so quickly you never got to see it.

  The problem is adapting to this new event-driven way of thinking. We don't want the program to do all the displaying of the splat and then go on to the next 1/60 of a second; we want it to set up the display, then let the frames pass while other things happen (including the user getting to see the splat).

  A good rule of thumb is **avoid looping an action that's supposed to take time, inside the main animation loop**. Just set it up, and let the main loop update it with successive frames.

  Another good rule is the Tip from designing the splat program, **keep parts of the main loop separate**: handle events (say), then display, then do updates.

So a way to fix this program is

```
while (SSDL_IsNextFrame ())
{
   //Events section
   ...
   if (mouseClick)
       framesLeftTillSplatDisappears = SPLAT_LIFETIME;
   ...

   //Display section
   //  display the splat
   ...

    //Update section
    --framesLeftTillSplatDisappears;
    ...
}
```

- **You can't get a new feature to work.** Try a program that *does* work (a sample program from the text or the Internet, or something you did earlier, or even a program with empty `main`) and make gradual changes until it's the new program.
- **You just added a new feature, and now nothing works.** Here are a few suggestions:
  - As in Chapter 1: **keep a trail of backups**, copies of your entire folder, as you make changes, so if something goes wrong and the sprites won't show, you can go back to an earlier version. It's more fun than pulling your hair out.
  - **Cut out all the code from a function that's misbehaving.** Then put half of it back. If the bad behavior returns, only put a quarter of it back; if not, add more code back in. Keep going till you've figured out what line is the problem.

- **Test to destruction.** If I absolutely can't figure what's wrong, I'll make a copy of the folder (maybe named "`ttd`"), make a backup copy of that, then remove code, especially code I think is irrelevant to the error. Is the error still there? If so, repeat, still making backups, until the program's so short there's nothing left but the error. If not, we may have found the problem! Still too complicated? Go to the previous backup, the one with the error, and only take out part of what removed the error. Whatever you do, you're homing in on the code that's the problem.

  Sometimes I have gotten down to two to three lines of code and determined the problem is a compiler bug. It happens. (Then I write the program a different way.) If it turns out to be something stupid, I'm happy to be done rather than hating myself for making a dumb mistake.

- **Identify differences between versions.** Maybe one has a feature you want, but a bug you don't. A precise report of differences can help you narrow down what you're interested in. In Unix, `diff file1 file2` lists the lines that differ. In Windows, **WinDiff** is a wonderful program from Microsoft (you may already have it) that does the same. Both work for individual files or entire folders.

- **Talk about the problem to someone who can really listen: a duck.** Maybe if you explain your problem to an expert, it'll become clear. Sure, but what if there's no expert handy? Talk to a rubber duck instead - seriously. Explain the problem in detail. As you do, you may find your solution. **Rubber ducky debugging** is a thing, and at present even has its own web site (`https://rubberduckdebugging.com/`).

For more tips, review the "Antibugging" section at the end of Chapter 9.

EXERCISES

In these and subsequent exercises, plan in advance, and use the debugger if anything goes wrong.

1. Make those balls bounce, as in Chapter 11…and have your mouse control a little player on the screen. Avoid the bouncing balls.
2. Make a space game: a UFO flies overhead, dropping missiles while you shoot back. You'll need an array of missiles.
3. Make a version of a fairgrounds duck shoot game. To make it interesting, you could have slow missiles (going straight from your crosshairs to the duck, but taking a second to get there).
4. Make a gun that can rotate, put it in the middle of the screen, and shoot bad guys coming from random directions.
5. Make your own game, either a copy of an existing arcade game or your own idea.

CHAPTER 13

Standard I/O and File Operations

We've had too much fun. It's time to get serious.

Or, maybe, it's time to learn how to program when you *aren't* using a graphics and game library. One reason is, you usually aren't. Another is that even if you were, you might want to access files (for loading a game level, say), and in C++ we handle files much as we do usual user interaction.

Standard I/O programs

Example 13-1 is a program that uses standard I/O. It may look familiar.

Example 13-1. "Hello, world!" using C++ standard I/O

```
//Hello, world! program, for _C++ for Lazy Programmers_
//      -- from _C++ for Lazy Programmers_

//It prints "Hello, world!" on the screen.
//  Quite an accomplishment, huh?

#include <iostream>

using namespace std;

int main ( )
{
    cout << "Hello, world!" << endl;

    return 0;
}
```


W. Briggs, *C++ for Lazy Programmers*, https://doi.org/10.1007/978-1-4842-5187-4_13

Here are the changes from SSDL's Hello, World!, starting at the bottom and working backward:

- It's time to come clean: `ssin` and `sout` are cheap knockoffs of the built-in `cin` (pronounced "C-in") and `cout` ("C-out") that come with the compiler. `cin` and `cout` don't work with the SDL window, so we needed a substitute. `cin` and `cout` are like `ssin` and `sout`, but (a) you can't set the cursor - you can only go down the screen, and (b) you can't set the font.
- We needed `main` to have arguments `(int argc, char** argv)` for compatibility with SDL; now they can be omitted.
- `using namespace std;`: `cout` is part of the "standard" namespace, and you have to tell the compiler to use it, or it'll complain it doesn't know what `cout` is.
- Instead of `"SSDL.h"`, we load `<iostream>`, which like `<cmath>` and `<cstdlib>` comes with the compiler. It defines `cin`, `cout`, `endl` (works like `'\n'`), and other things.

Compiling in Microsoft Visual Studio

It's easiest to make a copy of the `basicStandardProject` in the repository's `newWork` folder and use that. But I'll describe how to make a standard project on your own anyway.

In Visual Studio 2017 and earlier, say File ➤ New ➤ Project. You should see something like Figure 13-1. On the left, go to Visual C++ or Visual C++ ➤ Other and select Empty Project.

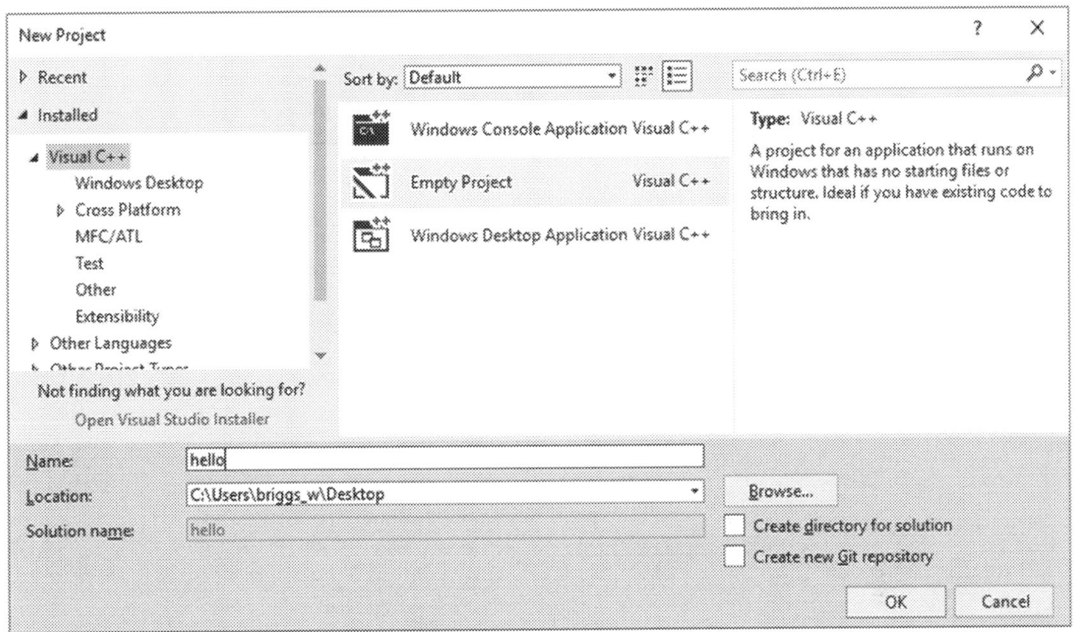

***Figure 13-1.** Making an Empty Project in Microsoft Visual Studio 2017*

In 2019, Create New Project, and select Empty Project from the list it shows.

Name and locate it what you like; click OK or Create.

The project really *is* empty (Figure 13-2), and we need `main`. Right-click Source Files and Add a New Item. Make it a C++ file (`.cpp`) of an appropriate name (Figure 13-3); I like `main.cpp`.

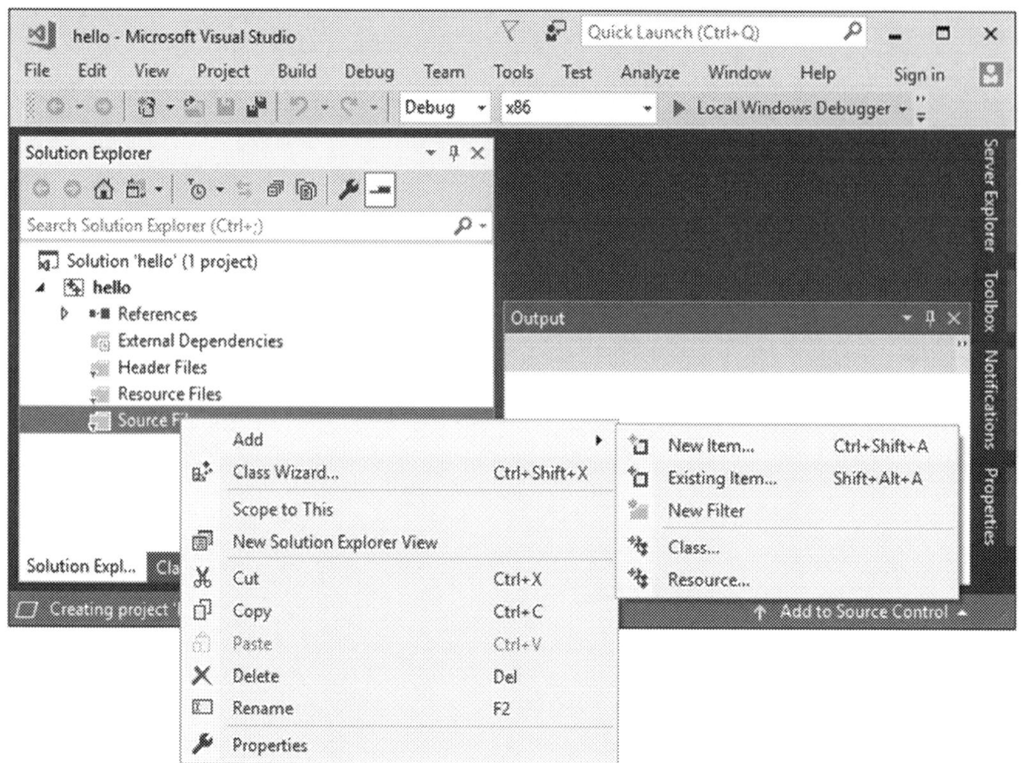

Figure 13-2. *Add New Item*

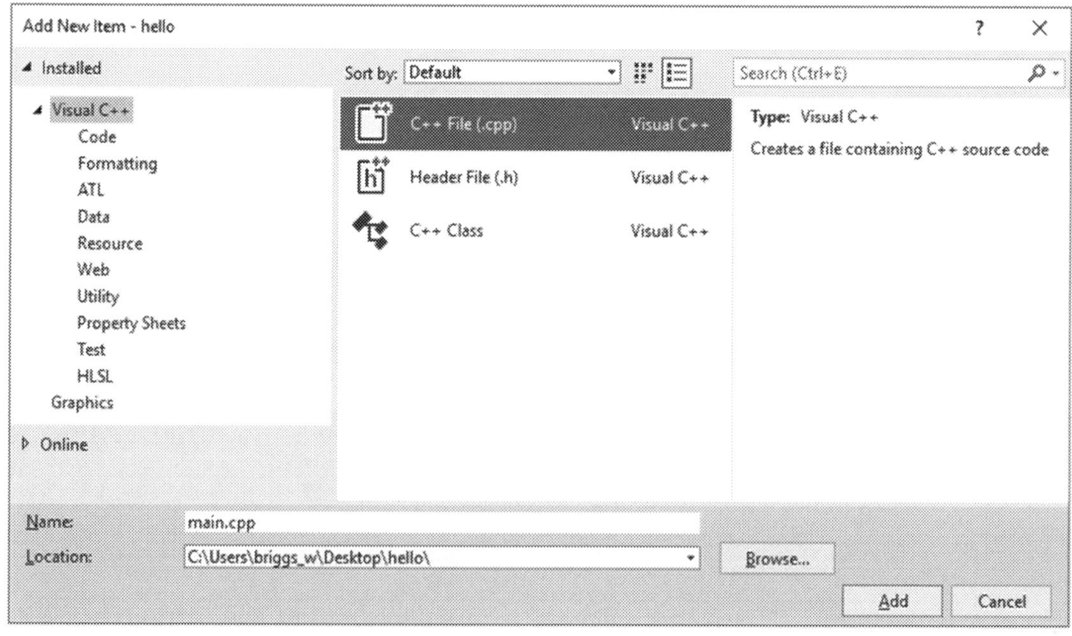

Figure 13-3. *Add New Item, cont'd*

In 2017 and earlier, ensure SubSystem is set to Console in Project Properties (Figure 13-4). We'll consider why in a moment.

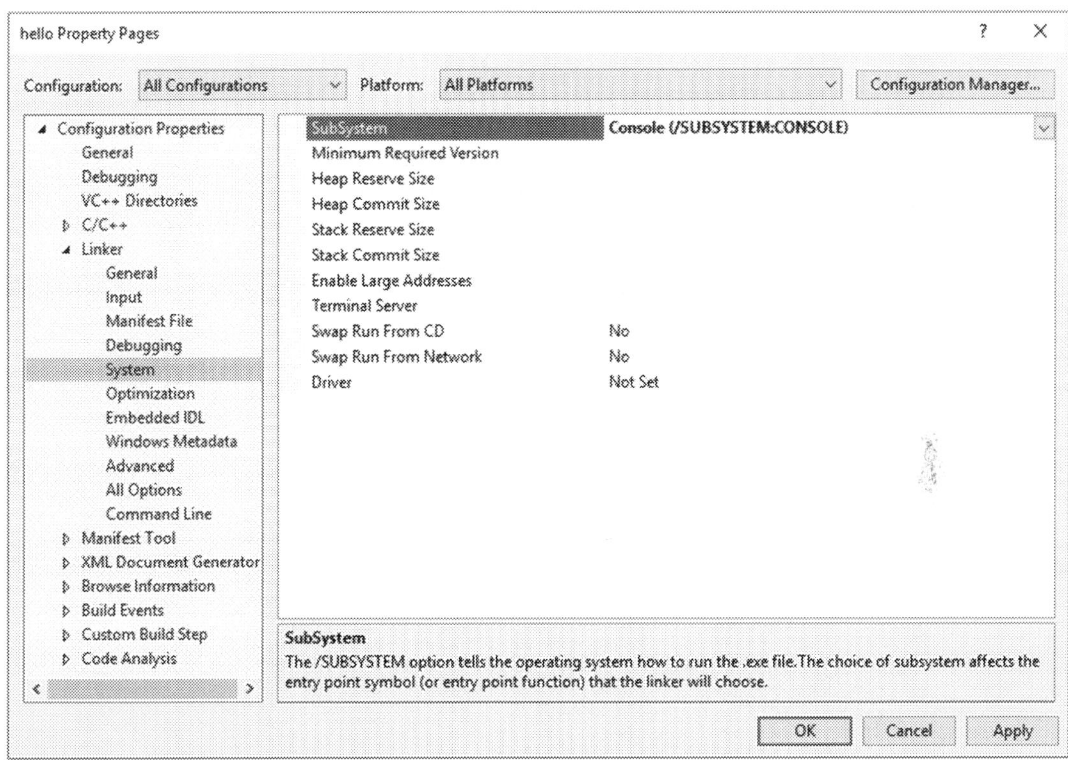

Figure 13-4. *Setting the SubSystem to Console*

Now you're ready to type your program – but not quite ready to run it. Read on.

Antibugging

Here are some new issues you may find moving to standard I/O with Microsoft Visual Studio. **The program closes before you have a chance to see anything.** Solutions:

- Under Tools ➤ Options ➤ Debugging, uncheck **Automatically close the console when debugging stops**. This will apply to all console projects in this compiler till you change it.

Programs created with my `basicStandardProject` are console programs. If you make your own Empty project, you can make it a console project thus: Project ➤ Properties; set Configuration Properties ➤ Linker ➤ System ➤ SubSystem to Console (Figure 13-4). If this stops working, Visual Studio may still be running previous copies of that or other programs. It seems it automatically closes all but the first regardless. Kill all other console windows and start a new one; or try restarting Visual Studio.

Or, add this line just before the `return`:

```
system ("pause"); //Make program wait for user
```

- **You find there are pch.h and pch.cpp in your project. What?** You must have created a Windows Console Application. You can ignore those files.
- **The compiler can't find a precompiled header.** Precompiled headers are a way to reduce compile time when you have very long header files. I don't think we need them at this point. To disable, go to Project ➤ Properties, then set C/C++ ➤ Precompiled Headers ➤ Precompiled Header to – wait for it – Not Using Precompiled Headers. Or make a new Empty Project.
- **_WinMain@16 can't be found.** I think you created a Windows Desktop Application project, not an Empty Project, by clicking the wrong thing in the boxes shown in Figure 13-1. Re-create the project, making sure it's an Empty Project.

Compiling with g++

```
g++ -g main.cpp -o myProgram
```

That's it. The `-g` means "support debugging with `gdb` or `ddd`"; the `-o` means "name my executable `myProgram`." You can leave off the `-o` option and the executable will be `a.out` or `a.exe`.

Or if you want, you can copy the `basicStandardProject` from the repository's `newWork` folder, and type `make`; we'll be doing that in Chapter 16 anyway. It names its executable `a.out`.

To run the program, enter `./myProgram` (Unix) or `myProgram` (MinGW).

To debug, use `ddd myProgram &`[1] (Unix) or `gdb myProgram` (Unix and MinGW). In MinGW, we used to `break SDL_main`; since there now is no `SDL_main`, `break main` instead.

Extra Why do we put ./ before the program name in Unix?

When you type a command, Unix looks through its list of directories, called the PATH, for the command you typed. If your current directory (known in Unix as `.`, a single period) isn't in the PATH, it won't find it, so if you type a.out to run your program, it won't find it.

I don't like that, so let's put `.` ("dot") in the PATH.

Suppose it's the first directory it checks. Then if a bad guy can get a malicious program into your directory and name it a common command like `ls`, he can get you to do awful things: you type `ls`, and it deletes the operating system or something:

```
cp myEvilProgram innocentUsersFolder
mv innocentUsersFolder/myEvilProgram innocentUsersFolder/ls
```

```
#now we wait for the innocent user to type ls
```

OK, so we'll make it the *last* directory checked. Now, if you type `ls`, Unix will look in `/bin` (or wherever), find the right `ls`, and run it.

But if the bad guy guesses what typos people make and names his evil program `sl`, and your fingers miss...he's got you.

I don't know how likely that last scenario is, but it's a reason to leave `.` out of the path if you're concerned.

---

[1]The & means "give me a command prompt again immediately; don't wait for `ddd` to finish." Optional but a good practice.

Antibugging

- **The debugger says no debugging symbols are found.** In ddd, it also gives a blank window. Compile again with the -g option or use my Makefile.

EXERCISES

1. Write a program which prints all 99 verses of "99 bottles of beer on the wall." In case you missed this cultural treasure, it goes like this:

```
99 bottles of beer on the wall
99 bottles of beer;
Take one down, pass it around,
98 bottles of beer on the wall!
```

The last verse is the one in which the last bottle is taken down.

Make sure your program prints neatly and handles the special case of 1 bottle of beer (not "1 bottles of beer").

File I/O (optional)

cin and cout as files

In a sense, we've been using files already – at least, two things that C++ considers to be files: cin and cout.

cin is an input file. It just happens to be an input file that gets its information from the keyboard as you type. cout is an output file: the output file that is your computer screen. A stretch of the definitions? Perhaps – but in this section I use cin and cout as *actual* files.

Getting the command prompt in Windows

To do this we'll need a command prompt. There's many ways to get it in Windows, depending on the version. Some are [Windows Key]-R, type cmd; Start Menu, type cmd; and Task Manager, File ➤ Run new task, type cmd.

Now you need to send it to the correct folder.

The lazy way: go to your program's folder in Windows, click the folder icon in the title bar, and copy the path it shows (Figure 13-5).

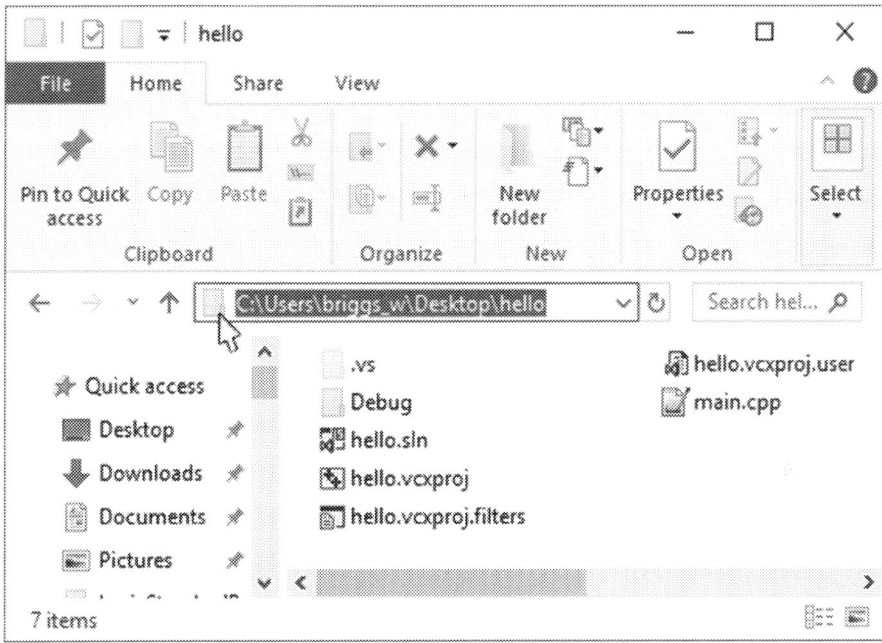

Figure 13-5. *Getting the path of your folder*

Is the drive you see in the prompt of the `cmd` window the same as in the address you just copied? If not, enter the new drive, probably `C:`. Either way, type `cd`, a space, and paste (Ctrl-V) the address. Hit Enter. Figure 13-6 shows the commands.

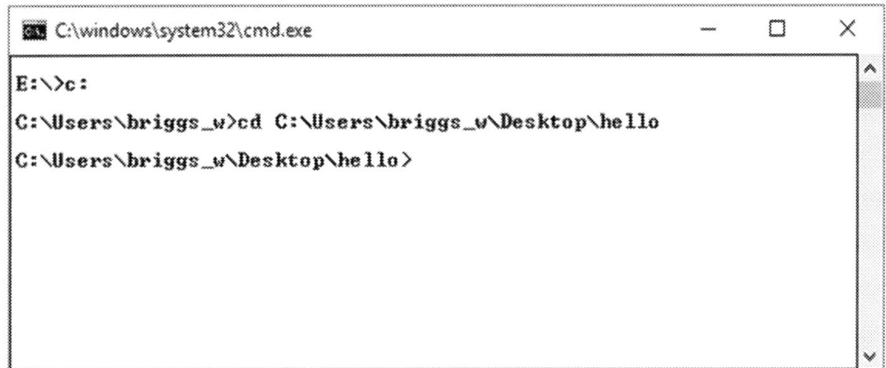

Figure 13-6. *Changing to your project's directory in* `cmd`

Visual Studio puts your executable, `<your project>.exe`, in a folder, probably `Debug`. Copy it to the same folder as your `.vcxproj` and it'll be able to find whatever files you put there.

Redirecting I/O at the command prompt

To make your program get input from `in.txt`, not the keyboard, type

```
myProgram < in.txt //The < goes from file to program; makes sense
```

To make it also send its output to `out.txt`, not the screen, type

```
myProgram < in.txt > out.txt
```

Try sending the Hello program's output to a file and see what you get.

while (cin)

I've heard the letters that appear most frequently in English text are, starting with the super-frequent E, ETAOINSHRDLU. Let's see if that's true by giving the program some huge text, maybe off gutenberg.org, and counting the frequencies.

```
make an array of frequencies for letters, all initially zero
while there are characters left
    read in a character //we won't prompt the user; it's all coming from a
    file
    if it's an 'A' or an 'a' add 1 to frequency for 'A'
    else if it's a 'B' or a 'b' add 1 to frequency for 'B'
    else ...
print all those frequencies
```

I know how to create arrays, add 1 to `int`s, and read in characters. But how do I know there are characters left?

`while (cin) ...` will do it. If you put `cin` someplace you'd expect a `bool`, it's evaluated to something like "if nothing has gone wrong with `cin`." The usual thing that goes wrong with `cin` is hitting the end of the input file. Example 13-2 shows the completed program.

Example13-2. Counting frequencies of letters in a text file

```
//Program to get the frequencies of letters
//      -- from _C++ for Lazy Programmers_

#include <iostream>

using namespace std;

int main ()
{
    //make an array of frequencies for letters, all initially zero
    enum { LETTERS_IN_ALPHABET = 26 };
    int frequenciesOfLetters[LETTERS_IN_ALPHABET] = {}; //all zeroes

    //read in the letters
    while (cin)                 //while there are letters left
    {
        char ch; cin >> ch;     //read one in
        ch = toupper(ch);       //capitalize it

        if (cin)                //Still no problems with cin, right?
            if (isalpha(ch)) //  and this is an alphabetic letter?
                ++frequenciesOfLetters[ch - 'A'];
                                //A's go in slot 0, B's in slot 1...
    }

    //print all those frequencies
    cout << "Frequencies are:\n";
    cout << "Letter\tFrequency\n";
    for (char ch = 'A'; ch <= 'Z'; ++ch) //for each letter A to Z...
        cout << ch << '\t' << frequenciesOfLetters[ch - 'A'] << '\n';

    return 0;
}
```

Try this with etaoinShrdlu `< in.txt > out.txt` and you'll get an `out.txt` file like

```
Frequencies are:
Letter Frequency
```

```
A       11
B       3
C       3
D       6
E       20
...
```

If the letters are coming from a file, `while (cin)` fails when we reach the end of file. But actual keyboard input has no end of file. You can simulate it by hitting Ctrl-Z and Enter (Windows), or Ctrl-D (Unix). *It must be the first character on the line, or it may not work.*

Reading in characters, including whitespace

New task: read in a file, every character, and capitalize everything.

This looks like it should work, but doesn't:

```
while (cin)                     //for each char in file
{
    char ch;  cin >> ch;        //read in char
    ch = toupper (ch);          //capitalize
    if (cin) cout << ch;        //cin still OK? Then print
}
```

With this input

```
Twinkle, twinkle, little bat!
How I wonder what you're at!
```

we get this output

```
TWINKLE,TWINKLE,LITTLEBAT!HOWIWONDERWHATYOU'REAT!
```

`cin >>` skips whitespace. Fine for user interaction and the ETAOIN SHRDLU program, but here we need whitespace.

Solution: `ch = cin.get();`. `cin.get()` returns the next character, even if it's space, tab (`\t`), or end of line (`\n`).

Example 13-3 reads in a file and produces an ALL CAPS version.

Example 13-3. Capitalizing a file, character by character.

```
//Program to produce an ALL CAPS version of a file
//      -- from _C++ for Lazy Programmers_

#include <iostream>
#include <cctype>              //for toupper

using namespace std;

int main ()
{
    while (cin)                //for each char in file
    {
        char ch = cin.get();    //read in char
        ch = toupper (ch);     //capitalize
        if (cin) cout << ch;   //cin still OK? Then print
    }

    return 0;
}
```

Antibugging

- **You told it to stop at the end of file, but it goes too far.**

```
/////////// get an average -- buggy version //////////////
double total = 0.0;     //initialize total and howMany
int  howMany = 0;

while (cin)               //while there are numbers in file
{
    int num; cin >> num; //read one in

    total += num;         //keep running total
    ++howMany;
}
```

Your input file is

```
1
2
```

and your average is...1.6667. Huh?

Trace it with the debugger. It reads in 1, adds it, increments `howMany`. Reads in 2, adds it, increments `howMany` again. Test for end of file with `while (cin)`; it keeps going.

But aren't we at the end of the file? Maybe not: there may be another `\n` or space or something.

So the program keeps going. It reads in the next number, and there isn't one, so it leaves `num` as 2, adds it again (!), increments again. An error is born.

It couldn't know there wasn't going to be another number till it tried to read it. So the solution is to **test the input file after every attempt to read, to ensure it didn't run out of input while reading**:

```
int num; cin >> num; //read one in

if (cin)              //still no problems with cin, right?
{
    total += num;     //keep running total
    ++howMany;
}
```

See the source code for a complete (and correct) version of this program.

EXERCISES

In all these exercises, use standard I/O:

1. Read in a sequence of numbers and print it in reverse order. You don't know how many, but you do know it's no more than, say, 100. (This way you can declare an array that's big enough.)
2. Count the characters in a file.
3. ...not including whitespace or punctuation.

Using file names

It's too much work to redirect I/O all the time. Maybe I have multiple input files – they can't all be cin. Or maybe I just want the program to remember the file name and not expect me to type it at the command prompt.

Say I have a game with angry robots wandering around trying to collide with my player. The player starts on the left side of the screen, and it's my job to get it to the right without any collisions.

It might make the game more interesting if I placed the robots in specific locations, designing each level successively tougher than the last. We'll start level 1 with three robots, so that's three locations.

If I got this from cin (way too annoying, but we'll change that in a minute), some of the code might look like Example 13-4.

Example 13-4. Code to read in several points from cin

```
//A (partial) game with killer robots
//  meant to demonstrate use of file I/O
//This loads 3 points and prints a report
//      -- from _C++ for Lazy Programmers_

#include <iostream>

using namespace std;

struct Point2D { int x_=0, y_=0; };

int main ()
{
                    //an array of robot positions
    enum { MAX_ROBOTS = 3 };
    Point2D robots[MAX_ROBOTS];

    int whichRobot = 0;
    //while there's input and array's not full...
    while (cin && whichRobot < MAX_ROBOTS)
    {
        int x, y;
        cin >> x >> y;              //read in an x, y pair
```

```
        if (cin)                      //if we got valid input (not at eof)
        {                             //store what we read
            robots[whichRobot] = {x, y};
            ++whichRobot;             //and remember there's 1 more robot
        }
    }

    for (int i = 0; i < MAX_ROBOTS; ++i)
        cout        << robots[i].x_ << ' '
                    << robots[i].y_ << endl;

    return 0;
}
```

Now let's make the program go get the file without me using >. Here's what I must do to use a named input file:

1. #include <fstream>, which has definitions I need.
2. ifstream inFile;. This declares my input file. ofstream is for output files.
3. inFile.open ("level1.txt");. Opening a file associates it with a filename and ensures the file is there.
4. Verify the file opened without error. If it's an input file, the error may be that the file doesn't exist or isn't in the folder you thought it was. If it's an output file, you may have a disk problem or a read-only file. Here's how to verify:

   ```
   if (! inFile) // handle error
   ```

5. Change cin to inFile wherever you want to use the new file. If it's an output file, change cout to outFile.
6. When done, close the file: inFile.close ();. This tells the operating system to forget the association between inFile and "input.txt" and thereby lets other programs that might need it, use it again. To be sure, when your program ends, all files it referenced will be closed – but it's wise to get in the habit of putting away your toys, I mean files, when you're done with them. Your mother would be proud.

Example 13-5 is the updated version of the program.

Example 13-5. Program that reads an input file and prints to an output file.

```
//A (partial) game with killer robots
//  meant to demonstrate use of file I/O
//This loads 3 points and prints a report
//      -- from _C++ for Lazy Programmers_

#include <iostream>
#include <fstream>  //1. include <fstream>

using namespace std;

struct Point2D { int x_=0, y_=0; };

int main ()
{
                    //an array of robot positions
    enum { MAX_ROBOTS = 3 };
    Point2D robots[MAX_ROBOTS];

                    //2. Declare file variables.
                    //3. Open the files.
                    //Here's two ways to do both; either's fine
    ifstream inFile; inFile.open("level1.txt");
    ofstream outFile ("saveGame1.txt");

                    //4. Verify the files opened without error
    if (!inFile)
    {
        cout << "Can't open level1.txt!\n"; return 1;
                    // 1 is a conventional return value for error
    }
    if (! outFile)
    {
        cout << "Can't create file saveGame1.txt!"; return 1;
    }

                    //5. Change cin to inFile, cout to outFile
```

```
    int whichRobot = 0;
    //while there's input and array's not full...
    while (inFile && whichRobot < MAX_ROBOTS)
    {
        int x, y;
        inFile >> x >> y;          //read in an x, y pair

        if (inFile)                //if we got valid input (not at eof)
        {                          //store what we read
            robots[whichRobot] = {x, y};
            ++whichRobot;          //and remember there's 1 more robot
        }
    }

    for (int i = 0; i < MAX_ROBOTS; ++i)
        outFile     << robots[i].x_ << ' '
                    << robots[i].y_ << endl;

                    //6. When done, close the files
    inFile.close(); outFile.close();

                    //can still use cout for other things
    cout << "Just saved saveGame1.txt.\n";

    return 0;
}
```

That worked: it saved saveGame1.txt in the same folder as the .vcxproj file (Visual Studio) or executable (otherwise).

The program erases whatever contents saveGame1.txt has when the program starts and replaces it with new contents.

You can have multiple input and output files in your programs. You can also pass files into functions:

```
void readFile (ifstream& in,  double numbers[], int& howManyWeGot);
void writeFile(ofstream& out, double numbers[], int  howMany);
```

EXERCISES

1. Write a program to determine if two files are identical.

2. Write and test functions to read from, and print to, a file of `Point2D`'s.

3. Roll 2 dice 100 times, and store the resulting sums in a file...

4. ...then load that file and print a histogram: a bar showing how many times you got 2, another showing how many times 3, and so on. Do this in SSDL (use `basicSSDLProject`; go ahead and use file variables; just don't expect `cin` and `cout` to work); or print X's across the screen showing how many times each value showed up (Figure 13-7).

```
2       : X
3       : XXXXXXX
4       : XXXXXXXX
...
```

Figure 13-7. *A histogram printed with X's*

5. Is the Earth getting warmer?

   There's a file `temperature.txt`[2] in the sample code for this chapter, which contains, for given years, year and estimated average global temperature. (The temperature given is degrees Centigrade relative to estimated average temperature for 1910–2000).

   So what can we learn from it?

   The degrees increase per year, which is

$$m = \frac{N\sum xy - \sum x \sum y}{N\sum x^2 - (\sum x)^2}$$

[2]Source: `www.ncdc.noaa.gov/cag/global/time-series`.

x is year and y is temperature. Σ x, read as "the sum of x," means "the sum of all the x's." m is the slope of the line y = mx+b that most closely matches the data.

How closely the yearly temperatures actually match this line. This is

$$R = \frac{N\sum xy - \sum x \sum y}{\sqrt{\left[N\sum x^2 - (\sum x)^2\right]\left[N\sum y^2 - (\sum y)^2\right]}}$$

If R is –1 or 1, then the correlation is strong. If R is near 0, it's very weak. Negative R means that the temperature is decreasing with time (but we'd know this already from m).

Write a program that reads the file and provides the user with degrees increase per year and R. What functions will you need? Test them enough to be sure you trust them before giving your answer.

Of course, correlation does not prove causality. For example, people who drink coffee ski more (let's say). Does this mean coffee causes skiing? Maybe it's that ski lodges give free coffee. Or maybe people who like to have fun are more likely to ski and drink coffee. For causality, we need a bit more (human) thinking.

6. Make your own cryptogram: a letter scheme, as in, A means R, B means D, and so on. Then encode a message using your encryption scheme. Also write a decryption program and verify everything works.

CHAPTER 14

Character Arrays and Dynamic Memory

Character arrays – a.k.a. "character strings," or text – are important for many tasks. This chapter shows how to handle them, and how to create those or other arrays when you don't know the size in advance.

Character arrays

We've been using char arrays from the beginning. Our "Hello, world!" quote from Chapters 1 and 13 is a character array, with contents as shown in Figure 14-1.

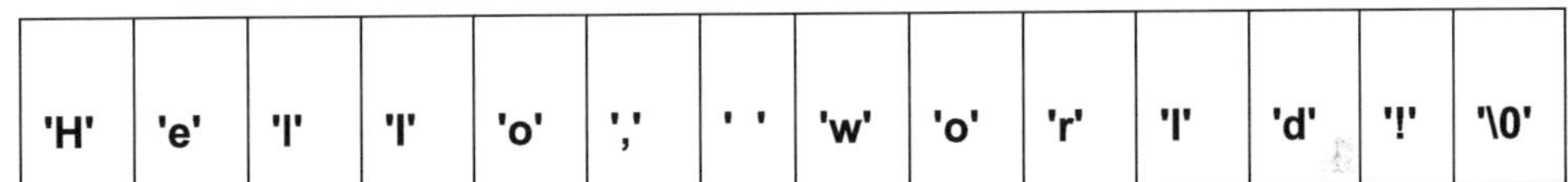

'H'	'e'	'l'	'l'	'o'	','	' '	'w'	'o'	'r'	'l'	'd'	'!'	'\0'

***Figure 14-1.** The contents of the "Hello, world!" character array literal*

'\0', the "null character," is a marker to tell C++ this is where our character string ends. cout stops printing not when it reaches the end of allocated space – it doesn't know or care how much space was allocated – but when it reaches '\0'.

Let's see what we can do with char arrays besides printing.

Here are two ways to **initialize a character array**.

```
char A[] = {'d','o','g','\0'}; //they both mean the same thing
char A[] = "dog";              //but this one's easier to read,
                               //  don't you think?
```


W. Briggs, *C++ for Lazy Programmers*, https://doi.org/10.1007/978-1-4842-5187-4_14

You can also **read a word into a character array** from `cin` or an input file. We'll need to be sure the array we declare has enough room for what's typed in. We do this by allocating way more characters than we're likely to need.

```
const int  MAX_STRING_SIZE = 250;
char  name[MAX_STRING_SIZE];
cout << "What's your name? "; cin >> name;
```

That code reads in one word. If you want to **read the entire line** (maybe you want to let the user enter both first and last names?), you'll want `cin.getline (name, MAX_STRING_SIZE);`.

We can **pass the array into a function**. In Example 14-1 we have a function that prints a question and gets a valid yes or no answer. We don't plan to change the array, so we pass it as `const`.

Example 14-1. A function that takes a `char` array as a parameter

```
bool getYorNAnswer (const char question[])
{
	char answer;

	do
	{
		cout << question;
		cin  >> answer;
		answer = toupper (answer);
	}
	while (answer != 'Y' && answer != 'N');

	return answer == 'Y';
}
```

Let's now find how long a character array is – not the allocated memory, but the part being used, up until the null character.

```
where = 0
while the whereth char isn't the null character (not at end of string)
  add 1 to where
```

Example 14-2 gives a complete version.

Example 14-2. The `myStrlen` function

```
unsigned int myStrlen (const char str[])
                                    //"strlen" is the conventional
                                    //   name for this function
{
    int where = 0;

    while (str[where] != '\0')      //count the chars
        ++where;

    return where;                   //length is final "where"
}
```

This and other functions are already provided in include file `cstring`. Table 14-1 lists the most commonly used.

Table 14-1. *Some `cstring` functions, simplified for clarity*

`unsigned int strlen (const char myArray[]);`	return length of character string in `myArray` (how many characters till the null character)
`void strcpy (char destination[], const char source[]);`	copy contents of `source` into `destination`
`void strcat (char destination[], const char source[]);`	copy contents of `source` to the end of `destination`. If you call `strcat` on arguments containing "Mr." and "Goodbar", the resulting destination will be "Mr.Goodbar"
`int strcmp (const char a[], const char b[]);`	return 1 if a comes after b in alphabetical order, as in `strcmp ("beta", "alpha")`; -1 if a comes before b, as in `strcmp ("alpha", "beta")`; 0 if they are identical

---

Note Microsoft Visual Studio may give a warning when it sees `strcpy` or `strcat` and others:

```
warning C4996: 'strcpy': This function or variable may
be unsafe. Consider using strcpy_s instead. To disable
deprecation, use _CRT_SECURE_NO_WARNINGS. See online help for
details.
```

`strcpy_s` and `strcat_s` are versions of `strcpy` and `strcat` which try to stop you from writing past the bounds of the array. Sounds wise, but this never caught on generally. I don't use them because I want code to be portable between compilers. Or maybe I just like living on the edge.

You can suppress the warning if you want: put this line at the top of any file that references `strcpy` and so on:

```
#pragma warning (disable:4996)
                          //disable warning about strcpy, etc.
```

Antibugging

- **In the debugger, you see your `char` array looking reasonable, but toward the end it's full of random characters.** That's OK: whatever's past the `'\0'` isn't printed or used anyway. You can ignore it.
- **You see reasonable characters in your `char` array being printed, then followed by extra garbage.** The string is missing its final `'\0'`. Solution: insert the `'\0'` at the end.
- **It acts like it's gotten some of your input, before you had a chance to type it.** (If using file I/O, it skips part of the file.) Here's an example:

```
do
{
    cout << "Enter a line and I'll tell you how long it is.\n";
    cout << "Enter: "; cin.getline (line, MAX_LINE_LENGTH);

    cout << "That's " << strlen (line) << " characters.\n";
```

```
    letsRepeat = getYOrNAnswer ("Continue (Y/N)? ");
}
while (letsRepeat);
```

First time through, you're good. Every time after that, when you say you want to do it again, it says your line length is 0 and asks if you want to continue.

Think of `cin` as providing a sequence of characters headed from keyboard to program, as in Figure 14-2.

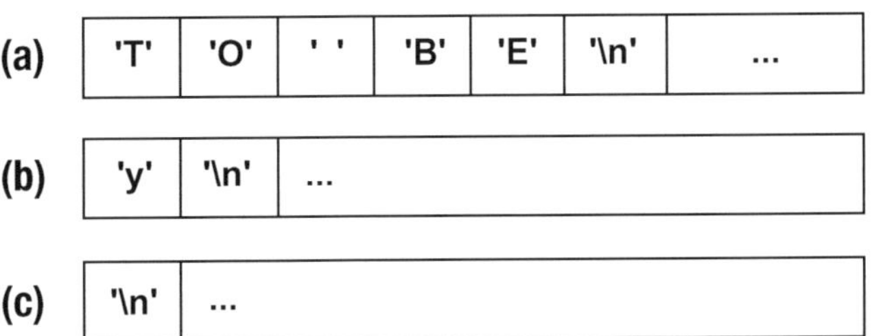

Figure 14-2. *The* `cin` *buffer, with whatever the user typed as its contents*

In (a), you've entered your first line, `TO BE`. `cin.getline` takes all that, up through the '\n'.

In (b), you've entered your response to the "Continue (Y/N)?" question.

In (c), `getYOrNAnswer` has done its input: `cin>>answer`. `answer` becomes `'y'`, and `getYOrNAnswer` is done.

We're ready to start the loop again and get more input...but look what was left in the `cin` buffer:[1] a string for `cin.getline` to read. It's an empty string, but it's still a string, because it ends with `'\0'`. So `cin.getline` won't wait for you to type; it goes right on and reads that empty string...and we're back in `getYOrNAnswer` being asked if we want to continue.

[1]Buffer: temporary storage, especially for I/O.

We need to dump that '\0' before cin.getline can be fooled. Here are two ways:

- cin.getline again, just to get rid of the '\0'.
- cin.ignore (MAX_LINE_LENGTH, '\n');. This ignores all chars, up through MAX_LINE_LENGTH or the first \n, whichever comes first.

I think let's put it in getYOrNAnswer: it's the function that asked the question that gave us trouble, so it should clean up after itself.

```
bool getYOrNAnswer (const char question[])
{
    ...

    cin.ignore (MAX_LINE_LENGTH, '\n');
                                          //dump rest of this line

    return answer == 'Y';
}
```

EXERCISES

1. Write and test myStrcpy, your own version of the strcpy function described in Table 14-1. (There is an answer later in this chapter.) To ensure it really is putting the '\0' at the end, let the destination array be filled with all X's (say) before you do the copy.
2. Write and test your version of strcat.
3. ...and strcmp.
4. Ask the user his/her name, and repeat it back. If the first letter is lowercase, capitalize it.
5. (Uses file I/O) Determine the average length of lines in a given file.
6. (Uses file I/O) Write a program which finds and prints words in common between two given files. Assume each word appears at most once in a file.

Dynamic allocation of arrays

Sometimes you don't know till the program runs how big an array should be. But this won't work:

```
int size;
//calculate size somehow
int A[size];//compiler will complain: size must be literal or const or enum
```

Here's what to do instead.

First, declare the array without allocating memory for its elements:

```
int* A;
```

A is not an int but an address of ("pointer to") ints, same as when we declared it with [ ]'s, only without storage for those ints yet.

Next, give it the memory it needs:

```
A = new int [size];
```

This asks part of C++, the "heap manager," to give us a chunk of that many ints. There's a whole heap o' memory available just for this, and the heap manager can give you chunks of it whenever you need. This is called "dynamic allocation" because it happens while the program is running. The way we've been doing it so far, with allocation at compile time, is "static allocation." (Memory allocated in these ways is called "dynamic" or "static.")

We use the array just as we would before. When done, we tell the heap manager it can have it back, thus:

```
delete [] myArray;
```

[ ] is a reminder to the heap manager that what you're throwing back is an array. If you forget the [ ], alas, the compiler won't tell you you screwed up – you have to remember yourself.

In summation: to "dynamically allocate" an array of any <type>:

1. <type>* myArray = new <type> [size];.
2. Use the array as you normally would.
3. delete [] myArray; when you're done.

It's easy to forget to `delete []`. Does it matter? Sure: if you keep allocating memory and never handing it back – if you keep doing a **"memory leak"** – the memory eventually runs out and the program crashes. Later we'll have a way of making deleting easier to remember.

Extra In 1992 Edmund Durfee, an artificial intelligence researcher, gave an invited talk to the National Conference on Artificial Intelligence (AAAI-92): "What Your Computer Needs to Know, You Learned in Kindergarten" – referencing the popular book *All I Really Need to Know I Learned in Kindergarten* by Robert Fulghum. Here's what Durfee said your computer needs from your early childhood education:

- Share everything.
- Play fair.
- Don't hit people.
- Put things back where you found them.
- Clean up your own mess.
- Don't take things that aren't yours.
- Say you're sorry when you hurt someone.
- Flush.
- When you go out into the world, watch for traffic, hold hands, and stick together.
- Eventually, everything dies.

Many of these are useful in operating systems. Maybe you have a program that hogs memory and CPU time, so that if you want to interact with a different program, you can't. (Share everything.) Or maybe it can only run if it takes up the whole screen. (Play fair.)

In the case of memory, we need with "Put things back where you found them." Just like with crayons and toys, it'll be easier to find what we need if we always put it back.

Example 14-3 shows how to use dynamic allocation.

Example 14-3. A program that dynamically allocates, uses, and deletes an array of `int`s

```
//Program to generate a random passcode of digits
//          -- from _C++ for Lazy Programmers_

#include <iostream>
#include <cstdlib> //for srand, rand
#include <ctime>   //for time

using namespace std;

int main ()
{
    srand ((unsigned int) time(nullptr));//start random # generator

    int codeLength;                       //get code length
    cout<< "I'll make your secret passcode. How long should it be? ";
    cin >> codeLength;

    int* passcode = new int[codeLength]; //allocate array

    for (int i = 0; i <codeLength; ++i)  //generate passcode
        passcode[i] = rand () % 10;      // each entry is a digit

    cout << "Here it is:\n";             //print passcode
    for (int i = 0; i < codeLength; ++i)
        cout << passcode[i];
    cout << '\n';
    cout << "But I guess it's not secret any more!\n";

    delete [] passcode;                  //deallocate array

    return 0;
}
```

Antibugging

The most common problem with dynamic memory is a program crash. What might cause it?

- **Forgetting to initialize.** If you haven't initialized `myArray`, its address points to some random location. It will almost certainly crash. Which is better than getting wrong output and not knowing it.

  Two ways to prevent this:

  ```
  int* A = new myArray[size];
                              //initialize as soon as you declare
  ```

  or

  ```
  int* A = nullptr;
                  //we'll initialize to something sensible later
  ```

  By convention, `nullptr` means "pointing nowhere, so don't even think about looking at any elements."

  In older programs it's not `nullptr` but `NULL`.

- **Forgetting to delete.** Do this long enough and the program will run out of memory and crash.

- **Forgetting to use the `[]` in `delete []`.** This causes "undefined behavior," which means it might crash, behave perfectly, or start World War III. I wouldn't risk it.

Other problems:

- **Incorrectly declaring multiple pointers on one line.** It's strange, but `int* myArray1, myArray2;` *doesn't* create two arrays. It creates an `int` array `myArray1` and another (single) `int myArray2`. Why so confusing? This is something left over from the C standard. Solution:

  ```
  int* myArray1;
  int* myArray2;
  ```

- **Using dynamic memory when you don't have to.** This isn't an error, but it leads to errors. Dynamic memory has more that can go wrong: you must remember to allocate with `new []` and deallocate with `delete []`. If you don't gain anything (say, if you know at compile time how big your array is), save yourself some work: allocate things the old way.

EXERCISES

1. Ask the user his/her name. You'll need a buffer long enough to store any reasonable name. Then store it in an array that's exactly long enough.

2. Ask the user how many stars to draw; generate an array of random stars; draw them. Use functions as needed.

3. (Uses file I/O) Write a program which first counts the lines in a file (see Exercise 5 in the previous section), dynamically allocates an array to store those lines, and reads them all in. Hint: you can open the file, count the lines, close it, then open again.

4. (Harder) Dynamically allocate a game board, like a chessboard but of variable size. I can't just allocate a 2D array, so we'll have to make do with a 1D array. Decide on its size and how to access the rowth, clmth location.

5. (Uses SSDL. Hard) Write your own bitmap: a dynamically allocated array, each of which contains the color of a pixel in the image. As in the previous exercise, we'll need to use a 1D array.

   Provide a render function: given the bitmap, a starting location on the screen, and the bitmap's width and height, display the bitmap at that location. To draw a pixel use `SSDL_SetRenderDrawColor` and `SSDL_RenderDrawPoint`.

   Would it be a good idea for bitmap to be a `struct`, containing the array plus width and height?

Using the * notation

We already use * to declare dynamically allocated arrays:

```
double* myArray = new double[sizeOfArray];
```

We can also use it to refer to individual elements. *A means A[0], because *A means "what A points to," and A points to the 0th element.

*(A+1) means A[1]. The compiler is smart enough to know that A+1 means the address of the next element. (Adding something to a pointer like this is called "pointer arithmetic.")

A[1] is easier to read than *(A+1) – so why do this new notation? One reason is to get you ready for what we'll be doing later with *.

Another is this interesting new way to traverse an array. Consider the myStrcpy function from Exercise 1 in the first section of this chapter.

```
void myStrcpy (char destination [], const char source[])
{
    int i = 0;

    while (source[i] != '\0')
    {
        destination[i] = source[i];
        ++i;
    }

    destination[i] = '\0'; //put that null character at the end
}
```

Here's a version that doesn't use [ ]'s.

```
void myStrcpy (char* destination, const char* source)
{
    int i = 0;

    while (*(source + i) != '\0')
    {
        *(destination + i) = *(source+i);
        ++i;
    }

    *(destination+i) = '\0'; //put null character at the end
}
```

Not clearly better, but it will work. Next we eliminate the use of i, and just update source and destination directly:

```
void myStrcpy (char* destination, const char* source)
{
    while (*source != '\0')
    {
        *destination = *source;
        ++source; ++destination;
    }

    *destination = '\0'; //put null character at the end
}
```

Will it work? Yes. Now we're adding 1 to source each time we go through the loop – so each time, it points to its next element. (Same for destination.) When source reaches the null character, the loop stops.

Remember that when testing conditions, 0 means false and everything else means true (Chapter 4). So while (*source != '\0') can be written as

```
while (*source) //if *source is nonzero -- "true" -- we continue
```

We can therefore write the function as

```
void myStrcpy (char* destination, const char* source)
{
    while (*source)
    {
        *destination = *source;
        ++source; ++destination;
    }

    *destination = '\0'; //put null character at the end
}
```

This is where I really should stop. It's readable when you get used to it, and it's short. But this is too much fun to quit now.

Recall the post-increment operator (as in X++) from Chapter 5. Y=X++; really means Y=X; X=X+1;. Get the value, then increment.

We can use it here for both destination and source – because we use their values to do assignment, then increment.

```
void myStrcpy (char* destination, const char* source)
{
    while (*source)
        *destination++ = *source++;

    *destination = '\0'; //put null character at the end
}
```

Also recall that the value of X=Y is whatever value was assigned – which in the case of `*destination++ = *source++` is simply `*source`. We want to continue as long as this is nonzero.

```
void myStrcpy (char* destination, const char* source)
{
    while (*destination++ = *source++); *destination = '\0';
}
```

This borders on evil and rude. I wouldn't want to write my code like this, but it *does* show the flexibility we get by using `*`.

Note * is called the "dereference" operator – since it takes a reference (address) of a thing and gives you the thing itself.

& is its opposite: the "reference" operator. It takes an object and gives you the address:

```
int  x;
int* addressOfX = &x;
```

I don't often use it in C++; it's more useful in C, which lacks our reference parameters. Which uses the symbol & as well. Which makes life more confusing. Ah, well. If * can mean dereference (`*addressOfX`) *and* multiply (x*y), I'd suppose & can mean more than one thing too.

Antibugging

- **The compiler gripes that you're initializing a** `char*` **with a string constant**, as in `char* str = "some string";`.

  Say `char str[] = "some string";` instead.

EXERCISES

In all these exercises, use * notation – no [ ]'s:

1. Write `strcmp`.
2. ...and do the same for our other basic character array functions.
3. Write and test a function `contains` which tells if one character string contains another. For example,

   ```
   contains ("'Twas brilling, and the slithy toves"
             " did gyre and gimble in the wabe",
             "slithy")
   ```

   would return true.
4. (Harder) Write a function `myStrtok` which, like the `strtok` in `cstring`, gets the next word ("token") in a character array. It might be called thus:

   ```
   char myString[] = "Mary Mary\nQuite contrary";
   const char* nextWord = myStrtok (myString, " \t\n\r");
                          //I use space, tab, return, and
                          //the less-used carriage return \r
                          //as "delimiters": separators
                          //between words
   while (nextWord)
   {
       cout << "Token:\t" << nextWord << '\n';
       nextWord = myStrtok (nullptr, " \t\n\r");
   }
   Expected output:
   Token:    Mary
   Token:    Mary
   ```

```
Token:    Quite
Token:    contrary
```

When you call it the first time for a given string, it should return a pointer to the first word. (If there isn't one, it returns `nullptr`.) Then, every time you pass in `nullptr`, it gives you the next word in the string you used earlier – returning `nullptr` when it runs out.

You'll want the `contains` function from the previous exercise. You'll also need a `static` local variable.

Just as with the compiler's `strtok`, you get to mangle the input string as you like. The usual way is to put `'\0'`, overwriting a whitespace character, wherever you want the currently returned token to end.

CHAPTER 15

Classes

Till now what we've covered has been essentially C with a few tweaks, notably `cin` and `cout`. Now it's time to add the thing that puts the + in C++: classes.

Writing classes

Here's a class type to store a calendar date.

```
class Date
{
      int days_;
      int months_;
      int years_;
};
...
Date arrival;//Variables of a class type are called "objects"
             //Using the term makes you sound smart at job interviews
```

We could have done that with a `struct`. As with `struct`s, we can declare variables of this type, pass them as parameters, get at the parts with "`.`", and so on – it looks much the same. But we're about to get new ways to reuse code and avoid errors.

The first way: I don't want `day_`, `month_`, and `year_` available to just any part of the program; they might get messed up. I'll have certain functions are allowed to access them, called **member functions**.

The object metaphor: private data, and member functions to access it. Consider objects in the physical world. An object – say, a rubber ball – has characteristics: maybe it's red, bouncy, has a certain mass and composition. You can't just set those characteristics to whatever you want when you want – can you set the color field on a real ball to be blue? Tell it to be light as a feather? Instead, the object itself affords ways you can interact with it.

W. Briggs, *C++ for Lazy Programmers*, https://doi.org/10.1007/978-1-4842-5187-4_15

You can't set the color field, but you can paint it. You can't change its mass directly, but you can do things that would alter the mass, like chopping it or burning it. You can't set its position to 90 kilometers straight up, but you can throw it and see how far it goes.

We'll make our classes the same way: with characteristics, and methods we decide are appropriate for interacting with those characteristics.

This is meant as a natural way of thinking about variables of class types: **objects**. (Thus the term "object-oriented.")

So what's something appropriate to do with a Date? For one thing, you can print it (Example 15-1).

Example 15-1. The Date class: a simple version

```
class Date
{
public:
      void print (ostream&);[1]

private:
      int days_;
      int months_;
      int years_;
};
...
Date arrival;
...
arrival.print (cout);
```

The public section is for things the outside world (such as main) can access: that is, main can tell a Date to print itself. The private section is for parts that only Date can access directly. (If you don't specify, it's all private – but it's good practice to specify.)[2]

[1]It's ostream&, not ostream, because the designers of iostream disabled copying of ostreams, presumably on the grounds that it makes no sense. If you forget, the compiler will remind you.

[2]And that's the only difference between a struct and a class: if you don't specify (which we always do, for classes), class members are private and struct members are public. But programmers usually use struct for small, simple groupings without member functions and with everything public. That's because structs existed in C before classes were invented, and that's how C uses them.

BNF for a class is roughly

```
class <name>
{
public:
  <function prototypes, variables, and types;
  usually prototypes, almost never variables>
private:
  <function prototypes, variables, types; usually variables>
};
```

Look at the print call in Example 15-1. Why aren't we telling arrival about day, month, and year? It already knows – it contains them! It doesn't know whether we want to print to cout or a file, so we do have to tell it that.

I didn't say *how* to print yet. Here's how.

```
void Date::print (std::ostream& out)
{
      out << days_ << '-' << months_ << '-' << years_;
}
```

The "Date::" tells the compiler, "This isn't just any function named print – it's the one belonging to Date."

When you call it

```
arrival.print (cout);
```

...whose days_ will it print? arrival's.

If you're using a truly programmer-friendly editor (I definitely include Microsoft Visual Studio's), you'll notice when you type in appointment: the editor lists available member functions (see Figure 15-1) – so far, just print, but we'll soon have more. You can click one and it'll paste it in for you. Add the opening paren and it'll remind you what kind of arguments it expects.

Same for Date::. It'll list available members.

If it doesn't, don't worry: sometimes the editor gets confused.

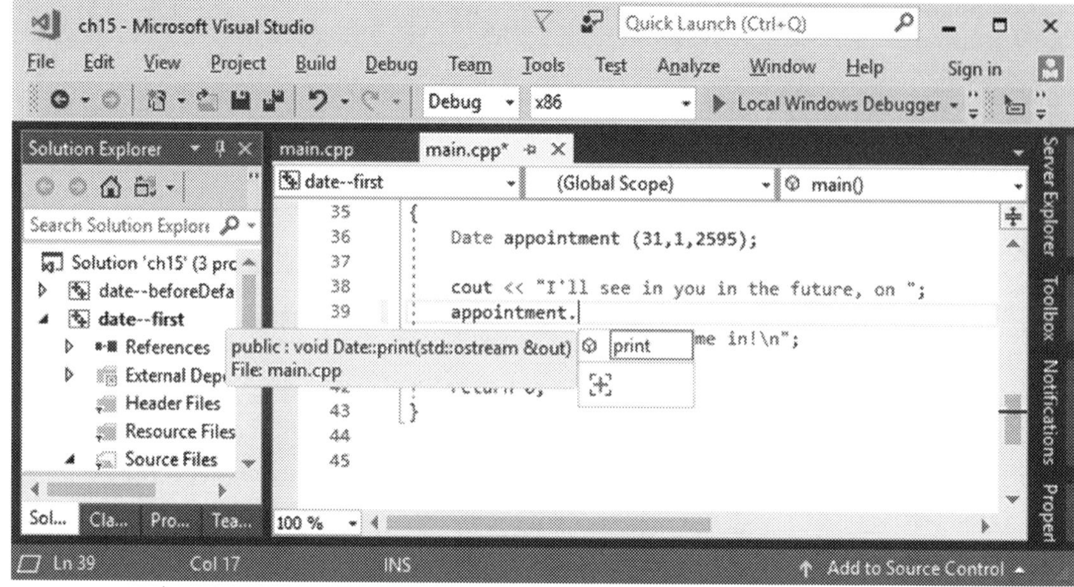

Figure 15-1. *Microsoft Visual Studio IntelliSense prompting with function prototype information*

Constructors

We already know it's wise to initialize variables. In classes, we have a special type of function called a **constructor** ("ctor," in a common abbreviation) which does this (see Example 15-2).

Example 15-2. The Date class and a program to use it

```
//A program to print an appointment time, and demo the Date class
// ...doesn't do that much (yet)
//  -- from _C++ for Lazy Programmers_

#include <iostream>

using namespace std;

class Date
{
public:
    Date (int theDays, int theMonths, int theYears); //ctor

    void print (std::ostream& out);
```

```
private:
    int days_;
    int months_;
    int years_;
};

Date::Date (int theDays, int theMonths, int theYears) :
    days_ (theDays), months_ (theMonths), years_ (theYears)
    //theDays is the parameter passed into the Date constructor
    //  function.  days_ is the member that it will initialize.
{
}

void Date::print (std::ostream& out)
{
    out << days_ << '-' << months_ << '-' << years_;
}

int main ()
{
    Date appointment (31,1,2595);³

    cout << "I'll see in you in the future, on ";
    appointment.print (cout);
    cout << " . . . pencil me in!\n";

    return 0;
}
```

The constructor's name is always same as its class. When you declare a variable of class `Date`, it calls this function to initialize member variables. (There is no return type; essentially a constructor "returns" the object itself.)

The second line of the function – `days_ (theDays), months_ (theMonths), years_ (theYears)` – tells it to initialize `days_` to be equal to `theDays` and so on. By the time we reach the `{}`'s, there's nothing left to do, so the `{}`'s are empty this time.

[3]You can also use {} notation: Date appointment = {2595,1,31};. It calls the same ctor.

You could instead initialize in the body of the function, using =:

```
Date::Date (int theDays, int theMonths, int theYears)
{
    days_ = theDays; months_ = theMonths; years_ = theYears;
}
```

but the member initialization syntax with the ()'s is more common, is less error-prone (see the Antibugging section), and is necessary in some situations, so it's lazier to get in the habit now.

To visualize how member functions interact with data members, consider this diagram of what happens in Example 15-2. main's first action is to allocate space for appointment and call its constructor (Figure 15-2), passing in arguments. I draw the constructor outside main, because it *is* a separate function...but it's part of appointment, so I'll unify it and the data members with the dashed line.

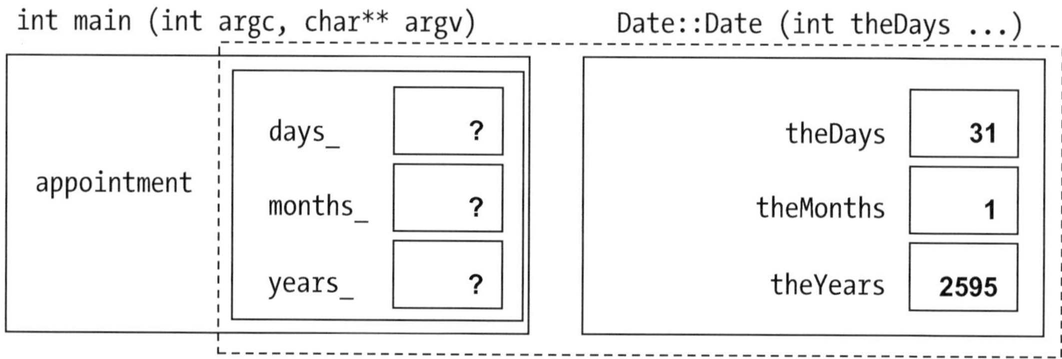

***Figure 15-2.** Calling the Date constructor*

The constructor copies theDays into days_, theMonths into months_, and theYears into years_ (Figure 15-3).

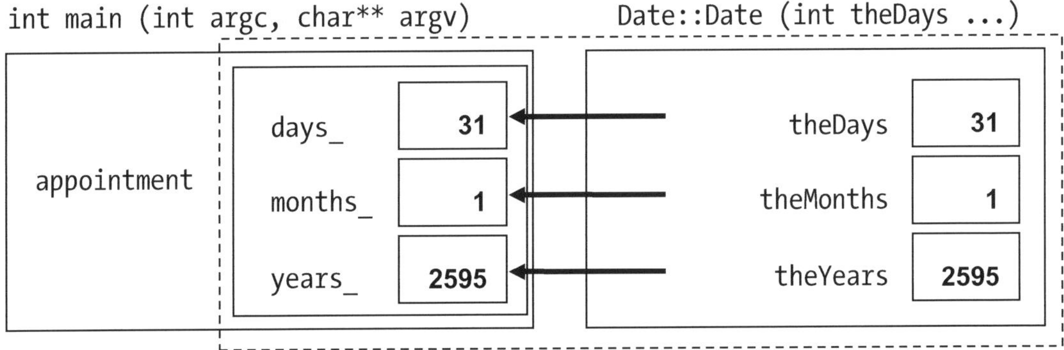

***Figure 15-3.** The `Date` constructor initializes `appointment's` data members*

When done, the constructor goes away (Figure 15-4).

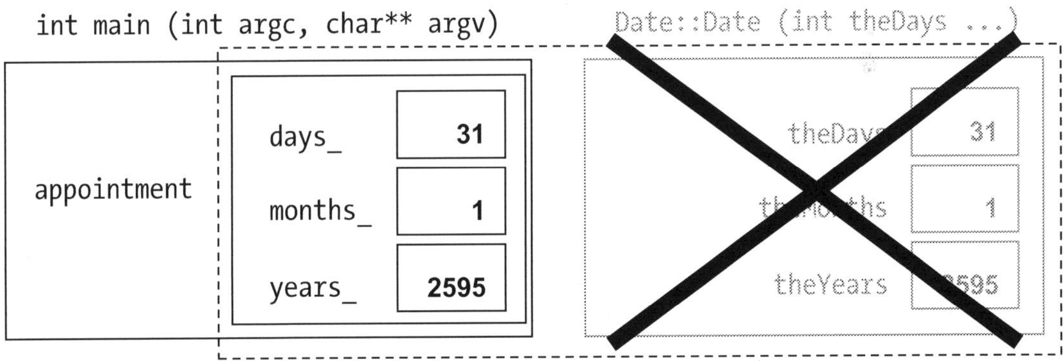

***Figure 15-4.** The `Date` constructor is finished*

This shows the different roles of (for example) member `days_` and constructor parameter `theDays`: `days_` is persistent, and remembers the day component of your appointment; `theDays` is a parameter `Date::Date` uses to channel information from `main` into `days_`, and goes away when `Date::Date` is done.

After this, `main` continues, printing `"I'll be getting up at "`, then enters `appointment`'s `print` function, which knows all about `days_`, `months_`, and `years_` (Figure 15-5).

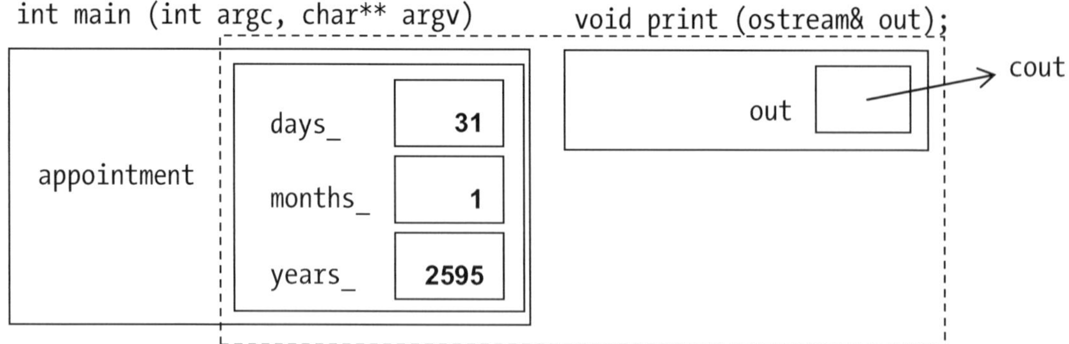

Figure 15-5. *Calling* `appointment's` `print` *function*

Golden Rule of Member Function Parameters Don't pass in the object's data members. The function already knows them.

Antibugging

- **The constructor is called, but data members never get initialized.** If we use this constructor

  ```
  Date::Date (int theDays, int theMonths, int theYears)
  {
      theDays     = days_;
      theMonths   = months_;
      theYears    = years_;
  }
  ```

  we'll get bizarre output, maybe

  ```
  I'll see in you in the future, on -858993460--858993460--
  858993460 · · · pencil me in!
  ```

  I have `days_` and `theDays` swapped, so I'm copying *from* the data member I wanted initialized (which apparently had -858993460 in it – with uninitialized variables, you never know) *to* the parameter that had the value I wanted (Figure 15-6).

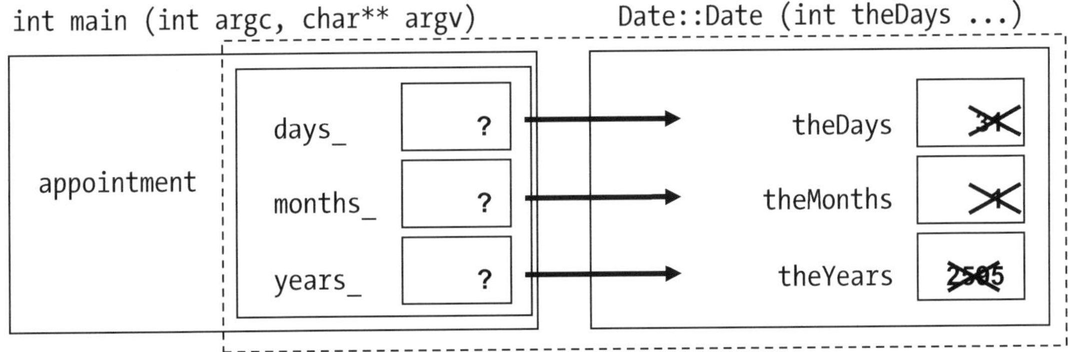

Figure 15-6. *A constructor that has it all backward*

This can't happen if you use the initialization method with ()'s before the {. It will report an error if you try to initialize the wrong thing.

```
Date::Date (int theDays, int theMonths, int theYears) :
    days_ (theDays), months_ (theMonths), years_ (theYears)...
```

EXERCISES

1. Write a `Time` class for remembering when to get up in the morning, when to nap, and so on. Include relevant data members, a print function, and an appropriate constructor.
2. Write and test a function `Time currentTime()`. It will call `time` (just as we do when initializing the random number generator), getting the number of seconds since January 1, 1970. We only care about the number of seconds since midnight. Convert that to seconds, minutes, and hours, and return the current `Time`. It is *not* a member of `Time`.
3. Augment the `Date` program with a function `Date currentDate ()` which calls `time`, as in the previous problem, and gets the current `Date`. The function is *not* a member of `Date`. Is my earlier assumption that time starts at January 1, 1970, correct on your machine?

4. (Harder) Add a function `Date::totalDays ()` which returns the number of days in the date since December 31, 1 BC. You'll need to handle leap years. A solution is in the book's sample code.

5. (Harder) Add a function `Date::normalize ()` which corrects if the `Date` has one or more fields out of range: for example, `Date tooFar (32, 12, 1999);` would make `tooFar` be the date 1-1-2000. It should be called by the ctor. A solution is in the book's sample code.

   Is there an easier way to write `normalize` and `totalDays`?

const objects, const member functions…

Consider this code.

```
const Date PEARL_HARBOR_DAY (7, 12, 1941);

cout << "A date which will shall live in infamy is ";
PEARL_HARBOR_DAY.print (cout);
cout << ".\n";
```

It's reasonable to consider `PEARL_HARBOR_DAY` a constant, since it can never change. (Unless you have a working time machine.) However, if we make it `const` the code will no longer compile. Why not?

C++ distinguishes member functions that can alter the object from those that can't. This is a way of preventing errors. If `print` is the sort of thing that can alter a `Date`, we shouldn't allow it to be called on a constant `Date`.

Since `print` *is* safe for `const` objects, we'll tell C++ thus:

```
class Date
{
    ...
    void print (std::ostream&) const;
    ...
};
```

```
void Date::print (std::ostream& out) const
{
      out << days_ << '-' << months_ << '-' << years_;
}
```

The word `const` after the `()`'s tells the compiler: this function is OK for constant objects. It also tells the compiler, when compiling `print`, to generate an error if any changes are made to data members.

It's sometimes tempting, if you get a lot of errors, to strip out the word `const` from your program entirely. It isn't a good idea. This feature does protect us from genuine errors.

Antibugging

- **You get errors about converting something from** `const`. Often this means you forgot a `const` at the end of a member function prototype (and the top line of its function body too).
- **It says your member function body doesn't match the prototype, but they sure look the same.** Check that they're both `const` or neither is.

...and `const` parameters

Suppose we want to pass a `Date` to a function `fancyDisplay`, which prints the time in some cute way.

```
void fancyDisplay (Date myDate, ostream& out)
{
      cout << "*************\n";
      cout << "* "; myDate.print (out); cout << " *\n";
      cout << "*************\n";
}
```

I didn't use `&` for `myDate`, so `myDate` itself isn't passed in, but a copy.

In a way, this is fine, because we don't want to alter `myDate`. But copying costs more than it did for a mere `int` – three times more, as it has three `int`s. As we create bigger classes, we may find it slows down our programs.

Here's a partial fix:

```
void fancyDisplay (Date& myDate, ostream& out);
```

This isn't perfect, because now we allow `fancyDisplay` to alter `myDate`! One more thing is needed.

```
void fancyDisplay (const Date& myDate, ostream& out);
```

Now `fancyDisplay` won't take the time to copy `myDate`, *and* can't alter it.

Golden Rule of Objects as Function Parameters If you want to change an object passed in as a parameter, pass it as `TheClass& object`.

If you don't, pass it as `const TheClass& object`.

Multiple constructors

There's no need to limit ourselves to one constructor. We may want other ways to create `Date`s:

```
Date d (21, 12, 2000);          //using our old ctor...
Date e (d);                     //e is now exactly the same as d
Date f;                         //now one with no arguments
Date dateArray [MAX_DATES];     //still no arguments
Date g (22000);                 //22,000 days -- nearly a lifetime
```

Let's take them one by one.

Copy constructors

`Date`'s copy constructor is the one that has as its sole argument another `Date`. We call it this because it makes a copy (duh).

```
Date::Date (const Date& other) :                    //"copy" ctor
    days_(other.days_), months_(other.months_), years_(other.years_)
{
}
```

This declaration uses it

```
Date e (d);
```

as does this:

```
Date e = d; //Looks like =, but it's really calling the copy ctor
```

The = form is called "syntactic sugar": something not really necessary that makes code more readable.

There's something else special about the copy constructor. If ever C++ needs to make a copy of a `Date`, it will call it **implicit**ly, that is, without you telling it to. Two examples:

```
void doSomethingWithDate (Date willBeCopied);
                              //I'd rarely do this, but if I did...
Date currentDate (); //No &, so it returns a copy
```

What if you don't write a copy constructor? C++ will make its best guess of how to copy, and that guess is sometimes dangerously wrong. A good rule: *always specify the copy constructor.*

Default constructors

```
Date::Date () :                               //"default" ctor
      days_ (1), months_ (1), years_ (1)      //default is Jan 1, 1 AD
{
}

...

Date f;
Date dateArray[MAX_DATES];
```

If you don't know how to initialize your Date, you tell it nothing, and it uses its **default constructor**: the one that takes no arguments. We also do this with arrays. So we always write the default constructor.

Tip When declaring an array of a class type, C++ uses the default constructor.[4]

Conversion constructors

This constructor call Date g (22000); needs Date to convert these way too many days to a more conventional day, month, year arrangement. I'll use function normalize from Exercise 5 earlier: if we give it 22,000 days, it'll convert that to 26 days, 3 months, and 61 years.

```
Date::Date (int totalDays) :              //conversion ctor from int
      days_ (totalDays), months_ (1), years_ (1)
{
      normalize ();
}
```

The normalize function, called by this and any ctor that needs it, should go in the private section. Date functions will call it when needed, so nobody else has to.[5]

A constructor with exactly one argument (not a Date) is called a **conversion constructor**, because it converts from some other type (like int) to the class we're writing.

You can also call it like this: Date g = 22000;.

Like with the copy constructor, if ever C++ needs a Date but you gave it an int, it will call this implicitly. Suppose you call void fancyDisplay (const Date& myDate, ostream& out); but pass in an int: fancyDisplay (22000, cout);. C++ will convert 22000 to a Date and fancyDisplay that Date. Nice!

---

[4]Unless you use {}'s, as in Date myDates[] = {{31,1,2595},{1,2,2595}};. But that's a lot of work.

[5]Functions in the private section are called "utility" functions since they perform tasks useful to the other, public functions. We don't really need the term, but using it makes me sound smart so of course I use it.

Summary

It is the responsibility of each constructor to make sure the data members are in some acceptable state. Unfortunately, C++'s basic types let you declare *them* without initialization. But we can construct our classes so C++ initializes all data members.

Because of the issues mentioned earlier, I recommend this guideline:

Golden Rule of Constructors Always specify default and copy constructors.

Antibugging

- **You declared an object, using the default constructor, but it doesn't recognize it.**

  ```
  Date z ();
  z.print (); //Error message says z is a Date() (?)
              //or at least isn't of a class type
  ```

  Using the ()'s made the compiler think you were declaring a prototype for a function `z` that returns `Date`. I mean, how could it tell that's not what was meant?

  The solution is to ditch the parens: `Date z;`.

- **"Illegal copy constructor" or "invalid constructor"** with this copy constructor prototype: `Date (Date other);`.

  Suppose the compiler let you call this function. Since there's no `&`, the first thing it would do is make a copy of `other`. How? By calling the copy constructor. Which means it has to make a copy of `other`. Which means it calls the copy constructor. And so on till you're out of memory.

  This is **accidental recursion**, that is, a function calling itself when you didn't intend it to. Good thing the compiler (Visual Studio or g++) catches the problem. Solution: use a `const &` parameter.

Default parameters for code reuse

We can save more work by telling C++ that if we don't give arguments to some of our functions, it should appropriately fill them in.

For example, I'm tired of specifying the `cout` in `myDate.print (cout);`. Isn't it usually `cout`? But I don't want to hard-code `cout` into the function, because I may later want to print to a file.

So I change the prototype:

```
void print (ostream& out = cout) const;
```

Now I can just say `myDate.print();`, and the compiler will think, "He didn't say, so he must want `cout`."

I have a constructor that takes three `int`s, one that takes one, and one that takes nothing. If I use defaults, I can combine these into one function:

```
class Date
{
public:
      Date (int theDays=1, int theMonths=1, int theYears=1);
            //Defaults go in the prototype
      ...
};

...

Date::Date (int theDays, int theMonths, int theYears) :
      days_ (theDays), months_ (theMonths), years_ (theYears)
{
      normalize ();
}
```

Now I can call it with zero to three arguments:

```
Date Jan1_1AD;
Date convertedFromDays   (22000);
const Date CINCO_DE_MAYO (5, 5);
Date doomsday            (21, 12, 2012); //Well, that didn't happen
```

I can do all the things I did with constructors I had before, but only have to write one constructor; and I got a new one free, that takes day and month.

This works for non-member functions too:

```
void printRatio (int divisor, int dividend, int base=10);
```

If some parameters have defaults and some don't, those with defaults go last. The compiler doesn't want to be confused about which arguments you intend to omit.

Date program (so far)

Here's what we have (Example 15-3). `fancyDisplay` now has a default parameter for `cout`.

I also added an enumeration type `Month` and prototypes for `isLeapYear` and two other functions. They relate to dates, but they're not members of `Date`.

I can make `Month` a member...but to refer to (say) `JUNE` I must write `Date::JUNE`, which is clunky.

It doesn't make sense for `isLeapYear` to be a member of `Date`. It doesn't need access to `Date`'s data members `days_`, `months_`, and `years_`. But especially, it's not something you do to a `Date`, but something you do to a year, which is an `int`. It belongs *with* `Date`, but it's not an aspect of `Date`, so I don't make it a member.

Example 15-3. Another program using the `Date` class

```
//A program to print an appointment time, and demonstrate the Date class
// ...doesn't do that much (yet)
//  -- from _C++ for Lazy Programmers_

#include <iostream>

using namespace std;

enum Month {JANUARY=1, FEBRUARY, MARCH, APRIL, MAY, JUNE,
            JULY, AUGUST, SEPTEMBER, OCTOBER, DECEMBER};

bool isLeapYear   (int year);
int  daysPerYear  (int year);
int  daysPerMonth (int month, int year);
```

```
                                //We have to specify year in case month
                                //  is FEBRUARY and it's a leap year
class Date
{
public:
    Date (int theDays=1, int theMonths=1, int theYears=1);
                                //Because of default parameters,
                                //  this serves as ctor taking 3 ints;
                                //  a new one taking days and months;
                                //  the conversion from int ctor;
                                //  and the default ctor

    Date (const Date&);         //copy ctor

    void print (std::ostream& out = std::cout) const;

    int totalDays   () const; //total days since Dec 31, 1 B.C.

    operator int () const { return totalDays (); }
private:
    int days_;
    int months_;
    int years_;

    void normalize  ();
};

Date::Date (int theDays, int theMonths, int theYears) :
    days_ (theDays), months_ (theMonths), years_ (theYears)
{
    normalize ();
}

Date::Date (const Date& other) :
    days_ (other.days_), months_ (other.months_),
    years_ (other.years_)
{
}
```

```
void Date::print (std::ostream& out) const
{
    out << days_ << '-' << months_ << '-' << years_;
}

//Date::totalDays and Date::normalize from earlier exercises
//  as well as isLeapYear, daysPerYear, and daysPerMonth
//  are omitted here, but they're in the book's sample code

void fancyDisplay (const Date& myDate, ostream& out = std::cout)
{
    cout << "*************\n";
    cout << "* "; myDate.print (); cout << " *\n";
    cout << "*************\n";
}

int main ()
{
    enum {MAX_DATES = 10};

    Date d (21, 12, 2000);          //using our old ctor...
    Date e = d;                     //e is now exactly the same as d
    Date f;                         //now one with no arguments
    Date dateArray [MAX_DATES];     //still no arguments
    Date g (22000);                 //22,000 days, nearly a lifetime

    cout << "This should print 26-3-61 with lots of *'s:\n";
    fancyDisplay (22000);           //tests conversion-from-int ctor

    return 0;
}
```

EXERCISES

1. Update the Time class to use what you learned in the rest of this chapter.

CHAPTER 16

Classes (Continued)

More things to make your classes work, and work well.

`inline` functions for efficiency

Consider the diagrams of what happens in function calls from Chapters 8 and 15. They show what the computer does. It creates a new copy of the function, an "activation record," containing everything the instance of the function needs, especially local variables. It copies parameters into a part of memory the function can access. It stores what it needs to know about the function it was in (the state of the registers in the CPU – if you don't know what that is, don't worry about it). Finally, it transfers control to the new function.

When done, it reverses the process: throws away the copy of the function with its variables and restores the state of the old function.

That's a lot of work on the compiler if you do it often. So what are we supposed to do? Stop using functions?

The solution is **inline** functions. An inline function is *written* as a function, behaves as a function as far as the programmer's concerned, and seems to compile as a function, but the compiler does something sneaky: it replaces the function call with a piece of code to do the same thing. Here's one way to make a function inline: just precede it with `inline`.

```
inline
void Date::print (std::ostream& out) const
{
      out << days_ << '-' << months_ << '-' << years_;
}
```


W. Briggs, *C++ for Lazy Programmers*, https://doi.org/10.1007/978-1-4842-5187-4_16

When you write this

```
d.print (cout);
```

the compiler treats it as though you'd said

```
cout << d.days_ << '-' << d.months_ << '-' << d.years_;
      //but there's no problem with these members being private
```

thus saving the overhead of the function call.

If a function is big enough, the time overhead isn't significant compared to time spent in the function itself. But `inline` introduces a new overhead: multiple copies of a big function expanded inline would take up a lot of memory. Here's how to know whether you should make a function inline.

Golden Rule of `inline`

A function should be inline if it

- Fits on a single line
- Contains no loops (for, while, or do-while)

`inline` is actually a *suggestion* to the compiler, not a command. The compiler will overrule you if it thinks the function shouldn't be inline. Fine by me: in this case, compiler knows best.

Here's a quick, easy way to make *member* functions inline: put the whole thing inside the class definition.

```
class Date
{
    ...

      void print (ostream& out) const
           //inline, because it's inside the class definition
      {
            out << days_ << '-' << months_ << '-' << years_;
      }

      ...
};
```

Access functions

Sometimes we want the rest of the world to be able to *see* our data members, but not alter them. It's like with a clock: you have to set it through appropriate controls (member functions), but you can *see* the time whenever you like.

This is how it's done:

```
class Date
{
public:
      ...

      //Access functions
      int days      () const { return days_;   }
      int months    () const { return months_; }
      int years     () const { return years_;  }
};
```

The way to call them is the same as with `print`: use a `.`:

```
cout << "It's been " << myDate.days ()
    << " days since I had fry bread!\n";
```

It's a good idea to use access functions when not changing data members, *even inside member functions*. Suppose I decide to dump `days_`, `months_`, and `years_` and have just one data member `totalDays_`, from which member functions can calculate days, months, and years, as needed. A function referring to `days_` will have to be rewritten! but not if it refers instead to `days()`, which will still exist.

And this is why we use underbars after data member names: `days_` and so on. It's why I used the funny names `theDays`, `theMonths`, and so on as parameters to the first ctor I wrote. If I did this:

```
class Date
{
public:
    Date(int days, int months, int years) :
        days(days),months(months),years(years)
    {
    }
```

```
    int days() const { return days; }
    ....
private:
    int days, months, years;
};
```

I'd have so many things named days I'd never sort them out![1] Nor would the compiler. The names need to be distinct.

Separate compilation and include files

By now our programs are long enough we should break them into multiple files. Here are good general rules for how:

- Let every class have its own file.
- Let every set of clearly related functions share a file. For example, if you were writing the trigonometric functions sine, cosine, tangent, and so on, you could put them together.
- Let main have its own file, possibly shared with functions called by main that would not be useful to other programs. If you're writing a program for poker, say, functions related to bidding might go in the file with main (since only poker does poker-style bidding), but functions related to shuffling and dealing a deck would go elsewhere (since many games involve decks).

In terms of getting it all to work, though, there's a problem. This new file will need to know certain things (such as the class definition!) – and so will main. This information needs to be shared.

Fortunately, we already know how to do this: include files.

[1]Or I could have a data member days and an access function getDays (); some use that convention. But I find myDate.getDays() harder to read than myDate.days().

What happens in separate compilation

Suppose you create these files: `myclass.h` ("h" as in "header"), containing the class definition; `myclass.cpp`, containing the member functions; and `main.cpp`, containing the main program. (I give the `.h` and `.cpp` files the same name as the class, in lowercase. Conventions vary; be consistent.) You include it like so:

```
#include "myclass.h" //<-- Use "" not <>; and let the file end in .h
```

Here are the stages the compiler goes through to build a program.

First, it **compiles** the C++ source files you created (Figure 16-1). When it encounters an `#include` directive, it stops reading the source file, reads the `.h` file you included, then goes back to the source file.

The compiler produces for each source file an "object" file in machine language.

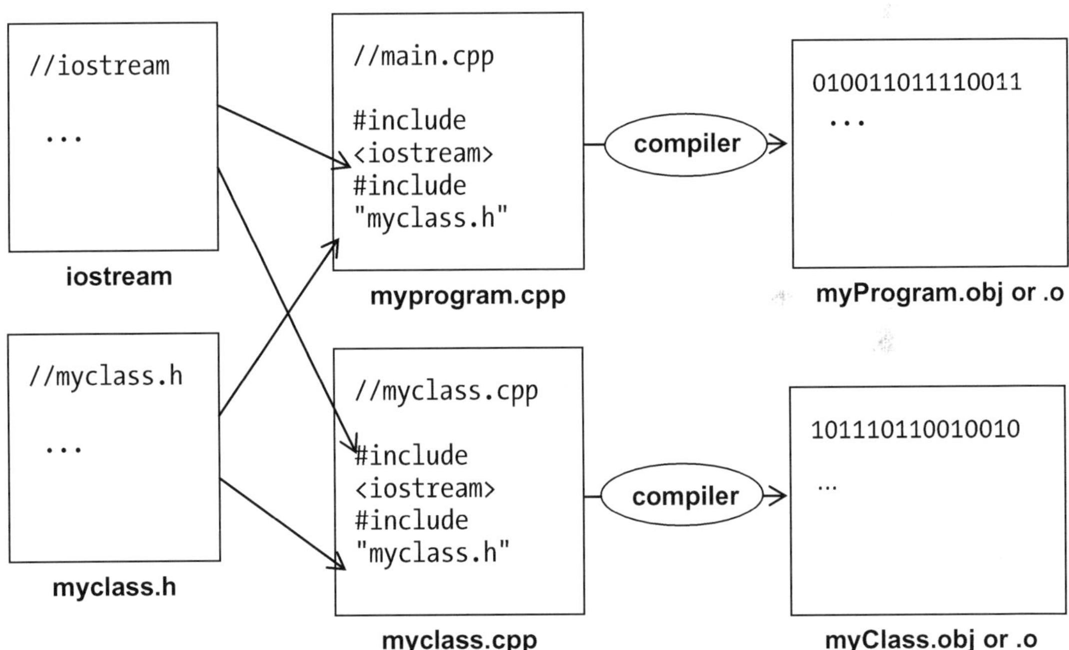

***Figure 16-1.** The compile stage of building a program*

If there are no errors, the compiler is ready to **link** (Figure 16-2). The object files know how to do what they do, but they don't know where to find function references, either from each other or from system libraries. The link stage "links" these files together by resolving the references and produces an executable file. The executable will end in `.exe` if you're using Visual Studio; Unix and MinGW are flexible.

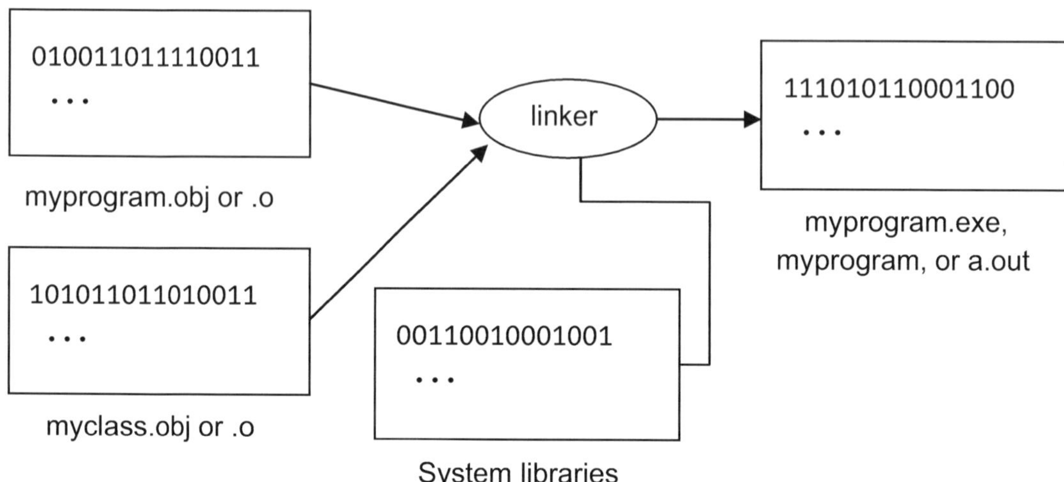

Figure 16-2. *The link stage in building a program*

Seeing this process enables us to understand precisely what should and shouldn't go into an include file.

Writing your .h file

Here's what should be in an include file (so far):

- Types, including class definitions and enumeration types
- Function prototypes and inline functions

Here's what shouldn't:

- Functions
- `const` or variable declarations

Here's why. If you put a function (or a declaration) in an include file, it will be included into different `.cpp` files. When you compile those files, you therefore get multiple copies of the same function. If this happens, when you call the function, the compiler won't know which copy to use, and it's not smart enough to realize they're identical. You'll get an error saying it has duplicate definitions.

Including a .h file only once

Suppose that `time.h` (from earlier exercises; it defines class `Time`) is needed for a new class `Stopwatch` (Example 16-1).

Example 16-1. `stopwatch.h.`

```
//stopwatch.h: defines class Stopwatch
//  -- from _C++ for Lazy Programmers_

#include "time.h"
class Stopwatch
{
private:
    Time start_, stop_;
};
```

We'll need to `#include "time.h"` so the compiler can declare `start_` and `stop_`. Then we get to `main.cpp`:

```
//Program that uses Stopwatches and Times
//            -- from _C++ for Lazy Programmers_

#include "time.h"
#include "stopwatch.h"

int main (int argc, char** argv)
{
      Time duration;
      Stopwatch myStopwatch;
      ...
}
```

When compiling `main.cpp`:

First, the compiler includes `time.h`, which defines class `Time`.

Then it includes `stopwatch.h`. First thing *that* does is `#include "time.h"`, which defines class `Time`. *Again.* The compiler complains: duplicate definition for class `Time`!

The solution is to tell the compiler to only read a `.h` file if it hasn't already been read. There's a commonly used trick: we define something in the `.h` file; then put something around the whole file saying, only read this if that you've never heard of it (Example 16-2).

Example 16-2. time.h

```
//Time.h: defines class Time
//  -- from _C++ for Lazy Programmers_

#ifndef TIME_H //"If not defined TIME_H..."
#define TIME_H

class Time
{
    ...
};

#endif //TIME_H
```

The first time through, it's never heard of `TIME_H`, so it reads the `.h` file. This defines class Time, and also `TIME_H`.

Next time, it's heard of `TIME_H`, so it skips to the `#endif`. Class `Time` doesn't get redefined. Mission accomplished.

Avoid `using namespace std;` in include files

`using namespace std;` shouldn't be in your include file. What if someone includes your file, but didn't want the `std` namespace? Wanted to define his/her own version of some `std` function? So that you won't need the `using` declaration, preface things from the C++ standard library – notably `cin` and `cout` – with `std::`, as in `std::cin >> x;`.

Constants in include files

So what about constant declarations? They're declarations, so they mustn't go in .h files.

If the constant is an integer or character, there's no problem: use enum.

```
enum { DAYS_PER_WEEK = 7};
```

If not, you can put a reference to the constant in the .h file, but put the constant itself into a .cpp file. We might have this reference in a .h file

```
extern const char GREETING [];
```

and have the constant itself declared in the appropriate source file:

```
const char GREETING[] = "Welcome to NerdFest 1.0!\n";
```

The **extern** keyword before a declaration tells the compiler, "This variable will be declared elsewhere - you'll find out where at link time."

Backing up a multi-file project

In Unix, to back up the directory myproject, enter this command:

```
cp -R myproject myprojectBackup1
```

In Windows, copy and paste the entire folder, ignoring anything that won't copy.

Antibugging

Circular includes make a strange error. Let's alter time.h so it needs Stopwatch.

```
#include "stopwatch.h"

class Time
{
    void doSomethingWithStopwatch (const Stopwatch&);
};
```

Let's say main.cpp includes stopwatch.h. This should define STOPWATCH_H, then include time.h. The first thing *it* does is include stopwatch.h again.

Since you already defined STOPWATCH_H, it won't go into that file again. It returns to time.h, finds the reference to Stopwatch, and generates an error, because we never got to a definition of Stopwatch!

An include file can include another – but they can't include *each other*.

Some fixes:

You can rethink whether that function should be in Time at all. Should Time really depend on Stopwatch? Shouldn't it be the other way around? (That's is the best answer for this code.)

If that doesn't work…you can refer to Stopwatch in Time without knowing what it is, as long as the code doesn't need details. Tell time.h only that Stopwatch is a class:

```
class Stopwatch;

class Time
{
        void doSomethingWithStopwatch (const Stopwatch&);
};
```

Problem solved.

Next problem: what if you have lots of files and can't remember where you put one of your functions?

- **Visual Studio.** Right-click the function name. "Go to Declaration" will take you to the prototype; "Go to Definition" will take you to the function itself if it's available.
- **Unix.** Though there are packages to help with this (ggtags for emacs is one), there's no guarantee they're on your system. This command is a quick-and-dirty[2] way to find the function and all references to it: grep functionIWant *.
- **MinGW.** I use Windows Grep – look for it online – to search for the function name.

[2]Easy not elegant.

Multiple-file projects in Microsoft Visual Studio

Adding new files. Go to the Project menu and select Add New Item.

Building the project. Build ➤ Build recompiles any files that have changed since the last build and links the project. Rebuild recompiles them all.

Or just run it; it will Build, then run, as before.

Extra Now that you've got multiple source files, you may want an easier way to clean up the extra files Visual Studio creates.

In the folder with your project, use Notepad or some other editor to create a file `clean.txt`. Here's what should be in it:

```
REM Erase folders you don't want -- here's my picks
for /r . %%d in (Debug,.vs) do @if exist "%%d" rd /s/q "%%d"

REM Erase other files -- here's my picks.
REM /s means "in subfolders too"
del /s *.ncb        REM used by earlier versions (before 2010)
del /s *.sdf        REM used by earlier versions (2010-2015)
```

Save your text file and change its name from `clean.txt` to `clean.bat`. (Can't see the `.txt`? Uncheck Hide extensions for known file types – see coverage of this in Chapter 1.) Click Yes on the warning dialog box in Figure 16-3.

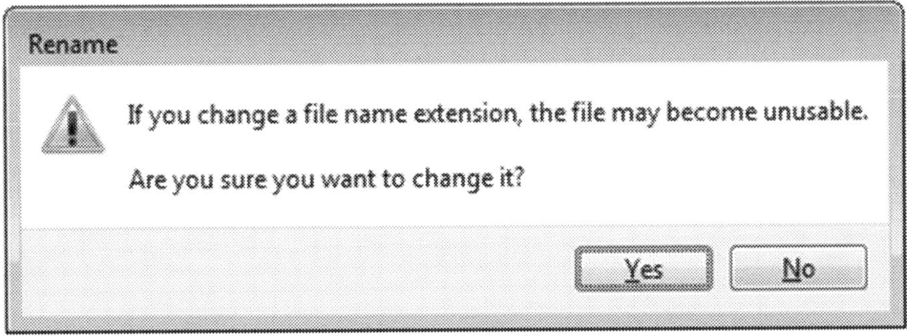

Figure 16-3. *Microsoft Windows' warning about changing a file extension*

...and get your new `clean.bat` file.

You can double-click this "batch" file – that is, a file of commands – whenever you want to erase the extra files. Be warned: `del` erases things permanently.

Multiple-file projects in g++

Command line: more typing, less thinking

You can build the program with this command:

```
g++ -g -o myprogram myprogram.cpp myclass.cpp
```

You can separate the compile and link stages:

```
g++ -g -c myprogram.cpp            //-c means "compile only -- don't link
g++ -g -c myclass.cpp
g++ -g -o myprogram myprogram.o myclass.o        //now link
```

Makefiles: more thinking, less typing

Makefiles keep track of what files in your project have changed. When you `make`, it'll only rebuild the parts it needs to. This cuts compile time. It's also nicer to type `make` than `g++ -g -o myprogram file1.cpp file2.cpp....`

Makefiles are far from easy, but they're essential for big projects, or those using lots of libraries, as we had earlier.

A simple version

Example 16-3. A simple Makefile

```
#This is a basic Makefile, producing one program from 2 source files

myprogram:  myclass.o main.o
            g++ -g -o myprogram myclass.o main.o

main.o:     main.cpp myclass.h
            g++ -g -c main.cpp
```

```
myclass.o:  myclass.cpp myclass.h
            g++ -g -c myclass.cpp

clean:
            rm -f myprogram
            rm -f *.o
```

The first line in Example 16-3 is a comment, because it starts with a #.

I'll take things out of order for simplicity. The line

```
main.o:           main.cpp myclass.h
```

says that to compile the `.o` (object) file for main, you need `main.cpp` and `myclass.h`. If either changes, `make` will rebuild `main.o`. (`make` detects changes based on modification times of the files.)

The next line, `g++ -g -c main.cpp`, is the command to compile it. If it fails, `make` stops so you can correct errors.

The lines for `myclass.o` are understood the same way.

Back to the top:

```
myprogram:  myclass.o main.o myclass.h
            g++ -g -o myprogram myclass.o main.o
```

This establishes that `myprogram` depends on `myclass.o`, `main.o`, and `myclass.h`, and tells how to create it. Since it's the first thing in the Makefile, this is what the computer tries to build when you type `make`.

`clean` is a convenient thing: if you say `make clean`, it'll erase `myprogram` and all `.o` files. The `-f` option is so it won't report an error if there aren't any, because that's not a problem.

A better version

The preceding Makefile was too much work: we had to specify each `.cpp` file and which `.h` files it depends on. We'll now create a Makefile (Example 16-4) that should work on most projects you'll encounter in the rest of this text and elsewhere.

Example 16-4. A Makefile for any project of .cpp source files – first attempt

```
# Makefile for a program with multiple .cpp files

PROG        = myprogram              #What program am I building?
SRCS        = $(wildcard *.cpp)      #What .cpp files do I have?
OBJS        = ${SRCS:.cpp=.o}        #What .o   files do I build?

$(PROG):      $(OBJS)                # Build the program
              g++ -o $@ -g $^

%.o:          %.cpp                  # Make the .o files
              g++ -g -o $@ -c $<

clean:                               # Clean up files
              rm -f $(PROG)
              rm -f *.o
```

First we define some variables. After that, we see that our program depends on the object files (as before). Note that variables take `$()` around them.

`$@` means "what is left of the `:` above?" and `$^` means "what's everything to the right?"

The section producing `.o` files makes one for each `.cpp` file. `$<` means "what's the *first* thing to the right?"

(If you want to know everything about how to use these weird-looking constructions, well, the Internet is yours. If you just want to find something that works...the Internet is still yours. That's how I do it: look up tutorials, and see what solves my problem.)

To see how these variables get translated into actual commands, type `make` – it'll print the commands as it executes them.

The Makefile still has one big thing wrong (besides looking like it's written in Egyptian hieroglyphics). It doesn't refer to any `.h` files. If you change a `.h` file, `make` won't know to recompile on that basis – and it should.

So we add a magical incantation to the end of the Makefile:

```
%.dep:        %.cpp                   # Make the .dep files
              g++ -MM -MT "$*.o $@" $< > $@

ifneq ($(MAKECMDGOALS),clean)         # If not cleaning up...
-include $(DEPS)                      #  bring in the .dep files
endif
```

The first section says: for every .cpp file we have, we need a .dep file, which will contain information on dependencies. The g++ -MM line generates it. The main.dep file might look like main.o main.dep: main.cpp myclass.h meaning "Remake main.o and main.dep whenever main.cpp or myclass.h changes." The -MT "$*.o $@" option specifies what's left of the :.

The reason we put main.dep there is so if anything changes in either main.cpp or myclass.h (say, we add another #include), main.dep gets updated too.

include $(DEPS) says include these rules into the Makefile. The initial - says don't report if there's an error, like the file not existing, as will happen the first time you run make after a clean. And the ifneq... thing says don't bother about .dep files if you're just about to clean them up anyway.

Yes, it's complicated, but them's the breaks.

Example 16-5 is our result. It should work unaltered for new projects unless you change the name of the executable.

Example 16-5. A complete Makefile. Copy into any folder you have a project in, and run by typing make

```
# Makefile for a program with multiple .cpp files

PROG            = myprogram              #What program am I building?
SRCS            = $(wildcard *.cpp)      #What .cpp files do I have?
OBJS            = ${SRCS:.cpp=.o}        #What .o   files do I build?
DEPS            = $(OBJS:.o=.dep)        #What .dep files do I make?

###########################################################

all: $(PROG)

$(PROG):     $(OBJS)                    # Build the program
             g++ -o $@ -g $^

clean:                                  # Clean up files
             rm -f $(PROG)
             rm -f *.o
             rm -f *.dep
```

```
%.o:        %.cpp                      # Make the .o files
            g++ -g -o $@ -c $<

%.dep:      %.cpp                      # Make the .dep files
            g++ -MM -MT "$*.o $@" $< > $@

ifneq ($(MAKECMDGOALS),clean)           # If not cleaning up...
-include $(DEPS)                        #  bring in the .dep files
endif
```

Antibugging

- **`Makefile:16: ** Missing separator. Stop.`**

  No joke: this is because on the specified line, you indented with spaces instead of tabs. Solution: snort, roll your eyes, whatever, and use tabs.

Final `Date` program

Examples 16-6 through 16-8 show the finished program for `Date`. `main` is a driver to test the class.

Example 16-6. `date.h`

```
//class Date
//        -- from _C++ for Lazy Programmers_

#ifndef DATE_H
#define DATE_H

#include <iostream>

enum Month { JANUARY=1, FEBRUARY, MARCH, APRIL, MAY, JUNE,
             JULY, AUGUST, SEPTEMBER, OCTOBER, DECEMBER};

bool isLeapYear   (int year);
int  daysPerYear  (int year);
int  daysPerMonth (int month, int year);//Have to specify year,
                                         //in case month is FEBRUARY
                                         // and we're in a leap year
```

```
class Date
{
public:
    Date(int theDays=1, int theMonths=1, int theYears=1) :
       days_(theDays), months_(theMonths), years_(theYears)
    {
        normalize();
    }
    //Because of its default parameters, this 3-param
    // ctor also serves as a conversion ctor
    // (when you give it one long int)
    // and the default ctor (when you give it nothing)

    //Default is chosen so that the default day
    // is Jan 1, 1 A.D.

    Date(const Date& otherDate) : //copy ctor
           days_(otherDate.days_),
           months_(otherDate.months_),
           years_(otherDate.years_)
    {
    }

    //Access functions
    int days        () const { return days_;   }
    int months      () const { return months_; }
    int years       () const { return years_;  }

    int totalDays() const; //convert to total days since Dec 31, 1 BC

    void print (std::ostream& out = std::cout) const
    {
        out << days_ << '-' << months_ << '-' << years_;
    }
```

```
private:
    int days_;
    int months_;
    int years_;

    void normalize  ();
};

#endif //DATE_H
```

Example 16-7. `date.cpp`, abbreviated for brevity. Function bodies are in the book's source code

```
//class Date -- functions
//  -- from _C++ for Lazy Programmers_

#include "date.h"

bool isLeapYear (int year)
{
       ...
}

int daysPerYear (int year)
{
    ...
}

int daysPerMonth (int month, int year)
{
    ...
}

void Date::normalize ()
{
       ...
}
```

```
int Date::totalDays () const
{
    ...
}
```

Example 16-8. A driver program for class Date

```
//A "driver" program to test the Date class
//  -- from _C++ for Lazy Programmers_

#include <iostream>
#include "date.h"

using namespace std;

int main ()
{
    Date t (5,11,1955); //Test the 3-int ctor

    //... and print
    cout << "This should print 5-11-1995:\t";
    t.print (cout);
    cout << endl;

    //Test access functions
    if (t.days () != 5 || t.months () != 11 || t.years () != 1955)
    {
        cout << "Date t should have been 5-11-1955, but was ";
        t.print ();
        cout << endl;
    }

    Date u = t;          //...the copy ctor
    if (u.days () != 5 || u.months () != 11 || u.years () != 1955)
    {
        cout << "Date u should have been 5-11-1955, but was ";
        u.print ();
        cout << endl;
    }
```

```
    const Date DEFAULT; //...and the default ctor
                        //I do consts to test const functions
    if (DEFAULT.days () != 1 || DEFAULT.months () != 1 ||
        DEFAULT.years () != 1)
    {
        cout << "Date v should have been 1-1-1, but was ";
        DEFAULT.print ();
        cout << endl;
    }

    //...and total days
    enum {DAYS_FOR_JAN1_5AD = 1462}; //I found this number myself
                                     //  with a calculator
    Date Jan1_5AD(1, 1, 5);
    if (Jan1_5AD.totalDays() != DAYS_FOR_JAN1_5AD)
        cout << "Date Jan1_5AD should have had 1462 days, but had "
             << DAYS_FOR_JAN1_5AD << endl;

    //Test normalization
    const Date JAN1_2000 (32, 12, 1999);
    if (JAN1_2000.days () != 1 || JAN1_2000.months() != 1 ||
        JAN1_2000.years() != 2000)
    {
        cout << "Date JAN1_2000 should have been 1-1-2000, but was ";
        JAN1_2000.print ();
        cout << endl;
    }

    cout << "If no errors were reported, "
         << " it looks like class Date works!\n";

    return 0;
}
```

The output is

```
This should print 5-11-1995:      5-11-1955
If no errors were reported, looks like class Date works!
```

See how I try to make the driver user-friendly: it gives as little output as possible if everything works. Less output to wade through when testing.

EXERCISES

In these exercises, use separate compilation; provide your classes with appropriate constructors, using default arguments where helpful, and access functions; use inline functions where possible.

If it turns out that nothing goes in the `.cpp` file (could happen), you don't need to write one.

1. Update the `Time` class to use what was covered in this chapter.

   Add a constant `Time MIDNIGHT`, and make it available to `main.cpp` using `extern`.

2. Add `Time` functions `sum` and `difference`, which return the sum/difference of this `Time` with another `Time`. Its return value is also a `Time`.

3. What do you want engraved on your tombstone? Make a `Tombstone` class, which contains a birthdate, a death date, a name, and an epitaph. In addition to a member function `print`, give it a `lifespan` function, which returns the duration of the person's life as a `Date`.

4. Make a class `Track`, which contains title, artist, and duration (a `Time`) of a piece of music.

   Now make a class `Album`, which contains a title and an array of `Tracks`. Include, among the other functions you know you'll need, a function `duration()` which is the sum of all the `Track`'s durations.

static members (optional)

Example 16-9 implements a class Car for a used car lot.

Example 16-9. A Car class, showing static members and a member that is a type

```
//Class Car, and a program to use it
//   -- from _C++ for Lazy Programmers_

#ifndef CAR_H
#define CAR_H

#include <iostream>

class Car
{
public:
    enum { MAX_NAME_SIZE = 50 };

    Car();
    Car(const Car &);
    Car(int theYear, const char* theMake, const char* theModel);

    void print(std::ostream&) const;

    const char* make () const { return make_;   }
    const char* model() const { return model_;  }
    int         year () const { return year_;   }

    static int  numCars()     { return numCars_;}
    void        buy    ()     { ++numCars_;     }
    void        sell   ()     { --numCars_;     }

private:
    char make_[MAX_NAME_SIZE], model_[MAX_NAME_SIZE];
    int  year_;

    static int numCars_;
};

#endif //CAR_H
```

I want to keep track of how many cars exist on my lot, so I have the data member numCars_. The word static here means "belonging to the entire class." Earlier it meant "local variable that persists even when you leave the {}'s it was declared in." C++ loves to recycle keywords.

I also want to let the external world see how many Cars there are, so I have a member function numCars(). It makes sense for numCars() to be static since it applies to the entire class. buy and sell could be static, but we may have other things to do with a particular Car in buying and selling it, so it seems clearer to leave them as ordinary member functions.

static functions can't be const. The compiler will remind you.

It would be nice if we could initialize numCars right there in the class definition... but we can't. We'll need to do it outside. It can't go in the .h file, because it's a variable initialization, and that's code. I put it in car.cpp (Example 16-10).

main shows us how to call static member functions (Example 16-11).

Example 16-10. A Car class – the .cpp file

```
//Class Car
//   -- from _C++ for Lazy Programmers_

#include <cstring>
#include "car.h"

int Car::numCars_ = 0;                   //initialize the number of Cars to 0
```

Example 16-11. A program to use the Car class

```
//A program that uses the Car class
//   -- from _C++ for Lazy Programmers_

#include "car.h"

using namespace std;

int main ()
{
    Car banzai (2020, "Ford",   "GT40");
    Car mudbug (1987, "Jeep",   "Wrangler");
    Car sport  (2000, "Toyota", "Corolla");
```

```
    cout << "Looks like we have "
         << Car::numCars () << " cars in stock!" << endl;

    return 0;
}
```

EXERCISES

1. Add a static data member, and an access function, to Tombstone (from the last set of exercises) for the number of Tombstones created.
2. Add a static data member, and an access function, to Date to keep track of the latest Date the program has yet seen.

CHAPTER 17

Operators

You may have seen this error:

```
char string1[] = "Hello", string2[] = "Hello";
if (string1 == string2) ...
```

This condition fails because == for arrays compares memory addresses, not contents, and the addresses differ.

This also causes problems:

```
string2=string1;
```

It copies not `string2`'s contents, but its address, to `string1`. `string1`'s contents are lost. This is wasteful and also error-prone:

```
string2[1] = 'a';       //string1 becomes "Hallo", though it
                        //wasn't even mentioned here!
```

So let's make our own string class, forcing the operators to do what *we* want, and never worry about this again.

Appendix B lists operators C++ lets us overload. Short version: almost any, but you can't make up your own.

The basic string class

```
class String
{
public:
      String (const char* other=""); //conversion from char* ctor;
                                     //  default ctor
      String (const String &other);
```


W. Briggs, *C++ for Lazy Programmers*, https://doi.org/10.1007/978-1-4842-5187-4_17

```
private:
      char* contents_;
};
```

I want my `String` class to handle strings of any length, so I'll use dynamic memory, as in Chapter 14.

Here are two reasonable ways to set the default:

- As `nullptr`. `nullptr` is by convention nothing, so this makes sense.

  If I do this, I'll need every function to check for `nullptr` before accessing `contents_`. Too much work.

- As a character array of length 1 containing only `'\0'`, that is, as `""` (the empty string). I'll use this.

I'll now write the constructors.[1]

```
String::String[2] (const char* other = "")//Conversion from char* ctor,
                                          //  and default ctor
{
    contents_ = new char[strlen(other) + 1];
             //The +1 is room for final '\0'
    strcpy(contents_, other);
}

String::String (const String &other)
{
    contents_ = new char[strlen(other.contents_) + 1];
    strcpy(contents_, other.contents_);
}
```

[1]If I don't, C++ will, like so:

```
String::String () { contents_ = nullptr; };
String::String (const String& other) { contents_ = other.contents_; }
```

So we'll end up using `nullptr`, which I'd decided against, and we'll share memory between `String`s so altering one alters the other. A perfect justification for the Golden Rule of Constructors.

[2]When discussing a member function, I'll usually start it with `String::` to clarify that it's a member. We omit `String::` when inside the class definition.

That's too much redundant code. Maybe I could get one constructor to farm out its work to another? Sure. This "delegated constructor" lets the other do all the work. Code reuse, less typing, yay.

```
String (const String &other) : String (other.c_str())     {}
```

Now I'll make some new functions. These go inside the class definition:

```
const char* c_str() const { return contents_;              }
int         size () const { return (int) strlen (c_str()); }
                      //Inefficient! Is there a better way?
```

Destructors

When using dynamically allocated arrays, we need `delete []` to throw back memory when we're done. But `contents_` is a private member of `String`, so `main` can't do it. Nor should it: it's `String`'s job. It needs a function to be called we're done with the `String`.

Enter the destructor (or, per common abbreviation, "dtor").

```
String::~String () { if (contents_) delete [] contents_; }
    //Why "if (contents_)?" Paranoia. Deleting nullptr gives a crash.
```

This function, named "~" plus the class name, is called automatically whenever the `String` goes away (e.g., when the `String` is declared inside a function and the function ends).

This is

- Less work: write it once and you're done.
- Automatic, so you won't forget.

Memory management just got a lot easier, as long as you remember the Golden Rule.

Golden Rule of Destructors

If you're using dynamic memory in a class, always write the destructor.

I'll add another Golden Rule. You can violate it, but it *does* reduce errors.

Golden Rule of Dynamic Memory

If possible, don't use it. If you must, try to hide it inside a class and clean up with a destructor.

Destructors could be used for other things at the end of a variable's lifetime...but I never do.

Binary and unary operators

```
bool String::operator== (const String& other) const
{
    return strcmp (c_str(), other.c_str()) == 0;
}
```

Using the == operator looks like this:

```
if (stringA == stringB)...
```

When the computer gets to `stringA == stringB`, it goes into the function `String::operator==`.[3] There are two `String`s used. The one on the left, `stringA`, is "this" one: the one that owns this `operator<` function. The one on the right, `stringB`, is the "other" one, the one passed in as a parameter.

When you refer to a member like `other.c_str()`, that's the `c_str()` that belongs to `other`. If you don't say who it belongs to, it belongs to "this" one – the one on the left.

This function will work for any class you write – just change the class name:

```
bool String::operator!= (const String& other) const
{
    return ! (*this == other);
}
```

[3]This whole operator business is syntactic sugar. You *could* call these functions the ugly way: `if (stringA.operator==(stringB))...`

These operators are **binary**: they need two Strings to work. A **unary** operator has only one argument, like the - ("unary minus") in (-myInt)+2 or the ! in if (! isReady). As an example unary operator, I'll write ! for the String class. ! myString will mean myString is empty.

```
bool String::operator! () const { return ! size(); }
```

With a unary operator, we don't have to wonder which String we're using. It's the only one we have: "this" one.

Golden Rule of Operators

If an operator has one argument, "this" object – the one whose members we can refer to without specifying whose they are – is the only object mentioned in the call of the operator.

If an operator has two arguments, "this" object is the one on the left of the operator in the call. The one passed as a parameter is the one on the right.

Operators don't have three arguments.[4]

EXERCISES

1. Make a Point2D class. You should be able to create points (specifying the coordinates, or defaulting to (0,0)), print them, and compare them. We won't provide < and so on for now (what does it mean, if point1 < point2?), but we can compare them with == and !=.
2. Make a Fraction class. You should be able to create fractions (specifying numerator and denominator, or defaulting to 0/1)), print them, and compare them with all available comparison operators.

---

[4]There's an exception: the ?: operator. Here is an example of its use:

```
cout << (x>=0 ? "positive" : "negative");
```

This means that if (x>=0) cout << "positive"; else cout << "negative";
I don't use it much. C++ won't let you overload it anyway.

Assignment operators and `*this`

How can we assign one String to another?

```
operator= (other)
    delete the old memory
    allocate the new memory, enough to hold other's contents
    copy the contents over
```

There's one more thing = always does: it returns something. We usually just call it like A=B; but this is also legal:

```
A=B=C;
```

Since = is processed right to left, this means

```
A=(B=C);
```

which really means that when doing B=C, assign the value of C to B, return the value you get, and send it across the = to A. So B=C must return whatever B becomes.

```
operator= (other)
    delete the old memory
    allocate the new memory, enough to hold other's contents, and
    copy the contents over
    return "this"
```

or

```
const String& String::operator=  (const String& other)[5]
{
    if (contents_) delete[] contents_;            //delete old memory
    contents_ = new char[strlen(other.c_str()) + 1]; //get new memory
              //The +1 is room for final '\0'
    strcpy(contents_, other.c_str());             //copy contents over
    return *this;
}
```

[5]See Exercise 3 for an interesting tweak on this algorithm.

this is defined whenever you're in a member function, as the memory address of "this" object. Since this is a pointer to the object, *this is the object itself. (We rarely use this without the *, though we can.) We wanted = to return what "this" object has become; now it does.

*this is *always* the thing to return from =. Since operators for +=, -=, and so on also return the newly altered object, they also return *this.

I think I'll rewrite the conversion ctor and operator= to extract the code they have in common and put it in a new function copy. Code reuse.

```
String::String (const char* other="") { copy(other); }

const String& String::operator= (const String& other)
{
    if (contents_) delete[] contents_; copy(other.c_str());
    return *this;
}

void String::copy(const char* str)
{
    contents_ = new char[strlen(str) + 1]; //get new memory
                                         //The +1 is room for final '\0'
    strcpy(contents_, str);                 //copy contents over
}
```

The other thing that most needs comment is ='s return type.

Suppose it were written thus:

```
String String::operator= (const String& other);
```

Since there's no &, it will call the copy constructor to make a copy of what it's returning. This takes time since it has to copy the array character by character. We can save time if we return not a copy but the thing (*this) itself.

```
String& String::operator= (const String& other);
```

But I don't want anything altering what's returned, so I add const.

```
const String& String::operator= (const String& other);
```

No security breach; no extra copy being made. Golden Rule time.

Golden Rule of Assignment Operators

Every assignment operator (=, +=, -=, etc.) should return `*this`.

...as a constant reference (e.g., `const String&`).

And here's another rule.

Golden Rule of =

Always specify =.

The reason is same as for copy constructors: *if you don't, the compiler will do it for you,* and it may do it in a stupid way. For `String` it will define it to copy the memory address. We were trying to get *away* from that.

Antibugging

A common mistake: putting `TheClassName::` in front of the wrong thing.

```
String::const String& operator=... //const is a member of String ?!
```

The error messages may be confusing or clear depending on the compiler. Either way the solution is to stick `TheClassName::` on the left end of the function name. `const String&` is the return type; `String::operator=` is the function name.

EXERCISES

1. Add = to the `Point2D` class from the previous exercises.
2. Add = to the `Fraction` class.
3. What happens in `String::operator=` if you say this: `myStr = myStr;`? Fix = to avoid the problem. My answer is in Example 17-2.

Arithmetic operators

Now we'll do an "arithmetic" looking operator: +. I think it's reasonable to define + to mean concatenation. If `word=="cat"` and `addon=="fish"`, then `word+addon` should be `"catfish"`.

We'll write += and +. Programmers using `String` may want either, and have reason to be annoyed if they have to guess which we provided.

```
operator+= (other String)
      remember the old contents
      allocate new contents, big enough that we can add other.contents
      copy the old contents into the new
      append other contents
      delete the old contents
      return *this
```

Order matters. If we delete the old contents before we use them, we'll lose what's in them.

```
const String& String::operator+= (const String& other)
{
    char* oldContents = contents_;

    contents_ = new char [size() + other.size() + 1];
            //1 extra space at the end for the null char

    strcpy (contents_, oldContents);  //copy old into new
    strcat (contents_, other.c_str());//append other contents

    delete [] oldContents;

    return *this;
}
```

Good enough. Now I can do `operator+` inline in the class definition. Shall I have it return `const String&` too?

```
const String& operator+ (const String& other) const
                                   //There's something wrong here...
{
    String result = *this; result += other; return result;
}
```

Let's see what happens when we call it.

Suppose, in main, we say copied = word+addon. First, we call operator+. It makes its result (Figure 17-1).

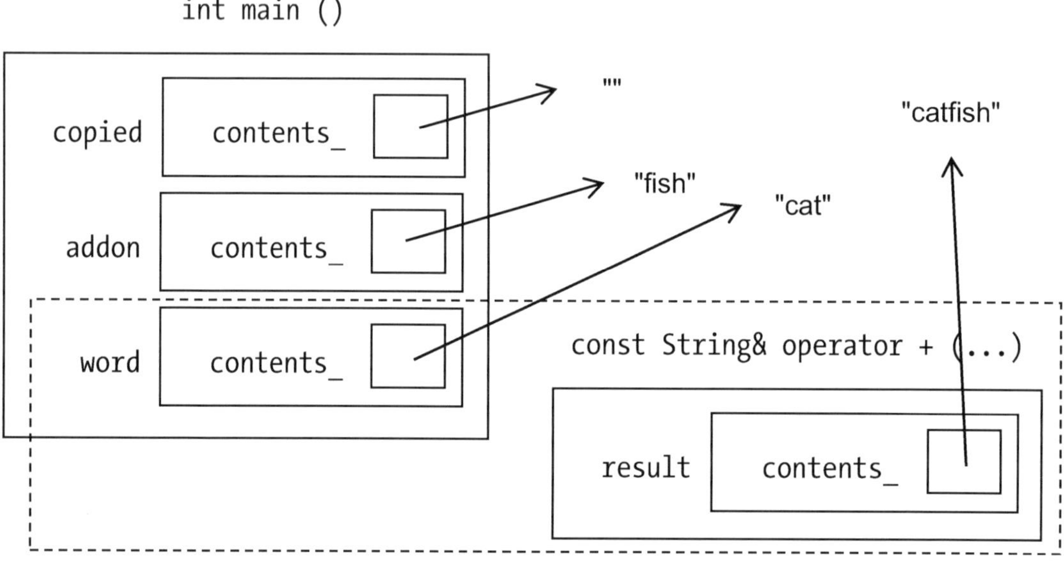

***Figure 17-1.** operator+ (flawed version) at work*

Then it returns its result and goes away (Figure 17-2). But result, being +'s local variable, is destructed when + completes, so what main gets no longer exists by the time it gets it. Using it would be a Bad Idea.

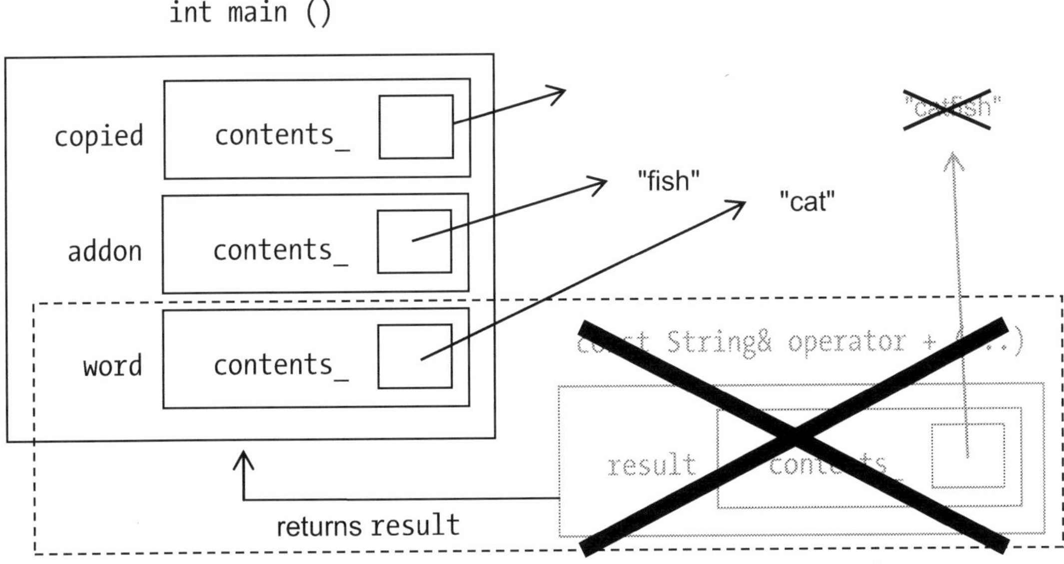

Figure 17-2. *operator+ (flawed version) returns its value*

The solution is to return a copy. It will persist till it's no longer needed.

```
String String::operator+ (const String& other) const //That's better
{
    String result = *this; result += other; return result;
}
```

Golden Rule of Returning `const &`

Local variables should not be returned with `const &`.

Things that will persist after the function returns, including `*this` and data members, may be. If they're of class types, they should be.

Why make + call +=, rather than the reverse? + makes two copies: local variable `result` and the copy made when we return. += has no locals and returns `const &`, so it's pretty efficient. If we made it call +, it would have to do extra copying.

+ should always be written as it is here, no matter if we're adding strings, numbers, or heffalumps (whatever they are). It can be copied into program after program.

EXERCISES

1. Add +, +=, -, and -= to Point2D. Also add *, *=, /, and /=. It may not make sense to refer to point1/point2, but it *would* make sense to refer to point1/2 – you'd divide both coordinates by 2 to get a new Point2D. So the "other" argument of *, *=, /, and /= would be int.
2. Add +, -, *, /, and +=, -=, *=, and /= to Fraction.

[ ] and ( )

Now we'll support the use of [ ]'s to access individual characters.

```
char  String::operator[] (int index) const { return contents_[i]; }
```

We're only half done, because though we can say

```
char ch = myString[0];
```

if we say

```
myString[0] = 'a';
```

the compiler will complain "l-value required."

This means (*very* roughly – I'm keeping it simple) that the thing left of the = (L for left) is not the sort of thing that *can* be left of =: it's not modifiable. If you want to alter myString, you need not a *copy* of the element but the element itself:

```
char& String::operator[] (int index)        { return contents_[i]; }
```

Won't the compiler get confused, having two functions identical but for return type? But they're *not* identical: one is const. So C++ will apply the const one to things that can't change and the non-const to things that can.

```
const String S ("Hello");
cout << S[0] << endl;       //OK; uses the const version of []

String T("Goodbye");
T[0] = 'Z';                 //Also OK; uses the non-const version, which
                            //  returns something that can be changed
```

Golden Rule of [ ]

If you define [ ], you need two versions:

```
<type>  operator[] (int index) const { ... }
<type>& operator[] (int index)       { ... }
```

The code between the { }'s will almost certainly be identical.

You can also add () operators. We might want to say `mystring (2, 5)` to get the substring containing characters 2 through 5. This is its prototype; see Example 17-2 for implementation.

```
String String::operator () (int start, int finish) const;
```

You can have () operators with different numbers of arguments. I don't use them because to me something like `mystring (2, 5)` isn't clear, but it's there if you want it.

EXERCISES

1. Add [ ] (`const` and non-`const` versions) to `Point2D`. `point1[0]` is the x coordinate, and `point1[1]` is the y coordinate.
2. ...or to `Fraction`. `myFraction[0]` is the numerator and `myFraction[1]` is the denominator.

>> and <<: operators that aren't class members

I also want to print `String`s using `>>` and `<<` with `cin` and `cout` or other files.

We can't write these operators as members. Remember that the thing on the left of an operator is always "this" object. But in `cout << myString`, the left operand is `cout`. If we wrote `operator<<` as a member of `String`, `cout` would have to be a `String`.

The fix is to make the operator a non-member:

```
                                //this goes OUTSIDE the class definition
ostream& operator<< (ostream& out, const String& foo);6
{
       ...
       return out;
}
```

I have it return ostream& because of when I chain <<'s together (as in cout << X << Y). The order of operations is (cout << X) << Y; that is, cout << X does its work, then returns its "value" of cout, so the next << has cout as its left operand and can be used to print.

This is my first attempt.

```
inline                                                      //in string.h
std::ostream& operator<< (std::ostream& out, const String& foo)
{
       out << foo.contents_; return out;
}
```

This won't compile. foo.contents_ is private.

We could return contents_ via an access function, but this is a more versatile solution:

```
class String
{
public:
   ...
   void print (std::ostream& out) const { out << c_str(); }
   ...
};
```

[6] In the programming language LISP and elsewhere, foo is used to name a variable when it's obvious what foo is. If two such "placeholder" names are needed, it's often foo and bar. It's a good bet this is from the military acronym "FUBAR," meaning roughly "Fouled Up Beyond All Recognition."

Some programmers consider foo and bar to be 3vil because they aren't descriptive, but I think I'd rather read foo than theString or rightHandSide.

```
inline
std::ostream& operator<< (std::ostream& out, const String& foo)
{
    foo.print(out); return out;
}
```

We just fixed the privacy violation in a way that will work for any class we ever write – a Good Thing. Let's handle `cin >>` similarly:

```
void String::read (std::istream& in);

inline
std::istream& operator>> (std::istream& in, String& foo) //no const!
{
    foo.read (in); return in;
}
```

`String::read` is trickier than `String::print`. Here's my first try.

```
void String::read (istream& in) { in >> contents_; }
```

Problem is, we don't know if `contents_` has enough space to store what's typed in. Solution:

```
class String
{
public:
    enum {BIGGEST_READABLE_STRING_PLUS_ONE    = 256};
                        //biggest string we can read, incl '\0'
    ...
};

void String::read  (std::istream& in)
{
    static char buffer [BIG_NUMBER_PLUS_ONE];
    in >> buffer;
    *this = buffer;
}
```

It's a hack – an inelegant solution – but it'll do well enough. If you're worried someone may enter more than 256 characters, make buffer bigger.

You *could* write other operator functions as non-members: pass in the object we were calling *this as the first parameter:

```
const String& operator=  (      string& left, const string& right);
bool          operator== (const string& left, const string& right);
```

We usually don't, because these functions clearly belong to String, and need access to private data members.

EXERCISES

In both exercises, if you're trying to read an int and the user types a char, your istream in gets caught in an error state and can't read further. You can fix it with in.clear ():

1. Add ostream << and istream >> operators for the Point2D class.
2. ...or the Fraction class.

++ and --

It wouldn't make much sense to say myString++, so I'll shift to the Fraction example from exercises.

myFraction++ should add 1 to myFraction. Recall there are two versions of ++: ++myFraction, meaning add 1 and return what you get, and myFraction++, meaning add 1 and return what you had before adding.

This is the pre-increment version:

```
const Fraction& Fraction::operator++ ()  //used for ++myFraction
{
      *this += 1;             //add 1 to this Fraction
                              //(Surely Fraction can convert from int?)
      return *this;
}
```

How can we distinguish the post-increment version? Not by name, or number of arguments...so C++ has a hack just for this:

```
Fraction Fraction::operator++ (int junk) //used for myFraction++
{
      Fraction result = *this;
      ++(*this);            //code reuse again
      return result;
}
```

The `int` argument here really *is* junk: it's just a placeholder, meant to distinguish this ++ operator from the other.

EXERCISES

1. Add both versions of ++ and -- to `Point2D`, and test. `myPoint++` would add 1 to the x_ component.
2. Add both versions of ++ and -- to `Fraction`, and test.

Explicit call to constructor

This works fine:

```
String A;
A =  "moo"; //conversion ctor creates a
            //String containing "moo", passes to =
A += "moo"; //conversion ctor creates another, passes to +=
            //now A == "moomoo"
```

Here's something that *wouldn't* work.

```
A = "moo" + "moo";
```

When C++ does the +, it has no idea you want the + that belongs to `String`, since neither operand is a `String`! So it'll use the + that goes with character arrays, adding memory addresses and setting `A` to something strange.

This works:

```
A = String("moo") + "moo";
```

The call to String here is an "explicit call to constructor." It creates a temporary String variable, never named; then C++ applies the operator+ call to it. When it's done with the unnamed String, it deletes it.

Here it is with Point2D:

```
myPoints[0] = Point2D (2, 5);
myPoints[1] = Point2D (3, 7);
...
```

EXERCISES

1. Write a program that declares five Point2Ds and prints them, without naming them as variables, by using explicit call to constructor.
2. Write a program that declares five Fractions and multiplies them, without naming them as variables, by using explicit call to constructor.

Final String program

Examples 17-1 and 17-2 show the complete String class; Example 17-3 tests it.

Example 17-1. string.h

```
//String class
//      -- from _C++ for Lazy Programmers_

#ifndef STRING_H
#define STRING_H

#include <cstring> //uses cstring functions all over

class String
{
public:
    enum {BIGGEST_READABLE_STRING_PLUS_ONE   = 256};
                         //biggest string we can read, incl '\0'
```

```
String (const char* other="") { copy(other);                    }
String (const String &other) : String (other.c_str())   {}
                    //a "delegated" ctor
~String()           { if (contents_) delete [] contents_;  }

//access function

const char* c_str() const    { return contents_;           }

//other functions, not operators

int       size () const { return (int) strlen (c_str()); }
                    //Inefficient! Is there a better way?
bool operator! () const { return ! size();               }

//comparison operators

bool operator< (const String& other) const
{
    return strcmp (c_str(), other.c_str()) <  0;
}
bool operator> (const String& other) const
{
    return strcmp (c_str(), other.c_str()) >  0;
}
bool operator<= (const String& other) const
{
    return strcmp (c_str(), other.c_str()) <= 0;
}
bool operator>= (const String& other) const
{
    return strcmp (c_str(), other.c_str()) >= 0;
}
bool operator== (const String& other) const
{
    return strcmp (c_str(), other.c_str()) == 0;
}
```

```
    bool operator!= (const String& other) const
    {
        return ! (*this == other);
    }

    //assignment and concatenation

    const String& operator=  (const String& other);
    const String& operator+= (const String& other);
    String        operator+  (const String& other) const
    {
        String result = *this; result += other; return result;
    }

    //[] and substring

    char  operator[] (int index) const { return contents_[index]; }
    char& operator[] (int index)       { return contents_[index]; }

    String operator () (int start, int finish) const;

    //I/O functions
    void read  (std::istream& in );
    void print (std::ostream& out) const{ out << c_str();        }
private:
    char* contents_;
    void copy(const char* str);
};

inline
std::istream& operator>> (std::istream& in, String& foo)
{
    foo.read (in); return in;
}
```

```
inline
std::ostream& operator<< (std::ostream& out, const String& foo)
{
    foo.print(out); return out;
}
#endif //STRING_H
```

Example 17-2. string.cpp

```
//class String, for char arrays
//      -- from _C++ for Lazy Programmers_

#include <cstring>
#include <iostream>
#include "string.h"

using namespace std;


const String& String::operator=  (const String& other)
{
    if (this == &other) return *this; //never assign *this to itself
    if (contents_) delete[] contents_; copy(other.c_str());
    return *this;
}

void String::copy(const char* str)
{
    contents_ = new char[strlen(str) + 1]; //get new memory
                                  //The +1 is room for final '\0'
    strcpy(contents_, str);                //copy contents over
}

const String& String::operator+= (const String& other)
{
    char* oldContents = contents_;

    contents_ = new char [size() + other.size() + 1];
            //1 extra space at the end for the null char
```

```
    strcpy (contents_, oldContents);  //copy old into new
    strcat (contents_, other.c_str());//append other contents

    delete [] oldContents;

    return *this;
}

String String::operator () (int start, int finish) const
{
    //This constructs the substring
    String result = *this;
    strcpy (result.contents_, contents_+start);
                //contents_+start is the char array that is
                //  "start" characters after contents_ begins
    result.contents_[finish-start+1] = '\0';
                //the number of chars in this sequence
                //  is the difference plus 1

    return result;
}

void String::read  (std::istream& in)
{
    static char buffer [BIGGEST_READABLE_STRING_PLUS_ONE];
    in >> buffer;
    *this = buffer;
}
```

The driver in Example 17-3 uses the function `void assert (bool condition)` which verifies `condition` is true – and if not, crashes the program. Good: if something's wrong, we'll know it.

Example 17-3. A driver for `String`

```
//Driver program to test the String class
//      -- from _C++ for Lazy Programmers_
```

```
#include <iostream>
#include <cassert>  //for assert, a function which crashes
                    //  if the condition you give is false
                    //used for debugging
#include "string.h"

using namespace std;

int main ()
{
                   //using consts to ensure const functions are right
    const String EMPTY;
    const String ABC ("abc");

    //Testing default ctor, conversion ctor from char*, ==, !=, !
    assert (EMPTY == ""); assert (! EMPTY); assert (! (EMPTY != ""));
    assert (ABC != "");                     assert (! (ABC == ""));

    //Testing c_str, size ...
    assert (strcmp (ABC.c_str(), "abc") == 0);
    assert (ABC.size() == 3);

    //Test >, >=, <, <=, !=,
    //We're doing lots of automatic calls  to conversion ctor
    //  from const char*, so that's tested too
    assert (ABC <  "abd");  assert (! (ABC >= "abd"));
    assert (ABC <= "abd");  assert (! (ABC >  "abd"));
    assert (ABC >  "abb");  assert (! (ABC <= "abb"));
    assert (ABC >= "abb");  assert (! (ABC <  "abb"));
    assert (ABC <= ABC);    assert (ABC >= ABC);

    //Test []
    String xyz = "xyz";
    assert (xyz[1] == 'y'); xyz[1] = 'Y';
    assert (xyz[1] == 'Y'); xyz[1] = 'y';
    assert (ABC[1] == 'b'); //const version
```

```
    //Test =, ()
    xyz = "xyz and more";
    assert(xyz(4, 6) == "and");

    //Testing copy ctor  ...
    assert (ABC == String(ABC));

    //Testing + (and thereby +=); =; also c_str
    String ABCDEF = ABC+"def";
    assert (ABCDEF == "abcdef");
    assert (strcmp (ABCDEF.c_str(), "abcdef") == 0);

    //Testing << and >>
    String input;
    cout << "Enter a string:\t"; cin >> input;
    cout << "You entered:\t" << input << endl;

    cout << "If no errors were reported, "
         << "class String seems to be working!\n";

    return 0;
}
```

EXERCISES

1. Using `assert` and explicit call to constructor, test your `Point2D` class.
2. ...or your `Fraction` class.

#include <string>

So here's what I've been hiding: C++ already has a string class, and you now know how to use it. You'll need `#include <string>`. The type is `string`, not `String`.

CHAPTER 18

Exceptions, Move Constructors, Recursion, and O Notation

One needful thing – a better way of handling error conditions – and a few very-nice-to-haves: more efficient copying ("move" functions), functions that call themselves (recursion), and a way to figure how time-efficient your functions are.

Exceptions

How should a program handle runtime errors? Some options:

- **The ostrich algorithm**. Simply hope the problem will never occur: your integers never exceed `INT_MAX`, your calls to `strcpy` never overrun the `char` array, and so on. We do it a lot, and it works! Shall we try it in software for a nuclear reactor? For verifying who gets access to your bank account? Oops.
- **Crash**. Avoid suggesting this one at the nuclear plant, too.
- **Print an error message**. Fine for your laptop; not so good for a microwave oven or smartwatch.
- **Return an error code**. Make your function return `int`, and if the return value is something that means "error" (-1 is conventional), something must have gone wrong. It's a lot of work, though, always checking the return value.

W. Briggs, *C++ for Lazy Programmers*, https://doi.org/10.1007/978-1-4842-5187-4_18

Different situations call for different resolutions. So we need an easy way to separate error detection, which wouldn't change, from error resolution, which would.

To illustrate the "exception" mechanism that does this, let's have an example. The **stack** is a data structure commonly used in computer science. (You've already encountered the Call Stack.) It's like a stack of cafeteria trays. All you can do with a stack without upsetting the cafeteria people is put a tray on top ("push" the tray), take one off the top ("pop" it), look at the top one, and notice whether the stack's empty. That, and (since this is C++) construct and possibly destruct it.

I'll be lazy (of course!) and avoid dynamic memory.

Here are problems we might encounter:

- We might try to push an item onto a stack that's already full ("overflow").
- We might try to look at the top item, or pop an item, from a stack that's empty ("underflow").

Member functions should only *notice* the errors, like `top` here:

```
class Stack                         //A stack of strings
{
public:
    class UnderflowException    {};    //An "exception class"

    ...

    const std::string& top () const
    {
        if (empty()) throw UnderflowException ();
        else return contents_[howMany_-1]; //the top element
    }
    ...
};
```

If all goes well `top` returns the last item in the `Stack`, the `howMany-1`th. But if the `Stack`'s empty, `top` creates an object of type `UnderflowException` using explicit call to constructor. Then it **throws** (reports) it.

(BNF version: `throw` <*some variable or value*>.)

If nobody knows how to handle the error, the program crashes, as it should. We've seen unhandled exceptions already, when we were trying to load an image with a misspelled filename, say, and SDL threw an exception. That may be all we need, for this or for overflows. Example 18-1 is the complete Stack class.

Example 18-1. A Stack class

```
//Stack class, with a limited stack size
//      -- from _C++ for Lazy Programmers_

#ifndef STACK_H
#define STACK_H

#include <string>

class Stack
{
public:
    class UnderflowException    {}; //Exceptions
    class OverflowException     {};

    enum {MAX_ITEMS = 5};

    Stack()                      { howMany_ = 0;  }
    Stack(const Stack& other)                      = delete;[1]
    const Stack& operator= (const Stack& other) = delete;

    const std::string& top () const
    {
        if (empty()) throw UnderflowException ();
        else return contents_[howMany_-1];
    }
```

[1]This says, "I'm not going to write this function, and neither is the compiler." Copying a stack seems insecure to me, and I definitely don't see a reason. So I save some effort.

```
    void push (const std::string& what)
    {
        if (full ()) throw OverflowException  ();
        else contents_[howMany_++] = what;
    }

    std::string pop   ()
    {
        std::string result = top(); --howMany_; return result;
    }

    bool empty () const { return howMany_ == 0;         }
    bool full  () const { return howMany_ >= MAX_ITEMS; }
    //Why not just see if they're equal?  howMany_ *can't* be
    //  bigger than MAX_ITEMS, can it?
    //  Not if I did everything perfectly, but...
    //  better to program defensively if you aren't perfect

private:
    std::string contents_ [MAX_ITEMS];
    int         howMany_;  //how many items are in the stack?
};

#endif //STACK_H
```

But if we want, we can make a function in the call stack know how to **catch** and handle what was thrown.

Think of the exception as a hot potato. The `if` statement throws it. If the function it's in knows how to catch it, fine. If not, it relays the hot potato, I mean, the `UnderflowException`, to whatever function called it, then the one that called that one, and so on. Each time, the function stops what it's doing and returns immediately, delaying only enough to throw away its local variables, destructing as necessary. This continues until we return to a function that can catch the error, or we exit the program with an error.

Let's say `main` is the function that we decided should handle the error. I'll equip `main` with a try-catch block (in Example 18-2). The `try` part contains what I want to do. The `catch` parts contain error-handling code for if something goes wrong.

Example 18-2. Code to catch an `UnderflowException`

```
int main ()
{
    Stack S;

    try
    {
        ...
        cout << S.top ();
        ....
    }
    catch (const Stack::UnderflowException&)
    {
        cout << "Error in main: there was a stack underflow.\n";
        cout << "Saving everything and quitting...\n";
        ... code that handles any cleanup we need to do ...
        cout << "Quitting now.\n";
        return;
    }
    //maybe a catch for Stack::OverflowException too

    return 0;
}
```

The structure of a `try`-`catch` block is

`try` *{ <do stuff> }*

`catch` *(<parameter>) { <error handling code> }*

*[and possibly more catches]**

So what *is* an `UnderflowException`? It's just what you see: an object of type `UnderflowException`, with no data members and no member functions. Is this stupid? Not at all. `throw`ing it tells `main` that an underflow occurred. What else *would* it want to know? I can't think of anything. If for some reason you *do* want your exception class to contain data members, functions, what have you, fine; `throw` and `catch` will work the same way. But I never do.

If you're in an exception's `catch` block and want to throw it again, say `throw` without any arguments.

Should you use exceptions?

Yes! They're ideal for letting the error handling be done wherever it should be, with minimal extra coding. I use them regularly. (I'll admit I rarely catch them. Maybe that's because I'm more into writing libraries than software for those nuclear plants.)

EXERCISES

1. Adapt the `String` class from the previous chapter to throw an exception if the indices passed to the `[]` operators, or the substring operator `()`, is out of range. Test to be sure it works.
2. Add and test a `Fraction` member function to convert to `double`; throw an exception if the denominator is 0.

Move constructors and move = (optional)

`String` is doing more work than it should, and that may slow us down. (OK, *I've* never noticed, but the C++ community is persnickety about efficiency.) Consider this code.

```
compoundString = str1+str2;
```

There is a temporary copy made in operator+, repeated below. It's when we return the `result`, passing a copy of that local variable. This calls the copy ctor, which contains a call to `strcpy`. The bigger the string, the longer `strcpy` takes.

```
String String::operator+  (const String& other) const
{
    String result = *this; result += other; return result;
}
```

Modern C++ has a mechanism whereby something can give up its memory to something else that needs it, avoiding the need for copying. Here it is, in Example 18-3.

Example 18-3. A move constructor for `String`

```
String (String&& other)          //The "move" constructor
{
    contents_ = other.contents_; //2 statements; no loops,
    other.contents_ = nullptr;   //  no strcpy. Cheap!
}
```

The && means "apply this function if the parameter is something that can give up its value and that's OK." That's surely true of `result`! So we take the contents from `result` (temporarily called `other` in the move constructor). We give it `nullptr` so when it hits its destructor, it won't `delete[]` the `contents_` it gave us.

The other extra work comes after we leave +, when the temporary copy it provides is copied by `operator=`, which also does a `strcpy`. We can save time if we just move that copy's contents into `compoundString`. Example 18-4 provides a new = operator with no `strpcying`.

Example 18-4. A move assignment operator for `String`

```
const String& String::operator= (String&& other) //move =
{
    if (this == &other) return *this; //never assign *this to itself

    if (contents_) delete[] contents_;

    contents_       = other.contents_; //no loops! no strcpy!
    other.contents_ = nullptr;

    return *this;
}
```

Because we have more options now, I want to supersede the old Golden Rules of Constructors, and of =, with this:

Golden Rule of Constructors and =

Either have one of the following:

- No ctors and no = specified (old-style structs, essentially)
- Default ctor, copy ctor, and = specified
- Default, copy, =, plus move ctor and move =

EXERCISES

1. Adapt Exercise 5 from Chapter 15, with its `Tracks` and `Albums`, to use dynamic memory. Then write a move constructor and move = for `Album`. Test with the debugger to be sure you're really using move functions when you should.

Recursion (optional; used in the next section)

Sometimes it's easiest to define something in terms of itself.

For example, consider the "factorial" function. 5! (read as "5 factorial") is 5*4*3*2*1 = 120. 0! and 1! are both 1; in general, n! is n*(n-1)*(n-2)...*2*1. (n-1)! is (n-1)*(n-2)*...*2*1; so n! = n*(n-1)!. The result gets big fast as you increase n.

This is an algorithm, then, for calculating n!.

```
if n is 0, return 1
else return n * (n-1)!
```

This reveals two general principles needed to ensure **recursion** – a function calling itself – will terminate:

- **There must be an ending condition.** Otherwise, recursion never ends (until the computer runs out of memory).
- **There must be progress toward that ending condition**, for the same reason.

Example 18-5. A simple recursive function

```
int factorial (int n) //maybe give it unsigned --
                      // and return unsigned long long?
{
      if (n == 0) return 1;
      else return n * factorial (n-1);
}
```

The reason recursion works is C++ creates a new copy ("activation record") for each invocation. Suppose your main program calls Example 18-5's `factorial` with an argument of 3.

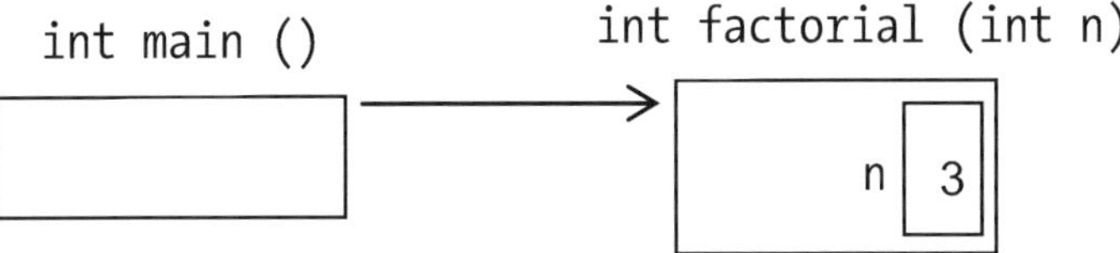

n isn't 0, so we have to call `factorial (n-1)`.

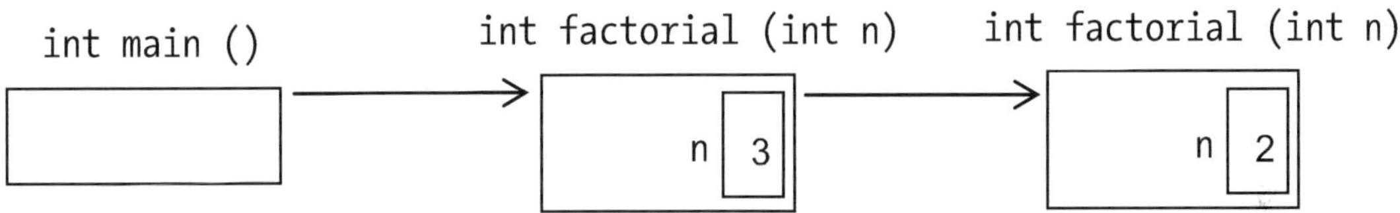

And again, and again, till we get a version of factorial that has n=0 and so doesn't recurse further. It will return 1 to the `factorial(1)` call.

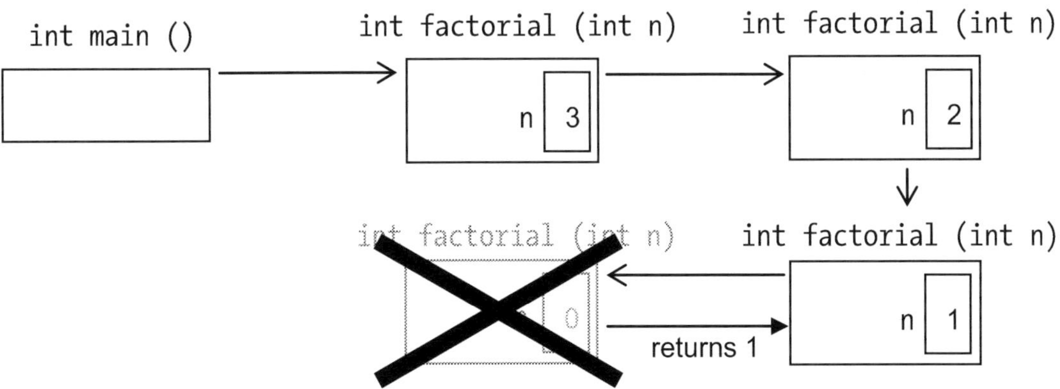

factorial(1), then, returns 1*factorial(0), which is also 1:

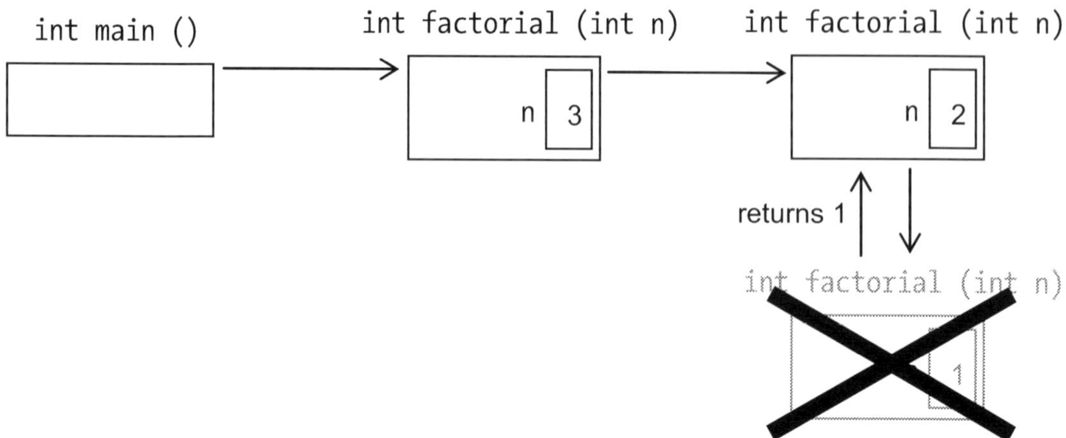

factorial(2) returns 2*factorial(1), which is 2:

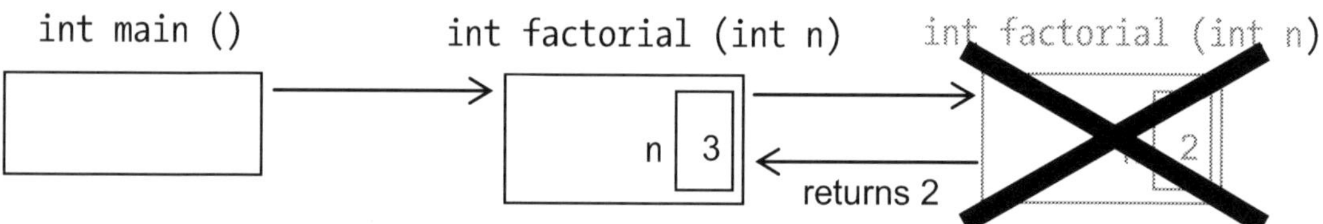

Finally, factorial(3) returns 3 times factorial(2), that is, 6.

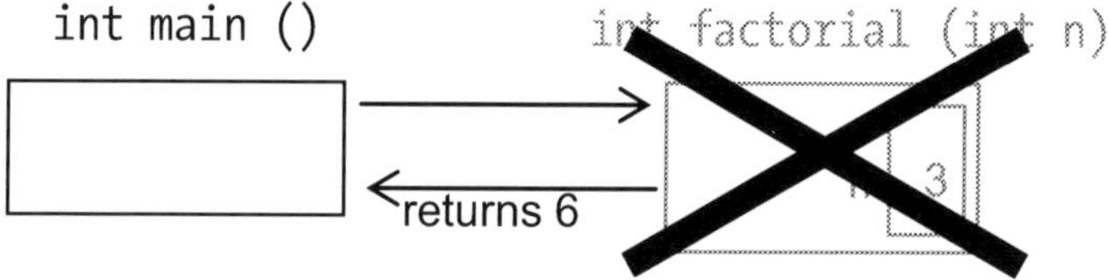

If you Debug in Microsoft Visual Studio a program with a recursive function, you can see copies of the function on the Call Stack (Figure 18-1). Click one to see its local variables.

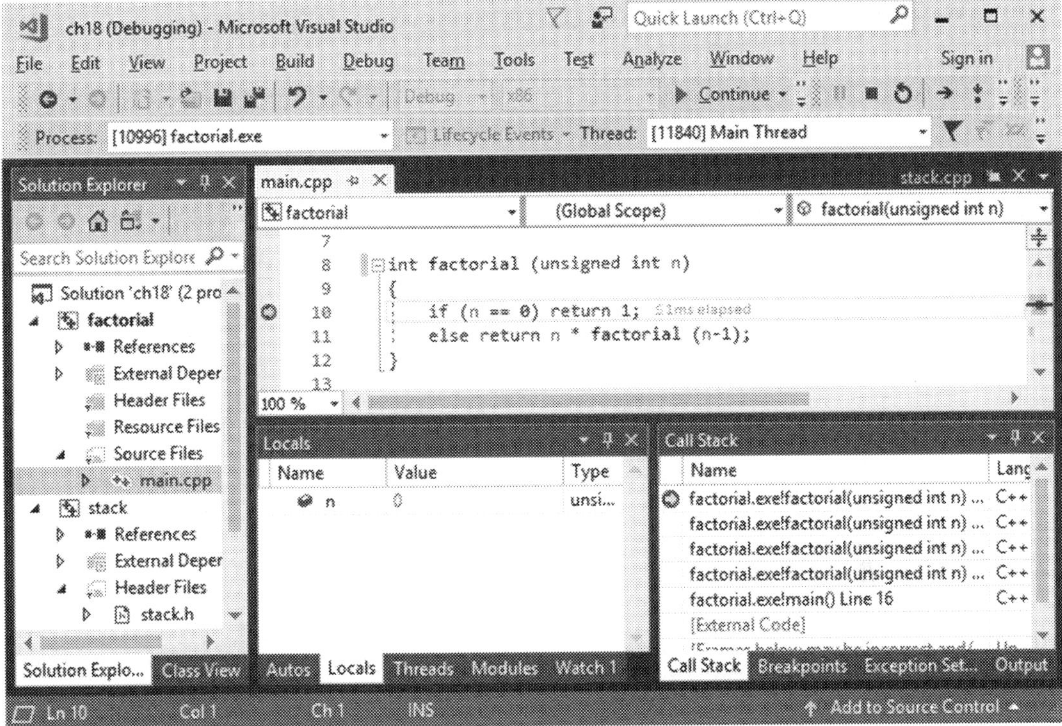

Figure 18-1. *The Call Stack in Visual Studio*

In ddd or gdb, `where` shows you the call stack. `up` and `down` take you between copies of whatever functions are on it – when you `print` a variable, it'll use the context of the copy you're looking at.

Because a recursive function has multiple copies, there's more work for the compiler using recursion than with our usual method of looping an action, that is, iteration. But it's sometimes easier to write functions recursively than with iteration.

Golden Rule of Recursion

Every recursive function must have, so it will terminate,

- A base case, in which there is no further recursive call
- Progress toward that base case in every recursive call

Antibugging

- **Your program churns a while, then crashes** saying "segmentation fault" or "stack overflow."

  Either you forgot the ending condition or you weren't making progress toward it. Using the debugger should help you figure which.

EXERCISES

1. The Fibonacci number sequence goes like this:

   ```
   Fibonacci (1) = 1
   Fibonacci (2) = 1
   Fibonacci (n) = Fibonacci (n-1) + Fibonacci (n-2) if n > 2.
   ```

   Use recursion to write the Fibonacci function and a program to test it.

2. Write and test a function `void indent (const char* what, int howMuch)` which prints the character string `what` after indenting `howMuch` spaces. If `howMuch` is 0, it just prints the string. If not, it prints a space and calls itself with `howMuch-1` spaces.

3. Write and test a recursive version of the pow function. `pow (a, b)` returns a^b.

4. Write and test a recursive function log which, given a positive integer `number` and an integer `base`, returns $\log_{base}$ (number). $\log_{base}$ (number) is defined as how many times you can divide number by base before getting to 1. For example, 8/2 gives 4, 4/2 gives 2, and 2/2 gives 1; that's 3 divisions; so $\log_2 8$ is 3. We won't worry about fractional parts: $\log_2 15$ is also 3, because (using integer division) 15/2 is 7, 7/2 is 3, and 3/2 is 1.

Algorithm analysis and O notation (optional)

Suppose we want to sort a list of names. I know! Let's generate all possible orderings of names, and stop when we get one that's perfectly ordered! Computers are fast, right?

```
while we haven't found an ordered sequence
   generate a new permutation of the elements
```

That's not much detail, but I already predict a problem. Suppose there are 4 elements. There's 4 possibilities for the first element. That leaves 3 possibilities for the next, which leaves 2 possibilities for the next, and 1 for the last: there are 4*3*2*1 possibilities: 4! So for N elements, we'll have N! orderings to consider. With N=100 that's 10^{158}. Computers are fast, but they aren't *that* fast.

Sometimes the algorithm is obviously a bad idea. Sometimes you don't realize how bad it is till you run it - unless you use **O notation**, so you can know what program *not* to bring to management and *not* what to spend your time writing.

Consider this code:

```
for (int i = 0; i < N; ++i)
    sum += array[i];
```

The initialization gets done once; the comparison, array reference, assignment, and increment are each done N times. We could say there are 1+4N things being executed.

What about some other snippet with a loop? Maybe it's a little different and we get, oh, 5+3N. Which one's faster, or are they the same? Hm.

We have a way of rating algorithms that greatly simplifies how we describe the time requirements and so helps us compare and evaluate them. It's called **O notation**. Here are the simplifying rules for O notation:

- If one addend is clearly smaller than another when the data set is large, discard the smaller one. So if we have 1+3N, we discard the 1 and get 3N.
- Discard constant multipliers. 3N becomes N.

The result is written as O(N). The preceding for loop is O(N), or "is of order N."

The simplification is justified. What we care about is what happens when the data set is large (small data sets are always easy). When N is large, 3N+1 is approximately 3N: the difference in 3,000,001 and 3,000,000 is negligible. We also don't care about constant multipliers. Whether N doubles from 3000 to 6000 or 3N doubles from 9000 to 18,000 – it's still doubling, and we want to know how increasing N degrades performance. This tells us.

A few examples. Consider this algorithm:

```
read in N                   1
read in M                   1
read in P                   1
add them                    1
divide by 3                 1
print the average           1
```

Each line is 1 action. Add 'em up and we have 6. We can discard constant multipliers; 6=6*1, so O(6)=O(1). This algorithm is of order 1: it'll take the same amount of time regardless of what values you give it.

Here's another:

```
for each element in an array     N x
      if this element is negative       (1
            change it to positive              + 1)
```

The last line is 1 action. The `if` statement that contains it is 1 more; O(2)=O(1). Because it's in a for loop, it will be done N times, where N is the length of the array. So this algorithm is O(N).

Here's another.

```
do
      for each successive pair of elements in an array
            if they are in the wrong order
                  swap them
while our last iteration of the do-while loop had a swap in it
```

This algorithm is a way to sort an array. Here's how it works. Consider an array of *Sesame Street* characters.

Kermit	Grover	Bert	Oscar	Piggy	Elmo

The first iteration of the preceding do-while loop does swaps, as needed, for each successive pair. Kermit should be swapped with Grover

Grover	Kermit	Bert	Oscar	Piggy	Elmo

and Bert

Grover	Bert	Kermit	Oscar	Piggy	Elmo

We keep moving through the array till we get to the end, swapping any wrongly ordered pairs.

Grover	Bert	Kermit	Oscar	Elmo	Piggy

It's still not in order, but we made progress. Here's what we get after another pass through the array:

Bert	Grover	Kermit	Elmo	Oscar	Piggy

Another:

Bert	Grover	Elmo	Kermit	Oscar	Piggy

And another:

Bert	Elmo	Grover	Kermit	Oscar	Piggy

This algorithm is called "bubble sort" because elements gradually "bubble" their way to correct positions. (And "bogo-sort" by people say it's 3vil because it's too slow. I don't know what they'd call the permutation method I had earlier, but it wouldn't be nice.)

How long will this algorithm take, in O notation? "If they are in the wrong order swap them" is O(1). We go through the entire array, making N-1 comparisons; so a pass through the array is O(N-1)=O(N). How many passes do we make? If we've got a very disordered array – say, if Piggy's in slot 0 and Bert is in the last slot – we'll need N-1 passes, since each pass moves an element at most 1 slot. $O(N(N-1))=O(N^2-N)=O(N^2)$.

$O(N^2)$ is called "quadratic time"; O(N) is predictably called "linear time." O(1) is "constant time." We try to avoid $O(2^N)$, "exponential time."

EXERCISES

1. What is the time in O notation for the function in Example 10-3, which returns the smallest number in an array?
2. ...for a function to determine if a word is a palindrome?
3. ...for a function to print all the elements in an NxN grid?
4. Write a function `intersection` which, given two arrays, finds all those elements in common and puts them in a new array. What is the time requirement, in O notation?
5. Write bubble sort and verify that it works.
6. Write a program that finds all primes up to some limit using the Sieve of Eratosthenes: You go thru and eliminate all numbers divisible by 2, then by 3, then by 4, and so on.

   What is the time requirement, in O notation?
7. What is the time required for Exercises 2, 3, and 4 from the previous section?

CHAPTER 19

Inheritance

The purpose of this chapter is to enable us to reuse code between similar classes.

The basics of inheritance

There's an unwritten rule that in a C++ intro text you must have an example using employee records, so here's mine (Example 19-1). It makes sense. I personally can't think of anything more exciting than employee records.

Example 19-1. Class Employee

```
//Class Employee
//      -- from _C++ for Lazy Programmers_

#ifndef EMPLOYEE_H
#define EMPLOYEE_H

#include <iostream>
#include <string>
#include "date.h"

class Employee
{
public:
    Employee () {}
    Employee (const Employee&) = delete;
    Employee (const std::string& theFirstName,
              const std::string& theLastName,
              const Date& theDateHired, int theSalary);
```


W. Briggs, *C++ for Lazy Programmers*, https://doi.org/10.1007/978-1-4842-5187-4_19

```
    const Employee& operator= (const Employee&) = delete;

    void print(std::ostream&) const;

    //access functions
    const std::string& firstName () const { return firstName_;    }
    const std::string& lastName  () const { return lastName_;     }
    const Date&        dateHired () const { return dateHired_;    }
    int   salary                 () const { return salary_;       }
    bool  isOnPayroll            () const { return isOnPayroll_; }
    int badPerformanceReviews    () const
    {
        return badPerformanceReviews_;
    }

    void  quit                   ()       { isOnPayroll_ = false;}
    void  start                  ()       { isOnPayroll_ = true; }
    void  meetWithBoss           () { ++badPerformanceReviews_;  }

private:
    std::string firstName_, lastName_;1
    Date dateHired_;
    int  salary_;
    bool isOnPayroll_;
    int  badPerformanceReviews_;
};

inline
std::ostream& operator<< (std::ostream& out, const Employee& foo)
{
    foo.print (out); return out;
}

#endif //EMPLOYEE_H
```

[1] `std::string` has a dtor. When does it get called? If you don't write a dtor for a class, C++ generates a default, which calls dtors of any members that have them. So `Employee`'s default dtor destructs the two strings. You don't need to plan for this – it's automatic.

Since I'm using the `Date` class, I'll need to copy `date.h` and `date.cpp` from the earlier chapter into my new project's folder. g++ users are done at that point; Visual Studio users right-click the project and say Add, Existing Item, and so on (Figure 19-1).

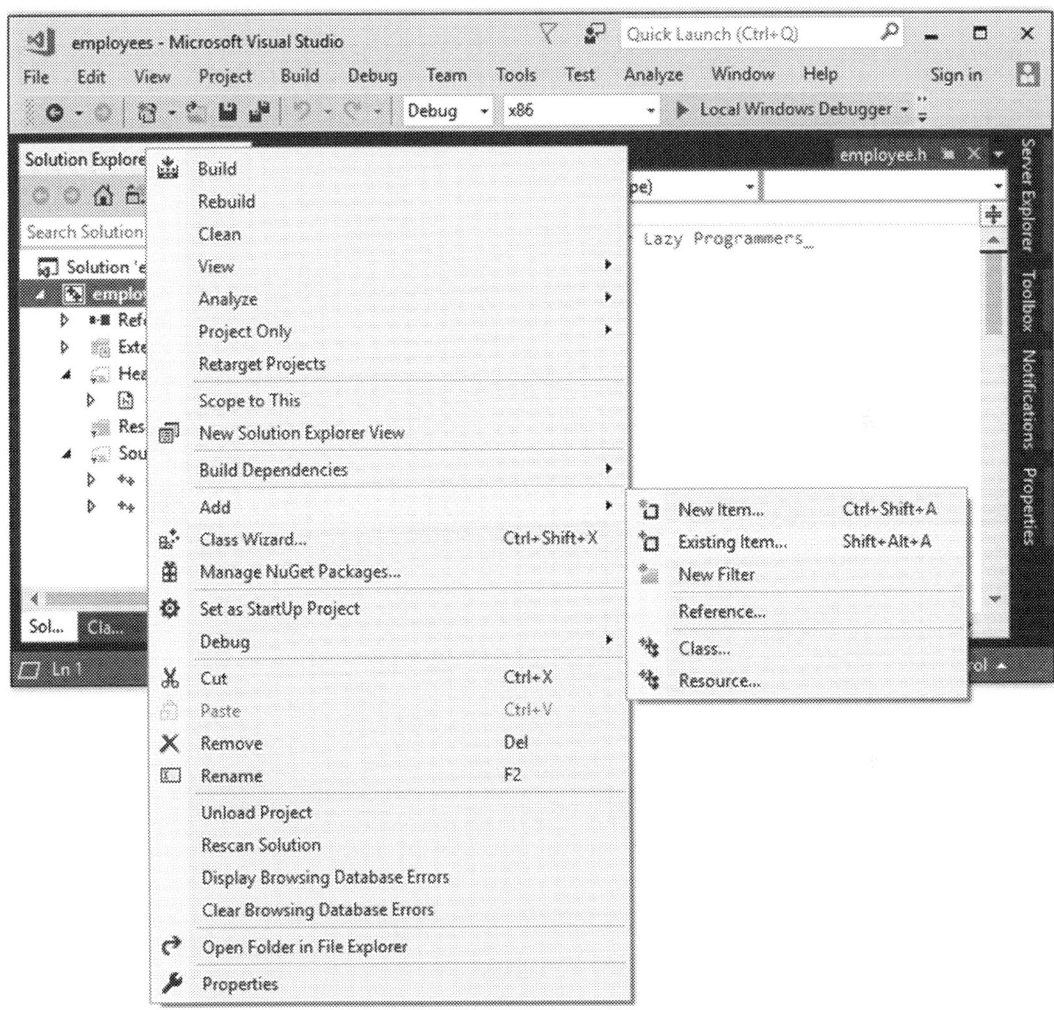

***Figure 19-1.** Adding existing items in Visual Studio*

Not all employees are the same. If what I read – especially in Scott Adams's *Dilbert* – is accurate, a manager is like any other employee, having a name and a salary, but with extra characteristics: the power to hire and fire, low IQ, and an obsession with tormenting employees.

It would be redundant to write a whole new class for Manager, repeating those parts also in Employee such as firstName, lastName, and salary. So instead we'll make Manager a subclass (or derived class, or child class) of Employee, as shown in Example 19-2. This is **inheritance**.

Example 19-2. Class Manager

```
//Class Manager
//      -- from _C++ for Lazy Programmers_

#ifndef MANAGER_H
#define MANAGER_H

#include "employee.h"

using Meeting = std::string;

class Manager: public Employee
{
public:
    Manager ();
    Manager (const Manager&) = delete;
    Manager (const std::string& theFirstName,
             const std::string& theLastName,
             const Date&   theDateHired,
             int           theSalary);
    ~Manager () { delete [] schedule_; }

    const Manager& operator= (const Manager&) = delete;

    void hire (Employee& foo) const { foo.start (); }
    void fire (Employee& foo) const { foo.quit  (); }
    void laugh()                const
    {
        std::cout << firstName() << " says: hee-hee!\n";
    }

    void torment (Employee&) const;
```

```
private:
    Meeting*    schedule_;
    int         howManyMeetingsOnSchedule_;
    void        copy (const Manager& other);
};

#endif //MANAGER_H
```

`class Manager: public Employee` means `Manager` is a subclass of `Employee`, and everything an `Employee` has a `Manager` has too (Figure 19-2). Don't worry about the word `public` yet.

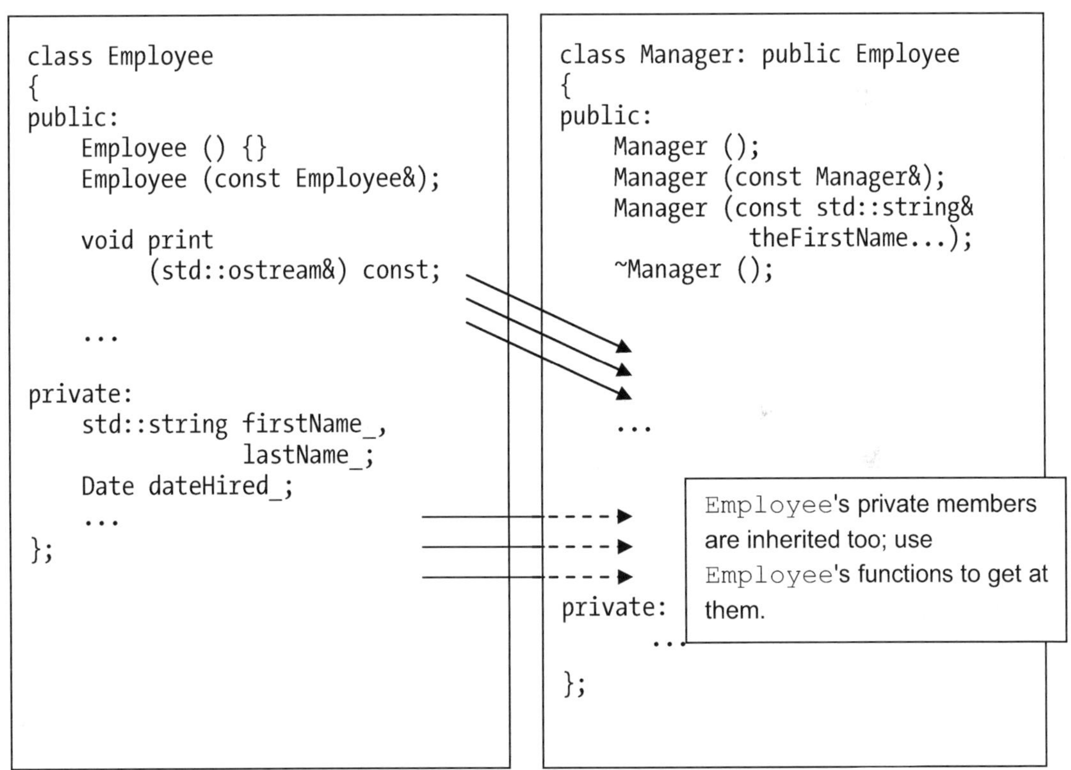

Figure 19-2. *How inheritance works. Everything that's in `Employee` is also in `Manager` – but if it's `private`, it won't be visible*

So this code is legal:

```
Manager  alfred ("Alfred E.", "Neumann", Date (10, 1,1952),
                  OBSCENELY_LARGE_SALARY);
//firstName, salary are inherited from Employee
cout << alfred.firstName() << " makes " << alfred.salary ()
     << " per month!\n";
```

We don't rewrite those functions – we just use them. Anything you can do with an `Employee`, you can do with a `Manager` – because a `Manager` *is* an `Employee`.

Constructors and destructors

We'll surely want to call `Employee`'s constructor when we write `Manager`'s. No problem: we'll use the same syntax we use to initialize data members.

```
Manager::Manager (const string& theFirstName,
                  const string& theLastName,
                  const Date& theDateHired,
                  int theSalary) :
      Employee (theFirstName, theLastName, theDateHired, theSalary),
      schedule_ (nullptr), howManyMeetingsOnSchedule_ (0)
{
}
```

The constructor does things in this order:

- The constructors after the ":" are called, parent class constructor first (even if you put it later).
- Whatever's between the {}'s gets done (in this case, nothing).

If you don't say what parent constructor to call, it will call the default.

When a `Manager` goes out of scope, its destructor is called first, then its parent's. (And then its grandparent's, if any, and so on.) You won't need to think about this – it's automatic.

EXERCISES

For these exercises, be sure that

- **Data members are private** (of course).
- Just for now, **there are no access functions**. This is to ensure that the subclass only accesses its own data, not its parent's. For example, to print, the subclass should call its parent's print function, then print its own data members.

1. An eyeglasses prescription (Figure 19-3) lists: **sphere** or power, **additional** correction for bifocals, and stuff for astigmatism (**cylinder**, **axis**). The two eyes are called "OD" and "OS" not "left" and "right," because what's cooler than calling your eyeballs weird Latin abbreviations?

   Write and test a class to contain, and neatly print, this information.

	OD	OS
Sphere	-3.00	-2.00
Additional	2.50	2.50
Cylinder	+0.25	+0.50
Axis	150°	70°

Figure 19-3. *An eyeglasses prescription*

   Write and test a subclass for contact lenses to contain and print that plus a little more: **back curvature** and **diameter**, numbers to ensure the lens comfortably fits the eyeball.

2. A child in special education may have an "IEP," an Individual Education Plan, to spell out what special needs exist and how the school will address them. Write and test a class for a student record (name, whatever else looks relevant) and a subclass for the record of a student with an IEP. You can let the IEP be a single string.

Inheritance as a concept

Subclasses are part of how we think outside the computer, too. In biology, *animal* is a subclass of *organism*, mammal is a subclass of *animal*, *human* is a subclass of *mammal*, and *ubergeek* is a subclass of *human* (Figure 19-4). In each case, the subclass has every characteristic of the superclass (or parent class, or base class), plus extra characteristics. An animal is an organism that can move; an ubergeek is a human who programs so well the gods themselves are impressed.

You aren't a *subclass* of human, because you aren't a class. You're an *instance* of human. (Apologies to my extraterrestrial readers.)

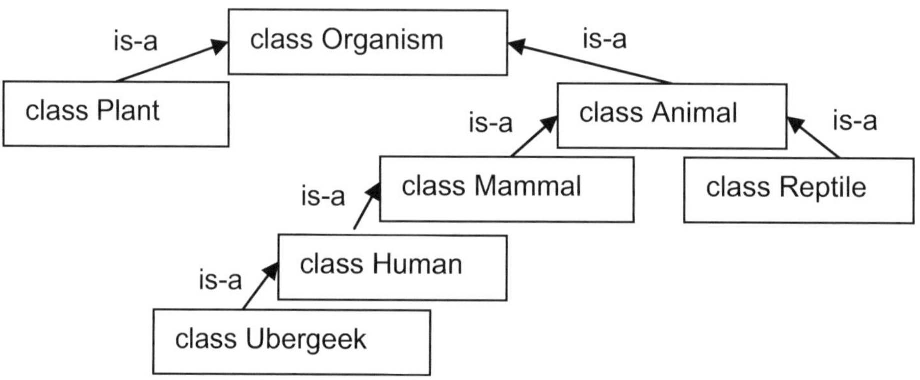

Figure 19-4. *A class hierarchy. An Ubergeek is a Human, which is a Mammal, and so on*

This is as good a point as any to mention a distinction commonly used in object-oriented thinking, between *is-a* and *has-a*.

An Ubergeek *is-a* Human (and a Mammal, etc.). An Ubergeek *has-a* computer. So when God created the Ubergeek, His code must have looked something like this:

```
class Ubergeek: public Human //an Ubergeek is-a human
{
      ...
private:
      Computer myComputer_;  //an Ubergeek has-a computer
};
```

So the things an `Ubergeek` *has* go in the private section. The thing that an Ubergeek *is* goes on that first line.

Figure 19-5. *Plato and Aristotle, the first two ever to have an argument about object-oriented programming. Sort of*

Extra Your local philosophy professor will probably want to shoot me for saying this, but object-oriented programming is so very…Platonic.

Plato considered classes ("ideals") to be what was ultimately real, and the particular instances – the objects or variables in our vocabulary – to be imperfect examples of that ultimate reality. So `Human` is the real thing; you and I are just instances.

In radical materialism – as far from Plato as you can get – classes aren't real; only material objects are. Of course, since radical materialism isn't a material object, that might be a problem, but lazy philosophy, unlike lazy programming, is beyond the scope of this book.

Aristotle considered things themselves to be real, and the classes to be their inherent natures. You're real, and `Human` is what you really are. He splits the difference.

However it works out in reality, C++ is Platonic: the class comes first. (You have to have the class definition before you can create a variable of that type.)

Classes for card games

People like to play cards on the computer, so let's make classes to help us build a variety of card games. Code reuse.

I'll provide in Example 19-3 class Card and give it things any class should have: default and copy constructors, operator=, access functions, and I/O. I also soup up the Rank and Suit enums from Chapter 10.

Example 19-3. The Card class (card.h). card.cpp is in the book's source code

```
//Card class
//   -- from C++ for Lazy Programmers

#ifndef CARD_H
#define CARD_H

#include <iostream>

//Rank and Suit: integral parts of Card

//I make these global so that I don't have to forget
// "Card::" over and over when I use them.
enum Rank {ACE=1, JACK=11, QUEEN, KING};
enum Suit {HEARTS, DIAMONDS, CLUBS, SPADES};
enum Color{BLACK, RED};

inline
Color toColor(Suit s)
{
    if (s == HEARTS || s == DIAMONDS) return RED; else return BLACK;
}

std::ostream& operator<< (std::ostream& out, Rank r);
std::ostream& operator<< (std::ostream& out, Suit s);
std::istream& operator>> (std::istream& in, Rank& r);
std::istream& operator>> (std::istream& in, Suit& s);

class BadRankException {};  //used if a Rank is out of range
class BadSuitException {};  //used if a Suit is out of range

//...and class Card.
```

```
class Card
{
public:
    Card (Rank r = Rank(0), Suit s = Suit(0)) :
        rank_ (r), suit_ (s)
    {
    }
    Card (const Card& other) { *this = other; }

    const Card& operator= (const Card& other)
    {
         rank_ = other.rank(); suit_ = other.suit (); return *this;
    }

    bool operator== (const Card& other) const
    {
        return rank() == other.rank () && suit() == other.suit();
    }
    bool operator!= (const Card& other) const
    {
        return !(*this==other);
    }

    Suit  suit () const { return suit_;            }
    Rank  rank () const { return rank_;            }
    Color color() const { return toColor (suit()); }

    void print (std::ostream &out) const { out << rank() << suit(); }
    void read  (std::istream &in );
private:
    Suit suit_;
    Rank rank_;
};

inline std::ostream& operator<< (std::ostream& out, const Card& foo)
{
    foo.print (out); return out;
}
```

```
inline std::istream& operator>> (std::istream& in,        Card& foo)
{
    foo.read  (in);  return in;
}
#endif //CARD_H
```

An inheritance hierarchy

A few games we might create:

FreeCell (Figure 19-6). At upper left are cells, each of which can store a single card; the upper right is foundations, each of which takes an Ace, then a 2, and so on, in the same suit; at the bottom are piles, randomly dealt. You can take a card from a pile or add a card to a pile if it's down in alternating color. For example, you can move a black 10 onto that jack of diamonds if you have one free.

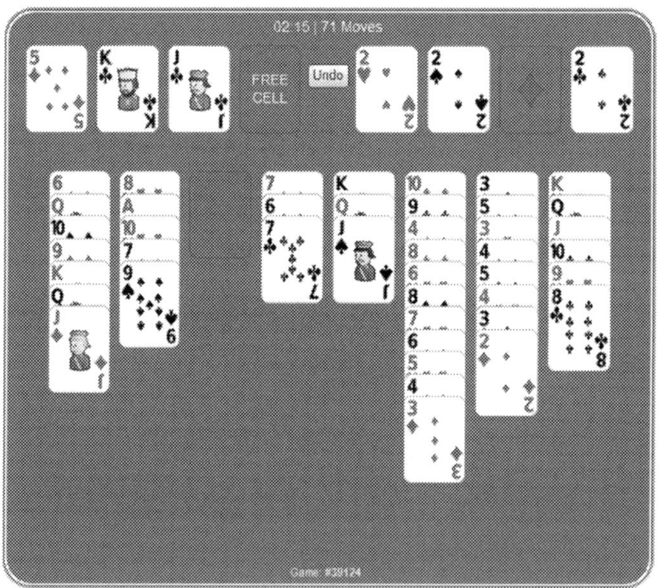

Figure 19-6. *FreeCell*

Klondike (Figure 19-7). Like FreeCell, it has foundations (top right); it also has a deck, a waste pile, and piles of its own type at the bottom.

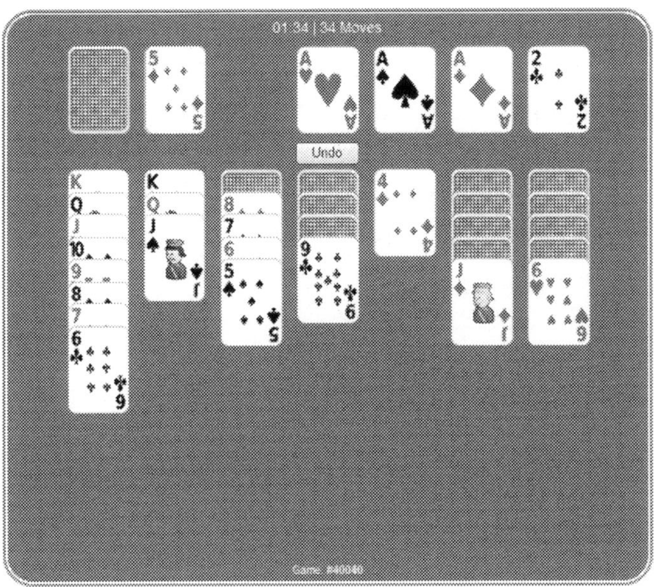

Figure 19-7. *Klondike solitaire*

Hearts, Spades, and other multiplayer games with a deck and hands. Common groupings include

- Deck: You can shuffle it and deal off the top.
- Waste (discard pile): You can put a card on top or take one off.
- Cell: Like Waste, you can add to a cell or take from the top – but there can only be one card.
- Foundation: All one suit, starting with Ace and going up.
- Hand: You can add to it and take out any card you want.
- FreeCell pile: Add a card, down in alternating color; take a card off.
- Klondike pile: More complicated; left as an exercise.

These all have two things in common: contents and a size. Do any have more in common?

I'd say that a Cell *is-a* Waste pile, because the way you interact with it is the same: add a card, take one off the top. It just has a restriction on size.

Beyond that I'd say no. You can't say Foundation is a special case of Deck, or that a Klondike pile is a special case of a Waste pile. (Some of this may be a matter of opinion.) But they all have this in common: they're all groups of cards. So we can have a `CardGroup` class and inherit from it. (A `Hand` is a `CardGroup` with nothing added, so we'll make `Hand` an alias for `CardGroup`: `using Hand = CardGroup;`).

So I propose the inheritance hierarchy in Figure 19-8, based on `CardGroup` (Example 19-4).

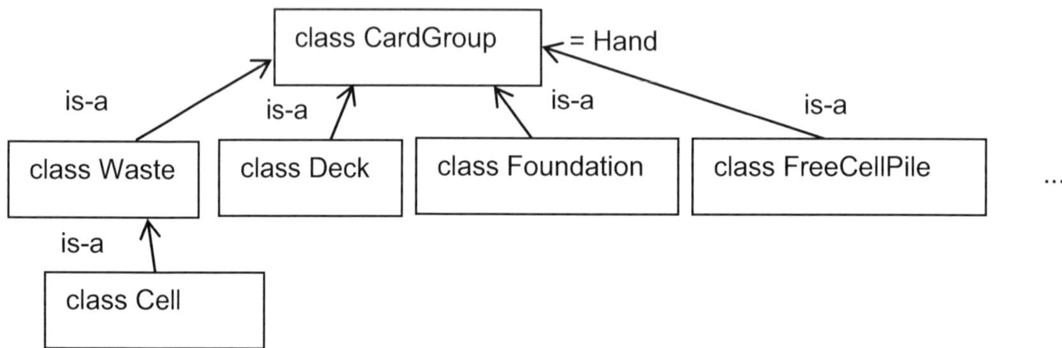

Figure 19-8. *A hierarchy of classes for groups of cards*

Example 19-4. `cardgroup.h`

```
//CardGroup class (for playing cards)
//  -- from C++ for Lazy Programmers

#ifndef CARDGROUP_H
#define CARDGROUP_H

#include <iostream>

#include "card.h"

class OutOfRange  {};          //Exception classes
class IllegalMove {};

class CardGroup
{
public:
    enum {MAX_SIZE = 208};     //if anybody wants to play a game
                               //  w/ more than 4 decks, change this.
```

```
CardGroup ()                       { howMany_ = 0;              }
CardGroup (const CardGroup& other){ *this    = other;           }
CardGroup (const Card& other)
{
    howMany_ = 0; addCard (other);
}

const CardGroup& operator= (const CardGroup&);
bool operator== (const CardGroup& other) const;
bool operator!= (const CardGroup& other) const
{
    return !(*this == other);
}

Card& operator[] (unsigned int index);
Card  operator[] (unsigned int index) const;

Card remove          (unsigned int index);
Card top             () const { return (*this)[size()-1];  }
Card removeTop       ()       { return remove (size()-1);  }

unsigned int size    () const { return howMany_;           }
bool         isEmpty() const { return size() == 0;         }
bool         isFull () const { return size() >= MAX_SIZE; }

//addCard does NOT check that it's legal to add a card.
//We need this for creating CardGroups during the deal.
void addCard (const Card&);

//makes sure the addition of the card is legal, then adds it
void addCardLegally (const Card& other)
{
    if (isFull ()) throw IllegalMove();
    addCard (other);
}

void print (std::ostream&) const;
```

```
private:
    unsigned int howMany_;
    Card contents_ [MAX_SIZE];
};

inline
std::ostream& operator<< (std::ostream& out, const CardGroup& foo)
{
    foo.print(out); return out;
}

using Hand = CardGroup;

#endif //CARDGROUP_H
```

private inheritance

Consider the `Waste` class. We shouldn't allow random access of `Waste` through the `[]` operators; you can only look at the *top* card of a `Waste` pile.

To restrict access, we change the type of inheritance:

```
class Waste: private CardGroup
{
...
```

This makes the `CardGroup`'s public members go in `Waste`'s private section (Figure 19-9).

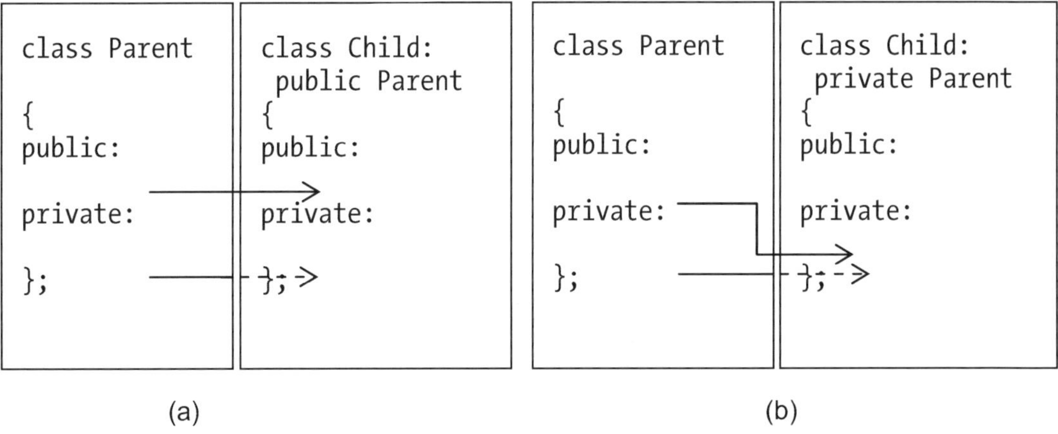

Figure 19-9. *Public (a) and private (b) inheritance. Use private if there's any inherited public member that must be kept private in the child class*

`operator[]` is now private – good – but there are public members of `CardGroup` that we *want* `Waste` to make available to the outside: `isEmpty` and `print`, for example. Since they're private, we make new public functions with the same names, that simply call the parent's functions, as in Example 19-5.

Example 19-5. Class `Waste`, in `waste.h`, using `private` inheritance

```
//Waste class
//      -- from _C++ for Lazy Programmers_

#ifndef WASTE_H
#define WASTE_H

#include "cardgroup.h"

class Waste: private CardGroup
{
public:
    Waste () {}
    Waste (const Waste&     other) : CardGroup (other) {}
    Waste (const CardGroup& other) : CardGroup (other) {}

    const Waste & operator= (const Waste& other) = delete;
```

```
    bool operator==         (const Waste& other) const
    {
        return CardGroup::operator== (other);
    }
    bool isEmpty        () const { return CardGroup::isEmpty ();  }
    bool isFull         () const { return CardGroup::isFull  ();  }
    unsigned int size   () const { return CardGroup::size ();     }
    Card top            () const { return CardGroup::top();       }
    Card removeTop      ()       { return CardGroup::removeTop(); }
    void addCardLegally (const Card& foo)
    {
        CardGroup::addCardLegally (foo);
    }
    void print (std::ostream& out) const{ CardGroup::print (out); }
};

inline
std::ostream& operator<< (std::ostream& out, const Waste& foo)
{
    foo.print (out); return out;
}
#endif //WASTE_H
```

Hiding an inherited member function

Waste has from CardGroup a member function isFull, true if the Waste has MAX_SIZE cards. Its child class Cell has a different version. If you call isFull on a Cell, which will it use?

Cell::isFull **hides** the inherited version. To use Waste's version, you must specify: myCell.Waste::isFull (). We wouldn't do anything so grotty outside the class, but we might inside a member function like Cell::addcardLegally in Example 19-6.

Example 19-6. `cell.h`

```
//Cell class
//  -- from C++ for Lazy Programmers

#ifndef CELL_H
#define CELL_H

#include "waste.h"

class Cell: public Waste
{
public:
    Cell ()                                     {}
    Cell(const Cell& other) : Waste (other)     {}
    const Cell& operator= (const Cell& other) = delete;

    //public inheritance, so all public members of Waste are here...

    bool isFull    () const {return ! isEmpty (); }

    void addCardLegally (const Card& card)
    {
        if (isFull ()) throw IllegalMove (); //Cell must be empty
        else Waste::addCardLegally (card);
    }
};

#endif //CELL_H
```

A game of Montana

Montana solitaire uses `Cell` and `Deck`, so it should be a good test of our hierarchy.

The rules: deal out all cards in a 4x13 grid of cells, remove the aces, and get a mess like in Figure 19-10.

Figure 19-10. *A game of Montana*

Your goal is to get 4 rows lined up from 2 to King, each with one suit.

The only valid move is to put a card into an empty cell. The card you put must follow whatever's on its left, in the same suit; for example, you can only follow 2♥ with 3♥. If it's in the leftmost column, you have to put a 2. A space following a King is unusable.

When you get stuck, redeal all the cards that aren't in sequences starting with 2 on the left, in suit. You get 4 deals.

A working program (with Deck removed – that's an exercise) is in the code accompanying the text; Examples 19-7 through 19-9 show the highlights.

Example 19-7. `montana_main.cpp`: a game of Montana

```
//A game of Montana solitaire
//  -- from C++ for Lazy Programmers

#include <cstdio>       //for srand, rand
#include <ctime>        //for time
#include "io.h"         //for bool getAnswerYorN (const char[]);
#include "montana.h"

int main ()
{
    srand ((unsigned int) time (nullptr)); //start rand# generator

    Montana montanaGame;
```

```
    do
        montanaGame.play ();
    while (getYorNAnswer ("Play again (Y/N)? "));

    return 0;
}
```

Example 19-8. montana.h

```
//class Montana, for a game of Montana solitaire
//  -- from _C++ for Lazy Programmers_

#include "gridLoc.h"
#include "cell.h"
#include "deck.h"

#ifndef MONTANA_H
#define MONTANA_H

class Montana
{
public:
    enum { ROWS = 4, CLMS  = 13};
    enum { NUM_EMPTY_CELLS =  4}; //How many empty cells in grid? 4
    enum { MAX_TURNS       =  4}; //How many turns allowed? 4

    class OutOfRange {};          //Exception class for card locations

    Montana                   ()                 {};
    Montana                   (const Montana&) = delete;
    const Montana& operator= (const Montana&) = delete;

    void play ();

private:
        //displaying
    void display            () const;
```

```
        //dealing and redealing
    void deal               (Deck& deck, Waste& waste);
    void cleanup            (Deck& deck, Waste& waste);
    void resetGrid          (); // make it empty

        //playing a turn
    void makeLegalMove      (bool& letsQuitOrEndTurn);
    void makeMove           (const GridLoc& oldLoc,
                             const GridLoc& newLoc);
    bool detectVictory      () const;
    void congratulationsOrCondolences(bool isVictory) const;

        //working with empty cells

    //store in emptyCells_ the location of each empty cell
    void identifyEmptyCells ();

    //which of the empty cells has this row and clm? A B C or D?
    char whichEmptyCell      (int row, int clm) const;

    //Is this a valid cell index? It must be 0-3.
    bool inRange(unsigned int emptyCellIndex) const
    {
        return (emptyCellIndex < NUM_EMPTY_CELLS);
    }

        //placing cards

    Cell&        cellAt(const GridLoc& loc)
    {
        if (inRange(loc)) return grid_[loc.row_][loc.clm_];
        else throw OutOfRange();
    }

    const Cell& cellAt(const GridLoc& loc) const
    {
        if (inRange(loc)) return grid_[loc.row_][loc.clm_];
        else throw OutOfRange();
    }
```

```
    //Is this location within the grid?
    bool inRange(const GridLoc& loc) const
    {
        return (0 <= loc.row_ && loc.row_ < ROWS &&
                0 <= loc.clm_ && loc.clm_ < CLMS);
    }

    //Can Card c follow other card?
    bool canFollow(const Card& c, const Card& other) const
    {
        return c.suit() == other.suit() &&
            c.rank() == other.rank() + 1;
    }

    //Can card c go at this location?
    bool canGoHere(const Card& c, const GridLoc& loc) const;

    //Is the cell at row, clm ordered at its location? That is,
    //    could we put it here if it weren't already?
    bool cellIsCorrect(int row, int clm) const
    {
        return ! grid_[row][clm].isEmpty () &&
               canGoHere(grid_[row][clm].top(), GridLoc(row, clm));
    }

    //data members
    Cell    grid_        [ROWS][CLMS];        //where the cards are
    GridLoc emptyCells_ [NUM_EMPTY_CELLS];  //where the empty cells are
};

#endif //MONTANA_H
```

Montana::play creates a new Deck and Waste every time it's called. You can see in it how they are used. Montana::makeMove shows how Cell can be used (cellAt returns the Cell at a given location).

Montana::makeLegalMove uses a try-catch block in case the input goes wonky.

Example 19-9. Part of `montana.cpp` (the rest is in the book's source code)

```
//class Montana, for a game of Montana solitaire
//  -- from C++ for Lazy Programmers

#include <iostream>
#include "deck.h"
#include "io.h"       //for bool getAnswerYorN (const char[]);
#include "montana.h"

using namespace std;

    //Playing the game

...

void Montana::play ()
{
    Deck  deck;
    Waste waste;
    bool  isVictory = false;

    resetGrid(); //prepare for deal by ensuring grid is empty

    for (int turn = 1; turn <= MAX_TURNS && ! isVictory; ++turn)
    {
        cout << "******************** New turn! "
                "*********************\n";

        //To test detectVictory func, uncomment setupForVictory,
        //comment out deal, and see if isVictory becomes true
        //setupForVictory(grid_, deck, waste);

        deck.shuffle ();              //Shuffle deck
        deal (deck, waste);           //fill grid with cards
                                      //  and remove aces
        identifyEmptyCells ();        //remember where the aces were
                                      //  in a list of 4 emptyCells_
```

```
        bool letsQuitOrEndTurn = false;
        isVictory = detectVictory(); //already won? Unlikely, but...

        while (! isVictory && ! letsQuitOrEndTurn)
        {
            display();
            makeLegalMove (letsQuitOrEndTurn); //play a turn
            isVictory=detectVictory();         //did we win?
        }

        cleanup (deck, waste);        //collect cards for redeal

        //If user won, we go on and leave loop
        //If we're out of turns, we go on and leave loop
        //Otherwise give user a chance to quit
        if (!isVictory && turn < MAX_TURNS)
            if (getYorNAnswer("Quit game (Y/N)?"))
                break;
    }

    congratulationsOrCondolences (isVictory);
}

void Montana::makeMove  (const GridLoc& oldLoc,
                         const GridLoc& newLoc)
{
    cellAt(newLoc).addCardLegally (cellAt(oldLoc).removeTop ());
}

void Montana::makeLegalMove (bool& letsQuitOrEndTurn)
{
    bool isValidMove = false;

    do
    {
        cout << "Move (e.g. A 1 5 to fill cell A with "
             << "the card at row 1, clm 5; q to quit/end turn)? ";
```

```
        //Which empty space will we fill -- or are we quitting?
        char letter; cin >> letter;
        if (toupper(letter) == 'Q') letsQuitOrEndTurn = true;
        else
        {
            int emptyCellIndex = toupper(letter) - 'A';

            try
            {
                //Which cell are we moving from?
                GridLoc from;  cin >> from;
                //Which cell are we moving to?
                GridLoc to = emptyCells_[emptyCellIndex];

                //If the empty cell exists, and is really empty...
                if (inRange(emptyCellIndex) && cellAt(to).isEmpty())
                    //if card to move exists, and move is legal...
                    if (!cellAt(from).isEmpty() &&
                        canGoHere(cellAt(from).top(), to))
                    {
                        isValidMove = true;
                        makeMove(from, to);
                        emptyCells_[emptyCellIndex] = from;
                    }
            }
            catch (const BadInput&) {}
                //reading GridLoc went bad -- just try again
        }
    } while (! isValidMove && ! letsQuitOrEndTurn);
}
```

EXERCISES

1. Write a subclass of class `Date` from earlier, adding a function `printInText`. It will print the `Date` not in numeric format (e.g., 12/12/2012), but in your favorite ASCII-using language: `doce de diciembre de 2012` (Spanish); `December 12, 2012` (English); whatever you like. What kind of inheritance will you use?

2. Write a subclass of `string` called `UnixFilename` that doesn't allow spaces – it immediately replaces them with _'s. And it won't let you interfere by changing the string's individual letters:

```
UnixFilename myFileName ("my file name");
                              //becomes "my.file.name"
myFileName[2] = ' ';          //forbidden
```

   What kind of inheritance will you use?

3. Write a `Reserve` class. It's a group of cards; the only legal move is to take a card off the top. What should it inherit from?

The next four exercises will be especially useful for the FreeCell game exercise in Chapter 21.

4. Write the shuffle algorithm for the `Deck` class. What is its time requirement in O notation? Can you get it down to O(N)?

5. ...and write the `Deck` class.

6. Write a `Foundation` class. A `Foundation`, remember, starts with ACE and goes up in suit, or it may be empty. Throw an exception if a call attempts to add an unsuitable card.

7. Write the `FreeCellPile` class. Throw exceptions as appropriate.

8. Write the `KlondikePile` class. A Klondike pile is like a FreeCell pile in that you can only add something going down by alternating color, but it's different in that you can add a *sequence* of such cards as long as the top card of the pile

matches that criterion. For example, if the top of a Klondike pile is a black king, you can put a sequence on it if that sequence starts with a red queen. You can also remove a sequence of cards from a Klondike pile, as long as it's down in alternating color.

So apparently you need to add and remove sequences. What class is a sequence? What class should your add-sequence and remove-sequence functions belong to?

Also, a Klondike pile has 0 or more cards at the bottom, face down. You can't move any sequence including a face-down card. If you remove all face-up cards, you can then expose the (face-down) top card.

Throw exceptions as appropriate.

The best way to be sure you understand the rules is to play the game, but I would never encourage anyone to find yet another way of wasting time at work.

9. (Involved, but not hard) Write a game of Go Fish (look online for rules).

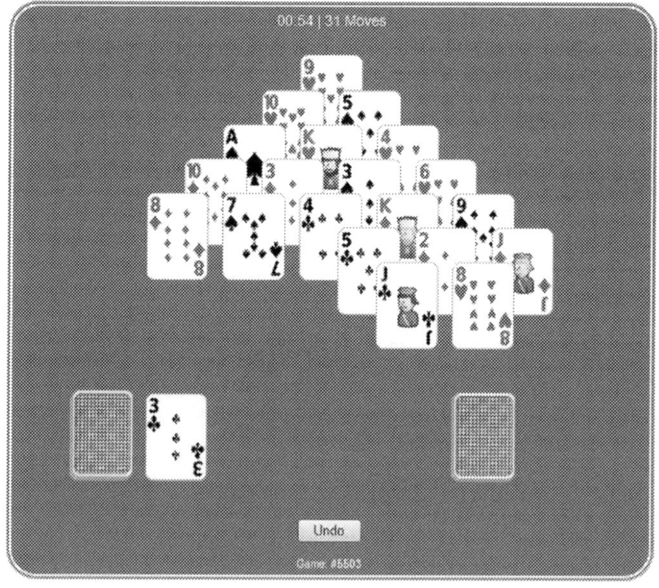

Figure 19-11. *Pyramid solitaire*

10. (Hard) Write the `Pyramid` class for `Pyramid` solitaire (see Figure 19-11; look online for rules).

11. Design a simple calculator class, that can have two numbers and can do the four basic functions +, -, *, and /.

    Now write an engineer calculator class that does all those things, but also does some other fancy things (say, square root and exponentiation). What kind of inheritance will you use?

CHAPTER 20

Templates

Would I write a function or class that takes `int`s, and another just like it except it takes `string`s, and another just like it except it takes `Ubergeeks`? That doesn't sound lazy! This chapter enables us to write it *once*, using templates.

Function templates

Recall this function for swapping `int`s, from Chapter 8:

```
void swap (int& arg1, int& arg2)
{
      int temp = arg2; arg2 = arg1; arg1 = temp;
}
```

That's fine for `int`, but what if I want `double`s? `string`s? Heffalumps? I don't want to write new versions for every type I encounter! Here's the fix.

```
template <typename T>
void swap (T& arg1, T& arg2)
{
      T temp = arg2; arg2 = arg1; arg1 = temp;
}
```

This is a **function template**: not a function in itself, but instructions on how to *make* a function once it knows what type we want.

The `template <typename T>` tells the compiler that this will be a template and that the thing that we expect to change is the type we're calling `T`. `T` is a sort of blank, to be filled in with a type when we decide what we want.

Example 20-1 shows how to use it.

W. Briggs, *C++ for Lazy Programmers*, https://doi.org/10.1007/978-1-4842-5187-4_20

Example 20-1. Using the `swap` function template

```
//Utterly useless program that uses a function template
//      -- from _C++ for Lazy Programmers_

template <typename T>
void swap(T& arg1, T& arg2)
{
      T temp = arg2; arg2 = arg1; arg1 = temp;
}

int main ()
{
    int    I = 10  , J = 20  ;
    double M =  0.5, N =  1.5;

    swap (I, J);
    swap (M, N);
    //swap (I, N); //No: can't figure what T should be

    return 0;
}
```

The compiler doesn't create *any* `swap` function until it gets to the line `swap (I, J);`. Then it notes that `I` and `J` are both `int`s, so it substitutes `int` for `T` in the template and creates a `swap` function that takes two `int`s.

On the next line, it generates a `swap` for `double`.

I put the function template *above* `main`. If the compiler can't see it before it's used, it won't know *how* to create the function – it won't have read the instructions yet. So the function template goes at the beginning of the program or in a `.h` file in place of the prototype.

In summation, to convert a function into a function template

1. **Put** `template <typename T>` **or such in front.**
2. **Change the type you were using to** `T` **or** `const T&`**.** If it's in a place where a class type would use a copy constructor – a return type or parameter without an `&` – `const T&` will prevent needless copying.
3. **Put the new function template where you had its prototype.**

Antibugging

- **Linking, the compiler says it can't find the function, but you can see it later in the program or in another** `.cpp` **file.** See Step 3.

Other possible mistakes:

- **Converting** `int` **to** `T/const T&` **when you shouldn't.** I have this code for searching an `int` array:

  ```
  bool contains (int array[], int howMany, int item)
  {
      for (int i = 0; i < howMany; ++i)
          if (array[i] == item)
              return true;
      return false;
  }
  ```

  and convert it to

  ```
  template <typename T>
  bool contains (T array[], const T& howMany, const T& item)
  {
      for (int i = 0; i < howMany; ++i)
          if (array[i] == item)
              return true;
      return false;
  }
  ```

  If it's an array of strings, it doesn't make sense for `howMany` to be `const string&`! It should remain an `int`.

- **Using an operator that doesn't work correctly for type** `T`**.** Suppose I try to compare two T's with != or use = – but T is an array. != and = don't work right with arrays.

```
template <typename T>
void copy (T& thing1, const T& thing2)
{
    if (thing1 != thing2) thing1 = thing2;
    ...
}
```

Or maybe I use the function template with a type that doesn't even *have* != or =. The template won't compile.

The usual fix is to use templates only with things that make sense. Classes you wrote (correctly) should be fine, because you wrote = and other relevant ops.

EXERCISES

1. Write and use a function template that will print an item of any type you give, surrounded by *'s.
2. Write and use a function template `prompt` which prints "?" before getting input with `cin`, then returns what it read as an & parameter. It should be able to read in any type `cin` can handle.
3. Write function template `sqr` to square a value of any numeric type.

The `Vector` class

Arrays are trouble. You can give an array an index of -2000 and it'll happily give you something dumb. If you declared an array to hold 50 elements but decide you want 51, too bad.

We can fix that by making a better-behaved array-like class called `Vector` (see Examples 20-2 and 20-3).

Example 20-2. vector.h, for a vector of ints

```
//Vector class:  a variable-length array of ints
//  -- from _C++ for Lazy Programmers_

#ifndef VECTOR_H
#define VECTOR_H

class Vector
{
public:
    class OutOfRange {};    //exception, for [] operators

    Vector ()   { contents_ = new int[0]; howMany_ = 0; }
    Vector (const Vector& other) { copy (other);         }

    ~Vector ()  { delete [] contents_;                   }

    const Vector& operator= (const Vector& other)
    {
        if (contents_) delete [] contents_; copy (other);
        return *this;
    }

    bool operator== (const Vector& other) const;
    bool operator!= (const Vector& other) const
    {
        return !((*this) == other);
    }

    unsigned int size () const { return howMany_;      }

    int  operator[] (unsigned int index) const;
    int& operator[] (unsigned int index);

    void push_back  (int newElement); //add newElement at the back

    void print (std::ostream&) const;
```

```
private:
    int* contents_;
    unsigned int howMany_;

    void copy (const Vector& other);
};

inline
std::ostream& operator<< (std::ostream& out, const Vector& foo)
{
    foo.print(out); return out;
}

#endif //VECTOR_H
```

It's a lot like String, only of course I can't use strcpy and so on.

Example 20-3. vector.cpp

```
//Vector class:  a variable-length array of ints
//       -- from _C++ for Lazy Programmers_

#include <iostream>
#include "vector.h"

bool Vector::operator==(const Vector& other) const
{
    bool noDifferences = true;

    //quit if you find a difference or run out of elements
    for (unsigned int i = 0; i < size() && noDifferences; ++i)
        if ((*this)[i] != other[i]) noDifferences = false;

    return noDifferences;
}

int  Vector::operator[] (unsigned int index) const
{
    if (index >= size ()) throw OutOfRange ();
    else return contents_[index];
}
```

```
int& Vector::operator[] (unsigned int index)
{
    if (index >= size()) throw OutOfRange();
    else return contents_[index];
}

//add newElement at the back
void Vector::push_back  (int newElement)
{
    int* newContents = new int [howMany_+1];
                                     //make room for 1 more...

    for (unsigned int i = 0; i < size(); ++i)
                                     //copy old elements
                                     // into new array...
        newContents[i] = contents_[i];

    newContents[howMany_] = newElement;  //add the new element...

    ++howMany_;                          //remember we have 1 more...

    delete [] contents_;                //throw out old contents_
    contents_ = newContents;            // and keep new version
}

//print Vector with []'s around it, spaces between
void Vector::print (std::ostream& out) const
{
    out << "[  ";

    for (unsigned int i = 0; i < size(); ++i)
        out << (*this)[i] << "  ";

    out << ']';
}
```

```
//Sort of like String::copy from Chapter 17, but w/o strcpy
void Vector::copy(const Vector& other)
{
    //set howMany to other's size; allocate that much memory
    contents_ = new int[howMany_ = other.size()];

    //then copy the elements over
    for (unsigned int i = 0; i < size(); ++i)
        contents_[i] = other[i];
}
```

Example 20-4 shows how you might use it.

Example 20-4. Using Vector

```
//Example with a Vector of int
//      -- from _C++ for Lazy Programmers_

#include <iostream>
#include <cassert>
#include "vector.h"

using namespace std;

int main ()
{
    Vector V;

    for (int i = 1; i < 11; ++i) V.push_back (i);

    cout << "Can you count to 10?  The Count will be so proud!\n";

    cout << V << endl;

    return 0;
}
```

So, it's safe (throwing an exception if we give a bad index), and we can add as many elements as we want.

Efficiency (optional)

In Chapter 22 we'll have another container for elements, the "linked list." So that we can decide which container we want for this or that task – and for practice with O notation – let's consider the efficiency (time requirements) of `Vector`'s member functions. (If you skipped O notation, skip the rest of this section.)

You might take time to decide for yourself what these functions will be in O notation.

OK, you're back. `Vector::copy`, which is used by `operator=` and the copy constructor, has a loop in it that iterates `size ()` times. `push_back` also has such a loop. Others just have some `if` statements. Table 20-1 shows the efficiencies of some functions, given N as the current array size.

Table 20-1. *Time required for some* `Vector` *functions*

Function	Efficiency (time requirement)
`size`	O(1)
`operator[]`	O(1)
`operator=`	O(N)
`copy constructor`	O(N)
`push_back`	O(N)

The bottom line: if you want to do something to the whole vector, the time required is O(N) – no big surprise. If you're just doing something with one element, the time required is O(1) – *except* `push_back`. That takes O(N) time, because you have to copy the old `contents_` into a new chunk of memory.

Oh, well. It's better than not having the flexibility. And there may be ways to make it quicker (see Exercise 3).

EXERCISES

1. What is the time required for `print`, in O notation?
2. Write pop_back. What is its time requirement? If it's not O(1), you're doing too much work!

3. (Harder) Rewrite `push_back` so that instead of reallocating every time you add a new element, it allocates enough for *ten* new elements – and only has to do this every tenth time. Does it change the time cost, in O notation? Do you think it's worth doing?

4. Write a class `Queue`. It's like a `Stack` except that you take items off the *opposite* end from where you add them. So you get them out in the same order you put them in.

   By convention, you "enqueue" onto one end and "dequeue" from the other.

   What is the time for enqueue, and dequeue, in O notation?

Making `Vector` a template

Am I going to write a brand new class depending on whether I want a Vector of integers, strings, or 1960's rock musicians? I'm a lazy programmer. There's no *way* I'll do that.

Enter the **class template**. A class template is essentially a set of instructions for making a class, just as a function template is instructions for making a function.

There's a simple list of changes we can make to convert `Vector` to be one and thus store different types:

1. **Change any `Vector` declaration to say what it's a `Vector` of.** In Example 20-5, `Vector` becomes `Vector<int>`. This is the *only* change we make in that file.

Example 20-5. Example 20-4, updated to use a class template for `Vector`

```
//Example with a Vector of int
//      -- from _C++ for Lazy Programmers_

#include <iostream>
#include <cassert>
#include "vector.h"

using namespace std;
```

```
int main ()
{
    Vector V<int>; //Step #1: Vector becomes Vector<something>

    for (int i = 1; i < 11; ++i) V.push_back (i);

    cout << "Can you count to 10?  The Count will be so proud!\n";

    cout << V << endl;

    return 0;
}
```

2. **Put the contents of** `vector.cpp` **into** `vector.h`**; erase** `vector.cpp`**.**

   It's the same as in the function templates section: until you *call* `push_back`, the version of `push_back` that works with `int`s doesn't exist. On that line, the compiler needs to know how to create the function, which means it needs the body of the function template. So the body has to be in the `.h` file.

3. **Put** `template <typename T>` **in front of**

   a. **The class definition**

   b. **Each function body** that's outside the class definition

4. **Replace** `int` **with** `T` **or** `const T&` **where appropriate**, as with function templates.

5. **Replace** `Vector` **with** `Vector<T>`

   a. **when it's part of** `Vector::`

   b. **any time you're not in the class**, as in

   ```
   std::ostream& operator<<(std::ostream& out,
                            const Vector<T>& foo);
   ```

   or

   ```
   Vector<T> somethingThatReturnsVector();
   ```

   If you put `Vector<T>` in too many places, no one will shoot you. But it doesn't work for constructor names.

Let's see what that gives us (Example 20-6).

Example 20-6. Changing Vector to a class template

```
//Vector class:  a variable-length array
//      -- from _C++ for Lazy Programmers_

#ifndef VECTOR_H
#define VECTOR_H

template <typename T>             //Step #3 (a): add template <typename T>
class Vector
{
public:
    class OutOfRange {};     //exception, for [] operators

    Vector ()   { contents_ = new T[0]; howMany_ = 0; }//#4: int -> T
    Vector (const Vector& other) { copy (other);      }

    ~Vector ()  { delete [] contents_;                }

    const Vector& operator= (const Vector& other)
    {
        if (contents_) delete [] contents_; copy (other);
        return *this;
    }

    bool operator== (const Vector& other) const;
    bool operator!= (const Vector& other) const
    {
        return !((*this) == other);
    }

    unsigned int size () const { return howMany_;      }

    const T& operator[] (unsigned int index) const;
                                                //#4: int -> const T&
          T& operator[] (unsigned int index);

    void push_back  (const T& newElement);   //#4: int -> const T&

    void print (std::ostream&) const;
```

```
private:
    T* contents_;                          //#4: int -> T
    unsigned int howMany_;

    void copy (const Vector& other);
};

template <typename T>                      //#3b: add template <typename T>
inline                                     //#5b: Vector->Vector<T>
std::ostream& operator<< (std::ostream& out, const Vector<T>& foo)
{
    foo.print(out); return out;
}

//#2: move contents of vector.cpp into vector.h
//   (still contained in #ifndef)

template <typename T>                      //#3b: add template <typename T>
bool Vector<T>::operator==(const Vector& other) const
                                           //#5a: Vector::->Vector<T>::
{
    bool noDifferences = true;

    //quit if you find a difference or run out of elements
    for (unsigned int i = 0; i < size() && noDifferences; ++i)
        if ((*this)[i] != other[i]) noDifferences = false;

    return noDifferences;
}

...

#endif //VECTOR_H
```

That's all there is to it!

Now you can use that `Vector` with base types of your choosing. In Example 20-7 we use it with `strings` and more.

Example 20-7. Using the new `Vector` template with `strings`

```
//Example with a Vector of string
//        -- from _C++ for Lazy Programmers_

#include <iostream>
#include <cassert>
#include <string>
#include "vector.h"

using namespace std;

int main ()
{
    //Setting up the band...
    Vector<string> FabFour;
    string names[] = { "John","Paul","George","Ringo" };
    enum { NUM_BEATLES = 4 };

    for (int i = 0; i < NUM_BEATLES; ++i)
        FabFour.push_back(names[i]);

    cout << "The Fab Four: " << FabFour << endl;

    //Trying other base types...
    Vector<int> V; for (int i = 1; i < 11; ++i) V.push_back(i);
    Vector<Vector<double>> Grid;

    return 0;
}
```

Antibugging

- **The compiler says you didn't write some member function of your class template, and you know you did.** Is everything moved into the `.h` file?
- **The compiler says your class template isn't a type.** Maybe you left off `<myBaseType>` from a variable declaration.

- **The compiler complains that you're using operator >> when you declared a Vector of Vectors:** Vector<Vector<int>> Grid;.

  Old compilers have this issue. Put a space between the closing >'s: Vector<Vector<int> > Grid;

EXERCISES

1. Convert Vector's push_back and copy to work with Vector as a template. My solutions are in the book's source code.
2. Adapt the Point2D class from Chapter 17's exercises to be a class template. You can now have Point2D's made from doubles, or ints, or floats, or any other reasonable type.
3. Convert class Queue from the previous exercises to be a template.
4. Rewrite CardGroup from the previous chapter as a subclass of Vector<Card>.
5. (Uses move constructors, etc.) Add a move copy constructor and move = to Vector. My answers are in the book's source code.

Unusual class templates

You can have more than one typename, as in Example 20-8.

Example 20-8. Class template pair, which allows you to specify two types, simplified from C++'s version in #include <utility>

```
template <typename S, typename T>
struct pair
{
    pair();
    pair(const S& s, const T& t);
    pair(const pair& other);

    //operators =, ==, !=, and others
```

```
        S first;
        T second;
};

int main ()
{
    pair<int,string> P (1, "C++ for Lazy Programmers");
    cout << "The number " << P.first << " C++ text EVER is "
         << P.second << "!\n";

    return 0;
};
```

You can make a template argument be a value, as in Example 20-9.

Example 20-9. A class template that allows you to specify an integer

```
template <int SIZE>
class Stack          //Stack of chars with at most SIZE elements
{
public:
        ...
        bool full  () const { return howMany_ >= SIZE; }
private:
        char contents_[SIZE];
        int  howMany_;
};

int main (int argc, char** argv)
{
        Stack<30> S;
        ...
}
```

EXERCISES

1. Using the Queue class template from the previous section, make a subclass PriorityQueue, in which each item has an attached priority. When you enqueue a new item, it goes ahead of all those in the Queue that have lower priority. You'll want pair.
2. (Hard) Make a class template BigInteger which acts as an integer of arbitrary size. Let the template parameter be the number of bytes (unsigned chars) you want in your BigInteger. Support all reasonable arithmetic operators and stream I/O.
3. Rewrite Montana to add a new option: undo. To support it, you'll need to keep a Vector of moves so you can undo your last move, the one before that, and so on until there are no more moves to undo. What information does a move contain? The Vector can be emptied when a new turn begins.

#include <vector>

I've kept something from you again; I've got to stop doing that. C++ already has an std::vector class template in #include <vector>. It isn't as cool as ours, because it lacks a built-in print function, but you can't have everything.[1]

std::swap and std::pair are also built in, in #include <utility>.

[1]Actually STL has good reason for not having a print function: how do you want it delimited? Commas? Spaces? Do you want []'s around it, <>'s, ()'s? STL's creators could work around it, and they have; we'll see how in Chapter 23.

CHAPTER 21

Virtual Functions and Multiple Inheritance

Virtual functions and multiple inheritance don't show up in most classes I write – but when I need them, I need them.

Virtual functions

Polymorphism is, essentially, using the same word to mean different things. We've been doing it all along. Consider the operator +. We use it for adding `int`s and for adding `double`s. And `string`s. These are conceptually similar, but they're done very differently by the machine.

Another example might be a function `start`, which could apply to a car, a plane, or a lawn mower. In each case, the body of the function will be different (turning a key, going through a flight check, pulling the crank cord). But the name is the same.

Consider classes we'll want if we're drawing 2D shapes on a computer screen: circles, rectangles, squares, and chunks of text, maybe. These have a lot in common: position, color, and the ability to be drawn and moved. We can call those common qualities "shape" qualities, and have a class `Shape` to hold them (Figure 21-1).

Figure 21-1 sets up the class hierarchy, and Examples 21-1 and 21-2 show some relevant class definitions.

W. Briggs, *C++ for Lazy Programmers*, https://doi.org/10.1007/978-1-4842-5187-4_21

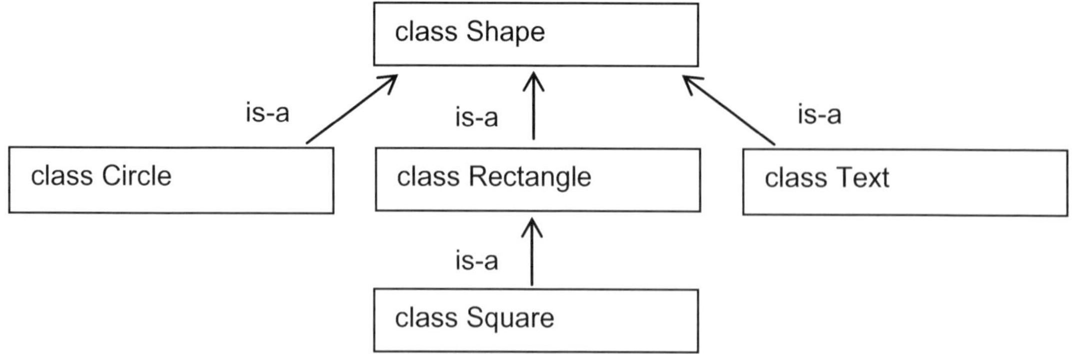

Figure 21-1. *A hierarchy of Shapes*

Example 21-1. shape.h

```
//Shape class, for use with the SSDL library
//              -- from _C++ for Lazy Programmers_

#ifndef SHAPE_H
#define SHAPE_H

#include "SSDL.h"

struct Point2D  //Life would be easier if this were a full-fledged
{               //  class with operators +, =, etc. . . . but that
    int x_, y_; //  was left as an exercise.
};

class Shape
{
public:
    Shape(int x = 0, int y = 0, const char* text = "");
    Shape(const Shape& other)          { *this = other;         }
    virtual ~Shape() { if (description_) delete[] description_; }

    //Color
    void  setColor(const SSDL_Color& c) { color_ = c;           }
    const SSDL_Color&  color   () const { return color_;        }
```

```
    //Access functions
    const Point2D&  location    () const { return location_;     }
    const char*     description() const { return description_;  }

    //Drawing
    void   drawAux() const;

    void   draw    () const
    {
        SSDL_SetRenderDrawColor(color()); drawAux();
    }

    //Moving
    void moveBy(int deltaX, int deltaY)
    {
        moveTo(location_.x_ + deltaX, location_.y_ + deltaY);
    }

    void moveTo(int x, int y)
    {
        location_.x_ = x;    //Point2D::operator= would help here!
        location_.y_ = y;
    }

private:
    Point2D    location_;
    SSDL_Color color_;
    char*      description_;  //Using char* not std::string helps
                              // illustrate how this chapter affects
                              // dynamic memory
    void copy(const char*);   //Used for copying descriptions
};

#endif
```

Shape contains what all shapes have in common, such as (say) color_. Notice function draw: it uses SSDL_SetRenderDrawColor to tell SSDL to start using the Shape's color, then calls drawAux, an "auxiliary" (helper) function that does the actual drawing. drawAux will be different for Circles (where it'll use SSDL_RenderDrawCircle), Texts (where it'll call SSDL_RenderText), and so on. Circle's drawAux is shown in Example 21-2.

Example 21-2. circle.h

```
//Circle class, for use with the SSDL library
//       -- from _C++ for Lazy Programmers_

#ifndef CIRCLE_H
#define CIRCLE_H

#include "shape.h"

class Circle: public Shape
{
 public:
    Circle () : radius_ (0)  {}
    Circle (const Circle& c) { *this = c; }
    Circle (int x, int y, int theRadius, const char* txt="") :
    Shape (x, y, txt), radius_ (theRadius)
    {
    }

    const Circle& operator= (const Circle& c)
    {
        Shape::operator=(c); radius_ = c.radius(); return *this;
    }

    int radius () const { return radius_; }

    void drawAux() const
    {
        SSDL_RenderDrawCircle (location().x_, location().y_, radius());
    }

 private:
    int radius_;
};

#endif
```

The code won't work: the compiler complains that `Shape::drawAux`, called in `Shape::draw`, was not written. It's right. `Circle`'s `drawAux` was written, but `Shape::draw` doesn't know anything about `Circle` functions.

What we need is a way to make `Shape::draw` call the *right* version of `drawAux`: `Circle::drawAux` for `Circle`s, `Text::drawAux` for `Text`s, and so on.

This is the fix: **`virtual functions`**.

Example 21-3. The Shape class, with a virtual function

```
class Shape
{
public:
        ...
        virtual void drawAux ();
        ...
};
```

In the version in Example 21-3, we tell the Shape class, "Whenever you call `drawAux`, use the child class's version, if there is one."

`Circle` needs to be told that its `drawAux` is overriding a virtual function, so we do that as well (Example 21-4).[1]

Example 21-4. The `Circle` class, with the `override` specifier

```
class Circle: public Shape
{
        ...
        void drawAux () const override;
        ...
};
```

[1]`override` was added to the standard in C++11. It isn't required, but it's a *very* good idea. It makes the compiler notice if you spelled the parent and child functions differently or gave slightly different parameter lists or `const` specifications.

Behind the scenes

Before, an object of a given class stored only data members (Figure 21-2). It didn't store member functions in memory with the object, as it would waste space.

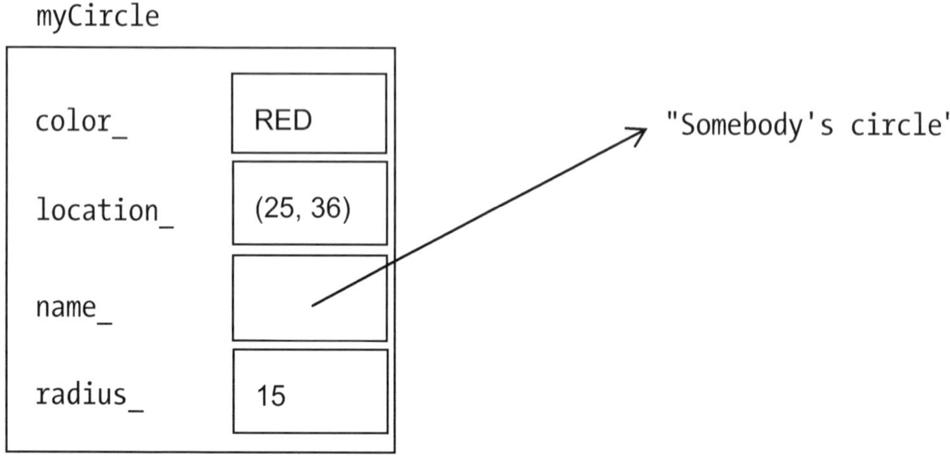

Figure 21-2. *A `Circle` object, before virtual functions*

But now the object also contains the address of any virtual function (Figure 21-3), so it remembers which version to call.

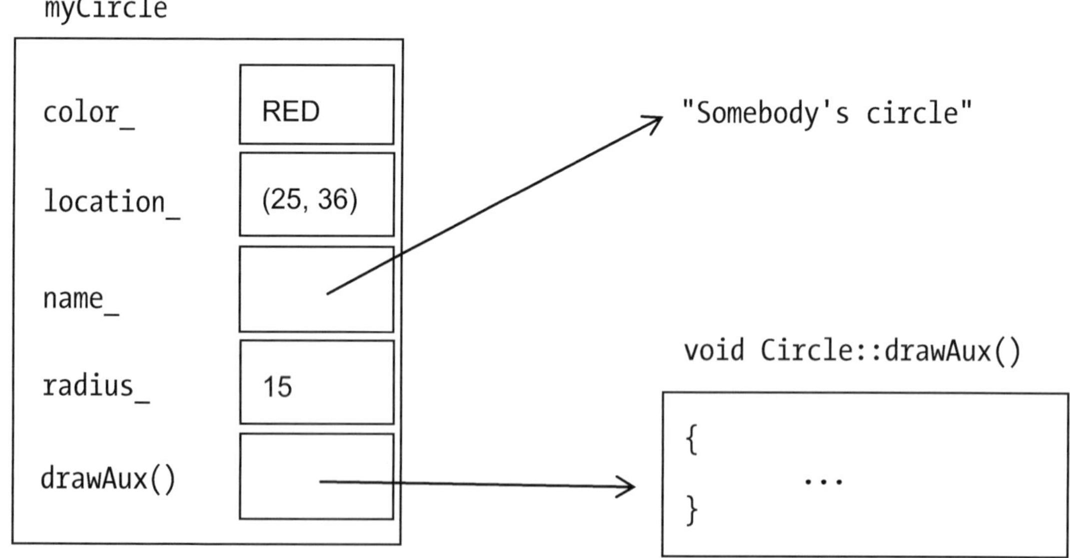

Figure 21-3. *A `Circle` object, using virtual functions*

We added some overhead: an extra pointer for the drawAux function in every Circle. But it's small overhead – nothing to be concerned about.

Pure virtual functions and abstract base classes

Next question: how do we write Shape::draw(), anyway?

Unless we specify what *kind* of Shape it is – unless it's a Circle or other subclass – there's no answer to that question. So we'll take the easy way out: we won't write it for Shape, but will instead tell the compiler, "You can't have a Shape that's just a Shape, and this function is why." Example 21-5 shows how that's done.

Example 21-5. The Shape class, with a pure virtual function. This makes Shape an "abstract" class

```
class Shape
{
public:
    ...
    virtual void drawAux ()=0;
    ...
};
```

By adding =0, we make drawAux a **pure virtual** function, and Shape into an **abstract class**, meaning one you can't use to declare variables:

```
Shape myShape;    //Nope, can't do this, the compiler will stop you
Circle myCircle;  //No problem: it's a shape, but it's also a Circle,
                  //   and we can drawAux Circles
```

Why virtual functions often mean using pointers

Example 21-6 shows something we might want to do with Shapes: put them into a vector, and do something (like draw()) to every Shape in the vector.

Example 21-6. An (unsuccessful) attempt to use a sequence of Shapes

```
//Program to show, and move, the Olympics symbol
//It uses Circle, and a subclass of Shape called Text
//          -- from _C++ for Lazy Programmers_

#include <vector>
#include "circle.h"
#include "text.h"

int main (int argc, char** argv)
{
    SSDL_SetWindowSize (500, 300); //make smaller window

    //Create Olympics symbol
    std::vector<Shape> olympicSymbol;
    enum {RADIUS = 50};

    //consisting of five circles
    olympicSymbol.push_back (Circle ( 50,  50, RADIUS));
    olympicSymbol.push_back (Circle (150,  50, RADIUS));
    olympicSymbol.push_back (Circle (250,  50, RADIUS));
    olympicSymbol.push_back (Circle (100, 100, RADIUS));
    olympicSymbol.push_back (Circle (200, 100, RADIUS));

    //plus a label
    olympicSymbol.push_back (Text (150,150,"Games of the Olympiad"));

    //color those circles (and the label)
    SSDL_Color olympicColors[] = { BLUE,
                             SSDL_CreateColor (0, 255, 255) /*yellow*/,
                             BLACK, GREEN, RED, BLACK };
    for (unsigned int i = 0; i < olympicSymbol.size(); ++i)
        olympicSymbol[i].setColor (olympicColors [i]);

    //do a game loop
    while (SSDL_IsNextFrame ())
    {
        SSDL_DefaultEventHandler ();

        SSDL_RenderClear (WHITE);      //clear the screen
```

```
        //draw all those shapes
        for (unsigned int i = 0; i < olympicSymbol.size(); ++i)
            olympicSymbol[i].draw ();

        //move all those shapes
        for (unsigned int i = 0; i < olympicSymbol.size(); ++i)
            olympicSymbol[i].moveBy (1, 1);
    }

    return 0;
}
```

This makes sense: create a sequence of Shapes, then draw them. But it won't work. One reason is that Shape is now an abstract class; since you can't create something that's just a Shape, you certainly can't create a vector of them.

The other reason is that olympicSymbol[0], for example, has enough room to store a single Shape. That means it has room for a color_, a location_, a description_, and a pointer to drawAux. Where will you store the radius_ for a Circle? The contents_ of the Text object? There isn't room!

To fix this, we need dynamic memory. Yes, I know: lazy programmers avoid dynamic memory, as it's error-prone and harder to write. But sometimes you have to have it. In this case, when you create a Circle using new, it'll allocate the amount it needs.

Example 21-7 shows how it's done. It's a little different from how we used dynamic memory before: then, we wanted an array, so we used []: char* str = new char [someSize], and delete [] str to clean up. This time, each time we allocate a Shape, we allocate *one* Shape. So we leave out the []'s: new Circle not new Circle []; delete not delete [].

We'll get more practice allocating/deallocating single elements in the next chapter.

Example 21-7. A program that successfully uses a vector of Shapes to display and move a complex symbol. Output is in Figure 21-4

```
//Program to show, and move, the Olympics symbol
//It uses Circle, and a subclass of Shape called Text
//          -- from _C++ for Lazy Programmers_

#include <vector>
#include "circle.h"
```

```
#include "text.h"

int main (int argc, char** argv)
{
    SSDL_SetWindowSize (500, 300); //make smaller window

    //Create Olympics symbol
    std::vector<Shape*> olympicSymbol;
    enum {RADIUS = 50};

    //consisting of five circles
    olympicSymbol.push_back (new Circle ( 50,  50, RADIUS));
    olympicSymbol.push_back (new Circle (150,  50, RADIUS));
    olympicSymbol.push_back (new Circle (250,  50, RADIUS));
    olympicSymbol.push_back (new Circle (100, 100, RADIUS));
    olympicSymbol.push_back (new Circle (200, 100, RADIUS));

    //plus a label
    olympicSymbol.push_back
        (new Text (150,150,"Games of the Olympiad"));

    //color those circles (and the label)
    SSDL_Color olympicColors[] = { BLUE,
                                   SSDL_CreateColor (0, 255, 255) /*yellow*/,
                                   BLACK, GREEN, RED, BLACK };
    for (unsigned int i = 0; i < olympicSymbol.size(); ++i)
        (*olympicSymbol[i]).setColor (olympicColors [i]);

    //do a game loop
    while (SSDL_IsNextFrame ())
    {
        SSDL_DefaultEventHandler ();

        SSDL_RenderClear (WHITE);      //clear the screen

        //draw all those shapes
        for (unsigned int i = 0; i < olympicSymbol.size(); ++i)
            (*olympicSymbol[i]).draw ();
```

```
        //move all those shapes
        for (unsigned int i = 0; i < olympicSymbol.size(); ++i)
            (*olympicSymbol[i]).moveBy (1, 1);
    }

    //Done with our dynamic memory -- throw it back!
    for (unsigned int i = 0; i < olympicSymbol.size(); ++i)
        delete olympicSymbol [i];

    return 0;
}
```

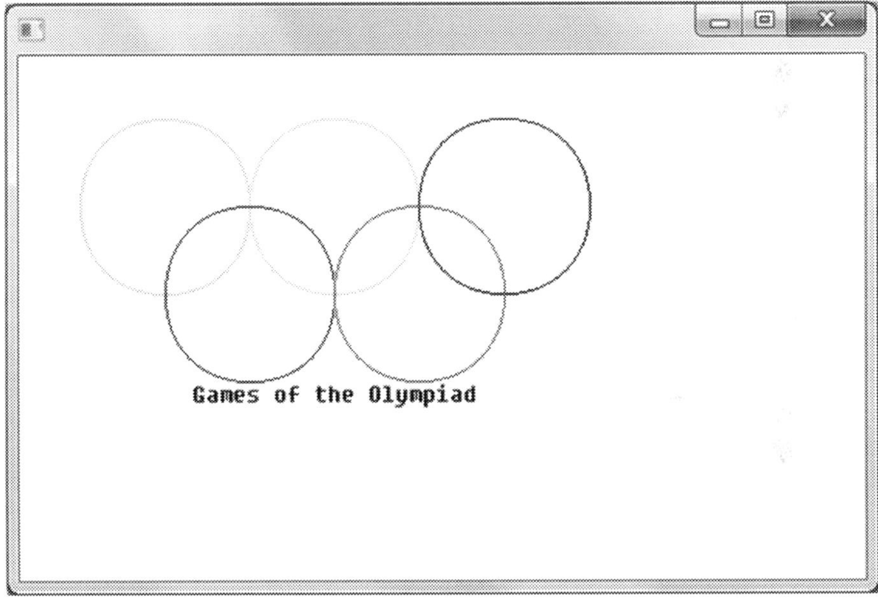

***Figure 21-4.** Output of the Olympic Symbol program in Example 21-7*

In this code, we maintain a vector not of Shape but of Shape*. Then, when we use new to create a Circle or Text, it can get us a chunk of memory the right size for that subclass.

Since olympicSymbol[i] is a pointer, we say not olympicSymbol[i].draw () but (*olympicSymbol[i]).draw ().[2]

[2]If all those parentheses make your pinkies tired, well, we get an easier way to write this in the next chapter.

Finally, as always when using dynamic memory, we throw back the memory with delete when we're done.

To be sure it *all* gets thrown back, we need the next section.

Virtual destructors

Consider the Text object used in Example 21-7, the one that contains "Games of the Olympiad." Example 21-8 shows an implementation of it.

Example 21-8. text.h

```
//Text class, for use with the SSDL library
//              -- from _C++ for Lazy Programmers_

#ifndef TEXT_H
#define TEXT_H

#include "shape.h"

class Text: public Shape
{
 public:
    Text (const char* txt = "")    { copy (txt);        }
    Text (const Text& other) : Shape (other)
    {
        copy (other.contents_);
    }
    Text (int x, int y, const char* txt = "") : Shape(x, y)
    {
        copy(txt);
    }
    ~Text () override { if (contents_) delete contents_; }

    const Text& operator=(const Text& other);

    const char* contents () const { return contents_; }
```

```
    void drawAux         () const override
    {
        SSDL_RenderText (contents_, location().x_, location().y_);
    }

 private:
    char* contents_;
    void copy (const char* txt);//used for copying contents
};

#endif
```

It uses dynamic memory to allocate its character array. Naturally when we're done, we'll need to throw it back. But the statement in main that should do this –

```
for (int i = 0; i < olympicSymbol.size(); ++i)
      delete olympicSymbol [i];
```

– doesn't. olympicSymbol [i] is a pointer to a Shape, not a Text; so it will only delete things that belong to the Shape. It doesn't know about Text's contents_.

The solution once again is to use the version of the destructor that *does* know: Text's version. And we do that by making Shape's destructor virtual and Text's an override:

```
virtual Shape::~Shape () { if (description_) delete[] description_; }

        Text::~Text  () override  { if (contents_) delete contents_; }
```

Now, when the destructor on a Shape is called, the Shape will know which version to call. If it's a Text, the destructor called will be Text::~Text () – which, when finished, then calls the destructor for parent class Shape, as destructors do whether they're virtual or not.

It's easy to forget, when you build an inheritance hierarchy, whether you used virtual functions in this or that class. And there's no way to know when you're writing the parent class that no descendant will ever use dynamic memory. So if there is any possibility anyone will allocate a subclass dynamically – and how would you know? – you should make the destructor virtual.

Golden Rule of Virtual Functions

(Usual version) If you're using virtual functions in a class hierarchy, make the destructors virtual.

(Stronger version) Since you don't know when you write a class what people writing subclasses will do...make all destructors virtual. Period.

I used `char* contents_` in Text, and `char* description_` in Shape, to make it obvious we'd need destructors. But if we'd used C++'s `string` class instead, the same thing would have happened: when you deleted a pointer to Shape that was actually a pointer to a `Text`, `delete` wouldn't know that it was really a `Text` and wouldn't know to tell `string contents_` to call *its* destructor. So you'd still need to give Shape a virtual destructor:

```
virtual Shape::~Shape ()                { }
```

Inheritance and move ctor/move = (optional)

If you write the move constructor and move = for Shape and its subclasses, you may find that Shape's works fine, but when you try to use it from `Circle`:

```
Circle (Circle&& c) : Shape (c) //Nope, not working right...
{
    radius_ = c.radius();
}
```

...it calls Shape's regular copy constructor instead.

When you use `Circle`'s move constructor, it's because C++ thinks the thing being copied is an "r-value," a thing that you can safely use up, mangle, and so on, as it's not going to be used again, so we're perfectly safe stealing its memory.

But while it's in the constructor, we need to keep it around till we're done, so its r-value-ness is taken away. So we call Shape `(c)` and it won't use the move constructor.

C++'s fix is to force it back to an r-value for that call:

```
#include <utility> //for std::move

...

Circle (Circle&& c) : Shape (std::move (c))
{
    radius_ = c.radius();
}
```

It works the same with move =:

```
const Circle& operator= (Circle&&       c)
{
    Shape::operator=(std::move(c)); radius_ = c.radius();
    return *this;
}
```

For more examples of move semantics (that's what they call use of move constructors and move =), please see the shapes project in the book's source code.

Antibugging

- **The compiler says your subclass's override function doesn't match any in the base class.** You may have left off a const on the function header, or spelled the function name differently, or given it a slightly different parameter list.
- **The compiler says your subclass is abstract, but it doesn't contain pure virtual functions.** For example,

  ```
  Circle myCircle;
  ```

  might complain that Circle is abstract - but you didn't put any virtual functions in it at all!

You may have forgotten to override the parent's pure virtual functions. This makes the subclass abstract too.

Or you may have forgotten to make the corresponding child class function an `override`, and its header didn't perfectly match the parent's (see the previous entry in this "Antibugging" section). Solution: add `override`.

EXERCISES

1. In this simple shooting game, a *powerup* is a target you can hit with a mouse click. The types of powerup – FlashyPowerup, MegaPowerup, or Wormhole – give different points and show different animations when you hit one (see Figure 21-5).

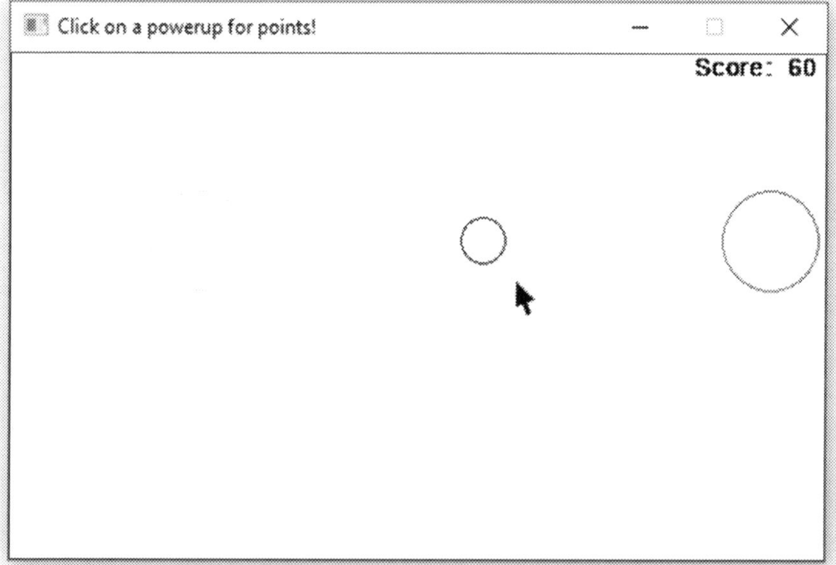

Figure 21-5. *The Powerup exercise, showing the "wormhole" animation*

In this chapter's section of the sample code, you'll find a partially written program for shooting powerups. It uses the `Shape` hierarchy. To get it working, you'll need to alter `main.cpp` to use pointers and add `virtual` and `override` in the right places in the `Powerup` class hierarchy.
I recommend making `Powerup` abstract, for the same reason as with `Shape`.

2. In the `CardGroup` class hierarchy from Chapter 19, add functions `isLegalToAdd` and `isLegalToRemove` to every subclass that might need them. (For example, `Cell::isLegalToAdd` returns true only if the cell is empty and `Cell::isLegalToRemove` only if it's not.)

   Let `CardGroup`'s `addCardLegally` call `isLegalToAdd`, using virtual functions so it calls the appropriate subclass version. No other class should have its own `addCardLegally`.

   Test to be sure the right functions are actually called. You may want some try-catch blocks.

3. (Bigger project) Expanding on Exercise 2, write a nongraphical FreeCell game. You should have an array or vector of `CardGroup` (`CardGroup*`, actually) including `FreeCellPiles`, `Cells`, and `Foundations`. Let the user specify which `CardGroup` to move a card from or to ("F1" for foundation 1, "P2" for pile 2, say). The `CardGroup` chosen knows, based on what subclass it is, which version of `isLegalToAdd` or `isLegalToRemove` to use:

```
CardGroup* from = askUserToPickCardGroup();
if (from->isLegalToRemove())
                    //can we take card from top?
    ...
```

Multiple inheritance

Consider the two classes in Example 21-9, made for a 3D graphics program.

Example 21-9. Classes `Object` and `Model`

```
class Object
{
public:
   Object ();
   Object (const Object&);
      ...
private:
   double velocity;
   double acceleration;
   Point3D position;
};

class Model
{
public:
   Model ();
   Model (const Model&);

   void load (const char* filename);
   void display () const;
      ...
private:
   vector<Triangle> Contents;
};
```

Class `Object` has position, velocity, and acceleration. It's for working with the laws of motion.

Class `Model` is something with a physical appearance. It's composed of triangles, which probably fit together to make an apparently solid object.

Can you have `Objects` that aren't `Models`? Sure. You might have a model in some other format, not using triangles – a sphere, maybe.

Can you have `Models` that aren't `Objects`? Sure. You could be using CAD/CAM to design products for manufacturing.

So a `Model` isn't an `Object` and an `Object` isn't a `Model`...but it makes sense to have something be both. I'll call that something `ModelObject` (Figure 21-6).

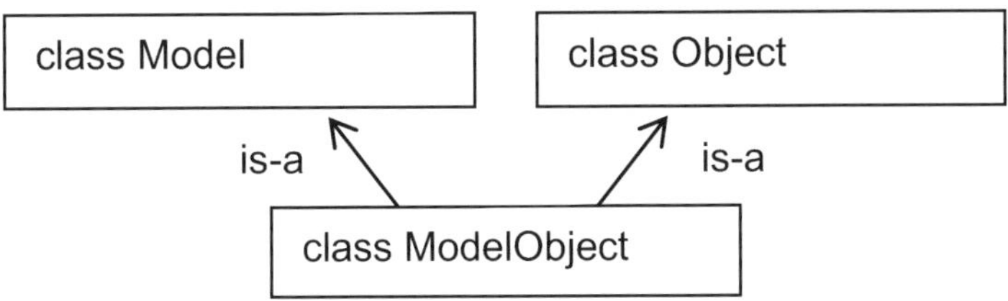

Figure 21-6. *Inheriting* `ModelObject` *from* `Model` *and* `Object`

Since `ModelObject` is a `Model` and an `Object`, it inherits the characteristics of both: it will have position, velocity, and acceleration like an `Object`, and the vector of `Triangles`, plus the `load` and `display` functions, from `Model`.

We can use public or private inheritance. `public` makes sense.

Example 21-10. Class `ModelObject`: an illustration of multiple inheritance

```
class ModelObject: public Model, public Object
{
public:
      ModelObject () {}
      ModelObject (const ModelObject& other)
            : Model (other), Object (other)
      {
      }
      ...
};
```

To call the parent constructors, use the ":" just as you do with ordinary inheritance; but this time, call both parent constructors (or use their defaults).

This isn't often needed, but when it is, it's convenient.

Antibugging

Suppose we make a role-playing game. In it we have class `Player`, with a `name_` and a number of `hitPoints_`. It also has a member function `takeAttack (int howMuch)` which reduces the hit points by a given amount.

We make two subclasses, `Fighter` and `Magician`. A `Fighter` has a member `attack`, which takes a `Player` and reduces its hit points. A `Magician` has a member `bespell`, which does a magic attack.

But some games let you make hybrid classes for your characters. We'll make `FighterMagician` a subclass of both `Fighter` and `Magician`. Now we have a class that can both `attack` and `bespell`. Cool.

But here's a problem. `Fighter` has members `hitPoints_` and `name_` (inherited from `Player`). `Magician` also has `hitPoints_` and `name_` (inherited from `Player`). So `FighterMagician` has two copies of `hitPoints_` and two copies of `name_`!

This is called the "diamond problem," for some reason. Maybe Figure 21-7 will give us a clue?

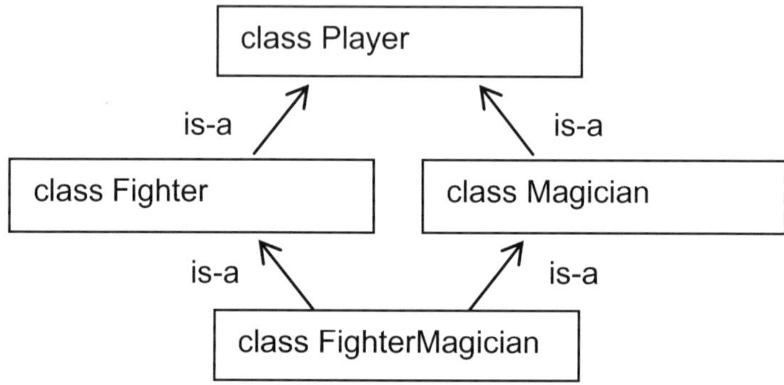

Figure 21-7. *The diamond problem in multiple inheritance*

We can't reason our way out of this one; C++ will have to help us. And it does: it lets us make `Fighter` and `Magician` "virtual" base classes, essentially saying, "Don't do that extra-copies-of-common-grandparent-members thing."

```
class Fighter:  virtual public Player ...
class Magician: virtual public Player ...
```

One more issue: since `Fighter` and `Magician` may call different Player constructors, which would lead to ambiguity, `FighterMagician` has to explicitly state what `Player` constructor it wants called, like so:

```
FighterMagician (const char* name) : Fighter ([some args]),
                                     Magician ([some args]),
                                     Player (name)
{
}
```

If we don't specify, the compiler will use the default.

EXERCISES

1. Write the classes from the preceding "Antibugging" section – `Player`, `Fighter`, `Magician`, and `FighterMagician`.

   Since you're not making a real game, to keep it simple, `attack` and `bespell` can both just pick random numbers to take from the opponent's hit points. It doesn't matter if the `FighterMagician` uses `attack` or `bespell` – just pick one in `main` for its method of fighting.

   Now let a `Fighter` (say) go up against a `FighterMagician`, and see who wins the match.

2. Using the `Shape` class, make a class `Composite` which is both a `Shape` (so it has a `location`, `virtual drawAux`, etc.) and a vector of `Shape*` (so it can be made of circles, texts, whatever). Be sure that your `Composite` can be created, moved, and displayed and is properly destructed.

   One tricky bit is that a `Composite` has two kinds of locations: the one inherited from `Shape` and the locations of all its subcomponents. Make your `move` functions update all locations.

3. If you did Exercise 1 in the section on virtual functions, you can extend it with a `PowerupSet` class, which is both a `Shape` and a vector of `Powerup*`. Be sure your `PowerupSet` can be created, drawn, and animated and is properly destructed. The functions in `main.cpp` that take `vector<Powerup>` (or some such) should be altered to take `PowerupSet`.

   `PowerupSet` has two kinds of locations: the one inherited from `Shape` and the locations of its subcomponents. Make your `move` functions update all locations.

CHAPTER 22

Linked Lists

One problem with the `Vector` class is the time it takes to add an element: O(N), where N is the number of elements already in the `Vector`.

So here's another scheme for maintaining a sequence that will be quicker to update.

What lists are and why have them

All around the city a group of superheroes is waiting. They have a scheme for notifying each other if their powers are needed: each has the phone number of another, who has the number of another, until the last one on the list, who has none. (See Figure 22-1.)

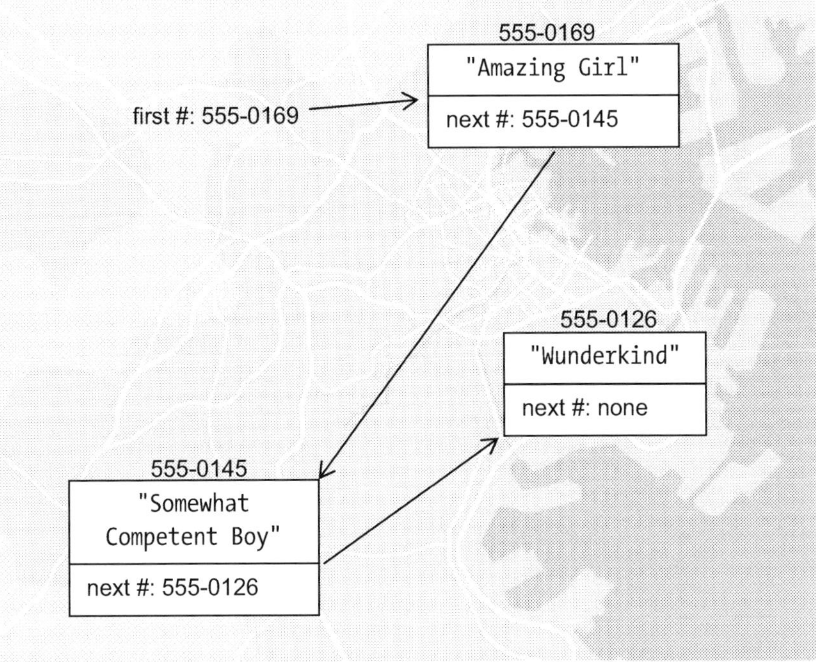

***Figure 22-1.** Our city, with three superheroes in a linked list. Amazing Girl is first, at 555-0169; Somewhat Competent Boy is at 555-0145; Wunderkind is at 555-0126*

W. Briggs, *C++ for Lazy Programmers*, https://doi.org/10.1007/978-1-4842-5187-4_22

In the computer, we don't use phone numbers, but memory addresses. This data structure holds the information each person has:

```
struct Superhero
{
      std::string name_;        //The Superhero's name
      Superhero*  next_;        //The address of the next Superhero
};
```

Remember, Superhero* means pointer to Superhero – where to find a Superhero in the computer's memory, just as Shape* meant where to find a Shape in Chapter 21. Wunderkind comes last and has "none" as her next phone number, so we'll set her next_ field to nullptr, C++'s special pointer that means "nothing."

Suppose we want to add another hero to the list. It's quick and easy: give him the number of the current first in the list. He'll put it into his next_ field. Then remember *his* contact information as the new first number (see Figure 22-2).

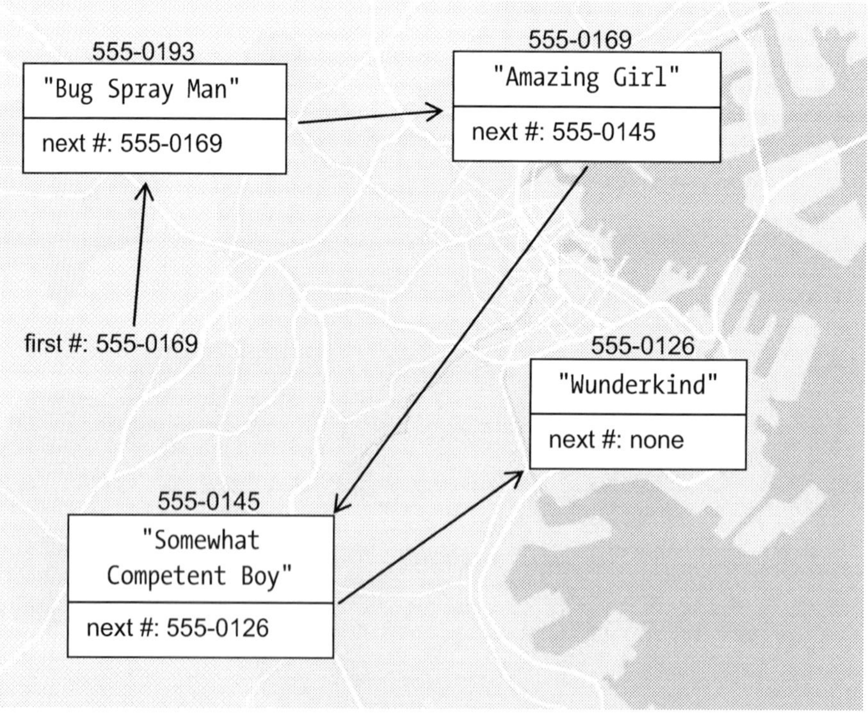

Figure 22-2. *The same linked list, after we add Bug Spray Man*

More formally, the algorithm is

```
create a new Superhero struct
put the name of the new person into the Superhero
put the pointer to the start of the list into the Superhero, as "next"
let the new start of the list be the address of the new Superhero
```

There's no loop here, and no recursion, so the time requirement is O(1). A big improvement over Vector's O(N)!

But suppose we want to look at the ith element (whatever i may be) – that is, use operator[]. How can we do this? With Vector, it was just contents_[index] – no loop, no repetition, and therefore O(1). Here, we have to go sequentially:

```
current position = start;

for j = 0; j< index; ++j
      current position = the address of the next Superhero;
      if we go off the end of the list, throw an exception;

return the name in the current position;
```

This *does* have a loop – and its time requirement is O(index). On average, that'll be O(N/2), or O(N).

Table 22-1 shows how you'll know which is better for a given task, Vector or List. If you do a lot of lookup (operator[]), Vector is quicker. If you do a lot of adding (push_back or push_front), List is quicker.

Table 22-1. *Time required for some Vector and List functions*

Function	**Efficiency (Vector)**	**Efficiency (List)**
operator[]	O(1)	O(N)
operator=	O(N)	O(N)
copy constructor	O(N)	O(N)
push_back	O(N)	not written
push_front	not written	O(1)

I often use Vector, because I find that I look into a sequence more often than I build it. If the sequence is small, it won't matter much. If it's huge, you should pay more attention to picking the best one.

Let's move now to writing the List. We'll drop the superhero analogy and make List a template (Example 22-1).

Example 22-1. The List class, first version

```
//class List:  a linked list class
//      from _C++ for Lazy Programmers_

#ifndef LIST_H
#define LIST_H

template <typename T>
class List
{
public:
    List ();
    List (const List <T>& other);
    ~List();

    const List <T>& operator= (const List <T>& other);

    bool operator== (const List <T>& other) const;

    int  size () const;
    bool empty() const;

    void push_front(const T& newElement);    //add newElement at front
    void pop_front ();                       //take one off the front
    const T& front () const;                 //look at front element

    void print(std::ostream&) const;
private:
```

```
    struct Entry¹
    {
        T      data_;
        Entry* next_;
    };

    Entry* start_;          //Points to first element in list
};
```

It's like Vector, except

- We use push_front not push_back.
- The data members are different.
- I left out operator[]. It's so inefficient that after years of grousing that *I don't care if it's inefficient just let me use it!* I've bowed to the community and left it out. We'll get a more appropriate way to access the members in the next chapter anyway.

Let's write some of those functions now, starting with the default constructor.

List<T>::List ()

It makes sense to have the default List be empty. How do we specify that a list is empty? By convention, this is true when the pointer start_ is nullptr. You could say that it points to nothing – because there's nothing in the list.

```
template <typename T>
class List
{
public:
    List () { start_ = nullptr; }
    ...
};
```

[1]One struct/class inside another? No problem: we've had classes inside classes before. But the struct's data members are public (by default). Is this a security risk? Not at all. They're still in List's private section..

void List<T>::push_front (const T& newElement);

When we begin push_front, we have the List as it was, containing start_; and a newElement. We need newElement added to the front, as shown in Figure 22-3.

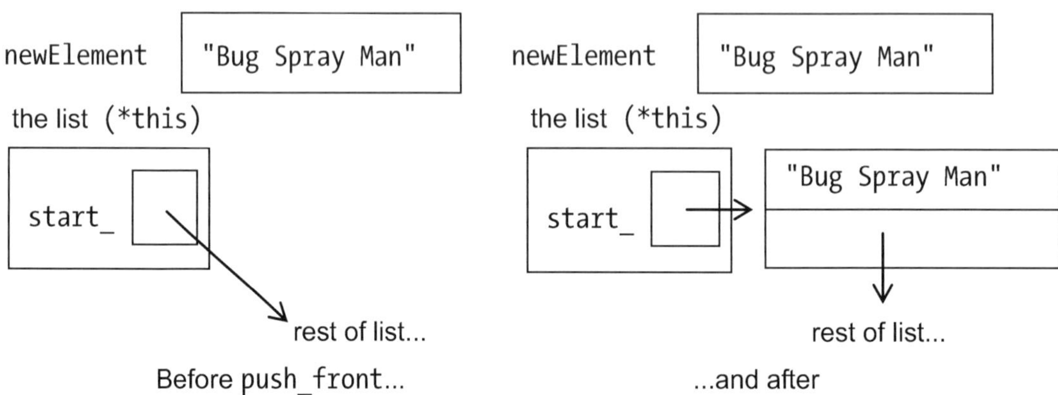

Figure 22-3. *Before, and after, adding a new element to a* List

Here's how to make that happen:

```
create an Entry
put the newElement into its data field
put the old version of start into its next field
put the address of the new Entry into start
```

Seems straightforward enough. Here it is in code.

```
template <typename T>
void List<T>::push_front (const T& newElement)
{
    Entry* newEntry    = new Entry; //create an Entry
    (*newEntry).data_  = newElement;//put newElement in its data field
    (*newEntry).next_  = start_;    //put old version of start
                                    //  in its next field

    start_             = newEntry;  //put address of new Entry
                                    //  into start
}
```

Let's take that line by line.

The first line, `Entry* newEntry = new Entry;`, uses dynamic memory to create the new `Entry`. Just as in Chapter 21 with new `Shape`s, we're only allocating one `Entry` at a time, not an array of them, so we don't need `[]`'s.

In the second line, `newEntry` is the address of the new `Entry`, so `*newEntry` is that `Entry` itself. `(*newEntry).name_` therefore is its `name_` field. The third line is similar.

The fourth line stores the address of `newEntry` in the `start_` field of the `List`, so we'll remember where to find it. Our new `Entry` now directs us to the rest of the `List`. If the `List` had elements, good; we'll see them. If the `List` was empty, then that pointer to the rest of the list is `nullptr`. Also good: we'll know that's the end.

void List<T>::pop_front()

...a function to take off the first element. Here's my first attempt. (For brevity I just show the code, but of course I'd write the algorithm first.)

```
template <typename T>
void List<T>::pop_front()
{
    if (empty()) throw Underflow();

    delete start_;                   //delete the item
    start_ = (*start_).next_;        //let start_go on to the next
}
```

(Remember that, as in Chapter 21, we use `delete` not `delete []` - because we used `new` without the `[]`'s, allocating not an array but a single `Entry`.)

So let's say we're taking Bug Spray Man off that list. Figure 22-4 shows what we start with.

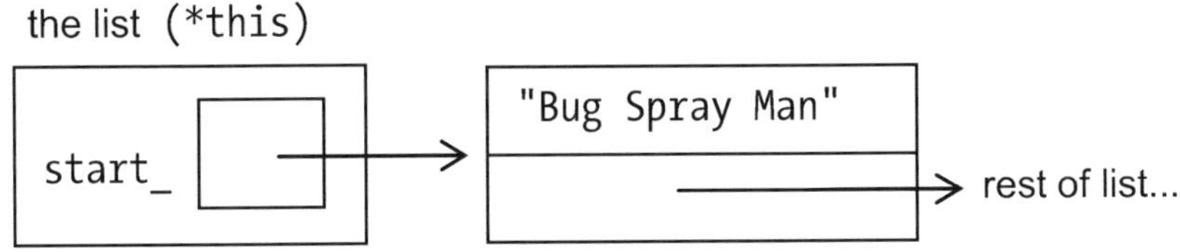

Figure 22-4. *Getting ready to pop_front*

I'll trace through the steps. Is it empty? No problem there. Now we delete what start_ points to, and get Figure 22-5.

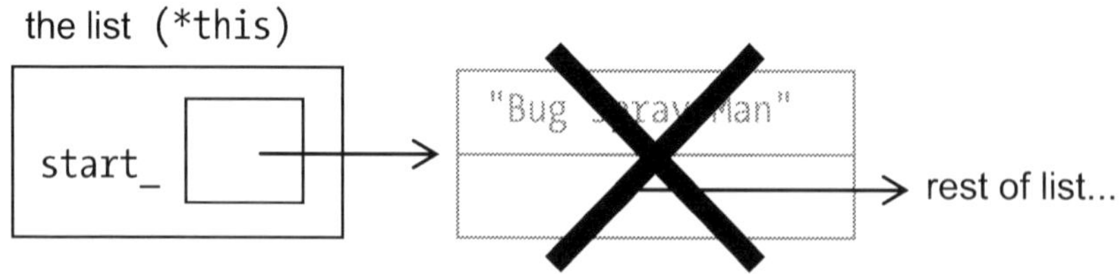

Figure 22-5. *We deleted the element in pop_front. Nope, that's not right....*

Then we access (*start_).next_. But what start_ pointed to has been deleted and no longer exists. The address of the rest of the list is gone. Crash!

Maybe we could do this in a different order: delete things only after we're *sure* we're done with them.

```
template <typename T>
void List<T>::pop_front()
{
    if (empty()) throw Underflow();

    Entry* temp = start_;       //store location of thing to delete
    start_ = (*start_).next_;   //let start_ = next thing after start_

    delete temp;                //delete the item
}
```

Now let's see how it goes.

We check for the empty condition; no problem.

We set temp equal to start_ (Figure 22-6).

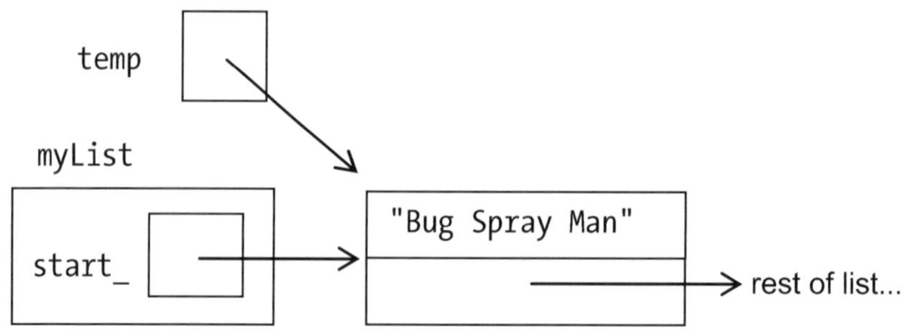

Figure 22-6. *Starting pop_front (again)*

We move `start_` to point to the rest of the list (Figure 22-7)...

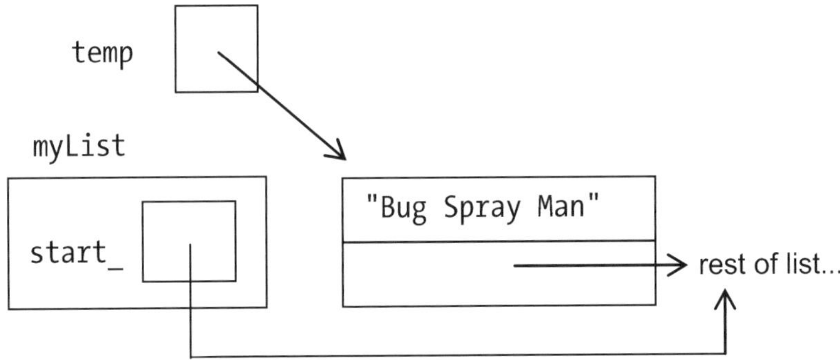

***Figure 22-7.** Setting `start_` to where it should go....*

...and we delete the `Entry` we no longer need (Figure 22-8).

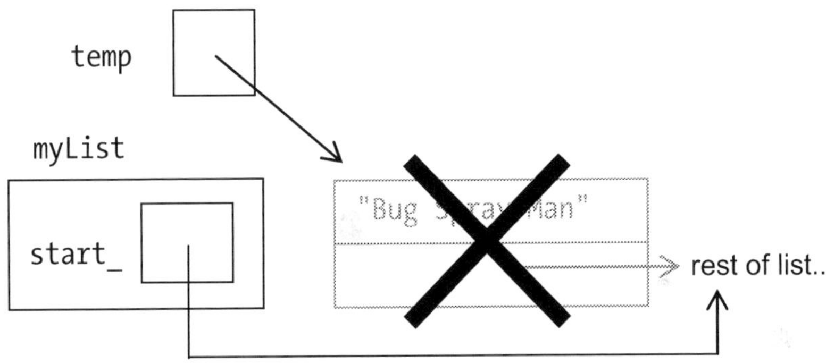

***Figure 22-8.** `pop_front` now works correctly*

When doing lists, I'm always drawing these boxes and arrows: without them, I'm bound to lose pointers, follow bad ones, and so on. So I get this Golden Rule.

Golden Rule of Pointers

When changing or deleting pointers, draw diagrams of what you're doing.

List<T>::~List()

Eventually we have to throw all those Entrys back.

I could write a while loop to delete them, making a diagram to make sure I don't lose any pointers, but...I'm a lazy programmer. Do I already have something to throw back Entrys safely? Sure: pop_front.

```
template <typename T>
List<T>::~List () { while (!empty()) pop_front(); }
```

Done.

->: a bit of syntactic sugar

Writing (*newEntry).next_ is wearing out my pinkies from using the shift key. Fortunately, C++ provides another way of writing exactly the same thing, easier to type, and a little easier to read:

```
newEntry->next_; //means (*currentPointer).next_;
```

So here's our new version of push_front.

```
template <typename T>
void List<T>::push_front (const T& newElement)
{
    Entry* newEntry = new Entry; //create an Entry
    newEntry->data_ = newElement;//put newElement in its data field
    newEntry->next_ = start_;    //put old version of start in
                                 //  its next field

    start_          = newEntry;  //put address of new Entry
                                 //  into start
}
```

More friendly syntax: pointers as conditions

We often need code like this

```
if (next_ != nullptr)...
```

or

```
while (next_ != nullptr) ...
```

Consider how conditions for `if` statements (and `for` loops, `while` loops, and `do-whiles`) work. The expression between the `()`'s is evaluated. If it evaluates to 0, that means false; anything else is true.

Well, `nullptr` is *kind of* like 0 – at least, it means "nothing." Nothing, false, 0, whatever. So you can write

```
if (next_ != nullptr)...
```

as

```
if (next_)...
```

"If `next_` isn't nothing; if there is a next thing..." is what this condition is saying. Use it if you find it convenient.

The linked list template

Example 22-2 contains completed versions of the preceding functions, plus a few others. Some are left as exercises.

Note how `operator=` is implemented. To set one list equal to another, you must throw away the old memory with `delete`; let `start_` be `nullptr`, meaning that the list is now empty; then copy the other `List`'s `Entry`s into this `List`.

Since we want to throw away the old memory...weren't we doing that already, in the destructor? Yes: so we make a function `eraseAllElements` that can be called by `operator=` *and* the destructor, for code reuse.

`createEmptyList` is another utility function for code reuse.

Example 22-2. `list.h`, containing the `List` class

```
//class List:  a linked list class
//    from _C++ for Lazy Programmers_

#ifndef LIST_H
#define LIST_H
```

```
template <typename T>
class List
{
 public:
    class Underflow  {};                        //Exception

    List ()                                      { createEmptyList();  }
    List (const List <T>& other) : List ()       { copy(other);        }
    ~List()                                      { eraseAllElements(); }

    const List <T>& operator= (const List <T>& other)
    {
        eraseAllElements (); createEmptyList(); copy(other);
        return *this;
    }

    bool operator== (const List <T>& other) const; //left as exercise

    int  size         () const;                 //left as exercise
    bool empty        () const { return size() == 0; }

    void push_front(const T& newElement);       //add newElement at front
    void pop_front ();                           //take one off the front
    const T& front () const;                     //left as exercise

    void print     (std::ostream&) const;       //left as exercise
 private:
    struct Entry
    {
        T       data_;
        Entry* next_;
    };

    Entry* start_;                               //Points to first element

    void copy(const List <T>& other);           //copies other's entries
                                                 //  into this List

    void eraseAllElements ();                    //empties the list
```

```
    void createEmptyList  ()
    {
        start_ = nullptr;                   //the list is...nothing
    }
};

template <typename T>
inline
std::ostream& operator<< (std::ostream& out, const List <T>& foo)
{
    foo.print(out); return out;
}

template <typename T>
void List<T>::eraseAllElements () { while (!empty()) pop_front(); }

template <typename T>
void List<T>::push_front (const T& newElement)
{
    Entry* newEntry = new Entry; //create an entry
    newEntry->data_ = newElement;//set its data_ field to newElement
    newEntry->next_ = start_;    //set its next_ field to start_

    start_          = newEntry;  //make start_ point to new entry
}

template <typename T>
void List<T>::pop_front()
{
    if (empty()) throw Underflow();

    Entry* temp = start_;   //store location of thing to delete
    start_ = start_->next_; //let start_ = next thing after start_

    delete temp;            //delete the item
}

template <typename T>
```

```
void List<T>::copy(const List <T>& other)
{
    Entry* lastEntry = nullptr;   //last thing we added to this list,
                                  //  as we go thru other list
    Entry* otherP = other.start_; //where are we in the other list?

    //while not done with other list...
    //   copy its next item into this list
    while (otherP)
    {
        //Make a new entry with current element from other;
        // put it at end of our list (so far)
        Entry* newEntry = new Entry;
        newEntry->data_ = otherP->data_;
        newEntry->next_ = nullptr;

        //If list is empty, make it start_ with this new entry
        //If not, make its previous Entry recognize new entry
        //  as what comes next
        if (empty()) start_           = newEntry;
        else         lastEntry->next_ = newEntry;

        lastEntry = newEntry;  //Keep pointer for lastEntry updated
        otherP = otherP->next_;//Go on to next item in other list
    }
}

#endif //LIST_H
```

Antibugging

When pointers go wrong, they *really* go wrong. You'll probably get a program crash.

Here are the worst and most common pointer-related errors:

- **Crash, from following a** `nullptr` – for example, saying `*myPointer` when `myPointer` is `nullptr`. The best preventative: before you refer to what a pointer points to (by putting the `*` in front or `->` after), always check:

  ```
  if (myPointer != nullptr) ...
  ```

  When pointers are involved, paranoia is a Good Thing.

- **Crash, from using a pointer that has not been initialized.** Solution: **always initialize every pointer**. If you don't know what to initialize it to, use `nullptr`. Then `if (myPointer != nullptr)...` will prevent the error (see previous paragraph).

- **Crash, from following a pointer that points to something that's been deleted.** Tracing what the code does with diagrams, as I did in previous sections, is the best prevention I know. Once you have a few functions that you trust, you can be lazy, as I was with `eraseAllEntries`: let a trusted function like `pop_front` do the scary work.

- **The program gets stuck in a loop.**

  ```
  Entry* p = start_;
  while (p)
  {
      ...
  }
  ```

  The problem here is I forgot to make the `while` loop go on to the next entry:

  ```
  p = p->next_;
  ```

  I am less likely to forget if I put it in the form of a `for` loop:

  ```
  for (Entry* p = start_; p != nullptr; p = p->next)...
  ```

EXERCISES

1. Write `List::front () const`. (This and the rest of these exercises except the last have answers in the next chapter's sample code.)
2. Write `List::size () const`. Can you make it work in O(1) time?
3. Write `List`'s member function `operator==`. Use the -> operator where appropriate.
4. Clean up the code a bit by giving `Entry` a constructor taking the data field and, optionally, the next field. This should help prevent the error of forgetting to initialize.
5. Write `List::print (std::ostream&) const`.
6. (Requires move ctors, move =) Give List a move constructor and move =.
7. (Harder) Add a data member `Entry::prev_`, so that you can traverse the list backward; and `List::rStart_`, so you'll know where to start. Also add `List` member functions push_back, pop_back, back, and `List::print_backwards`.

#include <list>

Yes, the linked list class is also built in. It lacks `print`. It lacks `operator[]`. On the other hand, it does have push_back – see Exercise 6 – and lots of other functions you can look up on your own.

So here's a problem: if you can't use [], how *can* you get to the elements of a list? It's pretty useless if you can't! Well, there is a way: it's called "iterators," and it's covered in the next chapter.

CHAPTER 23

The Standard Template Library

Should every programmer make his/her own vector class, list class, and so on? Oh, of course not. So some time back the Standard Template Library (STL) was developed and put into the standard. In STL you'll find containers like list and vector; strings, as we already use them; and commonly needed functions like swap, find, and copy.

You'll also find an annoying emphasis on efficiency. I say "annoying" because STL promotes efficiency by *disabling* things you may want to do that are inefficient. For instance, if you want to use operator[] with a list you can forget it: it takes too long (O(N) time). If you want that, the makers of STL reasoned, you can use a vector. They're right. But I still get to be annoyed.

We've got to get at the elements of a list somehow. How? Let's deal with that now.

Iterators

operator[] for list doesn't exist. Entry* is private. What can we do?

STL's list class provides **iterators**: things that say where we are in the list, and can traverse it. Example 23-1 shows what you can do with them.

Example 23-1. Using iterators

```
//doSomethingTo each element of myList, from beginning to end
for (list<T>::iterator i = myList.begin(); i != myList.end(); ++i)
      doSomethingTo (*i);
```


W. Briggs, *C++ for Lazy Programmers*, https://doi.org/10.1007/978-1-4842-5187-4_23

The `iterator` type is a member of `list<T>` like our `Entry` struct, only publicly available. As shown, it often starts at `begin ()`, that is, the start of the list, and keeps going till it reaches the `end ()` (Figure 23-1).

`end()` refers not to the last element, but to one *past* the last element. We use it to see if we're going too far, and we test this using != rather than <. (Whether one iterator is less than another is not defined – but whether they're equal is.)

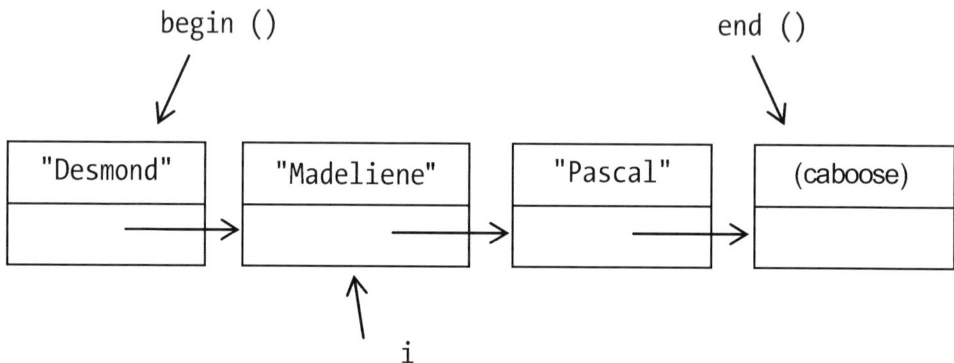

Figure 23-1. *A list, with its `begin()` and `end()` access functions, and an iterator `i` denoting the second element. `end()` is one step past the last element*

`++i` and `i++` work as expected: they take you to the next element.

To get not the iterator but the thing it's referring to, put the * in front, as in Example 23-1.

That's all there is to it!

Is your reaction something like "But what *is* an iterator?"?

Formally, it's just as described: it's a thing that refers to an element in the list, and when you say ++, it goes to the next element.

Informally…it's not exactly a pointer, but it does point to something. You can use * with it, and ->, just as you would with a pointer. But ++ means go to the next element in the list, *not* the next memory address, as it would with a pointer. Think of it as a souped up pointer if you like – or a finger you can put on an entry, and can move to the next when you like – but what it really is is a class, something like in Example 23-2.

Example 23-2. An iterator class for `List`

```
template <typename T>
class List
{
public:
    class BadPointer{};                    //Another exception class
    ...

private:
    ...

    Entry* start_;                         //Points to first element
    Entry* end_;                           //...and the caboose

public:
    class iterator                         //An iterator for List
    {
    public:
        iterator(const iterator& other)  : where_(other.where_) {}
        iterator(Entry* where = nullptr) : where_(where)        {}

        const iterator& operator= (const iterator& other)
        {
            where_ = other.where_;
        }

        bool operator== (const iterator& other) const
        {
            return where_ == other.where_;
        }
        bool operator!= (const iterator& other) const
        {
            return !((*this) == other);
        }
```

```
        const iterator& operator++()    //pre-increment, as in ++i
        {
            if (where_->next_ == nullptr) throw BadPointer();
            else where_ = where_->next_;
            return *this;
        }
        iterator operator++ (int)       //post-increment, as in i++
        {
            iterator result = *this; ++(*this); return result;
        }

        T& operator* ()
        {
            if (where_->next_ == nullptr) throw BadPointer();
            return where_->data_;
        }

        T* operator->()//Yes, this really is how you do it. It works!
        {
            if (where_->next_ == nullptr) throw BadPointer();
            return &(where_->data_);
        }
    private:
        Entry* where_;
    };

    iterator       begin() { return iterator(start_); }
    iterator       end  () { return iterator(end_  ); }
};
```

And now we can get to the List's contents without taking it apart.

...with `vector`, too

`list`s *need* iterators. But STL provides them for `vector` and other containers, and STL mavens recommend using them. Why?

- **Easy rewriting of code.** Consider these two versions of code with a `vector`:

  ```
  for (int i = 0; i < v.size(); ++i)
        doSomething(v[i]);
  ```

  and

  ```
  for (vector<T>::iterator i = v.begin(); i != v.end(); ++i)
        doSomething(*i);
  ```

  I write this and later think, no, I see now `vector` isn't the way to go; `list` is better.

  If I used the first version, I've got major changes on both lines. If I used the second, all I have to do is change `vector` to `list`.

- **Some member functions of `vector` already require iterators**. `insert`, for instance.

- **Generic programming.** Suppose there's something you may want to do with a container – any container.

  ```
  ... find(digits.begin(), digits.end(), 7); //Is a 7 in there?
  ```

  Since the version for `list` must have iterators, the version for `vector` has iterators too. That way you can learn one way to call the function and it'll work regardless of your choice of container. The section on `algorithm` later in this chapter introduces a few of many such functions STL provides.

But if you do use `int index` for `vector`s as before, the sky won't fall.

const and reverse iterators

Often using an iterator gives an unexpected type conflict. Consider this code:

```
class EmptyList {};                    //Exception

template <typename T>
double findAverageLength(const List<T>& myList)
{
      if (myList.empty()) throw EmptyList();

      double sum = 0;
      for (List<string>::iterator i = myList.begin();
           i != myList.end();
           ++i)
            sum += i->size();

      return sum / myList.size();
}
```

The compiler gives an error message that boils down to: vec is `const`, but you're using an `iterator` with it, and that's a type conflict.

This is how STL prevents you from using an iterator with a `const` container and doing something that alters the container. The solution:

```
template <typename T>
double findAverageLength(const List<T>& myList)
{
      if (myList.empty()) throw EmptyList();

      double sum = 0;
      for (List<string>::const_iterator i = myList.begin();
           i != myList.end();
           ++i)
            sum += i->size();

      return sum / myList.size();
}
```

That's all it takes.

If you prefer you can go through the container backward (note the rbegin and rend – the same as begin and end, only in reverse):

```
for (list<T>::reverse_iterator i=myList.rbegin();
      i !=myList.rend();
      --i)
    doSomethingTo (*i); //myList must be non-const
```

...or do backward *and* const:

```
for (List<string>::const_reverse_iterator i = myList.begin();
     i != myList.end();
     ++i)
    sum += i->size();
```

To know which to use:

- To go through the container, use an iterator.
- If the container is const, use const_iterator.
- If you're going backward, stick reverse_ in there somewhere.

To get comfortable with iterators, I recommend doing Exercises 3 and 4.

Antibugging

- **You get an error message too long to read:**

  ```
  conversion from 'std::__cxx11::list<std::pair<std::__cxx11::basic_
  string<char>, std::__cxx11::basic_string<char> > >::const_
  iterator' {aka 'std::_List_const_iterator<std::pair<std::__
  cxx11::basic_string<char>, std::__cxx11::basic_string<char> > >'}
  to non-scalar type 'std::__cxx11::list<std::pair<std::__
  cxx11::basic_string<char>, int> >::const_iterator' {aka 'std::_
  List_const_iterator<std::pair<std::__cxx11::basic_string<char>,
  int> >'} requested
  ```

Rip out things that don't look important. This get us

```
conversion from list<pair<string, string >>::const_iterator to
list<pair<string, int>>::const_iterator requested
```

My mistake is now obvious: I forgot what I wanted a `pair` of. *Way* easier to read.

- **You get pages of error messages, reporting errors in system libraries.** Look for your own filename(s) in the messages and focus on those.

EXERCISES

1. Using iterators in a for loop, write a function `reverse` which returns a reversed copy of a `List` you give it.
2. Now write it so that instead of passing a `List`, you pass in two iterators, its `begin ()` and its `end ()`.
3. Add a `const_iterator` class to `List`.

   You'll need new `const` versions of `begin` and `end`, to return `const_iterator` instead of `iterator`.
4. In the last chapter, there was an exercise for equipping a `List` to be traversed backward. Using that, incorporate `reverse_iterator` and `const_reverse_iterator` into the `List` class.
5. Using iterators in for loops, write functions to convert back and forth between STL `lists` and `vectors`.

Getting really lazy: ranges and `auto`

This works for traversing a container:

```
for (vector<string>::const_iterator i = myVector.begin();
     i != myVector.end();
     ++i)                          //A lot of typing...
     cout << *i << ' ';
```

This works too:

```
vector<string> myVector; ...
for (const string& i : myVector) //a "range-based" for loop
    cout << i << ' ';    // <-- no *: i is an element, not an iterator
```

And this works for arrays:

```
int myArray[] = { 0, 1, 2, 3 };
for (int  i : myArray)  cout << i << ' ';
```

Great, but I'm even lazier now. Let the compiler figure out the element type.

```
for (auto i : myArray)  cout << i << ' ';
                       //Overkill? I *did* know it was an int...
for (auto i : myVector) cout << i << ' ';
```

You can use `auto` for any variable declaration where the compiler can figure out the type – that is, where the variable is being initialized. We do have to give it *some* help: it won't apply &'s unless we tell it.

```
for (auto& i : myArray) i *= 2; //without & it won't change the array
```

That also applies if we want the & to prevent needless copying:

```
for (const auto& i : myVector) cout << i << ' ';
```

I use `auto` when type names are so long I think my fingers will fall off (`vector<vector<int>>::const_reverse_iterator` – aigh!). I think it *is* overkill for `int`.

initializer_lists (optional)

One thing I was sorry to give up, going from arrays to more sophisticated containers, was the bracketed initializer list, as in `int array [] = {0, 1, 2, 3};`. Initializing element by element is more trouble.

But we can use {} lists with our own classes too (and of course it's built-in for STL). This code illustrates doing this with Vector.

```
#include <initializer_list> //for std::initializer_list

template <typename T>
class Vector
{
public:
    Vector (const std::initializer_list<T>& other);
    ...
};

template <typename T>
Vector<T>::Vector(const std::initializer_list<T>&  other) : Vector ()
{
    for (auto i = other.begin(); i != other.end(); ++i)
        push_back(*i);
}
```

std::initializer_list has iterators built in, so this'll work. Then again, since it has iterators built in, so will this simpler version:

```
template <typename T>
Vector<T>::Vector(const std::initializer_list<T>&  other) : Vector ()
{
    for (auto i : other) push_back(i);
}
```

EXERCISES

1. Since std::initializer_list has begin() and end(), but not rbegin() and rend(), if you want to use it to initialize a List, List will need push_back. Create List::push_back if you haven't already, and give List a constructor that takes an initializer_list.

algorithm (optional)

Many things you'll want to do with containers are in the include file <algorithm>. Here's how to find an element in a container named digits. It can be list, vector, whatever.

```
auto i = find(digits.begin(), digits.end(), 7);
if (i != digits.end()) cout << "Found a 7!\n";
```

find searches the range from digits.begin () up until digits.end (). It returns an iterator referencing the first element equal to 7. If there is no such element, it returns digits.end().

Here's how to copy the contents of one container to another. They can be different types of container.

```
copy(digits.begin(), digits.end(), back_inserter(newContainer));
```

Or maybe just copy the ones that match some criterion? We can pass in a function:

```
bool isEven (int i) { return i % 2 == 0; }
...
copy_if(digits.begin(), digits.end(), back_inserter(evens), isEven);
```

Most of these functions should work for any container type. sort(digits.begin(), digits.end()); does what you think it does. (Operator < for its elements will need to be defined.) But if you want to sort a list, you'll have to use its member function: myList.sort ();. Go figure.

STL containers don't overload the << or >> operators for I/O. Understandable, since we all may want different ways to print or read in containers, but it's still a pain. STL provides another way to print, weirdly named:

```
copy(evens.begin(), evens.end(), ostream_iterator<int>(cout, " "));
```

int is what we have a list of; cout is where it's going, and " " is what to print after each element. " " is likely better than (say) ", " which will give us a comma after the last element, too. You'll need to #include <iterator>.

There are more; an Internet search will get you what you need. cplusplus.com and cppreference.com are good places to start.

The erase-remove idiom

How about removing things we don't want from the container – say, take out all the evens? This look promising. I assume digits is 1 2 3 4 5 6 7 8 9.

```
remove_if (digits.begin(), digits.end(), isEven);
```

digits is now 1 3 5 7 9 6 8 9. Huh?

We have to read the fine print. Wherever you look it up online, you'll find that remove doesn't actually remove anything: it moves unwanted elements to the end of the sequence and returns an iterator to where the new end should be. So why's it called remove? Beats me.

The hack is to use another function to chop it off at the new end. erase(iter1, iter2); erases everything from iterator iter1 up to iter2, so we can use that to do the erasing:

```
erase (remove_if (digits.begin(), digits.end(), isEven),
       digits.end());
```

I'm sorry to expose you to that evilness, but now that you have the hack you can use it as needed.

Antibugging

- **You add or remove elements while in a for loop and get a crash.** When you do anything to change the contents of your container, bets are off regarding iterators already in the container. Consider this code:

  ```
  for (auto i = digits.begin(); i != digits.end(); ++i)
      if (isEven(*i))
          digits.erase (i);     //erase element referenced by i
                                //(different "erase")
  ```

  The problem is that after you erase whatever's at i, i points to a nonexistent element. The loop increments i and gets to another nonexistent element at who-knows-where, and your program fails. (It *might* work.)

erase returns an iterator referencing the next element after the deleted one, so you can do this, even if it's ugly:

```
for (auto i = digits.begin(); i != digits.end(); )
                                                    //no ++ here!
   if (isEven(*i))
      i = digits.erase (i);     //erases *i and moves i
                                //  to next location
   else
     ++i;
```

Or you can use the erase-remove hack, I mean idiom:

```
digits.erase (remove_if (digits.begin(), digits.end(),
                         isEven),
              digits.end());   //Isn't it lovely?
```

Tip If a function alters the structure of the container (like erase), it may invalidate the iterators. Declare iterators again as needed, or find a function that does what you want in one call so you won't care.

EXERCISES

1. In the string "SoxEr776asdCsdfR1234qqE..T12Ci-98j0apqwe0DweE" there is a secret code. Use an `<algorithm>` function to extract only the capital letters and read the code.

2. (Uses file I/O) First, make a file of strings. Then make two copies of it. In one, alter the order and the capitalization of some of the strings. In the other, replace some of the strings.

   Now write a program that can read two files into vectors or lists and, using STL functions, tell if the files are different, ignoring order and capitalization. Use an STL function not covered in this chapter (so you'll need an Internet search) that change a string to all caps or all lowercase. To find what's in one sequence but not the other, consider this algorithm:

```
for each element in sequence 1 (using iterators)
   use the "find" function to see if it's also in sequence 2
```

3. Do the preceding problem, but instead of using `find` and a loop, use `set_difference` (also not covered in this chapter). And `erase`.

CHAPTER 24

Building Bigger Projects

One day you may want to build a bigger project. This chapter introduces some useful tools: namespaces, conditional compilation, and the construction of libraries.

Namespaces

Suppose I write a library for geographical information, to be used for maps, making voting districts, whatever. I make some classes: maps, vectors (XY pairs used for graphics), regions, and more.

Then I notice that I can't compile because map and vector already mean something in C++. OK. Call 'em GeoLib_map, GeoLib_vector, and so on, like with SDL and SSDL functions.

And I'm using a third-party library, which happens to define region as something else...this is getting tedious. Is there a shortcut?

Sure. Make a **namespace** GeoLib and put everything you want the world to see in it, as in Figure 24-1.

```
//geolib_map.h

#ifndef GEOLIBMAP_H
#define GEOLIBMAP_H

namespace GeoLib
{
    class map {...};
}

#endif //GEOLIBMAP_H
```

```
//geolib_map.cpp

namespace GeoLib
{
    map::map ()
    {
        ...
    }

    ...
}
```

```
//geolib_vector.h

#ifndef GEOLIBVECTOR_H
#define GEOLIBVECTOR_H

namespace GeoLib
{
    class vector {...};
}

#endif //GEOLIBVECTOR_H
```

Figure 24-1. *A namespace can contain code from different files*

W. Briggs, *C++ for Lazy Programmers*, https://doi.org/10.1007/978-1-4842-5187-4_24

Programmers can now type GeoLib::map or std::map, and the compiler will know which they mean.

If they get tired of typing GeoLib:: over and over, they can use using:

```
using GeoLib::region;
              //you can omit the GeoLib:: in GeoLib::region

using namespace GeoLib;
              //now *all* GeoLib members can have GeoLib:: omitted

using namespace std;
              //now all std:: members can have std:: omitted too
              //If the compiler gripes, you can still use GeoLib::
              // or std:: to clarify which you want
```

To illustrate construction of namespaces, Examples 24-2 and 24-3 show the creation of a namespace Cards; Example 24-5 uses it.

It's a matter of debate whether using namespace <whatever>; is 3vil. It's more typing, but you can easily resolve name conflicts by adding <whatever>::. I say use it as you like in the privacy of your own .cpp files, but don't mess up others' by putting it in .h's they may include.

Conditional compilation

Now I'm using my GeoLib code, and I'm finding my calculations are wrong, wrong, wrong. It's hard to tell which functions are screwing up. I want to generate a report of those calculations so I can check them:

```
map::area(region) thinks area of block group 6709 is 672.4
dist to center is 356.2
map::area(region) thinks area of block group 6904 is 312.5
dist to center is 379.7
...
```

I don't want this printed *all* the time – just when debugging.

So I create a #define in a .h file that every other file includes (Example 24-1).

Example 24-1. A `.h` file containing `#define DEBUG`, for conditional compilation

```
//debugSetup.h

#ifndef DEBUGSETUP_H
#define DEBUGSETUP_H

#define DEBUG                 //Yes, that's the whole thing

#endif //DEBUGSETUP_H
```

I use it wherever I have debugging information to print

```
#ifdef DEBUG
    cout << " map::area(region) thinks area of block group "
         << bg->id() << " is " << bg->area() << endl;
    cout << "dist to center is "
         << distance (region.loc(), bg->loc()) << endl;
#endif
```

and comment or uncomment the `#define DEBUG` depending on whether I want to see this.

Libraries

Libraries come in two flavors, **static** and **shared**. A static library's code is brought right into the executable at link time; the shared library is in another file, loaded at runtime. So the static library is said to be quicker to run (I've never noticed a difference) and you don't have to worry where your shared library got moved to as it's always right there in the executable. But shared saves space, as many programs can use the same code, and is more easily updated.

I lean toward shared. It's common for Unix and seems to help with portability between compiler versions. But both are fine.

I'll try it both ways here, for both compilers. For my example I'll use the card games code from Chapter 19, with generally useful classes (`Card`, `Deck`, etc.) going into the library. The Montana game will use that library.

You might create some other library as you go. See Exercises at the chapter's end, or choose your own.

g++

Static libraries

To create a static library, compile the object files as usual

```
g++ -g -c deck.cpp
...
```

then link with

```
ar rcs libcards.a deck.o card.o cardgroup.o
                                  #ar for "archive"; rcs is needed flags
```

Shared libraries

The shared library needs object files "relocatable" in memory, so compile them like this:

```
g++ -g -fPIC -c deck.cpp #PIC: "position independent code." All righty then
```

In Unix, shared libraries end in `.so`, so link like this:

```
g++ -shared -o libcards.so  deck.o card.o cardgroup.o
```

Windows uses the extension `.dll`, so for MinGW, type this:

```
g++ -shared -o libcards.dll deck.o card.o cardgroup.o
```

Linking

g++ needs to know where to find the includes files, where to find the library files, and what libraries to use.

We tell it by flags:

- `-I<name of directory>` to find include files;
- `-L<name of directory>` to find library files;

- `-l<library>` to say what libraries we want linked in. Library names have an initial `lib`, and the extension `.a`, `.so`, or `.dll`, stripped off, as here:

```
g++ -o a.out -g montana.o io.o montana_main.o \¹
    -I../cardLibg++ -L../cardLibg++ -lcards
                                    #uses libcards.<something>
```

You can have as many copies as you want of any flag.

Running

If you used a static library, you can just run the program now (`./a.out`).

If it's dynamic, the system needs to know where to find it. Solutions:

- Bribe the system administrator to put the `.dll` or `.so` file in the system path. This makes sense if multiple programs use it and your program's important enough.
- Copy the `.dll` or `.so` to the folder with the executable. Good for a single project; not so good if you have lots of folders and therefore lots of copies.
- Set the environment variables so the system can find it. This is what I did with SSDL, and you can see it in the scripts in the folders (`runx`, `runw`, `gdbx`, etc.) The command is like this:

```
export LD_LIBRARY_PATH=../cardLibg++ #Unix
PATH="../cardLibg++:$PATH"           #Windows
```

[1]\ means "continue on the next line."

Makefiles

These long commands get tedious to type repeatedly, so they're bundled into Makefiles in the chapter's source code: one type for building the library, one for building a program that uses the library, and in the latter's folder, scripts to point the system to the library's path.

Edit the first Makefile to pick the kind of library to create, then edit all of them for paths, executable names, whatever you like.

Microsoft Visual Studio

Static libraries – The easy option

To build a static library in Visual Studio 2017, select File ➤ New ➤ Project, then Visual C++ ➤ Windows Desktop ➤ Static Library. In 2019 click Create New Project and scroll through a list.

When it creates the project, it expects you to use "precompiled headers."[2] You can

- **Support this by putting a line at the start of each source file**: either

  ```
  #include <stdafx.h>
  ```

  or

  ```
  #include "pch.h"
  ```

  depending on which the new project provides you with. It must come before any other includes or your code won't compile.

If you don't want to have to do all that, you can fix it in one step:

- **Eliminate precompiled headers** thus: under Project ➤ Properties, for All Configurations/All Platforms (top row), set Configuration Properties ➤ C/C++ ➤ Precompiled Headers ➤ Precompiled Header to Not Using Precompiled Headers. You can ignore the files the compiler gave you with the project.

[2]Microsoft Visual Studio and g++ both have this method of helping with compile times. The idea is that instead of recompiling a .h file anew for each source file you include it in, you can reduce compile time by compiling it once. I haven't felt the need, but with STL, header files do seem to keep growing, so...

Projects that use your library need to know where to find its include files. Under Project Properties for All Configurations/All Platforms, set Configuration Properties ➤ C/C++ ➤ General ➤ Additional Include Directories appropriately (see Figure 24-2).

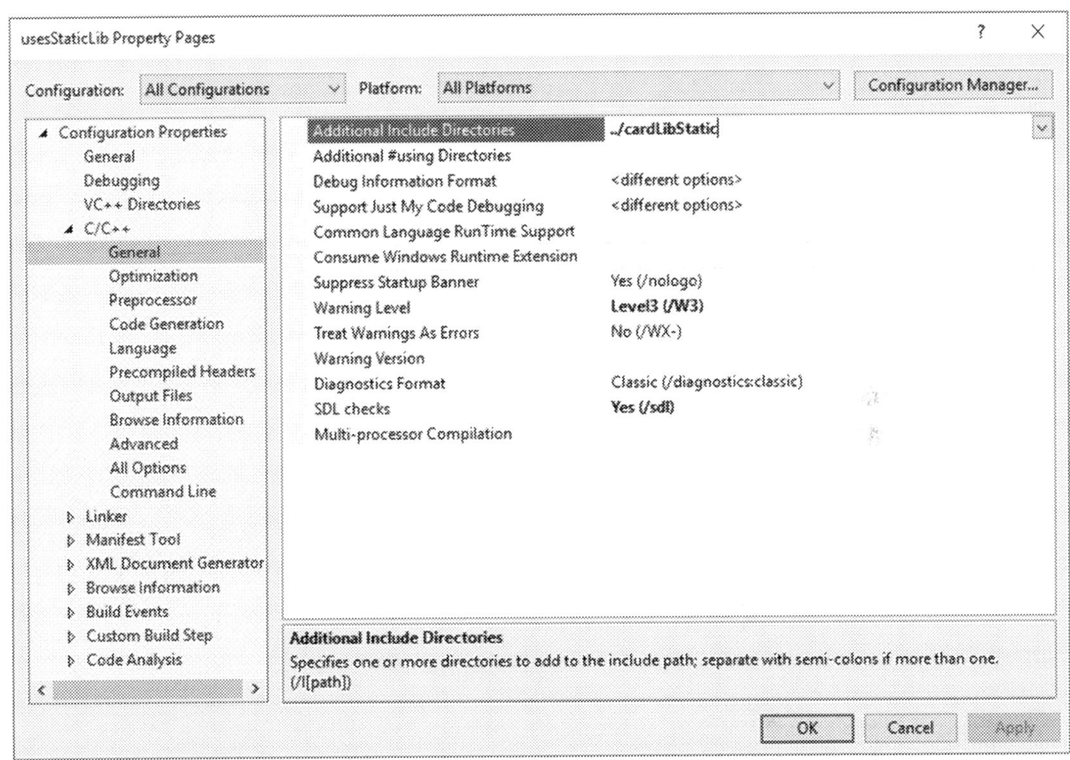

Figure 24-2. *Telling a project where to find library include files, in Visual Studio*

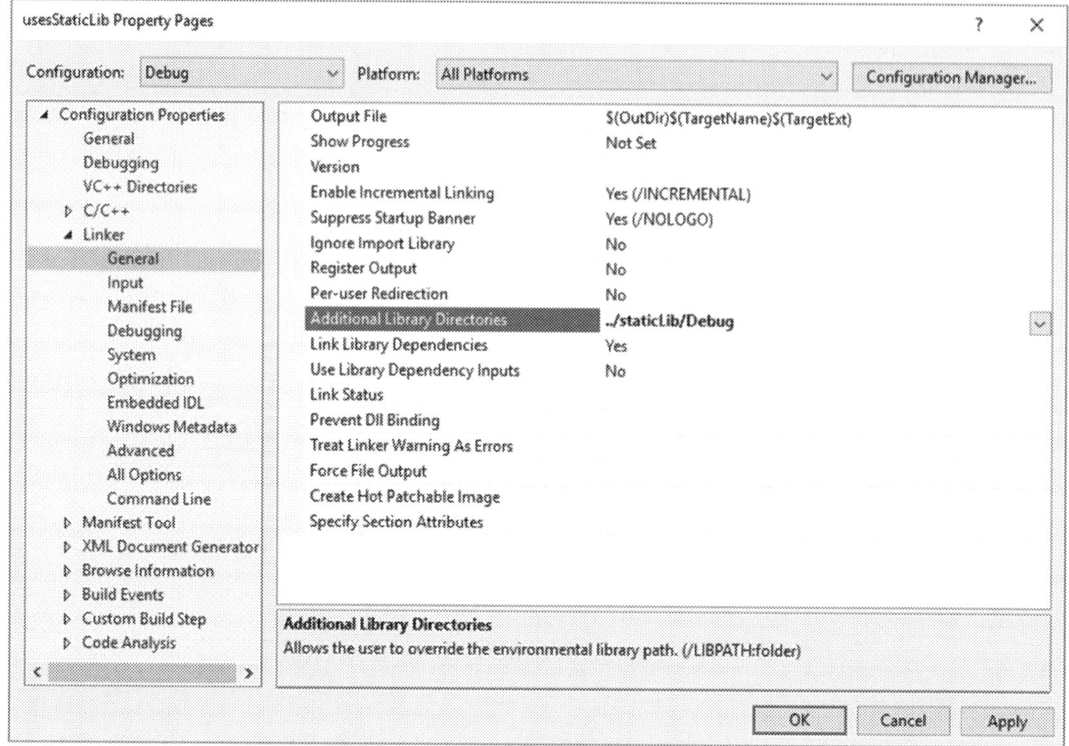

Figure 24-3. *Telling the project where to find your library, in Visual Studio*

Add your library's path to Configuration Properties ➤ Linker ➤ General ➤ Additional Library Directories (Figure 24-3). Its location will differ between configurations and platforms; it'll probably contain `Debug` or `Release` if you're doing x86/Win32, or `x64/Debug` or `x64/Release` if not. I suggest starting with Debug and x86.

Now you must tell it *what* the library is. Under Project Properties, All Configurations/All Platforms, add the name of the library under Configuration Properties ➤ Linker ➤ Input ➤ Additional Dependencies (Figure 24-4). It'll be `<your library project>.lib`.

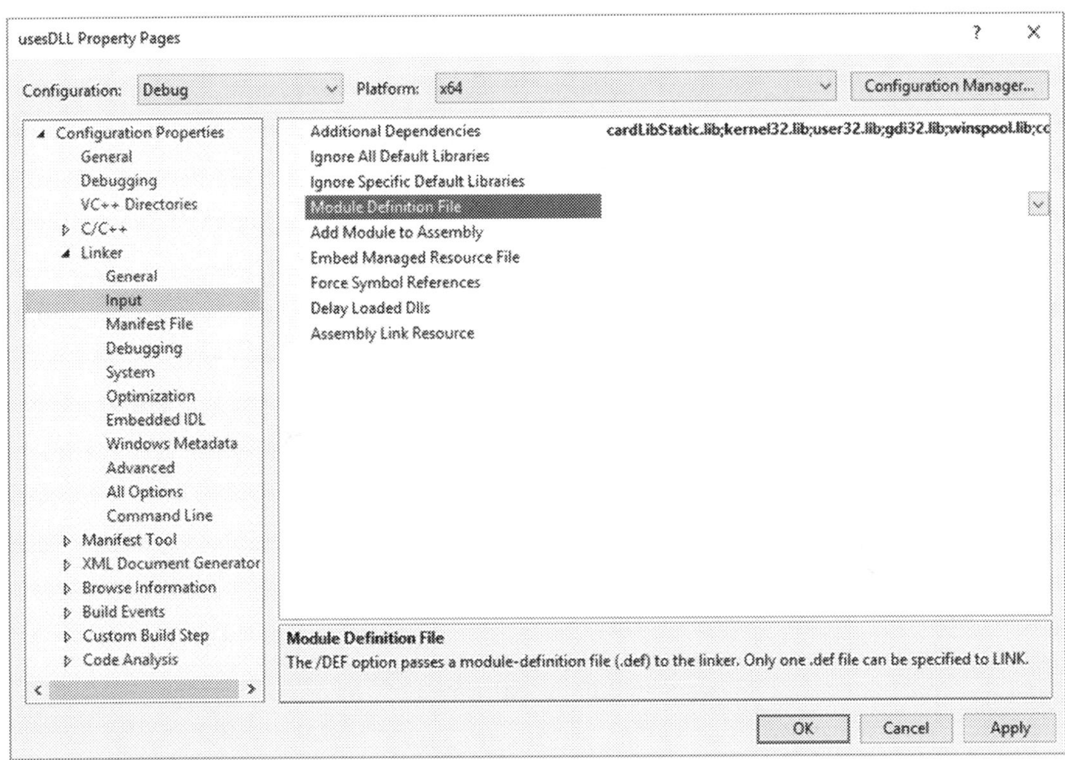

Figure 24-4. *Adding a library dependency in Visual Studio*

Dynamic Link Libraries (DLLs) – the not so easy way

To make your own DLL, go back through the previous section, but for project type select Dynamic Link Library instead of Static Library.

Now that that's built...

When directing new programs to use your library, when you tell Project Properties about the library (Figure 24-4), it'll still be <your project>.lib. I thought we were creating a DLL? Yes, but we're really creating two things: the .dll, which contains the runtime code, and a .lib file that tells the program at compile time, "you'll get to import these things from a DLL later."

This is where it gets weird. When the compiler sees a prototype, it needs to know if it's going to be compiling and exporting it (because it's compiling the library) or importing it from a DLL (because it's compiling a program that uses the library). The way to say this is to prepend to the prototype either `__declspec(dllexport)` or `__declspec(dllimport)`. `__declspec` means "I'm about to tell you something about this function" and `dllexport`/`dllimport`, well, that's obvious.

So are we supposed to write two versions of each prototype, one for import and one for export?

This common hack means we won't have to:

1. Write a .h file like in Example 24-2.

Example 24-2. A .h file to help with DLL projects

```
//Header to make DLL functions import or export
//  -- from C++ for Lazy Programmers

#ifndef CARDSSETUP_H
#define CARDSSETUP_H

# ifdef IM_COMPILING_MY_CARD_LIBRARY_RIGHT_NOW
#  define DECLSPEC __declspec(dllexport)
# else
#  define DECLSPEC __declspec(dllimport)
# endif //IM_COMPILING_MY_CARD_LIBRARY_RIGHT_NOW

#endif //CARDSSETUP_H
```

   Now DECLSPEC means "this is to be exported" *or* "this is to be imported"...depending on whether we're compiling the library or using it. Just right.

2. In each .cpp file in the library, write this #define:

   ```
   #define IM_COMPILING_MY_CARD_LIBRARY_RIGHT_NOW
   ```

   That's how it'll know what DECLSPEC should be.

   This must be done before any .h files related to your project (so they can use it) and after #include <stdafx.h>/#include "pch.h", if we're using that (because that always comes first).

3. Put DECLSPEC before everything being exported from the .cpp files.

4. ...and before the corresponding prototypes in the .h files, too. They have to match.

Files will look something like Examples 24-3 and 24-4. Example 24-5 shows how to use `Cards` members in a `montana.h`; in `montana.cpp`, I just said `using namespace Cards;` and made no other changes.

Example 24-3. Parts of `card.h`, set up to make a DLL, and forming a namespace

```
//Card class
//  -- from C++ for Lazy Programmers

#ifndef CARD_H
#define CARD_H

#include <iostream>
#include "cardsSetup.h"

namespace Cards
{
    enum Rank { ACE = 1, JACK = 11, QUEEN, KING };
    enum Suit { HEARTS, DIAMONDS, CLUBS, SPADES };

    DECLSPEC std::ostream& operator<< (std::ostream& out, Rank  r);
    DECLSPEC std::ostream& operator<< (std::ostream& out, Suit  s);
    DECLSPEC std::istream& operator>> (std::istream& in,  Rank& r);
    DECLSPEC std::istream& operator>> (std::istream& in,  Suit& s);

    class Card
    {
    public:
        Card(Rank r = Rank(0), Suit s = Suit(0)) :
            rank_(r), suit_(s)
        {
        }
        Card(const Card& other) { *this = other; }

        DECLSPEC void read(std::istream &in);
    private:
        Suit suit_;
        Rank rank_;
    };
```

```
    inline
    std::ostream& operator<< (std::ostream& out, const Card& foo)
    {
        foo.print(out); return out;
    }

    inline
    std::istream& operator>> (std::istream& in, Card& foo)
    {
        foo.read(in);  return in;
    }
}
#endif //CARD_H
```

Example 24-4. Part of card.cpp, set up to make a DLL, and forming a namespace

```
//Card class
//  -- from C++ for Lazy Programmers

#include "stdafx.h" //or maybe its #include "pch.h"
#include <iostream>
#define IM_COMPILING_MY_LIBRARY_RIGHT_NOW
                   //see setup.h. Must come before card
                   // related includes, after stdafx/pch.h if any
#include "card.h"

using namespace std;

namespace Cards
{
    DECLSPEC void Card::read(std::istream &in)
    {
        try { in >> rank_ >> suit_; }
        catch (BadRankException&)
                                  //if reading rank_ threw an exception
        {
```

```
            in >> suit_;       // consume the suit as well
            throw;             // and continue throwing the exception
        }
    }

    DECLSPEC istream& operator>> (istream& in, Suit& s)
    {
        ...
    }

    ...
}
```

Example 24-5. Part of montana.h, showing use of namespace Cards

```
//class Montana, for a game of Montana solitaire
//   -- from _C++ for Lazy Programmers_

#include "gridLoc.h"
#include "cell.h"
#include "deck.h"

#ifndef MONTANA_H
#define MONTANA_H

class Montana
{
public:
    enum { ROWS = 4, CLMS  = 13};

    Montana   () {};
    void play ();

private:
    //dealing and redealing

    void deal                   (Cards::Deck& deck, Cards::Waste& waste);
    void cleanup                (Cards::Deck& deck, Cards::Waste& waste);

     ...
```

```
    //data members
    Cards::Cell grid_       [ROWS][CLMS];     //where cards are
    GridLoc     emptyCells_ [NUM_EMPTY_CELLS];//where empty cells are
};

#endif //MONTANA_H
```

If that goes well, there's one more thing to set in the program that uses your library: it needs to find the DLL at runtime.

The easiest way is to copy the DLL into the project folder. Or put it in the system PATH (which may require Administrator access).

If that's not what you want, go to Project Properties (Figure 24-5), and set Configuration Properties ➤ Debugging ➤ Environment. It needs an update to the PATH variable, without forgetting the old PATH…if the location of the DLL is `..\cardLibDLL\Debug`, you can give it `PATH=..\cardLibDLL\Debug\;%PATH%`.

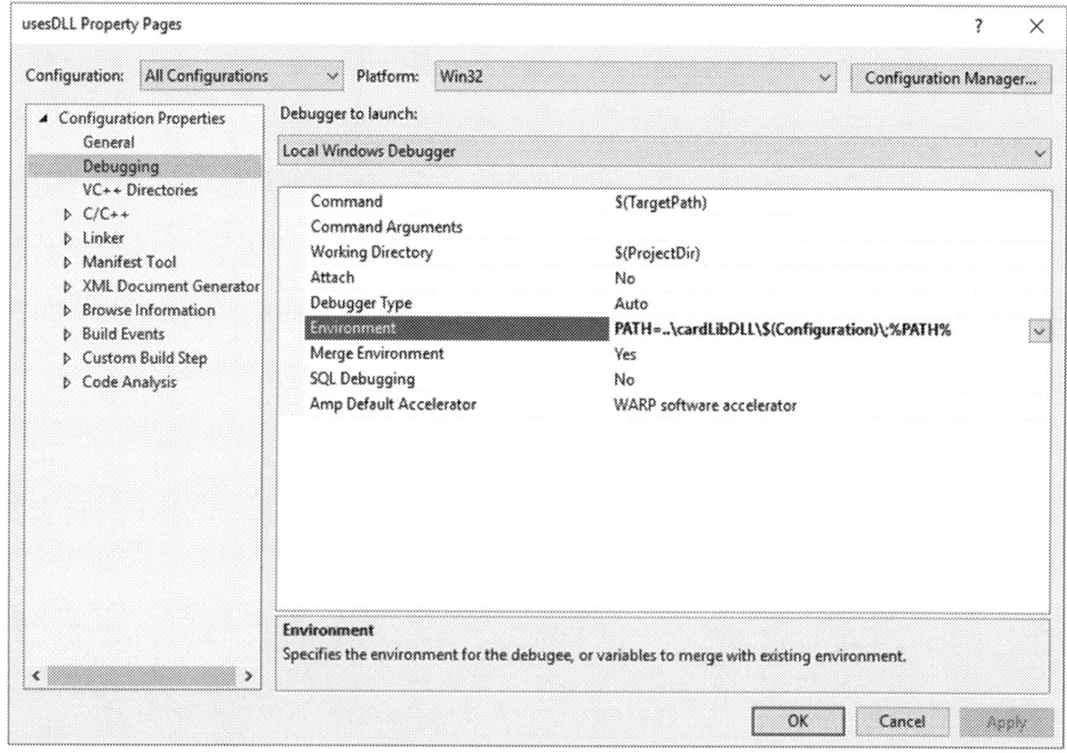

***Example 24-5.** Setting the PATH in Visual Studio*

Antibugging

- **You make changes to Project Properties, but they have no effect.** It's easy to overlook the top line of the Project Properties window (Figure 24-5). Sometimes you correct one configuration, but you're using another. I prefer to edit All Configurations, All Platforms, wherever possible.
- **The compiler complains that common things like `cout` don't exist.** Put `#include <stdafx.h>` or `#include "pch.h"` before other includes or stop using precompiled headers; see the beginning of this section.
- **At runtime, the program can't find the DLL.** But you set the PATH variable, as earlier.

  If it's not a typo in the PATH, maybe you erased the `.user` file. This is what contains the environment information. Recreating it should solve the problem.
- **At runtime, the program can't start; the error message isn't clear.** Maybe your program's Platform (Win32 or x86 v. x64) doesn't match the DLL's.

EXERCISES

1. Put `PriorityQueue`, `List`, `Time`, `Fraction`, or some other class you did in previous exercises, into its own library, and link it to something that uses it.
2. Make a library named `shapes` (in a namespace `shapes`), using the `Shape` hierarchy from Chapter 21, extending it as you like; and link it into a program that uses the `Shapes`. You'll need to adapt the Makefile or .vcxproj in `basicSSDLProject` to help with SDL/SSDL includes and library files.

CHAPTER 25

History

C++ is descended from Simula 67, credited as the first object-oriented language, and C, which is basically what this book covered before classes. Just for the fun of it, let's look them over – and also Smalltalk, also credited as the first object-oriented language. Maybe you'll write another first object-oriented language someday.

Simula 67

Designed for simulations, Simula 67 contained classes, inheritance, and virtual functions. It didn't get much use. The best guess is that it didn't get much use because it didn't get much use: that is, it was not widely propagated, so there was no snowball effect, no virtuous cycle of compilers, people wanting programmers who knew it, people learning it, and so on. But it (largely) had the ideas that distinguish C++ from C.

Smalltalk

So did Smalltalk. Smalltalk was the first popular language of this type. Though C++ got its ideas on high-level organization from Simula 67, it's only fair to grant Smalltalk – which also inherits from Simula – a place here.

In the 1970s, Alan Kay, a newly graduated PhD from the University of Utah, could foresee that before long computers wouldn't be only for universities, government agencies, and major companies: even your dear old grandma might well have one. Your dear old grandma probably wouldn't be willing to program it in FORTRAN, though, unless she's a professional programmer. Like my kids' grandma.

So Smalltalk was developed: a language with an easier way of thinking and better organization than other languages of the day. Smalltalk came with its own environment (like Visual Basic and Python, if you know either of these languages), and a lot of overhead for the computer in terms of graphics, and this, plus to a lesser extent its

W. Briggs, *C++ for Lazy Programmers*, https://doi.org/10.1007/978-1-4842-5187-4_25

sometimes quirky syntax,[1] limited the language's appeal. Looks like grandma won't be programming in Smalltalk, either, even if she *is* a professional programmer. (The opposing view can be explored at `www.smalltalk.org`.)

(On the other hand, Smalltalk did popularize the object-oriented paradigm, and inspired Steve Jobs with its graphical user interface to say: let's have that on our Apple computers.[2] And thereby windowing systems spread.)

The way to make this user-friendly programming environment, Kay and his colleagues thought, was to use familiar metaphors: objects and classes, thus making an "object-oriented" programming language.

It may not have taken over the world, but it's taken over your desktop: menus, windows, and so on are object-oriented concepts – structures with their own internal states, reacting to messages sent (such as mouse clicks and keystrokes) in ways determined by what classes of things they are.

What "object-oriented" is

As Smalltalk (and the rest of the world) would define it, "object-oriented" means that a language has[3]

- Encapsulation, that is, private sections.
- Inheritance.
- Polymorphism: Virtual functions, operator overloading, and function overloading.
- Dynamic binding: This is what we do with the `new` command to allocate memory. A truly object-oriented language uses dynamic binding for all variables. This is less efficient, so C++ only does it when necessary.

C++ has these but doesn't require that you use them. In Smalltalk, everything is an object. Most languages are hybrids like C++.

---

[1]Consider a simple for loop in Smalltalk: `1 to: 10 do: <some action>`. This sends to the number 1 a message saying "do `<some action>` until iterations reaches 10." Send a message to 1? I like it. But it's, well, counterintuitive.

[2]Steve Jobs, *Triumph of the Nerds*, Part III.

[3]Some would add "open recursion." I wouldn't, and C++ doesn't need it.

C

Meanwhile, back at the ranch (specifically, at AT&T Bell Labs), someone had adapted a much more bare-bones language called BCPL (Basic Combined Programming Language) into also bare-bones languages imaginatively named B, and then C. (If progress had continued in the same direction, the one after would presumably have been P.) C was a tough-guy language, in which people not only suffered a steep "learning curve" (i.e., it was relatively tough to learn), but ended up saying phrases like "learning curve." And wrote things like `while (*a++=*b++);` and thought it was cool.

But C was certainly efficient – efficient enough that you could write operating systems in it. The Unix operating system predates C, but came to be written in C. C didn't have to be pretty as long as it was that effective.

It's apparently not true that C was an April Fool's joke designed to see just how crabbed and difficult a language could be and have people not catch on. But you may start to wonder if you drop by `www.ioccc.org`, the web site of the International Obfuscated C Code Contest, where programmers compete to have the most confusing and reader-hostile code. I particularly liked the one in which the program was shaped to look like Dr. Seuss's *The Cat in the Hat*.

C++

The ideas in Simula 67 found a receptive audience with my hero Bjarne Stroustrup, who had the idea to make a hybrid language between C and Simula, getting the efficiency of C and the organization of Simula. He had good reason. He'd written a simulator for a distributed software system in Simula, and liked its ease of organization and ability to detect type errors – better than the error checking of Pascal, he thought, which was too limiting. However, compiling and running the program showed a lot of inefficiency, so he converted to BCPL – admiring the increased speed, but missing the features he'd left behind.[4]

And so C with Classes, and later C++, came to be.

[4]Stroustrup, Bjarne. 1993. "A History of C++: 1979–1991," Section 2 (C with Classes).

C++ has been a resounding success. There is some dispute as to which of its modern competitors are descendants and which are merely amazingly similar (like its sibling Objective C, which appeared about the same time). But if we consider merely "languages which look like C (even down to the level of using == for compare, say), have objects, and came later," we have to include Java, JavaScript, PHP, Python, C#, and Ruby.

Standards

C++ came out in the mid-1980s with much of what you've seen here. As time went by, the community added exceptions, templates, the Standard Template Library, and other features.

For a decade in this century, programmers used the International Standards Organization's C++98 standard or the similar C++03 from 2003 (ish). But there was an interest in resolving perceived problems, including inefficient creation and destruction of classes (that's why we now have move constructors) and a lack of pointer safety. C++11 – initially called C++0x because they didn't know what year it would come out – began the process of resolving these issues, with C++14 and C++17 giving further changes.

Some of C++'s big new features relative to 10 years before include move constructors, lambda functions, `enum class`, `auto` variables, range-based for loops (`for (auto thing : sequence)`), smart pointers, `constexpr`, and structured bindings (`auto [a, b] = <something that's two values>`).

Stats vary, but I'm seeing C++ as the third most popular programming language, after Java and C. When you chose this language, you chose well.

CHAPTER 26

Esoterica (Recommended)

These are all extras, but fun and useful ones. To provide a little practice and familiarity, some build on others, so I suggest taking them in order.

sstream: using strings like cin/cout

To me this is one of the most useful new features: for file I/O, for sending print output to graphical displays, and for nontrivial user input.

Suppose you want to print details of a game to your heads-up display, centered at the top.

```
Points: 32000  /  Time left: 30.2  /  Mood: Annoyed
```

You could calculate the width of each label and each value (good luck doing that with a variable-width font) and from those calculate the location to print each item...if you do, turn in your lazy programmer badge right now.

Or you could do a lot of conversions and string concatenations and send that to `SSDL_RenderTextCentered`, as in the following. Once more, turn in that badge.

```
string finalString = string ("Points: ")
          + int2String (points) //How *do* you convert int to string?
          + "/ Time left: "     // Something tells me it's not easy
          + double2String(time) // and double is going to be worse.
          + " / Mood: " + mood;
SSDL_RenderTextCentered(finalString, SSDL_GetWindowWidth()/2, 10);
                                //10 pixels down
```

If we send variables of other types, like `Point2D`, we'll need more conversion-to-string functions. That's a lot of work.

W. Briggs, *C++ for Lazy Programmers*, https://doi.org/10.1007/978-1-4842-5187-4_26

Enter the stringstream. It's like cin, cout, and a string all rolled into one. You can write to it then extract the string produced; or put a string in and read from it.

To construct a string using <<, do the following:

1. #include <sstream>.
2. Declare a stringstream.
3. Print to the stringstream using <<.
4. Access the string you've constructed using the str () member function.

If you want to use it again, you can reset its contents to "", as in myStringStream.str("").[1]

Example 26-1 uses stringstream to send text to SSDL_RenderTextCentered. Output is in Figure 26-1.

Example 26-1. A rudimentary heads-up display (HUD) using stringstream

```
//Program that uses stringstream to center
//   multiple things on one line
//       -- from _C++ for Lazy Programmers_

#include <sstream>                          //Step #1: #include <sstream>
#include "SSDL.h"

using namespace std;

int main(int argc, char** argv)
{
    int points = 3200;                     //Some arbitrary data to test
    double time = 30.2;                    // printing to HUD
    char mood[] = "Annoyed";

    stringstream out;                       //#2: Declare a stringstream
    out << "Points: " << points << "   /   Time left: "
```

[1]stringstream also as a clear function, but be not deceived: it clears error flags, not the contents.

```
                                        //#3: Print to stringstream
        << time << "   /   Mood: " << mood;

    string result = out.str();          //#4: Access with str()
    SSDL_RenderTextCentered(result.c_str(),
                            SSDL_GetWindowWidth()/2, 10);

    SSDL_WaitKey();            //Wait for user to hit a key
    return 0;
}
```

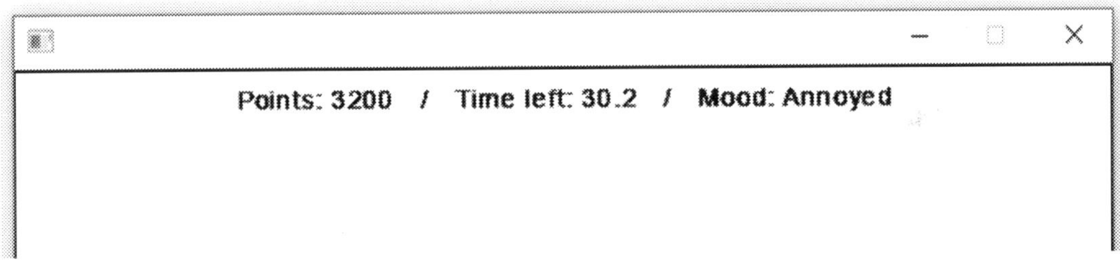

***Figure 26-1.** Output of the `stringstream` program*

You can also use `stringstream` as a source of input: set the string using `str`, and then extract from it using `>>`:

```
dataLine.str ("Flourine  0.52 0.63");
dataLine >> elementName >> firstReading >> secondReading;
```

Using `stringstream` for input involves these steps:

1. `#include <sstream>`.
2. Declare a `stringstream`.
3. Initialize the `stringstream` with the `str ()` member function.
4. Read from the `stringstream` using `>>`.

If there's a possibility you ran out of input, you can call `clear()`, as in `dataLine.clear()`, to clear error flags before reuse. Table 26-1 summarizes the `stringstream` functions you're likely to use the most.

Table 26-1. Commonly used `stringstream` functions, simplified

`stringstream& operator<< (stringstream&, const SomeType& thingToPrint);`	print to the stringstream's contents
`stringstream& operator>> (stringstream&, SomeType& thingToRead);`	read from the stringstream's contents
`string stringstream::str () const;`	return the stringstream's contents
`void stringstream::str (const string&);`	set the stringstream's contents
`void stringstream::clear ();`	clear any error flags you might have set while reading from or writing to stringstream

EXERCISES

1. Suppose we have a set of files: `file1.txt, file2.txt...file100.txt`. Use `stringstream` to construct the filename for the xth file.
2. Write and test a function template that takes in a variable, prints it to a string, and returns the string.
3. Initialize a character array with text containing words and numbers, then read its parts appropriately into variables using `stringstream`.
4. (Uses file I/O) Read in a file of numbers, ignoring everything after a comment marker #. Here's how: read in a line; discard anything after any # you find; then read in all numbers from what's left and push them into a vector.

`iomanip`: formatted output

Suppose you want to print tables in columns. `'\t'` is clunky – your best option is the **manipulator** `setw`, which is found in the `iomanip` include file.

```
cout << setw(10) << Thing1 << Thing2 << "\n";
```

This prints Thing1 right-justified in 10 spaces. (Thing2 is unaffected.) If Thing1 is too big, well, it goes over. If you want it left-justified, do this:

```
cout << left;
cout << setw(10) << Thing1 << Thing2 << "\n";
```

left is a message we're sending to cout saying left justification is now on. Set it back to default with cout << right;.

This will help with printing floating-point numbers neatly:

```
cout << setprecision (2);
```

Like left, setprecision continues to have effect until you change it to another value. The default is 6.

Example 26-2 uses these manipulators to neatly print statistics on two familiar planets.

Example 26-2. Program to neatly print a table of astronomical data using iomanip

```
//Program to print temp, pressure for Venus and Earth
//      -- from _C++ for Lazy Programmers_

#include <iostream>
#include <iomanip>  //for setw and setprecision

using namespace std;

int main ()
{
    //constants related to spacing on the page
    const int      PLANET_SPACE =    10;
    const int        TEMP_SPACE =    15;
    const int    PRESSURE_SPACE =    15;

    //planetary temperature and pressure
    const double      VENUS_TEMP =   464;
    const double VENUS_PRESSURE = 92000;
    const double      EARTH_TEMP =    15;
    const double EARTH_PRESSURE =  1000;
```

```
    //Right-justify, and use 1 (fixed) decimal point precision
    cout << right << fixed << setprecision (1);

    //Print the headers
    cout    << setw (PLANET_SPACE)  << " "
            << setw (TEMP_SPACE   ) << "Average"
            << setw (PRESSURE_SPACE)<< "Surface"    << endl;
    cout    << setw (PLANET_SPACE)  << " "
            << setw (TEMP_SPACE   ) << "temperature"
            << setw (PRESSURE_SPACE)<< "pressure"   << endl;
    cout    << setw (PLANET_SPACE)  << "Planet"
            << setw (TEMP_SPACE   ) << "(degrees C)"
            << setw (PRESSURE_SPACE)<< "millibars" << endl;
    cout    << endl;

    //Print the data
    cout    << setw (PLANET_SPACE)  << "Venus"
            << setw (TEMP_SPACE   ) << VENUS_TEMP
            << setw (PRESSURE_SPACE)<< VENUS_PRESSURE << endl;
    cout    << setw (PLANET_SPACE)  << "Earth"
            << setw (TEMP_SPACE   ) << EARTH_TEMP
            << setw (PRESSURE_SPACE)<< EARTH_PRESSURE << endl;

    cout    << "\n...I think I'll just stay home.\n\n";

    return 0;
}
```

Here's the output:

```
              Average        Surface
          temperature       pressure
 Planet   (degrees C)      millibars

  Venus         464.0        92000.0
  Earth          15.0         1000.0

...I think I'll just stay home.
```

Other iostream manipulators are in Table 26-2. To use those manipulators that take arguments, like `setw` and `setprecision`, you'll need to `#include <iomanip>`. More detail on how to use these follows the table, but you will rarely need them; `setw` and `setprecision` usually do all I need.

***Table 26-2.** Partial list of `iostream` manipulators. Defaults are in bold*

Manipulator	Meaning	Persistence
columns and justification		
`left/right/ internal`	when filling with the fill character after `setw`, add your padding on the left/**right**/inside the value (see explanation in this section)	until changed
`setfill (char fillchar)`	when filling after `setw`, use character `fillchar`. Default is `' '`	until changed
`setw (int width)`	print the next thing using `width` characters, filling in with the fill character. If the next thing requires more room, give it what it needs. Default width is **0**	next thing printed only
flushing output		
`flush`	go ahead and print anything in the print buffer (see explanation in this section)	immediate
`unitbuf/ nounitbuf`	sent print buffer to output immediately/**not immediately** after a << operation (see explanation in this section)	until changed
numeric representation		
`defaultfloat`	uses default format for floating-point numbers (see explanation in this section)	until changed
`fixed`	used fixed format for floating points: exactly as many digits right of the decimal point as `setprecision` specified, and no exponent	until changed
`hex/oct/dec`	read and print integral values in hexadecimal/octal/**decimal**	until changed
`scientific`	use scientific format for floating point: exactly one digit left of the decimal point; exactly as many digits to the right as `setprecision` specified; and an exponent part, such as e+003	until changed
`setbase (int base)`	set base to 8, **10**, or 16	until changed

(continued)

Table 26-2. *(continued)*

Manipulator	Meaning	Persistence
`setprecision (int p)`	set precision of floating-point printing to p. Default is **6**	until changed
`showbase/ noshowbase`	print integral values with/**without** a preceding h if they're in hexadecimal format	until changed
`showpoint/ noshowpoint`	show/**don't show** decimal point when printing floating points	until changed
`showpos/ noshowpos`	print positive numbers with/**without** initial "+"	until changed
`uppercase/ nouppercase`	print the e in scientific notation and x in hexadecimal base, in uppercase/**lower**case	until changed
set/reset flags		
`setiosflags (int flags)`	set formatting flags. This function duplicates, by setting those flags, the effects of other manipulators in this table[2]	until changed
`resetiosflags (int flags)`	unset (clear) formatting flags	until changed
whitespace in input		
`skipws/noskipws`	**always skip**/don't skip whitespace in upcoming input, stopping at first non-whitespace character	until changed
`ws`	skip whitespace in upcoming input, stopping at the first non-whitespace character. Not needed if `skipws` is already on	immediate
Other		
`boolalpha/ noboolalpha`	print/read bool values as "true" or "false"/**as 1 or 0**	until changed
`endl`	print end-of-line (`'\n'`) character and `flush`	immediate
`ends`	print null (`'\0'`) character	immediate

[2]Search for `fmtflags` on `www.cplusplus.com` for a complete list of formatting flags.

`left, right, internal.` `left` and `right` say, put fill characters so as to left- or right-justify the value printed. With `internal`, if the value printed is a number with a preceding + or - sign, the sign is printed on the left, the number on the right, and fill characters are added between. If the value printed is anything else, internal justification works like right justification.

`showpoint`. If you're using fixed format for floating point – or default – and it's showing nothing right of the decimal place, it won't show the decimal place either, unless you `cout << showpoint`. For example, by default, 350.0 shows up as `350`, but if you `cout << showpoint`, it'll have a `.` at the end, as in `350.`

`scientific` format has one digit left of the decimal point, exactly as many digits to the right as specified by `setprecision`, and an exponent: for example, `6.023e+023`, which means 6.023×10^{23}, or `3.14159e+000`, which means 3.14159×10^{0}, or 3.14159, or π.

`fixed` format has no exponent and, like scientific, as many digits right of the decimal point as was specified by `setprecision`.

`defaultfloat` considers precision to be the maximum number of digits in the number, right or left of the decimal point – a maximum that may be overridden for large numbers. (If precision is 4, the number 12345.2 will be printed as 12345 – overriding the maximum of 4 so you can read the number.) It may omit trailing 0's; 6.1500 may be printed as 6.15, even if the precision is more than 3.

(Best not to think too much about `defaultfloat`; it's for when you really don't care.)

`flush, unitbuf`. When you print something, it may not immediately appear on the screen. `cout << flush` makes whatever's waiting to be printed, show up now. `cout << unitbuf` says to do that every time something is printed.

When you print an `endl`, the line gets flushed anyway, so this usually isn't worth bothering with.

EXERCISES

1. Use `setw` and anything else you might need to print a form that someone might fill out – possibly an application (taking in name, address, etc.), possibly something more interesting. You decide.
2. Print an 8x8 grid, like a chessboard.
3. Print a table showing the number of times you fell down per year, starting at age 2 and ending at your current age. I hope it's dropped somewhat. Make it neat.

4. Print a table of the cost of various items at your surf shop: surfboard, surfboard bag, huaraches, whatever. The `.`'s in the dollar amounts should line up.
5. Print a table of the weights of the preceding items.
6. Using scientific notation, print the probability, in any given year, of these events: there is a major political scandal; life spontaneously forms on Mars; a comet hits the Yucatan Peninsula and makes us go the way of the dinosaurs; something more interesting than programming in C++ happens (the lowest probability, of course). Use scientific notation. Make the numbers up – that's what everyone else does.

Command-line arguments

The example and exercises in this section, like most programs using command-line arguments, require file I/O (see Chapter 13).

Especially in the Unix world, it's sometimes necessary to give arguments to the program. Unix and MinGW users know this well: you've typed variants of `cd myFolder`, `g++ -o a.out myprogram.cpp`, and `gdb a.out`.

Suppose you want a program to check text files for differences. The command might look like: `./mydiff file1.txt file2.txt`

You'll need to change the first line of `main`: `int main (int argc, char* argv[])`

`argc` ("argument count") is the number of arguments, and `argv` ("argument vector," but it's an array, not a `vector`) is an array of character arrays, each containing one argument, starting with the program name.

So if your command is `./mydiff file1.txt file2.txt`, `argc` will be 3, and `argv` will contain the values shown in Figure 26-2.

`argv[0]`	`"difference"`
`argv[1]`	`"file1.txt"`
`argv[2]`	`"file2.txt"`

Figure 26-2. *Possible command-line arguments*

Example 26-3 shows code for the program.

First, it ensures we have a reasonable number of arguments. If something goes wrong, it's conventional to tell the user what was expected. argv[0] is always the program name. (We don't hard-code it as " ./mydiff," in case we change the program name later.)

cerr is like cout, but it can't be redirected with >, so it's useful for error messages. But cout's OK too.

Example 26-3. diff.cpp: a program using command-line arguments

```
//Program to find the difference between two files
//  -- from _C++ for Lazy Programmers_

#include <iostream>
#include <fstream>
#include <cstdlib> //for EXIT_FAILURE, EXIT_SUCCESS
#include <string>

using namespace std;

int main (int argc, char** argv)
{
    //Did we get right # of arguments? If not, complain and quit
    if (argc != 3) //3 args: 1 program name, plus 2 files
    {               //On failure, tell user what user should've entered:
        cerr << "Usage: " << argv[0] << " <file 1> <file 2>\n";
        return EXIT_FAILURE;
    }

    //Load in the 2 files
    ifstream file1(argv[1]), file2(argv[2]); //open files
    if (! file1) //On failure, say which file wouldn't load
    {
       cerr << "Error loading " << argv[1] << endl;
        return EXIT_FAILURE;
    }
    if (!file2) //On failure, say which file wouldn't load
    {
        cerr << "Error loading " << argv[2] << endl;
        return EXIT_FAILURE;
    }
```

```
    string line1, line2;

    while (file1 && file2)      //While BOTH files are not finished
    {
        getline(file1, line1); if (!file1) break; //read lines
        getline(file2, line2); if (!file2) break;

        if (line1 != line2)    // if lines differ print them
        {
            cout << "<: " << line1 << endl; //< means "first file"
            cout << ">: " << line2 << endl; //> means "second file"
                                            //this is conventional
        }
    }

    //If either file has more lines than the other, print remainder
    while (file1)
    {
        getline(file1, line1);
        if (file1) cout << "<: " << line1 << endl;
    }
    while (file2)
    {
        getline(file2, line2);
        if (file2) cout << ">: " << line2 << endl;
    }

    return EXIT_SUCCESS;
}
```

To run this, type `./mydiff file1 file2`. Visual Studio users will likely find the executable in `Debug/` or `Release/`.

Debugging with command-line arguments in Visual Studio

If you just hit Debug in the Visual Studio environment, it runs as if it has no arguments, which it doesn't. To fix this, go into Project Menu ➤ Properties ➤ Configuration Properties ➤ Debugging, and add your arguments to Command Arguments (Figure 26-3).

The command-line arguments are stored in the `.user` file. If you delete it, you'll have to add them again.

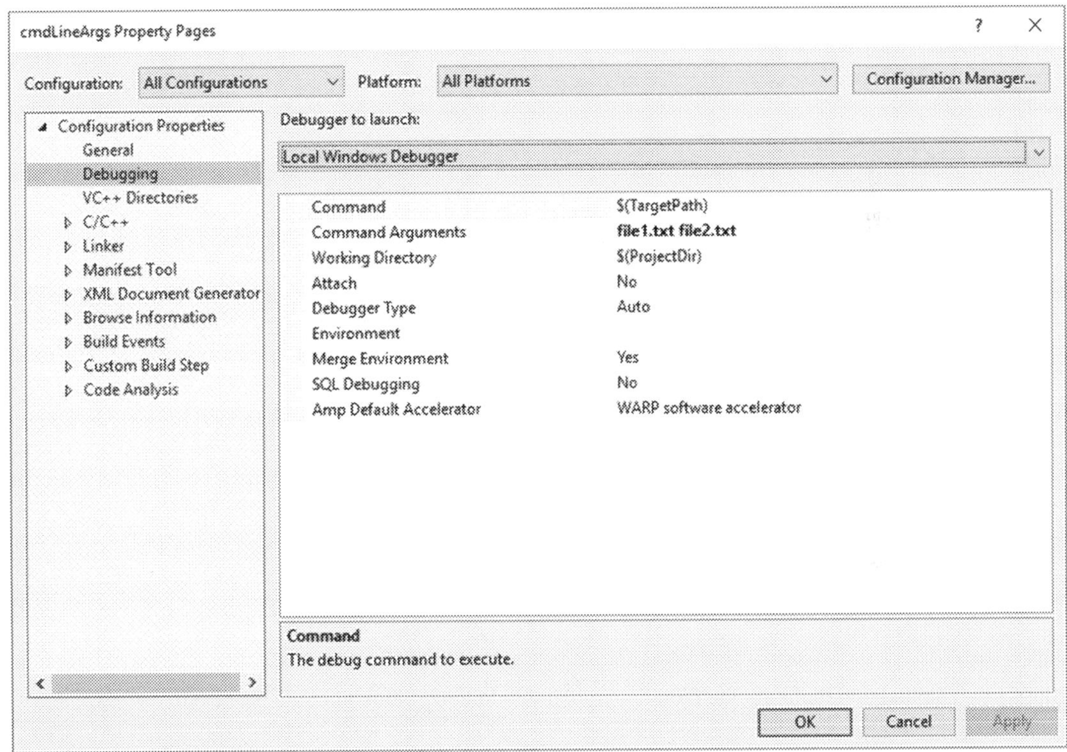

Figure 26-3. *Setting Command Arguments in Microsoft Visual Studio*

Debugging with command-line arguments in Unix

Whether in ddd or gdb, at the prompt, type

```
set args file1.txt file2.txt
```

and you're there.

EXERCISES

1. Write a program `grep`, a simplified version of the Unix utility. It should repeat all lines from standard input that have a given word. So if you have a file `input.txt` with lines

   ```
   alpha
   beta
   alphabet
   ```

   then the command `grep alpha < input.txt` should print this on the screen:

   ```
   alpha
   alphabet
   ```

2. To the previous exercise, add an option `-n` which, if present, directs `grep` to print the line number of each line of output. (Flags starting with - are common for Unix commands.) Given the preceding input, the command `grep -n alpha < input.txt` should print on the screen:

   ```
   1: alpha
   3: alphabet
   ```

3. Write a program `getcolumns` which, given input with numbers in columns, prints to standard output a version with only those columns. For example, if you call `getcolumns 0 3` and get input like this

   ```
   1900    -0.06    -0.05    -0.05    -0.08    -0.07    -0.07
   1901    -0.07    -0.21    -0.14    -0.06    -0.2     -0.13
   ...
   ```

   `the output should show only columns 0 and 3:`

   ```
   1900    -0.05
   1901    -0.14
   ...
   ```

   I recommend using `stringstream`. `iomanip` wouldn't hurt either.

static_cast et al

Short version: wherever you once said newtype (value), say static_cast<newtype> (value):

```
double dbl = double (intVal);
```

becomes

```
double dbl = static_cast<double> (intVal);
```

and

```
((ChildClass*) (parentClassPtr))->childClassFunction ();
```

becomes

```
(static_cast<ChildClass*> (parentClassPtr))->childClassFunction ();
```

Why? So that when you try to say

```
int* intArray = static_cast<int*> (myFloatArray); //huh?!
```

the compiler won't let you. Pointer safety.

I don't recommend the other **casting operators** C++ offers, and wouldn't blame you if you went on to the next section.

Still here? OK. Here are the other types:

- const_cast<type>. This enables you to add or take away constness:

  ```
  ((const_cast<const MyClass*> (someVar ))->print (cout);
                                          //adds constness
  ((const_cast<      MyClass*> (someConst))->alterMeInSomeWay();
                                          //takes it away
  ```

  ...but you can't safely apply it to something that was originally declared const. You *can* apply it to something that was passed in as a const parameter.

  I avoid this. If it's non-const, what can I do with a const that I can't do with a non-const? Not much. If it's const, I really shouldn't break that security.

- `dynamic_cast<type>`. This lets you cast things around an inheritance hierarchy if there are virtuals involved. I've never used it.
- `reinterpret_cast<type>`. This isn't quite "anything goes" – it doesn't affect `const`ness, and it can't cast things it can't figure out – but it can do weird things like the casting `myFloatArray` to the `int*` above. I've never used it either.

But maybe I *have* used the last one without knowing, back when all we had was the older, simpler cast `<type>()`. When you do that, C++ tries these types of cast in order:

- `const_cast`
- `static_cast`
- `static_cast` then `const_cast`
- `reinterpret_cast`
- `reinterpret_cast` then `const_cast`

looking for one that will work. If it fails, you can't do the cast.

In my view we use `static_cast`, not the old-style cast, primarily so it doesn't make its way to `reinterpret_cast` without us knowing.

Defaulted constructors and =

Earlier in the book, I avoided using the defaults for constructors and operator=, on the grounds that sometimes C++'s guess is wildly wrong: specifically, it copies array addresses rather than their contents.

But sometimes it's exactly right. We can save a little time with the `Card` class from Chapter 19:

```
class Card
{
public:
    Card            ();
    Card            (const Card& other) = default;
    Card& operator= (const Card& other) = default;
    ...
```

```
private:
    Rank rank_; Suit suit_;
};
```

If we're going to take C++'s defaults, we'd better know what they do! It's something like this:

- In the default (no argument) constructor, default-construct all the parts. `Card () {}` would do that anyway, so I can just leave it.
- In a copy ctor, copy parent classes and members with whatever you got (copy ctor for classes, = for basic types).
- In =, call = on all parts.

The use of = explains why it won't work right for arrays - but is fine for many other things.

`constexpr` and `static_assert`: moving work to compile time

If I can shove some of the work over to compile time, runtime will be faster. That wouldn't be the worst thing in the world.

`constexpr`, despite its name, really means "do this at compile time," though as such it tends to make things constant. Here's one use:

```
constexpr int THE_WITCHING_HOUR=3; //could've done this with enum
constexpr double PI = 3.14159;     //but not this
```

And another: `constexpr` functions. Example 26-4 has several.

Example 26-4. Class `Card`, using defaulted ctors and `constexpr`

```
//Card class
//   -- from C++ for Lazy Programmers

#ifndef CARD_H
#define CARD_H

#include <iostream>
```

```
//Rank and Suit: integral parts of Card

//I make these global so that I don't have to forget
// "Card::" over and over when I use them.
enum Rank {ACE=1, JACK=11, QUEEN, KING};
enum Suit {HEARTS, DIAMONDS, CLUBS, SPADES};
enum Color{BLACK, RED};

std::ostream& operator<< (std::ostream& out, Rank r);
std::ostream& operator<< (std::ostream& out, Suit s);
std::istream& operator>> (std::istream& in, Rank& r);
std::istream& operator>> (std::istream& in, Suit& s);

class BadRankException {};  //used if a Rank is out of range
class BadSuitException {};  //used if a Suit is out of range

inline
constexpr Color toColor(Suit s)
{
    if (s == HEARTS || s == DIAMONDS) return RED; else return BLACK;
}

//...and class Card.

class Card
{
public:
    constexpr Card(Rank r=Rank(0), Suit s=Suit(0))
        : rank_(r), suit_(s)
    {
    }
    constexpr Card            (const Card& other) = default;
    constexpr Card& operator= (const Card& other) = default;

    constexpr bool operator== (const Card& other) const
    {
        return rank() == other.rank () && suit() == other.suit();
    }
```

```
    constexpr bool operator!= (const Card& other) const
    {
        return !(*this == other);
    }

    constexpr Suit  suit () const { return suit_; }
    constexpr Rank  rank () const { return rank_; }
    constexpr Color color() const
    {
        return toColor(suit());
    }

    void print (std::ostream &out) const { out << rank() << suit(); }
    void read  (std::istream &in );
private:
    Suit suit_;
    Rank rank_;
};

inline std::ostream& operator<< (std::ostream& out, const Card& foo)
{
    foo.print (out); return out;
}

inline std::istream& operator>> (std::istream& in,       Card& foo)
{
    foo.read  (in);  return in;
}

inline
constexpr Card JOKER(Rank(-1), Suit(-1));
                                 //works in later implementations of C++17

#endif //CARD_H
```

I won't go into fine detail, but you can make a function (member or not) constexpr if it's simple and relies on other parts that can be constexpr.

One thing I like here is the declaration of JOKER above. With inline constexpr I can put constants in my .h files without also having to initialize them in a .cpp somewhere: I'm done in one line.

Note At time of writing, compilers aren't quite ready to call inline constexpr's part of their implementation, but you can set a flag and they'll take it. This flag is also needed in some sections later in this chapter.

g++: add the -std=c++17 flag to the g++ command.

Visual Studio: set Project Properties ➤ C/C++ ➤ Language ➤ C++ Language Standard to /std:c++17.

...or use the Makefile or .vcxproj file that comes with source code for this section.

Now let's see test our Card functions – but let's do it at compile time, with this code:

```
//Test some Card functions...
constexpr Card ACE_OF_SPADES         (ACE, SPADES  );
constexpr Card COPY_OF_ACE_OF_SPADES(ACE_OF_SPADES);

static_assert (ACE_OF_SPADES ==COPY_OF_ACE_OF_SPADES,
                "Copy ctor or == failed");
static_assert (COPY_OF_ACE_OF_SPADES.rank() == ACE &&
                COPY_OF_ACE_OF_SPADES.suit() == SPADES,
                "Copy ctor or access functions failed");
static_assert (toColor(SPADES) == BLACK,
                "toColor failed");
static_assert (COPY_OF_ACE_OF_SPADES.color() == BLACK,
                "Card::color failed");
static_assert (JOKER.rank() == Rank(-1) &&
               JOKER.suit() == Suit(-1),
        "JOKER access functions or initializations failed");
```

`static_assert (condition, message)` takes a condition it can verify at compile time, plus a message of what its failure might mean, and lets you know of problems at compile time rather than runtime. In Visual Studio it'll tell you while editing, which is even nicer.

User-defined literals: automatic conversion between systems of measurement

On September 23, 1999, the US space probe Mars Climate Orbiter was lost near Mars. Apparently the part of the program that dealt with achieving orbit had some calculations in metric and some in English measurements. The program crashed and NASA never got anything from its $327M spaceship. Oops.

I totally relate. Every time I write a program with trig functions, I use degrees and C++ uses radians.

NASA didn't write their software in C++17 because it didn't exist yet, but if they had, they could have had the computer convert automatically as needed between systems. Here's how:

1. Write an operator to convert from your unit to some unit you want the calculations done in – I'll convert miles to meters:

   ```
   long double operator"" _mi  (long double mi)
   {
       return mi * 1609.344; //1 mi = 1609.344 meters
   }
   ```

   You *do* need the leading _.

2. Call it thus: **10_mi**. C++ treats this as passing 10 to the `"" _mi` operator.

In BNF, the operator looks like this (though you can add qualifiers to it like `constexpr`):

<return-type> `operator "" _`*<operator name> (<parameter list>)*
{
  <body>
}

Using it is like this: *<value>_<operator name>*, no spaces.

Example 26-5 uses this with constexpr – why not? – for a few simple calculations.

Example 26-5. A program using user-defined literals

```
//Program to use user-defined literals
//      -- from _C++ for Lazy Programmers_

#include <iostream>
#include <cmath>

using namespace std;

constexpr double PI = 3.14159;

//"Literal" operators

constexpr
long double operator"" _deg (long double degrees)
{
    return degrees * PI/180;
}
constexpr
long double operator"" _deg (unsigned long long degrees)
{
    return degrees * PI/180;
}

constexpr
long double operator"" _m   (long double  m) { return m;            }
                                                   //1 m = 1 m (duh)
constexpr
long double operator"" _mi  (long double mi) { return mi * 1609.344;}
                                                   //1 mi = 1609.344 m
int main ()
{
    cout << "The speed of light is 186,000 miles per second.\n";
    cout << "In metric, that's ";
```

```
    cout <<      186'000.0_mi[3]   << " meters per second --\n"
         << "   should be about " << 300'000'000.0_m  << ".\n";

    cout << "Oh, and sin (30 deg) is about 0.5: "
         << sin(30_deg) << endl;

    return 0;
}
```

Output:

```
The speed of light is 186,000 miles per second.
In metric, that's 2.99338e+008 meters per second --
   should be about 3e+008.
Oh, and sin (30 deg) is about 0.5: 0.5
```

Two peculiarities regarding parameters:

- The parameter list must be one of the sets in Table 26-3. Mostly I use `long double`.
- It won't do implicit casting between types (though it's flexible about modifiers like `unsigned` or `long`). If you give it `186000_mi`, it will fail, because it expected `double` not `int`. Either add `.0` or write an operator that expects an integer type.

Table 26-3. *Possible parameter lists for user-defined literal operators*

`unsigned long long`	`long double`
`const char*`	
`Char`	`const char*,     std::size_t`
`wchar_t`	`const wchar_t*,  std::size_t`
`char16_t`	`const char16_t*, std::size_t`
`char32_t`	`const char32_t*, std::size_t`

[3]You can use these "digit separators" to make numbers easier to read. I'll grant that apostrophe looks weird here, but comma was busy with other things.

EXERCISES

Using user-defined literals, made `constexpr` if possible:

1. Mars's air pressure is about 6.1 millibars and Earth's is about 14.7 pounds per square inch. Venus's is about 9.3 MPa. Look up these units online for conversions, and calculate how many times more pressure Venus has than Earth, and Earth than Mars.

2. Using weights the user provides for 3 objects in pounds, kg, and stone, figure which is heaviest.

Lambda functions for one-time use

STL's function `sort` can take a third argument, a comparison function that returns `true` if the first argument is less than the second. Suppose we want to sort cities by name, *and* by population:

```
bool lessThanByName (const City& a, const City& b)
{
    return a.name()             < b.name();
}
bool lessThanByPop     (const City& a, const City& b)
{
    return a.population() < b.population();
}
...
sort (cities.begin(), cities.end(), lessThanByName);
sort (cities.begin(), cities.end(), lessThanByPop);
```

If a test is only going to be used once, maybe I'm too lazy to create a complete function for it. I can do this instead:

```
sort(cities.begin(), cities.end(),
     [](const City& a, const City& b)
     {
         return a.name() < b.name();
     });
```

This is called a "lambda" function, a term borrowed from the mathematics by way of the LISP programming language. The [ ] is a way of saying "the function name goes here, except I'm not bothering with a name this time."

Lambda captures

It gets weirder. Suppose I want to instead order my Citys by their distance from a particular location. I can't pass in that location as a third argument - sort expects a two-argument comparison function! But I can tell the lambda, "Bring this variable in from outside":

```
const City DELHI ("Delhi", 25'703'000, { 28_deg, 77_deg });

sort(cities.begin(), cities.end(),
     [&DELHI](const City& foo, const City& bar)
     {
         return distance(DELHI, foo) < distance(DELHI, bar);
     });
```

I put an & with it to say, send in by reference - don't make a copy. You can't put const & at this point, but since DELHI is const, it won't alter it.

I can leave the & out if the lambda needs to see but not alter a value, and copying isn't costly:

```
//Find out if some bad letter is in my city's name
auto findBadLetter =
    find_if(name.begin(), name.end(),
            [badLetter](char ch) { return ch == badLetter; });
```

Table 26-4 shows what things we can put between the []'s. Usually we don't need anything. But we can list specific variables, with or without &. We can also say, with = or &, "let everything in." "Everything" here means variables that aren't global (ack!) and aren't static.[4] Globals and static locals can be referred to anyway, without being listed in the [ ]'s.

[4]The correct term is "automatic variables."

Table 26-4. *Lambda captures. These go between the [ ]'s of a lambda function, to allow access to non-static local variables that are not the lambda function's parameters. They can be combined:* `arg1, &arg2, this`

`arg1 [, arg2...]`	use arg by value in the lambda function
`&arg [, arg2...]`	use arg by reference (changing it in the lambda function changes it outside as well)
=	use all available variables by value
&	use all available variables by reference
`this`	use members of current object. If in a non-const function, they can be modified

(I think it's better to specify exactly what can go into the function – avoid bare & and =.)
Example 26-6 is the city-sorting program.

Example 26-6. A program to sort cities, using lambdas. Parts are omitted for brevity but are in the source code

```
//Program that uses lambda functions to order cities
//  by different criteria
//      -- from _C++ for Lazy Programmers_

#include <iostream>
#include <cmath>  //for sin, cos, asin, sqrt
#include <vector>
#include <string>
#include <cassert>
#include <algorithm>

using namespace std;

    //constexprs
constexpr double PI = 3.14159;

    //...including user-defined literal operators
constexpr
```

```
long double operator"" _deg(unsigned long long deg)
{
    return deg * PI / 180;
}
constexpr
long double operator"" _mi(long double  mi)
{
    return mi * 1609.344;    //1 mi = 1609.344 m
}

    //types
struct PointLatLong
{
    long double latitude_, longitude_;
};

class City
{
public:
    City(const std::string& n, int pop, const PointLatLong& l) :
        name_ (n), population_ (pop), location_(l)
    {
    }
    City             (const City&) = default;
    City& operator= (const City&) = default;
    const std::string& name     () const { return name_;       }
    int population              () const { return population_; }
    const PointLatLong& location() const { return location_;   }
private:
    std::string  name_;
    int          population_;
    PointLatLong location_;
};

    //function prototypes
double distance(const PointLatLong&, const PointLatLong&);
```

```
inline
double distance(const City& xCity, const City& yCity)
{
    return distance(xCity.location(), yCity.location());
}

////Functions for use without lambdas:
//bool lessThanByName(const City& a, const City& b)
//{
//  return a.name() < b.name();
//}
//bool lessThanByPop(const City& a, const City& b)
//{
//  return a.population() < b.population();
//}

int main()
{
    //Some prominent party spots
    vector<City> cities =
    {
        {"London",          10'313'000, { 51_deg,  -5_deg}},
        {"Hamburg",          1'739'000, { 53_deg,  10_deg}},
        {"Paris",           10'843'000, { 49_deg,   2_deg}},
        {"Rome",             3'718'000, { 42_deg,  12_deg}},
        {"Rio de Janiero", 12'902'000, {-22_deg, -43_deg}},
        {"Hong Kong",        7'314'000, { 20_deg, 114_deg}},
        {"Tokyo",           38'001'000, { 36_deg, 140_deg}}
    };

    //Without lambdas:
    //sort(cities.begin(), cities.end(), lessThanByName);
    //sort(cities.begin(), cities.end(), lessThanByPop);

        //Print those cities in different orderings:

    cout << "Some major cities, in alpha order :       ";
    sort(cities.begin(), cities.end(),
```

```
    [](const City& a, const City& b)
    {
        return a.name() < b.name();
    });
for (const auto& i : cities) cout << i.name() << " / ";
cout << endl;

cout << "Ordered by population:                    ";
sort(cities.begin(), cities.end(),
    [](const City& a, const City& b)
    {
       return a.population() < b.population();
    });
for (const auto& i : cities) cout << i.name() << " / ";
cout << endl;

cout << "Ordered by how far they are from Delhi:  ";
const City DELHI("Delhi", 25'703'000, { 28_deg, 77_deg });

sort(cities.begin(), cities.end(),
    [&DELHI](const City& a, const City& b)
    {
        return distance(DELHI, a) < distance(DELHI, b);
    });
for (const auto& i : cities) cout << i.name() << " / ";
cout << endl;

cout << "Ordered by how far they are from LA:     ";
const City LA ( "Los Angeles", 3'900'000, {34_deg, -118_deg} );

//& will work here -- but &LA would be a little more secure
sort(cities.begin(), cities.end(),
      [&](const City& a, const City& b)
    {
        return distance(LA, a) < distance(LA, b);
    });
for (const auto& i : cities) cout << i.name() << " / ";
cout << endl;
```

```
    //And something to illustrate the use of lambda capture by value:
    //Does Los Angeles have an 'x' in it?
    char badLetter = 'x';
    assert(find_if(LA.name().begin(), LA.name().end(),
        [badLetter](char ch) { return ch == badLetter; })
        == LA.name().end());

    return 0;
}
```

EXERCISES

In all of these – of course – use lambda functions. I'm referencing functions I have not put in the text; look 'em up on Internet as needed:

1. Use the `for_each` function to capitalize every element of a container of strings.
2. Use the `count_if` function to see how many integers in a container are squares of integers.
3. Use `all_of` to verify that every string in your container contains some substring, to be given by the user.
4. Sort the preceding `City`s by latitude.

Structured bindings and `tuple`s: returning multiple values at once

In Chapter 7 I may have given the impression that a function can only return one thing. If so…I lied.

We can already return a `pair`, `vector`, or `list...` but here's an easy way to return multiple things without all that overhead. Example 26-7 shows how it looks.

1. `#include <tuple>`. A tuple is a sequence of values, possibly of different types; it's what we'll return.

2. **Let the function return** auto. It's actually returning std::tuple <firstType,secondType,...>, but why not let the compiler figure that out?

3. **Return your values with** return std::make_tuple (value1, value2, ...);.

4. **Store the return value in a "structured binding":**

   auto [variable1, variable2, ...] = functionCall (...);

   This declares variable1 and so on and initializes them from what your function returned.

5. At time of writing, until some future upgrade, **tell the compiler you really want to use the C++17 standard**. See the Note in the constexpr section.

Example 26-7. Using structured bindings to get multiple values through a return statement

```
//Program to calculate the quadratic formula
// (using structured bindings and tuples)
//      -- from _C++ for Lazy Programmers_

#include <iostream>
#include <cmath>    //for sqrt
#include <tuple>    //for tuple stuff    //Step #1: #include <tuple>
#include <cassert>

using namespace std;

//If auto's going to work in main, we need the
// function body *here*. Else there's no way main
// can know what type is to be returned

                                      //#2: return auto
auto quadraticFormula(double a, double b, double c)
{
    int numroots = 0;
```

```
    double root1 = 0.0;
    double root2 = 0.0;

    double underTheRadical = b * b - 4 * a*c;
    if (underTheRadical >= 0) //If we have to sqrt a neg #,
                              // no solution. Otherwise...
    {
        root1 = (-b + sqrt(underTheRadical)) / (2 * a);
        root2 = (-b - sqrt(underTheRadical)) / (2 * a);

        if (root1 == root2) numroots = 1; else numroots = 2;
    }
                                    //#3: return a tuple
    return std::make_tuple(numroots, root1, root2);
}

int main ()
{
    //Get user input
    cout << "Enter the a, b, c from ax^2+bx+c = 0: ";
    double a, b, c;  cin >> a >> b >> c;

    //Get the results
                                    //#4: store result in auto[...]
    auto[howMany, r1, r2] = quadraticFormula(a, b, c);

    //Print the results
    switch (howMany)
    {
    case 0: cout << "No solution.\n";                      break;
    case 1: cout << "Solution is "   <<r1<<endl;           break;
    case 2: cout << "Solutions are " <<r1<<' '<<r2<<endl; break;
    default:cout << "Can't have "    <<howMany<<" solutions!\n";
    }

    return 0;
}
```

This new ability, plus what we know from earlier, leads to an updated version of the Golden Rule on this topic in Chapter 8.

Golden Rule of Function Parameters and `return` (Version 2)

- If a function provides a value
    - If it's small, return it. For multiples, return a tuple.
    - If not, pass by &.
- If it takes a variable in and changes it, pass by &.
- If it takes it in and doesn't change it,
    - If it's an object, pass as `const TheClass&` object.
    - Else pass by value (no &).
- If it's a move constructor or move =, pass by &&.

...except arrays are passed in as parameters, with or without `const` depending on whether the contents are to change.

You can also use tuples other places, sort of like `pair` only with different numbers of elements. To get at the parts, whether to change them or use them, use `std::get<>()`:. Put which element you want between the `<>`, and the tuple between the `()`:

```
std::tuple<int, double, double> myTuple
  = std::make_tuple(0, 2.0, 3.0);
assert(std::get<0>(myTuple) == 0); //check the 0th value
std::get<0>(myTuple) = 1;          //set the 0th value
```

Fine if it saves you time. But it's not even half as cool as the thing with `auto [...] =`.

EXERCISES

1. Write a function `sortedTriple` that takes in a tuple of three elements, puts them in order, and returns the new version. Let `main` use `auto [...]` to store the values.

2. Write a function which, given a `vector`, returns the maximum, the minimum, the average, and the standard deviation, all in a tuple. Standard deviation is sometimes defined as $\sqrt{\Sigma(x - average\ x)^2 / N}$.

   Now write one that does the same thing for a `list`. Generic programming, yeah. Let `main` use `auto [...]` to store the values in each case.

Smart pointers

One motivator behind recent updates in C++ was to stop pointer errors from blowing up our code. Good luck with that! But there are improvements.

unique_ptr

A main workhorse is `std::unique_ptr`. It maintains a pointer, lets you use it, and deletes it automatically when it goes out of scope. Yes, you can break it, but you have to *try*. It's usually initialized with `make_unique`, which takes an argument to initialize a base type variable you want a pointer to, or constructor arguments for an object you want created:

```
#include <memory>
...
std::unique_ptr<int >     p1 = std::make_unique<int>(27);
        //new int ptr, value 27
std::unique_ptr<Date> pDate = std::make_unique<Date>(1, 1, 2000);
        //Put the arguments for Date's constructor in
        //   and make_unique will take care of it
```

Or it takes the size of an array you want created:

```
std::unique_ptr<char[]> myChars = std::make_unique<char[]>(100);
```

After that use it as you normally would a pointer:

```
*p1 = 2; cout << *p1;
myChars[5] = 'A';
pDate->print(cout);
```

You can get at the pointer inside with `get()`:

```
strcpy (myChars.get(), "totally unique");
```

No need to remember cleanup; it'll delete itself. And there's no confusion over who does the delete, because `unique_ptrs` don't share memory (thus the word "unique").

You *can* tell it to delete immediately:

```
p1.reset(); //the memory is deleted, and p1 now thinks it's nullptr
```

and maybe reset it to something else you want:

```
p1.reset (new int); //takes ownership of the new int --
                    // is responsible for deleting later
```

Why do any of this?

- Error prevention: so you don't forget to initialize or delete, and so you don't forget and use a pointer that has been deleted – it's automatically set to `nullptr`, so you can't.
- Exception safety: when you leave a function, it calls destructors on all local variables. Raw pointers – the kind we've been using – don't have destructors, so their memory won't be thrown back, but `unique_ptrs` do throw theirs back in their destructors. So if you throw an exception, using `unique_ptr` prevents memory leaks.

Most pointers in my code are in classes' private sections, so although I may not be exception-safe, I think they're fairly secure otherwise. But let's see if `unique_ptr` can save us any trouble.

I'll start with the Olympic symbol program from Example 21-7. It contains a `vector` of not `Shape`s but pointers to `Shape`, and must, since they're actually pointers to subclasses of `Shape`. Example 26-8 shows the new version of `main`.

Example 26-8. The Olympic symbol program from Example 21-7, now using `unique_ptr`

```
//Program to show, and move, the Olympics symbol
//It uses Circle, and a subclass of Shape called Text
//      -- from _C++ for Lazy Programmers_

#include <vector>
#include <memory> //for unique_ptr
#include "circle.h"
#include "text.h"

int main (int argc, char** argv)
{
    SSDL_SetWindowSize (500, 300); //make smaller window

    //Create Olympics symbol
    std::vector<std::unique_ptr<Shape>> olympicSymbol;
    enum {RADIUS = 50};

    olympicSymbol.push_back
        (std::make_unique<Circle>( 50,  50, RADIUS));
    olympicSymbol.push_back
        (std::make_unique<Circle>(150,  50, RADIUS));
    olympicSymbol.push_back
        (std::make_unique<Circle>(250,  50, RADIUS));
    olympicSymbol.push_back
        (std::make_unique<Circle>(100, 100, RADIUS));
    olympicSymbol.push_back
        (std::make_unique<Circle>(200, 100, RADIUS));

    //plus a label
    olympicSymbol.push_back
        (std::make_unique<Text>(150,150,"Games of the Olympiad"));

    //color those circles (and the label)
    SSDL_Color olympicColors = { BLUE,
                    SSDL_CreateColor (0, 255, 255) /*yellow*/,
                    BLACK, GREEN, RED, BLACK };
```

```
    for (unsigned int i = 0; i < olympicSymbol.size(); ++i)
        olympicSymbol[i]->setColor (olympicColors [i]);

    //do a game loop
    while (SSDL_IsNextFrame ())
    {
        SSDL_DefaultEventHandler ();

        SSDL_RenderClear (WHITE);   //clear the screen

        //draw all those shapes
        for (const auto& i : olympicSymbol) i->draw ();
                                          //ranged-based for loops ftw!
        //move all those shapes
        for (const auto& i : olympicSymbol) i->moveBy (1, 1);
    }

    //No longer needed:
    //for (auto i : olympicSymbol) delete i;

    return 0;
}
```

I'm not exactly excited at the work I saved, but I guess it's better than making a slew of errors as mentioned previously.

Let's see what it'll do inside a class. Shape has a `char` pointer `description_`. In real life I'd just use a `string`, but this should help us see what `unique_ptr` does for us when a class must have a pointer (as, in fact, the `string` class must). Examples 26-9 and 26-10 show the new version of Shape.

Example 26-9. The Shape class from Example 21-1, now using `unique_ptr` (`.h` file)

```
//Shape class, for use with the SSDL library
//      -- from _C++ for Lazy Programmers_

#ifndef SHAPE_H
#define SHAPE_H

#include <memory> //for unique_ptr
#include "SSDL.h"
```

```
struct Point2D  //Life would be easier if this were a full-fledged class
{               //  with operators +, =, etc. . . . but that
    int x_, y_; //  was left as an exercise.
};

class Shape
{
 public:
    Shape(int x = 0, int y = 0, const char* text = "");
    Shape(const Shape& other);
    Shape(Shape&&) = default;
    virtual ~Shape() {} //No need to delete contents_ -- handled!

    const Shape& operator= (const Shape& s);
    Shape& operator= (Shape&&) = default;

    ...

    const char*     description() const { return description_.get(); }

    ...

 private:
    Point2D    location_;
    SSDL_Color color_;
    std::unique_ptr<char> description_;
    char* copy(const char*); //used for copying descriptions
                             //altered from original for clearer use
                             // with the new description_, but
                             // it's not really new stuff
};

#endif
```

Example 26-10. The Shape class from Example 21-1, now using `unique_ptr` (`.cpp` file)

```
//Shape class, for use with the SSDL library
//   -- from _C++ for Lazy Programmers_
```

```
#include "shape.h"

//ctors
Shape::Shape(int x, int y, const char* text)
    : description_(copy(text))
{
    location_.x_ = x; location_.y_ = y;
}

Shape::Shape (const Shape& s) :
    location_ (s.location()),
    color_    (s.color   ()),
    description_(copy(s.description_.get()))
{
}

//I no longer have to write the move ctor

// ...or the move = operator

//operator=
const Shape& Shape::operator= (const Shape& s)
{
    location_ = s.location();
    color_    = s.color   ();
    description_.reset (copy (s.description_.get()));
    return *this;
}

//copy, used by = and copy ctor
char* Shape::copy (const char* text)
{
    char* result = new char [strlen (text) + 1];
    strcpy (result, text);
    return result;
}
```

The main advantages I find are

- No need to write any code in the destructor – `description_` knows how to delete itself. I also don't have to fool with deleting memory in `operator=` or the copy constructor.
- I can now use defaults for the move functions. `location_` and `color_` use their copy ctors (`location_`'s is the default, but that's fine if the members are just `int`s); `description_` knows how to copy itself with move. Not writing move constructor and move = saved me about eight lines of coding.

shared_ptr

A `unique_ptr` owns its memory, and nobody else should alter or deallocate it.

A `shared_ptr` lets other `shared_ptr`s own the same memory. It maintains a record of how many `shared_ptr`s are using it (this is "reference counting"), and only when that number drops to 0 does the memory get deleted.

Here's a possible use: I have a 3D model I can load from a file. These things tend to be large. If I have 20 monsters of the same type, I don't want 20 copies of all that graphics data!

So I put the graphics data in one object of type `GraphicsData` and create an `Instance3D` object for every instance of the monster. Let them share their `GraphicsData`.

```
class GraphicsData
{
    ...

private:

    ... lots of graphics info...
};

class Instance3D
{
    ...

    Point3D location_;
    shared_ptr<GraphicsData> _modelInfo;
};
```

I'd hate to have all the monsters wiped out, the model graphics info therefore erased, and then have to load it again when I start the next level. I'll probably keep a copy in `main ()` to preserve it.

`shared_ptr`'s reference counting sometimes has a problem that A refers to B refers to A (or a longer chain), so the number of references never drops to zero and nothing ever gets deleted. `weak_ptr` is a way of dealing with that problem, not covered further here.

Antibugging

The main problem I find with smart pointers is forgetting the `get()`:

```
strcpy(myChars, "totally unique"); //should be myChars.get()
```

EXERCISES

1. Rewrite the `String` class (use Chapter 18's so it'll have move copy and move =) to use `unique_ptr`.

Bit twiddling: &, |, ~, and

Many libraries, SDL and its helpers, for example, require you to set some of their features with individual bits,[5] and report features the same way. Let's see how to work with that.

To start up the SDL_Image library, you call `IMG_Init`, which takes a single argument of type `int` telling it what image formats to support. How? `SDL_Image.h` provides **flags** (bits with assigned meaning): `IMG_INIT_JPG` is 1, `IMG_INIT_PNG` is 2, `IMG_INIT_TIF` is 4, and so on. We have to combine them into that one `int`, bit by bit (no pun intended).

...	0	0	0	0	0	1	0	1
...	128	64	32	16	8	4	2	1

Figure 26-4. *How an `int` sent to `IMG_Init` is laid out: reading right to left, we have bit 1, bit 2, bit 4, and so on. This one's set to support jpgs and tiffs (bits 1 and 4)*

[5]A bit is a binary (base 2) digit, 0 or 1, the smallest possible piece of information. I don't know how we got this far without that term.

A sequence of bits (Figure 26-4) can be viewed as a number (stored in binary, usually printed in decimal), a character, image data...or, as in this case, just a string of bits.

We have operators – "bitwise" operators – that help us manipulate the bits:

- Bitwise or, as in x | y. Each bit in x | y will be 1 if it's 1 in either x *or* y (Figure 26-5 (a)).

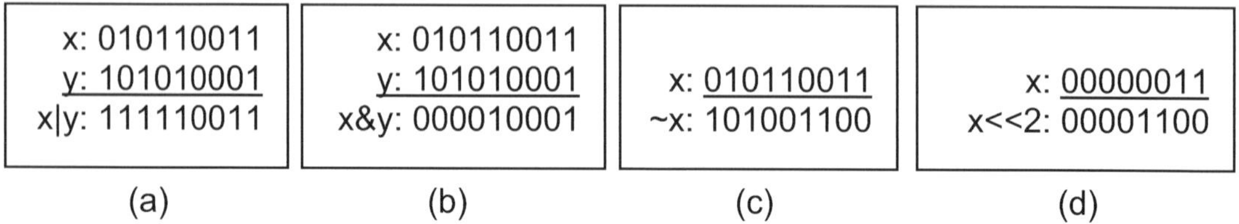

Figure 26-5. *Bitwise arithmetic*

- Bitwise and, as in x & y. A bit in x & y will be 1 if it's 1 in both x *and* y (Figure 26-5 (b)).
- Bitwise not, as in ~x. All the bits are flipped, or reversed (Figure 26-5 (c)).
- And we can move the bits left or right with shift operators << and >> (now doing double duty for stream I/O and bit manipulation). x << 2 has all the bits in x shifted left two bits (Figure 26-5 (d)).

Now we can see how to construct the `int` to send to `IMG_Init`. `flags = IMG_INIT_JPG | IMG_INIT_TIF` gives us

```
IMG_INIT_JPG: 000000001
IMG_INIT_TIF: 000000100
       flags: 000000101
```

and we pass it in it like this: `IMG_Init (flags);`.

To play with this more, I have an example of a super-simplified oven (Examples 26-11 and 26-12). You can set it to bake and/or broil (that's 1 bit each). I want finer control of the two burners on top, so I let the rightmost 2 bits control the right burner; the next 2 bits left of those control the left burner. The values they can take are 00 for off, 01 for low, 10 for medium, and 11 for high.

I also have a "fire" condition: if both burners are on high and the oven's set to bake *and* broil.

Example 26-11. Program that uses bit twiddling to set and use flags, part 1

```
//Program that controls a Super-Simple Demo Oven (SSDO) with flags
//       -- from _C++ for Lazy Programmers_

#include <iostream>
#include <cassert>

class SSDO  //A Super-Simple Demo Oven
{
public:
    enum FLAGS
    {
        RIGHT = 0b00000011,  //This is how to write in binary in C++:
        LEFT  = 0b00001100,  //  precede with 0b or 0B
        BAKE  = 0b00010000,
        BROIL = 0b00100000
        //Top two bits are unused
    };

    enum Condition
    {
        OFF = 0b00,
        LO  = 0b01,
        MD  = 0b10,
        HI  = 0b11,
    };

    enum
    {
        RIGHT_BURNER_OFFSET= 0, //starts at right end of flags
        LEFT_BURNER_OFFSET = 2, //starts 2 bits left
        FIRE = 0b00111111
    };
```

To turn on bake or broil, I use bitwise or, `|`, on a member variable `flags_` (see Figure 26-6 (a)): `flags_ = flags_ | BAKE;`.

```
          flags_: 01000011
            BAKE: 00010000
   flags_ | BAKE:01010011
```

(a)

```
          flags_: 01010011
           ~BAKE: 11101111
   flags_ & BAKE: 01000011
```

(b)

Figure 26-6. *Turning the BAKE bit on and off in the super-simple oven*

To turn it off, I need to keep all other bits unchanged but set that to 0. This'll do it: get a number in which all bits are 1 except BAKE, and "and" that with `flags_` (Figure 26-6 (b)): `flags_ = flags_ & ~BAKE;`.

Setting a burner is tougher because it's not just 1 bit. I still need the & and ~, but I need to take that `Condition` – `OFF`, `LO`, `MD`, or `HI` – and shift it to the right position for the given burner.

To set the left burner on `HI`, say, I clear out the left burner bits as I did with `BAKE` using ~ and & (Figure 26-7 (a)). Then I take `HI`, `0b11`, and shift it left 2 bits with << to get `0b1100`. I use bitwise or to put them together.

```
                  flags_: 01001011
                   ~LEFT: 11110011
            flags_&~LEFT: 01000011
                   HI<<2: 00001100
   flags_&~LEFT | HI<<2: 01011111
```

(a)

```
                 flags_: 01111111
                   FIRE: 00111111
          flags_ & FIRE: 00111111
         flags_ == FIRE: false (?!)
  (flags_ & FIRE) == FIRE:      true
```

(b)

Figure 26-7. *(a) Turning the LEFT burner on; (b) checking the FIRE condition*

I determine if the oven's catching fire – that is, if everything's on, and burners are on high – by saying `(flags() & FIRE) == FIRE`. If I just say `flags()==FIRE` it might not work, because I don't know what those two unused leftmost bits are (Figure 26-7 (b)). Defensive programming.

Example 26-12. Program that uses bit twiddling to set and use flags, part 2

```
//We're still in class SSDO's public section...

//ctors and =
SSDO()                { flags_ = '\0';    }
```

```
SSDO(const SSDO&)                    = delete;
const SSDO& operator= (const SSDO&) = delete;

//the controls
void    setBake() { flags_ |= BAKE;    }
void  clearBake() { flags_ &= ~BAKE;   }
void   setBroil() { flags_ |= BROIL;   }
void clearBroil() { flags_ &= ~BROIL;  }

void    setRightBurner(Condition c)
{
    flags_ &= ~RIGHT;
    flags_ |=
        static_cast<unsigned char>(c << RIGHT_BURNER_OFFSET);
          //The static_cast makes it obvious I *know* I'm
          // changing between types Condition and unsigned char
}

void   setLeftBurner  (Condition c)
{
    flags_ &= ~LEFT;
    flags_ |=
        static_cast<unsigned char> (c<< LEFT_BURNER_OFFSET);
}

void clearRightBurner()              { setRightBurner(OFF); }
void clearLeftBurner ()              { setLeftBurner (OFF); }

//access functions
unsigned char flags  () const        { return flags_;       }
bool isSelfCleaning  () const
{
    return (flags() & BAKE) && (flags() & BROIL);
}
bool isFireHazard    () const  //they're all on, high!
{
    return  (flags() & FIRE) == FIRE;
}
```

```
private:
    unsigned char flags_; //I only have a few bits;
                          //  don't need a whole int
};

using namespace std;

int main ()
{
    SSDO myOven;

    //Turning the oven completely on; now it's in self-cleaning mode
    myOven.setBake();
    myOven.setBroil();
    assert(myOven.isSelfCleaning());
    assert(myOven.flags() == 0b00110000);

    //Playing with the right burner, checking the result...
    myOven.setRightBurner   (SSDO::LO);
    myOven.clearRightBurner ();
    assert ((myOven.flags() & SSDO::RIGHT) == 0); //()'s needed!

    //I probably shouldn't do this...
    myOven.setRightBurner   (SSDO::HI);
    myOven.setLeftBurner    (SSDO::HI);
    if (myOven.isFireHazard())
        cout << "Cut the power and call the fire department!\n";

    return 0;
}
```

On the last `assert`, I needed the `()`'s before the `==`. If I didn't have them, it would parse that expression as `myOven.flags() & (SSDO::RIGHT == 0)`, which would be weird.

Now we should be able to set flags to send information to libraries that use them, and get such information back; or use them in libraries of our own.

Antibugging

- **Wrong answer to a bit manipulation expression, but you don't see how.** Maybe you used `&&` for `&`, or `||` for `|`. I certainly do that. Or (as earlier) maybe you need some `()`'s.

EXERCISES

1. Write a function to determine if a number is odd or even, by checking one of its bits.
2. Write a function that prints a number in binary by checking its bits. You may want `sizeof`.
3. Write a function that finds the $\log_2$ of an `int`, using `>>`, not `/`.
4. Write a function to tell if a sequence of bits in a number is symmetric (like 11000011 but not 11010011).

CHAPTER 27

Esoterica (Not So Recommended)

These features exist; they can be useful in rare circumstances; I hardly ever use them.

protected sections, protected inheritance

Consider the class in Example 27-1. Phone has a member numCalls_ which keeps track of all calls made, ever, by any Phone. There's a function to change it, but it's private, because we really should only update numCalls_ when making a call ().

Example 27-1. The Phone class

```
class Phone
{
public:
    void call() { /*do some stuff, and then */ incNumCalls(); }
    static int numCalls() { return numCalls_; }

private:
    void incNumCalls   () { ++numCalls_;       }
    static int numCalls_;
};
```

But now we've reached the dawn of human civilization and there are MobilePhones. When they make calls, they need to increment that number too. They can't access Phone::incNumCalls(); it's private. And we already decided for good reason not to make it public. What else can we do?

W. Briggs, *C++ for Lazy Programmers*, https://doi.org/10.1007/978-1-4842-5187-4_27

C++ provides another section: **protected** (see Example 27-2). The outside world can't see it (like private) but it's visible to child classes. Problem solved.

Example 27-2. Phone and `MobilePhone` share a family secret via `protected`

```
class Phone
{
public:
    void call() { /*do some stuff, and then */ incNumCalls(); }
    static int numCalls() { return numCalls_; }

protected:
    void incNumCalls   () { ++numCalls_;      }

private:
    static int numCalls_;
};

class MobilePhone : public Phone
{
public:
    void call() { /* do stuff w cell towers, and */ incNumCalls(); }
};
```

`protected` also gives us a new type of inheritance. Let's say when you do a mobile call, you need some extra security. So in `MobilePhone` I'll ditch the old `call` and add a new function `secureCall`.

```
class MobilePhone : <public? private? something else?> Phone
{
public:
    void secureCall()
    {
        makeSecure ();
        /* do cell tower stuff */
        incNumCalls();
    }

    void makeSecure (); //however that's done
};
```

With public inheritance (Figure 27-1), things are as public in the child class as they were in the parent. No new restrictions on access are added.

But that lets the outside world use the insecure, inherited `call` function on a `MobilePhone`. Maybe private inheritance, as in Figure 27-2, would be better? Looks like it.

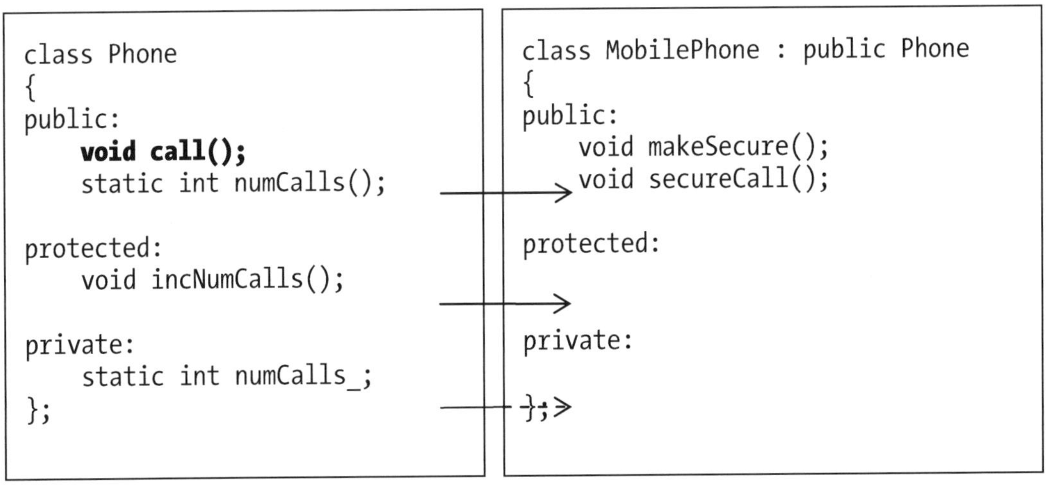

```
class Phone
{
public:
    void call();
    static int numCalls();

protected:
    void incNumCalls();

private:
    static int numCalls_;
};
```

```
class MobilePhone : public Phone
{
public:
    void makeSecure();
    void secureCall();

protected:

private:

};
```

Figure 27-1. *Public inheritance with a protected section*

```
class Phone
{
public:
    void call();
    static int numCalls();

protected:
    void incNumCalls();

private:
    static int numCalls_;
};
```

```
class MobilePhone : private Phone
{
public:
    void makeSecure();
    void secureCall();

protected:

private:

};
```

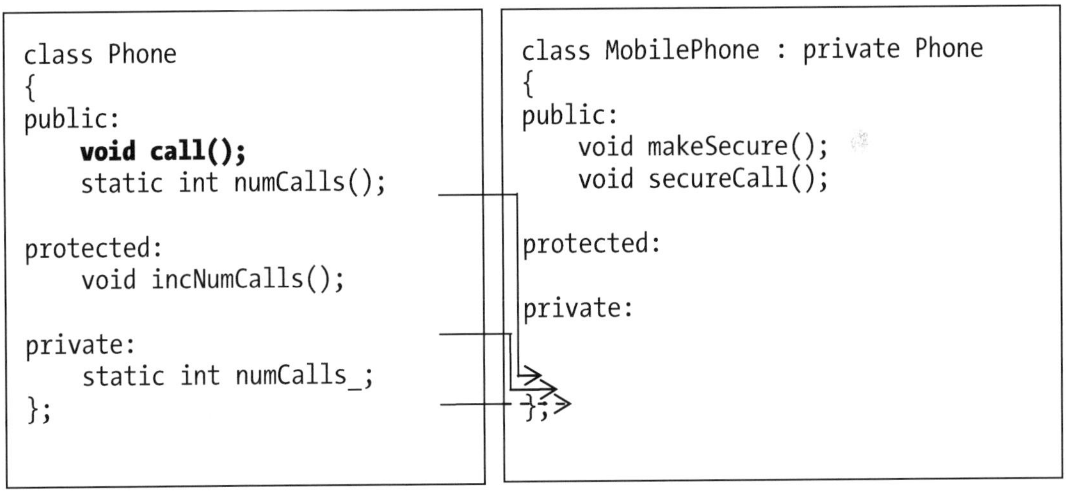

Figure 27-2. *Private inheritance with a protected section*

Now I'll add a subclass of MobilePhone: a SatellitePhone. It does its calling differently:

```
class SatellitePhone : public MobilePhone
{
public:
    void secureCall()
    {
        makeSecure ();
        /* do satellite stuff */
        incNumCalls();
    }

    //makeSecure is inherited and public
};
```

Problem: SatellitePhone can't use incNumCalls. Private inheritance put it in MobilePhone's private section.

We can use protected inheritance, as in Figure 27-3. It's just like public inheritance except that inherited public members become protected.

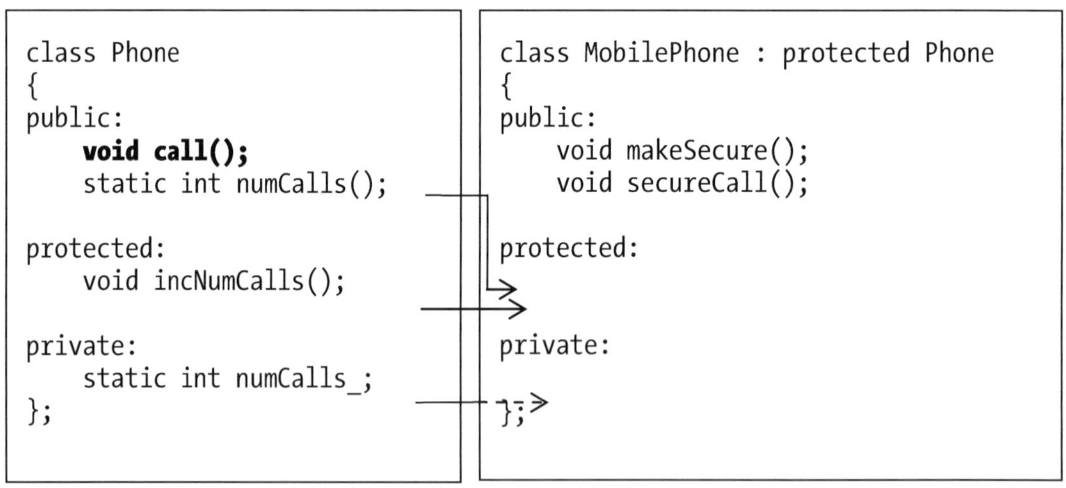

Figure 27-3. *Protected inheritance and a solution to SatellitePhone's problem*

Now the subclasses are secure, and all classes access `incNumCalls()` as needed.

```
Phone P;             P.call();
MobilePhone MP;     MP.secureCall();
SatellitePhone SP; SP.secureCall();

assert(Phone::numCalls() == 3); //Assertion will succeed
```

It doesn't at all matter whether you use private or protected inheritance until you have a grandchild class. Even then it probably won't matter. I almost never need protected sections or protected inheritance.

Template specialization

You won't often need this either, but when you do...

Suppose I have a `Vector` (Chapter 20's `Vector`) of `Superhero*`. (Likely I'm doing something with subclasses of `Superhero`, as with the `Shapes` of Chapter 21.) `Superheros` are printable with `<<`, so `Vector::print` should work fine:

```
template <typename T>
void Vector<T>::print (ostream& out) const
{
      for (int i = 0; i < size(); ++i)
            out << (*this)[i] << '/';
}
```

I add `Superheros` Somewhat Competent Boy, Amazing Girl, and so on, then print like so:

```
cout << superheroes << endl;
```

and get this:

```
0x2fc7f80/0x2fc7fa0/0x2fc7fc0/0x2fc6de8/
```

What fun. Why's it so strange?

It did what we told it. We gave it a `Vector` of pointers and told it to print them, and sure enough, it printed pointers, which are memory addresses.

We'll add a new version of `Vector::print` so if the element type is `Superhero*` it will print the `Superhero` instead (Example 27-3).

Example 27-3. A template specialization

```
template<>
void Vector<Superhero*>::print (ostream& out) const
{
    for (unsigned int i = 0; i < size(); ++i)
        out << *((*this)[i]) << '/';
}
```

The `template<>` at the beginning says this is a **specialization** of a template: we're not telling C++ how to print *any* `Vector`, just `Vector`s of `Superhero*`.

Here's our new output:`Somewhat Competent Boy/Amazing Girl/Superpolite Man/Wunderkind/`

For more on template specialization, see *The C++ Programming Language* by Bjarne Stroustrup, or the Internet.

EXERCISES

1. Write a function `printBase3` that prints an `int` in base 3. Then write a specialization of `Vector<T>::print` that prints all `int`s in base 3.
2. Write a function `isOrdered` that returns `true` if a `std::pair`'s `first` is less than (<) its `second`.

   ...except if first and second are `const char*`, in which case it uses `strcmp` to evaluate.

`friend`s, and why you shouldn't have any

This section's example uses file I/O (Chapter 13).

Consider a program that uses maps. It reads in several `Area`s, like the ones in Figure 27-4, each of which has a name and bounding box (how far the `Area` extends north, south, west, and east). It then reports which `Area` is furthest north. Examples 27-4 and 27-5 show source code, with some code omitted for brevity.

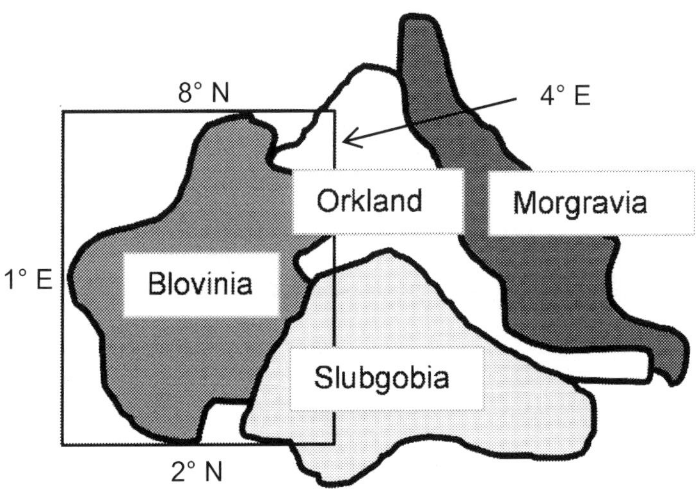

Figure 27-4. *A four-Area map, with a bounding box shown on one Area*

Example 27-4. `area.h`

```
//Class Area
//Each Area is read in as
//  <north bound> <south bound> <west bound> <east bound> <name>
//  as in
//  8 2 1 4 Blovinia
//...and that's what an Area contains

//      -- from _C++ for Lazy Programmers_

#ifndef AREA_H
#define AREA_H

#include <string>

class Area
{
public:
    enum Direction { NORTH, SOUTH, EAST, WEST };
    enum           { DIRECTIONS = 4 };

    Area () {}
    Area (const Area& other);
```

```
    const Area& operator= (const Area& other);

    void read  (std::istream& in );
    void print (std::ostream& out) const { out << name_; }

private:
    double boundingBox_[DIRECTIONS];
        //the northernmost, southernmost, etc., extent of our Area
        //bigger numbers are further north
        //bigger numbers are further east
    std::string name_;
};

inline
bool furtherNorthThan (const Area& a, const Area& b)
{
    return a.boundingBox_[Area::NORTH] > b.boundingBox_[Area::NORTH];
}

#endif //AREA_H
```

Example 27-5. findNorthernmostArea.cpp

```
//Program to read in regions from a file, and tell which
//  is furthest north.
//      -- from _C++ for Lazy Programmers_

#include <iostream>
#include <fstream>
#include <vector>
#include "area.h"

using namespace std;

int main ()
{
    vector<Area> myAreas;
```

```
    ifstream infile("regions.txt");
    if (!infile)
    {
        cerr << "Can't open file regions.txt.\n"; return 1;
    }

    while (infile)                //read in Areas
    {
        Area area; infile >> area;
        if (infile) myAreas.push_back (area);
    }

    //find the northernmost Area
    int northernmostIndex = 0;
    for (unsigned int i = 1; i < myAreas.size(); ++i)
        if (furtherNorthThan (myAreas[i],myAreas[northernmostIndex]))
            northernmostIndex = i;

    //print it
    cout << "The northernmost area is "
         << myAreas [northernmostIndex]
         << endl;

    return 0;
}
```

I know I've written clear, well-commented code here (and I'm humble too), so I won't explain further. But when furtherNorthThan tries to access boundingBox_, the compiler complains of a privacy violation. It's right: boundingBox_ *is* private.

C++ **friends** are a fix for this. If a function is so closely associated with a class that it may as well be a member – but it isn't convenient to make it one – you can give it access to all members, including the private ones, just as though it were. Here's how: somewhere in class Area (I put it at the top so it's always the same place), put a friend declaration for the function (Example 27-6).

Example 27-6. A `friend` for `Area`

```
class Area
{
    friend bool furtherNorthThan (const Area& a, const Area& b);
    ...
};
```

Now the program should compile fine, and report that Morgravia is furthest north.

You can also make a class a `friend`:

```
class Area
{
    friend class OtherClassITrust;[1]
    ...
```

Or make some other class's member function a friend:

```
class Area
{
    friend void OtherClassIPartlyTrust::functionIFullyTrust();
    ...
```

Is this a good idea?

According to Marshall Cline and the C++ Super-FAQ,[2] yes. He argues that a `friend` function is part of the public interface just as a public member function is. It doesn't violate security, but is just another part of it.

I see his point, but I can't think of an example that can't be done another way. In Example 27-4, we could replace

```
bool furtherNorthThan (const Area& a, const Area& b);
```

with

```
bool Area::furtherNorthThan (const Area& b) const;
```

That's what we do with operators like `<`. Why not this too?

[1]If the other class has already been declared, you can leave out the word `class` here.

[2]At time of writing, `https://isocpp.org/wiki/faq/`.

I used to make stream I/O operators >> and << friends of the classes they printed/read; now I have them call member functions print and read. Using friend might be easier, but not by much.

If you want it, use it as experts suggest: for things tightly connected to the class in question, so they can be considered part of the class's interface to the world. I'm betting it won't be often.

User-defined conversions

Should we add a way to implicitly cast from String to const char* as needed? Makes sense: many built-in functions expect a char*, and you might prefer myInFile.open (filename); to myInFile.open (filename.c_str()), especially around the 100th time you type it. So we'll add it (Example 27-7).

Example 27-7. String, with a user-defined cast operator

```
class String
{
public:
    ...
    const char* c_str    () const      { return contents_;            }
    operator const char* () const      { return c_str ();             }
        //will implicitly cast from String to const char*
    ...
};
```

Works fine for that call to myInFile.open. Then we try a simple string comparison:

```
if (str1 == "END")
    cout << "Looks like we've reached the END.\n";
```

It no longer compiles – gives complaints about ambiguity or too many overloads.

It's right: there are now *two* ways to match the arguments of operator ==: implicitly convert "END" to another String, and compare with String's == and implicitly convert str1 to a char* with the cast operator and use char*'s ==.

The solution is to put the word explicit in front of the function:[3]

```
explicit operator const char* () const { return c_str (); }
```

Now we can cast, but we have to *say* we want to cast:

```
myInFile.open ((const char*) filename);
```

It works, but did we gain anything over saying filename.c_str()?

I never seem to find a way to use this feature that is both safe and time-saving. Maybe you will.

EXERCISES

In each exercise, better use explicit to avoid ambiguity.

1. Add a cast-to-double operator to the Point2D class from earlier exercises. The double version of a Point2D is the magnitude: $\sqrt{x^2 + y^2}$.

2. Add a cast-to-double operator to the Fraction class. The double version of 1/2, for example, is 0.5 (of course).

[3]You can also put explicit in front of other functions sometimes called implicitly, like copy and conversion constructors, to disable implicit calls – but I never do.

CHAPTER 28

C

If you know C++, you almost know C. Experience with C gets you another brag – one character long, so it should fit! – on your resume. C is popular for operating systems and embedded systems, and there are a lot of libraries in it.

C is essentially what we covered before getting to classes, excluding

- SDL/SSDL
- `cin` and `cout`
- & parameters
- `bool` (use `int` instead)

There are no classes, exceptions, overloaded operators, templates, or namespaces. `struct`s exist but don't have member functions or public/private/protected sections (it's all public).

There are smaller differences, including

- Casting looks like this: `(int) f`, not this: `int (f)`.
- `struct S {...};` does declare a `struct` named `S`, but to declare a variable of that type requires an extra word:

  ```
  struct S myStruct;
  ```

cplusplus.com and cppreference.com, despite the names, are good resources on C as well as C++.

W. Briggs, *C++ for Lazy Programmers*, https://doi.org/10.1007/978-1-4842-5187-4_28

Compiling C

In **Visual Studio** you can't select "C file" as something to add to your project, but you can select C++ file and name yours `<something>.c`. The compiler will treat it as a C file. Compile and run as usual.

In **Unix** or **MinGW**, name your program `<something>.c` and compile with the `gcc` command, which works like g++ only for C files.[1] The sample code has this built into its Makefiles.

Example 28-1 is the obligatory "Hello, world!".

Example 28-1. "Hello, world!" in C

```
/*
Hello, world! -- again!  This time in C.
            from _C++ for Lazy Programmers_
*/

#include <stdio.h>

int main ()
{
      printf ("Hello, world!\n");

      return 0;
}
```

Some things to note:

- Comments in C are `/*like this*/` not `//like this`. (Visual Studio allows the `//` comments, but it's non-standard.)

[1] If you want both C++ and C files in the same project, that'll work, but there are tricks required. You'll need to put `main` in a C++ file; link using g++ not gcc; and for any C include files to be used in a C++ file, wrap the include thus:

```
extern "C"
  {
  #include "mycheader.h"
  }
```

For more on this, at time of writing, see the C++Super-FAQ, `https://isocpp.org/wiki/faq/mixing-c-and-cpp`.

- Include files, belonging to the system or not, end in `.h`. Those C++ inherits from C have the initial `c` taken back off: `stdlib.h` not `cstdlib`; `math.h` not `cmath`.
- We print with `printf`; more on that in the next section.

I/O

All these I/O functions are in `stdio.h`.

printf

Instead of `cout >>`, C has the function `printf` ("print-f," meaning "print with formatting").

```
printf ("Ints like %d, strings like %s, and floats like %f -- oh, my!\n",
        12, "ROFL", 3.14159);                        /* %d is for "decimal" */
```

will print

```
Ints like 12, strings like ROFL, and floats like 3.141590 -- oh, my!
```

The `%` sequences are placeholders in the "format string" (`"Ints like %d..."`), showing where to put each successive argument. You can have as many arguments as you want. The most common `%` sequences are `%d` for decimal integer, `%f` for fixed floating point, and `%s` for string, that is, character array. `%%` means "just the `%` character."

There are modifiers you can put inside them; for example, `%.2f` puts 2 digits right of the decimal point.

scanf, and the address-of (&) operator

`scanf` ("scan-f") replaces `cin >>`, and looks like this:

```
scanf ("%f %s", &myDouble, myCharArray);
```

`&` means "take the address of." C and C++ both have this operator, but C uses it all the time. `scanf` needs to know where `myDouble` is so it can alter it (more on that in the next section). It doesn't need the address of `myCharArray` because `myCharArray` *is* an address.

Visual Studio gives a warning if you use scanf, or some other functions in this chapter, that the function is unsafe, just as it does with some cstring functions (see Chapter 14). Example 28-2 shows one way to disable the warning if that's your preference.

Example 28-2. printf and scanf

```
/*
Program to test C's major standard I/O functions
        -- from _C++ for Lazy Programmers_
*/

#include <stdio.h>

/*Disable a warning about scanf, etc., in Visual Studio */
#ifdef _MSC_VER
#pragma warning (disable:4996)
#endif

int main ()
{
    float number;            /* number we'll read in and print out  */
    int   age;               /* your age                            */
    enum {MAXSTR = 80};      /* array size                          */
    char  name [MAXSTR];     /* your name                           */

        /* A printf showing float, and use of % sign                */
    printf ("%3.2f%% of statistics are made up on the spot!\n\n",
            98.23567894);

        /* printfs using decimal, hex, and char array               */
        /* %02d means pad number to a width of 2 with leading 0's   */
    printf ("%d is 0x%x in hexadecimal.\n\n", 16, 16);
    printf ("\"%s\" is a $%d.%02d word.\n\n", "hexadecimal",
            5, 0);
```

```
        /* Scanf needs & for the variables it sets */
    printf ("Enter a floating-point number:  ");
    scanf ("%f", &number);
    printf ("%g is %f in fixed notation and %e in scientific.\n",
            number, number, number);
    printf ("...in scientific with a precision of 2:  %.2e.\n\n",
            number);

        /* ...except arrays, since they're already addresses      */
    printf ("Enter your name and age:  ");
    scanf ("%s %d", name, &age);
    printf ("%s is %d years old!\n\n", name, age);

    return 0;
}
```

This is what the output might look like:

```
98.24% of statistics are made up on the spot!

16 is 0x10 in hexadecimal.

"hexadecimal" is a $5.00 word.

Enter a floating-point number: 2
2 is 2.000000 in fixed notation and 2.000000e+000 in scientific.
Here it is in scientific with a precision of 2: 2.00e+000.

Enter your name and age: Linus 7
Linus is 7 years old!
```

Table 28-1 gives a partial list of format codes for `printf` and `scanf`.

***Table 28-1.** Format codes for `printf` and `scanf`*

% Sequence	Meaning
%d	integer in decimal format
%o	integer in unsigned octal
%x/%X	integer in unsigned hexadecimal. Hex 1f will show up as 0x1f/0X1F
%c	character
%s	character array
%f	fixed point floating point
%e/%E	scientific notation floating point. The E will be uppercase if you say %E
%g/%G	Like %f or %e, whichever gives shorter output. The E (if any) will be uppercase if you say %G
%p	pointer
%%	the % character itself

`fprintf` and `fscanf`; `fopen` and `fclose`

File I/O in C uses variants of `printf` and `scanf`. Consider this code:

```
FILE* file = fopen ("newfile.txt", "w");           /* open file */
fprintf (file, "Avogadro's number is %.4e.\n", 6.023e+023);
fclose  (file);                                    /* close it  */
```

To open the file for writing, we call `fopen` ("f-open"), give it the filename, and `"w"` meaning "write" (to an output file). The file information is stored in a pointer of type `FILE*`.

Closing the file is simply sending the file pointer to `fclose`, as earlier.

In between, adapt your `printf`s to `fprintf`s by adding the `file` as the first argument.

If you want to read instead or write, open the file with `"r"` for "read" and adapt `scanf` similarly:

```
file = fopen ("newfile.txt", "r");
fscanf (file, "%s %s %s %e", word1, word2, word3, &number);
fclose (file);
```

If successful, fscanf and scanf return the number of arguments you gave. If the number is different, something went wrong. Probably you reached the end of file. Test for that like so:

```
while (1)                                   /* while true */
{
    if (fscanf (file, "%d", number) != 1) break;
    ...
}
```

Example 28-3 illustrates the use of these functions.

Example 28-3. fprintf, fscanf, fopen, and fclose

```
/*
Program to test C's major standard file I/O functions
        -- from _C++ for Lazy Programmers_
*/

#include <stdio.h>

/*Disable a warning about fopen, etc., in Visual Studio */
#ifdef _MSC_VER
#pragma warning (disable:4996)
#endif

int main ()
{
    FILE* file;              /* a file to write to or read from     */
    float number;            /* number we'll read in and print out  */
    enum { MAXSTR = 80 };    /* array size                          */
    char junk [MAXSTR];      /* a char array for reading in (and thus
                                    discarding) a word              */

        /* printing to file. The number gets 4 digits of precision */
    file = fopen ("newfile.txt", "w");
    printf  (      "Avogadro's number is %.4e.\n", 6.023e+023);
    fprintf (file, "Avogadro's number is %.4e.\n", 6.023e+023);
    fclose  (file);
```

```
    /* reading from a file                                         */
file = fopen ("newfile.txt", "r");
fscanf (file, "%s %s %s %e", junk, junk, junk, &number);
                     /* Read in 3 words, then the number we want */
fclose (file);
printf ("Looks like Avogadro's number is still %.4e.\n", number);

return 0;
}
```

The file will contain `Avogadro's number is 6.0230e+023.` and the output to the screen will be

```
Avogadro's number is 6.0230e+023.
Looks like Avogadro's number is still 6.0230e+023.
```

sprintf and sscanf; fputs and fgets

A few more I/O functions

- **sscanf ("s-scan-f")** reads from a character array. If `myCharArray` is `"2.3 kg"`, we can say

  ```
  sscanf (myCharArray, "%f %s", &myDouble, myWord);
              /* myDouble gets 2.3, myWord gets "kg" */
  ```

  In C++ we'd have said

  ```
  sstream myStringStream (myCharArray);
  myStringStream >> myDouble >> myWord;
  ```

- **sprintf** prints to a character array:

  ```
  sprintf (myCharArray, "%s %f", name, number);
  ```

  In C++ we'd have said

  ```
  sstream myStringStream;
  myStringStream << name << number;
  string myString = myStringStream.str();
  ```

- **fputs and fgets**. fputs (myCharArray, file); prints the given char array to a file. fgets (myCharArray, max, file); gets a line of input from file, no more than max characters including the '\0', and stores it in myCharArray.

If you want to use keyboard and display instead of files, do it like so: fputs (myCharArray, **stdin**); and fgets (myCharArray, max, **stdout**);.

Example 28-4 illustrates the use of these functions.

Example 28-4. A program using sprintf, sscanf, puts, and gets

```
/*
Program to test sprintf, sscanf, fgets, fputs
        -- from _C++ for Lazy Programmers_
*/

#include <stdio.h>

/*Disable a warning about scanf, etc., in Visual Studio */
#ifdef _MSC_VER
#pragma warning (disable:4996)
#endif

int main ()
{
    while (1)                   /* forever, or until break... */
    {
        enum {MAXLINE=256};     /* array size for line        */
        char line [MAXLINE];    /* a line of text             */
        enum {MAXSTR = 80};     /* array size for word        */
        char word [MAXSTR];     /* your word                  */
        int  number;            /* a number to read in        */

        /* get an entire line with fgets; on EOF quit         */
        printf("Enter a line with 1 word & 1 number, EOF to quit: ");
        if (! fgets  (line, MAXSTR, stdin)) break;
```

```
        /* repeat line with fputs                                  */
        printf("You entered:  ");
        fputs (line, stdout);

        /* Use char array as source for 2 arguments                */
        if (sscanf (line, "%s %i", word, &number) != 2)
            fputs ("That wasn't a word and a number!\n", stdout);
        else
        {
            /* Print using sprintf and puts                        */
            sprintf(line, "The name was %s and the number was %i.\n",
                    word, number);
            fputs  (line, stdout);
            /*
            If this weren't a demo of new functions, I'd have said:
              printf ("The name was %s and the number was %f.\n",
                      name, number);
            */
        }
        fputs ("\n", stdout);  /* add blank line to separate */
    }

    fputs ("\n\nBye!\n", stdout);

    return 0;
}
```

Sample output:

```
Enter a line with 1 word and 1 number, EOF to quit:
You entered:  Mila 18
The name was Mila and the number was 18.

Enter a line with 1 word and 1 number, EOF to quit:
You entered:  Catch 22
The name was Catch and the number was 22.

Enter a line with 1 word and 1 number, EOF to quit:

Bye!
```

Summary

In Table 28-2, if I don't give the meaning of what's returned by a function, it's because with that one we rarely care. With fgets, fopen, and the scanf family, we do.

***Table 28-2.** Common stdio functions in C*

printf and variants	
`int printf (const char* formatString, ...);`	print to screen arguments after formatString, as specified by formatString
`int fprintf (FILE* file, const char* formatString, ...);`	same as printf but prints to file
`int sprintf (const char* str, const char* formatString, ...);`	same as printf but prints to str
scanf and variants	
`int scanf (const char* formatString, ...);`	read arguments after formatString as specified by formatString. Returns EOF if it reaches EOF before reading any; else # of arguments successfully read
`int fscanf (FILE* file, const char* formatString, ...);`	same as scanf but reads from file
`int sscanf (const char* str, const char* formatString, ...);`	same as scanf but reads from str
opening/closing files	
`FILE* fopen (const char* filename, const char* fileMode);`	open, and return pointer to, file specified by filename. The most common fileModes are "r" (read), "w" (write), and "a" (append)
`int fclose (FILE* file);`	close the file

(continued)

Table 28-2. (*continued*)

reading/writing strings	
`int fputs (const char* str, FILE* file);`	print `str` to `file`
`char* fgets (char* str, int max, FILE* file);`	read `str` from `file`, reading at most `max-1` characters (so `str`'s size should be `max` or greater). Returns `NULL` on failure.

Antibugging

- `scanf` **fails for lack of &:**

  ```
  scanf ("%f %s",  myDouble, myCharArray);
  ```

  should have been

  ```
  scanf ("%f %s", &myDouble, myCharArray);
  ```

  It's easy to forget the &'s, and the compiler may not warn you.

Parameter passing with *

C doesn't have & parameters, but like C++, it considers other parameters to be unchanged by a function call. Uh-oh.

```
void swap (int arg1, int arg2)²
{
    int temp = arg1; arg1 = arg2; arg2 = temp;
}

int main ()
{
    int x, y;
    ...
    swap (x, y);  /* x, y will not be changed */
    ...
}
```

Instead C expects the programmer to send in the *address* of the argument:

```
int main ()
{
    int x, y;
    ...
    swap (&x, &y); /* x's and y's addresses are sent, not x and y */
    ...
}
```

The function takes that address and uses * to refer to the thing it points to, which *can* be altered.

```
void swap (int* arg1, int* arg2)
{
    int temp = *arg1; *arg1 = *arg2; *arg2 = temp;
}
```

---

[2]If you run across a function with its parameters defined after the initial ()'s:

```
int f (thing1, thing2)
  int thing1;
  float thing2;
  {
   ...
```

...you've run across the old Kernighan and Ritchie (K&R) standard. May it accept its honored place in history and stop showing up in people's code.

It works! But it's clunky, and it introduces a maddeningly common error: forgetting the *'s.

Example 28-5 uses it (and doesn't forget the *'s).

Example 28-5. Program using parameter passing with *'s in C

```
/*
Program to do statistics on some strings
        from _C++ for Lazy Programmers_
*/

#include <stdio.h>  /*for printf, scanf*/
#include <string.h> /*for strlen       */

/*Disable a warning about scanf, etc., in Visual Studio */
#ifdef _MSC_VER
#pragma warning (disable:4996)
#endif

void updateLineStats (char line[], unsigned int* length,
                      float* averageLineLength);

int main ()
{
    printf ("Type in a line and I'll reply. ");
    printf ("Type the end-of-file character to end.\n");

    while (1)   /* forever (or until a break) ... */
    {
        enum { MAXSTRING = 256 };      /* max line length    */
        char line [MAXSTRING];         /* the line           */
        int  length;                   /* its current length */
        float averageLineLength;

        /* get line of input */
        if (!fgets (line, MAXSTRING, stdin)) break;

        /*do the stats. We send addresses, not variables, using &*/
        updateLineStats (line, &length, &averageLineLength);
```

```
        /* give the result  */
        printf ("Length of that line, ");
        printf ("and average so far: %d, %.2f.\n",
                length, averageLineLength);
    }

    return 0;
}

void updateLineStats (char line[], unsigned int* length,
                      float* averageLineLength)
{
    static int totalLinesLength = 0;    /*have to remember these */
    static int linesSoFar = 0;          /*  for next time        */

    *length = (unsigned int) (strlen (line));
                                        /*length is a pointer, so*/
                                        /*  *length is the length*/

    /* fgets included the final \n, but I won't count that:      */
    --(*length);

    ++linesSoFar;
    totalLinesLength += *length;

    *averageLineLength = /* and averageLineLength needs its *, too*/
        totalLinesLength / ((float) linesSoFar);
}
```

Output:

```
Type in a line and I'll reply. Type the end-of-file character to end.
alpha
Length of that line, and average so far: 5, 5.00.
bet
Length of that line, and average so far: 3, 4.00.
soup
Length of that line, and average so far: 4, 4.00.
```

Antibugging

- **"<variable> differs in level of indirection" or "cannot convert from <type> to <type>*" or "makes pointer from integer without cast."** There are many ways to complain, but the bottom line is it's hard to remember to put the &'s in the function call and even harder to remember the *'s *every! time!* you use the variable passed in. I never found a fix. At least you know that's a likely culprit for what goes wrong; and the compilers seem pretty good about warning us.

Dynamic memory

Forget `new`, `new []`, `delete`, and `delete []`: C's dynamic memory is simpler, if uglier:

```
#include <stdlib.h>                  /* for malloc, free          */

...

<type>* myArray = malloc (myArraySize * sizeof (<type>));
              /* allocate a myArraySize element array of <type> */

...use the array...

free (myArray);                      /* throw it back             */
```

There's no destructors to help you remember to free things – you're on your own. Example 28-6 adapts Example 14-3, an earlier program using dynamic memory, to C.

Example 28-6. A C program using dynamic memory

```
/*
Program to generate a random passcode of digits
        -- from _C++ for Lazy Programmers_
*/

#include <stdio.h>
#include <stdlib.h> /* for srand, rand, malloc, free */
#include <time.h>   /* for time                      */
```

```
/*Disable a warning about scanf, etc., in Visual Studio */
#ifdef _MSC_VER
#pragma warning (disable:4996)
#endif

int main ()
{
    srand ((unsigned int) time(NULL));/* start random # generator */
                                      /* NULL, not nullptr       */

    int codeLength;                   /* get code length          */
    printf ("I'll make your secret passcode. "
            "How long should it be? ");
    scanf ("%d", &codeLength);

                                       /* allocate array          */
    int* passcode = malloc(codeLength * sizeof(int));

    for (int i = 0; i < codeLength; ++i)/* generate passcode      */
        passcode[i] = rand () % 10;    /* each entry is a digit   */

    printf ("Here it is:\n");          /* print passcode          */
    for (int i = 0; i < codeLength; ++i)
        printf ("%d", passcode[i]);
    printf("\n");
    printf("But I guess it's not secret any more!\n");

    free (passcode);                   /* deallocate array        */

    return 0;
}
```

EXERCISES

Do the exercises from Chapters 13 and 14, excluding those that use SSDL, in C.

CHAPTER 29

Moving On with SDL

By using SSDL you've gone most of the way toward becoming an SDL programmer. To learn new things to do with SDL, you can

- Dump SSDL and get a tutorial on SDL. You'll see a lot that you recognize. Many SSDL functions are SDL functions with an "S" stuck on the front (as in, `SDL_PollEvent` became `SSDL_PollEvent`). Usually SDL functions need one more initial argument, often of type `SDL_Window*` or `SDL_Renderer*`, two types you'll learn right away. You can usually guess what'll be needed (hint: functions with "Render" in the name probably need `SDL_Renderer*`). Or...
- Keep SSDL, but extend with more SDL features – say, joystick support.

Either way it'll be useful to look behind SSDL to what it's been hiding from you. Let's start with initialization and cleanup code.

The typical SDL program has a version of `main` that looks like Example 29-1.

Example 29-1. A simple SDL program

```
//An SDL program that doesn't do anything interesting
//      -- from _C++ for Lazy Programmers_

#include <iostream>
#include "SDL.h"
#include "SDL_image.h"
#include "SDL_mixer.h"
#include "SDL_ttf.h"
```


W. Briggs, *C++ for Lazy Programmers*, https://doi.org/10.1007/978-1-4842-5187-4_29

```
int main(int argc, char** argv)
{
    //initialization

    enum { DEFAULT_WIDTH = 640, DEFAULT_HEIGHT = 480 };
    if (SDL_Init(SDL_INIT_EVERYTHING) < 0) return -1;

    SDL_Window* sdlWindow
        = SDL_CreateWindow("My SDL program!",
                           SDL_WINDOWPOS_UNDEFINED,
                           SDL_WINDOWPOS_UNDEFINED,
                           DEFAULT_WIDTH, DEFAULT_HEIGHT,
                           0); //flags are 0 by default
    if (!sdlWindow) return -1; //nope, it failed

    //defaults below:
    // rendererIndex shd be -1 (pick first renderer that works best)
    // rendererFlags should be 0
    int rendererIndex = -1;
    int rendererFlags = 0;
    SDL_Renderer* sdlRenderer
        = SDL_CreateRenderer(sdlWindow, rendererIndex,
                             rendererFlags);

    if (!sdlRenderer) return -1;//nope, it failed

    SDL_ClearError();           //Initially, no errors

    static const int IMG_FLAGS  //all available types
        = IMG_INIT_PNG | IMG_INIT_JPG | IMG_INIT_TIF;
    if (!(IMG_Init(IMG_FLAGS) & IMG_FLAGS))  //start SDL_Image
        return -1;

    if (TTF_Init() == -1) return -1;         //...and SDL_TTF

                                             //...and SDL_Mixer
    int soundInitialized = (Mix_OpenAudio(88020, MIX_DEFAULT_FORMAT,
                                  MIX_DEFAULT_CHANNELS, 4096) != -1);
    if (!soundInitialized) SDL_ClearError();
```

```
            //if it failed, we can still do the program
            //  -- just forget error

    //STUFF YOU ACTUALLY WANT TO DO GOES HERE

    //cleanup
            //If sound system started, close it
    if (soundInitialized) {Mix_AllocateChannels(0);Mix_CloseAudio();}
    TTF_Quit();
    IMG_Quit();
    SDL_DestroyRenderer(sdlRenderer);
    SDL_DestroyWindow(sdlWindow);
    SDL_Quit();

    return 0;
}
```

Writing code

In SSDL, the initialization code in Example 29-1 is done by `SSDL_Display::SSDL_Display`. There are simplifications. One biggie is: we can't throw an `SSDL_Exception` without SSDL (!), so instead we deal with failure to launch with `return -1;`.

See what it does: initializes SDL (this must be done first); creates the window (good!); creates a "renderer," needed to draw or paste images; and initializes SDL_Image and SDL_TTF, needed for image and fonts. If anything goes wrong, we give up, because you can't really go on without these things.

It also supports sound by initializing SDL_Mixer's `Mix_OpenAudio`. In SSDL this is done by `SSDL_SoundSystem`'s constructor.

The `//cleanup` code shuts down the helper libraries, kills the window and renderer, and finally shuts down SDL. In SSDL this is done by `SSDL_SoundSystem`'s and `SSDL_Display`'s destructors.

I obviously prefer my way, for organization, neatness, and not having to type all that code in every new program; but since we're looking at the messy guts of it all, I guess we'll leave it in `main` as game programmers often do. At least I'm not using global variables.

So can we get a program that will actually do something? Sure, but first let me talk about what else SSDL has been covering up:

- Many SSDL types represent SDL types, usually pointers.
  - SSDL_Color is essentially an SDL_Color (duh).
  - SSDL_Display is essentially an SDL_Renderer* and an SDL_Window*. (If you care how the SSDL_Display gets passed into SDL functions that want these types, see SSDL inline functions for handling windows or rendering.)
  - SSDL_Font is a TTF_Font*.
  - SSDL_Image is an SDL_Texture*.
  - SSDL_Music is a Mix_Music*.
  - SSDL_Sound is a Mix_Chunk* and an int (for channel).
  - SSDL_Sprite is an SDL_Texture* plus a lot of fields to be sent to SDL_RenderCopyEx in a complicated call (see SSDL_RenderSprite).

  These classes exist mostly to protect beginners from pointers, and everyone from having to do his/her own dynamic allocation and cleanup.
- Besides RGB, SDL_Color has an "alpha" member which also ranges 0 to 255. 0 means completely transparent and 255 means completely opaque. To use it, you'll need SDL functions with "blend" in the name.
- Forget ssin and sout; you'll use TTF_RenderText_Solid (see SSDL_Display::RenderTextLine).
- SDL is always using dynamic memory, but you can't use new and delete: SDL and its helpers provide their own allocation and deallocation functions, for example, SDL_CreateTexture and SDL_DestroyTexture; TTF_OpenFont and TTF_CloseFont. You have to use them.

OK, so let's do something, cheating by seeing how SSDL did it. I'll put an image on the screen and wait for someone to hit a key. Hoo-ah!

I'll use `SSDL_LoadImage` and `SSDL_RenderImage` for the image (searching for these in the SSDL code – they've got to be there somewhere). If you're following along by searching yourself – please do! – you'll see I leave out calls to `SSDL_Display::Instance` (that's just there to ensure the initialization code gets called first, and we did that already). We won't stretch the image, so I'll omit references to `stretchWidth` and `stretchHeight` and use the image's actual size. I rename variables as needed. With a little more cleanup, I get the code in Example 29-2, which goes immediately after the `//initialization` code in Example 29-1.

Example 29-2. Displaying an image in SDL

```
//Draw an image, and wait for a response

SDL_Surface* sdlSurface = IMG_Load("media/pupdog.png");
if (!sdlSurface) return -1;

SDL_Texture* image = SDL_CreateTextureFromSurface
                              (sdlRenderer, sdlSurface);
if (!image) return -1;
SDL_FreeSurface(sdlSurface);

SDL_Rect dst;                //dst is where it's going on screen
dst.x = 0; dst.y = 0;

SDL_QueryTexture(image, nullptr, nullptr, &dst.w, &dst.h);
                             //get width and height of image
SDL_RenderCopy(sdlRenderer, image, nullptr, &dst);
```

Waiting for a key...I find `SSDL_WaitKey`, then the thing that it calls, then the things *it* calls, and eventually get the monstrosity in Example 29-3. It goes right after the image-display code in Example 29-2.

Example 29-3. Waiting for a keystroke in SDL

```
    //Waiting for a key

    SDL_Event sdlEvent;

    SDL_RenderPresent(sdlRenderer);       //display everything

    bool isTimeToQuit = false;
```

```
while (!isTimeToQuit)
{
    if (SDL_WaitEvent(&sdlEvent) == 0) return -1;

                                    //handle quit messages
    if (sdlEvent.type == SDL_QUIT) isTimeToQuit = true;
    if (sdlEvent.type == SDL_KEYDOWN
        && sdlEvent.key.keysym.scancode == SDL_SCANCODE_ESCAPE)
      isTimeToQuit = true;

    if (sdlEvent.type == SDL_KEYDOWN) //Got that key? break
        break;                        // (break, not return!)
}
```

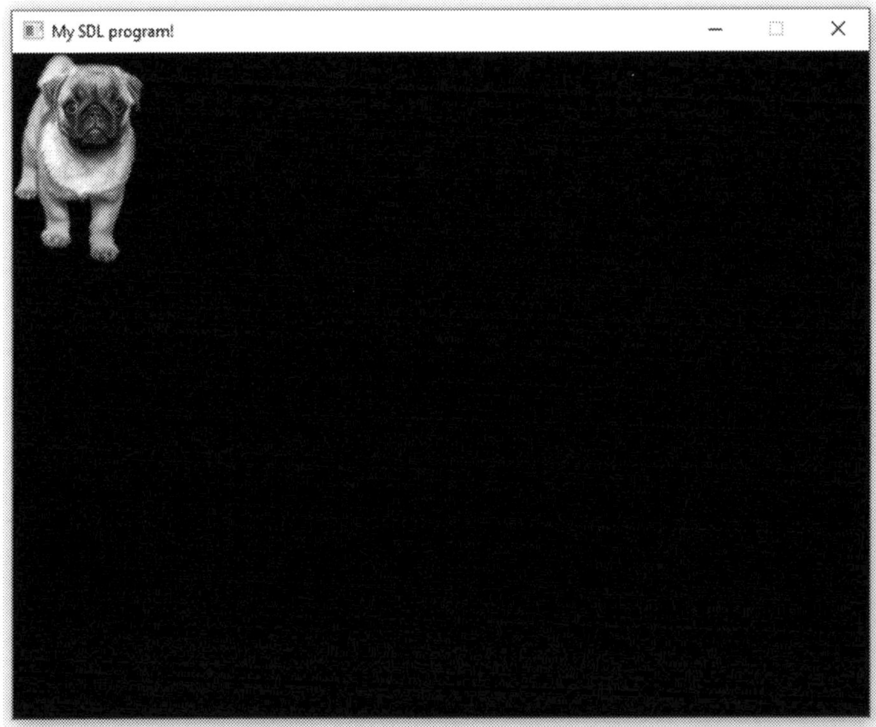

Figure 29-1. *The SDL program from Examples 29-1, 29-2, and 29-3. Was it worth it?*

Well, what do you know, it works (Figure 29-1). And it only took me 100 lines!

Admittedly, I wrote some awful code there: everything's in `main`. But I already did my good coding (I hope) in building the SSDL library. If I were going to write *good* code, I'd have just said

```
int main (int argc, char** argv)
{
    const SSDL_Image PUPPY = SSDL_LoadImage("media/pupdog.png");
    SSDL_RenderImage(PUPPY, 0, 0);
    SSDL_WaitKey();

    return 0;
}
```

Game programs have been notorious for bad practices: long functions like this one, global variables, pointers out the wazoo. As you start programming SDL, you can show everyone how to do it right.

Compiling

In Unix or MinGW: take an SSDL-capable `Makefile` for your platform (MinGW or Unix) and remove all references to SSDL.

In Microsoft Visual Studio: take an SSDL-capable project (`.vcxproj`, `.vcxproj.filters`, and `.vcxproj.user`), load it, and remove all references to SSDL – that is, under Project ➤ Properties, Configuration Properties:

- C/C++ ➤ General ➤ Additional Include Directories: take out the path to SSDL includes.
- Linker ➤ General ➤ Additional Library Directories: take out the path to SSDL libraries.
- Linker ➤ Input ➤ Additional Dependencies: take out ssdl<whatever it is>.lib.

Then compile, and run, as you would an SSDL project.

Further resources

I think the best reference is libsdl.org. Documentation on SDL_Image, and others, is there; you just have to find it (I do a web search for what I want and it'll take me there). And it's hard to beat Lazy Foo' (lazyfoo.net) for tutorials.

APPENDIX A

SDL/SSDL Setup Issues

Instructions for using SDL and SSDL with this book are in the source code: essentially, download the source code, make a copy of `basicSSDLProject` (keeping it in the same folder), and build and run with your compiler. You shouldn't need to read this appendix unless something goes wrong, or you are curious how to go further.

Unix

g++

g++ should already be installed when you installed Unix! And there are different Unix distributions with different command sets, so I can't give a definitive answer on installing g++ beyond "consult your Unix distribution." But if `apt-get` exists in your world, you may want `sudo apt-get install build-essential` or `sudo apt-get install g++` (and maybe other packages). `sudo yum install <package>` is another possibility.

SDL

Installing SDL is a sysadmin's job. I'd refer you to the SDL site, but when I went there they referred me to my Unix distribution site…which actually makes sense. But I'll try to help anyway. Relevant packages at time of writing include `libsdl2-dev`, `libsdl2-image-dev`, `libsdl2-mixer-dev`, and `libsdl2-ttf-dev` (`apt-get`); or `SDL2-devel`, `SDL2_image-devel` `SDL2_mixer-devel`, and `SDL2_ttf-devel` (`yum`).

W. Briggs, *C++ for Lazy Programmers*, https://doi.org/10.1007/978-1-4842-5187-4

SSDL

To get SSDL working, you must build it. Go to the book's sample code and follow instructions there (look for README's). You can leave `libssdl.so` where you find it; the `Makefiles` in the sample code know where it is as long as you don't move any directories.

The code repository has scripts in it to run and debug your SSDL programs. This is because Unix won't know where to find `libssdl.so`. That's fine – use the scripts – but if you don't want to use them, copy `libssdl.so` to the same directory you find SDL2 programs (you'll have to be sysadmin) or into the directory with your project. Then you can run your program thus: `./a.out`; and debug it thus: `gdb a.out` or `ddd a.out`.

Making your own Makefiles

If you want to create your own projects, look into the Unix `Makefile` of any of the SSDL projects in the sample code, and do something similar. If you want just the command-line version, run `make` and see what commands it produces, likely something like so:

```
g++ -c `sdl2-config --cflags` -I../../external/SSDL/include main.cpp -o main.o
g++ -o a.out -g main.o `sdl2-config cflags` I../../external/SSDL/include
  lssdl  lSDL2main -lSDL2 -lSDL2_image -lSDL2_ttf -lSDL2_mixer -L../../
external/SSDL/unix
```

Yowza.

Antibugging

- **You get a message that says the system can't find an include file or library.**

  Maybe it's not there. See earlier in this appendix for notes on installation. **Or maybe it's looking in the wrong place.** Make sure your folder is in the `newWork` folder of the book's source code, and it should be able to find SSDL. The `Makefiles` in the source code use the `sdl2_config` command, which knows path information; if `sdl2-config --cflags --libs` can't find things you need, you may want to reinstall.

MinGW

g++

To install g++ and other needful things, at time of writing, tell the MinGW Installation Manager (`mingw-get.exe`) to install, at least, `mingw32-gcc-g++-bin`, `mingw32-gdb-bin`, and `msys-make-bin`.

SDL and SSDL

These are in the code repository that accompanies the book. Keep your folder either where it was (if it's my sample code) or in the source code's `newWork` folder (if it's yours) and the MinGW `Makefile` should know where both SDL2 and SSDL are.

The code repository has scripts to run and debug your SSDL programs. This is because Windows won't know where to find the various `dll` files associated with SDL2. If you can put them in your folder or in a place that's on Windows's PATH, or alter the PATH variable so that it knows where to find them, you won't need the scripts: you can run your program by typing `a.out` or debug it by typing `gdb a.out`.

Making your own Makefiles

If you want to create your own projects, look into the MinGW `Makefile` of any of the SSDL projects in the sample code, and do something similar. If you want just the command-line version, run make and see what commands it produces. It will look long and scary.

Antibugging

- **You can't compile because of missing includes or library files.** See Chapter 1: your project folder may not be in the source code's `newWork` folder.
- **It can't find SDL2's `dll`s.** Run with `bash runw`, not `a.out`.
- **You get a runtime error about a `dll` file.**

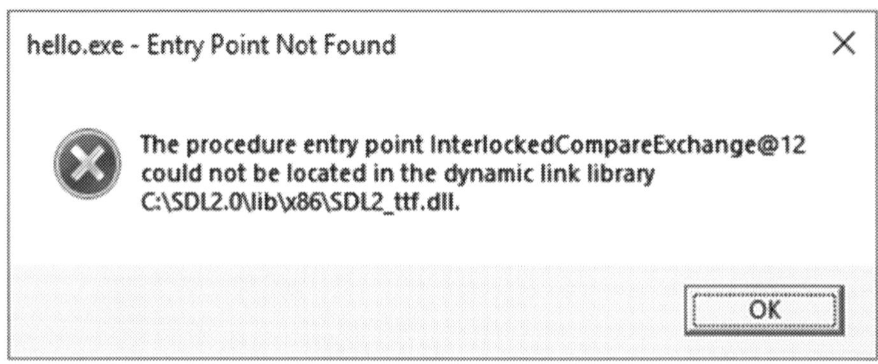

Figure A-1. *A Windows* `dll` *error*

This likely results from a conflict between one of the `dll`'s that SDL2 and its helper libraries use and another installed on your machine. The elegant fix is to find the conflicting copy, and, whichever program is using it: update it; uninstall it; remove it from the system path; or move it to later in the system path than SDL2. Of course, it may make the other program not work. Oops.

A quicker and safer, if less efficient, solution is to copy SDL2's `dll`'s from wherever it keeps them and put them in the folder with your project. That way it'll find *them* first.

Microsoft Visual Studio

SDL/SSDL

These libraries are in the code repository that accompanies the book. Keep your folder either where it was (if it's my sample code) or in the source code's `newWork` folder (if it's yours), and the Visual Studio project should know where both SDL2 and SSDL are.

If you want to run them without using the compiler…it's inefficient, but you can copy all SDL2's various `dll`'s into the folder with the executable before running. Or, if it makes sense, copy them some place Windows already looks for `dll`'s: some place in the PATH.

Making your own project files

There's a lot to be done to make your own Visual Studio project file work with SDL2 and SSDL…and here it is. Create an Empty Project, and under Project ➤ Properties, Configuration Properties:

- Be sure you're editing either All Configurations (top left) or at least the one you intend to use, probably Debug; and the All Platforms or the relevant platform (top middle), probably Win32.
- Under Debugging ➤ Environment, set the PATH to include wherever SDL2's `dll`'s are stored. In the repository, that's `PATH=..\..\external\SDL2\lib\x86;%PATH%`. If they're already installed somewhere in the PATH, you can omit this step. This, by the way, is stored in `<your project>.vcxproj.user`, so erasing that file will erase this information.
- C/C++ ➤ General: set Additional Include Directories to find SDL2's and SSDL's includes; I did it like this: `..\..\external\SDL2\include;..\..\external\SSDL\include`
- C/C++ ➤ Code Generation ➤ Runtime Library should show /MTd (for Debug) or /MT (for Release).
- Linker ➤ General: set Additional Library Directories to find the libraries. I did it like this: `..\..\external\SDL2\lib\x86;..\..\external\SSDL\libvs\Win32`
- Linker ➤ Input ➤ Additional Dependencies should include those libraries. Mine looks like so: `ssdl_$(Configuration).lib;sdl2.lib;SDL2main.lib;sdl2_image.lib;sdl2_ttf.lib;sdl2_mixer.lib;%(AdditionalDependencies)`. The `$(Configuration)` means "put `Debug` here if we're doing Debug mode, `Release` here for Release mode".
- Linker ➤ System ➤ Subsystem should be Windows.
- ...and add whatever source files you want to the project - `main.cpp` sounds good - and go.

Antibugging

- **You can't compile because of missing includes or library files.** See Chapter 1: your project folder may not be in the source code's `newWork` folder.

- **You get a runtime error message about a `dll` file.** Maybe you erased the `.user` file, which tells Visual Studio where to look. If not, see the previous "Antibugging" section under MinGW.

Sound

If sound isn't working at all, see one of the earlier sections in this appendix. But if the quality is a problem, read on.

First, the obvious. Is sound working for other programs? Pull up YouTube and play something. Is it all sound files, or just one? If it's just one, there may be a problem with the file or its format. If you know what you're doing, download a tester program for SDL_Mixer and verify you're getting reasonable sound, thus detecting whether it's an SDL or an SSDL problem.

Or it may help to change the numbers used to initialize SDL_Mixer's `Mix_OpenAudio`. SSDL has two ways:

- Put this line at the top of your file that has `main` in it:

  ```
  SSDL_SoundSystemInitialize
                          initializer(88020, MIX_DEFAULT_FORMAT,2, 4096);
  ```

  then start altering the numbers (see below).

  This method may change if SSDL goes into a new version.

- Edit those same numbers in SSDL itself. You can find them as defaults in the `Instance` member function of `SSDL_SoundSystem`.

The first argument, `frequency`, usually seems to be a multiple of 22005 Hz. Too small and it may cause static; too large and it may skip.

There's a list of possible values for the second argument, `format`, in the SDL_Mixer documentation online, currently at `www.libsdl.org`; play with them to see which sounds best.

The third arguments, `channels`, should be 1 (mono) or 2 (stereo).

The fourth is `chunksize`. I see multiples of 1024 used.

Any sufficiently wrong number may cause the music not to play.

I found no benefit in changing the last two arguments, but could improve sound by stumbling onto the right format and having a high enough frequency.

APPENDIX B

Operators

Associativity

Unary operators (as in -a) are evaluated right side first (perhaps because there is no left side).

Assignment operators (as in A=B) are evaluated right side first, then left.

All other operators are evaluated left to right.

Precedence

Here are the groupings of C++ operators from highest precedence (evaluated first) to lowest.

::
. -> [] () ++ (post-increment) -- (post-decrement) typeid C++-style cast (<type>())
++ (pre-increment) -- (pre-decrement) unary operators: ~ ! & * - + new, new[] delete, delete [] _Alignof/alignof sizeof C-style cast (<type>)
.* ->*

(*continued*)

W. Briggs, *C++ for Lazy Programmers*, https://doi.org/10.1007/978-1-4842-5187-4

<table>
<tr><td>* / %</td></tr>
<tr><td>+ -</td></tr>
<tr><td>>> <<</td></tr>
<tr><td>< <= => ></td></tr>
<tr><td>== !=</td></tr>
<tr><td>&</td></tr>
<tr><td>^</td></tr>
<tr><td>|</td></tr>
<tr><td>&&</td></tr>
<tr><td>||</td></tr>
<tr><td>?:</td></tr>
<tr><td>assignment operators: = += -= *= /= %= ^= &= |= <<= >>=</td></tr>
<tr><td>throw</td></tr>
<tr><td>, (comma)</td></tr>
</table>

Overloading

These are the operators available for overloading in C++:

- arithmetic: + - * / % ++ --
- logical: & | !
- bitwise: && || ~ ^
- << >>
- assignment: = += -= *= /= %= ^= &= |= <<= >>=
- comparison: > >= < <= == !=
- -> ->*
- [] ()
- new new[] delete delete[]
- User-defined literals ("" _<identifier>)
- , (comma)

APPENDIX C

ASCII Codes

dec	hex		dec	hex		dec	hex		dec	hex	
0	00	null character	32	20	space	64	40	@	96	60	`
1	01		33	21	!	65	41	A	97	61	a
2	02		34	22	"	66	42	B	98	62	b
3	03		35	23	#	67	43	C	99	63	c
4	04		36	24	$	68	44	D	100	64	d
5	05		37	25	%	69	45	E	101	65	e
6	06	acknowledge	38	26	&	70	46	F	102	66	f
7	07	bell	39	27	'	71	47	G	103	67	g
8	08	backspace	40	28	(	72	48	H	104	68	h
9	09	horizontal tab	41	29	)	73	49	I	105	69	i
10	0A	line feed	42	2A	*	74	4A	J	106	6A	j
11	0B	vertical tab	43	2B	+	75	4B	K	107	6B	k
12	0C	form feed	44	2C	,	76	4C	L	108	6C	l
13	0D	carriage return	45	2D	-	77	4D	M	109	6D	m
14	0E		46	2E	.	78	4E	N	110	6E	n
15	0F		47	2F	/	79	4F	O	111	6F	o
16	10		48	30	0	80	50	P	112	70	p
17	11		49	31	1	81	51	Q	113	71	q
18	12		50	32	2	82	52	R	114	72	r
19	13		51	33	3	83	53	S	115	73	s

(*continued*)

W. Briggs, *C++ for Lazy Programmers*, https://doi.org/10.1007/978-1-4842-5187-4

dec	hex		dec	hex		dec	hex		dec	hex	
20	14		52	34	4	84	54	T	116	74	t
21	15		53	35	5	85	55	U	117	75	u
22	16		54	36	6	86	56	V	118	76	v
23	17		55	37	7	87	57	W	119	77	w
24	18		56	38	8	88	58	X	120	78	x
25	19		57	39	9	89	59	Y	121	79	y
26	1A		58	3A	:	90	5A	Z	122	7A	z
27	1B	escape	59	3B	;	91	5B	[	123	7B	{
28	1C		60	3C	<	92	5C	\	124	7C	|
29	1D		61	3D	=	93	5D	]	125	7D	}
30	1E		62	3E	>	94	5E	^	126	7E	~
31	1F		63	3F	?	95	5F	_	127	7F	delete

APPENDIX D

Fundamental Types

Type	Example literal values
bool	true, false
char	'A', '\0', '0', '\n'
unsigned char	'A', '\0', '0', '\n'
signed char	'A', '\0', '0', '\n'
char8_t[1]	u8'A', u8'\u7E'
char16_t	u'A', u'\u3053'
char32_t	U'A', U'\u3053', U'\U000096e8'
wchar_t	L'A', L'\xff00', L'0', L'\n'
float	2.71828F, 6.023E23F
double	2.71828, 6.023E23
long double	2.71828L, 6.023E23L
int	-42, 42
signed int	-42, 42
unsigned int	42U
short int	-42, 42
signed short int	-42, 42
unsigned short int	42U
long int	-42L, 42L

(*continued*)

[1]char8_t isn't supported by g++ until version 9, or current versions of Visual Studio. It's part of the standard, but…I wouldn't, yet. Use char.

W. Briggs, *C++ for Lazy Programmers*, https://doi.org/10.1007/978-1-4842-5187-4

Type	Example literal values
`signed long int`	`-42L, 42L`
`unsigned long int`	`42UL`
`long long int`	`-42LL, 42LL`
`signed long long int`	`-42LL, 42LL`
`unsigned long long int`	`42ULL`
`void`	No values

APPENDIX E

Escape Sequences

Symbol	Meaning
\"	Quote (")
\'	Single quote (')
\?	Question mark (?); rarely used
\\	Backslash (\)
\<up to 3 digits>	The digits form an octal (base 8) number; the escape sequence is the corresponding character. For example, '\101' is 'A', ASCII 65. \0 is commonly used as the "null" character (see Chapter 14)
\a	Alert (often a beep)
\b	Backspace (rarely used)
\f	Form feed (rarely used)
\n	New line
\r	Carriage return (rarely used)
\t	Tab
\u<4 digits>	The Unicode character or characters corresponding to the 4 hexadecimal digits used; not used in this book
\u<8 digits>	The Unicode character or characters corresponding to the 8 hexadecimal digits used; not used in this book
\v	Vertical tab (rarely used)
\x<digits>	The 1 or more digits form a hexadecimal number, and the value is the corresponding character. For example, '\x5A' is 'Z', ASCII 90

W. Briggs, *C++ for Lazy Programmers*, https://doi.org/10.1007/978-1-4842-5187-4

APPENDIX F

Basic C Standard Library

The following are commonly used functions from standard libraries incorporated from C. For a complete listing, go online, possibly to `www.cplusplus.com`.

cmath

Trigonometric functions	
`double sin  (double angle);`	sine
`double cos  (double angle);`	cosine
`double tan  (double angle);`	tangent
`double asin (double angle);`	arcsine
`double acos (double angle);`	arccosine
`double atan (double angle);`	arctangent
`double atan (double x, double y);`	arctangent (x/y)

Exponential functions	
`double exp   (double num);`	e to the num power
`double log   (double num);`	base e log of num
`double log10 (double num);`	base 10 log of num
`double pow   (double b, double p);`	b to the p power (b^p)

W. Briggs, *C++ for Lazy Programmers*, https://doi.org/10.1007/978-1-4842-5187-4

Other functions	
`double abs (double num);`	absolute value
`int abs (int num);`	absolute value
`double sqrt (double num);`	square root

cctype

Classifying functions	
`int isdigit (int ch);`	return whether ch is a digit ('0'...'9')
`int isalpha (int ch);`	return whether ch is a letter ('A'...'Z' or 'a'...'z')
`int isalnum (int ch);`	return whether ch is either of the above
`int islower (int ch);`	return whether ch is lowercase (false for non-letter characters)
`int isupper (int ch);`	return whether ch is uppercase (false for non-letter characters)
`int isspace (int ch);`	return whether ch is whitespace (' ', '\f', '\n', '\r', '\h', or '\v')
`int ispunct (int ch);`	return whether ch is punctuation: not space, letter, or digit

Conversion functions	
`int tolower (int ch);`	return the lowercase version of ch. If ch is not a letter, returns ch
`int toupper (int ch);`	return the uppercase version of ch. If ch is not a letter, returns ch

cstdlib

`double atof (char* text);`	return the first `float` or `double` in the text
`int atoi (char* text);`	return the first `int` in the text
`void srand (unsigned int seed);`	starts pseudo-random number generation, starting the pseudo-random sequence with `seed`
`int rand ();`	return the next pseudo-random number in a range `0...RAND_MAX`
`RAND_MAX`	maximum number returned by `rand`

APPENDIX G

Common Debugger Commands

Microsoft Visual Studio

- To set a breakpoint, or "stop sign," click just past the left margin on the line you want. To erase it, click the red circle. You can put breakpoints anywhere in code.
- To start debugging, Start Debugging (F5) or otherwise run the program. Function keys require holding down "Function" or "Fn" on some keyboards.
- To stop debugging, Stop Debugging (Shift-F5) or otherwise stop the program.
- To go down one line, Step Over (F10).
- To go into a function, Step Into (F11).
- To step out of a function, Step Out (Shift-F11).
- To go to a particular line, right-click and choose Run To Cursor (Ctrl-F10)
- To see the value of a variable, look to the lower left, and select the Autos or Locals tab, or select Watch 1 and type it in.
- You can do calculations of a formula by typing in the formula into Watch1.

W. Briggs, *C++ for Lazy Programmers*, https://doi.org/10.1007/978-1-4842-5187-4

gdb/ddd

`break`	set breakpoint on current line
`break <line number>`	set breakpoint on line in current file
`break <function>`	set breakpoint for current function, e.g., `break myFunc` or `break myFunction (int, int, int)`
`clear <function-name>`	clear breakpoint on function
`continue`	keep running to the next break (if any)
`delete <number>`	delete breakpoint #<number>
`down`	go down the call stack (toward current line)
`finish`	finish the current function
`help`	help. It really does help!
`info locals`	
`print <expression>`	
`quit`	
`run [<arg1> <arg2>...]`	run the program in the debugger
`set <variable>`	change the value of a variable
`set args <argument>*`	set command-line arguments (`argv`)
`step`	go to the next line in execution
`up`	go up the call stack (toward main)
`watch <variable>`	set the debugger to break if the value of variable changes
`where`	show the current call stack

Many of these commands can be abbreviated; for example, `c` means `continue`.

Commands can often be repeated simply by hitting return (`next` and `step` have this property).

To quit, type `quit`.

APPENDIX H

SSDL Reference

In the following listings, if you don't understand the explanation for an entry (say, if you don't know what "Mix_Music" means), that may be something you won't need until moving from SSDL to SDL.

Updating the screen

`void SSDL_RenderPresent();`	render whatever is presently drawn; that is, update the screen. Automatically called by `SSDL_Delay`, `SSDL_IsNextFrame`, `SSDL_WaitEvent`, `SSDL_WaitMouse`, and `SSDL_WaitKey`

Added types

`struct SSDL_Color {  int r, g, b, a; };`	same as `SDL_Color`, but with constructors. Fields mean red, green, blue, and alpha (opacity) and range 0–255
`class SSDL_Exception;`	an exception thrown by SSDL functions
`class SSDL_Font;`	a wrapper for `TTF_Font*`
`class SSDL_Image;`	a wrapper for `SDL_Texture*`, as used by the `SDL_Image` library
`class SSDL_Music;`	a wrapper for `Mix_Music*`
`class SSDL_Sound;`	a wrapper for `Mix_Chunk*` and associated channels
`class SSDL_Sprite;`	an `SSDL_Image` with added capabilities

W. Briggs, *C++ for Lazy Programmers*, https://doi.org/10.1007/978-1-4842-5187-4

Clearing the screen

`void SSDL_RenderClear ();`	clear the screen to current erasing color
`void SSDL_RenderClear (const SSDL_Color& c);`	clear screen to color c

Colors

`const SSDL_Colors` include BLACK, WHITE, RED, GREEN, BLUE.

`SSDL_Color SSDL_CreateColor (int red, int green, int blue, int a=255);`	create and return a color. Max value for each parameter is 255. `alpha` (transparency) defaults to 255 (completely opaque)
`void SSDL_SetRenderDrawColor (const SSDL_Color& c);`	set drawing, including text, to use color c
`void SSDL_SetRenderEraseColor (const SSDL_Color& c);`	set erasing (backspacing, clearing of the screen) to use color c
`SSDL_Color SSDL_GetRenderDrawColor();`	return current drawing color
`SSDL_Color SSDL_GetRenderEraseColor();`	return current erasing color

Drawing

`void SSDL_RenderDrawPoint (int x, int y);`	draw a point
`void SSDL_RenderDrawPoints (const SDL_Point* points, int count);`	draw points
`void SSDL_RenderDrawLine (int x1, int y1, int x2, int y2);`	draw a line
`void SSDL_RenderDrawLines (const SDL_Point* points, int count);`	draw lines between points

`void SSDL_RenderDrawRect (int x, int y, int w, int h);`	draw a `w` by `h` rectangle with its upper left at (`x, y`)
`void SSDL_RenderDrawRect (const SDL_Rect& rect);`	draw a rectangle
`void SSDL_RenderDrawRects (const SDL_Rect* rects, int count);`	draw `count` rectangles
`void SSDL_RenderFillRect (int x, int y, int w, int h);`	draw a filled rectangle
`void SSDL_RenderFillRect (const SDL_Rect& rect);`	draw a filled rectangle
`void SSDL_RenderFillRects (const SDL_Rect* rects, int count);`	draw `count` filled rectangles
`void SSDL_RenderDrawCircle (int x, int y, int radius);`	draw a circle
`void SSDL_RenderFillCircle (int x, int y, int radius);`	draw a filled circle

Images

`SSDL_Image SSDL_LoadImage (const char* filename);`	return an `SSDL_Image` loaded from `filename`
`void SSDL_RenderImage (SDL_Image image, int x, int y, int stretchWidth=0, int stretchHeight=0);`	display `image` positioned with its top left corner at `x`, `y`. If `stretchWidth` and `stretchHeight` are specified, it makes the image fill a rectangle with that specified width and height

(continued)

`void SSDL_RenderImageEx (SDL_Image image, const SDL_Rect& src, const SDL_Rect& dst, double angleInDegrees = 0.0, SDL_RendererFlip flipValue = SDL_FLIP_NONE);`	display the portion of `image` bounded by `src` rectangle in the image, stretched or shrunk as needed to fill `dst` rectangle on the screen. Image will be rotated by `angleInDegrees`, and flipped either not at all (`SDL_FLIP_NONE`), horizontally (`SDL_FLIP_HORIZONTAL`), vertically (`SDL_FLIP_VERTICAL`), or both (`SDL_FLIP_HORIZONTAL | SDL_FLIP_VERTICAL`). Called by `SSDL_RenderSprite`
`int SSDL_GetImageWidth (SDL_Image image);`	return `image`'s width
`int SSDL_GetImageHeight (SDL_Image image);`	return `image`'s height

Mouse, keyboard, and events

`int SSDL_GetMouseX();`	provide current X of mouse
`int SSDL_GetMouseY();`	provide current Y of mouse
`int SSDL_GetMouseClick ();`	return whether mouse is clicked, and if so, which button: `SDL_BUTTON_LEFT`, `SDL_BUTTON_MIDDLE`, `SDL_BUTTON_RIGHT`, and some others (see SDL documentation online)
`bool SSDL_IsKeyPressed (SDL_Keycode whichKey);`	return whether a given key is currently pressed. Keys are `SDL_Keycode`s, not `char`s; see Chapter 12 or SDL documentation online
`int SSDL_PollEvent (SDL_Event& event);`	return true if there is an event in the event queue, and put its information into `event`. Called again, it goes on to next event

`void SSDL_WaitEvent (Uint32[1] eventType, SDL_Event& event);`	refresh the screen and wait for an event of the given `eventType` (or a quit event)
`int SSDL_WaitMouse ();`	refresh the screen and wait for mouse click; returns which button
`SDL_Keycode SSDL_WaitKey ();`	refresh the screen and wait for a key hit. Return value is the key hit but is usually ignored
`void SSDL_DefaultEventHandler ();`	read all events on queue, and process the quit events

Music

In the following table, each function parameter or return type shown as `SSDL_Music` may actually be of type `Mix_Music*` – but you can ignore that and pass in `SSDL_Music`.

If a function doesn't have music as an argument, it works on what's currently playing.

`void SSDL_FadeInMusic (SSDL_Music m, int loops, int ms);`	fade in music over `ms` milliseconds, and play for specified number of times. -1 means repeat forever
`void SSDL_FadeInMusicPos (SSDL_Music m, int loops, int ms, double pos);`	...do the same, starting at position pos. What `pos` means depends on file type
`Mix_Fading SSDL_FadingMusic();`	return whether music is fading in or out. Return values are `MIX_NO_FADING`, `MIX_FADING_OUT`, `MIX_FADING_IN`
`void SSDL_FadeOutMusic (int ms);`	start music fading out over `ms` milliseconds

(continued)

[1]A `Uint32` is an `int` of a particular size. It's used here for consistency with SDL. You can ignore that and just think of it as `int`.

`Mix_MusicType SSDL_GetMusicType (const SSDL_Music music);`	return file type of music. See SDL_Mixer documentation online for details
`void SSDL_HaltMusic ();`	halt music
`SSDL_Music SSDL_LoadMUS (const char* filename);`	load music from filename
`void SSDL_PauseMusic ();`	pause music
`bool SSDL_PausedMusic ()`	return whether music is paused
`void SSDL_PlayMusic (SSDL_Music m, int loops=-1);`	play music for specified number of times. -1 means repeat forever
`bool SSDL_PlayingMusic ()`	return whether music is playing
`void SSDL_ResumeMusic();`	unpause music
`void SSDL_RewindMusic();`	rewind music; works on some file types
`void SSDL_SetMusicPosition (double position);`	start music at given position. How (and whether!) it works depends on file type
`int SSDL_VolumeMusic (int volume=-1);`	set the volume, which should be 0 to `MIX_MAX_VOLUME` (128), and return the new volume. If volume is -1, it only returns the volume

Quit messages

`void SSDL_DeclareQuit ();`	post a quit message. Rarely used, as SSDL handles this itself. This tells `SSDL_WaitEvent`, `SSDL_WaitKey`, `SSDL_WaitMouse`, and `SSDL_IsNextFrame` not to wait
`bool SSDL_IsQuit ();`	check whether a quit message has been posted
`void SSDL_ToggleEscapeIsQuit();`	turn on/off whether hitting the Escape key constitutes a quit message. Default is on

Sounds

In the following table, each function parameter or return type shown as SSDL_Sound may actually be of type int (representing a sound channel) – but you can ignore that and pass in SSDL_Sound.

`int SSDL_ExpireSound (SSDL_Sound snd, int ms);`	cause the sound to halt after ms milliseconds
`int SSDL_ExpireAllSounds (int ms);`	cause all sounds to halt after ms milliseconds
`void SSDL_FadeInSound (SSDL_Sound& sound, int repeats, int ms);`	fade in sound over ms milliseconds, repeating the specified number of times. If repeats is -1, it repeats forever
`void SSDL_FadeInSoundTimed (SSDL_Sound& sound, int repeats, int ms, int duration);`	same as above, but play for at most duration milliseconds
`int SSDL_FadeOutSound (SSDL_Sound snd, int ms);`	fade out sound over ms milliseconds
`int SSDL_FadeOutAllSounds (int ms);`	fade out *all* sounds over ms milliseconds
`Mix_Fading SSDL_FadingChannel (SSDL_Sound);`	determine if the sound is fading. Return values may be MIX_NO_FADING, MIX_FADING_OUT, or MIX_FADING_IN
`void SSDL_HaltSound (SSDL_Sound);`	halt sound
`void SSDL_HaltAllSounds ()`	halt all sounds
`SSDL_Sound SSDL_LoadWAV (const char* file);`	load sound from file. Despite the name, some formats other than WAV are supported. See SDL_mixer documentation online
`void SSDL_PauseSound (SSDL_Sound);`	pause sound

(continued)

`void SSDL_PauseAllSounds ()`	pause all sounds
`void SSDL_PlaySound (SSDL_Sound sound, int repeats=0);`	play sound one time plus specified number of repeats. -1 means repeats forever
`void SSDL_PlaySoundTimed (SSDL_Sound sound, int repeats, int duration);`	same as above, but plays at most `duration` milliseconds
`void SSDL_ResumeSound (SSDL_Sound);`	resume sound if paused
`void SSDL_ResumeAllSounds ();`	resume all paused sounds
`bool SSDL_SoundPlaying(SSDL_Sound)`	return whether the sound is playing
`bool SSDL_SoundPaused (SSDL_Sound)`	...or paused
`int SSDL_VolumeSound (SSDL_Sound snd, int volume=MIX_MAX_VOLUME);`	set volume of sound, from 0 to `MIX_MAX_VOLUME`, which is 128; return the volume. If volume argument is -1, it only returns the volume
`int SSDL_VolumeAllSounds (int volume=MIX_MAX_VOLUME);`	...or do the same for all sounds

Sprites

Miscellaneous	
`void SSDL_RenderSprite (const SSDL_Sprite& s);`	draw sprite at its current location
`void SSDL_SpriteFlipHorizontal ( SSDL_Sprite& s);`	flip sprite horizontally
`void SSDL_SpriteFlipVertical (SSDL_Sprite& s);`	...vertically
`bool SSDL_SpriteHasIntersection (const SSDL_Sprite& a, const SSDL_Sprite& b);`	return whether sprites a and b intersect

Get	
`int SSDL_GetSpriteX    (const SSDL_Sprite&);`	return sprite's x position on screen
`int SSDL_GetSpriteY    (const SSDL_Sprite&);`	...and y
`int SSDL_GetSpriteWidth (const SSDL_Sprite&);`	return sprite's width as it will appear on screen
`int SSDL_GetSpriteHeight (const SSDL_Sprite&);`	...and height
`int SSDL_GetSpriteOffsetX(const SSDL_Sprite&);`	return x part of sprite's offset (see Chapter 11)
`int SSDL_GetSpriteOffsetY(const SSDL_Sprite&);`	...and its y component
`int SSDL_GetSpriteClipX (const SSDL_Sprite&);`	return x component of the starting point of the sprite in its image file
`int SSDL_GetSpriteClipY (const SSDL_Sprite&);`	...and its y component
`int SSDL_GetSpriteClipWidth (const SSDL_Sprite&);`	...and its width
`int SSDL_GetSpriteClipHeight (const SSDL_Sprite&);`	...and its height
`bool SSDL_GetSpriteFlipHorizontal (const SSDL_Sprite&);`	return whether sprite is flipped (mirrored) horizontally
`bool SSDL_GetSpriteFlipVertical (const SSDL_Sprite&);`	...and vertically
`double SSDL_GetSpriteRotation (const SSDL_Sprite&);`	return sprite's rotation in degrees; default is 0

Set	
`void SSDL_SetSpriteLocation (SSDL_Sprite& s, int x, int y);`	set sprite's location on screen
`void SSDL_SetSpriteSize (SSDL_Sprite& s, int w, int h);`	...and its size
`void SSDL_SetSpriteOffset (SSDL_Sprite& s, int x, int y);`	...and its offset
`void SSDL_SetSpriteClipLocation (SSDL_Sprite& s, int w, int h);`	...and where it starts in its image file
`void SSDL_SetSpriteClipSize (SSDL_Sprite& s, int width, int ht);`	...and the size of the part of the image file it uses (default is all)
`void SSDL_SetSpriteRotation (SSDL_Sprite& s, double angle);`	...and angle of rotation

Text

In the following table, each function parameter or return type shown as SSDL_Font may actually be of type TTF_Font* - but you can ignore that and pass in SSDL_Font.

`sout << thing;`	print `thing` on the screen. `thing` must be printable
`ssin >> thing;`	read variable `thing` from the keyboard. `thing` must be readable
`void SSDL_SetCursor (int x, int y);`	position the cursor at x, y for the next use of `sout` or `ssin`
`SSDL_Font SSDL_GetCurrentFont();`	return current font
`SSDL_Font SSDL_OpenFont (const char* filename, int point);`	create a TrueType font from `filename`, and `point`

`SSDL_Font SSDL_OpenSystemFont (const char* filename, int point);`	same, but loads from the system fonts folder
`void SSDL_SetFont (const SSDL_Font& f);`	use `f` as the font for `sout`, `ssin`, and Render functions except where specified (see the following functions that render text)
`void SSDL_RenderText (const T& thing, int x, int y, const SSDL_Font& font = currentFont);`	print `thing` (which may be any printable type) at position x, y, using `font` if specified, otherwise using current font, which may be changed with `SSDL_SetFont`
`void SSDL_RenderTextCentered (const T& thing, int x, int y, const SSDL_Font& font = currentFont);`	print `thing`, as above, centered on x, y

Time and synchronization

See also "Mouse, keyboard, and events."

`void SSDL_Delay (Uint32 milliseconds);`	refresh the screen and wait this many milliseconds
`void SSDL_SetFramesPerSecond (Uint32 FPS);`	set the number of frames per second `SSDL_IsNextFrame` will wait. Default is 60
`bool SSDL_IsNextFrame ();`	refresh the screen and wait for the duration of the current frame (since the last time `SSDL_IsNextFrame` was called) to pass

Window

`void SSDL_GetWindowPosition (int& x, int& y);`	get window's x, y position
`void SSDL_GetWindowSize (int& width, int& height);`	...and size
`const char* SSDL_GetWindowTitle ();`	...and title
`int SSDL_GetWindowWidth ();`	...and width
`int SSDL_GetWindowHeight();`	...and height
`void SSDL_MaximizeWindow ();`	expand window to maximum size
`void SSDL_MinimizeWindow ();`	minimize window to icon size
`void SSDL_RestoreWindow ();`	restore window that was made full screen, or minimized, to normal size
`void SSDL_SetWindowPosition (int x,int y);`	put window at x, y on computer screen
`void SSDL_SetWindowSize (int w, int h);`	set window's width and height
`void SSDL_SetWindowTitle(const char* t);`	set window's title

References

Briggs, Will. 2019. *C++ for Lazy Programmers.* Self-referential citation.

cplusplus.com. 2019.

cppreference.com. 2019.

Cline, Marshall, Bjarne Stroustrup, et al. 2019. C++ Super-FAQ. `https://isocpp.org/wiki/faq`.

Durfee, Edmund H. "What Your Computer Really Needs to Know, You Learned in Kindergarten." In Proceedings of the Tenth National Conference on Artificial Intelligence, pages 858-864, July 1992.

Goldstine, Herman H. 1972. *The Computer from Pascal to von Neumann.* Princeton Univ. Press, Princeton, NJ.

The International Obfuscated C Code Contest. 1984-2016. `https://www.ioccc.org/`.

PBS. 1996. *Triumph of the Nerds,* Part III. Transcript is available at `http://www.pbs.org/nerds/part3.html`.

Persig, Robert. 1974. *Zen and the Art of Motorcycle Maintenance.* Morrow Quill, pp. 278-280.

Simple Direct Media Layer (SDL). 2019. `https://www.libsdl.org/` and `https://wiki.libsdl.org/`.

Stonebank, Michael. 2001. UNIX Tutorial for Beginners. `http://www.ee.surrey.ac.uk/Teaching/Unix/`

Stroustrup, Bjarne. 2013. *The C++ Programming Language.* Addison-Wesley.

Stroustrup, Bjarne. 1993. "A History of C++: 1979-1991." Proceedings of the Second ACM History of Programming Languages conference (HOPL-2). Also at `http://www.stroustrup.com/hopl2.pdf`.

Sung, Phil, and the Free Software Foundation. 2007. A Guided Tour of Emacs. `https://www.gnu.org/software/emacs/tour/`.

W. Briggs, *C++ for Lazy Programmers*, https://doi.org/10.1007/978-1-4842-5187-4

United States Department of State, Office of the Under Secretary for Public Diplomacy and Public Affairs. 2012; accessed 2019. Identity and Marking Standards. https://eca.state.gov/files/bureau/state_department_u.s._flag_style_guide.pdf.

United States House of Representatives. Accessed 2019. United States Code, TITLE 4—FLAG AND SEAL, SEAT OF GOVERNMENT, AND THE STATES. http://uscode.house.gov/view.xhtml?path=/prelim@title4/chapter1&edition=prelim.

Index

Symbols

A

W. Briggs, *C++ for Lazy Programmers*, https://doi.org/10.1007/978-1-4842-5187-4

H

I, J

K

L

M

N

O

P

Q

R

W, X, Y

Z

Printed in the United States
By Bookmasters